EKISTICS

CONSTANTINOS A. DOXIADIS

EKISTICS

AN INTRODUCTION TO THE SCIENCE
OF HUMAN SETTLEMENTS

NEW YORK

OXFORD UNIVERSITY PRESS

1968

TO EMMA

my companion on the road

CONTENTS

CONTENTS ANALYSIS

x

BOOK TWO: FACTS

BOOK FOUR: ACTION

ILLUSTRATIONS

The dates given on plans of settlements refer to the physical form of these settlements on these dates or in these centuries.

The dates given of plans of settlements designed by the author and Doxiadis Associates, or the Athens Center of Ekistics, refer to the year in which these plans were first conceived.

Several plans concerning cities of the future and related projections—especially in the larger units of Megalopolis and Ecumenopolis—are general sketches only, intended as a first approximation of the evolution to be expected. Their detail varies according to the progress of research work on the project in question. The author intends to present in forthcoming publications the more comprehensive plans now being prepared.

xviii

xxiv

ACKNOWLEDGEMENTS

Acknowledgements are due to all those who helped me learn about human settlements, their problems, and their solutions. They are many, in many villages and cities around the world; some are dead and some alive, they are those who build human settlements and those who live in them.

Special acknowledgements are due to all the authors and publishers mentioned here and listed in detail, who were kind enough to give me permission to quote or use material belonging to them. I am particularly grateful to Mr. Paul Delouvrier, Commissioner General of Paris, Professor Kenzo Tange, Professor Eiichi Isomura, Professor Jean Gottmann, Mr. Christian Zervos, Professor Emrys Jones, Mr. J. Travlos, The National Capital Planning Commission of Washington D.C., and the Egnsplansekretariatet for Storkøbenhavn.

I want to thank the Athens Center of Ekistics and the office of Doxiadis Associates for a very considerable amount of data and plans that I have used from their research and projects.

I also want to express my acknowledgements to the architects, Mr. A. Tombazis and Miss C. Spyropoulou for supervising the drawing and standardising of all the plans and Mr. G. Papageorgiou, and Mr. C. Gartsos for contribution in this effort; the painter Mr. Iannis Tsarouchis for preparing one drawing, Mr. N. Avronidakis, Mr. G. Perpinias, Miss L. Iossifoglu, Miss E. Caliata, and Miss C. Doxiadis for having helped at different stages with the collection of the data and the editing of the manuscript; and Miss A. Capsalis and Miss A. Patsy for their help with drafting many of the plans. This book could not have come to be without the contribution of several other draughtsmen and typists who helped considerably with their skilled work.

I also owe particular acknowledgements to my old friend Mr. J. Papaioannou for his collaboration in all matters related to projections of different phenomena into the future, to Professor J. Tyrwhitt of Harvard University for her reading of the first text and her constructive comments, and to Miss E. M. Horsley and Miss Georgina Bannister of The Hutchinson Publishing Group of London for their continued interest and support.

I owe very particular acknowledgement to another old friend, Professor Maurice Kilbridge of Harvard University, who had the patience to go through the final manuscript in a very critical way and help me to approach the reader in a way that can be better understood by people from many fields of knowledge.

The Architectural Press, Robert Auzelle, C. V. Barnes, Biblo & Tannen, Inc., Professor C. Blegen, George Braziller, Inc., The British School of Archaeology at Athens, the Cambridge University Press, Centre National de la Recherche Scientifique, F. E. Coleman, Compagnie Centrale d'Etudes Industrielles, P. Dikaios, Vincent Fréal et Cie, Armin von Gerkan, the *Geographical Review*, F. Gibberd, J. W. Graham, Walter de Gruyter & Co., Paul Hamlyn Publishers, the Highway Research Board Bulletin, L. Hilberseimer, the Johns Hopkins Press, M. K. Kovaios, Pierre Lavedan, the Macmillan Company, Inc., the Oxford University Press, Penguin Books Ltd., Steen Eiler Rasmussen, D. S. Robertson, D. M. Robinson, Soprintendenza alle Gallerie ed alle Opere d'Arte, the Technical Chamber of Greece, Paul Theobold & Co., A. M. Voorhes, Werner Verlag, the Zoological Society of London.

PREFACE

I am sitting at the top of a tower on the island-fortress of Bourtzi in the Gulf of Argolis, in Southern Greece, in the centre of the large bowl formed by the mountains of this ancient land. Southwards the mainland is very close to me, only a few hundred metres away; and then the land opens like a huge spiral to the east, more so to the north, still more to the west; until in the south-east the gulf opens towards the Aegean Sea . . . But here the horizon is closed by the distant mountains of the Peloponnesus. It seems as if I am in the middle of a great lake, in the centre of a continent.

Acronauplia, the fortress of the city of Nauplion, first capital of modern Greece, is very close to me. On the sea front there is a modern tourist hotel; then, to the left, there is the city of Nauplion, with churches and mosques rising out of it, and overlooking it all, the Frankish and Byzantine fortress of Palamidi. At the foot of the hills, dominated by a big church is spread out the more recent expansion of the city of Nauplion, built after the liberation of Greece. Over to the east, lies a plain where the soil from these hills has been accumulating over thousands of years. It is surrounded by barren hills crowned with small churches. To the north-west stretches the wide and fertile plain of Argolis, its green broken only by modern factories, and by the Acropolis of Tiryns, thousands of years old. To the north one can see an extension of the plain inland, then the city of Argos with Larissa, its Acropolis, backed by the high barren mountains of the Peloponnesus.

It is here, in the middle of a landscape which has been inhabited for thousands of years by Man, and which bears everywhere evidence of millennia of habitation by people who came from the north, the south, the east and west, with their civilisations, their religions and their cultures, that I sit to start the writing of this book, right in the middle of a big workshop which humanity has left for those who want to deal with the problems of human settlements (fig. 1).

Thirty-six years have gone by since I first started planning and designing houses and buildings as a student at the Technical University of Athens, and thirty-three years since I prepared the first plans of dynamic settlements without publishing them, hoping that I could do more work on them and learn more about such phenomena. Twenty-six years

have gone by since I returned to Athens from Albania, where I had been fighting with the Greek Army, and in passing through the devastated cities and villages I realised that I was unable to help give them a new life, on the basis of my studies in architecture, engineering, and planning. Twenty-six years have gone by since I started working, lecturing and writing in a systematic way towards a comprehensive approach to the problems of cities and villages that is, since I began developing *Ekistics* as the science of human settlements.

I dedicated these years to the effort of understanding human settlements better and promoting the development of a discipline and a science which would help us in meeting their problems. I wrote several articles and books, some of which have been published. I would especially like to mention *Ekistic Analysis*, which was written in 1943 and published in 1946, *Ekistic Policies for the Reconstruction of the Country with a 20-year Programme*,[1] which was written in 1944 and published in 1946, as well as an *Ekistic Geography of Greece*, and other books which are still in manuscript form. I wrote these books during the years of the foreign occupation of Greece in the last world war, when I could study and think, but not build. Then came the liberation and reconstruction and I decided that action was more imperative, both for the countries which needed it badly and for me who had to learn.

It was during these years that I had the opportunity to work first for Greece and then—from 1951 on—for several other countries on all continents upon problems of human settlements ranging from architecture to national programmes and plans, and at the same time on other problems which were directly connected with human settlements, such as economic development, education, art and technology.

During these years I was lucky enough to have the opportunity of working with many people and various governments on many important cases of different kinds. I could work and talk with, and offer suggestions to, all types of people concerned with these problems. In several cases I failed; in others I succeeded. Thus I gradually started learning. More recently the four Delos Symposia held on the island of Delos in the Aegean Sea in 1963, 1964, 1965 and 1966, gave me the opportunity to discuss these problems with many

1

Acronauplia

the fortress of the city of Nauplion showing Bourtzi, the small island in the middle of the gulf

leading scientists, artists, technologists, humanists and administrators from all over the world. During these meetings we all agreed that we need a new approach to the problems of human settlements.

All these years I have felt it my duty to present in a systematic way the knowledge which I have acquired in this field. This feeling of duty has been counterbalanced by my knowledge that, although we need a unified approach to the problems of human settlements and although I have been working hard to achieve it, I have made only a few first steps in this direction. The question, therefore, arose in my mind as to whether I was entitled to speak at this early stage of the development of my knowledge with any certainty about the science of human settlements.

The consciousness of how little I know in this field would have restrained me from writing at all in the hope that I should be able to do much better later in my life. However, the opposing feeling, that whatever I have gained may be of some value to others even if they manage to prove that I am wrong (since in this way somebody else will guide us to the first necessary steps), together with the feeling that many of us are more concerned with protecting ourselves against the possibility of being proved wrong, rather than expressing our real views and contributing to progress, have persuaded me to present my ideas in this field.

Although I could have perhaps waited for several more years before writing this book, there are two reasons why I am writing it now: the first is that we are all mortal, and the second is the necessity of putting my ideas in writing while I still have time to defend them and, by so doing, become involved in the debate and the exchange of views which will lead to the discovery of the true solution of these problems. So this book is written only as the beginning of a process leading towards a systematic knowledge of the science of human settlements. In many parts of this book I would have liked to add much more—had I the data and the knowledge—but I do not believe that it is worth waiting, since I agree with

Vannevar Bush that: 'Fortunately, scientific endeavour does not have to be perfect to yield results'.[2]

In 1963 I felt that I was under the obligation to start a process which would have to be continued by many others in order to gradually become a corporate task. So I started to write again after 19 years, not only on projects, which I had been working on continuously, but also on ideas and theories. My first publication was *Architecture in Transition* (1963), then *The New World of Urban Man*, a series of lectures and discussions with Dr. Truman Douglass (1965), *Urban Renewal and the Future of the American City* (1966), and *Between Dystopia and Utopia* (1966).[3]

Since 1964 I have been writing *Ekistics* which was delayed mainly because I found that I had to redraw all the plans of all settlements in order to unify their presentation and allow for comparisons which could lead to an understanding of their nature. It was at that time that I made the discovery that most of the available plans were published without even an indication of their scale. The first manuscript was completed in 1964 when this introduction was first written, the second in 1965 and the third and present one in 1966. Each manuscript is more mature than the previous one and this shows how much we can learn with every day that passes, how early a stage this is in the development of systematic knowledge of human settlements.

This book—*Ekistics*—should be regarded as an outline of my personal experience, and an introduction to the total effort which has to be made. It will be followed by a series of studies dealing with certain specific aspects of Ekistics, the relationship of Ekistics to other disciplines, such as economics and aesthetics, a mathematical Ekistic theory and several other aspects of human settlements of the past, present and future. I hope that the publication of this volume will initiate controversies about the goals and the methods which have been used and also will cause reactions that will precipitate an exchange of views: these conditions are urgently needed to guarantee some progress in the realm of human settlements, a progress which is indispensable for the happy and free survival of Man.

It has been difficult for me to discover whom to thank for the knowledge I have acquired. There are so many people who have helped me to open my eyes and see this great human problem. My memory takes me back to my mother, who died when I was eight; she used to take me with her to the refugee camps where she supervised the cooking for the thousands of people fleeing to Greece from other countries. I think that she gave me my first lessons in the social aspects of life. My memory also takes me back to my father whom I would hear late at night discussing with friends his plans to house the refugees at a time when he was not only a practising pediatrician but also the Minister for Refugee Rehabilitation, and who, through his example, taught me how to look into the human aspects of a problem before tackling the techno-logical ones. I recall all my teachers, some of whom have managed to transmit to me the meaning of history and geography, the meaning of people and places. Among architects there is Professor D. Pikionis who, during long walks through Greece and at the Technical University, explained to me the aesthetic values of our surroundings. I also recall colleagues during my service for governments—Greek and foreign—who, whether supporting or fighting my ideas, always managed to teach me some truths. I remember thousands of collaborators who, working with me in different agencies and offices around the world, have contributed through long hours to the understanding of the problems of human settlements. I cannot forget Lewis Mumford, who with his works and writings has helped me greatly in the understanding of the intricate problems of human settlements, and Arnold Toynbee who first through his numerous books and articles, and, more recently also through conversations has helped me to understand the process of evolving human affairs and who had the kindness and patience to read the section referring to ancient cities and comment on it.

Finally my thoughts take me to those who have suffered so much because of the lack of proper settlements, and have forced me to open my eyes to this great problem. They were always the same, men, women and children, regardless of whether they lived in the ranchitos of Caracas, or the mountains of Asia; or whether they were the peasants of the African jungle, the nomads of the deserts of the Middle East, the refugees of Karachi, the commuters of New York or the nomadic dwellers on the outskirts of our big metropolitan areas. They were always the same men, women and children, for they were always human beings. To all those who suffered under inhuman living conditions, and made me suffer with them, I owe my greatest gratitude.

For those who will not understand my attitude towards the people who are living and suffering in human settlements, the people who, as a whole, know much more about what they want in their lives than experts do, I would like to mention a recent incident in Rio de Janeiro where I presented a plan for the elimination of the slums, the 'favelas', of that city. Upon completion of my presentation, somebody asked me: 'But if there are to be no "favelados", who will compose the sambas?'.

I could not answer that question; and as long as I am not able to do so, I will know that we are only beginning our study of the science of human settlements.

CONSTANTINOS A. DOXIADIS
March, 1967

3

INTRODUCTION

'Science proves nothing absolutely. On the most vital questions, it does not even produce evidence.

But is all the labor of science vain to the thinker, the seeker after a sure harbor, amid the mystery, evil, cruelty, majesty, that surrounds us? By no means. Science here does two things. It renders us humble. And it paints a universe in which the mysteries become highlighted, in which constraints on imagination and speculation have been removed, and which become ever more awe-inspiring as we gaze.'

VANNEVAR BUSH

THE CRISIS

Towards Disaster

Human settlements are no longer satisfactory for their inhabitants. This is true everywhere in the world, in under-developed as well as developed countries. It holds true both for the way of living of their inhabitants and for the forms we give to the shells of the settlements trying to satisfy their needs. And it is true whatever our aspect of the problem.

Economically speaking, this is so, since many of the inhabitants of human settlements do not have the means to satisfy their basic needs, and they either remain homeless, as in cities like Calcutta, or live in houses of very low quality, as in parts of many urban areas around the world and in almost all rural areas with very few exceptions. From the social point of view Man appears to be lost in the big cities, and feels abandoned by progress in many small towns and villages. On the political level, new types of societies and new types of people have not yet found their corresponding political institutions. From the technical point of view we see that most settlements do not have the facilities indispensable to their proper functioning, in spite of the technological achievements of our era. And finally, it also holds true aesthetically: we need only look around at the ugliness of human settlements of the present to be convinced of this.

It should certainly be mentioned that some areas exist in which conditions appear satisfactory. But we have to re-member that these belong mostly to cities of the past (we cannot include Venice, which is a fossil, as a satisfactory city of the present), or else they are inhabited by very small groups —mostly of high income—although even there one wonders whether conditions are really humanly satisfactory or whether they simply seem so from the outside because of the huge amounts of money expended on the individual houses.

If we do not realise how bad the situation is, if we have become accustomed to chaos, we need only ask ourselves why we tend to visit and admire those settlements of the past which have retained their values—like Venice, or even small villages, while we do not care to visit—driving through is not visiting—settlements of the present day, even those where people believe they are living happily, as in Beverly Hills. In settlements which have survived unaltered from old times, the contemporary visitor can participate in their life and feel satisfied. In new settlements he is able to admire only the great investment and some physical results achieved. Few would choose to spend their free time in these settlements.

The unsatisfactory conditions of our settlements are be-coming worse with every passing day, and we have no reason at all to believe that we are creating better conditions for tomorrow. This we can understand better if we look into the different elements of the human settlements one by one.

The elements

We will start with Man. He is unhappy in his settlements today and is growing more so as the time passes, even if he is not always conscious of the source of his unhappiness. He is no longer in proper relation or in balance with the other elements of the settlement: Society, which he has formed; the Networks of facilities that serve him; the Shells he has built; and Nature within which they are built. He is becoming a displaced person within his own settlement. Due to the lack of social cohesion within his group there is reason to believe he is becoming more neurotic and psychotic. Due to a lack of contact with the physical shell of the settlement, Man gradually feels himself to be a displaced person; the car has displaced him from his own public space, his square, his street. He is no longer free to move around in his own habitat, and

5

for the first time in human history he is in greater danger in the centre of his cities than in the open countryside. Noise, odours, and contaminated air force him to try to find refuge in the depths of buildings. He no longer participates in the life outdoors, the public life of the settlement.

At the same time, further out, his natural habitat is being spoilt and Man is gradually losing those areas which afforded him natural values, and allowed his senses to enjoy the environment. Thus, alienated from natural surroundings, displaced from the cultural surrounding, and lost amid the complicated social structure which he has himself created, urban Man feels all the more helpless. His only desire is to desert the urban settlement, temporarily, over week-ends and holidays, or even permanently, or perhaps try to create a utopia on its outskirts and escape there, only to find out soon that he has not solved his problems, but has simply transferred them to a different surrounding, merely changing the nature of some.

We need only think of the situation of our houses in relation to our cars to understand why some people prefer travelling to arriving. It is characteristic of Man's dissatisfaction with his permanent habitat and his desire to escape to a new type of surrounding, even if it is an escape provided by a means of transportation, and even if it turns him into a semi-nomad who finds greater happiness and comfort in his car than in his home. Is this not evident in the fact that many people, although living in slums, buy brand new cars?

The community is facing even more difficult problems. An increase in members of a settlement which is not developing in accordance with the needs of its community leads to its disintegration. Despite the spread of settlements into the countryside, we see no sign that this is the best way of facing the problems of a suffering community.

The physical shells of our settlements clearly demonstrate the continuous disintegration from which they are suffering. Think of the millions of settlements left behind by evolution, the millions of villages whose physical wealth is disintegrating because all the investment is flowing towards new centres, the tens of thousands of small cities whose location and structure correspond to an economy of the past and which are now losing the vitality that once kept them intact and in good shape. Then think of the reverse side, of new expansions of the big urban areas, where residence, industry, transportation and many other functions are mixed together irrationally so that no part of the settlements can function properly and assume its appropriate shape and form. Finally, we must think of the centres of our cities, overcongested, overbuilt and then cut by the traffic engineer's surgical knife into many pieces; slicing up the old texture without creating a new one worthy of the name.

Many of our settlements are decaying, many are being abandoned, and, though new parts of some of them or even completely new settlements are emerging, there are very few we can be proud of as being better than the ones we had in the past; even when this appears to be true, we find that only very small parts of those settlements can be considered really successful.

But this is not all. It is not only the physical shell of the settlement that deteriorates. There is something worse. By allowing our settlements to expand the way they do, we spoil values of greater importance: we spoil Nature, which is the container of our life. This is true in many ways. First, we take more and more valuable land and build on it haphazardly, thus upsetting the balance which exists. Then we alter the countryside by way of many projects such as highways and dams. From the aesthetic viewpoint, we need only look at quarries opened in the mountains, at transmission lines, at power stations and water towers, and so many other constructions, to realise the extent to which we are destroying the natural setting of human settlements (fig. 2).

This is not only true from the aesthetic point of view. If we only remember how many forests have been cut down or burned and how many mountains and hillsides have lost their topsoil, or have been completely eliminated, as, for example the hill in the centre of Rio de Janeiro where the first settlement was created, we can realise the parallel to the aesthetic disaster: we are causing a loss of natural resources. And this is also true of many other resources which we cannot see. It has recently been estimated that the probable length of life of all mineral reserves is such that 'in not more than half a century we shall be faced with a material shortage which cannot be served by present-day technology'.[1] Rachel Carson, in *Silent Spring*, also quotes Albert Schweitzer's warning: 'man will end by destroying the earth'.[2] While this may seem an exaggeration to some people today, it may well be a mere statement of fact in some decades.

While spoiling land, water and air in this manner, we are also destroying many other expressions of nature, such as wild flowers, insects and birds. And in this way, as Aldous Huxley has exclaimed, 'we are losing half the subject matter of English poetry'.[3] This is also why Prince Bernhard of the Netherlands, speaking several years ago at the Wild Life Fund dinner in London, said:

'We are dreaming of conquering space. We are already preparing the conquest of the Moon. But if we are going to treat other planets as we are treating our own, we had better leave the Moon, Mars and Venus strictly alone.'

And he continues:

'We are poisoning the air over our cities; we are poisoning the rivers and the seas; we are poisoning the soil itself. Some of this may be inevitable. But if we do not get together in a real and mighty effort to stop these attacks upon Mother Earth, wherever possible, we may find ourselves one day—one day soon, maybe—in a world that will be only a desert full of plastic, concrete and electronic robots. In that world there will be no more "nature"; in that world man and a few domestic animals will be the only living creatures. And yet, man cannot live without some measure of contact with nature. It is essential to his happiness'.[4]

6

2

Man destroys the natural setting of his settlements

It can certainly be argued that Man does not need some parts of nature to live in, but this cannot be proved, while it can be proved that Man needs uncontaminated air and water in order to survive. In the future we may try to create an artificial habitat where we will be completely separated from any contact with the natural elements, but before that we should ask ourselves if it is reasonable to spoil the natural habitat we have in order to create an artificial one, whether this will be a better one and whether we will be happier in this artificial habitat.

There is no question today that the crisis we face is leading us towards a disaster, not only due to the unbearable situation created within human settlements, but also due to the grave dangers created by technology which expands only in certain directions without any reasonable interconnection of these expansions into a better and uniform system. We have completely overlooked the necessity of conserving our resources until we can create better ones. This is also valid of the man-made landscape. How many satisfactory settlements have we destroyed without replacing them with better ones, without even knowing whether we can replace them?

Destroying the values created by Nature and Man is today our most characteristic action in 'building' human settlements.

The causes

The crisis has many causes: the unprecedented increase of population, the tremendous rate of urbanisation (the urban population of the world is increasing by 4 to 5 per cent

per year), the huge increase of the average per capita income, the unexpected, unforeseen and non-systematic technological progress, and the social and political impact that these forces have had on the life of Man.

Thus the basic components of human settlements—people and buildings and machines—have increased at an unprecedented rate. But the need has also expanded in a different way. Now architecture is a necessity for everybody, whereas in the past it was needed only for the well-to-do classes, and even earlier only for monuments, only for the kings and gods.

These changes have caused a great development in human and natural resources, a development which is accelerated with the passage of time. Therefore, a fourth dimension, the dimension of time, has become a vital factor in our problems.

FAILURE TO RESPOND

In quantity: lagging behind

In the past changes were slow in taking place. This is why Man was able to follow them without difficulty, adjusting himself, his thoughts, his creations and his settlements to the changes. This slow evolution looked natural to him and he followed the changing demands and built the appropriate settlements almost unconsciously. During the latest phase of development, however, the rate of change has increased so much that Man has been unable to follow it, adjust himself and produce accordingly.

Man had developed the habit of looking ahead a certain

7

3

Man's ability to foresee his needs

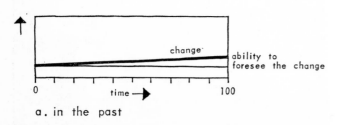

a. in the past

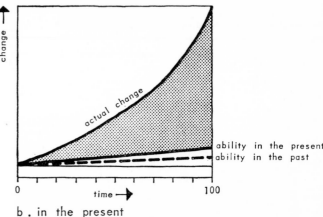

b. in the present

number of years, and foreseeing his needs—let us say up to the end of his life or through the next generation. This meant foreseeing very small changes. In our days, however, the same changes take place not in 30 or 50 years but in one or two, and consequently Man is caught unprepared. By the time he has finished a building his needs and the ability of the structure to serve them have changed (fig. 3).

Thus, when the population grew and economic and social evolution speeded up, the production of urban wealth did not adjust to the increasing population, much less to the economic and social progress which had been achieved. In many cases urban wealth was not being produced at the same rate at which economic and social evolution was taking place. As a result the gap between development as a whole and the quantity of material urban wealth has increased. Consequently, supply and demand have diverged more than before, and this gap is increasing. In the past, Man had only to achieve a synthesis of a few elements, mostly of people, buildings and nature; now he must achieve a synthesis of a much greater number of units in these elements, in addition to all kinds of machines.

The crisis has already started, and we should expect it to get worse since at present, in order to define it, we are comparing a low supply of urban wealth to the present scale of demand. This scale of demand is not accurate, however. It is suppressed below its real level because for centuries urban populations have adjusted themselves to the relatively low supply of existing urban wealth. This created a certain image of those needs which should be satisfied by an urban settlement. In the past, for example, the best that a citizen could expect from a settlement was a good house in a good neighbourhood, and this was actually sufficient, making everybody feel quite satisfied. What we may fail to realise, however, is that this good house in a good neighbourhood may have no constant value, for within a changing urban organism the neighbourhood may quickly change into a slum. Even if it retains its value, its inhabitants may not be satisfied as they may have to spend long hours commuting to their place of work; they may have to send their children to distant schools;

they may practically never be able to attend a concert or theatre as was possible in small cities in the past. These are the reasons why, although the gap between the supply of urban wealth and the demands for it may not look so bad today, we should expect the situation to get much worse, for as soon as Man begins to realise that his real needs are not properly served, that a new type of life creates new needs and that the urban goods which could satisfy him in the past will no longer satisfy him in the future, he will make much greater demands on his urban setting (fig. 4).

Human settlements have lagged behind in the quantity of urban goods offered to people. This is going to get much worse in the years to come. In order to face this situation we need to make a much greater effort.

In quality: confusion of ideas

Compared with what happens to the quality of our settlements, the wide gap that exists in the quantitative evaluation of the situation looks relatively satisfactory as quantity can at least be measured and achievements can be properly evaluated. But as soon as we think of the quality of human settlements, we find ourselves in great difficulties and the situation is much worse. We cannot even define what we mean by better quality; there is such a confusion of ideas in this field.

This confusion is both absolute and relative. In some instances we can be certain that original concepts have become confused and that people have been following the wrong policies and acting in the wrong way. Consider, for example, the imposition of certain building code standards which result in the creation of a much smaller number of houses with the justification that the house should either be of a certain high standard or not be built at all. The result is that people are in fact living in sub-standard houses, or are forced to live miles from the city which has imposed these building codes in order to satisfy some quite often abstract conception of satisfactory conditions underlying the regula-

4

the supply of urban wealth lags behind economic and social progress

the crisis is already here and the problems increase

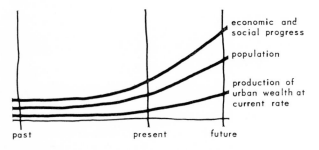

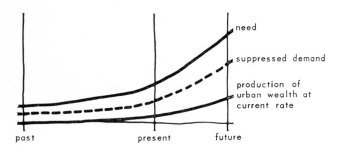

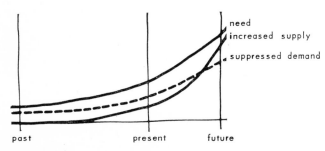

tions. Consider the confusion over density. In the same city where, for the sake of low density, some people in newer areas are forced to live at greater distances apart than they can afford, others are at the same time forced to live in worse conditions in some older areas. Consider the over-expansion of a city where, due to the reaction against the unhealthy, over-packed, old central areas, over-expansion has led to the other extreme, to many suburbs which have been created around the city, forcing people to travel unjustifiable distances every day. We must also think of many utopian attempts like the ones to pack people together in small cities in order to relieve them of the supposed evils of the villages, with no

consideration of the fact that these people were living by necessity in small villages as this allowed them to be within walking distance of their work and their activities. These are cases in which confusion has caused Man to revert to the wrong kind of solutions.

There is also another aspect of confusion, arising from the need for new solutions created by new conditions. Since there has been no systematic approach to reach new solutions, many people have, by necessity, attempted to solve the problems in their own individual way by projecting their own needs as the needs of the community. Because of a lack of goals, systems and criteria, no one has been able to demonstrate convincingly that these solutions are either right or wrong, or even that some are easier or more practical than others in this era of transition. Such confusion prompts many people to propose utopias. Planners, architects or engineers having to act in city building, propose, and quite often implement, projects which are neither convincing nor properly thought out. I would like to mention that this is not true only of unimportant projects created by unknown builders, but it can apply also to such experimental projects as Le Corbusier's *Unité d' Habitation* in Marseilles which has been highly controversial and has produced such adverse statements as Lewis Mumford's, 'an egocentric extravagance, as imposing as an Egyptian pyramid, which was meant to give immortality to a corpse, and—humanly speaking—as desolate'.[5] I mention this extreme case of a project by an outstanding architect and the comments of an outstanding thinker to show how great is the lack of a systematic approach to urban problems today (fig. 5).

As a result of this confusion of ideas and the enormity of the problems, we have not witnessed a systematic mobilisation of the indispensable intellectual resources; on the contrary, we see the exact opposite. I think that the overspecialisation of our era, when almost everyone is concerned with only one aspect of the problem of human settlements, such as architecture, engineering, urban sociology, anthropology, etc., and in some cases with only very detailed aspects of it, such as religious architecture, school buildings, etc., is a way of escape from the whole problem. In a similar way, some professionals have escaped not only to the relief offered by overspecialisation, but physically in space, by moving to countries going through earlier phases of development, in the hope that they would there be able to contribute much more. Nevertheless, they have overlooked two important considerations: first, that the gap between supply and demand, quantity and quality in these developing countries, is even larger, and second, that the obligations we have towards developing countries make our task much more difficult and our role much more delicate than when dealing with the more developed ones. In this way, many grave mistakes have been made in the developing countries by people of good intentions but low skills. Humanity has failed even in details because it lacks an understanding of the whole, and it has also failed in

9

5

architecture is passing through a phase of transition

no agreement can be reached even on such buildings as Le Corbusier's Marseilles apartment block (1947-1952). Many people, for instance Lewis Mumford, express great doubts as to its rationality

the less developed countries because it has overlooked the fact that their problems are actually more complicated.

We can now ask ourselves whether this confusion can be overcome or not. Three possible assumptions can be made about this point.

a. This situation is inevitable, as long as the city's structure is confused. People's minds cannot do better and we are being led to disaster.

b. This situation is not inevitable; it is a transitional one and conditions will be ameliorated in the natural course of time.

c. This situation is not inevitable; it is up to the people to change it.

We have no reason to believe that assumption *a.* is valid. Man is not completely conditioned by his city but only to a certain extent and this does not take place immediately. Human minds have so far been able to operate within confused cities, since they can isolate themselves from their immediate surroundings and think in a broader and, if necessary, in an abstract frame.

We have no reason to believe that assumption *b.* is valid. The city is not created by chance, it is created because of

certain reasons and it is created by Man. He has to act in order to change it.

Our concern, our discussions and studies, this book all indicate that assumption *c.* is a reasonable one. We are in the process of changing our outlook; if we succeed we can overcome the confusion.

Without coordination

The fact that we moved into overspecialisation and tried to find an easy way out has left us no overall coordination of our efforts. We are not able to coordinate those experts who could tackle even some aspects of the problem. We have had to deal with specialists who are involved in human settlements, but who continue to look at the problem in their own way: the architect at the buildings, the planner at the two-dimensional layout of the city, the engineer at the public utilities and structures, the administrator at the local government problems, and the economist and social scientist at their own particular interests. Since each man developed his interests in one direction, the total of Man's efforts could not lead anywhere; the situation grew more and more confused (fig. 6).

In this way each one has pursued his own goal, failing to mobilise and coordinate the other available resources. Very little has been drawn from geography, even less from anthropology, ecology, biology and many other disciplines. Through this lack of coordination Man has succeeded in overlooking the possible contribution of sciences, disciplines, technologies and arts which up to now have not been directly associated with the problems of human settlements, even though he could have learned a lot about methods and techniques from them.

6

every specialist looks at the settlements in his own way

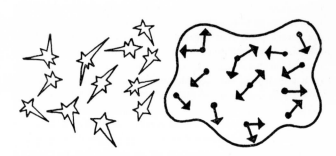

without coordination the system moves nowhere

7

a very small percentage of the Earth's population has all the required services in our contemporary settlements

Without adjustment

The lack of coordination for an overall conception and the lack of coordination of our efforts have also prevented each discipline and each group of experts from making the necessary adjustments to the new requirements of our time. For example when trying to estimate how many settlements provide their inhabitants with all the required facilities, we find that no more than perhaps 20 per cent of the total population of the Earth has proper community facilities. This percentage does not refer to quality of life at all. It is exactly in this 20 per cent of all people that the quality of life is most questionable. If we want to estimate the percentage of people who are provided with community facilities and who have a satisfactory type of life, it is questionable whether we will find more than a very small percentage (fig. 7).

To exemplify how different professions have failed to adjust to their new tasks, it seems pertinent in this connection to mention the attitude of two basic professions which could greatly contribute to the solution of the problems of human settlements, the professions of the economist and the engineer.

The economist in today's era of development, has to face such enormous problems of overall economic development that he has not specialised properly in Ekistic problems, the problems of human settlements. It seems still harder for him to realise that these problems are probably the most important

section of the overall economic activity of a country and this is true in spite of the fact that today, in the most developed economies 30 or 40 per cent of the total capital investment goes into projects in urban areas, while in certain under-developed countries this investment may exceed 90 per cent. This is so, in the latter case, since almost the entire investment effort takes place within the urban settlements, because little industry and few other kinds of productive projects exist to attract economic activity outside them. And yet up to now the subject of Ekistics has not been the main object of study of any major school of economics, but only a by-product of other economic phenomena.

Engineers also have not yet realised that the creation of urban settlements is one of their basic duties. They look at their task as a completely auxiliary one, and they limit themselves to serving the architect in connection with his structures and the town-planner in connection with community facilities. It is only recently that the traffic engineers have taken some responsibility for solving one of the major problems of our cities, automobile traffic. But their attempts to do so, due to the lack of an overall conception, have often done more harm than good to urban settlements; for in solving traffic problems, they have sometimes created new ones of various kinds, which have eventually led to a vicious circle and to disaster for the very settlements they were attempting to serve.

It is also interesting to note that due to the failure of the specialists to adjust themselves, even those who are responsible for the overall effort within human settlements, such as city officials and mayors, have failed to face the problems properly. They have been deprived of the possibilities they had in the past of dealing with the whole. It seems that this deprivation is twofold. On the one hand, they have been confined within the administrative city limits of the past, although the cities themselves have expanded far beyond them. In this way they have been geographically limited to only a part of the total living organism that these cities constitute. On the other hand, due to the great importance of some cities, new authorities have been superimposed and have taken over several of the functions for which the traditional authorities were previously responsible. Thus, the city officials are still limited within the cities of the past while living in the cities of the present and trying to build the cities of the future.

An example of failure

All these factors: lagging behind in quantity, a confusion of ideas, the lack of overall conception and coordination, the lack of the ability to adjust, have led to our failure to face the contemporary problems or to contribute constructively to their solution. As an example of how great this failure is, I will mention the architect's failure. This is the profession with

Introduction

8

the architect's influence in space

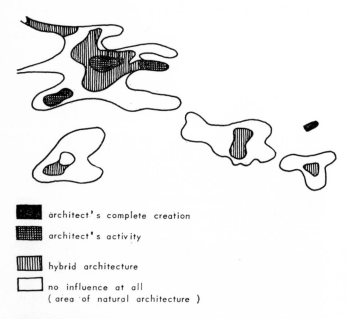

■ architect's complete creation

▨ architect's activity

▥ hybrid architecture

▢ no influence at all
(area of natural architecture)

which I started my life and I beg to be excused by my fellow architects for drawing everybody's attention to our failure. Also I hope that the experts from other professions which have also failed in this respect will be able to apply what I say to their own sphere, in order to understand where they, too, have fallen short. They can be assured that this failure on the part of architects is only one of many cases which show similar, if not even greater, failures in other fields. Some of the disciplines and professions which should have been very much involved in the problems of human settlements have not become interested at all, whereas the architects at least are worrying and are trying to contribute to the solution of their problems, even if they are not equipped to tackle their new dimensions and character.

If architects are not convinced of their own failure in facing the total problem of human settlements and if they cannot reach this conclusion by rational analysis, they should not overlook the fact that humanity today, instead of referring to the great architects and great builders, refers only to the engineers and scientists. When it is said that 'we are used to the really spectacular excitements of the engineers with their radar and rockets; and the life and death excitements of the doctors, the biological engineers, in their white coats'[6]; it is meant for those who admire the engineering (special) achievement and not the total architectural (synthesis) creation. Is this not characteristic of our problem? The hero is the specialist and not the one who achieves a synthesis—since no one has succeeded in doing so.

I shall start with the quantitative effort of the architect. If

we first attempt to examine the influence exercised by the architect, we will easily discover that the impact he has is not very significant. In practice architecture, as conceived and carried out by architects, is so limited quantitatively that it has no significant influence over the total creation. Even where it is of high quality, the creation is very often limited to a single building which loses enormously by its connection with the surroundings. Thus, a building which alone might have increased the importance of architectural creation will be lost in unimportant surroundings. We must always remember that architecture cannot be limited to the building itself, since in this way it would become an architecture of interiors or even decoration, while it should be connected positively with the surroundings.

Apart from that, the quality of architecture is such that even its direct product is questionable in many instances. Architects themselves have not really decided in which direction they want to go. Do they follow Le Corbusier or Mies van der Rohe? Are they interested more in individual aesthetic expression or in prefabrication? But even when good architecture as taught in good schools is spread all over the world, it becomes mixed with another type of architecture, which we can call natural architecture, created by the people themselves independently of the influence of the trained architect. As a result we have an additional 'hybrid architecture', or as it is called in some places 'builder's architecture', a cross between the architect's architecture and natural architecture. This confuses the situation enormously (fig. 8).

Since the architect usually operates only in a certain part of the world and there only in the central part of urban areas, if we take the total creation in the field of architecture as a single cone, his influence is quite small, and limited to the top (fig. 9). Even in countries such as England where the architect has a greater impact, his influence probably does not reach beyond 40 per cent of the total of the buildings erected, while his quantitative impact in the whole world is much smaller, perhaps of the order of 2 to 5 per cent.

It seems, therefore, that in spite of the good quality of a small proportion of architectural creation, the overall result—quantitatively and qualitatively—is a very poor and very limited architectural output.

Thus, the number of buildings created and the quality of the work done show that the architect, as we understand him today, has failed in his mission. He has confined himself to certain buildings and has been unable, in practice, to contribute significantly to the effort for better human settlements. Judging from the significant contribution of the architectural profession to the formation of human settlements in the past, one is led to expect much more from the architect of today. How can the architect justify his existence today when the average man knows that architects do not serve him either directly (more often than not, his house is not built by an architect), or indirectly, since architects seldom contribute much to the creation of a better human habitat as a whole.

But before carrying the argument any further, let me recapitulate the reasons why I feel so strongly about this failure. These are:

o in quantitative terms, the architect is not in charge of more than a minute fraction of the total creation of urban space, because very seldom is he given the chance to create an urban area with full professional responsibility for the entity and not for some buildings only;

o in qualitative terms, a very large part of even this limited activity is of a low order, either due to the forces of inertia or due to a misunderstanding of the architect's role;

o worthwhile architectural achievement is limited to some few good buildings. However, these do not form public architectural space in the human settlements as their effort is largely lost, sometimes even in their immediate neighbourhood.

The fact that, in a very few buildings, architects have managed to create new concepts of architecture and through them contribute to the creation of a better way of living, and the fact that, in even fewer cases, architects have managed to create satisfactory groups of buildings, where architectural space *has* been created, although very satisfactory for those who achieved this level of creation, are not sufficient to justify the activity of architects in general. In these circumstances, the architect is faced with the alternatives of either being confined to his buildings or deciding that it is his duty to play a leading role in the field of human settlements. Taking up the first challenge will mean that he will have to let others decide for him how to locate his buildings best; pursuing the second alternative will necessitate a re-definition of his role and his task, and a decision as to how far he is prepared or should be prepared to go.

In order to achieve his new goal, the architect will have to understand that he cannot play God, as Socrates accuses him of doing in Paul Valéry's *Eupalinos*.[7] On the contrary, he must understand that he is only building the walls that limit the space which is inhabited, and therefore conditioned, by Man. But he must also understand that this is a very important task indeed!

NECESSITY TO RESPOND

Clearing the confusion

It is quite clear that our failure to respond applies both in quantity, where we lag behind the demand, and in quality, where our confusion neither allows us to have any settlements of quality at all nor even to know what quality is and how to supply it. The problems are apparent in all elements of settlements. The crisis is serious. But as with every crisis, this one also creates opportunities. The problems we have to face also create possibilities for new solutions. The great forces

9

the architect's influence on the world's total architectural creation

a. one part of the world

b. only the urban part of this part

c. only the central part of the urban part

d. this is finally the influence throughout the world

the need for coordination among the individual professions and sciences involved in Ekistic affairs

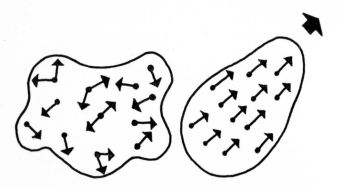

instead of letting
everyone continue
along his own road
without coordination

we need coordination
which leads to a
total positive gain

which have caused our problems—population, economic development, social change, intrusion of the machine—are at the same time forces which can help us face them.

If we think more systematically about this problem, we come to the conclusion that although the problem is not caused only by a confusion of ideas, it cannot be faced unless we can clear this confusion, and understand how to face it properly. By necessity this has to be the first step. In order to make it we must try to discover the real situation, the real problems and the best methods to cope with them; for it is only if we are armed with knowledge that we can respond and act properly.

Coordination in conception and practice

The confusion of our ideas is due to a lack of an understanding of the overall problem of human settlements, and to our inability to adjust our disciplines, technologies and professions to such an approach.

At this point we must remember that in the past, due to the slow rate of evolution and due to the fact that Man had been living for thousands of years in the same type of human settlements, first during the phase of agricultural economy in villages and then in small cities, he had managed to acquire the experience that enabled him to give the proper shape and form to human settlements. Every citizen was aware of the content, structure and form of the overall settlement, and every one could protest against solutions which were not in line with the common conception of what the settlement was and what needs it was supposed to serve.

In periods necessitating immediate action, such as the

period of colonisation of ancient Greek cities when new settlements were created, competent persons, who had managed to acquire such experience as existed in their era, took the leadership and created cities which corresponded to the requirements of their time. Hippodamos of Miletus, according to Aristotle, represents this type of personality—a man able to comprehend the experience of his era and express it in the cities he designed.

Yet, this natural understanding of problems and solutions in human settlements in their totality, no longer exists, due to the greatly increased rate of evolution of practically all phenomena related to human settlements. This understanding is what we have to regain before proceeding any further. Unless we are able to conceive and achieve a coordinated view of the total problem of human settlements, as people did in the past, we will certainly fail, since well intentioned action not guided by such an overall conception may even do harm to settlements, as recent bitter experience has shown. To understand why coordinated conception is the prerequisite for all subsequent work on the problem, we need only to remember the uncontrolled growth and change of human settlements which has resulted from the expansion of highways and the 'surgery' imposed by traffic considerations, a growth and change which very often create more problems than they solve.

It is only when we have an overall, well-coordinated conception that we can proceed in practice, in a coordinated way, in order to set goals and implement policies, programmes and plans for human settlements. Only then can we hope that implementation will make as much sense as conception and that proper conception will lead to the solution of the problems. Instead of letting each profession follow its own road towards the understanding and the solution of the problems of human settlements, we should provide a common system which will bring the different views together and by coordination lead them to positive gains (fig. 10).

Re-examination and adjustment

While we are trying to bring about coordination in conception and practice, we should remember that much work is being done on the solution of problems of human settlements. However, much of this work is not only un-coordinated, but is also very weak in itself. In spite of that, myths have been created about its importance and validity. One of these myths states that the transfer of slum dwellers into new quarters contributes to the solution of the problems created by their habitat. What is forgotten is that the new solution is frequently very inhuman; and although the new solution is perhaps much more healthy for the body of Man, people may not be satisfied with it, may not consider it a solution of their own, and may decide not to adopt and participate in it. The other facets of people, their feelings and desires as members of a community have been forgotten. Very often people are completely alienated from the settlement in which they find themselves because of the unexpected and unfamiliar solution offered to them by experts who, however well-meaning they may be, know little about the lives and aspirations of the dwellers. This is true even if the new houses of a slum clearance project are created on the old site, which does not happen very often. More often than not the displaced people suffer from a need to readjust themselves not only to a surrounding based on alien considerations, but also to a completely new area of the town, which is very often separated by great distances from the area in which they formerly lived and where they had their relatives, their connections and affiliations.

Another myth is related to the optimum size of cities. By transferring to the present day certain images of the past, when cities were confined within walls which set maximum limits to space and population, many people are still trying to discover an optimum size for the modern city which, if nothing else, is completely unrealistic.

If we think of all the work now in progress—the efforts to construct a new urban framework, the work on traffic amelioration (by this we very often mean only car traffic), etc.—we see that in attempting to arrive at a proper conception of the problems of human settlements and their solution, we should also be prepared to re-examine all theories which influence the policies and programmes now under way. In doing so, we should not forget that not only does the problem become more complicated, but also quite often we have fewer opportunities and fewer choices. We should understand that it is time—and we are already late—to readjust our own knowledge, technologies and professions in a coordinated way to the new conceptions regarding the problem.

Ekistics

The attempt to arrive at a proper conception and implementation of the facts, concepts and ideas related to human settlements, and the attempt to re-examine all principles and theories and to readjust the disciplines and professions connected with settlements, led to the need for a special discipline of human settlements, the discipline of *Ekistics*. The creation of this discipline must be conducted in a systematic way, for without objectivity and a systematic approach that defines goals, criteria and methods, it will be impossible to achieve a coordination of knowledge related to human settlements, much less the coordination of ideas which can lead to the conceptions needed to guide development. I, therefore, believe that the only way to meet the crisis in human settlements and to respond properly to it is the creation of the discipline of Ekistics.

The present book is an introduction to this discipline. It is only the beginning since the problems we are facing are not only multiple, but also acutely urgent, characteristic of the

critical situation which human settlements have now entered. If we wait for the proper development of a science of human settlements, we may find ourselves overwhelmed by the rising tide of the problems. We may even lose the battle for such a science since humanity may find no use of systematic theoretical thinking in a period of panic tension.

This is the reason why, while proceeding on the long march towards a completely systematic development of the science of Ekistics, we must also develop theories and systems of ideas which will help us to overcome the immediate problems. In order to make sense, this has to be based on the best knowledge acquired at every stage. Therefore, such provisional systems of ideas will have to be revised very often and continually take latest developments into account. The urgent need for such systems of ideas is imposed by the fact that we must proceed at once to practice these ideas without waiting for the full development of the science of Ekistics, but it is also necessary and useful in order to test the development of an overall theory of Ekistics. Thus, whenever possible, we should develop specific systems of ideas which can be implemented and tested, and which can be used as feed-back forces that can continuously modify the initial assumptions.

Since one of the major problems we face is the merging of settlements into much larger and complicated organisms, we at the Athens Center of Ekistics have been working on an attempt to foresee where human settlements are going in the future. It seems that they will merge into ever larger groupings which one day, a century or two from now, will become a continuous universal settlement, the universal city or Ecumenopolis. Simultaneously with this book I have been working on another called *Ecumenopolis: the Settlement of the Future*, which should provide a useful demonstration of how an overall theory of human settlements can be applied to some of the specific problems of our era, and another one: *Building our Cosmos*, which sets a general framework for our future action.

At the same time, my book, *Urban Renewal and the Future of the American City*, is an attempt to demonstrate how a general system of ideas can be related to a specific type of problem, such as the problem of planned urban renewal. In *Architecture in Transition*, I tried to show how we can achieve a readjustment of thinking within a specific discipline —architecture—in relation to the general discipline, science and theory of Ekistics. In my contribution to *The New World of Urban Man* and my lectures *Between Dystopia and Utopia* I discussed these matters in terms connecting them with other points of view.

With these seven books: *Ekistics, an Introduction to the Science of Human Settlements, Ecumenopolis: the Settlement of the Future, Building our Cosmos, Urban Renewal and the Future of the American City, The New World of Urban Man, Architecture in Transition* and *Between Dystopia and Utopia*, I hope to provide the reader with a general system of ideas and examples of how these ideas can be implemented in specific cases. I hope to give him the opportunity for thought, comment and criticism, so that he can gradually build his own theories about the whole, about the parts and about his own role vis-à-vis this great problem.

THE PRESENT STUDY

Outline

The present study begins with a preface explaining why I have written this book and expresses my gratitude to the people who have opened my mind to the problems and have contributed consciously or unconsciously to their understanding.

The preface is followed by an introduction in which I describe the crisis in human settlements, our failure to respond and the necessity to do so. This connects the present book with the historic moment we are passing through. In this way it links the general subject matter, the science of human settlements, with the special problems of the second part of the 20th century.

Following the introduction, the text is divided into four books, which are subdivided into 13 chapters. These books are not essentially concerned with the special problems of the present. They attempt to present a science, a body of systematic knowledge which is necessary, and which must be developed regardless of the particularly critical period through which we are now passing.

The first book is given to human settlements and to Ekistics as a science. It presents the subject matter of settlements and their classification, the need for Ekistics, its relation to other sciences, its subdivisions, its methodology and perspectives, and its experts, the Ekisticians. It closes with an attempted projection showing the future perspectives for Ekistics.

The second book deals with Ekistics as a descriptive science and contains the chapters on analysis as a static description of human settlements, their evolution, their pathology and finally the diagnosis of their conditions and problems. In a different presentation evolution might perhaps have preceded analysis of the present situation; we could have started with primitive settlements and followed their evolution to the present. This would have been chronologically proper, but it would not have allowed the reader to connect his present conception of problems in human settlements with the evolution he would be following.

The third book deals with Ekistic theories. It goes beyond description and attempts to identify the principles of the development of human settlements. It starts with a discussion of the phenomena we learn from analysis and evolution and attempts to describe them in a systematic way. It ends with a first attempt at a basic Ekistic theory which tries to explain the causes of these phenomena and the regularities which govern them.

The fourth book deals with Ekistics as a prescriptive discipline and contains the chapters on Ekistic therapy, development and the new tasks ahead for Ekistics, and on Ekistic practice.

In this way we move from the description of phenomena to a theory about them, and to the development of a prescriptive approach to action. This effort closes in an attempt to connect practice with theory and to answer the next natural question: how can we use the body of knowledge presented by this book in a practical way?

Material used

In Ekistics we cannot isolate ourselves in a laboratory in order to study problems under ideal conditions by isolating the necessary phenomena and following their evolution. This can be done in most other sciences, but not in Ekistics which studies the human settlements that consist of Nature, Man, Society, Shells and Networks. They are too big to be enclosed in a laboratory; they live too long to be studied in one researcher's lifetime. However, in Ekistics, we do have one big laboratory containing many cases created by humanity over thousands of years on the surface of the Earth, from which we can draw the necessary material.

This is the material I have used to study Ekistics: the human settlements of the past and the present. Sometimes I have been obliged to study hundreds of examples in order to understand them, while in other cases just a few dozens, or even fewer, sufficed, since there was either no necessity for further studies, or no great number of examples available. This is the reason the validity of my findings is not consistent in all cases nor all aspects. It is easier, for example, to draw conclusions about the Shells and the Networks of the settlements of the past than about Man and Society.

In all cases presented I have used drawings and plans most of which were prepared for this purpose, rather than photographs. There are three reasons for this. A photograph presents a great number of phenomena and does not allow us to isolate easily the special aspect to be studied while a drawing can stress the phenomena which must be emphasised and omit those which are not of interest to our study. In this way we can—by abstraction—present a specific phenomenon or a specific aspect of the settlement. Yet I still do not know how to present an entire settlement in one drawing. The most successful presentation, perhaps, would be a three-dimensional projection of all elements on a two-dimensional drawing, as in an Indian carpet (fig. 11). However, this would only be valid for the Ekistic micro-scale.

Photographs, including air-photographs, are of very great importance for the study of individual cases since they give excellent and revealing details. However, if I had used them in this general study they would definitely have confused the presentation. I would have had to use many more pictures than I have used plans and explain at length the difference between their individual and general characteristics. On the other hand,

11

a three-dimensional projection on a two-dimensional drawing   Indian carpet (seventeenth century)

drawings and plans can be prepared in the same way in which a laboratory staff prepares its specimens for demonstration purposes—they colour and photograph only those ingredients which have particular meaning.

Nearly all drawings and plans had to be redrawn especially for this book so that the phenomena studied could be presented in an identical way. Special attention was given to the inclusion of the scale of each plan, a point which is often neglected; without the notion of scale the phenomena we study and the conclusions we reach are of little value and can even be misleading. Discussions about the form of settlements are ridiculous if we do not speak of a particular scale. A circular settlement can be excellent if it is an independent unit covering a defined open or enclosed space, and unreasonable if it is one community of a system containing many more. Henry Moore rightly states that 'there is a right physical size for every idea'.[8] Attention was also given in presenting the orientation of every settlement shown; North points up in all plans.

In my effort to be as explicit as possible, I have very often reconstructed theoretical models using abstracts from different characteristic cases because, due to the great variation of phenomena, it would have been difficult to select just one example. On other occasions I have strengthened a specific case in order to make my point clearer and of a more general applicability. In such cases I have not given the name of the original example since it would be misleading.

However, when I thought that a specific example would be more interesting than a theoretical model I have used them. If in this effort I have used quite a number of Greek examples; this is not intended to mean that similar cases from other countries were not of universal value—I always made sure of their validity before presenting them—but rather that I wanted to be completely sure that I was not misinterpreting the causes of the phenomena because of any lack of knowledge of the details in each situation. This I was more often able to do for the Greek examples, since although I have been working in several countries of the world and know some of their cases quite well, I still believe that I know the Greek situations better. In this way the chances for misinterpretation of phenomena are reduced.

In the fourth book, of prescriptive Ekistic action, when illustrating the transition of settlements into the future, I have mostly used programmes and plans of settlements I was personally involved with, because I know them better, and because the future evolution of these settlements appears closer to the course I believe we must follow. In this respect the majority of the cases illustrating the future do not represent the total human effort of the present but my own convictions.

Since the whole study is inspired by a certain theory, the examples of new proposals which are mentioned are only those which correspond to it and, as is natural, these are examples drawn from my own activity. A few examples are mentioned which are not derived from my own work. They are presented either for a demonstration of a different point of view, in which case related comments are made on them, or because they coincide with the theory and illustrate it by a greater variety of cases.

Impersonal and personal approach

It becomes quite clear that whereas in the first three books I present Ekistics as an impersonal science and draw conclusions from what exists and has been done by humanity up to now, in the fourth book I do not attempt to present anything other than my own convictions about the course we should follow, based on what we have learned until now.

In a few cases when dealing with certain aspects of growth I had to use and criticise examples not related to my personal beliefs and efforts, such as the plans proposed for Washington D.C. and Copenhagen. For quite some time I could not decide whether I should criticise any specific plan or not, but I came to the conclusion that being polite is less important than the obligation to point out the weaknesses of a proposed solution. Only when we discuss these subjects in a detached way can we contribute to progress. If we want to turn our efforts into a science, then we must speak openly about the different theories and the different solutions proposed. To avoid this would mean to take the roads which would be diverging from a point of total human knowledge, without any hope of contributing to an understanding of the problems and the solutions we are offering. The criticism of new ideas has nothing to to with the great respect we have for the people who developed them, as they are pioneers of new developments. My attitude is derived only from the desire to learn more and to contribute further to progress by an open discussion. This is the spirit in which this book has been written.

This whole study has the limitations of its author. My training as an architect, engineer and physical planner allows me to speak with some certainty about related aspects of human settlements and about such fields as biology, anthropology, sociology, economics, administration and natural sciences. I am trying to bring the experience gained through these sciences into closer contact with our subject and I am, therefore, trying to simplify some phenomena and to present them in the vocabulary of the general reader.

In my efforts to speak about human settlements by using the experience of several disciplines, I have not attempted to answer those specific problems which are of concern only to special disciplines. I am thinking, for example, of the question I am often asked in the United States, why do I not deal with the racial problem? I am now convinced that what is basically wrong with human settlements in our era is that we can conceive neither of a way of life nor of its expression in a total settlement. If we can solve this problem we will find the road which leads to the solution of all partial problems regardless of how grave or how difficult they are.

This is what I am trying to do by way of this study, and to this basic aspect, the Ekistic one, I limit myself.

BOOK ONE

THE SUBJECTS AND THEIR STUDY

'Science is compounded of fact and logic'
J. BRONOWSKI   *The Common Sense of Science*

This book defines our subject which is human settlements and our studies of them; it describes the facts with which I am dealing and the logic which guides this study. It is divided into two chapters corresponding to facts and logic, subject and study.

CHAPTER ONE

THE SUBJECT—HUMAN SETTLEMENTS

THE SUBJECT AND ITS COMPONENTS

Human settlements and their elements

Human settlements are, by definition, settlements inhabited by Man. In this respect, the word 'human' defines the kind of settlements (human and not animal) and at the same time conveys a goal: human settlements should satisfy 'Man'.

By definition, the human settlement consists of:
- the content, or Man, alone and in societies;
- the container, or the physical settlement, which consists of both natural and man-made or artificial elements.

These two parts, when taken together, make up the human settlement whose largest possible dimensions are defined by the geographic limits of the Earth's surface. The total surface of the Earth, the largest possible container for Man, is, for all practical purposes, the whole cosmos of Man, the cosmos of the *anthropos*, the *Anthropocosmos*.

Such a definition of the human settlement implies that it is not merely three-dimensional but four-dimensional. Man and Society change continuously and, by so doing, create functions which, unlike Shells (which *can* be conceived in three-dimensional terms), require a fourth dimension, that of time, in order to be carried out. A three-dimensional conception of a settlement is very like a film which suddenly stops and arrests all the figures in their movements. A still photograph of a building looks real only if there are no human figures in the picture; if people have been arrested in the process of walking in front of the building, then the picture is frozen, unreal.

A human settlement needs both categories of elements in order to come into existence. Man alone or in groups, if not settled anywhere cannot be said to form a settlement or even a part of one. Once he does settle somewhere, even temporarily, we have a temporary, elementary settlement, in which a pattern of relationship between Man and his container comes into existence for a certain period of time (one day, many days, or one season) regardless of whether the container is a natural one (a cave), or one made by Man (a tent or a building). Of course Nature alone, without Man, cannot be said to form a settlement or even a container, since it has no human content. Even a man-made settlement, if no

longer inhabited by Man, cannot be considered a human settlement—it is only the corpse or the abandoned shell of a settlement, which must be considered as dead as any other corpse. Naturally, some people do call a dead settlement a 'settlement', but this is no more correct than calling the shell of a snail, a 'snail'. The term is used in many such cases for reasons of simplicity, but it is not accurate and should be used with care to avoid confusion. The purpose of this work is to study human settlements on our Earth, and more specifically in the Anthropocosmos.

The two basic elements of human settlements, the content and the container, can be further subdivided into five elements:
- Nature, providing the foundation upon which the settlement is created and the frame within which it can function.
- Man.
- Society.
- Shells, or the structures within which Man lives and carries out his different functions.
- Networks, or the natural and man-made systems which facilitate the functioning of the settlement, as for example roads, water supply, electricity, etc.

The basic difference between Shells and Networks lies in the fact that Shells provide cover for functions while Networks constitute them. We can have Shells covering Networks; we can have a geodesic dome covering an airfield, which is a part of an air-transportation network, as a bridge is part of a road network.

When speaking of Nature, I used the word 'presently' because at the beginning of the evolution of human settlements, and even, in a few cases, today, Nature itself has provided not only the foundation but also the full container, as occurs in periods during the past when men live in caves. Even today certain functions are carried out deep inside the Earth. For obvious reasons the present study deals only with man-made settlements.

The definition of the settlement as consisting of two categories of elements is well expressed in certain languages which distinguish between the Shells and their contents. In Greek, for example, we have the 'polis' and the 'demos'. In Latin we have 'urbs' and 'civitas'. In many other languages these terms are confused, and very often the term meaning 'shell' is also used to describe the contents. In English a

12

the elements of human settlements

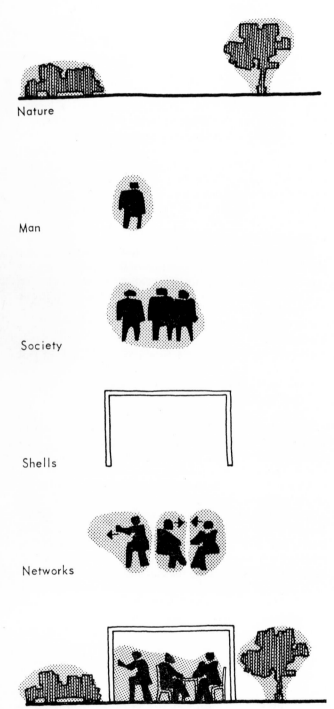

Nature

Man

Society

Shells

Networks

human settlements

correct distinction would be between the city and its citizens, or citizenry. Very often, however, the close interrelationship of the two elements causes us to include one term in the other; for example, when we say 'the whole city rose to its feet', we really mean the citizenry, or the contents of the city, and not the Shells.

I think I should mention at this point the fact that some of the popularly used divisions of settlements into their elements are not very helpful. One such division is into place, work, family (Le Play's *lieu, travail, famille*) and another (Patrick Geddes) place, work, *folk*. The fault lies in that the three components are not of the same nature; some are physical components (place, family, *folk*) and others are merely their functions (work). They do not belong in the same dimension, and, therefore, should not be used as subdivisions, with a uniform value, if the subject is to be covered in a systematic way.

The combination of Man, the content, and his container, forms the human settlement, and a balanced combination forms a successful settlement. The interrelationship of the two elements is very close. Man builds the Shells and thus creates the container which holds human activity. Although, technically speaking, the Shells are just a skin covering human functions and human space, this can also be said to express the conditions of the life it encloses. We can, therefore, frequently judge a human settlement by its physical aspects, that is, by its Shells and Networks in the same way a doctor often judges the condition of his patient by his appearance, even if the disease is one that acts internally.

Although in practice the study of human settlements is often limited to either the contents or the container, this is wrong, since the essential nature of human settlements involves both elements, and the proper study of settlements is the study of the interrelationship of these elements. The study of human settlements must not revolve primarily around their elements—these are the objects of study for the different disciplines—but around the relationships between these elements, since it is these relationships which bring the settlement into existence.

Unless we understand the interplay between Nature and Man, Networks and Society, Shells and Nature, and so forth, we cannot understand the human settlement and our conclusions will be as wrong as if we had studied the cardiovascular system of Man without reference to the digestive system and the whole body. It is only the holistic approach to human settlements that can illuminate our subject.

Chronologically speaking, the settlement can be presented as follows: Nature is the container, Man arrives in it, and forms social groups which function as a society (fig. 12). The social group, in its need for protection, finally creates the Shells and then, when it becomes larger and more complex, Networks.

In order to have a proper picture of a settlement we must find the correct spatial relationship between its elements in function. In the case of Man we can contain his functions in a space forming a bubble around him, as Edward Hall has defined in his studies of Proxemics.[1] We will also use bubbles to contain those who serve him (animals and machines). Then we will be able to visualize the Shells which cover this system of bubbles (fig. 13). If the functions take place within an enclosed building, then the Shells will have to take these three-dimensional moving bubbles into consideration and provide the proper space for them. The result will be a building, whose dimensions are defined by the dimensions of Man as related to his functions, and not by Man alone. If the functions take place in an open urban space, the Shells will express their space in three dimensions as a street or a square although we often recognise only two of these dimensions. If a function can be clearly defined, then it can be clearly shaped and limited. If a function does not need a building as a recreation in a park, for example, it can still be spatially defined in the same way.

If we study these relationships in a systematic way we will see that there are many different aspects of an Ekistic subject and its problems (fig. 14). Combining the five elements of human settlements first taken two by two we have ten combinations; by threes we have again ten combinations; by fours we have five, and by fives one combination. So we have a total of twenty-six combinations each defining a different Ekistic relationship of the elements.

To these we must add the relationship of each element to itself as, for example, the relationship of Man to himself—how he manages to isolate himself within the human settlement surrounding him. So by adding these other five combinations to the previous twenty-six, we arrive at a total of thirty-one combinations.

13

Man and some functions

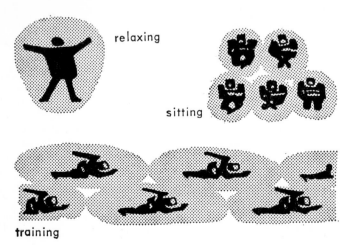

relaxing

sitting

training

14

the five elements of human settlements can be combined in twenty-six ways

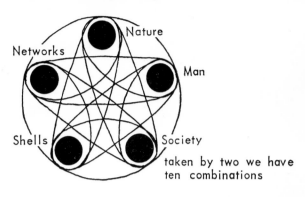

taken by two we have
ten combinations

taken by three we have
ten combinations

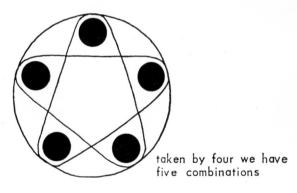

taken by four we have
five combinations

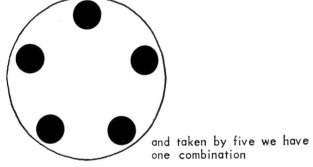

and taken by five we have
one combination

function and structure

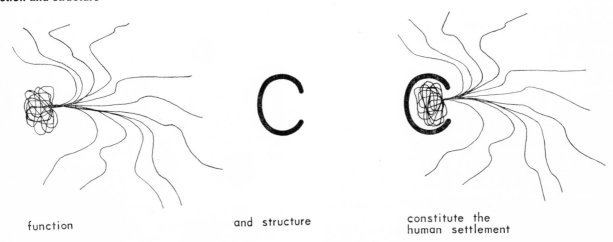

function   and structure   constitute the
human settlement

Aspects of human settlements

One of the gravest mistakes made in the study of human settlements is considering them as consisting of the container only (Nature, Shells and Networks) and thus depriving them of the fourth dimension, time, and of their life which is expressed in functions. In this respect, we are making the same mistake as the medical science, which for centuries had concerned itself with the human body, and studied its structure mainly through anatomy, but overlooked its functioning, which could be studied through physiology, until the time when modern medicine established the coordinated study of functions and structure.

Architecture in the 19th and the beginning of the 20th century overlooked the notion of functions and concentrated on structures and even more on forms. The result was the formalistic impasse which persisted until the movement for modern architecture broke through and set architecture free once again. Characteristically, the Charter of Athens, drawn up by Congrès Internationaux d'Architecture Moderne in 1933, introduces the four functions—dwelling, recreation, work and transportation)[2], as one of its basic points. Although the classification of transportation as a function similar to the others is wrong (see p. 27), the emphasis on functions is the right one and has helped in a proper understanding of architecture.

The only way of understanding the human settlements properly is by looking at their different aspects separately and then by studying their interconnections in forming a whole. To achieve this we have to separate function from structure since even though we start out with functions, which are expressed by structures, we gradually find ourselves with structures which have created so many commitments that they necessarily define the functions. In time we cannot separate one from the other and become confused. Winston Churchill expressed it very well when he said 'We shape our buildings and they shape us'.[3]

In actual life we *are* interested in functions, in living, working, running, walking; but these are not easily expressed physically; therefore, we tend to think of a settlement in terms of its Shells, even though what really matters are the men who live in it or use it in another way. Only when we are able to see the paths of Man instead of the Shells will we have a picture of his settlement which approaches reality (fig. 15). Paul Valéry wrote once, 'I think now of the trace made by man in the small space where he moves every day'.[4] It would be very important for us if we tried to look at these traces instead of just the walls and roads (fig. 16).

It is also wrong to present the function by a static picture of the elements which constitute it. In the same way in which it is wrong to mistake the Shells for the function. To speak of a density of 10,000 persons per hectare (4000 persons per acre) in a public square is not enough. We cannot form a judgement, unless we make clear whether this square is used for political gatherings—in which case the density is normal—or for open air shopping—when it is too high. The correct way of speaking about this density is by illustrating the function of the people; this can be done successfully if we present the human movements over a certain period of time, of seconds, minutes or hours, depending on the situation (fig. 17).

Only a correct analysis of the functions explains a settlement, as I will illustrate by one example. The small Greek town of Ermioni has an excellent harbour, but most of the local boats are kept outside it, and because of the rough sea are drawn up onto the sand. This seems unreasonable until we learn that the harbour is very good for visiting boats, but not satisfactory for the local fishermen who have to go out daily and do not want to have to sail around the peninsula. The

16

function and structure

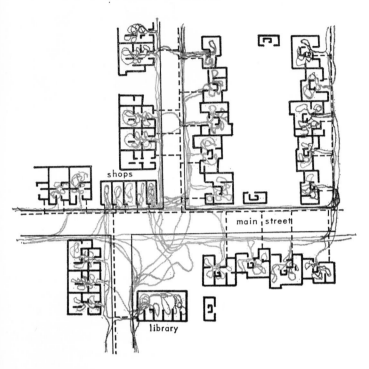

────── pedestrian movement
---- power, water and other networks

shops

main street

library

town is built in such a way as to serve those who are connected with the harbour as well as the local fishermen (fig. 18).

Human settlements and their parts

There is also some confusion about the extension of human settlements. If we assume the Shells to be the entire settlement, we are not only making the mistake of limiting the settlement to one of its elements, but we are limiting it geographically, as well, and are losing perspective and possibly being misled in our conclusions. The result of this limitation is confusion concerning the concept of the geographic extension of a human settlement. Is a human settlement only the built-up space created by Man for his uses? Is it only the covered space? If so, a house is a settlement and its garden is not, or the house and the garden are a settlement, but the part beyond the garden walls is not. And even assuming that all these and the streets as well belong to the settlement, can we also say that a park within the city is a part of it? If so, can we extend the boundaries of the settlement into the open countryside? Is a natural park part of a settlement?

In order to handle such problems, we must go back to the elements of human settlements. If we remember that these include Man and Society and their action, as well as the container within which this action is performed, we can conclude that all the space, natural or man-made, used by Man, is a part of the settlement. Actually, even a natural park, if it is to be visited by Man, must have roads, or at least paths, following the easiest line of connection, or the most interesting route. Thus, the space of a settlement accommodates all functions of Man, and can be recognised by his imprints on Nature.

We can then draw the general conclusion that the entire space inhabited by Man is a part of the human settlement. This is actually the entire 'Ecumeni' (in Greek Οἰκουμένη), the settled part of the Earth. Such a definition leaves only small parts of the Earth, and perhaps in the future no parts at all, without human settlements. But it is the only definition which can have general validity. The settlement of a city differs from the settlement of a village, as does a park from a farm, but the difference lies only in the intensity of settlement or habitation, the degree to which Man leaves his imprint on Nature. This degree helps us to classify human settlements, but does not change their nature as such.

It is true that by studying human settlements we concentrate our attention on those parts of terrestrial space which are more intensively used or developed. These are the built-up areas of the settlements where we have dense expressions of certain functions. This is also why, when we study human settlements or their functions and their interrelationship, we study the lines of transportation that connect them. Their proper study requires the analysis of their relationship with the surrounding space. A village, for example, can never be understood, if it is not seen as the nodal point of a functioning community which may cover forests and fields or sea and lakes. Certainly, people, when preparing the plan of a village, tend to present the areas of intense use, the built-up area, or perhaps a park, much more than the cultivated area, especially if it contains no special features, such as roads, or is very uniform, a vast olive grove, for example, or a vast wheat field. Plans tend to concentrate on the denser physical expression of the use of space. This does not mean, however, that the settlement can disregard its connection with the surrounding space. When, for example, we have a field of corn and we draw in the paths leading to it, or the canals and the system of irrigation, this does not mean that we are concerned merely with paths or canals—it means that we are concerned with the total interrelation and we are expressing this concern by studying each of the special elements in space. We need to remember that in building a house, the architect has studied the use of the entire space of the dwelling, even though his plan may show only the walls enclosing blank rooms. Similarly, the town-planner has studied the entire space of a city, even though his plan may show only roads or building blocks.

On whatever scale we examine a human settlement, be it

25

17

function and density

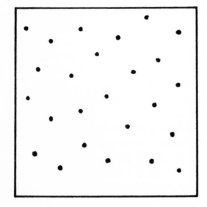

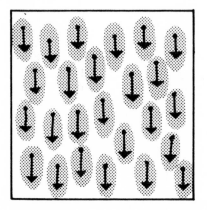
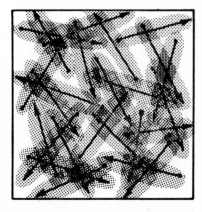

density alone
is not enough

but connected with functions shows that it is
normal for gathering but not for shopping because
in the second case the movements conflict

18

Ermioni

a city with boats outside the harbour

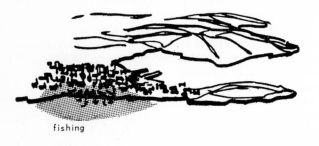

fishing

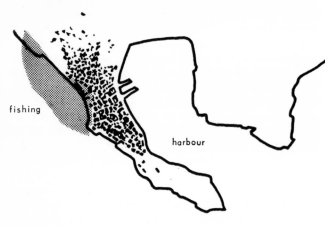

fishing

harbour

because it has two functions served by
both sides of the peninsula

a small house, a village, a minor city or a major region containing a metropolis and other cities, we will discover that the entire area constitutes a human settlement. There are a few exceptions, in major regions of the world such as the Polar Zones, or the Amazon jungle, or deserts where men cannot possibly dwell. There are also some minor regions which are not habitable, and thus do not belong to the category of human settlements. All others are by nature human settlements of different categories developed to varying degrees in accordance with their peculiar intensity of use (fig. 19). At the same time, though, we must remember that if town-planners are not concerned with the division of fields or the canals, other professions are, and in several countries they speak of settlements when new farm land is being subdivided.

Although the anatomy of human settlements will be presented more extensively in the chapter 'Ekistic Analysis', it is necessary to deal at this point with their basic parts and establish a terminology which will help the reader to avoid confusion resulting from the use of many terms in different ways. I use this opportunity to emphasise the fact that one of the basic weaknesses of our field is that it does not have an overall accepted terminology. For those who may find this unimportant I would like to mention the words of the doctor and teacher Ernest Southard as quoted by another doctor and psychiatrist, Karl Menninger: 'Perhaps I believe that the world can get forward most by clearer definition of fundamentals. Accordingly, I propose to stick to tasks of nomenclature and terminology, unpopular and ridicule provoking though they may be'.[5]

19

the nature of human settlements

grid 200 x 200m

a. in a farm the whole area is a human settlement

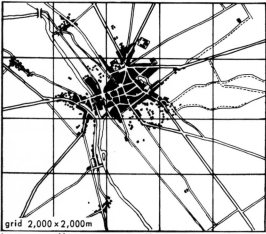

grid 2,000 x 2,000m

b. in a village or a small city the whole area is a human settlement

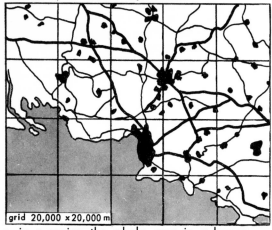

grid 20,000 x 20,000 m

c. in a region the whole area is a human settlement

Composite human settlements of all sizes consist of four categories of basic parts as shown in fig. 20. They are:

o the homogeneous,
o the central,
o the circulatory,
o the special.

I speak of composite human settlements, consisting of more than one house, because single houses need not necessarily have a central part and separate special parts.

These parts may change when the scale is different, but they are always present. For example, if we look at a village, we can recognise the following characteristic parts: The homogeneous parts, consisting of the fields; the central parts, or built-up village; the circulatory parts, consisting of roads and paths within the fields; and the special parts, i.e., a monastery contained within the homogeneous part. If we look, however, at the central or built-up part of the village, we again recognise a homogeneous part, consisting of the houses, a central one, with the church and shops, a circulatory one, with the streets, and a special part, which might contain a school building (fig. 20).

That this fundamental division of composite settlements into parts has not been universally recognised is the cause of much confusion. An instance of this has already been mentioned in the case of the Charter of Athens, where transportation is considered a function equal to dwelling, recreation and work, when it is a part of a settlement situated within its space serving the other functions.

Each part of a settlement can be again subdivided into others until we are left with the smallest unit, the room which necessarily consists of at least two parts, the homogeneous and the circulatory, and sometimes of special parts, certain pieces of furniture, for example, and more seldom of a central part.

On the basis of the previous explanations we are now able to recognise the fact that a settlement consists, not only of a built-up part, but also of the homogeneous and circulatory parts surrounding it. If we take into consideration all parts of a settlement, then we have the overall settlement or whole settlement. If, on the other hand, we take into consideration only the central part of the overall settlement then we are dealing with the built-up settlement consisting of densely built Shells and Networks. This distinction between an overall settlement and a built-up settlement is a basic one, and to disregard it, as we often do, and consider the part to be the whole, is to commit a grave mistake.

Ekistic units

The recognition that the wide range of human settlements can contain units as small as a room or as large as major parts of the Earth forces us to look into the problem of dimensions.

Since settlements consist of several elements, we can define

27

20

parts of human settlements

any settlement
consists of:

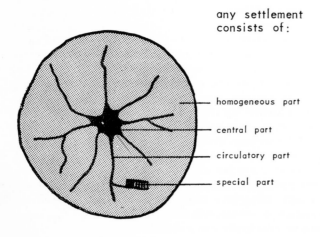

— homogeneous part

— central part

— circulatory part

— special part

a village consists
of:

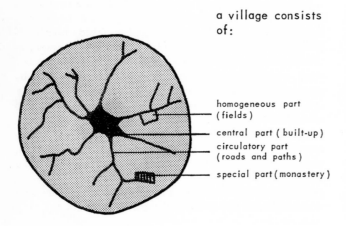

— homogeneous part
(fields)

— central part (built-up)

— circulatory part
(roads and paths)

— special part (monastery)

the built-up area
of the village
consists again of:

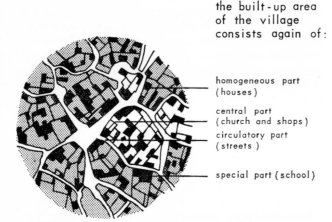

— homogeneous part
(houses)

— central part
(church and shops)

— circulatory part
(streets)

— special part (school)

their dimensions by defining the dimensions of their elements. If we consider the two elements, Man and Society, we can define the size of the settlement by the number of people living in it. Thus, we may have settlements ranging from the one-man settlement, which may be either part of a major settlement or an isolated one (for example, a light-house with one operator or a remote railway station with one employee), to settlements of tens, hundreds, thousands, millions and, lately, even tens of millions of people.

If we turn to the element of Nature, we can define the size of the settlement by the extent of the space which is covered either by the whole settlement, or by the intensely developed part of it, or by its built-up part only. This distinction may also serve in the case of Networks. Finally, if we turn to the element of the Shells we can study physical dimensions, which can be expressed either in areas or in volume. So, in the case of all the elements, we have touched upon the space covered by settlements.

If we now turn to the activity and the functions of a settlement we can also define it by way of its dimensions. For example, a settlement can show a small or large degree of economic activity—it can be the centre of a certain degree of productive activity, or an administrative centre of a certain degree of administrative importance, etc.

In this study we are dealing with terrestrial space in connection with human settlements, although we may soon have to deal with extra-terrestrial space as well. The terrestrial space used by Man is three-dimensional space in which height and depth add the third dimension, not as an auxiliary, but as an indispensable component of the space. If, however, we limited the dimensions of human settlements to three, we would be making a great mistake, for their space is not simply three-dimensional. Since human settlements cannot be said to exist without their functions and without people, they cannot be separated from the fourth dimension, that of time. Deprived of this, they lack the dynamic element of motion and evolution. In the absence of time, we are incapable of understanding the nature of human settlements. It is easy to explain why this fourth dimension is indispensable to the study of human settlements. When we spoke of Man's functions as an essential aspect of human settlements, recognising that they are the aspect relating Man (the content) to the Shells (the container), we necessarily introduced the concept of time, for Man needs time in order to live, and his functions require time in order to take place. Therefore, human settlements consist of and require four dimensions to be properly understood (fig. 21).

In practice we see human settlements of all sizes, ranging from a room to cities of tens of millions of people. But if we try to find out where it is that big settlements end (the whole settlement, not just the built-up part), we are at a loss. What are the financial boundaries of London, or the political boundaries of Washington or Moscow? There are none for their influence covers the Earth.

21

human settlements consist of and require four dimensions in order to be properly understood

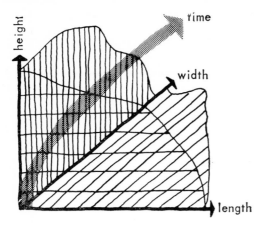

When we try to classify the settlements according to their dimensions, we will soon realise that they do not belong to easily definable categories of sizes but spread over the whole spectrum of possible sizes. Any such division will, therefore, have to be somewhat arbitrary, but it must also be an inherently satisfying and reasonable one.

Such a division has been worked out on the basis of empirical experience and is presented in a logarithmic scale. ...mallest unit of measurement is Man. He does not form a ...ment in himself since he is one of its elements, but he ...have a shell (his clothing is the smallest possible human ...and personal furniture plays the same role) and he is the ...and indispensable unit of measurement. The second ...est unit is a normal room. From this we go to a dwelling, a group of several dwellings, a small neighbourhood, a neighbourhood, a small town, a town, a city, a metropolis, a conurbation, a megalopolis, an urban region, an urbanised continent, until, finally, we reach the largest conceivable space for a settlement, which is the whole Earth.

This *Ekistic Logarithmic Scale* (ELS) can be presented geographically in several ways as shown in fig. 22. One way is on the basis of the areas covered by the different units, in this case it is the Area ELS or, if two-dimensional, the ELS Area Grid. Another way is on the basis of the number of people corresponding to each unit; in this case it is the Population ELS or the ELS Population Grid.

These two presentations of the scale show that the basic relationship of most of the consecutive units is in approximation to the ratio of 1 : 7. Accordingly we are led to the creation of a typical ELS for documentation purposes, the Documentation ELS, and the corresponding ELS Documentation Grid where all units are equal and represent the logarithms of a series with a base of 7. This scale has proved very useful in practice.

The ELS consist of 15 Ekistic units ranging from Man to Ecumenopolis and these units in turn belong to four basic groups (fig. 23):
- minor Shells, or elementary units (man, room, house);
- micro-settlements, the units smaller than, or as small as, the traditional town where people used to and still do achieve interconnection by walking;
- meso-settlements, between the traditional town and the conurbation within which one can commute daily;
- macro-settlements, whose largest possible expression is the Ecumenopolis.

The ELS can be used as a basis for the measurement and classification of many dimensions in human settlements. The same scale could also be used for those disciplines and sciences concerned with problems of terrestrial space, such as geography and regional science (fig. 23).

If we now combine a logarithmic scale for measuring space, in which the surface of the settlement is presented on one plane and a corresponding logarithmic scale of heights on another, ranging from one room to several hundred floors, we arrive at a form of presentation which can give a complete picture of the division of terrestrial Ekistic space in physical dimensions. But then we must combine this with the fourth dimension, time, to present the concept of all functions in human settlements in a single diagram (fig. 24).

Once we have an Ekistic Logarithmic Scale of terrestrial space on one side, and the various elements of human settlements on the other, we can combine them to form two-dimensional scales. Thus, by having, on the ELS, the dimensions of settlements on the one axis and the number of humans on the other, we can compare numbers of people in space. If we add to the same scale the scale of automobile transportation we can compare density of functions within space. In the same way, we can compare automobiles with population in order to define the interrelationship of people to them in every part of the scale, and so forth (fig. 25).

On the basis of experience, I propose a series of scales according to Ekistic units which we will call *Physical Ekistic Scales*. The resulting chart shows that for every Ekistic unit there is a corresponding physical scale by which we can best study the subject matter. Experience has shown, however, that in order to carry out these studies successfully, we must use several related scales. For example the study of a room requires a scale of 1 : 20, but it must also be studied at 1 : 50, in order to see it in connection with other rooms, and, if possible, at 1 : 100, in order to show its connection with larger groupings of rooms, whether these are within the same house or in a group of houses and apartments; and for similar reasons, also in a scale of 1 : 10, and perhaps 1 : 5 (fig. 26). Similarly, a typical town should be studied on 1 : 5,000 scale, but the correct implementation of the study will also require the scales 1 : 1,000 and 1 : 500, for detailed drawings, and possibly 1 : 10,000 and even up to 1 : 50,000 to show the relationships of this unit to the surrounding terrestrial space.

29

Ekistic Logarithmic Scales (graphic interpretation)

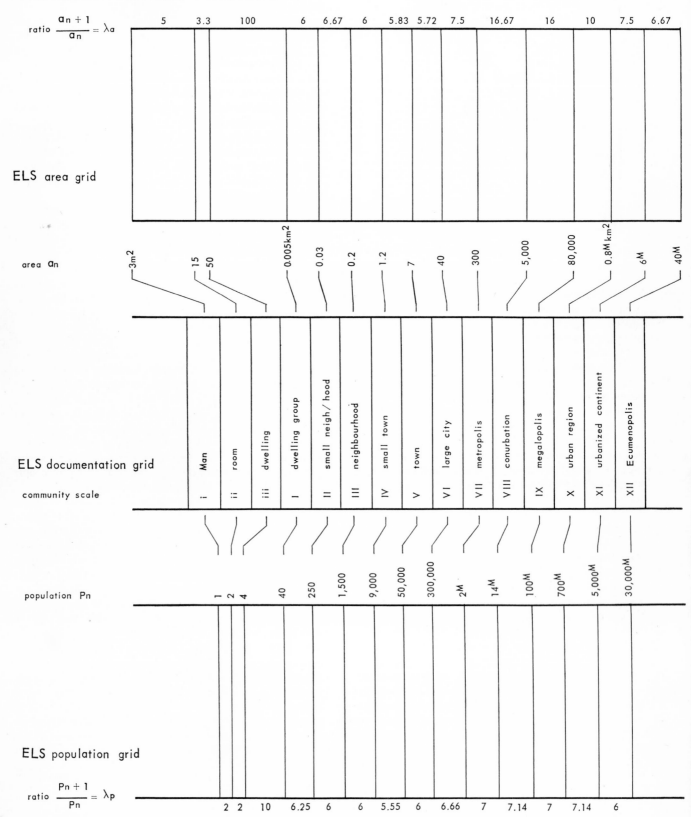

23

Ekistic Logarithmic Scale of terrestrial space and Ekistic units

settlements	elementary units of human settlements			communities of composite human settlements												
	micro - shells			micro - settlements				meso - settlements				macro - settlements			
	micro-micro-space			micro-space				meso-space				macro-space			
	micro-micro-scale			micro-scale				meso-scale				macro-scale			
community scale	i	ii	iii	I	II	III	IV	V	VI	VII	VIII	IX	X	XI	XII
level scale	1	2	3	4	5	6	7	8	9	10	11	12	13	14	15

ELS documentation grid

Man · room · dwelling · dwelling group · small neigh/hood · neighbourhood · small town · town · large city · metropolis · conurbation · megalopolis · urban region · urban continent · Ecumenopolis

24

terrestrial space

expressed in a three dimensional Ekistic Logarithmic Scale

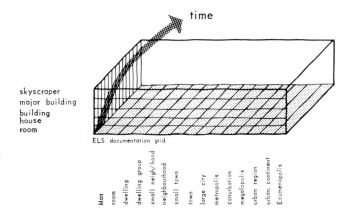

skyscraper
major building
building
house
room

ELS documentation grid

Man · room · dwelling · dwelling group · small neigh/hood · neighbourhood · small town · town · large city · metropolis · conurbation · megalopolis · urban region · urban. continent · Ecumenopolis

The most suitable physical scales for each Ekistic unit, as well as a suitable range of scales are shown in fig. 26. Without such charts the studies undertaken may easily slip out of focus, either by overlooking the most appropriate physical scale at which a phenomenon should be studied, or by overlooking the necessity of using related major and minor scales to incorporate the Ekistic unit under study into the terrestrial space around it.

An analysis of all the physical scales necessary to present all Ekistic units from Man to Ecumenopolis shows that we need a total of 24 scales, ranging from 1 : 1 to 1 : 50,000,000. Since Ekistic space can be subdivided into 15 Ekistic units, we ask ourselves why the range between the scales 1 : 1 and 1 : 50,000,000 should not be covered by 15 rather than by 24 scales, in which case the ratio between consecutive scales would be closer to 1 : 2·64, that is $\sqrt{7}$, rather than 1 : 2 and 1 : 2·5 which is what we have now. But this would have meant using scales which would be impractical since they would not be based on the decimal system which has many other advantages. Therefore, the 24 scales of 1 : 1 to 1 : 50,000,000 appear, upon final analysis, to be the most practical ones and the ones corresponding to most of the scales now in use. The above scales were used for the illustrations of the present study, but, since the plans had to be reduced to fit the page size, they have been presented graphically so that the reduction would not decrease the readability of the subject.

CLASSIFICATION AND ORDER

Need of classification

Human settlements are so numerous and so different from each other that any attempt to study or understand them is meaningless unless we classify them in an orderly way. Certainly this has been generally understood, but the classifications now in existence have three basic deficiencies. First, they differ from profession to profession; geography, economics and town-planning, for example, each classify settlements in radically different ways. Second, they do not cover the spectrum of settlements; the smaller and the largest units especially being overlooked. When we speak of 'town', 'city', and 'metropolis', we can be reasonably sure that the meaning of these words will be understood, although several countries have different definitions even for these units, but when we come to 'neighbourhood', or 'megalopolis', the meaning is not the same for everybody. Furthermore, several units of the spectrum are not covered by any name at all.

The third deficiency is that several basic methods of classification that have proved very useful for other disciplines, have not been used at all for human settlements. As an example I mention the complete absence of classifications based on dynamic morphology. When, ten years ago, I discussed the basic difference between static and dynamic settlements, which concept has always been indispensable in my work on cities, it was thought that I was introducing a new 'fashion' to our subject. It is quite characteristic that even today most of the studies in physical planning present human settlements classified by their structure, with the greatest emphasis laid on their physical design, and with distinctions between the grid-iron and other patterns. All this at a time when not a single major settlement can conceivably belong to such a simple category.

But other sciences have made great progress in this field.

25

phenomena interpreted on Ekistic Logarithmic Grids

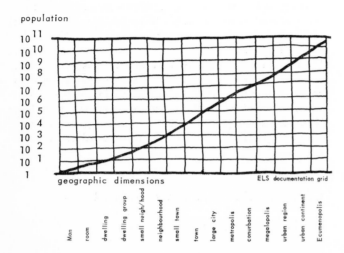

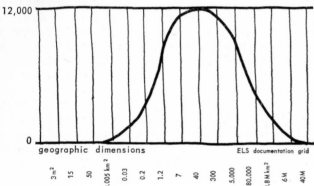

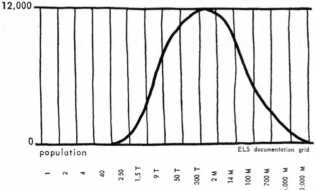

Mathematics certainly came first and then, especially after the beginning of the scientific revolution in the seventeenth century, one science after another proceeded on the same path making at first only attempts at systematic classification, then new proposals, new efforts, then use of these methods, until gradually, by trial and error, a system emerged as the most useful one. There may be many acceptable systems but what is important is to find the more practical ones, those which can help us to understand the subject matter, its laws and its evolution.

J. Bronowski, in *The Common Sense of Science* gives an excellent description of the process of classification and the search for order and its importance when he speaks of the contribution of Linnaeus in botany.

'The best example of the new order which was being discovered in the non-mathematical sciences is botany. It remains to this day the creation of a number of observers, among them the Swedish naturalist Linnaeus, who set out in the eighteenth century the system of classification by species and families on which it still rests. What kind of order was Linnaeus looking for? Why did his order seem so plainly more reasonable than, say, a grading of flowers by their colours?

This is the most difficult question in science. The notion of *order* cannot be defined on any ground except its success. It cannot be put into a science in advance at all. It is not obviously silly to classify flowers by their colours; after all, the bluer flowers do tend to be associated with colder climates and greater heights. There is nothing wrong with the system, in advance. It simply does not work as conveniently and as instructively as Linnaeus's classification by family likenesses.

Order is the selection of one set of appearances rather than another because it gives a better sense of the reality behind the appearances. Science is an orderly language for describing some events and predicting others like them. The order is a selection of appearances. And any selection itself implies and imposes, an interpretation'.[6]

It is J. Bronowski whom I will quote once again to show the roads that proper classification opened towards the understanding of evolution.

'The geologists and the fossilhunters had been tapping away for a hundred years before they pieced together the single story of the earth's crust. The story astonished and alarmed the religious world of the early nineteenth century. Fifty years later the careful botanical and animal observations fell into place as suddenly and as uncomfortably. Linnaeus had classified these observations by what I have loosely called family likenesses. Now Darwin gave ground for the view that they were literally family likenesses; the creatures have them in common because they have a common ancestry—they come from the same family. The likenesses were no longer merely a method of classification, they were suddenly seen as the living footprints of their historic causes'.[7]

And later: 'Science begins with the belief that the world is orderly or better, that it can be made orderly by human

26

physical scales

the range of most suitable scales for each Ekistic unit

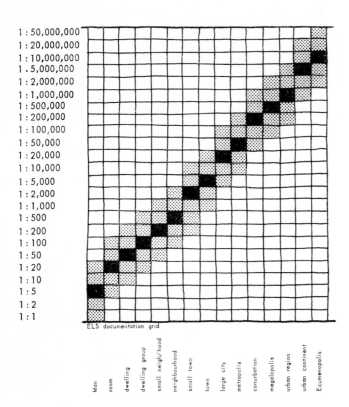

1 : 50,000,000	
1 : 20,000,000	
1 : 10,000,000	
1 : 5,000,000	
1 : 2,000,000	
1 : 1,000,000	
1 : 500,000	
1 : 200,000	
1 : 100,000	
1 : 50,000	
1 : 20,000	
1 : 10,000	
1 : 5,000	
1 : 2,000	
1 : 1,000	
1 : 500	
1 : 200	
1 : 100	
1 : 50	
1 : 20	
1 : 10	
1 : 5	
1 : 2	
1 : 1	

ELS documentation grid

Man, room, dwelling, dwelling group, small neigh/hood, neighbourhood, small town, town, large city, metropolis, conurbation, megalopolis, urban region, urban continent, Ecumenopolis

arrangement. This arrangement consists of putting things in groups, not of identical things, but of things which seem to be or behave alike. I say behave alike because the activity of ordering is not carried out, as Adam is said to have named the creatures, merely by sitting still and calling out likely words. It is an experimental activity of trial and error. We must from the outset underline its empirical nature, because there is no test for what is like and what is unlike except an empirical one: that the arrangement of things in these groups chimes and fits with the kind of world, the kind of life which we act out'.[8] All fields of knowledge which gradually become scientific pass through a stage of effort towards a systematic classification in spite of the resistance that is sometimes made to this effort. A recent example from the field of psychiatry is given by Karl Menninger in 'The Urge to Classify', a chapter of his book, *The Vital Balance*.[9] It is revealing to those who feel the need for involvement in this effort. It is imperative that we classify human settlements; for without a successful classification scientific progress in this field is impossible.

Types of classification

There are many possible methods for classifying human settlements. Most of them correspond to methods now in use, sometimes very successfully, by other sciences. Some basic types of classification are indicated here by categories. What we should keep in mind is that we may need even more in the future.

One category is based on sizes which can be measured by way of the sizes of the five elements and their combinations. Such is the classification by numbers of people, or by the geographic extent of the area covered, or by combinations of these sizes, like the combination of numbers and areas expressed by densities.

A second category is based on the location of the settlements—whether they are in plains or on mountains, near the sea coast or the rivers, in deserts or forests, etc.

A third category depends on relationships between settlements within space, and it can be either a hierarchical, or a non-hierarchical one. A railway station may supply several settlements with products (these settlements are dependent on it), but it may be smaller or larger than the settlements served by it.

A related category is that based on physical forms; it has been used more than any other, and is still being used. But it misleads those relying on it if they forget that the form is only the expression of content, function and structure, all of which are much more important than the form itself.

We can also have classifications based on the five elements of human settlements, Nature, Man, Society, Shells and Networks, and their subdivisions.

Other categories are based on functions which are very important to an understanding of the meaning and the role of settlements. They reveal the nature, the specialisation and the *raison d'être* of the settlements. They can be based on activity (economic, social, for example), their performance, or their special role (as dormitories, old-age residences, better for child-rearing, and so forth).

The time dimension expressed in the age of settlements, their place in the continuum—past, present, future—their relative static or dynamic character, the whole process of their growth, provides the basis for yet other categories of classification. Similar to the previous categories are those based on phases of evolution ranging from nomadic to agricultural.

There are classifications based on the degree of society's conscious involvement in the settlement's creation—natural and planned settlements. These have been used quite often but not in a way that reveals causal mechanisms or leads to an understanding of the process of development.

The ability of society to act simply in a descriptive or prescriptive way can provide the basis for other categories of classifications. Still others can be based on the institutions, legislative, administrative, and so forth, which society has created for settlements. In the same way we can base

E

classifications on all or some of the factors which play an important role in the life of settlements—the labour force of the building industry, the building materials, the financing of the construction of Shells or Networks, etc. Combinations of several methods can lead to even more elaborate and more difficult classifications. Such a one is a classification by functions, their relationship to sizes, structures and forms.

Finally, we reach the point of asking ourselves which classification is of the greatest importance. This cannot be answered until we define the goals of settlements, and in this I cannot do better than remember what Aristotle said about the goal of a city being to make its citizens happy and safe. This alone can be our ultimate goal and by way of it we can define the criteria according to which we can measure the quality of the settlements. The quality of our way of life, measured in terms of happiness and safety, is the basis for a classification of settlements in accordance with the value they have for Man. Even if this is very difficult for us to achieve, we have to attempt it.

Some basic classifications

In order to illustrate the meaning and the importance of the different kinds of possible classifications, I will present some basic ones and some phenomena related to them.

○ *by Ekistic units*

A classification by Ekistic units is not only fundamental but also practical, since settlements can be well defined subjects, being, more often than not, geographically distinct units. If, however, we want to proceed on the basis of this method, and study not only the units of settlements, but their subdivisions, the task is not easy at all. However, in spite of complications, it is of great importance. In order to make it possible to select large or small units, major or minor settlements, the whole or parts of settlements, we can use the term *Ekistic units*, by which we mean either distinctly separated settlements or relatively homogeneous parts of settlements.

Such a division can usefully be based on the Ekistic Logarithmic Scale, comprising the previously described Ekistic units. A practical presentation of the phenomena related to such a division can be shown on a matrix which we have previously called the Ekistic Grid whose horizontal dimension is the basic logarithmic scale of Ekistic units. If the phenomena to be studied are the Ekistic units with no reference to other divisions of the material, the matrix can represent the entire territory covered by human settlements. In this case the vertical dimension can represent the different degrees of the special phenomena which are studied, either in absolute figures or as percentages of the whole (fig. 27).

On the basis of such a classification, we can speak of settlements and of Ekistics of various scales. Micro-space

classification by Ekistic units and corresponding knowledge

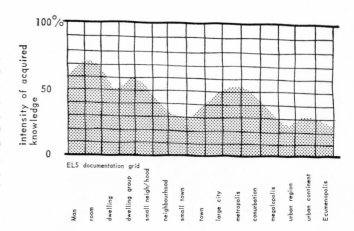

comprises Man, the room, the dwelling, the dwelling group, the small neighbourhood, and the neighbourhood. In many respects, it coincides with architectural space, although it goes beyond what is commonly considered as such. Ekistics of the middle scale is the next category, consisting of the small town, the town and the large city. This again coincides in many respects with town planning, city planning or urbanism. Finally, we have Ekistics of the macro-scale which begins with regional planning and ends with continental or terrestrial planning.

The division into the Ekistic units is no longer as clear as it was in the past. In our days cities have occasionally spread across the boundaries of regions and merged with one another into megalopolitan areas. Such expansion has obscured the original city boundaries and made the distinction of the Ekistic units much more difficult. This, however, does not mean that these categories of Ekistic units, representing demographic and geographic dimensions which correspond to certain functions, do not exist. It simply means that the effort to find a proper division for the material is more difficult than in the past when small cities had distinct physical limits. This is one of the tasks of Ekistics.

○ *by Ekistic elements*

Another important classification is by the five Ekistic elements, Nature, Man, Society, Shells and Networks. To achieve such a classification all elements must be taken into consideration. Man is a visual animal and is apt to give greater consideration to what he can see clearly. This is one of the reasons why, although many people understand that settlements consist of five elements, they are eager to speak only about what can be clearly seen—the physical aspects of the settlements. There can be no question of the importance of Nature and the Shells, nor of the need to handle many phenomena of the human settlements by designing their physical elements. However, this is no reason to confine our interest and attention to the Shells. We must keep in mind that the Shells are only the outward manifestation of the other elements of the settlement. Once Rodin was asked how he managed to handle the surface of his statues so well and he answered, 'The surface? I do not know; I always work inside the marble'.[10] This is how we must look at the form, shape and appearance of human settlements. We must recognise the Shells as the membrane that covers the real life of the settlement, the life of the people, their society and their functions. We must understand that we have to deal with phenomena consisting of five elements, although we can see only one of them.

Each of these elements can be subdivided once more—for example, the element of Nature can be subdivided into:
○ water
○ climate
○ geology
○ geomorphology
○ flora
○ fauna, etc.
and the Shells can be subdivided into:
○ residential buildings
○ public buildings
○ educational buildings
○ building techniques
○ physical layout, etc.

The following systematic subdivision of knowledge related to the five elements is now being used by the documentation centre of the Athens Center of Ekistics and has proved very useful even though it may still need further development on the basis of continued experience.

EKISTIC ELEMENTS

Nature

1. Geologic resources
2. Topographical resources
3. Soil resources
4. Water resources
5. Plant life
6. Animal life
7. Climate

Man

1. Biological needs
   (space, air, temperature, etc.)

2. Sensation and perception
   (the 'five senses')
3. Emotional needs
   (human relations, security, beauty, etc.)
4. Moral values

Society

1. Population composition and density
2. Social stratification
3. Cultural patterns
4. Economic development
5. Education
6. Health and Welfare
7. Law and Administration

Shells

1. Housing
2. Community services
   (schools, hospitals, etc.)
3. Shopping centres and markets
4. Recreational facilities
   (theatre, museum, stadium, etc.)
5. Civic and Business Centres
   (town hall, law-courts, etc.)
6. Industry
7. Transportation centres

Networks

1. Water supply systems
2. Power supply systems
3. Transportation systems
   (water, road, rail, air)
4. Communication systems
   (telephone, radio, TV, etc.)
5. Sewerage and drainage
6. Physical layout (Ekistic plan).

Such a classification by elements is fairly simple, and in many respects necessary, but it can be dangerous if it misleads us into looking at the settlement solely on the basis of such a division. The danger becomes even greater if we consider that experts coming from various fields of knowledge will be inclined to look mainly into the elements of their interest. Although people speak about the whole settlement, the discipline they represent becomes quite apparent from the element with which they deal. Social scientists are concerned with Man and Society, engineers are usually occupied with certain Networks, such as roads, geographers are more interested in Nature, and architects and physical planners deal mostly with the Shells. Yet settlements consist of all these elements, and Ekistics must study them simultaneously to find

28

classification by elements combined with Ekistic units

a. elements and units of interest

b. several elements in detail and units of interest

their interrelationship. This is why the classification of the settlements and Ekistic subject matter by elements should not be used unless we can focus our attention on the whole settlement, and this can be achieved more easily if we properly coordinate this classification with the more basic one by Ekistic units.

How can we separate Man from the society he lives in, be it a family or a nation? How can we look into the question of a house without taking into consideration its relation to the man who lives in it and the family he lives with? This is why we must use a two-dimensional grid, in which the vertical units can always help us to understand the meaning of the horizontal ones (fig. 28).

On this two-dimensional grid, we can present the knowledge already acquired through the disciplines gradually merging into Ekistics. One value of such charts is to show that our knowledge of the different elements varies enormously, particularly among the Ekistic units. I will give some examples. If we consider the shells of human settlements, we find that we know much about their small units, the single dwelling and the architecture of a single house or of a group of such dwellings. When, however, we move into the realm of shells in a big city or region, we realise that we know much less; in fact, we realise that we are only beginning to learn. If, on the other hand, we consider Nature, we find that we know more about the sub-soil and the surface of the soil, than we do about climate, air and water.

If we consider some of the aspects of man-in-society, we

find that once again we know more about the minor Ekistic units. In production, we know more about small and middle scale units, and in transportation more about larger rather than smaller units. On the other hand, we have studied leisure mostly with regard to the small Ekistic units. For special functions such as education, religion and defence, we may know more about some units and less about others. We know more about the problems of Man and Society in minor units than in major ones, since they have only now started participating in the life of major Ekistic units which in turn have only lately been formed. How can we be expected to know anything about the behaviour of Man or Society in a megalopolis, when it is now taking shape for the first time? By these methods we can first estimate our knowledge of the problem we are dealing with, then attack the sectors we have missed and gradually reach the point of insight into the real issues that should be our concern.

○ *by Ekistic functions*

This is a very important classification, since our basic interest in a settlement lies in the functions that it carries out, but it can be a misleading one since there are always many functions being carried out in every settlement, even in every small unit of a settlement. Such functions may be of primary importance, as is living, sleeping, producing, or of auxiliary importance, as is moving from one place to another.

29

classification by evolutionary phases combined with Ekistic units

nomadic settlements

agricultural settlements

urban - agricultural settlements

towns and cities

metropolis

ELS documentation grid

Man / room / dwelling / dwelling group / small neigh/hood / neighbourhood / small town / town / large city / metropolis / conurbation / megalopolis / urban region / urban continent / Ecumenopolis

Classifying settlements as industrial or commercial, for example, is difficult. It is much wiser to speak of percentages of participation of different functions in the activity of the settlement but even this sometimes becomes impossible. How can we separate into functions the space within a dwelling, that is, the space meant for living, the bedroom for example, from the space dedicated to production, the kitchen, or the study? Even if we wish to and are able to separate rooms by functions, how can we separate the functions within every single room? How can we disregard the fact that in a single living room we may have residence, recreation, transportation (the movements of Man), and production (studying or knitting)? We should be aware of these difficulties, since they complicate our effort. But they are not enough to deter us from our task, which is to attempt to classify settlements by their functions as well as by other means.

○ *by evolutionary phases*

Such a classification can be based either on a macro-scale of history, by classifying the settlements as nomadic, agricultural, urban, urban-industrial, and so forth, or on special historic micro-scales, by looking into a specific area at a limited period of time. In this case, we may recognise in Africa, for example, the pre-colonial settlements, the first colonial ones (fortresses), the second colonial settlements, the settlements of the period of independence. But we can use this procedure even with minor time units, and classify the settlements by phases of development. Even minor chronological differences between phases, will be physically manifest in the change in the appearance of the Shells. A better understanding of this classification can be achieved if we combine it with the Ekistic units, since we will immediately recognise a basic rule of evolution (fig. 29). The greater the economic activity of a period, the larger the settlements.

○ *by factors and disciplines*

An important classification especially useful in preparing plans of action is by factors which contribute to the creation, maintenance, operation and function of human settlements. Such factors can be money and financing, the organisation of labour, the building industry, land tenure, legislation, etc. It is, therefore, quite useful to be able to classify the whole subject matter by factors as well. This can be successful, provided the basic unit of study, that is the Ekistic unit, is not neglected. Otherwise such a classification may prove misleading.

I shall give one illustration to demonstrate how we can classify our subject matter by factors, and, at the same time incorporate such a classification into the broader one by Ekistic units. Let us assume that a study of the overall economic situation has convinced us that the country in question can afford to and is willing to invest in a proper programme for the renewal of human settlements. This alone unless broken into Ekistic units, will be completely misleading even if we work it out on the basis of national estimates. However, if we take into consideration the Ekistic units, we may well prove that although such action is possible for certain units such as large metropolitan areas, it is difficult in the case of cities, and perhaps impossible or unnecessary in the case of small rural communities and villages. Only when we divide a factor into Ekistic units, can we be sure it has helped us to understand the problem better (fig. 30).

Related classifications are those dealing with the involvement of society, descriptive or prescriptive action, human

30
**classification by factors and disciplines combined
with Ekistic units**

a. factors and Ekistic units

b. disciplines and Ekistic units

institutions, and so forth. Such classifications can be based on disciplines such as economics, social sciences, political and administrative sciences, technical and cultural disciplines, or their subdivisions. This classification is often imperative, for it is frequently necessary to study the subject from the point of view of one discipline, for example, the overall economic point of view. This may be required to incorporate the image of human settlements into the overall view of the economic status of a region or a country, which in turn may be necessary to define an economic policy for development in relation to human settlements. The same is true when it is required of us to define social and educational policies or to take action in such fields as transportation, technology, culture and art. Again, as previously discussed a classification by disciplines can be fruitful and constructive only if the basic classification by Ekistic units is not overlooked (fig. 30).

A system of classification

It has become apparent that the possibilities of classification of our subject matter are many and usually very interesting and promising. This is quite natural if we remind ourselves that other disciplines, dealing with phenomena consisting either of one element or of several, also rely on several types of classifications; however, the fact that it is natural does not mean that our task is made any easier. We have to classify the settlements, and we must use several classifications, but we also have to use a system that will help us make sense out of the totality of possible classifications. This system must involve using as few classifications as possible—those most useful; and it must also provide for using additional ones as required in different cases at each phase of our endeavour.

A prerequisite for the successful implementation of any

from a distance it seems as if the bell tower served as an aesthetic focus point for the country road

however from close up one discovers that the bell tower simply served as a point of reference for the surveyor in aligning the country road.

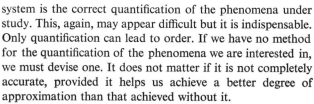

system is the correct quantification of the phenomena under study. This, again, may appear difficult but it is indispensable. Only quantification can lead to order. If we have no method for the quantification of the phenomena we are interested in, we must devise one. It does not matter if it is not completely accurate, provided it helps us achieve a better degree of approximation than that achieved without it.

A second prerequisite for a system of this sort, is that it forms a frame to include all possible ways of studying a human settlement. No part, element or aspect should be overlooked. No statement about human settlements can help us to understand the real issues, rather than some of their external expressions only, unless it is complete. And no system can help us unless it includes, or allows the inclusion of, all dimensions of our subject. For instance, it is pointless to say that the ancient Greeks could build very important monumental buildings if we do not at the same time point out that this was related to the fact that their residences were very modest, and that the most important part of Ekistic investment, at the time, was in monumental buildings and fortifications. Our system should allow classification, not only on the basis of aesthetic quality, but also on the basis of expenditure for different categories of Shells.

It may seem pedantic to require this coverage of the spectrum of phenomena for every Ekistic study. However, I cannot see how a study can otherwise be Ekistic. Regardless of what aspect is overlooked, the study is apt to arrive at the wrong conclusions on that account. This frequently happens. I have seen many studies dealing with human settlements whose conclusions were completely wrong because one or more factors required for the creation of a settlement had been overlooked. For example: I had heard of the aesthetic necessity which led the road builders of southern Spain to

design the roads connecting cities and villages in such a way, that in driving toward them one would always be facing the bell towers of the churches. This I considered quite reasonable until, during a visit to Spain, I noticed that although many of the country roads led towards the bell towers, and one was quite impressed by them when driving through the countryside, these same roads entered the city or the village in a way that did not allow one to see the bell tower any longer. Had these roads been designed this way for aesthetic reasons, these same reasons would have been even more valid within the city itself. However, the fact that the roads did not lead from the entrance of the city directly to the bell tower in a way allowing people to see it continuously meant there was no aesthetic reason underlying the design of the country roads towards the bell towers. It became clear that it was not aesthetics that had led to this solution, but the very practical consideration of the men who designed the roads, who used the bell tower as the most characteristic element to direct the alignment of the country roads (fig. 31).

It may well be argued that the road-builder or the surveyor was unconsciously following an aesthetic rule in selecting the bell tower as a centre for his synthesis. This can certainly be argued, for it is quite possible to be unconsciously influenced by aesthetic rules. However, we know first that this rule did not operate within the city itself, although it would have been natural for it to be valid there as well, and, second, that the apparent reason for which the roads were designed in this way was a practical necessity for an easier topographical survey.

In this case, as in others, if we look at the problem from every point of view, we will discover the real causes which influenced the creation of the settlement. If, however, we look at the settlement from only one point of view, we may ascribe a certain phenomenon to, for instance, aesthetic causes, when its true origin may have been technological.

Of all possible categories of classifications one is basic and must be used, even for the proper employment of the others. This is the classification by Ekistic units. Human settlements are our subject matter and unless we use them as our units there is going to be confusion. This classification is so important that we must begin and end every study with the Ekistic units.

The Ekistic units have been classified as the 15 categories presented in the Ekistic Logarithmic Scale. They can be assembled or divided into different groups. One such grouping is that comprising systems of settlements of a higher order, and single settlements, rural and urban ones:

- o The first and most important of all is the group of Ekistic systems, expressed in Ekistic regions. Having concluded that functions and activities constitute very important characteristics of settlements, we must also realise that they can be understood only on a regional basis. This is so because most settlements play a regional role, and there are very few, limited within their own boundaries. In order, therefore, to have a true picture of an Ekistic unit, we must start with the most important category of all, its Ekistic system.

- o Next we have a wide category of rural settlements. Contained in this, are the agricultural and fishing settlements, and others whose life depends on the collection of natural produce or the cultivation of land. The reason we select them as a second group is because of their fundamental and elementary functions. Actually, the other settlements still rely on them for their existence.

- o Finally, we have the urban settlements, which include all those whose functions are basically non-agricultural and non-rural.

Classification of settlements by Ekistic unit is easier after a proper quantification of the phenomena related to them. This does not present problems for small isolated settlements, but it is very difficult if these settlements are, physically, parts of major complexes; it presents even more problems in the case of growing settlements which absorb others. This is a basic reason why such a study and classification has to begin with Ekistic systems, since they give us insight into the units of different orders.

Experience has shown that after this basic classification of settlements, come three more which are also indispensable. These are the classifications by element, functions and evolutionary forces. The study of the elements shows that we can classify them in several ways. For instance, we may classify them in accordance with the order of their historical creation: Nature, Man, Society, Shells and Networks; or on the basis of the initiative for action: Man, Society and Nature being selected, Shells and Networks created; or again on the basis of initiative: Nature, functions derived partially from Nature, Man attracted by these functions, Society formed by Man,

Shells and Networks created by Man. But even more important are the definitions of the criteria by which we judge situations and phenomena. These criteria will help us judge whether an action related to Nature, for example, will guarantee that the natural elements will retain their present characteristics, or spoil these values without creating new ones.

In considering Man, we must ask ourselves whether an action will make him happier, more secure and more able to develop himself according to his best interests. The same applies when dealing with Society, Networks and Shells. We must make sure that these different elements are in balance with each other, since it is this balance that creates a successful human settlement.

Classification by functions can help us to understand the importance of settlements. For example, functions can define the numbers of men to be attracted, the types of societies to be developed, the selection of the location, and in many respects the Shells.

Classification by evolutionary forces is indispensable since it enables us to understand the real importance the functions have for the life of the settlements. To achieve this we must go as far back as possible and understand the evolutionary trends and their causes; it is only then that we will be able to understand the present and try to foresee the future.

We can now attempt to define the order in which we should take action so as to achieve systematic classification. First we should quantify all phenomena, aspects, and so forth, that we need, as far as we are able. We should then proceed to classifications, taking them in the following order:

- o by Ekistic units
- o by Ekistic elements
- o by Ekistic functions
- o by Ekistic evolutionary forces
- o by other categories in accordance with needs and possibilities.

These classifications have been limited to a certain degree of accuracy, the next phase may be to proceed to classifications based on more detailed studies. This depends on the purpose of the classification, on the degree of accuracy which is required, and on actual possibilities of implementation of such new methods.

Such classifications can be facilitated by the use of a standard Ekistic grid on which we inscribe two of the classifications (for example, units and elements). The coordinated use of several such sheets, each representing one subdivision of the classification will lead us to the formation of a three-dimensional system (fig. 32).

Specific information can be presented in these grids by areas of different shades or colours. On any one of them, we then have a graphic presentation of the special phenomenon described on it. If we want to compare it with others, we need only select the charts which we want to relate. If, on the other hand, we want to study a subject in a different way, for instance, by following one Ekistic unit throughout the various

three-dimensional systems of classification

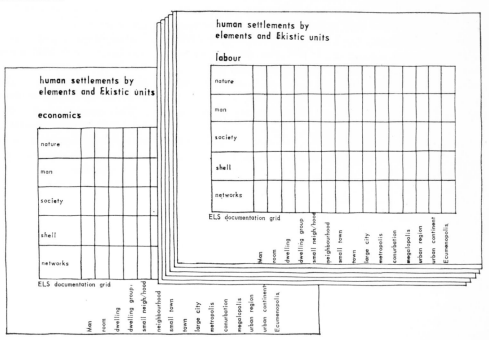

aspects presented on different charts (disciplines, factors, and so forth), we can do so by looking at the corresponding columns in all charts. The same procedure will be applicable when we want to look at all the elements in different phases, or to look at one element throughout all the charts. If we want to go into a detailed historical study, we can once again use one or more charts for every period of interest depending on the details we want to study. Following this procedure we can build a system of general classification of the subject matter.

THE NATURE OF HUMAN SETTLEMENTS

Cells or organisms

The previous analysis of the subject matter, its components and its classifications, allows us now to approach the important question of the nature of human settlements. Where can we place them within the inorganic or the organic world, natural or social? And what is their nature as biological individuals— are they simple or complex, are they cells or organisms?

I think that the answer to the first question is evident because human settlements consist of the five elements, three of which (Nature, Man, Society), at least, are organic. Human settlements belong to the organic world. If one or more of these three elements disappeared, human settlements would

not exist any more. For the same reasons I think that human settlements are a social phenomenon, even though they contain many elements which belong in the natural world. There can be no doubt, I think, that human settlements are very complex biological individuals. If only we think how many complex organisms (human beings, animals, trees, transportation networks, and so forth), they contain and how many combinations of these exist, we will recognise the complexity of these settlements.

The answer to the fourth question—whether, they are cells or organisms—is a more complicated one and requires greater attention. Cells are biological individuals of a lower order, while living organisms, such as Man, are biological individuals of a higher order since they consist of many biological individuals of a lower order.

Human settlements then, which consist of many biological individuals of this higher order, can be neither cells nor bodies nor organisms. There are many reasons which justify this statement quite apart from the inner reasoning that led us to it.

There is one basic difference between natural organisms and human settlements. As far as we know, natural organisms are not the product of conscious thought but of natural, unconscious processes; and they are not inhabited by conscious inhabitants. In this respect, human settlements are much more complex than natural organisms since they are inhabited by the conscious beings who have created them. More specifically, plants do not decide about their fate, and cannot even control their movements in space. Animals can make decisions about their acts, but only up to a certain degree, as for example, about their movements in space. But neither plants nor animals can control their physical transformation. Human settlements, on the other hand, can make decisions about their fate, though not about their movement in space (although even this is possible for nomadic settlements) and can definitely make decisions about their transformation and expansions.

Bertrand de Jouvenel when dealing with the political bodies in his book *The Pure Theory of Politics*, speaks of their analogies with human bodies and draws our attention to the existing contrasts:

'There is a most striking contrast between the object studied by medical science, the body of man, and the object of political science, the body politic. In the former case only the integrated whole has value in our eyes, the component cells are expendable; not so in the case of the body politic, where the whole is justified by its components, real persons. But the contrast goes further. Human bodies, are built on the same model, not so political bodies'.[11]

Plants cannot defend themselves if exterior forces decide on their elimination. Animals can defend themselves by fleeing or fighting, and, if wounded, can retire until healed. Human settlements can defend themselves, and even if completely destroyed can be reborn, if the functions they were performing were necessary ones.

Like all natural organisms, human settlements are born, grow, age and die. However, unlike natural organisms, they do not die by necessity; through conscious renewal processes they may live forever. Like natural organisms, human settlements grow by their own forces and by action taken within the first cells created by their inhabitants. Unlike natural organisms they do not grow only by the addition of new cells similar to the initial ones.

The great difference between human settlements and natural organisms is that settlements are the product of both natural and conscious forces and thus their evolution can be guided, while natural organisms are the result of natural forces only and their evolution cannot be guided except within very narrow limits.

Biological individuals of a higher order

If human settlements are neither cells nor bodies nor organisms, but organic biological individuals, we have to ask ourselves to what category they belong. For an answer we look to evolution and history.

Evolution on our planet commenced when the first cells formed multi-cell organisms by multiplying themselves. Out of the inorganic, came the organic one. Plants and animals were born from cells and the Earth was covered by these two categories of natural organisms until one of the last of the animal species was able to begin conscious action in transforming nature.

When Homo sapiens started settling in a permanent way on this Earth, he created a new kind of biological individual, that of human settlements, much larger than animals and plants and very different from them, but still in many respects comparable to these natural organisms.

Thus, some thousands of years ago, these new man-made biological individuals came into being. Nevertheless, they are very young when compared to the first organisms created by Nature which are now estimated to be three and a half billion years old. Human settlements appear, therefore, to be the youngest organisms with which Man has to deal. In terms of age, we are dealing with a category of young biological individuals which is different from cells and bodies and consists of many of them. We are, therefore, entitled to consider them as biological individuals of a higher order than cells and organisms.

Sir Julian Huxley has proposed the classification of cells as biological individuals of a first order, bodies as biological individuals of a second order, and human societies together with colonies of hydroids and beehives, as biological individuals of a third order. He also remarked that:

'In terms of biologically higher and lower, there is thus a radical difference between cells and human beings. Both are biological individuals which form part of more complex individualities. Cells are first-order individuals, bodies second-order ones, and human societies (like hydroid colonies or beehives) third-order ones. But whereas the individuality of the body of a higher animal, be it cuttlefish, insect or vertebrate, is far more developed than that of its constituent cells, that of a human society is far less so than that of its individual units.'[12]

This classification seems a practical and wise one, but still I must make a few remarks which may illuminate this question further. First, I think that the complete biological individuals of his third order are not human societies, but human settlements. If we deprive the society of its physical settlement it is doubtful whether it can survive. The complete biological individual is the whole human settlement which started by being a small roofless society which could not survive and develop except by settling. Individuals of his second order, that is animal or human bodies can develop and have done so without needing a settlement. Human societies *need* the settlement in order to organise themselves, and even in order to operate. How can the ten million people of London operate as a society within an area of 40 miles square without all the existing networks of transportation, communications, and facilities?

Secondly, and here I move to ground with which I am far less familiar, how can we be certain that cells are the biological individuals of a first order? Is it not possible that we may someday discover others of an even lower order?

Thirdly, the statement that human societies are less developed than the biological individuals, the organisms, that form them, is, I think, correct when limited to the present. But when we witness the technological progress of our day—the possibility, for example, of regulating traffic by a computerised system; the new potentialities for organisation being opened by expanding science and technology—are we not entitled to say when we look towards the future, that the situation may become reversed and these biological individuals of a higher order become more developed than the plant, animal and human organisms?

Let us remember that since human societies, or human settlements, are the youngest biological individuals, it is not strange that they should be so primitive in relation to other natural organisms created over a much longer period. Their primitiveness in fact is such, that many people are not prepared to classify them in the same category of organisms as plants and animals. And they are right. For although in many ways it does help to compare them with natural organisms so as to draw useful conclusions about several of their problems, one must avoid the very grave mistake of considering them to be the same type of organisms as those created by Nature.

If we keep these basic differences in mind, we can draw useful conclusions by comparing the parts of the organisms which have similarities, such as the supply and sewer systems with the digestive ones, the electronically controlled traffic with the nervous systems of animals, and so forth. This is as far as we can go.

The fact, however, that human settlements are so primitive, bound to one place like lichens sticking to rocks, should not deter us from recognising that they must become much more elaborate in order to help humanity survive in the new era it has entered, where technological forces generate new and much more complicated situations.

We can now state some hypotheses about the nature of human settlements:

a. They are complex social, organic, biological individuals.
b. They are two orders higher than cells and one order higher than bodies.
c. They are in a primitive phase of their development—at a lower level than the bodies which form them.

These hypotheses entitle us to expect human settlements either to transcend the primitive phase and reach higher levels of development and organisation, or to disappear as has happened to many plants and animals in the evolutionary process.

CHAPTER TWO

THE STUDY OF HUMAN SETTLEMENTS

THE SCIENCE OF EKISTICS

Our knowledge of human settlements

This is not the first time that Man has dealt with human settlements. It may, therefore, be useful to examine how he faced his problems in the past. Actually, he has been handling these problems for thousands of years—very roughly speaking for about ten thousand years in villages, and five to six thousand years in towns; and, for as far back as we know, he has always set the same goals for his life in a city. We have Aristotle's word for that. If this is so, then how has Man dealt with the problems of the study and creation of human settlements, and why are we now seeking new methods and solutions for old problems?

For several thousands of years, Man lived in villages. The demand for community services was very small, and we have no reason to believe that the villages failed to provide the services they were expected to provide for Man. Then, about five to six thousand years ago, Man started to build cities. Conditions in these cities must have been quite satisfactory for quite a long period. This may seem a strange assumption when we consider the technological progress achieved very recently in cities—the progress of sanitary facilities for example, or even the large capital investments in cities made in recent years. However, if we consider that more and more people are being killed or maimed in traffic accidents; if we remember how difficult it is today to move from one part of the city to another without wasting time and effort and without getting tired and exasperated; if we remember that racial and social problems are increasing and reaching critical proportions, that the delinquency rate is very high; and if, finally, we recognise that our settlements usually do not create a proper environment for a better life, we may conclude that conditions were more satisfactory in the past. This is especially true when we take into consideration the lower expectations of Man in earlier times.

In the past, settlements were certainly poor and technologically much less developed than today, but so was the whole of mankind. Expectations were, therefore, lower than at present. From the point of view of health, conditions in the

larger cities were in several respects less hygienic in the past, especially in the poorer sections; but contemporary cities do cause diseases for body and mind. In many villages, on the other hand, conditions were not greatly different from what they are today. Life in the cities and towns, so far as we can judge, was better organised, more unified and more homogeneous. Certainly a reason for this was that the cities were much smaller than they are today. Until the eighteenth century, most cities of the various civilisations of the world did not exceed fifty thousand inhabitants. It was only on rare occasions that they reached higher figures, and, on the whole, only for very short periods. Beginning in the eighteenth century, however, cities started to attract several hundred thousands of inhabitants, so that around 1800 Man witnessed the emergence of London as the first million-inhabitant city of the contemporary era.

Thus, with small populations and no mechanical means of transportation, most cities of the past, even the larger ones, did not exceed about two kilometres in length (fig. 33) and could be crossed on foot in not more than about twenty minutes. These cities had yet another characteristic: most of them were surrounded by walls for long periods of their existence so that, either their population could not increase, or the increase was so small that it could be absorbed inside the existing walls. Only seldom, and with intervals of whole centuries between, did it become necessary to expand the area of the towns and build new walls. In the Byzantine city of Constantinople, one of the largest cities before the eighteenth century (fig. 34), created by Constantine the Great in the fourth century, enlargement was necessary only once; it was carried out by Theodosios II in the first half of the fifth century.

Because their physical dimensions were small and their development slow, these towns were built on a human scale. Man walked freely inside them from one end to the other without meeting obstacles. He walked about the town feeling at home in it, enjoying it, hating it, admiring it, criticising it, living in it, so that it gradually became for him a kind of work of art in which he was deeply involved. This was the beginning of a long love affair between Man and art, as expressed by the town in which he lived. To realise this better, let us remember that the Acropolis of Athens was built over a long period of

ancient Greek cities

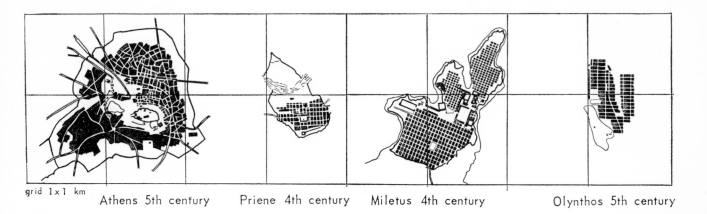

grid 1 x 1 km   Athens 5th century   Priene 4th century   Miletus 4th century   Olynthos 5th century

years and during several different phases of Athenian history. And we also remember that many important towns did not change in size over long periods of their history. Michelangelo, for instance, grew up and lived the greatest part of his life in Florence, a town that was essentially static. He walked its streets and its squares, and had time to think and let ideas ferment in his mind as to where statues or monuments were needed. The statues and monuments which he created were therefore linked with the town and with its inhabitants. When he placed his David at the Piazza de la Signoria, people came at night and stuck notes of praise or disapproval on the statue. Town, square and Man were all interconnected to form a unified entity.

In these towns which were, as we like to say, technologically undeveloped in relation to modern ones, but small and on a human scale, a man could walk about, comprehend, assimilate, become integrated. If a new idea in architecture was implemented, it could be established only if public opinion accepted it, because a new house was one of the very few being built in one year. Naturally, it would become the centre of attention and criticism, and, if it seemed to be good and to contribute to progress, other people copied it. If it was ugly, society did not accept it, and the house was ignored; no one copied it and little by little it was forgotten. Thus, through small experiments, small mistakes were corrected and improved. Through trial and error, architecture and the city developed.

In a way, each man was an expert on the subject of his town. If a town had only two-storey houses, nobody would lightly and without good reason have dared to build a three-storey house. Everyone knew that the masons were not accustomed to it, that the people would revolt against such a construction, since everybody was used to the idea that all people lived in similar types of houses, and that only public buildings or

buildings dedicated to God could distinguish themselves from the others by location, height and investment. There was no necessity even for the common man to possess any special knowledge in order to know exactly what type of house was acceptable in every street and neighbourhood, and to know that public buildings should give a special character to every settlement and every section of it.

We can see then that most of the towns of the past were created by their inhabitants in a collective, slow, systematic and not always conscious collaboration, which ensured survival of the best elements already in existence. This was a collective knowledge, which for many people could have been conscious, but for many others was certainly unconscious. As for the few towns, which were created as such from the beginning, or the parts of towns which did not grow by themselves but were given shape by leaders and craftsmen, these as well had to be in harmony with the traditions created by the people, traditions which demanded that a man of talent express them in more elaborate, official and monumental forms.

When Hippodamos organised the Greek town and planned Miletus, when the Roman planners spread their new towns over their empire, when the Renaissance artists redeveloped the Italian cities, when the Khan-I-Meamaran, or the master-builders of the Great Moguls, created Fatehpur-Sikri and Agra, or the Chinese emperors, Peking, they were all expressing, in an organised, official and monumental way, the trends and traditions which had been created throughout the centuries by the inhabitants of all the villages and small towns they had known in their parts of the world. The ability to grasp such tendencies and the talent to express them in more official forms were necessary in order to lead from the modest achievements of everyday architecture to an artistic and

34

the expansion of Byzantine Constantinople

▬•▬ old walls of the small city

•••••• walls of Septimus Severus built before the creation of the Byzantine Empire (A.D. 196)

▬ ▬ ▬ walls of Constantine the Great built in A.D. 325 when Constantinople became the capital of the Byzantine Empire

▬▬▬ walls of Theodosius built during the first half of the fifth century

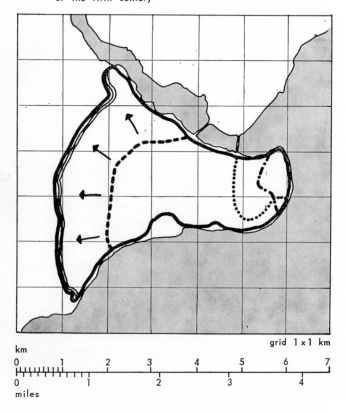

grid 1 x 1 km

km
0 1   2   3   4   5   6   7
0   1   2   3   4
miles

extraordinary creation. That is how the important built-up areas in many towns were created in the past. For us today these are model cities, with qualities that induce us to stay in them as long as possible. This is true not only for the famous ancient and medieval cities, but also for less known settlements of the past that through the years grew gradually and naturally into works of art.

I must repeat: for about ten thousand years Man has lived in villages, and for more than five thousand years in small urban settlements whose size and slow growth permitted the creation of continuous and compact settlements, and endowed these with values which remain important even today. Man created in these static settlements suitable shells and environment for an organised human life. In almost all these settle-

ments, the five elements (Nature, Man, Society, Shells and Networks) were in complete balance. And even when they did slip out of balance, the divergency was small, and could be brought back into balance without a major effort.

Then, beginning in the eighteenth century, continuing through the nineteenth, and especially in the twentieth century, the picture changed completely. The elements of human settlements are now developing individually at such different paces that the balance between them is lost. Man is developing demographically, culturally and intellectually. Society is growing and becoming more complex. The Networks of the settlements are being multiplied and complicated. Nature is being spoilt; the air and the water are being polluted; precious resources are being destroyed. The Shells which have to cover all these elements and connect them into a rational whole, can no longer catch up with these developments. The changes are too numerous, and they take place too fast.

The magnitude of the change can be clearly seen, for example, in the form of the city and the factors influencing it, the landscape, functions and also the inhabitants. The inhabitants, for many thousands of years, had been limited to human beings and some domestic animals. Then, in the nineteenth century, the advent of the railway had a great effect on the city, although it was able to exert a major influence only on its form, making it spread along the lines of its tracks. But, in the twentieth century, the city is inhabited by both humans and *machines*, mostly cars. Let us see how the latter influence the form of the city. Man moves at a speed of about five kilometres an hour (three miles per hour), just as he did in ages past, but cars, even in urban areas, move at speeds of up to two hundred kilometres per hour (125 miles per hour). These speeds, however, are not constant, since on many occasions cars cannot, and should not, move at speeds higher than the speed of Man. So, in addition to the original inhabitant, whose speed is constant and uniform, we now have a second one, whose speed fluctuates from five to two hundred kilometres an hour. This fluctuation depends on two factors: an exogenic one, imposed by the form and paving of the streets and traffic regulations; the other endogenic resulting from Man's personal desire to use different speeds. While in the past the structure and form of the city was largely influenced by the movement of Man, now it is influenced by the movement of Man and machine (fig. 35). Furthermore, we now have to reckon with the constantly changing maximum speed of the machine which depends on external causes, such as the design and condition of the roads on which it is moving, or internal ones, such as mechanical improvements which increase its power and speed.

We can also foresee that this potential speed is going to increase continuously, especially when new road designs are accepted and new cars, perhaps radar driven, are in use. We now have to reckon with the form of the city controlled both by Man's slow constant speed and the changing speed of the car and other machines, a speed whose maximum is still un-

35

the changing city under the influence of:

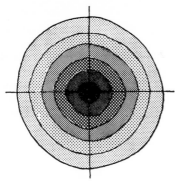

the constant factors of the past

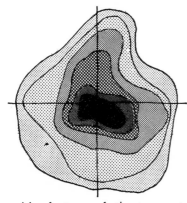

the changeable factors of the present

known. In the past one constant speed factor influenced the shape of the city, but now we have many factors moving at many different speeds and the variety of combination of movements in speed, direction, facilities, and so forth, has become very great. Therefore, we cannot move toward the study of the structure and form of the city without first thoroughly reconsidering the whole system of phenomena and ideas which influence our way of life and the settlements we build for our life.

This increase in the dimensions and the problems of our cities, as well as the increase of the order of complexity within them, comes at a time when human and social sciences are not sufficiently developed. Fred L. Whipple stated lately that they are in the phase in which the natural sciences were when the telescope was developed.[13] At the same time scientists, natural and social, are tending towards overspecialisation, and consequently losing sight of the whole phenomenon they are dealing with. This is true not only of scientists, but also of the attempts of Man to face the contemporary problems of his settlements. In the first complex settlements of the nineteenth century, and even more in the twentieth-century settlements, Man lost the ability to comprehend the totality of a human settlement, to understand and analyse it, and to create a synthesis out of its many elements. The natural ability which Man acquired in the past, of understanding the evolution of his settlement, of adjusting himself to it and developing it in a way that preserved its existing balance or else creating a new one, has now been lost.

Responsibilities have now been split in many ways. We have a multitude of specialists each trying to solve the existing problem separately. The town-planner is very often no more than a designer of two-dimensional plans with a few three-dimensional conceptions; the architect can do no more than take a plot of land and build on it and cannot assume the responsibility of the urban space finally produced—he can always throw the blame on the town-planner, or building regulations or attitudes of the neighbours; the civil engineer has been confined to taking care of underground parts of the town rather than what appears on the surface, with the exception of the structural cores of major buildings; the urban economist is simply interpreting urban economic phenomena; the sociologist is only analysing social problems, etc. The traffic engineer confines himself to existing trends, though very often he has to act as a surgeon, cutting open but not healing the city. The artist hides himself in the buildings, as there is seldom place for his work outdoors any longer. But who is it who deals with the whole? Who is seeing to the balance between Man, Society, Networks, Nature and Shells?

The gap between Man and his ability to cope with the problems of human settlements is already very big and is constantly increasing. In our course towards extreme specialisation in dealing with the problems of settlements, we have missed the main purpose for which settlements were created: human happiness, the happiness Man finds in the balance between himself and the other elements of his settlement. With every passing day, we are losing more of our ability to face the problem of human settlements in a synthetic way, because the more specialised we become, the more we move away from an understanding of the overall problem, and the more we forget the need for synthesis.

One may ask how we can say that it is only today that we have really lost the ability to face these problems holistically when humanity started to lose this ability in the eighteenth century and more definitely at the beginning of the nineteenth century. It would appear that most of the people now living were born without it. However, I believe, I can insist that the loss of this ability is a continuous process and that we are still losing it, on the following grounds. First, under the influence of many new forces, we are undoubtedly losing this ability in the big cities, although we have, to some degree, maintained it in our villages and small towns, some of which remain under constant, slow development. Even a specialist who fails in a big city may sometimes give a natural and logical solution for the problems of small centres. Therefore, in a way, we still possess these abilities, because we have some small towns and villages that are not under the influence of big, uncontrollable forces, and they can help us to understand correct solutions. Even the most uneducated people, if they give these matters enough thought, will not lightheartedly spoil a small town where everything is still in balance, and even if they do try, it is certain that they will meet with resistance from the inhabitants, unless the latter have already been deformed in their judgment by the nearness of a big city.

Second, I would attempt to answer this assertion in the manner of the aborigines of Australia who, when asked why they put their children in the water of rivers or lakes to swim soon after they are born, replied that they must do so before their children forget how to swim, implying that we have certain natural abilities which we run the danger of losing when life guides us in certain other directions. The ability of our forefathers to produce a synthesis on a certain scale must still exist in us because good examples of their activity still survive, but we are losing it because we are ignoring the various dimensions of the present problem and the need to develop this ability to meet the new requirements of our times.

Faced with the present problems and the present failures, the experts have retreated to their own corners to meet the problems either through separate sciences, such as economics, sociology, administrative sciences, technical and cultural disciplines, or by looking into a special aspect of the problem like transportation, housing or community facilities. As a result, modern architecture, which could contribute enormously to the creation of better cities, has not done so. Physical planning has been limited largely to regulative rather than creative action, regional planning is lost in theoretical research, and the overall problem has been practically abandoned.

It was only in the twentieth century that the first attempts at a better understanding or solution of this problem were made. Patrick Geddes tried to understand the total situation by extending his research to include several fields of knowledge and several areas of the world.[14] It was not, however, until the years between the two World Wars that specific attempts were made at a better understanding. Some of these attempts were directed towards achieving a knowledge of what was happening, ranging from the micro-scale of Brinckmann's *Platz und Monument*[15] and Camillo Sitte's analysis of old cities,[16] to the enlightening macro-scale efforts of Walter Christaller[17] to understand the interrelationship of settlements in space and the existence of certain networks.

While one group of people dedicated its efforts to an analysis of existing conditions, an analysis leading to a better understanding of the problem of human settlements, and thus limited itself to discovering the causes of our problems, another group, mostly architects, turned its attention to the creation of new forms of cities. In continuation of the efforts already made towards an escape from the existing suffocating cities (the most characteristic example being the garden city movement), there were architects who tried to solve the problems by submitting their own solutions. These efforts are characteristic of the desire of a large number of people to provide immediate solutions to complex problems. But the architects failed to analyse the problems in depth and to understand their cause, partly because they did not have enough facts, and, consequently, they failed in their efforts to find a real solution. They did not act in a scientific way. They did not recognise the changing nature of their subject. On the contrary, most tried to develop a new form of the city by basing their ideas on varying interpretations of the image of the habitat they had from the past. As could be expected, only very few managed to get a glimpse of the forms of the settlements to come, since they had insufficient knowledge to lead them to basically different solutions.

Among these attempts, which were necessarily confined to a relatively narrow field as a result of the limitations imposed by the professional backgrounds and training of their authors, we must mention the work of Le Corbusier. His efforts around 1930 to conceive the 'radiant city' are characteristic of great courage, which is even more impressive if we consider how very little knowledge existed at that time about the problem of human settlements and the limitations imposed on the solutions, especially in the fields of economics and the other social sciences. At about the same time thinkers in other fields turned their attention to the city, and here I should mention Lewis Mumford's very important effort to throw light on the problems and the crisis through his deep knowledge of many of the forces that shape human settlements.

In the post-war period, especially since the fifties, attempts to solve the problems of human settlements by the creation of new cities and the amelioration of existing ones were made. Characteristic of these the 'New Towns' especially prevalent in England, Sweden and the U.S.S.R., the building of new capital cities such as Chandigarh, Brasilia, Islamabad, and others; also efforts at urban reconstruction in Europe and urban renewal in the U.S.A. Although these efforts constitute important experiments in city building, they have not and cannot enrich our knowledge and our experience to the degree necessary to meet the present need.

Need of Ekistics

In order to meet the confused situation in the field of human settlements we need a unified approach. Such an approach is necessary for the following practical reasons:

- human settlements are unique biological individuals, they are entitled to a field of knowledge concerned only with them;

- unless this comes about it is impossible for Man to achieve an understanding of, much less a solution to their problems.

This second point may be argued by those who, following contemporary trends, are in favour of interdisciplinary collaboration. They are right in trying it in many fields including human settlements, but they are wrong if they think that interdisciplinary collaboration alone can fill the gaps which exist in this field of human knowledge. The reason is that we are dealing with such a complex subject that unless the total professional effort of a man over his lifetime is dedicated to the whole, the holistic aspect of human settlements, there is little hope of his becoming an expert in this field. Even if he does so, the road is long and life short. Let us not waste the time we have by trying simply to coordinate the multitude of important but dispersed areas of knowledge.

A simple illustration is necessary to demonstrate how complex the subject is and how meaningless it would be to try to deal with it by the simple coordination of a round table discussion. Settlements consist of five elements which can be studied through many disciplines in many ways. We can classify the knowledge we have about them into five basic categories—economics, social sciences, political sciences, technological disciplines and cultural disciplines. If we make a two-dimensional grid, combining the five elements and the five major categories of disciplines, we see that there are 25 nodal points on the grid, and we reach the conclusion that there are 25 ways of looking at our subject. This is true, but we are wrong if we conclude that there are only 25 ways of looking at the subject (fig. 36).

If we combine one element with one discipline, we have 25 combinations. But if we combine all the elements with all the disciplines as we must, then we will have 1,023 or $2^{10}-1$ combinations. If we assume, though, that the right combinations are those of the nodal points (e.g. Nature studied through economics, with Man studied through political disciplines) we will have 33,554,431 or $10^{25}-1$ combinations. All these calculations are based on the existence of one man only. If we consider that there are three people, then we will have 35 nodal points, which means, on the basis of the first assumption 4,095 or $2^{12}-1$ combinations, and on the basis of the second one $2^{35}-1$ or billions, etc.

It is quite clear that only a unified field of knowledge can save us from complete confusion. This is the field of Ekistics, and it is with Ekistics that I deal in this part of the book, leaving the question of whether it is a discipline or a science and that of its relationship to technology and art for later. Ekistics as a discipline needs a definition of its subject which I have already done, and of its vocabulary and its methods, which I do throughout this book.

In trying to define the goals and objectives of Ekistics, we must decide how we want to face the problem—in terms of the dimensions of the subject, or in terms of its nature, through a certain field of knowledge, or in terms of our own intent. It is quite natural that, at this early stage of the study, we should face certain difficulties in terms of definitions, delineation of subjects, setting of goals and methodology.

36

elements and sciences in the study of human settlements

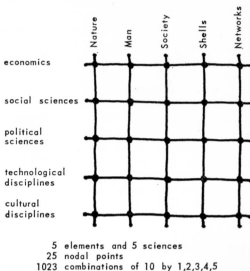

5 elements and 5 sciences
25 nodal points
1023 combinations of 10 by 1,2,3,4,5
33,554,431 combinations of the 25 nodal points

This is no reason, however, why we should avoid the real issues. At this present stage, we have an obligation to examine the problems even if we may have to refine and even modify our definitions later on. It is only by clarifying our goals at the beginning that we can hope to achieve the necessary progress and evolution of ideas. Our duty is to start a process and follow a road, however faint it may be. The important thing, is to be on the march. It is the fact that we are on the march and that we are aiming towards agreed goals that justifies our effort. It is only natural that while on the march we will constantly re-align our route; later we may even re-define our goals when we can see them more clearly. But what is inexcusable is to forget that we are on the march towards a goal, or to lose precious time discussing unimportant or less urgent issues. We must first define the goals and the general directions we should follow in order to reach them, then start to march. Details of the march can be worked out while we are on the move.

The goal of Ekistics as the study of human settlements, in terms of dimensions, is to develop a system and a methodology:

o to study all kinds of settlements, irrespective of size, location, etc., in order to draw general conclusions about them;

o to study each as a whole, without excluding any of its elements in order to illuminate the knowledge of the field and to solve the specific problems of the settlement under study.

F

It is only by studying all kinds of settlements that Ekistics can draw general conclusions which can be of importance to each individual settlement. For example, in zoology, it is necessary to study all kinds of animals in order to understand each different kind; only after a general theory of species was developed, could each one be placed in its proper perspective. The following is valid for every field of knowledge dealing with many related items: in order to be complete, it must incorporate all species, from the most elementary to the most developed.

By extending our field of study to all kinds of settlements, we include some which, although contemporary, belong to a different historical era. These can range from settlements which have remained at a very primitive level, as in parts of New Guinea and in the most undeveloped parts of Africa and the Amazon basin, to others which have existed throughout the entire historical period of human settlements. These extend our study in time, and help us to understand the evolution of human settlements better.

I must repeat: if we study Man alone or Society alone, if we study the Shells or the Networks alone, we cannot understand the whole subject, which is the human settlement. The role of Ekistics is to study human settlements in a coordinated, interdisciplinary way. Hence Ekistics is a new field of scientific knowledge, comprising the existing disciplines and sciences which study human settlements from their own point of view, and some which have not studied them at all, although they should have done so since certain aspects of the phenomena of human settlements belong to their disciplines. In our endeavour to study Ekistics we must remember that even though we have to study and learn many things, our main obligation is to study the gaps between elements and between disciplines; here is where the weakness lies. If we fill the gaps the whole system will operate as one complex entity in a synergetic way.

By defining the goal of the study of human settlements as the knowledge of all their types, and the approach as an interdisciplinary one, we confine Ekistics to the limits of a descriptive science. This might be enough to satisfy those interested in knowledge only, but it is not enough for those who are interested in creating better human settlements. To enlarge our goal, we must also assign a prescriptive role to Ekistics. Whether this is still within the realm of science, or whether at this point it becomes art, is a matter of further study and definition. At this point it is only important to state that Ekistics must cover both the descriptive and prescriptive aspects of the field of human settlements.

If we assign a prescriptive role to Ekistics, we have to define its goal. The basic goal of Ekistics is to create human settlements which will make their inhabitants happy and secure, as Aristotle expressed it. There have been attempts to define this in many different ways. Gradually, however, and regardless of the viewpoint from which people look at this problem, it is widely recognised today that settlements must be 'human'

not only in content but also in quality; they should provide for the well-being and satisfaction of their inhabitants.

This turns us back to statements like Protagoras', who said that, 'Man is the measure of all things'.[18] In our era, we are beginning once again to understand this basic truth, which remains valid in spite of the conquest that has been accomplished since then of wider spheres of the universe through knowledge. John Dewey tells us that, 'Humanity is not, as once thought, the end for which all things were formed; it is but a slight and feeble thing, perhaps an episodic one, in the vast stretch of the universe. But for man, man is the centre of interest and the measure of importance'.[19]

Once we are able to turn our attention back to Man, as the measure of the satisfaction which can be provided by human settlements, we can state that the goal of Ekistics is to achieve the best balance between Man and the physical settlement; Man and Society on the one hand, and Nature and the man-made settlement on the other.

Such a goal raises many questions relating to Man's happiness, well-being and satisfaction. These are difficult questions to answer. May I draw attention to only one aspect of well-being, that of health, in order to show how delicate is the problem we are dealing with. The World Health Organisation tried in 1946 to define health. Its definition covers quite a wide field and raises another set of problems, since it reads, 'Health is a state of complete physical, mental and social well-being and not merely the absence of disease or infirmity'.[20] Thus, health alone requires the satisfaction of many human needs, and human settlements must satisfy all these needs plus many others, such as cultural ones.

Such definitions also raise other and different questions: how far does a settlement satisfy human needs, some of which were found in the distant origins of Man while others are contemporary and are changing continuously? Are we going to set ourselves the goal of satisfying Man as a relic of the past, or Man as he is now developing? Which man do we have in mind? The type of man who is becoming a modern centaur (I refer to those creatures found in many advanced countries that are half-man, half-car), or the man foreseen by Orwell in *1984*,[21] or by Huxley in *Brave New World*[22] or in *Island*[23]? I think that human settlements should satisfy the man who is continuously developing into a better species. Therefore, our aim should be to provide the best continuous balance between Man and his habitat. The more perfect this balance, the greater his satisfaction (fig. 37).

If we look at our problem from the point of view of Man, the content of human settlements, Man the inhabitant, we will see that the greater his adaptation to the habitat, the greater his happiness. If we look at the same problem from the point of view of Ekistics, we will reach the conclusion that human settlements best serve their objective when they give Man the best chance to adapt to his habitat, provided, of course, that the adaptation is to his benefit.

Therefore, a goal of Ekistics as a prescriptive science is to

37

Man and his habitat consisting of natural and man-made elements

assist Man in being happy and safe within his settlements by creating conditions of balance between the elements of the settlements, so that he can adapt himself easily to the requirements imposed by the settlement as a whole, and in a way that will help him develop according to his own intentions.

When we set a balance between the elements of human settlements, as a goal for Ekistics, we are dealing by necessity with:
o Nature, which is being spoilt;
o Man, who is changing;
o Society, which is changing;
o the Shells, which must be created;
o Networks, which are changing.

We are creating Shells, but we do not know how much they contribute to the creation of a better Society, better Networks or even a better Man. Only one thing is certain: if we absolve Ekistics from the duty of producing an environment of better quality, we run the great risk of contributing to the deterioration of Society, to the deterioration of Man himself, and to the destruction of natural wealth. Therefore, Ekistics, as a prescriptive science, must aim at creating a balance which will be to the benefit of Man.

Discipline or science?

The fact that we need the knowledge of Ekistics does not necessarily mean that Ekistics can be considered a science. Some people will even question the possibility of having a science of human settlements. But many also question that geography and anthropography, for example, are sciences. Perhaps we should simply ask ourselves if it actually matters when and how the graduation ceremony into the world of sciences, so to speak, takes place. Is medicine a science? Some say yes, others no. Even if the answer is yes, when did medicine become a science? With Hippocrates, or before him, or after, or perhaps during the seventeenth or the nineteenth centuries? And how are we certain that even if we call medicine a science today, when basic discoveries still lie ahead, the people in future centuries will agree that medicine was a science in the twentieth century? Perhaps they will say that it became a science only in the twenty-first century, when, let us say, mental diseases were first related to chemical elements, and cured in a corresponding way. Perhaps at this point we must clarify what we mean by 'science'. I think that we can agree with J. Bronowski when he states that science 'is not the blank record of facts, but the search for order within the facts';[24] or that '...science is an activity of putting order into our experience';[25] and that 'The purpose of science is to describe the world in an orderly scheme or language...'.[26]

If we think in such terms about science I believe we will have no difficulty in calling Ekistics a science. Certainly some people who use narrower definitions of science may not be satisfied, but I do not believe that we should dwell more on terminology at this point. 'Science' is a relative term which may be accepted by a certain group of people and denied by others, accepted in one era and denied in another. Contemporary scientists agree today on a different interpretation of science, since Francis Bacon is quoted by Loren Eiseley as saying that science was 'not a belief to be held but a work to be done',[27] or since Bronowski is quoted by Theodosius Dobzhansky as saying that 'science is nothing else than the search to discover unity in the wild variety of nature—or more exactly, in the variety of our experience'.[28] In a practical way, which should be the real concern for all of us, what matters is the definition of our goal and our determination to move towards it. It is the dynamic action in this field which should interest us, not the static definition, the value of which is purely semantic and symbolic and has a greater meaning only when it helps us set a goal.

It can also be argued that at such an early stage of the evolution of this new category of biological individuals, the human settlement, there is a danger that the scientific theories to be developed about it may not be correct. But this is of little importance, since we know now that in physics, for example, great progress was achieved by way of initial theories which were not correct—Newton's law of gravity is not truly 'correct'—but it provided the means for a better study of the phenomena which led to even better theories. This is what Hans Selye meant when he said that 'Our facts must be correct. Our theories need not be if they help us to discover important new facts'.[29]

Hence the big question arises whether we have enough facts. To this my answer must be that the facts are certainly available; the many thousands of human settlements which exist today and the shells of those which existed in the past provide us with a great laboratory filled with facts. We have only to open our eyes, and not close them and try to 'invent' new settlements.

And this is not all that we have to say. We should also be aware that in order to classify Ekistics as the science of human settlements, it is not enough to depend on its content, which can be clearly defined; we should concentrate on the effort which Ekistics must make to attain its goals.

The science of human settlements has indeed a very difficult task ahead: to cover the complete field of human activity in settlements. As we have said, it cannot be limited to analysis; it must advance to policies, programming and planning, in order to be able to help Man to survive. And it has to go even further. It must become a guide for the implementation of the right ideas. At the same time it must cover many aspects previously covered by other related disciplines, not in order to replace them, but in order to bring them together in defining the framework within which all disciplines related to human settlements can operate. Architecture and traffic engineering, for example, cannot operate individually—this has already proved disastrous for many cities. They must be incorporated into the science of human settlements so that architecture can be correctly related to urban traffic as well as to urban economics, and such other disciplines as influence it directly.

Once we have determined that Ekistics cannot be limited to the realm of a descriptive science but must transcend it and become prescriptive as well, once we have determined that what we demand from Ekistics is not knowledge only but also directives for action, we begin to touch upon a very delicate problem, delicate especially for those schools of thought which want all 'sciences' to limit themselves to studies of existing phenomena and laws. I do not believe that at this formative stage of the science of Ekistics we should lose ourselves in an attempt to be exact about terminology and definitions. I think that we should be prepared to admit that when Ekistics enters into prescriptive action, it may not be using the same scientific methodology it used when describing phenomena or in discovering the laws of Ekistics. Therefore, we must be aware from the beginning that to be successful in the new discipline of Ekistics we must first work as *scientists*, and that we will be free eventually to work as technicians and artists in the actual formation of better human settlements only if our basis is scientific knowledge.

So in general terms, the discipline of Ekistics as the science of human settlements can be divided into:

- Ekistics as a descriptive science, and
- Ekistics as a prescriptive science, or a technology and art, whose purpose is the creation of human settlements.

And one final argument—today, there is a tendency to develop new sciences and this gives rise to criticism from some quarters, based on two points:

- that we have too many sciences. The answer to this is quite simple. Why not? If through a large number of sciences we can gain more knowledge and attain better conditions of life, why should we hesitate in having as many sciences as necessary? On the other hand, if having too many sciences is dangerous, because it creates a chaotic situation, then, Ekistics, by providing connecting links between sciences is helping Man put order into the chaos that has resulted from too many uncoordinated sciences.
- that a science has to be developed completely before it can be recognised as such. But we must remember that complete development entails protracted effort over a long period of time.

In the meantime, we should not hestitate to call Ekistics a science since this will help us to specify what it should eventually prove to be. After all, it has to start somewhere. Rachel Carson quotes Professor Carl R. Swanson in this respect:

'Any science may be likened to a river. It has its obscure and unpretentious beginning; its quiet stretches, as well as its rapids; its periods of drought, as well as of fullness. It gathers momentum with the work of many investigators as it is fed by other streams of thought; it is deepened and broadened by the concepts and generalisations that are gradually evolved'.[30]

Science, technology and art

Once we agree that Ekistics includes elements of science, technology and art, it is necessary to distinguish between these three. We must think once again of the distinction between descriptive and prescriptive sciences. Cosmology, for example, is a descriptive science, because it tries to discover the laws which govern the cosmos, and it seems, has no hope, at least in the foreseeable future, of effecting any changes in the realm of the cosmos. Ekistics, on the other hand, searches for laws which govern the settlements on the surface of the Earth, but also prescribes courses of action by which one may reasonably hope to change the nature, shapes and forms of settlements.

In Ekistics we must start out with science, but then we have to proceed to action. This action may be wise if it is based on the knowledge and understanding of facts, on science. In this way our knowledge will move from descriptive science to prescriptive disciplines, and will be based on theory and experience which will feed back its information, to contribute towards a better theory. In this way we will achieve a better

38

Ekistic terrestrial space and Ekistic disciplines

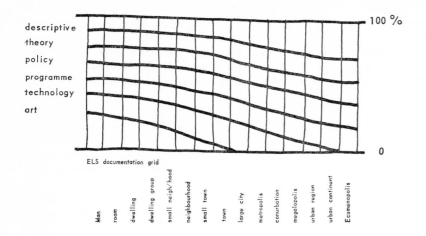

total conception of phenomena on the basis of which policies and programmes can be developed. Only at this stage will technology and creative art become reasonably practicable in this field.

We start with a descriptive science from which we develop theory and move into synthesis, and in this way define our policies and programmes, and develop technologies and arts. The further we move from description and theory into the field of prescription, the further we move from the field of pure science into the fields of technology and art. It is not quite clear where the line can be drawn between science and technology. What is important to Ekistics is the understanding that in order to attain its goal the whole range, from descriptive science to theory and from prescriptive science into technology and art, is necessary, regardless of where the lines of distinction are drawn. In the field of Ekistics, as in so many other fields, pure science and technology are very closely related; their aims are different, but not necessarily their subjects. To quote Sir Robert Watson-Watt, 'modern science is essentially concerned to do only in order to know' and 'technology is essentially concerned to know only in order to do'.[31] We can no longer think of technique without seeing it in its proper relation to science, and without actually basing it on science. In science lies our greatest hopes for new techniques in human settlements, and we should agree with René Dubos when he says 'there is reason to believe that science can develop techniques conducive to greater adaptability and yet compatible with the value of civilised life'.

Figure 38 shows the relationship of Ekistic space with disciplines. Horizontally Ekistic space is shown going from small to large units. Vertically the scope of Ekistic knowledge is shown—it begins with descriptive science, goes to theory, policy making, programming, technology and ends with art.

We must include the full range from descriptive science, theory, policy making, programming to technology since we deal in all these ways with each unit of Ekistic space. Only with visual art can we set limitations, for visual art cannot extend beyond Man's senses (beyond the limit of his senses there is no question of aesthetics, and, therefore, no question of visual art). This is why the diagram presented the role of the artist and the range of this role. His most intense field of activity is in the minor units of Ekistic space—the room, the building, the small community and perhaps even the city. In every other aspect, however, we should always be aware that Ekistics deals with the whole surface of the Earth.

Ekistics has to be prescriptive since its intention is to shape human settlements in the best possible way. It is also a descriptive science, and its additional task of having to solve problems, considered by some a weakness in a science, may, on balance, prove a source of strength, since quite often theory only acquires significance when used to achieve synthesis. This can be considered an argument for the position that people who are interested in synthesis only see analysis through the bias of technology and art. This is often true and is the reason why those keenly interested in synthesis, technology and art, must acquire the ability to look at their problems in a scientific way to be sure they have not overlooked factors and laws indispensable to the understanding of existing situations, which are the best workshop and the foundation for any future solutions. On the other hand scientists must acquire the ability of artists to create values through science; and this task they will learn from art, while the methods they use will be scientific.

Only if we act in this way—combining the knowledge of existing situations as seen by the scientist and the artist with the ability to synthesise and devise solutions—again as seen by both—can we be sure that we will have an opportunity to control and verify our findings and serve the discipline of Ekistics in both its descriptive and prescriptive functions. We should not forget that in all great eras of humanity, arts and science developed together; artists and scientists could understand each other and laymen could understand them both.

I think we can now reach a conclusion. Both descriptive and prescriptive Ekistics have the human settlement as their subjects of study. They do not differ in their approach to Ekistic problems, since both the Ekistic technologist and the artist must have scientific knowledge and scientific attitude. Descriptive and prescriptive Ekistics differ only in phasing, since the one precedes the other, and not in subject or intention. The intention of both is to learn the truth of a situation and to act according to the laws already known and those yet to be discovered.

One of many sciences

To be better understood, Ekistics must be seen in relation to other sciences. This is a much more difficult task now than it was a generation ago, for not only are new sciences being created, but also the traditional divisions into natural and social sciences and beliefs about the systematic classification of science are undergoing constant change. In spite of these difficulties, we need to consider how Ekistics is connected with other sciences so that we can draw conclusions about its methods and its future.

Since Ekistics is the science of human settlements, and since it must bring into balance the five elements which have already been discussed, it must be a science based on a knowledge of both the natural and the social sciences. It is useful to remind ourselves of the three phases of evolution as described by Sir Julian Huxley. We have proceeded beyond the cosmological and the biological phases and now find ourselves in the psycho-social one, when 'Mental activities are more important than are material'.[32] It is strange that although we are in this phase and studying human settlements, humanity has practically lost the ability to adjust to what it has created in order to serve all human needs, including Man's psychological needs.

Although human settlements are subjects of both the natural and human sciences, we find that they do not follow the rules of either of them, but adhere to much more complicated rules of their own. This is quite natural since human settlements contain elements of both natural and socio-human sciences. For example, human settlements are in some respects like other living organisms: they have a heart, they have a body, they are born, they can grow, decline and die; they are fed and they discard waste matter; they have a circulatory system, they have cells, and so forth.

On the other hand, unlike other living organisms, they sometimes grow without limits, merging together into new

units which are of a higher order than the elements of which they consist. Unlike other organisms, their death is not unavoidable but can be regulated or postponed forever by the action of Man. Their circulatory system is not oriented towards one heart only, but towards many centres, a hierarchical and complex system of hearts. Unlike animals they develop mainly in one plane; and they develop in squares and hexagons which remind one much more of crystals or beehives than of the animal world, although sometimes many similarities can be found.

This indicates that human settlements must be considered as phenomena with special characteristics which cannot be classified entirely in the category of social and human or of natural sciences, though they certainly relate to several phenomena studied by these sciences. The elements of Man and Society within human settlements have much in common with the same elements as studied by other social sciences. But when we think of their relationship to the form of the city or to movements within the city, such a study becomes related to natural sciences much more than to human ones. How Man settles and establishes a connection with a certain landscape is related to a human desire, but is expressed as a phenomenon created by Man for Man on the basis of natural laws. The way traffic flows in and out of a settlement is more a phenomenon of the natural than of the human sciences, although congestion may well be due both to natural and human factors.

Thus, human settlements, which are the product of many natural and socio-human forces, follow much more complicated rules which must be studied, without there being necessarily any attempt to identify them with the rules and laws of natural or socio-human sciences. It is easier for us to foresee where the oceans are going to be a few centuries from now than where the people are going to settle—foreseeing is easier for natural than for social phenomena (fig. 39a). Because human settlements consist of elements of both sciences, predictions about them differ from case to case depending on the type of settlement and the relative importance of its elements. Also we can foresee with much greater ease where a city will expand within two or three generations (especially if the landscape has some characteristic features which impose natural laws), than what the attitude of the inhabitants of that period will be. Also we can foresee with greater ease the developments within large Ekistic units which depend considerably on natural laws, rather than within smaller Ekistic units which depend more on human behaviour (fig. 39b).

Although Ekistics is influenced by both the natural and social sciences, we can rely more on the findings of the natural sciences, since they deal with more specific phenomena, and are, on the whole, more advanced. The social sciences provide a weaker link. Therefore, when the findings of Ekistics are equally based on findings of the natural and the social sciences, they inevitably include the weaknesses of the latter. This is

39

chances of foreseeing developments because of the nature of phenomena

a. in accordance with natural and social sciences

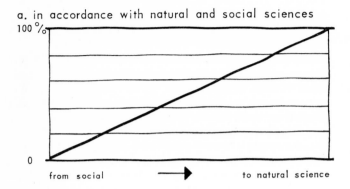

b. in accordance with Ekistic units

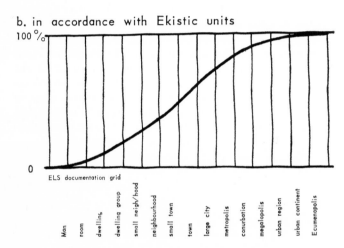

why, while making the maximum use of other sciences, Ekistics must open its own roads and develop its own theories.

The fact that we can speak with relative certainty about some natural phenomena, and less about social ones, and that we will soon have the ability to solve certain technical problems (it will be much easier, for example, to find the best systems of transportation networks than to understand the social phenomena in a city) intensifies the danger of overlooking the essence of Ekistics, which is the balance between all elements, and of proceeding with solutions based solely on the requirements of the physical elements of the settlements (the landscape, the Networks, and the Shells). While trying to find the best solutions for the physical elements, we must keep in mind that it is not the specific physical solution that is of interest to Ekistics, but rather the best balance achievable between this solution and all the elements and functions of the settlement, especially Man, and Society.

When we try to place Ekistics among scientific and other disciplines, we discover that it is connected with them in many

ways and in many directions. The simplest way to present this relationship is to connect Ekistics to the broad categories of economics, the social sciences, the political sciences, administration, technical and cultural disciplines and art, as a central circle closely connected with the others into a system (fig. 40). But such a presentation isolates our phenomenon from the whole field of human knowledge. If we want a better presentation we must show Ekistics as one circle connected directly with five, and through them with many more (fig. 41a). This presentation is realistic also in another sense in that it shows the gaps which exist in the fabric of knowledge. Although I do not agree with those who state that 'in some ways, for all its diversity, science is narrower now than it has ever been before',[33] I think that the gaps are many and present many great dangers. If we consider Man as the centre of a system, the picture of our knowledge looks like an expanding asteroid, which expands in some directions more than in others (fig. 41b). The systems have many gaps which are surrounded by knowledge and which are gradually filling up, and many more between the outgoing radii which have to be closed by ring-like connections.

Common effort among the related sciences will enable us to locate Ekistics correctly, not only from the point of view of the subject with which the different sciences deal, but also from the point of view of the goals they are trying to attain. We have defined Ekistics as a science whose goals are the creation of settlements for human satisfaction and happiness. As such, it leads us back to humanism. We are being led back to humanistic ideals. However, this time we must reach them through science. Humanistic ideals have always been largely quality-oriented, whereas the scientific method requires a quantitative approach.

40

Ekistics and the sciences directly contributing to it

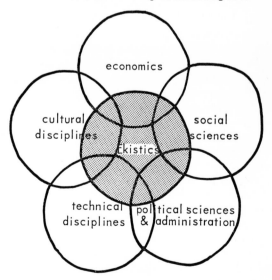

41

Ekistics and human knowledge presented in two dimensions

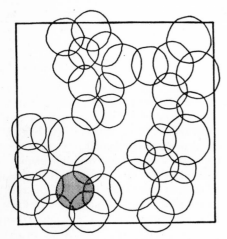

a. Ekistics within the system of cycles of human knowledge

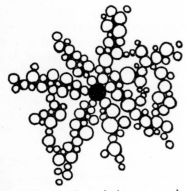

b. total human knowledge expands in a radial way

In Ekistics we now confront a new goal-oriented type of problem which other sciences are eventually going to face. How can we attain the goal of Man's satisfaction through a balance of the five elements of the human settlements (fig. 42)? This is a humanistic goal which in previous eras was aimed at and attained, either consciously or otherwise, in the realm of human settlements.

In stating that the problem of human happiness was approached and solved in the past, I should explain that I do not mean this in an absolute way. I do not mean that the settlements of the past were ideal, and I do not believe that we should search for our future utopias in the past. Utopias never have been built, and they cannot ever be. René Dubos is right when stating, 'Perfect harmony between man and his environment would have existed only if there had been a time when the world was stable and ideally suited to human needs.

But the Golden Age is only a legend, and it will not come to pass in a utopian future.'[34]

I am fully aware of many deficiencies in the settlements of the past—deficiencies in political structure and in social structure, which quite often led to human misery; and deficiencies in social, political and sanitary conditions which we today would consider unbearable. When I bring up the past, I mean simply that, in spite of many such deficiencies, human settlements represented a solution which was in many respects much closer to the demands of Man than are our present settlements. My reference is mainly to values existing in the settlements of the past which we today have lost. They were based on the interrelationship between the five elements of settlements, which, I think, were then in much better balance than they are in the settlements of today.

But one danger we must avoid, that of trying to specify Man's ultimate goal. We should not forget that 'it is futile to hope that the environment can be controlled sufficiently to assure passive health and happiness'.[35] Utopias are not goals to be attained but goals to be dreamed of. But when we combine reason with the dream we conceive the Entopias—the in-places towards which we should be heading. We will not lose ourselves in utopias if we concentrate on Ekistic problems in the manner which Karl Popper calls 'piece-meal social engineering' when he says, 'The piece-meal engineer will adopt the method of searching for and fighting against the greatest and most urgent evils of society rather than searching for and fighting for its greatest ultimate good'.[36]

42

the goal of Ekistics is to achieve a balance between the elements of human settlements in order to guarantee happiness and safety for Man

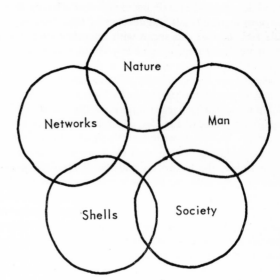

DISCIPLINES OF HUMAN SETTLEMENTS

Old and new disciplines

Human settlements were not created yesterday; the disciplines dealing with them are quite old. Geographers have always been interested in human settlements; architects have always built the Shells of the settlements; city planners have been interested in planning and creating order in cities; historians have contributed by providing monographs of certain villages and cities. Therefore, the disciplines concerned with human settlements can be considered as old as any other disciplines. But the disciplines of architecture and city planning, which concerned themselves specifically with settlements as such, have never covered the total problem—have never concerned themselves with all the elements of human settlements.

The current crisis in human settlements and the obvious inability of the disciplines traditionally concerned to handle it in a satisfactory way has caused other disciplines to enter the field. Some of them—economics, sociology, anthropology, psychology, medicine—are already greatly concerned with specific aspects of settlements. There is also a dawning interest in biology, ecology, mathematics and other disciplines. It is too early to say how much each of these disciplines can contribute to the problem. Indeed, success or failure depends not only on the content, objectives and methods of a discipline, but also on the people who try to develop them and the conditions which excite them. One thing seems certain, even at this early stage; the field of human settlements is so extensive, the problems so difficult, and the knowledge so limited, that there is an imperative need for contribution from all sources. In Ekistics which deals with the problems of human settlements as a whole, we must welcome every possible contribution and incorporate it into a total body of knowledge to arrive at the best possible results.

To conclude, it is not so much our duty to express value judgments on the disciplines concerned with human settlements, although this must also be done to help us clarify our ideas, but to create a framework within which these disciplines can contribute to the totality and gradually merge with the others to form a rational whole. This is the scope of our efforts.

Urban geography, regional science and Ekistics

Three disciplines or sciences are particularly concerned with human settlements as a whole: urban geography, regional science and Ekistics. The oldest of them by several thousand years is geography, which has been dealing with settlements in a systematic way through its branch of urban geography. Its main limitation is that it has been concerned with the description of human settlements, although at times geographers have gone beyond description into prescription and defined policies and action. Such was probably the case with

43

Ekistics, regional science and geography viewed as to their intent

Ekistics

analysis and definition of problem

synthesis of overall concept

regional science

analysis and definition of problem

synthesis of overall concept

geography

analysis and definition of problem

Deinocrates, the geographer who accompanied Alexander the Great as his consultant and probably guided him in the creation of the many 'Alexandrias'. However, urban geographers as a group have not in the past been interested in prescriptive action in a systematic way, though it should be mentioned that it was a geographer, Walter Christaller, who, in his 'Central Place Theory' (*Die Zentralen Orte in Süddeutschland, 1933*),[37] initiated a wide interest in questions of a rational location of settlements in space. Although recently some geographers have shown interest in prescriptive action, this has not taken the form of a broad movement, and has not led to any systematic prescriptive approach to the problems of human settlements.

A new effort towards a rational understanding of the effects of prescriptive action in locating functions in space has, during the present generation, been undertaken by regional science which has made several efforts to define mathematical laws relating Ekistic functions to each other.

Here we can find a distinction between Ekistics and regional science on the one hand, and geography on the other. Ekistics and regional science are both descriptive and prescriptive, while geography has always been a purely descriptive science, although in the last generation some attempts have been made to turn it into a prescriptive science as well. Actually, it might be said that Ekistics is an extension of urban geography into the realm of prescriptive science, while regional science is an extension of economic geography into the realm of prescriptive science.

If we wanted to classify the knowledge of these sciences from the point of view of intent, we would have the following

57

44

**Ekistic terrestrial space studied by Ekistics,
regional science and geography**

descriptive	analysis																		
	problem definition																		
theory																			
prescriptive	synthesis																		
	policy																		
	programme																		
	technology																		
	art																		

ELS documentation grid

Man · room · dwelling · dwelling group · small neigh/hood · neighbourhood · small town · town · large city · metropolis · conurbation · megalopolis · urban region · urban continent · Ecumenopolis

- Ekistics
- regional science
- geography

by dimensions and intent of discipline

45

**a region as seen by geography, urban geography,
regional science and Ekistics**

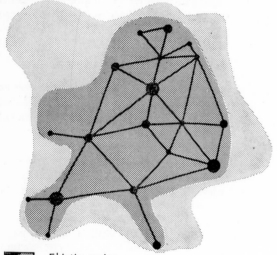

- Ekistic region
- geographic region
- region of regional science and urban geography

picture: descriptive science must precede any other aspect of it; it must study the phenomena through analysis and through the definition of problems (fig. 43).

As these three disciplines all deal in a broad and systematic way with the problems of human settlements, I believe it is useful to make a comparison of them so as to find how they can be built to form the overall body of knowledge on human settlements (fig. 44).

Geography studies terrestrial space as a whole without distinguishing between its elements. It is then divided into urban geography, transportation geography, and so forth, only for purposes of more systematic study. Urban geography divides space into regions and into units of certain sizes. In this respect the terminology of urban geography is similar to the terminology of regional science and Ekistics. Urban geography also states that within every region there are nodal and non-nodal areas. The nodal areas are settlements and the non-nodal areas accommodate certain functions— agriculture, fishing, mining, industry, and so forth—which justify the existence of nodal areas.

Regional science also is concerned with the problem of space which it divides into regions separated into parts for purposes of a more systematic analysis. For instance, when it speaks of a transportation network within a certain region, it is referring to it as a phenomenon closely related to production or residence.

Ekistics is concerned with all types of human settlements. Human settlements occupy terrestrial space. In every area of human settlements we have the built-up part, a system of lines of transportation and communication, and nodal points. This is as true in a small settlement, such as a house or a farm, as in a large one, such as a metropolitan area. What makes terrestrial space of interest to Ekistics is simply the fact that it has been settled.

46

Ekistic elements as seen by geography, urban geography, regional science and Ekistics

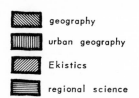

geography

urban geography

Ekistics

regional science

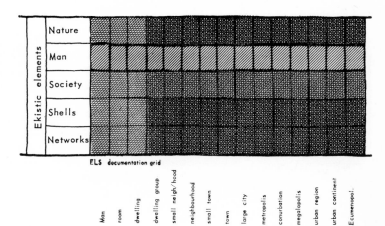

Thus we find that all three sciences or disciplines are concerned with terrestrial space that has been settled, while space that is completely without settlements is the subject only of natural geography (fig. 45). If space has been settled, it concerns urban geography because it is a geographic phenomenon, regional science because it contains economic functions and Ekistics because it is a human settlement. Thus all three disciplines have the same subject matter although it is defined in a different way by each.

From the point of view of the dimensions of the subject matter, urban geography covers all terrestrial space. In practice, this means from the micro-scale of small settlements to the surface of the Earth. In this respect, the physical dimensions are rather well defined and cover the whole Earth and different scales of phenomena related to Man. Theoretically, urban geography from a certain point of view can also be concerned with single buildings when describing the nature of the smallest human settlement.

Regional science covers the macro-scale of terrestrial space, from the unit of the small town upwards, and studies with intensity the problems of economics and production (fig. 46). Actually, regional science itself does not define its starting point. However, if we read studies carried out in regional science we can assume that it uses the community as its smallest unit. It is stated that, 'systems with which regional science might be concerned may be as small as a community or as large as the world'.[38] Here we have a definition of space which is vague as to the lower limit, and we do not know exactly what the term 'community' stands for. The definition is specific with regard to the upper limit if by 'world' we mean the Earth, and non-specific if we mean the space beyond it as well.

The concept of 'region' in regional science is elusive,

according to Isard.[39] Gernsey, on the other hand, defines regional science as 'a social science which deals with the analysis of areal groupings of physical, biological and societal phenomena'.[40] Here we must remark that this description of regional science only has meaning if related to the action of Man, that is, to the human settlement; otherwise it remains a purely theoretical concept. Actually, the term 'region' is the weakest part in the terminology of regional science. 'Region' is a term with no specific meaning, and in this respect I agree with Isard that it is elusive. A 'region' is a unit of space, and as such it cannot be used to determine a discipline. For example, if we take it that the unit of the naval forces is the fleet, we cannot speak of the science of the fleet or the discipline of the fleet, but only of naval discipline. We define a subject by its content and not by its units.

Ekistics covers all terrestrial space with greater intensity, although up to the present it has concerned itself with the more densely settled parts. Theoretically, and also by definition, if a process of production could be achieved in a certain area without depending on any type of human settlement—for instance by sowing a large area and collecting its products by plane, without anyone ever setting foot on the ground—Ekistics would not be concerned with it at all. Since this cannot happen, because even fishing—production on the seas—relies on some nodal points of the coastal areas, Ekistics is by necessity concerned with all terrestrial space ranging from the single room to the Ecumenopolis.

We can now state that while the subject matter of all three disciplines is practically the same, that is terrestrial space used by Man, from the point of view of the scale of the subject matter, urban geography and Ekistics are concerned with all terrestrial space while regional science is only interested in the macro-scale aspect of it.

47

**terrestrial space by disciplines and Ekistic units
as handled by urban geography, regional science
and Ekistics**

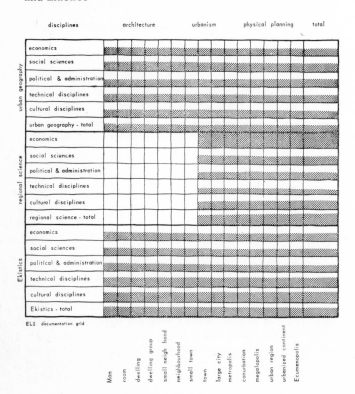

ELS documentation grid

One more point should be made. When we speak of space we mean, of course, terrestrial space, since we are not yet aware of the conditions and laws which may govern extra-terrestrial space and its relation to the disciplines with which we are dealing. It is quite possible that some of the principles used in terrestrial space, or perhaps all of them, are also valid in extra-terrestrial space, but I do not believe that at this stage we should be concerned with that. There is every hope that, if we manage to develop the principles governing the formation of terrestrial space as settled by Man, we will facilitate their eventual transfer into a broader realm in order to enlighten the efforts of Man in settling extra-terrestrial space. In any case, Man can have an excellent foundation for the conquest of extra-terrestrial space in this knowledge and control of terrestrial space and its problems.

Other disciplines of settlements

In order to have a clearer view of the three disciplines with which we are dealing, we must see how they relate to other disciplines and to activities within the settlement. This can first

be done by relating the three disciplines with the other disciplines and the Ekistic units, then with functions and Ekistic units, and finally, with other disciplines and functions.

If we look at terrestrial space by disciplines and by Ekistic units as handled by urban geography, we find that it tends to deal with the whole space-spectrum in covering the economic, social, political, administrative, technical and cultural aspects. Regional science covers terrestrial space in relation to other disciplines and Ekistic units in different ways and with different intensity in each case. Here the coverage begins from the small town upwards. When dealing with economics it is intensive and becomes weaker when dealing with cultural disciplines. In the fields of architecture, urban and physical planning, the coverage up to now has been weak in the case of economics and sociology and intensive in technical and cultural disciplines. Ekistics until now may also have been weak in the same fields, though perhaps not as much so; by definition, however, it is concerned equally with all these disciplines (fig. 47).

To define better the way in which these disciplines deal with the subject matter in relation to other disciplines, we can look at the relevant periodical publications. Based on personal impression, urban geography appears to be especially concerned with the broader categories of economics, social sciences, political sciences and administration.

In dealing with regional science, we can study the proceedings of the Regional Science Association (U.S.A.). On the basis of these proceedings it is quite clear that regional science has done much more work through abstract mathematical model construction than any other science in this field. From the point of view of its relation to other disciplines, we find from the first five volumes of the proceedings (1955–59) the following percentages of subject matter which show quite clearly where the centre of gravity lies.

Economics (mainly regional economic analysis)	62·9 per cent
Geography	5·7 per cent
Regional science (generally)	15·2 per cent
Physical planning	6·7 per cent
Political aspects	3·8 per cent
Social sciences	3·8 per cent
Transportation	1·9 per cent

Ekistics, on the other hand, has tried to cover wider aspects through methods of empirical analysis. Only lately has it begun to use mathematical models related to the dynamic growth of settlements, and other phenomena. Through empirical analysis it has managed to learn more about the interrelationship of functions within settlements and the contribution which can be expected from other disciplines and fields of knowledge. If we study the number of articles published in *Ekistics*,[41] a journal inspired by the need to collect all useful information leading to the formation of the science of Ekistics, we will note the following percentages of subject matter for the period 1955–1964.

terrestrial space by functions and Ekistic units as handled by urban geography, regional science and Ekistics

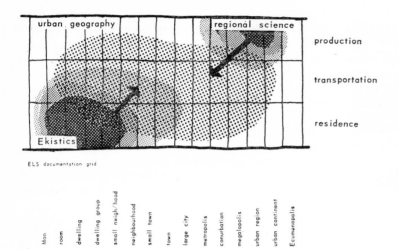

urban geography   regional science

production

transportation

residence

ELS documentation grid

Ekistics

Man / room / dwelling / dwelling group / small neigh/hood / neighbourhood / small town / town / large city / metropolis / conurbation / megalopolis / urban region / urban continent / Ecumenopolis

Economics	17·5 per cent
Geography	5·5 per cent
Political—administrative	6·0 per cent
Social sciences	19·5 per cent
History and anthropology	3·5 per cent
Architecture—engineering— city and regional planning	48·0 per cent

If we now look into terrestrial space as handled by the same disciplines in relation to functions and Ekistic units, we will find that while theoretically all three disciplines aspire to deal with all functions, in practice urban geography, while covering the total subject, has not worked with equal intensity on all functions and units, nor in a prescriptive way. Regional science has been concerned much more with production and transportation on a macro-scale; and Ekistics has been mainly concerned with residence, and more actively so in the middle- and micro-scales (fig. 48).

In order to have a better grasp of the relationship of the three sciences dealing with terrestrial space and its specific functions with the other disciplines, we must compare the present achievements and tendencies of these disciplines, separately and together (fig. 49). From such a comparison we see that urban geography tends to cover all related disciplines and functions in a similar way but with lower intensity in some cases. Regional science is more concerned with the aspects of production and less with transportation and residence. It is concerned primarily with economic problems, then with social, administrative, technical, and last with cultural and aesthetic problems.

Ekistics, up to now, has been concerned with a part of the economics of production, a larger part of the economics of transportation and an even larger part of the economics of residence and human settlements. Ekistics looks more closely into the social and cultural aspects of production, transportation, residence and the shells of settlements.

From the previous analysis we see that Ekistics, although directed at human settlements, is obliged to include large parts of the problem of production since that is the concern of several disciplines. It must include an even greater part of the problem of transportation, which cuts through many other disciplines, and finally it must cover the total aspect of residence and the shells of human settlements. The conclusion is quite clear. There are many functional aspects of space which can just as well be covered by other disciplines. It is, however, the role of Ekistics to cut through them and provide the synthesis necessary for an approach to problems of terrestrial space within human settlements; it is this synthesis which constitutes Ekistics' main task. In doing this, Ekistics is in no way supposed to relieve other disciplines, such as economics, of the responsibilities it has of defining and solving its own special problems. Ekistics has a basic role, and that is to provide the links between all special problems, thus formulating the total problem for the benefit of human settlements. To achieve this it must study all special problems as long as and so far as they contribute to the overall one—for example, in economics, it is not concerned with currency but with location theory.

Having described human settlements in terrestrial space as

49

terrestrial space by functions and Ekistic units
as handled by urban geography, regional science
and Ekistics

disciplines	production	transportation	residence	synthesis of functions
economics				
social sciences				
administration				
technical disciplines				
cultural disciplines				
urban geography				
economics				
social sciences				
administration				
technical disciplines				
cultural disciplines				
regional science				
economics				
social sciences				
administration				
technical disciplines				
cultural disciplines				
Ekistics				
economics				
social sciences				
administration				
technical disciplines				
cultural disciplines				
all three disciplines				

they are handled by different disciplines, we can now recapitulate and make a general statement (fig. 50). Human settlements have yet to be studied as a whole. Only several of their elements have been dealt with so far in different ways and for different lengths of time by the related disciplines.

If we look at terrestrial space we will find that it is only with regard to the smallest Ekistic units, that is the room, the house, the dwelling and the town, that we have satisfactory knowledge, bringing Man into balance with Society, Nature, the Shells and Networks. When we move to Ekistic units of a larger order, the balance which exists between the different elements of the settlements is much poorer, and when we move on to metropolitan areas, the balance is negligible.

If we look at each element of the settlements separately, we will find that the Shells have existed for many thousands of years. Nature has been dealt with appropriately only in minor settlements. A lot of work has been done on Networks but again only for minor settlements. Only very recently has work for some Networks in the larger settlements been done, particularly for such networks as traffic. Problems of Society have only lately been dealt with in relation to major settlements, and this is more true for the middle scale than it is for the micro-scale. Finally, the concern for Man, with all

his problems of health including his psychic health, began later, and these problems were dealt with more in minor Ekistic units than in larger ones.

We can therefore conclude that a practical goal for Ekistics is to fill the gap in knowledge and action which exists in the whole spectrum of terrestrial space covered by human settlements, and, further, to ameliorate the services provided by all disciplines, in the segments already covered, by coordinating the findings and action to form a synergetic whole.

Beginning of a new era

Apart from the three disciplines with which we have already dealt, many other disciplines and sciences are moving into the realm of human settlements. At the same time disciplines already concerned with human settlements which have in the past overlooked the role they could play, are now moving in to regain the lost ground.

In the first category we should mention biology, which now begins to be concerned with the fate of the human species in its settlements. Biologists are becoming interested in Man, in this new phase of his life as a captive of the man-made landscape. Ecology also begins to be much more interested in Man and his fate in his habitat which, though called the cradle of civilisation, may well become Man's grave. Those who study human settlements are beginning to use the experience of ecology and draw from its knowledge. Actually, they are now drawing more from this experience than from the natural sciences. Although the relationship is not direct, people dealing with human settlements are also beginning to learn from the general experience of such disciplines and sciences as zoology, astronomy and cosmology.

There is an increasing interest on the part of ecology, as by other sciences, in moving towards an interdisciplinary approach. Characteristically, F. Fraser Darling, taking over as president of section D (Zoology) of the British Association for the Advancement of Science, made this point very clearly.

'As a corollary, I think that ecological research must become more and more the effort of teams of workers; the single worker will continue to discover beautiful expressions of phenomena, but the syn-ecological studies in depth of habitats and communities which we need today demand far more than what one man can compass. Ecological studies are not designed *ad hoc* to solve land-use problems but to discover truth, and this high scientific approach must be jealously guarded, but thereafter ecologists can have a social conscience and apply their discoveries to the problems of land-use by man. The teams I envisage are not collections of specialists, if they are to be successful, but, to borrow Tensley's expression, organic entities.'[42]

However, the greatest movement, a turning of interest to the field of human settlements, has been in the social sciences, especially in those directly related to Man and his health.

50

**human settlements as handled by all disciplines
together by elements and Ekistic units**

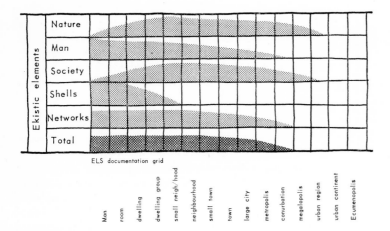

The increasing interest of health experts in human settlements is a result of the evolution in medicine and psychiatry, which has gradually led to an increased interest in Man not only from the point of view of medicine and psychiatry but also from biological, psychological and social aspects. The publication *The Urban Condition*,[43] in which social scientists and psychiatrists play a big role, shows that disciplines related to the first two of the five elements of human settlements (Man and Society) are beginning to mobilise their resources. The road they have to follow is long, since these experts, although able to understand problems and solutions usually overlooked by people concerned mainly with the problems of the Shells of human settlements, have not been prepared at all to look either at the container—the landscape on which the Shells are being built—or at some of the functions of the settlements.

Architects, engineers and planners now generally realise the limitations of their own disciplines as far as the human settlements are concerned. We are witnessing an important movement in many of these disciplines to bring them back to the course which will serve the human settlement as a whole. In my book *Architecture in Transition* I speak of the necessity for architecture to find its proper role within the realm of human settlements.[44]

All this means that Ekistics can expect much greater help and enlightenment from those disciplines seriously concerned with its problems, as well as from many other disciplines which did not contribute in the past but are now desiring to contribute to the solution of the problems of human settlements. We can also expect a movement for reform in several disciplines which have recently strayed from the right course. Such considerations and expectations allow me to predict that we are at the beginning of a new era which has come into

being since World War II. In this phase Ekistics will in fact become a science of human settlements, and in its effort it will rely on a very large group of disciplines directly or indirectly concerned with human settlements.

Participation in Ekistics

The fact that so many other disciplines are inclined to participate in the solution of the problems of human settlements creates an obligation to study their relationship to Ekistics in order to appreciate their role in the formation of this new science.

Taking the whole spectrum of terrestrial space divided into Ekistic units and trying to find the role of other disciplines within this spectrum, we arrive at the following diagram (fig. 51). The influence of cultural-aesthetic disciplines on Ekistics is very strong in micro-space which can be seen and conceived by Man with all his senses. When, however, we move to the larger units which Man cannot so easily perceive with his senses, either because his sight is blocked by buildings and natural features, or because it is simply beyond the limits of senses, the impact of the cultural-aesthetic disciplines on Ekistics decreases. When we reach such areas as the metropolis, Man's senses no longer help him to see, feel or conceive. At the end of the scale the impact of the aesthetic disciplines is negligible.

Similarly we can find that political disciplines only have importance beyond the unit of the neighbourhood, an importance which grows gradually and attains a very high degree of influence when we reach the level of the national state where national-political issues prevail on major decisions.

63

51

Ekistic space as handled by various disciplines

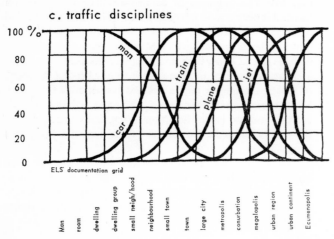

a. cultural - aesthetic disciplines

b. political disciplines

c. traffic disciplines

If we select one of the technical disciplines, let us say that dealing with traffic, we find that whereas traffic based on human or animal force (walking or riding) is of great importance in the building complex and the neighbourhood, it is practically of no importance in the scale of the large city, and of decreasing importance in the even larger areas, where transportation relies more on railways and airplanes.

We can now select architecture as one of the disciplines concerned with terrestrial space and see how it operates within it on different levels. Architecture, in Ekistic space, is one of the disciplines containing technological as well as cultural-aesthetic elements. On the basis of the previous considerations, architecture participates in the entire spectrum of the micro-scale. Its importance decreases in the middle scale, and becomes practically nil in the macro-scale. This means, among other things, that the patterns defining architectural space are those based on the two systems of axes crossing at right angles. I would refer those who are not familiar with architecture, to *Architecture in Transition*.[45] In the middle scale and especially in the macro-scale the prevailing pattern is the large scale natural one of hexagons.

In the past, when the technological and economic forces were not so powerful, the space of architecture was limited to a minor part of the spectrum. It was not only unnecessary but impossible as well for Man either to create the big architectural complexes of today, or pay for them. Today, because of the amounts Man can invest, he has the ability to impose patterns on large spaces. We can expect that in the future this space will comprise a larger sector of the whole spectrum, although it will gradually reach certain limits beyond which terrestrial space will be shaped by the natural pattern imposed by geography and economics[46] (fig. 52).

From such examples we see that the degree of participation of several disciplines in Ekistics varies in accordance with the order of the Ekistic unit, its importance, and the phase of its evolution. By this technique we can define the role of other disciplines within Ekistics, and in this way throw light on our subject. By doing so we can both assist the disciplines presently concerned with Ekistics as well as those which ought to be concerned.

SUBDIVISION OF EKISTICS

By human settlements

The simplest and most basic way of subdividing Ekistics is the subdivision by human settlements. While discussing them in Chapter One I suggested several ways in which they could be classified—by physical size and formation, by elements, functions, evolution. There are as many ways of subdividing Ekistics as there are of classifying settlements. We can have for example Ekistics of the Shells, or of minor cities, or again of rural and urban settlements, and so forth.

patterns within Ecumenopolis

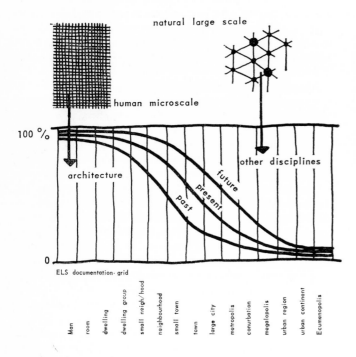

ELS documentation·grid

All these methods can be useful, depending on the scope of our study. I have tried them in specific cases and found that there is no reason at all for excluding any of them. The question which arises, as in many similar cases, is which subdivision can best serve every goal that we set, and the answer to this is a matter of judgement and experience.

A basic conclusion that I draw from experience is that if we have to subdivide Ekistics on the basis of the classification of human settlements, there are two practical ways of doing so.

- When we deal with large settlements it is useful to subdivide Ekistics by broad categories of settlements, combining units and corresponding basic functions. Such, for example, is the division by Networks, and rural and urban settlements which I used in Chapter One.
- If, on the contrary, we are dealing with small settlements then it is better to subdivide them by the elements and disciplines through which we can study them.

By fields of knowledge

On other occasions a division by fields of knowledge is more practical. This is the division which I used in the present study. We began with facts. This is the descriptive part of Ekistics which must be further subdivided into analysis of existing situations, and study of the evolution and the pathology. We can close by a diagnosis of the conditions.

Then we can move into Ekistics as a theory, draw conclusions about the general principles governing the phenomena, and through them build a whole theory of settlements and use it for the synthesis. The last basic part deals with Ekistics as a prescriptive discipline, with conceptions, goals, policies, programmes and plans and their implementation. With such a division we can, on the one hand, cover the entire field from abstract research to actual construction and operation of human settlements, and on the other avoid the confusion between facts, theories and action, between existing situations, our interpretations of them and our opinions as to what should be done.

One important point to remember is that in such a subdivision attention should be paid to the difference between the structure and the function of a settlement. If we look into medicine we will discover that the great step was taken when it moved from anatomy, or studying the structure of the body, to physiology, or studying its operation. Ekistics has to make this step. We may draw the following analogy.

order and structure: anatomy
cause and function: physiology.

Since human settlements are living biological individuals, we must study them in their normal healthy conditions, and also when they are suffering. In this respect we have the subdivisions of physiology dealing with healthy settlements, and pathology dealing with suffering ones.

It must have been noticed that I often use medical terms. The reason is obvious: settlements are alive and present many characteristics in common with human bodies. But they are not human bodies. There is the danger of following the parallel too far. This is a danger inherent in every parallel we draw not only between two such dissimilar entities as the human body and the human settlement, but also between two similar entities as with two settlements. This danger is no reason why we should avoid drawing parallels with medicine which are so useful, provided we know the limitations of their use. In this respect we must remember that medicine is dealing with natural organisms whose maximum achievements have been genetically predefined while Ekistics is dealing with organisms whose future is only partially predefined—it can be changed by Man.

A method of subdivision

The selection of the method of subdivision of Ekistics depends on our purpose. We can say that subdivision by settlements is better or worse than by fields of knowledge. We usually need both at the same time, and we can also have all sorts of combinations. In practice we need at least a two-dimensional division; one dimension is based on settlements while the other is based on fields of knowledge. Sometimes we use

G

the subdivision by fields of knowledge first and then a sub-subdivision by settlements, by elements, sizes, and so forth. This is useful in studies of major content as is this book. In other cases we may subdivide first by settlements and then by fields of knowledge. This occurs more often in specific case studies.

METHODOLOGIES FOR EKISTICS

Empirical method

Throughout history the study of human settlements, analysing as well as building them, has been mostly empirical. People are inclined to build, having as a basis the image of the settlements in which they live. Consciously or not, they study only the settlements in existence, and project their past into the future. At times people have thought in a systematic way of how settlements should be built and have designed ideal cities. Such proposals, however, have very seldom been implemented since they were Man's conception and were either altogether unrealistic and utopian or contained many such elements. Regardless of whether they were good or bad, there was no way of convincing others that the proposed settlements would be better than those in existence.

Hence, even the new settlements that have been created from time to time have for all practical purposes been a continuation of those already in existence. This is why in periods of crisis for human settlements, humanity has been unable to cope with new problems; it has continued along its old road, with no guiding theory and no method providing for the systematic adaptation of existing settlements to new demands.

This empirical method of study is that used in geography. Geography starts with the direct observation of existing phenomena, then proceeds to classifying and understanding them. This method has by necessity given us knowledge of static settlements of a minor scale. Thus, our total experience gained by the empirical method has been related to small-scale and relatively static Ekistic units.

The fact that in moments of crisis humanity has been misled by the empirical method does not mean that it is of no use. On the contrary, it is a very basic method for studying human settlements and should be used as much as possible. The weakness of the empirical method is that it cannot be of much help in new situations, especially when prescriptive action is required. Indeed it can even lead to disaster, for the greater the changes, the less its value, if we rely on it. This is why we find ourselves today at an impasse; we are facing a crisis, yet the purely empirical method, which we have been relying on, is unable to help us.

In order to cope with the situation Man faces today we need to use, in addition to empiricism, theoretical methods developed in a rational way.

Need of all methods

Now we ask ourselves what method or methods should we use in Ekistics? If Ekistics is to become a science, then it must rely on both empirical and abstract theoretical methods, it must rely on facts and thoughts, on facts and reason, facts and logic. A complete system of methods of research and study would include:

- empirical study of human settlements,
- empirical comparative study of non-human settlements,
- abstract theoretical study and development of a hypothesis,
- experimental study to test hypotheses,
- feed-back process to allow for the continuous correction of the experience gained from all previous methods.

The above methods cannot always be implemented in the same way for all Ekistic units or for each element of an Ekistic unit. On many occasions we shall rely on one method more than on others. If, for example, we are studying Man, it will be much more appropriate to rely mainly on the empirical method, less on the empirical comparative method, to a very small degree on the experimental method, and hardly at all on the abstract theoretical method.

If, on the other hand, we are dealing with the functions of traffic, we shall find that the first method will show up several weaknesses and problems; then we will be able to use the empirical comparative method probably only to a minor extent, and will have to rely greatly on the theoretical abstract method which can help us build models for traffic solutions to be tested by the experimental method.

For the empirical comparative studies we must consider all the sciences which can show us the way to useful conclusions, such as ecology and biology. It is much more difficult to draw useful conclusions from the natural sciences. But, although the creation of human settlements is really more in the realm of human and social sciences, we have to use so much material deriving from natural sciences in setting the foundations of our work and in constructing the shells, that we should learn as much as possible of their methodology.

It is in the field of abstract theoretical studies that we must really break completely new ground in the study of human settlements. In our rapidly changing era I would even venture to say that without abstract theoretical studies we shall never be able to understand what exactly is happening in human settlements. Up to now there has been great reluctance to use such techniques for the benefit of human settlements. This is why we are still unable to distinguish between several phenomena and study them properly, and consequently proceed to a different kind of synthesis. Ekistics must venture into this field and carry out as many theoretical studies as possible.

Ekistics must also develop abstract-theoretical models as has been done in other fields of which the closest to our case is regional science. It is because of its concentration on this approach that regional science has had some difficulty in

53

abstract theoretical connection (A B) and empirical one (A C B)

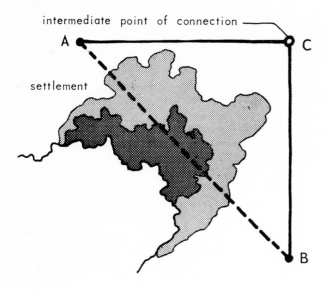

We can also proceed with the method of adopting new assumptions. If, for example, we were to assume that human settlements are not going to be inhabited by humans but by modern centaurs, we would come to understand which factors are related to all human qualities and which to only some of them. With modern centaurs as the inhabitants of the settlements, notions of distance would change, since centaurs move much faster than men. The economics of the settlement would remain the same if the centaurs produced a higher income to balance their higher needs. The aesthetics of the settlement might also remain the same, though possibly on a different scale, since centaurs have a larger stride than men. Such a wild venture into the impossible helps us understand what might happen, if we change the human element.

We have an old Greek poem which says:

> On horseback to the church he goes,
> on horseback to the ikons bows,
> on horseback from the priest's hand
> the holy bread he takes.[47]

It is a poem about brave men who, during the wars of liberation, so as not to be caught unprepared by the enemy, and, I imagine, to prove their bravery as well, went everywhere on horseback—a revival of the ancient centaurs. I am under the impression that we are now developing into a new type of centaur; I have not as yet heard of people entering their bedrooms in cars, but cars have intruded practically everywhere else; I have heard there are even drive-in churches. People are gradually becoming legless and developing a different attitude to life. The automobile has become an extension of their bodies.

The use of all these methods should be systematic, whatever is tried being considered an experiment. Conclusions should be drawn continuously from whatever is actually happening, and the proper feed-back process should be worked out in advance so as to lead to a continual improvement of the process. Without feed-back, we cannot achieve a really scientific approach and will never learn how to build better settlements.

A natural feed-back system existed in the settlements of the past. As mentioned earlier, in the small cities of the past, the leaders, the builders, and even the common men, knew what could be done, since whatever was attempted by one person was immediately learned by the others. The results were discussed by everybody in the market place, the coffee shops or tea-houses. If the effort proved successful, it was repeated, if not it was rejected. Today, because of the magnitude of the information necessary for such a process, the feed-back operation is limited and unsatisfactory. Consider the failures that have occurred with prefabricated houses. Many countries, developed as well as underdeveloped, are still trying to solve their housing problems by way of factories producing prefabricated houses. If we had had better feed-back it would have been possible to predict their eventual failure. Even in the absence of good economic studies, the failure of those who

proceeding towards synthesis. The role of Ekistics should be easier, since experience in human settlements has been basically empirical. Having followed the empirical road, we have already acquired the necessary experience to proceed to a synthesis where small scale Ekistic units are concerned; we do not yet have the data to do this for the larger Ekistic units. Regional science, on the other hand, having based all its findings on abstract mathematical models, can give solutions regardless of the Ekistic unit it is dealing with, but such solutions are of more a theoretical than practical value and are usually limited to certain aspects of the phenomena, particularly economic aspects. Hence, regional science still has to acquire the ability of proceeding to a synthesis, taking into account all the other disciplines, elements and factors which compose the Ekistic phenomenon.

I will venture to give a simple example of how these two methods can be compared in practice. Let us assume that we have to solve a traffic problem, namely to connect points A and B (fig. 53). A theoretical model will show that the straight line connection is the answer. In practice, however, we may have to reckon with so many forces of resistance to development between A and B that today the answer can only be given empirically with the line A–C–B. Even though an economic study may prove that the line A–B is preferable, we may have good reasons to avoid it. These reasons can be either of a practical-political nature, or of a social nature. For instance, a highway joining A and B may have to divide an existing community and defeat one of the basic rules of Ekistics, to respect every settlement consisting of human interests and human groupings.

first tried to produce large numbers of prefabricated houses should have served as a warning to the others. Yet this did not happen; further evidence of how much more difficult it is to learn today in spite of the existence of the many media of information. The amount of information to be transmitted has grown so much that even the very exceptional media at our disposal fail to keep us fully informed.

Dangers and traps

All the methods described above are indispensable. We can learn from the methodology developed by other sciences and we have new equipment, especially computers, which enable us to deal with a great variety of factors. However, the use of computers even though important and indispensable, should not be considered easy. The fact that the natural sciences have been able to make the greatest use of computers is not coincidental. Although they can deal with complicated problems, they have a much smaller number of variables than social sciences, and these, in turn, have fewer variables than human settlements.

The great difficulties encountered in using computers to solve social and political problems serves to warn us how much more difficult it is to use them in Ekistics. In human settlements we must reckon with almost all the variables of social sciences plus many of the variables of the natural disciplines. Sir Robert Watson-Watt has said,

'In the language of simple mathematics or physics, the question can be answered—to the satisfaction of nobody— by stating that in political problems the number of independent variables is vastly greater than in any of the problems that mathematicians or physicists would set themselves.'[48]

I am sure that at the time Sir Robert made the above statement he had not yet been exposed to the even more complicated problems of Ekistics.

Some efforts have already been made to collect and interpret data on human settlements by computers. Efforts have also been made to solve certain problems of human settlements by community development programmes worked out on a systems approach. Such efforts, however, have only dealt with a few of the variables. They have for example, never dealt with aesthetics. Furthermore, answers have been some-what theoretical and their contribution has usually been limited to the location of certain functions, nodal points and lines of communications. So far no answers have been given to such questions as, how such locations, even if they are the right ones, should be inter-connected to form a total system, taking into consideration such other requirements as that for rectangular house plots or for right-angle crossings at least at the scale of the smaller Ekistic units. Yet these are important as we cannot, with impunity, forget that in human settlements we must deal with creation, which should satisfy us from every point of view, as well as with the economic

functioning of a whole area. The efforts made so far have certainly been important—they have laid out a course, and must be studied carefully. Several have laid the foundations for future accomplishments. But they are still a long way from what could be called the interpretation, much less the solution, of the problems of human settlements as a whole.

In my travels I have seen many city officials confused by the lack of data; and others confused by too much data. New possibilities that open to us as a result of new methods and equipment cannot solve problems unless we have first managed to conceive the solution ourselves by hard thinking. Only when we have reached this point can we use assistance from the outside. In this respect modern techniques, which facilitate the gathering, storing and processing of information, can be a great trap for those who are now struggling to understand and cope with the present situation.

My conclusion is not that we should refrain from using computers; on the contrary, their use should be one of our foremost tasks; but we must use them wisely, taking into consideration the magnitude of the questions we have to answer—their importance and priority. However, we should be prepared for many difficulties and failures since not only is the number of variables large but, at least at present, we are unable to foresee exactly how certain variables of social and human importance, such as those related to aesthetic satisfaction, can be fed satisfactorily into computers. Similarly, how can we go about putting into the computers the conscious, or very often unconscious, demands of billions of people for a better life, a better way of building their settlements and greater opportunities? It is clearly a very complicated task indeed to detect such demands, measure them and find a way of expressing their proper value.

However, despite the difficulties encountered, I personally believe that we shall lose control of the more complex settlements now being built unless we are able to feed all the useful information into computers, and that, in order to do this, we must proceed systematically from partial problems towards problems of the whole. Even so, at the start we are bound to meet with failures and therefore must be prepared for a long period of hard effort until results begin to be apparent. We must undertake this task immediately as there is no hope for correct measurements and calculations unless we do so. With patience and the right system we can almost certainly achieve results.

But this is not the only danger and trap in the use of new methods. I have seen experts get confused and lost because they turned to new approaches and new concepts for help they could not get. This danger exists not only for Ekistics. Many fields suffer from an eagerness to learn more from other disciplines. Characteristically the authors of the study, *The Mighty Force of Research* wrote:
'There are dangers, of course, in overworking any concept, no matter how helpful. Some psychologists who originally encouraged their colleagues to study information theory and

to apply it in their experiments now feel that the theory is frequently misapplied by psychologists—and almost inevitably misapplied by sociologists'.[49]

The dangers and the traps are many—they are caused by the failure to recognise one basic truth: that the understanding and the solution of the problems of human settlements do not lie outside its domain but inside it and cannot be achieved by the contributions of donors and by mechanical devices; all these have to be mobilised by those who understand Ekistics, mobilised on the basis of a plan leading to the attainment of goals.

Criteria

The right methodology, in order to be successful, needs defined criteria. It is by these that we will judge the phenomena of human settlements, decide about their value and develop a system of measurements. To define the criteria is one of the most difficult aspects of our work, for any decisions taken must be related to many other questions raised throughout this book. I do not believe, therefore, that we can at this stage attempt to establish criteria of universal validity, since they may be assumed to have a greater value than is possible, even though I intend to deal with my understanding of this problem based on my own experience in forthcoming publications. Hence, at this stage, I can say only that the criteria ultimately to be developed should:

o cover all six categories of phenomena that we have mentioned, i.e., the five Ekistic elements, and their synthesis;

o be judged on the basis of universal and local value, as well as in relation to the notion of time and change.

We certainly need criteria for all elements as well as for their synthesis, since without them we cannot arrive at soundly based value judgments. For example, we may have a settlement which is completely adjusted to its natural environment; it has respected the natural values, be they vegetation, the sub-soil or the surface of the Earth; the water has not been polluted and the air has remained clean. In this settlement, however, Man may not be satisfied; Networks may be inadequate, and the Shells may be completely unsatisfactory from the economic point of view. Indeed we can anticipate a situation in which all elements are developed to a relatively satisfactory degree, but where there is still no proper synthesis.

Our task is complicated even further by the prior existence of specific criteria which have either a universal or a local importance. If we had only to look for universal criteria, the task might be easier. However, we find there is a need to keep a balance between these universal ones and criteria of local validity. For example, criteria regarding the successful incorporation of a new industrial plant into the outskirts of a big city where the natural setting has already been greatly altered, will be completely different from those related to the incorporation of the same plant in the open countryside or in a small settlement, which has not yet been altered by any major projects. In the first case, a proposition of levelling a large area by eliminating hillocks of a height of 20 feet or so may be justified by the fact that the plant will be constructed near a highway which has already cut through hills 30 feet high. However, such levelling may not be justifiable in an agricultural community where no other projects have required such levelling or such cutting into the ground. In this latter case a satisfactory solution may demand construction of the plant on two or three levels or shifting it to a nearby plan in order to avoid destroying the natural characteristics of the existing landscape.

Another example may be cited, more closely related to the technological policies in human settlements. In a country of high income it may be mandatory that dwellings for the lowest income groups each be equipped with a bathroom and a modern kitchen. This may easily be considered among the criteria for a satisfactory dwelling. However, in a country of low income, the corresponding criteria may limit the demand to the existence of a cold water shower and a separated space for cooking equipped with a smokeless stove.

Regarding economic criteria, in certain countries, an economically satisfactory dwelling for certain income groups may be considered one whose cost is equal to two and a half or three times the annual income of the family concerned, including the proportional cost of community facilities. In another country, a satisfactory dwelling may only be possible at a cost equal to four times the annual income of the family. The latter case is likely to be true for families moving from a rural into an urban environment, with incomes of unskilled workers.

What is also of great importance and should not be overlooked is the change in criteria effected by time. What is satisfactory today may not be so tomorrow. There is an imperative necessity for the continuous reappraisal of all criteria.

In conclusion, it is clearly necessary that we work out criteria, which will give satisfactory answers to questions concerning the various elements separately as well as their synthesis, by combining both universal and local factors at every given moment. This will have to be done independently in every specific case, taking into consideration all requirements as well as the all-important element of time.

PERSPECTIVES FOR EKISTICS

Grim outlook

Every expert in fields related to human settlements who seriously examines his own knowledge of his discipline must admit the present inefficiency of the approach and the

forces shaping human settlements

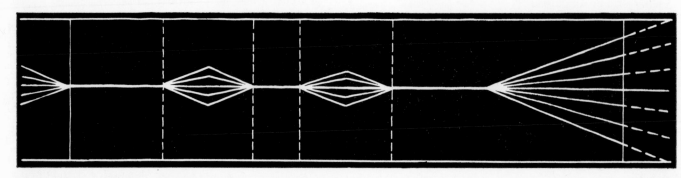

and knowledge of human settlements

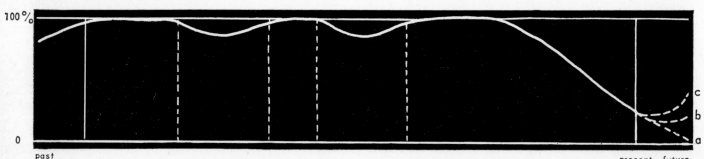

methods, as well as the lack of classified experience in dealing with these problems and the consequent need for a much greater effort in understanding the real issues with which we are dealing. These failings become even more serious when we consider the overall problem of human settlements and not merely single aspects of it. I think it is symptomatic that people avoid this major issue of the overall problem. This is quite natural; people who already feel frustrated by the problems of their own sector avoid going further and examining the whole. However, it has to be faced and we must be quite frank in admitting that today in the field of human settlements we know very little, and that we are very badly equipped to face the problems that already confront us.

We have already suggested that the knowledge which Man has acquired in this field over the last ten thousand years—knowledge which started accumulating, in regard to rural settlements some ten thousand years ago, and in regard to urban ones some five to six thousand years ago—had proved quite sufficient until the last two centuries. The fluctuation of the curve of knowledge as related to performance, during this period was probably very small since the changes from one civilisation to another and from one culture to another were on a relatively minor scale. Probably the only major dislocation occurred when Man first started to build urban settlements. It is natural to assume that he only succeeded after a number of

failures. During the last two centuries, however, Man has lost his assurance. Since then his knowledge of human settlements has been decreasing, reaching what is perhaps its lowest point in our days. I cannot believe that at any other time humanity could have known as little about one of its main problems—its own settlements—as we know today (fig. 54). This knowledge is, I think, still decreasing relative to the problem (curve *a*); there is a great need for this trend to change to *b* and *c* but even so the curve will continue to have a downward trend for some time.

As a parallel to this statement we must state that no matter how great the need for a science of Ekistics, such a science cannot be developed from one day to the next. We must truthfully admit that at this moment we cannot know the future of this science nor how it will be possible to build up this whole body of knowledge, much less bring its different aspects into balance. It is too early to shape it. The only thing we can say, however, is that we are beginning to understand the Ekistic problems of our era, and that we are in a position to lay down some basic principles which will guide our work, trace a road for our actions in the future and help develop the science.

Not only is our knowledge decreasing relatively but we do very little to increase it. As an example of how underdeveloped is this sector of learning. I would like to mention some data given by Richard Llewelyn-Davies and Peter Cowan in an article about research in Great Britain in the field of human settlements.[50] On the basis of data included in the report of the National Economic Development Council, they estimate that the proportion of net output devoted to research and development by the Building and Construction Industry is about 0·16 per cent versus a corresponding 2·6 per cent devoted to the same purpose by the Manufacturing Industry. These are quite characteristic figures and I do not know of any country where the situation is better for the Building Industry as a whole. On the contrary, I think that the situation is worse in most of the countries that I know of, although we do not have exact data. If we now take into consideration that advances are more apparent in the fields for which much more is spent for research and development, we can clearly understand one of the reasons why the progress in the field of human settlements is so unsatisfactory. No one expects, of course, that the Building and Construction Industry should conduct the full range of Ekistics research. But improved Shells are certainly as important to human settlements as improved products are to industrial production. And in this respect the Building and Construction Industry makes a very poor showing.

At the outset we must be aware that the immediate future will present even greater difficulties than the present. Even if we develop theories we must recognise the danger that the time lag between theory and practice may be growing. When we are not aware of the magnitude of a problem we tend to be more confident in attacking it, even if we are badly equipped to do so. But once we begin to realise the scale of the issues before us we may lose confidence in attacking even relatively simple ones. This is not all. As long as we have no balanced, overall system with which to tackle these problems, we can be fairly sure that we will make unequal progress in different sectors of our interest. Progress in traffic technology, for example, may continue to move ahead at a much higher speed than progress in other sectors, which will enlarge the gap already existing between several of the disciplines and factors which influence Ekistics, and this will decrease our ability to cope with the overall problem.

It is characteristic that many studies which are being carried out today tend to overlook several important aspects of the overall Ekistic problem, especially those related to the culture of human settlements. Many of these studies do not even touch upon the problem of the final form and shape of the settlement, which is the most important problem in conceiving the Shells. Although the Shells are only one of the five elements of the settlement, we cannot conceal the fact that, from the point of view of implementation they are most significant, for without them we cannot have a satisfactory human settlement, only an accumulation of the other elements in space.

The present situation is such that many people have lost their courage in this field and have become sceptical about the possibility of a rational approach. Several large educational institutions which want to deal with this problem have not yet dared to do so, while a good many foundations which have been supporting related programmes are gradually losing interest in them. This is partly due to the overall difficulties and partly to the failures which are only natural in an era such as ours, since we have not yet been able to create a systematic approach to the overall Ekistic problem. Hence, I feel that the immediate future for human settlements and Ekistics is grim. It is better to know this now in order to avoid undue pessimism and disappointments later.

Optimistic outlook

In spite of this grim picture, there are good reasons for some optimism. Even though we have not yet developed a system, it is definitely possible to do so. Since the system got out of balance because of forces released by Man, it should not be beyond Man's power to develop a system of control over them. History shows that this can be done. Man has done it in the past; he did it when he first created villages and again when he moved into cities. Therefore it is reasonable, although I admit daring, to conclude that this achievement can be repeated. Whenever in the past a society wanted to conquer broad terrestrial areas, it had the wisdom to organise its own space satisfactorily. Otherwise it retreated into forms requiring the lowest skills or organisation. It was the good organisation of the mainland of Greece that permitted the Macedonians under Alexander the Great to expand their rule as far as the Indus Valley. It was the sound political, administrative, legal and military organisation of Rome that permitted the Roman legions to create the extensive Roman empire. It was the same with both the Spanish and the British empires. Man now has to conquer what remains of non-settled land in terrestrial space—the desert, the jungle, the high mountains and the polar zones—and he is already beginning to think seriously of the conquest of extra-terrestrial space. But a successful expansion of the space settled by Man cannot be achieved unless we better organise the space which has already been settled. We cannot expand successfully by disorganising our own base . . . unless we become nomads. But then we are not conquering the new space; we are simply devastating it—if we can reach it.

These seem good reasons for organising our efforts but they are not enough to convince us that this can be done successfully. The progress made in several other sciences—the very great progress in technology which goes side by side with the development of new systems and new approaches, together with the development of persons of high intellectual calibre in much greater numbers than at any previous time—lead us to believe that, given the necessity to organise our settlements we will be able to mobilise our forces and develop the proper approaches. In spite of the grim present situation and outlook, it is possible to be optimistic once we decide to mobilise our resources, and once we understand the present situation

71

55

**knowledge and control of human settlements
three assumptions for the future**

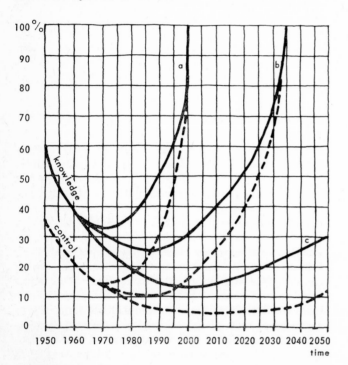

properly. There is no reason for believing that once we understand the magnitude of the problem we cannot cope with it. For even though we can foresee many difficulties, we cannot foresee any factor that, given proper time, we will not be able to contend with. The entire question is: when can we start to cope with it? Because if we do not act now, in which case we shall be heading towards disaster, humanity, when it eventually recovers from the disaster, will still have to face this problem. Therefore, the question for us is not whether we will abandon the idea of a systematic approach to human settlements forever, but whether we will abandon it long enough to witness a disaster first and act afterwards. The grim prospect is that we will allow ourselves to be led towards disaster. The optimistic one has as its basis the timely recognition of the crisis, and preparation for strong enough action which will change the present course.

Into the unknown

If we look back at human history and try to present the forces shaping human settlements graphically, we find that when the forces were small and the elements of human settle-

ments were in balance Man could achieve a synthesis by bringing the different views together; he could focus his whole effort and find good solutions. There were some periods, probably when the first villages or the first cities had to be built, when some of the forces got out of control, spreading into a wide spectrum, and the situation became very critical until humanity once again acquired the ability to bring these forces into focus and create a synthesis. At present we are in such a phase, with these forces spread out so widely that we do not know how to handle them.

If we think of Man's knowledge of human settlements, we will see that in periods lacking in balance this knowledge was low; but when knowledge in relation to the complexity of the problem was again built up, a balance was achieved until, in a subsequent crisis, Man again lost the ability to understand the situation, so that again it got out of control, and so on. At Present we are at a relatively low point of knowledge (fig. 55).

Where do we go from here? We do not really know. We may turn downhill, keep at the same level or even turn upwards. I wish I could say that we might follow an upward movement; unfortunately I cannot—those forces now shaping human settlements continue to get out of control. Therefore even if we make a great effort, we may only be able to keep our knowledge at the same level, which means that we will progress at the same rate as the increase in deterioration of the situation. However, it is much more probable that in the immediate future we will not be able to increase our knowledge as quickly as the situation deteriorates, and thus we must be prepared for a downward movement regardless of how great an effort we make. It will require some time, one or two decades perhaps, for us to know enough to catch up with the deterioration. But then our efforts will have a much greater impact, and hopefully we shall be in a position to turn back the forces now spreading uncontrollably and, perhaps a generation from now, get them once again under control.

I would like to add one more note about the prospects, as I now see them after 36 years of experience in the field of human settlements. I now believe that our knowledge, though it is decreasing in relation to the magnitude of the problem and will continue to do so for some years, could be increased by the end of the present decade. This can only happen if by then we have become fully cognisant of the real difficulties we are facing, and of the real crisis we are in. A conscious recognition of this crisis would, in my opinion, result in an upward turn of the curve of knowledge. But this turn upwards of the curve ('c') in figs. 54 and 55 is only possible if we start immediately to implement a proper programme for the recognition of the crisis (fig. 55). In this event, movements like the one started by the Delos group[51] are likely to prove of great importance.

If the curve of knowledge begins to turn upward, we can expect that the nineteen-seventies will witness the development of the first recognised theories which can give us a hope that in the eighties elaborate experiments can be tried out on a big scale on the basis of these theories and that these can be intensified in the nineties. If this happens we can hope that by the year 2000 a level of knowledge concerning the problems of human settlements will be reached which will be satisfactory for future action.

The level of controls over human settlements is at present below the level of our knowledge. This is natural, since our decline in knowledge has resulted in a much greater decline in Man's control over the human habitat. Due to this, and because it is very difficult to regain control quickly even when we know what it is we want to do, we can expect the curve of control to continue to move downward for some years. A move upward may only occur a decade after the curve of knowledge has turned up. Therefore, we cannot hopefully expect Man to start improving his control over human settlements until around 1980. However, this will not necessarily be a satisfactory level, for the present level of control is very low, and is almost certain to become even lower. Depending on how drastically Man decides to act, we can expect him to raise the curve of control from its downhill movement so that by the year 2000 he should be in firm control of the situation. If the action taken is not as drastic as it should be, a sufficient level of control may be reached only in the first decade of the next century, or even later.

To sum up: we are, at present, moving into the unknown, and the probabilities are that the forces shaping human settlements will continue to be out of control for some time to come. Our knowledge of the total situation in relation to the dimensions of the problem is likely to decrease for quite a number of years, but then we can hope it will catch up with the situation, and, once it does, the forces will gradually be brought under control.

So, at the present stage, having no control of the overall situation, it is impossible to express an opinion about such basic issues as the value of our present types of settlements for the future. It is quite likely that, a few generations from now, it will become clear that our present rural and urban settlements represent only a primitive version of the human settlements to come, which will be quite different and much more complicated. Our present settlements, may, therefore, be looked upon, a few generations from now, as simply the crude ancestors of a new type of settlement—the universal or Ecumenic settlement. Our lack of knowledge in this regard should not make us pessimistic. It should be an additional spur compelling us to face our problems in a more systematic and scientific way, without any prejudice as to what form of settlement or what form of life is best for the man of tomorrow, excepting one basic criterion—the creation of settlements which will enable Man to be happy and secure. The fact that we are moving into the unknown compels us to acquire the ability of foreseeing where we are going, and to 'invent the future'[52], as Dennis Gabor says. It also compels us to do something more—to build the future.

Laying the foundations

We are facing a grave situation. Though it cannot be solved it must be solved. There is only one way to proceed. Knowing that we need time in order to cope with it, we must now start to lay the foundations for much more systematic work. These foundations will consist of a system, a method, proper criteria and a science. This must be our first undertaking.

I have already ventured to suggest that this can be achieved within the next few decades. It will require enthusiasm and the coordinated effort of many countries, among many disciplines. I have also mentioned that a small group of people, gathered on the island of Delos, initiated a movement to create a unified approach. The first step was the issuing of the Declaration of Delos, in 1963. But such isolated instances are not enough. What is necessary is a much greater mobilisation of resources. Every one of us must understand that there is a need for organising and coordinating our forces. The problem is very complicated and unless we build up a system that allows us to learn as much as possible from each other as soon as possible, and unless we work on the basis of an overall plan which will minimise wasted time and effort, it will be very difficult to face the problems successfully. This is why I think that the basic foundation for the successful implementation of an effort to know and to control human settlements must be the creation of an international network guaranteeing the most rational mobilisation of all resources which can be of help in the solution of such a great problem. Individual efforts are not enough. The formation of a system is the prerequisite for the timely solution of this great problem, and this can only be achieved when we have the means to contact each other all over the world in seconds, when we can let each other know the latest findings of our research within the same day. We have no reason to believe that the creation of an international system for the mobilisation of all resources required to face the problems of human settlements is not possible. I firmly believe that it *is* possible and that it can be done within the next few years. If we can lay the foundations for this in the sixties, the system can be in operation by the early seventies and then improve upon itself continuously until by the end of the century it can serve its purposes and help Man to be in control of his environment.

Such an outlook is not grim; it is in fact, quite optimistic, and I believe it can be realised. But even this optimistic, yet realistic, prospect means a generation of intense action, without the assistance of completely accepted and detailed scientific equipment. What will happen in this interval?

We have to become reconciled to the fact that until Ekistics is so well developed that it can influence the evolution of human settlements in a scientific way, judgement plus experience acquired in the past must continue to guide us in the creation of human settlements. In order, however, for this natural and acquired knowledge to be used in the best way, we must now decide to approach all our problems with

73

56

contribution of several professions to Ekistics
and their relationship to Ekistic units

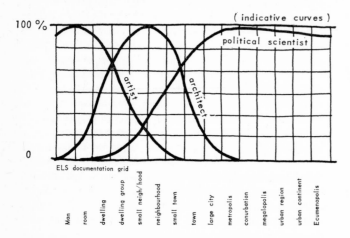

scientific detachment; without trying to create 'styles' or trying to create human settlements as we imagine we would like them to be. There is only hope in this direction if:

○ we build on the experience which humanity has accumulated by using it with the greatest possible respect;

○ we become scientific in our approach to what we must respect and what we must change.

We have said that up to now, those dealing with problems of human settlements have based their action on the descriptive and empirical approach, founded on observation of the achievements of the past and, indeed, on their repetition. We must now learn to take the synthetic approach, which has been the foundation for many of the achievements of the physical sciences. This does not mean that we must abandon the descriptive or empirical approach. On the contrary, in order to achieve our aims, we must use both the descriptive and empirical approach as well as the synthetic one, to the best of our abilities.

THE EKISTICIAN

One or many

We have a difficult task ahead—that of developing a system of knowledge and a science, of learning it and using it. As in every other field, we need the experts, the Ekisticians. Today we do not have them. Those closest to this science are the town-planners, who have the right training—not only in micro-scale but in all units of our space. But good town-planners are few and their impact is small; since the field has not been developed, its methods have no overall recognition and acceptance, and crucial decisions on the

life and death of cities are being taken before the problem reaches the town-planner's office.

We need many Ekisticians who understand the real problem and will be dedicated to the subject as a whole, who will understand that their subject is the whole spectrum of human settlements as living phenomena of the highest order and not some aspects of settlements or some of their parts or sub-systems.

But, if we need many Ekisticians for the overall universal task, for every single project, big or small, how about the development of the subject matter itself? Can one type of expert cover the whole ground or do we need many who will collaborate in order to solve the problem? We can even ask ourselves who is going to carry out this work and who is going to lay the foundations? Is the work going to be done by one expert or by many, since we have spoken repeatedly of an interdisciplinary approach? Where there is need for a science there is need for an expert.

We have certainly spoken of an interdisciplinary approach, but not of a multi-disciplinary one. We need the Ekistic expert to connect and unite the many disciplines capable of influencing human settlements to form the one which can guide all our efforts.

My answer to these questions is the following. We need *one* science—Ekistics—and therefore we need one expert only— the Ekistician. There can be no misunderstanding on this point. What we need is the synthesis of knowledge; this cannot be achieved by a computer nor in the space between the brains of the collaborating experts. If the issue which has to be faced each time is small, then one Ekistician is enough to handle it. Solving the problems of a small village or a small town is a task for one man. If the subject is large then there may be a need for many Ekisticians—but they must all be Ekisticians. If a surgical operation is small, one surgeon can carry it out; if it is big the chief surgeon will need assistants, but these assistants will have to be surgeons not dentists. We need Ekisticians, and in every case we need the chief Ekistician, the one person, the leader of the group, who will have responsibility for the final synthesis. As in the case of every group effort, there is a necessity for leadership, and this will be assumed by the one who not only has the strength to be a leader, but is also a more able synthesiser— an expert who can conceive the total picture with knowledge of all its aspects.

This does not mean that we do not need other experts who may not be Ekisticians, architects, engineers, economists, geographers, mathematicians, systems analysts, programming experts, etc. The larger the subject the greater the numbers necessary. In a surgical operation we need in addition to the doctors, the anaestheticians, the nurses and other assistants. All of them have to contribute in their own way within the proper unit and at the proper phase. How this can be done is shown by fig. 56 which presents the role of several experts in relation to the Ekistic units

57

architects and Ekistics

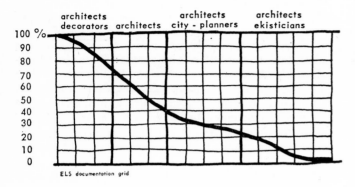

ELS documentation grid

degree of participation of architects in Ekistics

of several sizes. In small units the artist plays a big role, in big ones it is the political expert who contributes more.

All these experts can either assist Ekistics, through their own disciplines, or become Ekisticians; but in this case it will be a second profession, even if it is acquired as an extension of the first one. We see therefore that in every one of the contributing professions we may have experts with different degrees of involvement in Ekistics.

Let us take one profession—architecture—and see how it can contribute to Ekistics. We must have architects who are also excellent Ekisticians and who can exercise control and leadership over an Ekistic project. We also need architect/urbanists, and a number of architects who will design, supervise and build single buildings. The latter need not know much about Ekistics but they must be well trained in urbanism and architecture respectively. Finally, there is a need for architects who specialise in interior decoration or in landscape design. These, especially if they are acting in small scale, need know even less about Ekistics than the architects responsible for the major groups of buildings and the architect/urbanists. Thus, in every profession dealing with human settlements, we will need those who will master the total system of knowledge of Ekistics and who will be responsible for the solution of the major Ekistic problems and, therefore, candidates for leadership of Ekistic teams, and those who will concentrate on specialist tasks and have to learn less about the whole field (fig. 57).

We can now go even further and say that on the basis of such considerations, on the basis of the contribution of architecture to Ekistics, we can proceed to a reform of the architectural profession. In the past, the architect, the master

builder, was in charge of all aspects of the creation of a human settlement which was small and consistent with his scale. Especially in contrast to what he does now, he was not only a designer but also a master mason, a master builder. He was in charge of the production of materials, their transportation, and the construction and completion of the building. He was also not the designer of a single building in the narrow sense, but the designer of a neighbourhood, a community—not necessarily because he was asked to design all the buildings of the community, but because he was aware of his responsibility towards the whole community, and not towards a single owner only.

If we look at the scale of the architect's participation in Ekistics we see that his participation is very extensive for the small units, quite important for the dwelling groups and the neighbourhoods and more limited in the larger Ekistic units. If we consider that architecture is the profession which can provide leadership for minor Ekistic units, then we have to train the architect to take leadership in these units. This means that architects have to recapture the experience which they had in the past and understand the many new forces which are entering in the field of production. Architects should cease to be fashion designers, tailors for suits made to order.

The greatest forces of the architect should be geared to the understanding of the easy, inexpensive, mass production of houses and buildings, and the impact this production will have on construction, and the problems that it poses in the need to avoid uniformity and at the same time create settlements which will be economic, and easily produced, but also at least as individual and interesting as those of the past.

We cannot tackle the immense tasks which lie ahead with old-fashioned methods. Architects have to adjust to their new task and develop a new technique in order to face the new problems. These new architects will be the architect-builders.

In addition to them, we will need a second specialty of architects—those who will expand their field in space and instead of looking at the problem of only one building, will be able to look at dwelling groups, at small neighbourhoods, major neighbourhoods, even small towns. These will be the architect-community creators.

We can look in this way at every profession and define the range of specialties which we will need, from the complete knowledge of the small units to the contribution of the big ones.

His characteristics

Who, then, is going to be the Ekistician? Among all the experts who deal with the problems of human settlements, the Ekistician should be the one who has the most interdisciplinary approach, who, regardless of his training in one specific discipline, can look at the problem in an inter-disciplinary way. He must be the one who can achieve a synthesis, which is indispensable for the understanding and solution of the problems of human settlements. No architect who maintains an attitude about the supreme importance of architecture, no social scientist or geographer or political scientist can become an Ekistician, unless he understands that Ekistics is really a new discipline requiring an understanding of other fields of knowledge connected with it.

Who can become an Ekistician? Needless to say the Ekistician should be a scientist, and should have the most advanced training possible. Since, however, Ekistics has not yet been fully developed, and since we must rely on a number of other sciences, are we in a position to know who is going to make the best Ekistician? In order to answer this question, we must look at it in different ways. First we must consider the experience of the past. Who were the best Ekisticians in the past? Even though Ekistics as such did not exist, we know that new human settlements were being built and existing ones being successfully remodelled. Who were the people who achieved this? History tells us of cases where the men who created the best cities were not architects only; some were artists, military engineers, geographers, statesmen or sociologists. The past does not lead us to any specific conclusion about the greater importance of any specific science as a foundation for Ekistics. From the past we learn that those who created cities were men of high calibre who distinguished themselves in their own profession, but did not represent *one* preponderant profession. Then suppose we turn to the present; what does our present experience show? We will once more find Ekisticians who come from different professions and disciplines. They may hold the post of mayor, director of planning, chief engineer or administrator of a city. They may be statesmen, administrators, architects, planners or engineers. There is perhaps a preponderance of architects and physical planners. If we look into the individual cases more carefully, we will find that the best known city builders who come from architecture are dealing with areas of fairly limited dimensions. Architects seem to be better at conceiving and designing physical dimensions which are directly or indirectly related to architectural design.

If we see Ekistics as the science of human settlements covering all of them on all scales and in all dimensions, I do not believe that we can express any opinion about the best type of Ekistician. If we are speaking only of dimensions of a lower order, then it is the architect who has a better basis for becoming an Ekistician. This is as far as we can go in answering the question. The important thing is that we must rely on people from all fields which can contribute to Ekistics. From among them we will get the best Ekisticians. These may come, in the minor units, from architecture, in the middle units from engineering, and in major units from geography or perhaps politics and economics; though one cannot, of course, exclude the possibility that people coming from other disciplines, not mentioned above, may distinguish themselves on the whole Ekistic scale or in parts of it. We must remember that the participation of every discipline is in the entire Ekistic scale, and thus find those people who will have greater chances of becoming better Ekisticians in some specific parts of it.

I do not believe that I have enough experience to determine which profession would provide experts with the best background for good Ekisticians. Much wider experience will be necessary before we can reach that point. On the other hand I do have some experience, which, such as it is, allows me to say that the question is not so much one of background of discipline, but one of the *type of person* that we need, the type of natural and acquired characteristics which the Ekistician must have.

Some people ask me whether we need a generalist or a specialist. Quite apart from the confusion that such terms may create, I do not think I could answer this question. Both the so-called generalist and the specialist become specialists where the whole of human knowledge is concerned. A few years ago during the first Delos Symposion Edward Bacon called the Ekistician 'a specialist in generalities'.

The real question, as I have come to learn is, more than any other, whether the expert has flexibility and the ability to develop his mind and understand the new tasks, the new problems and the new solutions. Even in existing disciplines 'in a world where everything changes rapidly, the practical facts learned in school soon become obsolete' as René Dubos stated lately in his excellent article 'Can Man Keep Up With History?'[53] This is much more true in the field of Ekistics where the changes are greater, and where we have learned so little. We need the type of person who will be prepared to learn every day of his life. We need people with flexible minds who, to use conventional terminology, will be experts in changing notions and changing situations, as opposed to those who are experts in static situations. What we need is the expert with the dynamic approach as opposed to the expert who sticks to what he has learned.

Finally, we need people who can combine theory with practice, people who can think at night and build during the day, people who are both the philosophers and the architects that are so ably made out to be opposites by Paul Valéry in his *Eupalinos*.[54]

In closing this discussion, we have to ask ourselves, since we cannot take a position regarding the necessary background for the future Ekistician but only regarding his abilities, whether there *is* a necessity for scientific or technical background or whether we could not turn any person into an Ekistician after proper training.

Personally I do not believe that this is possible. It may be possible in the future when Ekistics will be fully developed into a well-shaped discipline and science; then we may have the opportunity to train people directly in Ekistics. We should be aware though that such training will take many years of formal education.

At present I think that it is much safer to have people entering the field of Ekistics after the right training in some other field in a well-established discipline, be it science, technology or art. I do not believe it is advisable to try and train people directly in generalities. Such a procedure holds great danger, namely, that if these are not the right types of people, those who can rise to the level of synthesis without a specific background, we should be prepared for many disappointments. The people concerned will become frustrated, and their contribution will be minimal.

As the situation stands at present I have seen people able to contribute to Ekistics only if they come from one well-developed profession and only if they have a very successful training in their own profession. The people who came to us desiring to 'put things together' without knowing which things they had to put together, without having learned how to put things together in a field more highly developed, were hopeless cases. My conclusion at this point is quite firm: in order to master Ekistics today, one must have a very good basic training in some other field.

His training

We now have to face the question of how an Ekistician can be trained. In order to facilitate an answer to this new, complicated and confusing subject I proceed with the clarification of the four basic questions: goals, levels of education, categories of experts and Ekistic units which they are able to serve.

Since the goals are usually expressed in very general terms, it is useful to make them much more specific by expressing them also in terms of the other three questions, as levels of education, categories of experts and Ekistic units. The goal of Ekistic education is the knowledge of the science of human settlements, i.e. a science which studies the five elements: Nature, Man, Society, Shells, Networks and their interrelationships. It is not the goal of education in Ekistics to create experts on any of these five elements, since this is the goal of other disciplines.

There are several levels of education for which we have to clarify whether we need or can have experts in Ekistics. These are the following: junior college, undergraduate, graduate, post-graduate, leadership and total (fig. 58). To the usual categories, of undergraduate, graduate or post-graduate studies, two more have been added. The junior college level has been added in order to answer the question of whether we can have people who would be able to work for small communities in the rural areas without having a full university degree. The leadership level has been added in order to face the question of whether we need people of a level higher than the usual post-graduate one, people who will provide the leadership in major efforts for human settlements.

We can now ask ourselves at which level should the training

58

education in Ekistics: definition of a policy

▓ areas to be covered (only indicatively shown)

of an Ekistician start. Should his training start at an undergraduate, graduate or even post-graduate level? I believe that, in this present phase, it is much safer to train Ekisticians at the graduate and post-graduate levels. I would be very much concerned if I had to train Ekisticians right from the undergraduate level. The reason is that with most people it becomes apparent whether or not they are capable of synthesis only after they have completed this level.

On the other hand we should not forget that we may need experts who can undertake Ekistic tasks in minor units only, let us say experts to deal with single villages or small neighbourhoods. These specialists, especially for the rural areas, may have to be trained at the junior college level or at the undergraduate level, provided they will be acting as technicians in this field under the leadership of Ekisticians.

The next questions are about the categories of Ekisticians and their specialisation within the field of Ekistics by elements, disciplines, phases of action and Ekistic units.

There are several ways in which we can define the categories of experts which will be needed for human settlements:

o division by the *elements* which are best known to the experts—this can be a division by experts coming from fields knowing more about Nature, Man, Society, Shells and Networks, or by experts who are most familiar with the synthesis of these elements;

o division by the *disciplines* from which the experts come and which they know more about, such as economics, social sciences, political sciences, administration, technical sciences, cultural disciplines, art, etc.;

o division by the *phase* of the work for which the experts are best fitted, such as analysis, definition of problems, development of policies, development of programmes, physical plans and designs, etc.

As the whole space available to Man on the face of this Earth can be divided into units of 15 sizes ranging from Man through room and house, to the whole Earth covered by Ecumenopolis, we can have a division of the experts into those who can cover the total or those who can deal with the micro-space such as houses and small neighbourhoods, or meso-space such as cities, or macro-space such as regions.

I do not believe that it is necessary at this point to define exactly how we want the experts to specialise within Ekistics. This is a question which depends much more on practical considerations than on theoretical desires. It is something that we will have to handle in practice with the understanding that we will need all types of persons in order to build the science of Ekistics.

Another question related to the training of an Ekistician is whether he should be trained in theory, or in practice, or in both. Again I believe he should be trained simultaneously in theory and practice. Unless he can see the theory, his practice will lose importance, and unless he practices

continuously, theory may remain quite vague. We must always keep in mind, though, that since we have not developed an Ekistic theory completely, it is much safer to base the training on practice, which, if nothing else, gives a realistic view of the Ekistic problems. People who will be given practical experience may not learn all there is to learn, but they will learn something; while people learning only theory may not be able to accomplish anything.

One last thing about education: since we know little about Ekistics at this point, we must rely on some general rules, valid in other sciences and technologies, and we must learn from the experience of the past.

Therefore, we reach the conclusion that Ekisticians must work as hard as possible in order to cover this vast unknown field. A body of acquired knowledge and an experience in training do not exist in a new science. In Ekistics we have a very small body of knowledge and practically no experience in training. The effort, therefore, on the part of those who enter this field will be much greater than that required of those in the process of learning a well developed discipline. Only those who are prepared to participate in the formation of this new discipline, and who do not expect to learn it from others but by seeking the truth themselves, should enter this field.

Ekistics needs people who understand its problems and who are inspired by its potential and the tasks it has to fulfil. Ekistics needs people who are ready to venture into the unknown in order to illuminate it, and—even in the face of failures and defeats—to conquer the terrestrial space which is Man's natural habitat and which must again become a truly human settlement. Ekistics needs people who do not '*know*' but '*learn*'; people who have decided that 'like health, learning cannot be acquired passively'.[55]

BOOK TWO

FACTS

'Our facts must be correct. Our theories need not be if they help us to discover important new facts.'

HANS SELYE *Stress*

The facts must be correct. This is why I separated them in a special book which is inspired by the desire to present facts in a descriptive way. This is not completely possible, because even the presentation of facts in a certain order is inspired by a theory. I have tried my best, however, to present facts which are not influenced by my own theories of action and methods for their study. This book contains four chapters:

CHAPTER THREE

THE SUBJECT—EKISTIC ANALYSIS

HUMAN SETTLEMENTS

Numbers and sizes

In this chapter I have tried to describe our subject as accurately as possible. I am deeply convinced that our facts must be correct. Many solutions which do not serve Man at all well—especially contemporary solutions—have failed because they have overlooked some facts and have had questionable interpretation of others. I have tried to approach this accuracy of description by way of common sense.

For this reason I have not followed any existing theory or classification. I studied the facts and let them guide me to an understanding of them. 'Common sense is not what we put into the world. It is what we find there.'[1]

I begin this effort with an attempt to define the actual dimensions of our subject matter, the number of settlements, of people who inhabit them and of the areas they cover. By so doing I differ radically from studies which give descriptions of only a few successful settlements; at first this was done for the really successful ones, and now it is being done for the fashionable ones as well. I also differ radically from studies which concentrate on the ailing settlements or their ailing parts. I do not believe that we can learn from the ailing parts, we can learn from the healthy ones, and we can complete our knowledge with the deviations from the normal conditions which prove the nature of the disease.

There are probably somewhat over 14,000,000 human settlements on this Earth. Among these there are three settlements with over 10,000,000 people. The total number of settlements over 1,000,000 is 141, over 100,000 is 1,460 and over 5,000 people is 32,700. In addition there are perhaps 10,000,000 composite rural settlements of all kinds and about 4,000,000 single family settlements. If, however, we take the dividing line between urban and rural settlements as being at the two thousand inhabitant level, and define an urban settlement as one with more than two thousand inhabitants, then there are about 92,200 urban settlements in the world and about 14,000,000 rural settlements (fig. 59). These figures are based on a study prepared by the COF Research Project, Athens Center of Ekistics, Athens Technological Institute.

The numbers of settlements are not indicative of the distribution of the population since their sizes differ enormously. Actually, 53·5 per cent of the population of the Earth still lives in rural settlements whose numbers, as defined above, represent 99 per cent of the total number of settlements (fig. 60).

In 1960 all the 14,000,000 had 1,625 million inhabitants, whereas the 92,200 urban ones had only slightly less—that is 1,335 million. These figures give us an average size of 208 inhabitants for all permanent settlements on the Earth, since even one-family separate settlements are considered distinct units. If we remove this category and take the average of the composite settlements with a permanent population of more than ten inhabitants, which number about 8,230,000, the average size of the Earth's permanent settlements is about 350 inhabitants.

Since we do not possess exact data for the minor settlements, we shall proceed to a detailed analysis of numbers and population considering those with more than 2,000 inhabitants. We find that although the numbers of settlements in every category between 2,000 and 10 million range from 59,500 to 3, the total population in each category is about 100 million; the only exception is the last category which has 41 million (fig. 61).

The distribution of settlements by size and the distribution of the total population by size of settlements varies among continents and countries. The extent of this distribution fluctuation from country to country can be seen in comparing Switzerland, as one of the most developed countries, with Greece, as one of those partially developed and Ghana, as a representative less developed nation (fig. 62). The differences are quite clear in the percentage of small settlements, which are many more in countries not technologically developed.

At this point, it may be worth estimating not only the number of settlements presently existing on this Earth, but the total number of settlements that have ever existed; making a distinction between those that existed in the past and the present-day settlements. It is difficult to make such an estimate, for many civilisations have disappeared completely, leaving us with very little data concerning them; on the other hand, there are a great number of settlements—urban and

H

59

number of settlements divided into basic categories

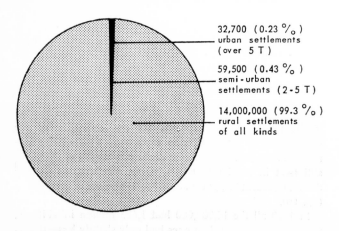

32,700 (0.23 %)
urban settlements
(over 5 T)

59,500 (0.43 %)
semi-urban
settlements (2-5 T)

14,000,000 (99.3 %)
rural settlements
of all kinds

60

populations of basic categories of settlements in millions (1960)

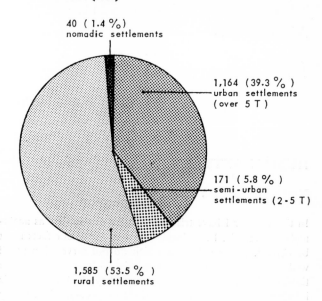

40 (1.4 %)
nomadic settlements

1,164 (39.3 %)
urban settlements
(over 5 T)

171 (5.8 %)
semi-urban
settlements (2-5 T)

1,585 (53.5 %)
rural settlements

rural—which may have existed from time immemorial and are still functioning today. Taking this into consideration, as well as the total population that has lived on this Earth since the beginning of civilisation (circa 4000 B.C.) which is of the order of 60,000 million, and ignoring the nomadic and semi-nomadic settlements, which are created for short periods of time only, we can conclude that the total of permanent settlements which have existed on this Earth since the dawn of civilisation cannot be more than twice the number of present-day settlements. This indicates a figure of, say, about 20 million of which more than 19 million are rural-agricultural settlements. Therefore, it is evident that when we deal with agricultural settlements, a species which has been reproduced on this Earth so many millions of times and of which we can still study some 14 million examples, that we can speak with some certainty about the phenomena related to them.

The corresponding figures for urban settlements are 92,200 for those existing at present, and perhaps 120,000 for all those that have ever existed. We should be able to speak with some certainty about a species which has been reproduced 120,000 times and of which 92,200 survive and can be studied in detail.

When we come to urban settlements of more than 20,000 inhabitants, 7,200 of which still survive and whose number throughout human history probably does not exceed 9,000, we can still deal with them with a certain amount of confidence. We have many examples of urban settlements created during various historical periods and still surviving.

When, however, we reach the number of settlements with over 100,000 inhabitants, where in fact we find the large category of dynamic settlements, we see that today their

number is not even 1,500 and it is questionable whether in the entire history of Man their total number exceeds 1,800. These numbers are quite limited, especially if we think of the dynamic settlements which have only lately started to grow and have completely transformed the initial static settlements that once composed their nuclei. About them we cannot speak with much certainty.

As for settlements with over one million people, there are 141 in existence today, and perhaps there have not been more than 150 in our entire history. This, together with the fact that the greatest concentration of such settlements is in a few countries of certain continents only, and that large areas of the world have only a few settlements of this category (lately created), leads us to the conclusion that we cannot speak with any certainty about these settlements.

Next we come to settlements with over two million people; there are only 65 today, and these are the first, for there have never been settlements of equal size in the past. All of them are recent, existing in only a few parts of the world and probably none of them have completed their cycle of evolution. Therefore, we are allowed to draw only tentative conclusions about them. The same is even more valid concerning settlements with more than ten million people which number only three (London, New York and Tokyo).

Finally, if we talk of the megalopolises, the first composite settlements which have tens of millions of people, we find only two in existence today, that is, the eastern American megalopolis, spreading from Boston to Washington D.C. with 37 million inhabitants, and the Japanese one of the area of Tokyo-Fukuoka with 65 million.[2] The former has just taken

61

world urban population classified as to size of settlement (1960)

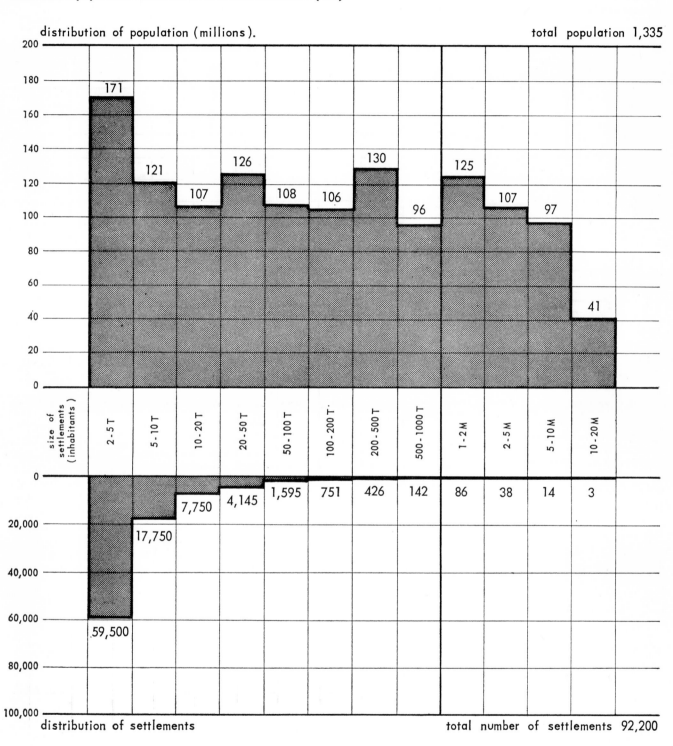

distribution of population (millions).   total population 1,335

	2-5 T	5-10 T	10-20 T	20-50 T	50-100 T	100-200 T	200-500 T	500-1000 T	1-2 M	2-5 M	5-10 M	10-20 M
population	171	121	107	126	108	106	130	96	125	107	97	41

size of settlements (inhabitants)

| settlements | 59,500 | 17,750 | 7,750 | 4,145 | 1,595 | 751 | 426 | 142 | 86 | 38 | 14 | 3 |

distribution of settlements   total number of settlements 92,200

83

urban population classified as to size of settlement
comparison in countries of different urbanisation

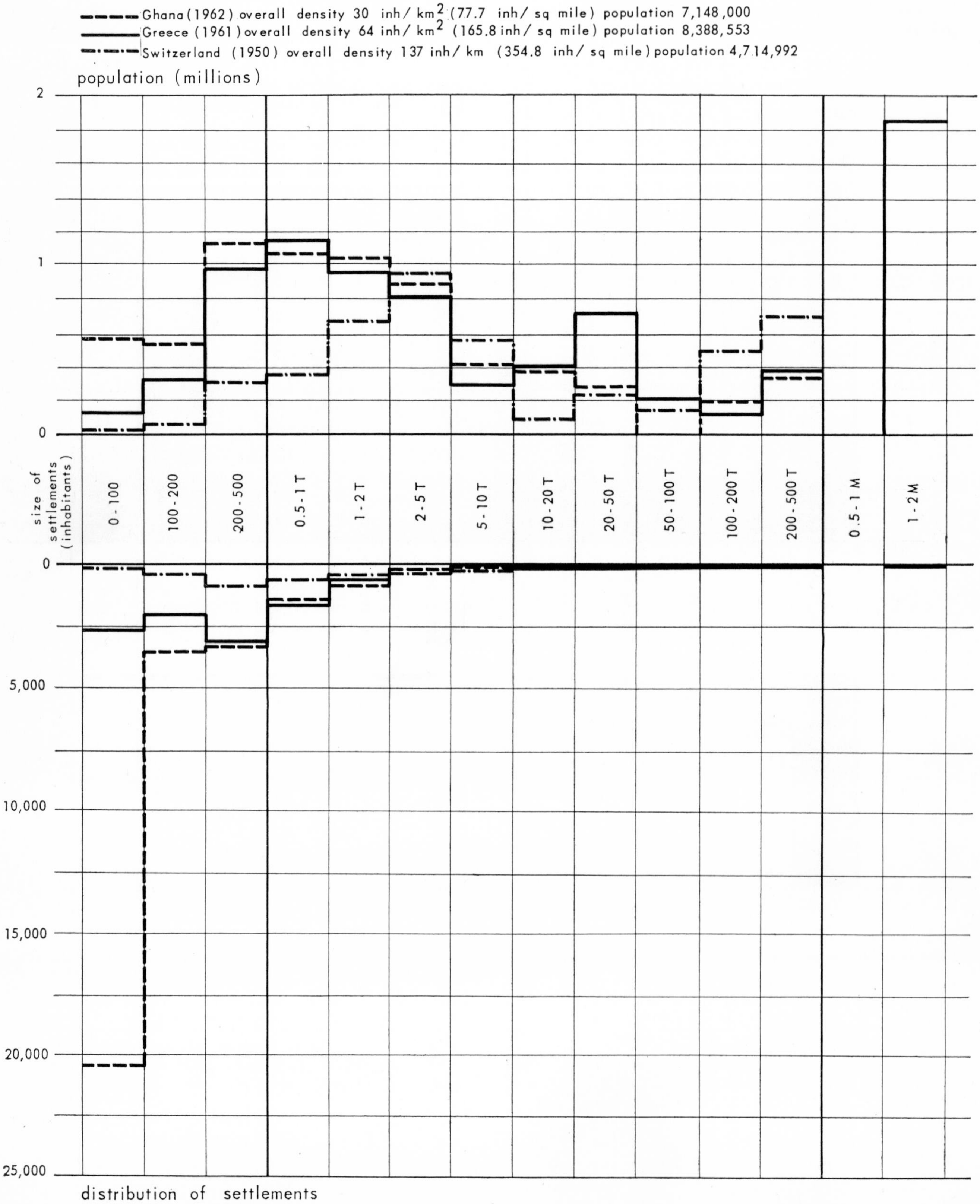

------- Ghana (1962) overall density 30 inh/ km^2 (77.7 inh/ sq mile) population 7,148,000
———— Greece (1961) overall density 64 inh/ km^2 (165.8 inh/ sq mile) population 8,388,553
—·—·— Switzerland (1950) overall density 137 inh/ km (354.8 inh/ sq mile) population 4,7.14,992

population (millions)

2

1

0

size of
settlements
(inhabitants)

| 0 - 100 | 100 - 200 | 200 - 500 | 0.5 - 1 T | 1 - 2 T | 2 - 5 T | 5 - 10 T | 10 - 20 T | 20 - 50 T | 50 - 100 T | 100 - 200 T | 200 - 500 T | 0.5 - 1 M | 1 - 2 M |

0

5,000

10,000

15,000

20,000

25,000

distribution of settlements

63

number of settlements

indicating the cumulative number of physically
separated settlements larger than the size mentioned.

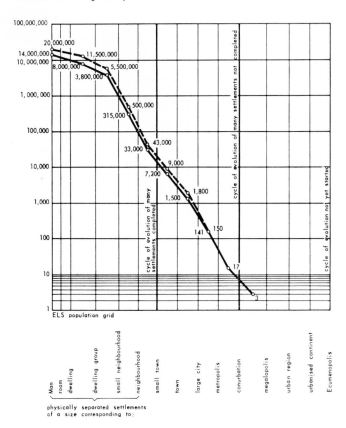

shape and was studied for the first time by the geographer
Jean Gottmann.[3] We are definitely unable to draw conclusions
of general validity about the megalopolises.

At this point, we can draw a chart showing how far we
can rely on the existing numbers of species in drawing
conclusions of general validity (fig. 63). From this chart, we
see that in the whole range of the Ekistic scale, we can speak
with some certainty about settlements of up to one hundred
thousand persons, and with diminishing validity about those
of a larger size, because in the latter case:
  ○ the number of the species is small,
  ○ their creation has taken place recently,
  ○ most of the settlements have not completed, and
  ○ some have only just begun, their life cycle.
On the basis of similar considerations and following
measurements of areas carried out by the Athens Center of

Ekistics, we are now in a position to talk about the surface
of the settlements, or the area of the Earth covered by them.
It is not possible to estimate the whole surface covered by
settlements, since even remote forests are settled in the sense
already explained; hence assumptions about their boundaries
are rather difficult. Even for the built-up areas of settlements,
definition of boundaries is complicated; nevertheless, an
effort has been made to estimate the areas considered built-up,
on the basis of the same criteria for all settlements. It was
found that the total surface of the built-up area in rural
settlements with a population below 2,000 was 135,000 sq. km.
(52,124 sq. mi.), the total surface of urban settlements was
223,000 sq. km. (86,100 sq. mi.) and the combined surface of
all human settlements was 358,000 sq. km. (138,224 sq. mi.).
This surface contains 0·875 per cent of the total surface of the
habitable part of the Earth, which is reckoned to be around
40,900,000 sq. km. (15,791,490 sq. mi.), for the year 1960[4]
(fig. 64).

On the basis of similar considerations, we can now estimate
the total investment in human settlements. Rural settlements
in 1960 had a total investment of around $778 billion, while
the urban ones had an estimated total of $3,471 billion, giving
a combined total value of about $4,249 billion, of which 18·3
per cent was in rural settlements and 81·3 per cent in urban
ones. If we remember that the total rural population is somewhat larger than the urban, we recognise that the total investment per urban inhabitant on the Earth is at present about
5½ times higher than the investment per rural inhabitant;
and if we compare this investment to the surfaces covered
by rural and urban settlements, we find that the investment
in the urban settlements per acre is about three times that
of the built-up part of rural settlements.

These figures do not necessarily show a difference in the
value these settlements hold for Man, from the point of view
of production and productivity in material goods or in other
values like art, attitude in life, etc.; in each case the difference
may be much larger or perhaps smaller than the one to six
per inhabitant or one to five per unit of surface. On the other
hand, the real difference in community or family cohesion,
in aesthetic values, in balance between all elements of a
settlement may be either smaller or larger in rural than
in urban settlements.

Species

○ *Similarities*

The Earth is covered by millions of human settlements. No
two of them are alike, but many of them have similar basic
characteristics which can be used to classify them into different
categories.

One classification is by size. There are single settlements
consisting of one farmhouse, one military camp, one

85

total area of urban settlements classified as to size of settlement (1960)

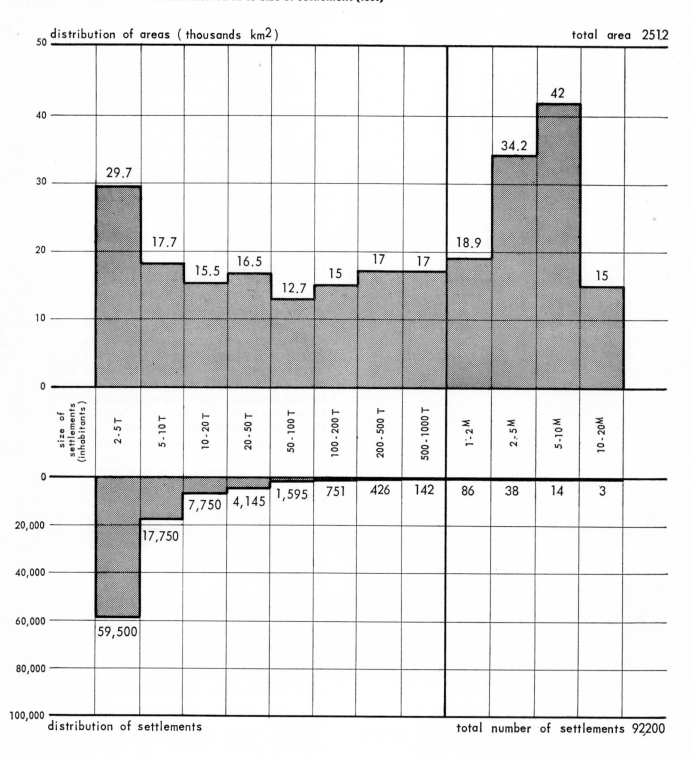

monastery, etc., and composite settlements consisting of many houses, camps and other functions. Classification by size in this sense does not refer to the number of people, buildings or functions included so much as to the number of units which form the settlement. Therefore, the farmhouse of a family in the open countryside, or a monastery enclosed by a wall and forming a cohesive compound unit is a single settlement, while a few farmhouses together, or even a small military camp, which has additions around it in the form of small houses built by merchants, are composite settlements. In a similar way settlements can be classified by the number of persons inhabiting them, by the number of families, or buildings, and so forth.

A second classification of settlements is based upon their permanency. We can have temporary settlements—tents or carts belonging to nomads, huts belonging to shepherds or fishermen—semi-permanent settlements—nomadic camps or army camps, which are not inhabited the year-round but only during certain periods. Finally, there are permanent settlements, inhabited the year-round. In another sense, we find settlements which are considered permanent because they are built with permanent materials (pukka settlements of India), or temporary because their shells consist of temporary materials (kutcha settlements). The fact that the shells of the settlement are permanent or non-permanent has some influence on the permanency of the settlement itself, but it is not so important a factor as that of the settlement being used the year-round. If this is the case there is good reason to believe that the settlement will gradually acquire permanent Shells. Settlements which are built of temporary materials, although inhabited the year-round, are usually in the first phase of becoming permanent settlements. It is the permanency of the settlement and not of the Shells that is the decisive factor.

Another classification is based upon the method by which settlements have been created. In this classification we have 'natural' settlements which have emerged by themselves, and planned settlements which have been built on the basis of a preconceived plan. There are very few planned ones in comparison to the total number of settlements; and even in the case of those originally built according to a plan, their subsequent development has seldom been based on the same plan. We know of no case where the builder of a settlement was able to foresee its total evolution and plan in advance for the developments to come. Hence, almost all settlements finally turn into 'natural' ones. Some have begun according to a plan, but very few still keep the characteristics of their original plan.

One of the most important classifications of settlements is that according to their basic function and purpose, for it is this that gives the settlement its most important characteristics and influences the other elements correspondingly.

Using these types of classifications we have the following categories of settlements:

o rural settlements such as nomadic, agricultural and others of a permanent or non-permanent nature, serving all types of primary production (fishermen's settlements, hunters' settlements, etc.);

o institutions, that is, settlements built for a specific purpose and for a specific group of people, which have, therefore, a characteristic location and shell. These can be governmental institutions (prisons, hospitals, etc.), military (camps, forts, etc.), or religious, as are monasteries—these follow their own laws, especially when they are isolated, and surrounded by open country;

o urban settlements; these fall into two major categories (mixed urban-agricultural settlements, and towns and cities), and perhaps into a third one, the metropolises (in case we have static metropolises which I do not know yet), and some minor ones. I do not mention the megalopolis, because the megalopolis is always dynamic in nature and as such belongs to another category;

o dynamic urban settlements; this category, although a very important one, has been generally overlooked up to now because it is the most recent. Dynamically growing urban settlements include Dynapolis or the dynamically growing city, Dynametropolis or the dynamically growing metropolis, and megalopolis which, as I have said, is always dynamic.

If we attempt to study the distribution of the entire range of human settlements by size and basic category on the Ekistic polygram, we reach the picture given in fig. 65. Nomadic settlements cover the small Ekistic units up to the size of a small neighbourhood. Agricultural settlements cover the whole range from the single family farm to a relatively large community. Mixed urban-agricultural centres start with the dimensions beyond the small neighbourhood and go up to four or five thousand people. Towns and cities start from two thousand people and reach up to fifty thousand, with very few exceeding this. Metropolises start from fifty thousand people on up, especially in countries of great technological development (like the U.S.A.). Dynapolises begin as cities which then turn into Dynapolises, etc.

o *Examples*

In order to present the whole range of the species in a systematic way I used a unified system of classification of their basic types. Combining the 'creation' and 'size' classifications, we find some characteristic examples of settlements from the earliest and most primitive ones to the most recent and developed. The most prevalent types of settlements around the Earth are still nomadic settlements, 'natural' agricultural villages, mixed urban-agricultural, towns and cities, metropolises and, recently, the various types of dynamic settlements. These settlements are presented in a series of eight characteristic examples. The scales of presentation

settlements classified as to their nature and population

	1	2	4	40	250	1.5 T	9 T	50 T	300 T	2 M	14 M	100 M	700 M	5,000 M	30,000 M
isolated settlements															
nomadic settlements															
agricultural settlements															
urban - agricultural settlements															
towns and cities															
metropolis															
Dynametropolis															
Dynamegalopolis															

ELS documentation grid.

Bottom axis: Man, room, dwelling, dwelling group, small neigh/hood, neighbourhood, small town, town, large city, metropolis, conurbation, megalopolis, urban region, urban continent, Ecumenopolis

have been selected in such a way as to allow comparisons of several settlements in the same scale and hence lead to an understanding of similarities and differences.

In nomadic settlements, the economy is usually based on cattle breeding; Man and Society are primitive and so are the community services. Nomads usually form self-governing communities and, although they have sometimes developed their own culture to a high degree, they are far behind technologically. The number of inhabitants in a nomadic settlement is small, usually not exceeding several score, even though there have been cases when numbers could be reckoned in the hundreds, and, in times past, nomadic settlements of some thousands have been formed. If I had to venture an estimate, I would say that the average nomadic settlement may have between fifty and a hundred inhabitants. Since these settlements are temporary, they hardly affect the natural environment at all; although they draw from the resources of the countryside—water, grass, wood—they seldom destroy these natural resources. Their shells are always temporary, either transportable or made of local materials having no permanency. Thus they leave practically no traces behind them, for even if some protective walls are built, they disintegrate easily. It is characteristic of nomads that either they do not limit their settlement by any kind of boundary, since they have no notion of land ownership, or they build a temporary barrier which, however, has no legal meaning since land is not owned by anyone, does not cost anything, and is abandoned after the season of temporary settlement is over. Thus, when they enclose a space with a fence they tend to adopt the most economic ratio of periphery to surface, that is a circle, and thus secure their possessions, usually cattle, in the easiest and most economic way (fig. 66).

The density of population in such areas is about one inhabitant per sq. km. or 0·01 inhabitant per hectare (0·004 inh/acre) for the whole inhabited area and approximately 100–150 persons per hectare (40–60 inh/acre) if we consider only the surface enclosed within the boundaries created by the inhabitants: that is, the nucleus or the part containing the shells of the settlement.

Agricultural settlements are inhabited by farmers or live-stock breeders and have their own local culture. The great majority of them are natural settlements, usually identified as villages. Their population is usually in the hundreds although some have only a few scores of people and others have more than a thousand. I would be inclined to state that the average village in the world has between one hundred and a thousand inhabitants. The functions of the community are related to primary production although there may be some commerce and handicrafts as well as elementary educational and social services. The built-up settlement is well adjusted to its natural environment. It is usually in a location protected from adverse climatic elements. If there is land which is not of high agricultural quality, it is likely that the nucleus or built-up part of the settlement is constructed on it. The pattern of the built-up settlement shows the existence of individual properties; land has a certain value, and, therefore, no land is left between private properties which may be big to allow for keeping livestock and growing vegetables. The built-up part is the most densely inhabited area, though there may well be some people belonging to the community who live on their farms outside of the nucleus. The Shells are permanent, usually well built from local materials. Average densities of such settlements are about 1·33 persons per hectare (0·53 inh/acre) for the whole area

66

nuclei of nomadic settlements

**average density of built-up area
150 inh/ha (60 inh/acre)**

**average overall density of area
utilised by inhabitants
0.01 inh/ha (0.004 inh/acre)**

Jkerra, Libya (1966)

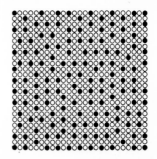

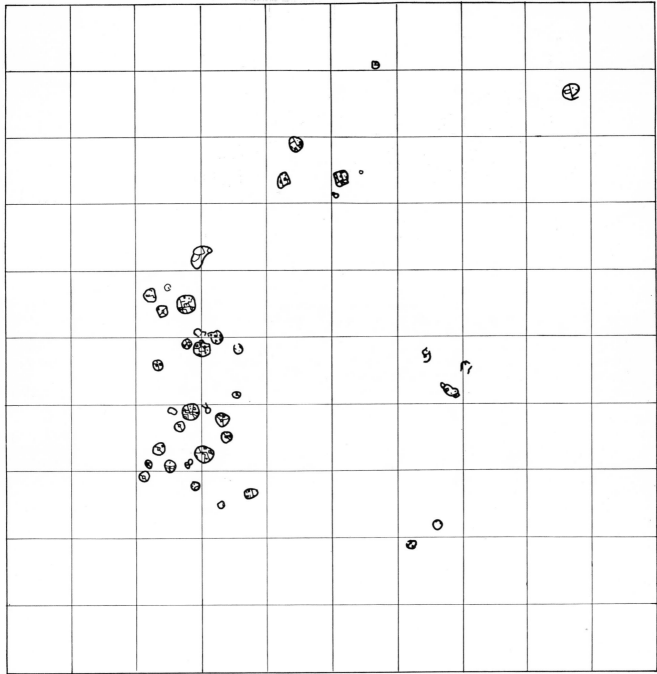

grid 100 x 100 m

67

nucleus of agricultural settlements

E. Pappas, Greece (1961)

average density of built-up area
80 inh/ha (32 inh/acre)

average overall density of area
utilised by inhabitants
1.33 inh/ha (0.53 inh/acre)

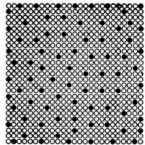

grid 100 x 100 m

metres

0   100   200   300   400   500   600   700   800   900   1000

0   500   1000   1500   2000   2 500   3000

feet

and approximately 80 persons per hectare (32 inh/acre) in the nucleus or its built-up part (fig. 67).

Mixed urban-agricultural settlements are agricultural villages with urban centres and are usually in the middle of a rural area that is not large enough to support a town, but still requires several urban services. Such services are, therefore, grafted onto one of the central agricultural settlements, and a hybrid settlement emerges. Its population is larger than that of the surrounding villages and the average may be between one and five thousand people. Man and Society are semi-agricultural, semi-urban the urban dwellers having been exposed to a strong influence from the agricultural majority, while the latter usually remain unchanged in the villages. The economy of the settlement is primary, secondary and tertiary as we may find small industries, commerce and trade, schools and some central administration. These urban-agricultural centres are the marketing centre of a system connecting them with the villages of the surrounding area. Their adjustment to the natural environment is almost the same as that of the agricultural settlements. The built-up area consists of two parts and two patterns which are merged together and inseparable. The central part, which usually contains all the urban functions, becomes a core of high density surrounded by the less densely and formally built agricultural part. It is quite clear that land properties have here a greater value than in the villages and in the urbanised commercial and business centre properties are smaller and much more densely built. The Shells, especially of the urban part, are more expensive, and of a more elaborate construction than those of the agricultural settlements. Density in these settlements varies from two to several tens of persons per hectare for the whole area and approximately 110 persons per hectare (44 inh/acre) in the built-up part (fig. 68).

Towns and cities were, with few exceptions, the only type of urban settlements existing on the Earth for five or six thousand years, until new types were born in the eighteenth century. They still form the largest group of urban settlements although several of them have now been transformed into new types of settlements. Their main characteristic is that they are static. This, in the past, was expressed by the fact that they were usually surrounded by walls, and even when they were not, they remained compact since no urban dweller could live out in the open countryside. These towns and cities are larger than the settlements already listed; they contain two to twenty thousand people and sometimes even up to fifty and a hundred thousand; but they seldom go beyond this. Only very few cities of the past are known to have had a population in the hundreds of thousands and these were the administrative capitals of empires—Rome, Constantinople, Peking and perhaps ancient Edo, the present-day Tokyo (fig. 69). These exceptional cases had little influence on the average town or city. In towns and cities Man and Society are both urban and almost all the economy is urban; the rural population, if there is any, is comparatively very small. These settlements

have superimposed their Shells on the natural landscape, but they have seldom spoiled it; usually they have respected its form, if for no other reason than economy. In most cases changing the form (to any great extent) of the surface of the Earth in an urban area was an impossible task. The financial possibilities of the earlier inhabitants were also limited by the fact that they usually had to carry out an economically and technologically big task, that is to protect their cities from enemies by the construction of defensive walls. The Shells of these cities are very compact; they are densely built and much more elaborate than almost all agricultural and semi-agricultural settlements. Their density varies from 150 to 350 inhabitants per hectare (60–140 inh/acre).

Growing cities have by their nature a lower overall density, as we can see in our contemporary cities, where modern developments, especially the introduction of the car, decrease the density even further. Present-day, medium size cities have a much lower density than the equivalent cities of the past because both density-decreasing factors (i.e. a more widely spread city and the car) have participated in their development. Their average density may be around 60 to 100 inhabitants per hectare (24–40 inh/acre); or an average of 75 (30 inh/acre). In the modern metropolis, both forces have entered into the picture even more; hence its density is of the order of 40 to 80 (16–32 inh/acre) or an average of 60 inhabitants per hectare (24 inh/acre).

Like the urban-agricultural settlements, towns and cities usually have one continuously developed centre, in most cases much more densely built than the rest. This is most apparent in the third dimension, the height of the buildings, and not always in the layout plan (figs. 70 and 71). In addition to this main centre or nucleus, they may show the beginnings of other secondary centres at nodal points in their circulatory system, which in larger cities may be quite important (figs. 72 and 73).

The metropolis is usually a major urban area with more than fifty thousand people, which, during a certain period, grew beyond its initial borders and incorporated other small settlements, both urban and rural, which existed around it. There were very few metropolises before the eighteenth century, when the cities first began to change into dynamic ones (Dynapolises) and to grow into Dynametropolises. I doubt if a single static metropolis exists today. Most of them are rapidly changing. Their sizes range from fifty thousand inhabitants to about ten million, and the average is around one to three million (fig. 74). The metropolis is a multi-centre urban settlement since, because of its physical dimensions, it can no longer be served by one centre (fig. 75). Though this is the main reason why it has more than one centre, there is another reason, a historical one; the metropolis has fused with other settlements and incorporated them along with their own centres (fig. 76).

The Dynapolis is the urban settlement which grows continuously. It was completely unknown before the eighteenth

68

urban-rural settlements

Karpenisi, Greece (1961)

average density of built-up area
110 inh/ha (44 inh/acre)

average overall density of area
utilised by inhabitants
2-40 inh/ha (0.8-16 inh/acre)

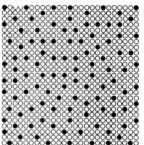

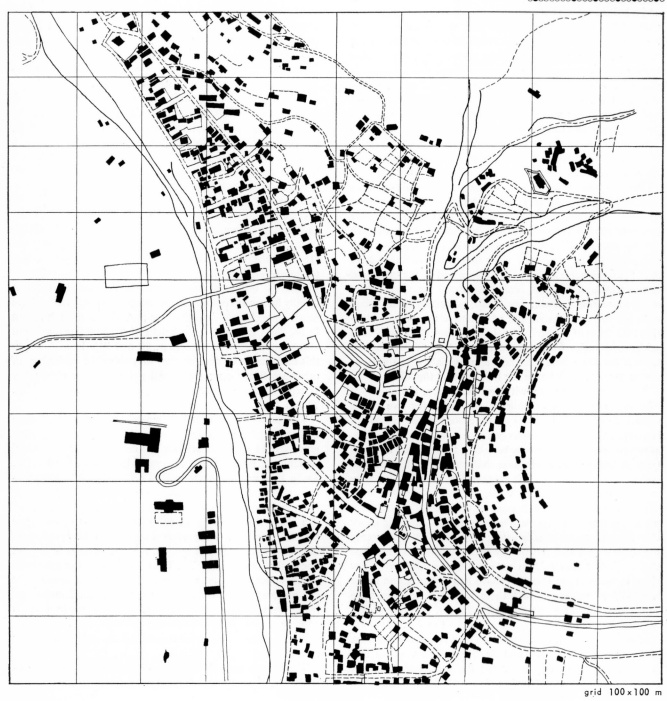

grid 100 × 100 m

metres

| 0 | 100 | 200 | 300 | 400 | 500 | 600 | 700 | 800 | 900 | 1000 |

| 0 | 500 | 1000 | 1500 | 2000 | 2500 | 3000 |

feet

the real areas of the three largest cities before the eighteenth century

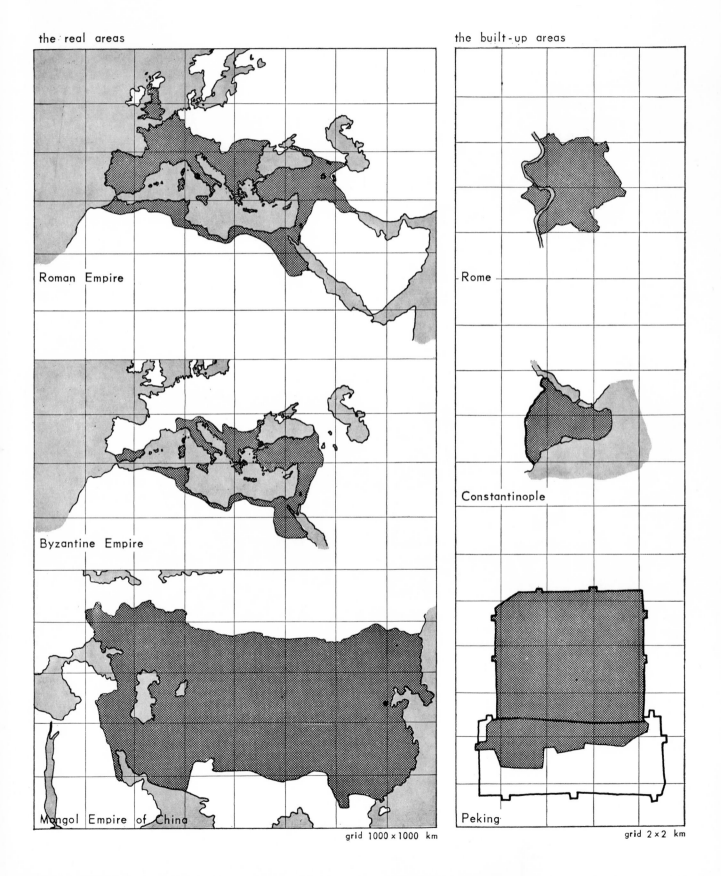

the real areas

Roman Empire

Byzantine Empire

Mongol Empire of China

grid 1000 × 1000 km

the built-up areas

Rome

Constantinople

Peking

grid 2 × 2 km

towns

average density of built-up area
150 inh/ha (60 inh/acre)

Larissa, Greece (1961)

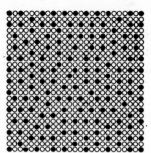

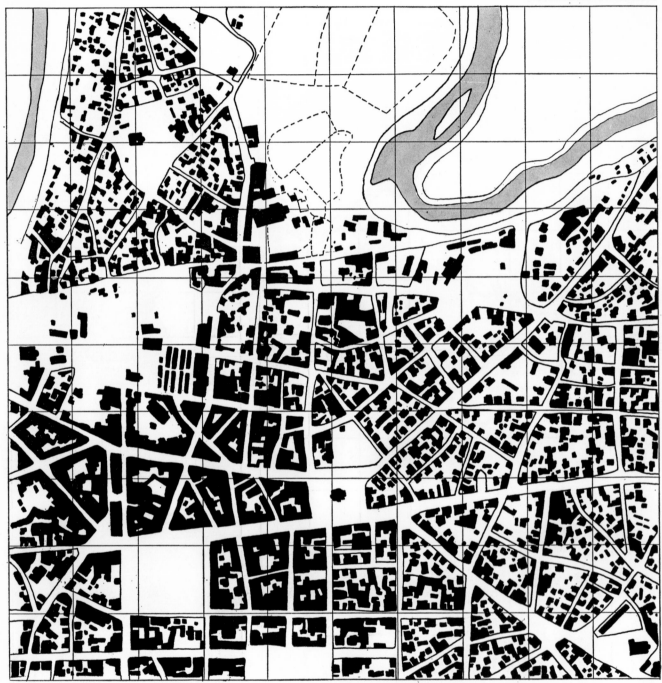

grid 100 x 100 m

metres

0	100	200	300	400	500	600	700	800	900	1000

0	500	1000	1500	2000	2500	3000

feet

71

towns

average overall density of urban area
75 inh/ha (30 inh/acre)

Larissa, Greece (1961)

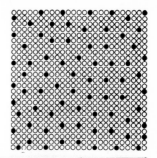

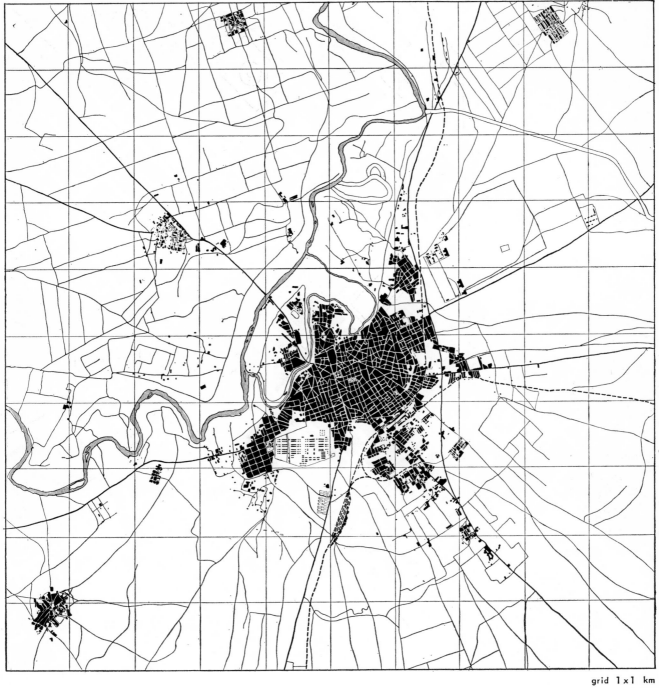

grid 1 x 1 km

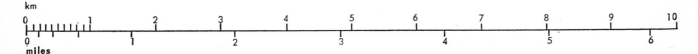

km

0   1   2   3   4   5   6   7   8   9   10

0   1   2   3   4   5   6

miles

72

cities

**average density of built-up area
180 inh/ha (72 inh/acre)**

Patras, Greece (1961)

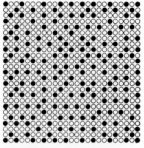

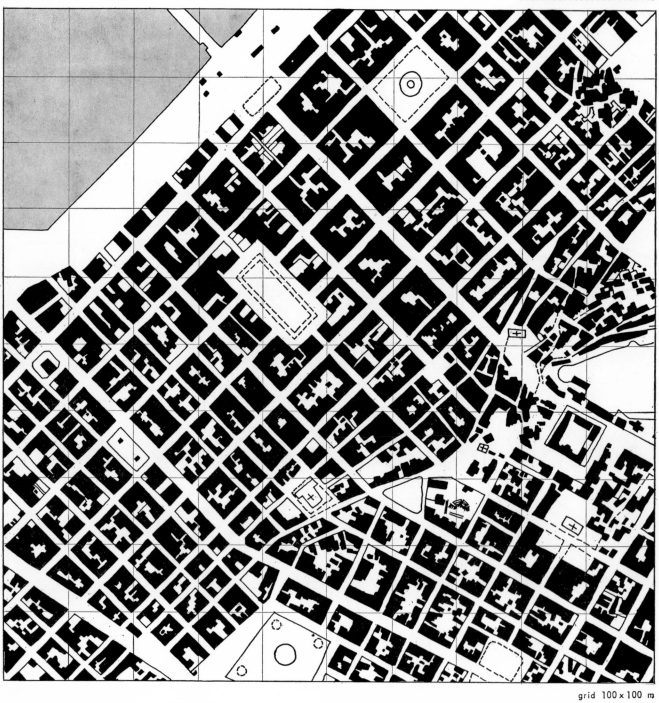

grid 100 x 100 m

metres

0   100   200   300   400   500   600·   700   800   900   1000

0   500   1000   1500   2000   2500   3000
feet

73

cities

average overall density of urban area
70 inh/ha (28 inh/acre)

Patras, Greece (1961)

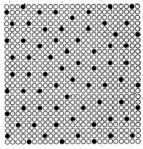

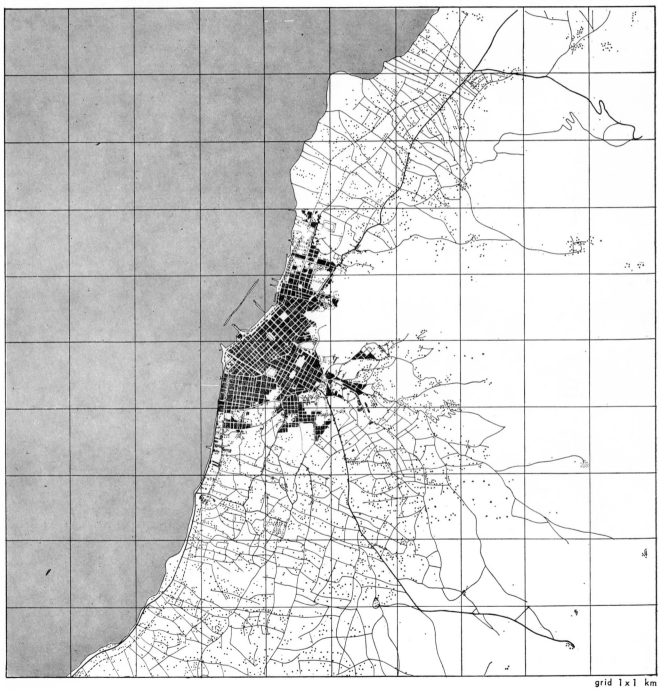

grid 1 x 1 km

km
0   1   2   3   4   5   6   7   8   9   10
0   1   2   3   4   5   6
miles

74

metropolis

average density of built-up area
100 inh/ha (40 inh/acre)

Athens, Greece (1964)

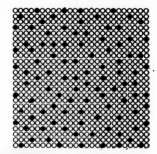

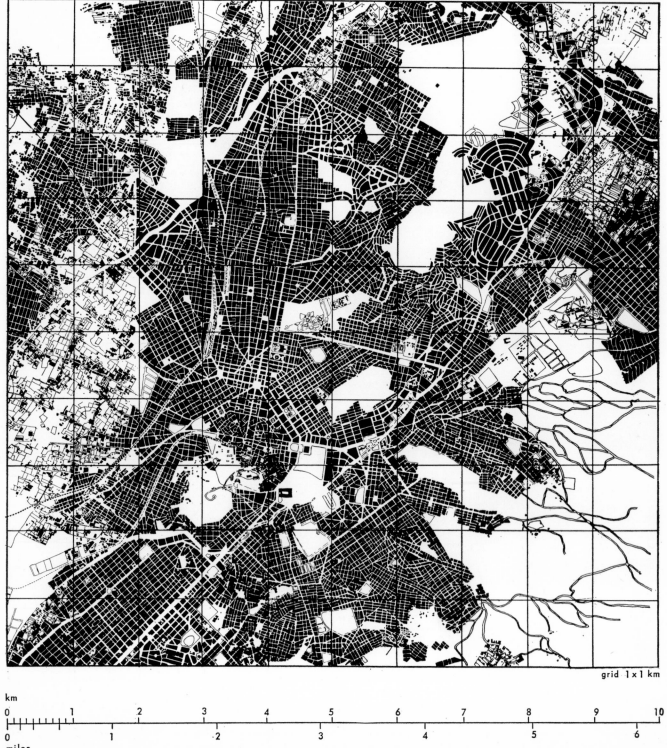

grid 1 x 1 km

km
0   1   2   3   4   5   6   7   8   9   10

0   1   2   3   4   5   6
miles

metropolis

**average overall density of metropolitan area
66 inh/ha (27 inh/acre)**

Athens, Greece (1964)

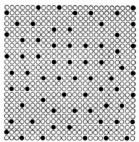

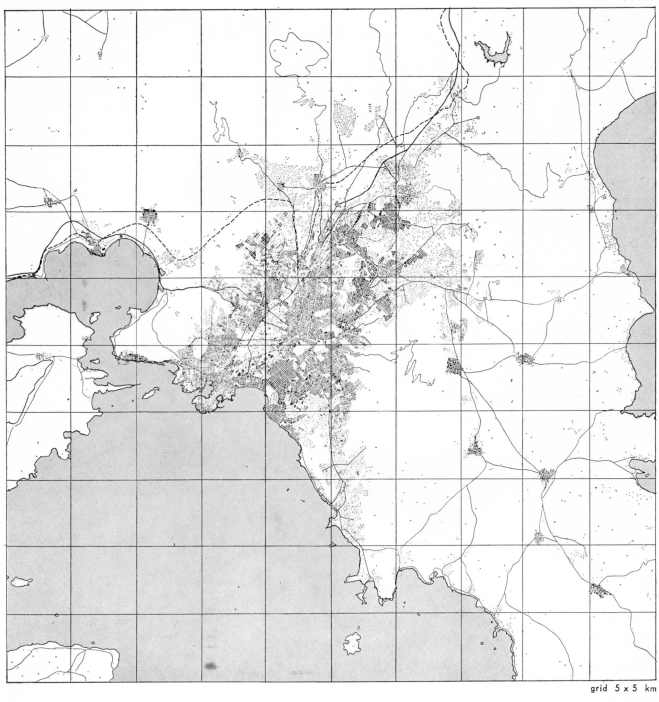

grid 5 x 5 km

km
0   5   10   15   20   25   30   35   40   45   50

0   10   15   20   25   30   35
miles

76

metropolis

**average overall density of metropolitan area
66 inh/ha (27 inh/acre)**

Athens, Greece (1964)

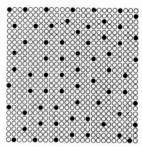

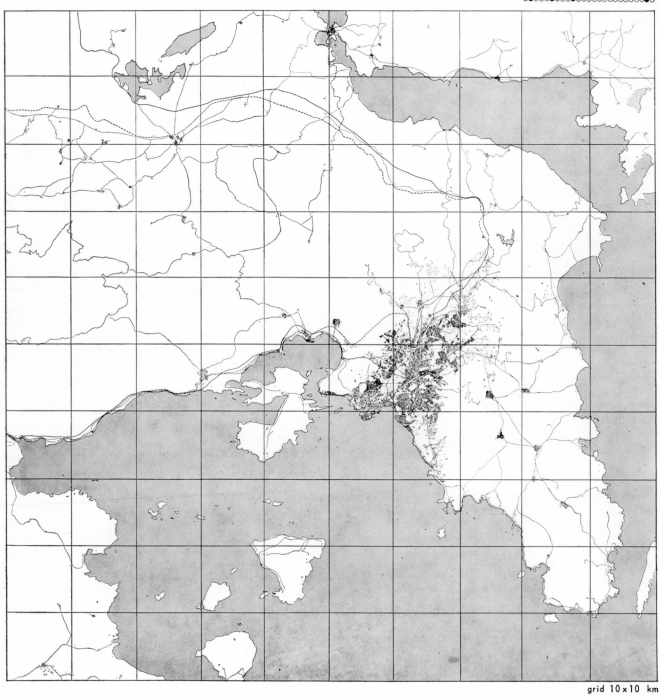

grid 10x10 km

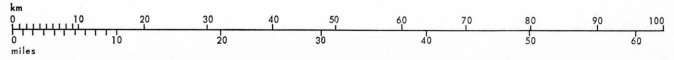

km
0   10   20   30   40   50   60   70   80   90   100

0   10   20   30   40   50   60
miles

century. Certainly some cities in the past grew at a high speed, but this lasted only for short periods, and only till they reached a certain limit, of a few thousands or a few score thousands of people. However, the present-day dynamic settlement, usually grows at an average of more than 3 per cent per year in population, and much more rapidly in investment and other economic aspects. Man and Society are living in a phase of very active development which is characteristic of every aspect of their life: economic, social, political, technological and cultural. When it was just a 'polis', a city, the present Dynapolis had a limited purpose—it was simply a military town, or a commercial centre, or an industrial town; but as a fullfledged Dynapolis it tends to attract additional interests and, in most cases, ceases to be specialised. Because of its rapid growth, practically always unplanned, Dynapolis spreads over the natural landscape with no respect for it—it spoils natural beauty and changes Nature all around it.

Dynametropolis is a metropolis which continues to exhibit constant growth, like the Dynapolis. Actually, Dynapolis very easily turns into a Dynametropolis since by growing constantly (unless it is in the desert or in a very sparsely populated hinterland) it spreads into other settlements. A Dynametropolis contains all the phenomena that characterise a Dynapolis, only intensified in scale and complexity. Nature gets spoiled and the entire structure goes out of control, while the Shells are uneven and inefficient, since even though it is much more expensive and much more elaborate, it is also unbalanced, and often contains very temporary, cheap and completely inadequate sectors (figs. 77, 78 and 79). In some respects the Dynametropolis contains examples of all types of settlements, including the nomadic, and the old and new agricultural ones.

The megalopolis is a very recent phenomenon. It has resulted from the merging of many metropolises. Its population is calculated in millions. It is distinct from the metropolis, either because its population exceeds ten million people, in which case it also covers a vast surface area, or because it has incorporated more than one metropolis. The megalopolis covers great areas at a present density from 2·7 persons per hectare (1·1 inh/acre) in the eastern American Megalopolis[5] to 8·6 in the Japanese Megalopolis[6] (figs. 80, 81 and 82). These densities must be viewed more critically than in other types of settlements, since the megalopolis is only now beginning to take shape and its future density may be much higher. The density of the first cities was almost certainly much lower than that of the later cities, and much closer to that of villages.

○ *Variations*

The eight examples of settlements which have been presented represent only in general characteristics the size, the function, the structure and the form of all settlements of their category. In practice we find that there are many variations of every species of human settlements, which depend on many variables leading to innumerable individual cases. I shall only attempt to give some characteristic examples to show how certain variables influence specific solutions in practice.

Natural conditions have an impact on built-up settlements though it is not as large as is often believed. The form of the landscape certainly imposes itself on the external shape of a settlement, though not on its internal structure; and climate dictates certain features in the micro-structure of the settlement (distances between houses for purposes of ventilation, form of the houses for the intake of air and exposure to the sun, etc.), but has little influence on its macro-scale.

Now let us take the variable, Man. We have no reason to believe that Man, in different cases, arrived at different types of solutions for his settlements when operating under similar conditions and working in a similar type of society. Furthermore, I do not believe that any differences can be attributed to race or religion. The only differences, which can be traced to a combination of factors related to the race and culture of Man, are details of architectural forms, and this is true only in the case of certain cultures that lived in isolation over long periods during which they elaborated their specific forms of architectural expression. However, such differences have never been so deeply-rooted as to influence the basic characteristics of human settlements at any major scale beyond architectural details.

This meant that the huts of the jungle dwellers in Asia, Africa or Europe were built according to the same rules, provided that the people that inhabited them had similar occupations—for instance cattle-breeding—lived in a similar landscape and climate and belonged to similar technological levels. In certain cases, I would go even further and say that, even under varying climatic conditions, huts of primitive people were often similar even though built with different materials. For example, the igloos of the Eskimos, are quite similar in conception to the straw huts of jungle tribes. In these cases, the people who created both types of dwellings belonged to similar technological levels, that is, they had not yet discovered more elaborate types of construction.[7]

If we take another variable—Society—it will once again be seen that similar types of societies, when all other conditions are equal, produce the same type of settlements. Fortresses in the north-western provinces of India near the Khyber Pass are not very different in conception and execution from fortresses in medieval Europe; and even the private family defence towers of some parts of the Peshawar plain have their counterparts in those parts of Italy and Greece where medieval settlements have survived. A different society, however, leads to different forms of settlements. Feudal settlements differ from the city-state settlements of ancient Greece, and the latter differ from Renaissance and industrial settlements. Society is perhaps the one cause of great differences

101

77

Dynamegalopolis

**average density of built-up area
120 inh/ha (48 inh/acre)**

London, England (1962)

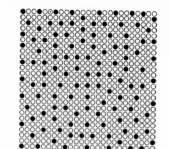

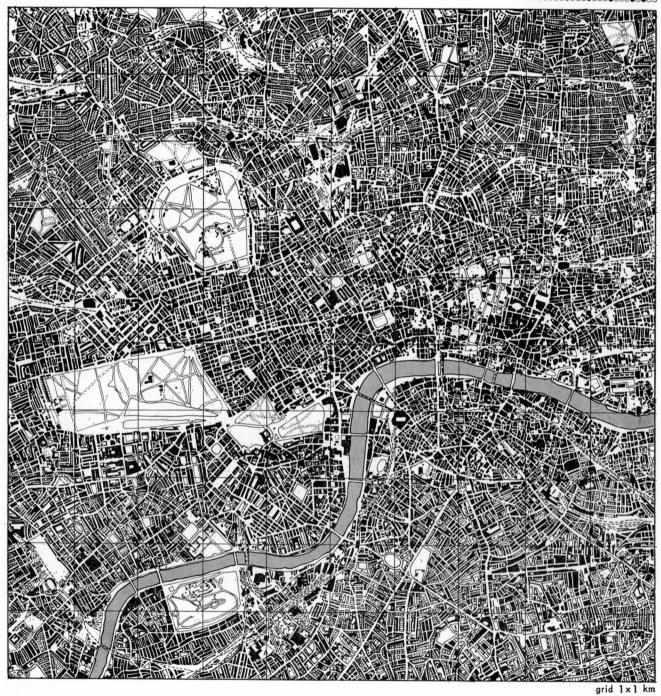

grid 1 x 1 km

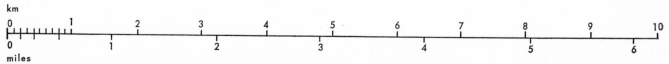

km
0   1   2   3   4   5   6   7   8   9   10

0   1   2   3   4   5   6
miles

78

Dynametropolis

**average overall density of metropolitan area
28 inh/ha (11 inh/acre)**

London, England (1962)

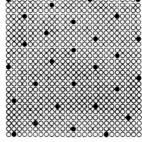

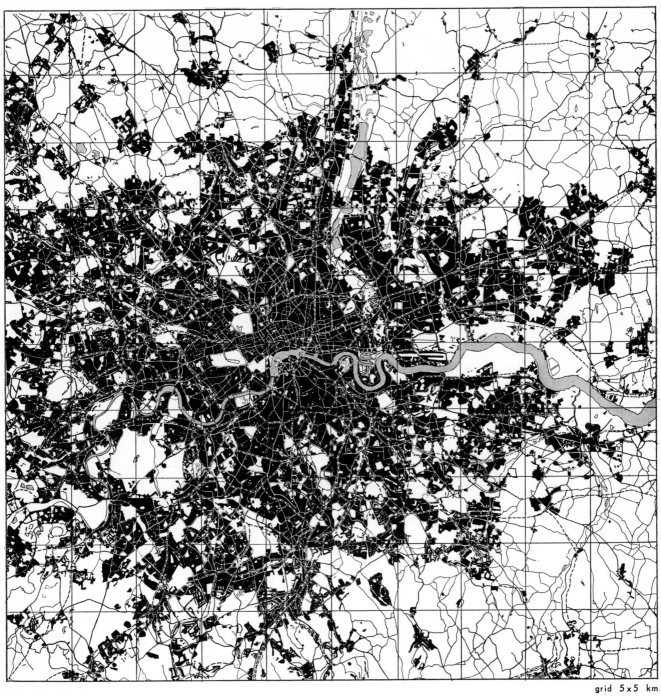

grid 5x5 km.

km
0   5   10   15   20   25   30   35   40   45   50

0   5   10   15   20   25   30
miles

79

Dynametropolis

**average overall density of metropolitan area
28 inh/ha (11 inh/acre)**

London, England (1962)

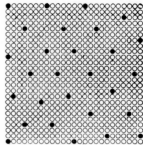

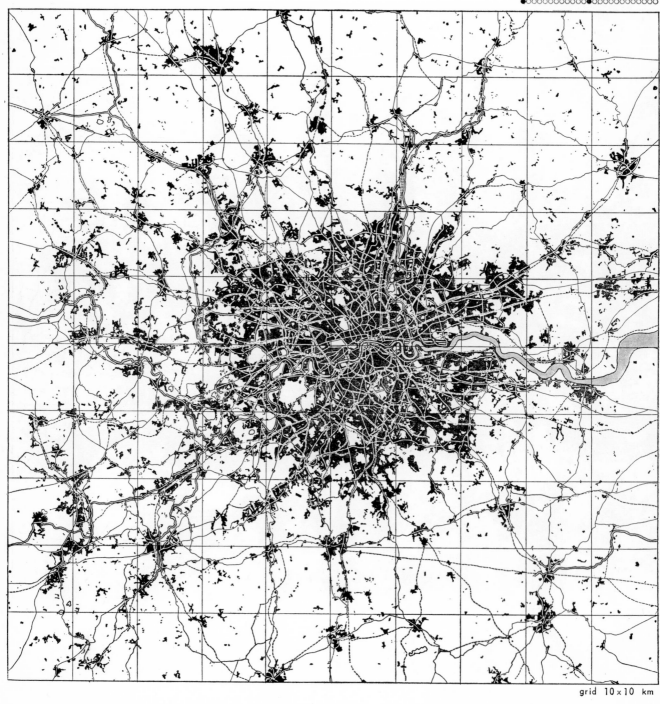

grid 10 x 10 km

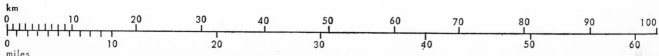

km
0   10   20   30   40   50   60   70   80   90   100

0   10   20   30   40   50   60
miles

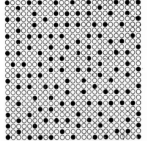

80

Dynamegalopolis

average density of built-up area
130 inh/ha (52 inh/acre)

New York, U.S.A. (1960)

grid 10×10 km

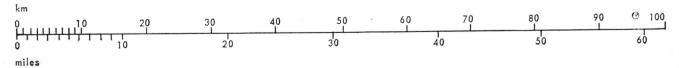

km

| 0 | 10 | 20 | 30 | 40 | 50 | 60 | 70 | 80 | 90 | 100 |

| 0 | 10 | 20 | 30 | 40 | 50 | 60 |

miles

81

Dynamegalopolis

average overall density of megalopolitan area
12 inh/ha (4.8 inh/acre)

megalopolis of the eastern seaboard, U.S.A. (1963)

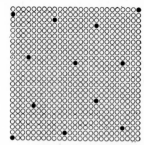

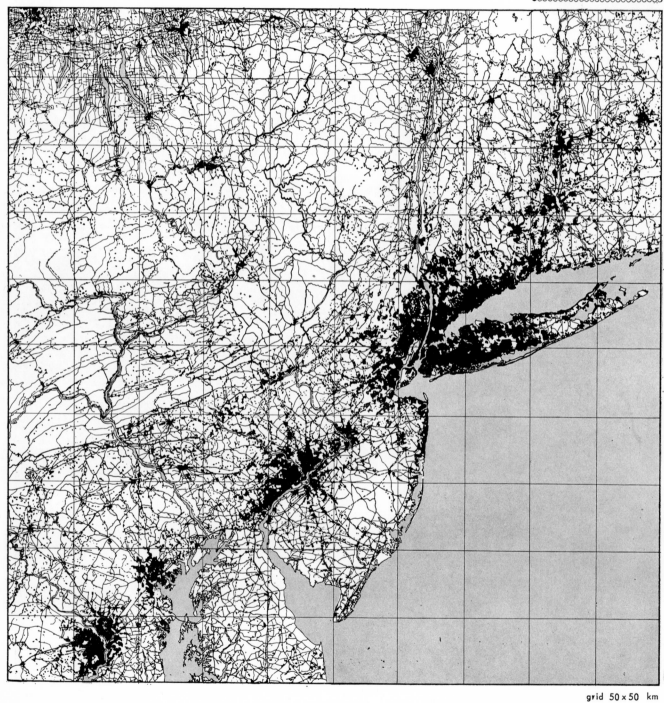

grid 50 x 50 km

km
0   50   100   150   200   250   300   350   400   450   500

0   50   100   150   200   250   300
miles

Dynamegalopolis

**average overall density of megalopolitan area
12 inh/ha (4.8 inh/acre)**

megalopolis of the eastern seaboard, U.S.A. (1963)

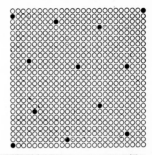

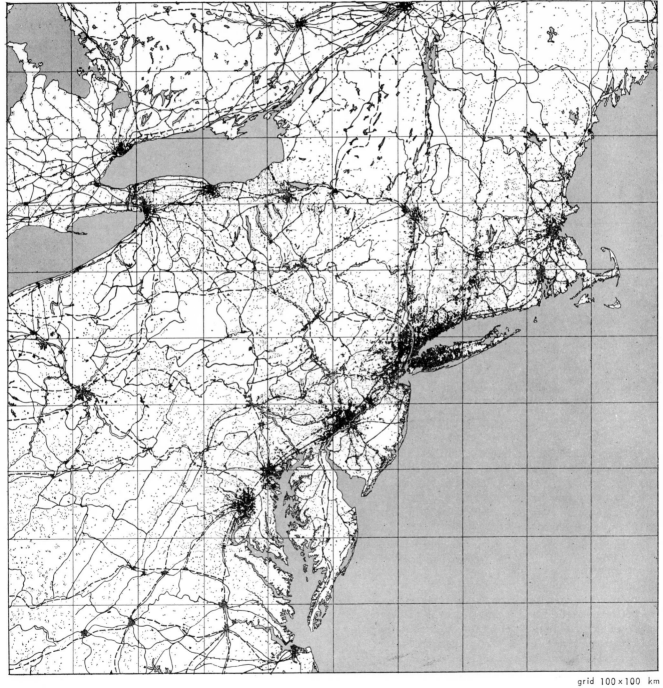

grid 100×100 km

km
0   100   200   300   400   500   600   700   800   900   1000

0   100   200   300   400   500   600
miles

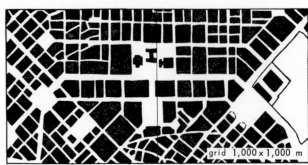

city

nomadic settlement

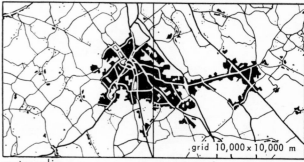

metropolis

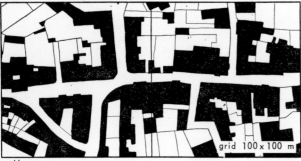

village

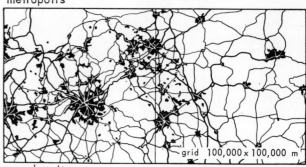

megalopolis

in settlements, though these differences are never due to the kind of people that created them, but to the social system they have formed. The above remarks about Society and its forms lead us to state that the economic purposes of human settlements are the main factor influencing their form. An agricultural settlement varies from an urban one, a commercial from an administrative one; and a composite settlement, serving many economic purposes together, is different in form from all the previous ones.

The Shells influence the overall settlement mainly in the micro-scale. The traditional structure of buildings based on two horizontal axes meeting at right angles and on horizontal slabs condition the three-dimensional form of all settlements with very few exceptions, especially in small settlements. No major change has taken place or has even been proposed, with the exception of the recent proposals by Buckminster

Fuller, to cover large parts of cities, like New York, with his geodesic shells.

Finally, if we consider the variable of Networks, we will see that at the beginning of the evolution of human settlements, Networks have played a very small role—if any at all—since they were very primitive (few water pipes and sewers), and followed the only Network which existed from the beginning, that of the roads. This Network again was in most cases a result of the types of Shells and not the condition for them. In the last two centuries, however, the situation has changed since railway lines, water supply systems, power lines, highways and all types of Network systems very often impose their structure on the human settlement, especially in the macro-scale. This influence becomes more important in the dynamic settlements, where more often than not the creation of the Networks precedes the creation of the Shells.

84

region with several types of areas

homogeneous, central, circulatory and special

Thessaly, Greece (1966)

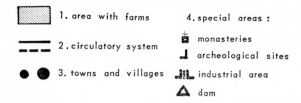

1. area with farms
2. circulatory system
3. towns and villages

4. special areas :
  monasteries
  archeological sites
  industrial area
  dam

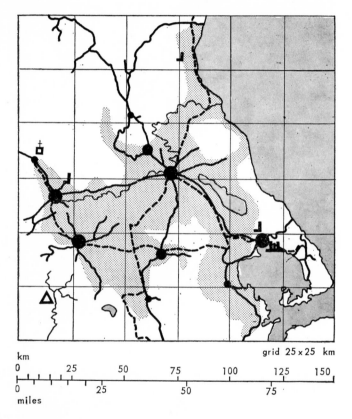

km
0   25   50   75   100   125   150

grid 25 x 25 km

0   25   50   75

miles

Such influence on the part of the Networks is valid in all countries and nations, since the rules defining them are all technological ones and hence of universal application. The only local factor that influences the Networks is the morphology of the landscape which may lead to different solutions, especially in the case of road networks which in turn influence the others.

We can perhaps draw one conclusion about the variations in the different forms of human settlements. They are mainly due to the economic purpose of the settlement, a big divergence of which may lead to big differences in the size, dimension, shape and structure of settlements. Differences in systems of political organisation, administration and defence

also have an impact but not as strong as that of economic purpose. Differences of Nature have an impact only in the micro-scale of the settlements and on its architectural details. Man, as an element of human settlements, does not lead to different solutions. All major differences with the exception of those due to the economic purpose of the settlement, are mainly in the micro-scale. In the middle- and macro-scale all settlements have similar characteristics that depend mainly on the variable of functions which, of course, comprises the incomes of the inhabitants and general economic conditions.

Anatomy

○ *Elements and parts*

Descriptive anatomy studies the structure of the settlements. Every settlement consists of five elements which exist in every part of it, like atoms within the molecule (fig. 274), and which are, however, combined in different ways to form four basic types of parts which are expressed as the four basic areas:
  ○ the homogeneous,
  ○ the central,
  ○ the circulatory,
  ○ the special.

The homogeneous areas are those which, in a study of the settlement at a certain scale showing its basic purpose, appear as its main part. For example, if the Ekistic unit is a farm with its installations, the homogeneous area is the farming area. If the Ekistic unit is a city, then the homogeneous part is the one covered by residences. If it is a metropolis then it is the one covered by broader residential areas (fig. 83).

Central areas are those serving other larger areas all around them with special functions, such as, markets, social or entertainment centres, and so forth.

The circulatory system is that which keeps the settlement going by providing movement of people, goods and information within it, as well as between it and other settlements. It is sub-divided into nodal points and circulatory lines. Nodal points occur where many lines of circulation cross each other, and circulatory lines are those on which movement takes place in opposite directions with no crossings.

Special areas are those which are neither homogeneous, nor central, nor part of the basic circulatory system. Such parts can be an army camp within a settlement, or a big factory, out of scale with the other functions among which it exists, or other types of areas or buildings differing from the homogeneous and the circulatory systems which contain them.

What is important to note about this division into four types of areas is that it is not limited to one scale only, as for example that of the whole city, but exists throughout the entire human settlement. If we look at it on a macro-scale, let us say a region, we will note the open countryside and the farms as the homogeneous areas, the cities and the villages

circulatory system: network of roads
France (1954)

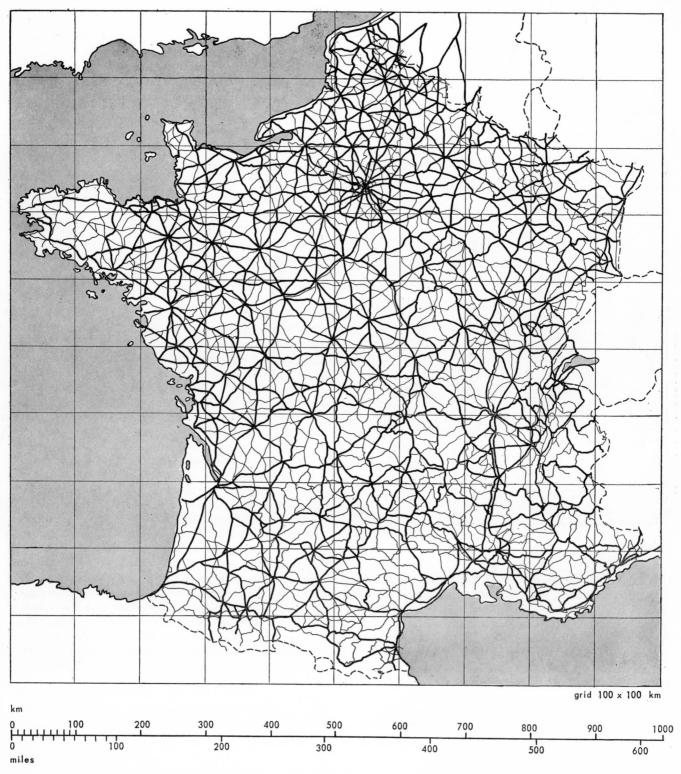

grid 100 x 100 km

km

| 0 | 100 | 200 | 300 | 400 | 500 | 600 | 700 | 800 | 900 | 1000 |

| 0 | 100 | 200 | 300 | 400 | 500 | 600 |

miles

86

circulatory system: network of railways
France (1954)

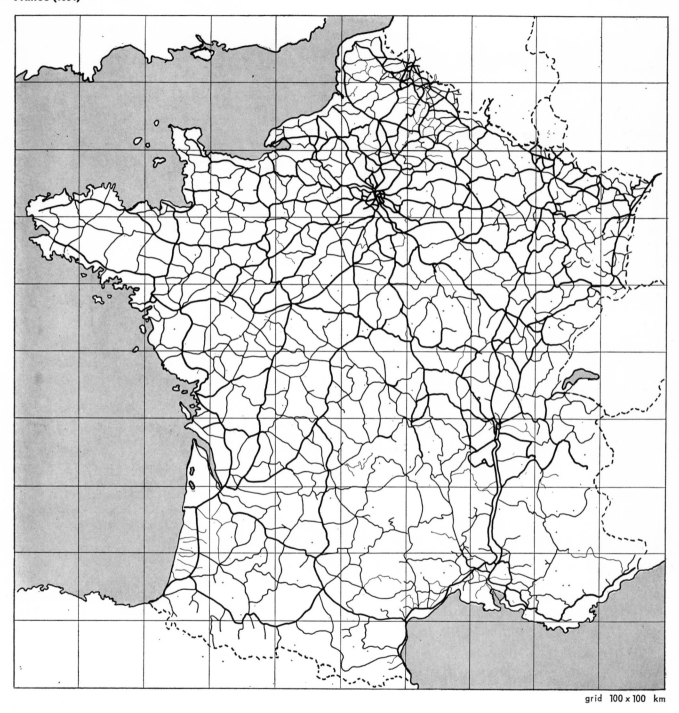

grid 100 x 100 km

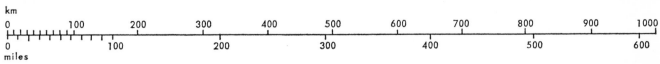

anatomy of areas considered as homogeneous

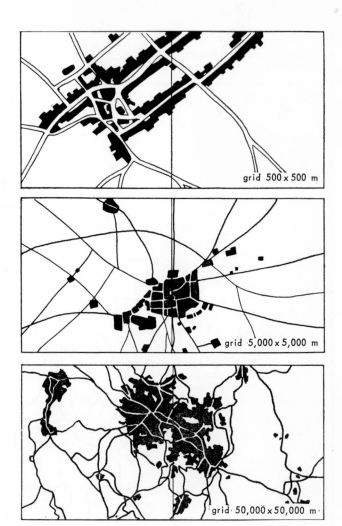

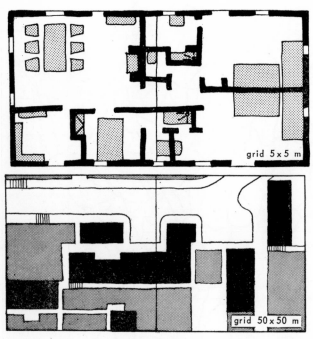

as the central ones, some major functions such as an industrial area, as the special parts and the highways, railways, canals and rivers as the circulatory lines (fig. 84).

A big region, like France, shows clearly the homogeneous areas—which may be different if we look from the point of view of the network of roads or that of railroads, the circulatory systems, or the combined systems, the central areas—which in the case of a region are many and of varying importance—and the special areas—in this case the international tourist zone near the southern and south-eastern frontiers of the country (figs. 85 and 86).

If we enter one of the residential areas of a city which up to now has been called homogeneous, we will discover that it consists of streets, crossroads, residences and some special functions, and if we enter one of the residences, we will find that it too consists of a circulatory system (entrances, corridors, etc.), a homogeneous area (living room, bedrooms, etc.) and special functions (bathroom, kitchen, etc.). Again, we can break down a homogeneous part, like the living room, into nodal points (the door and other key parts of the living

room), circulatory lines, homogeneous areas and special functions (fireplace) (fig. 87).

So we see that the so-called homogeneous area exists in a certain scale of observation, since whenever we speak of a settled area, its homogeneous part can be broken down into very small components, as far as the parts of a single room. In a bedroom, for example, it is really only the bed which is the homogeneous area while the space around it between the furniture belongs to the circulatory system. We can conceive all Ekistic space as an entire organism covered by a circulatory system beginning from the broad lines of world communications and entering into every single room. In the same way in living organisms, the blood circulation must infiltrate all parts of the body although we only can see it clearly in the basic arteries.

A study of the anatomy of human settlements shows that in their more primitive types, all similar functions are carried out by the same organs. For example, in a nomadic settlement there is hardly any important central point. There are homogeneous areas, a circulatory area (the open space between tents and compound walls of the different nomads), but it is difficult to recognise any point of nodal importance. In a primitive village we have a circulatory system and a nodal point, but on this nodal point—the village square— we have all kinds of functions from marketing to production (it is here where they will produce new furniture or dry the wool), entertainment, leisure, political and religious meetings, etc. In cities, functions begin to vary, and we may well have one circulatory system for pedestrians, another one for bicycles, another for cars or trucks and different railway lines for transportation of goods. Here the central square is no longer used for all types of functions, but is limited to marketing, entertainment, political, religious or social meetings.

In a metropolis the central square is not necessarily conducive to shopping any more, since it has probably been taken over by car traffic although some of it may survive. Other functions have found their own special locations; there are streets and squares for shopping, or even specialised regions for fresh foods or flowers or luxury goods. The circulatory system has been specialised even further, and there are specific areas for off-street parking apart from parking on circulatory lines, there are broad railway areas permitting the railway to come right to the centre of the city and airports taking care of the entire connection with other areas.

Another consideration of the atanomy of human settlements shows that at the very beginning there is only homogeneous Nature. Then we have the homogeneous Shells. They are both homogeneous, but the Shells contain the elements of the circulatory system. In a homogeneous area the paths of the people converge towards the Shells, and thus a primitive circulatory system and an even more primitive nodal-central point is added. From these we move to settlements where, in addition to homogeneous areas and a circulatory system, a central area takes concrete shape. In the last phase we have special areas. From then on settlements develop more and more specialised functions and organs, as do animals and plants.

Although settlements prove to have many common characteristics with plants and animals, they also have some basic differences. Whereas animals and plants are predetermined and limited in size, human settlements are not. The former have one central organ, one heart, one stomach, not repeated on any other scale, while human settlements are much more composite and have a hierarchical repetition of many functions in many organs throughout their body. Finally, while in animals and plants the whole circulatory system tends towards one centre only and is therefore an open circuit, in human settlements there are two types of circulatory systems: one connecting the parts to the centre and the other connecting the parts to one another thus creating a closed circuit (fig. 88).

In dealing with human settlements we must be aware of these resemblances and differences with animal life. They can help us enormously in understanding many aspects of the func-

tioning of the body of human settlements. The differences are such, however, that we can never transfer a solution from animal or plant life to human settlements without critically judging whether or not there is a possibility of comparison.

The above may lead us to believe that a comparative study of human settlements may have great value, provided we understand that organic life is one, inorganic phenomena are quite different and settlements yet another type of life. Comparisons can be very important if we are aware of their possibilities and limitations, and disastrous if we overlook them.

The study of the structure of settlements has led me to conclude that throughout their total structure, they always consist of four parts: homogeneous, central, circulatory and special. It is worth seeing how these parts are related to the five basic elements of the settlements. If we present on a diagram the elements of the settlements and the parts of their structure in two dimensions, we can come to very interesting conclusions about their relationship (fig. 89). Beginning with Nature, we can state that when it is homogeneous, it is either non-settled, or, if settled, has lines of circulation and central and special functions so small that they do not disturb its character as homogeneous Nature. In other words, homogeneity is the prevailing characteristic of a natural landscape; the other parts can only be of secondary importance.

If we now consider Nature in the central part, we recognise a certain antithesis. By necessity Nature must play a secondary role. However, it can play a very important role in special parts. For example, Nature can be the prevailing characteristic in a cemetery or in sports grounds. Finally, in the circulatory system, Nature becomes of secondary importance again.

Such a comparison of the relationship between elements and structural parts can lead to useful conclusions about the formation of the parts and the importance of the elements in them. Man, for example, acts and behaves in a different way if in a homogeneous area, a central area, a special area or a circulatory one. We must plan for him in a different way in each. In a homogeneous area Man can rest, while in a central area he carries out special functions and his position is that of power, control or service. Man behaves differently in a special area, depending on the special function of this area. Finally, Man finds himself in the circulatory part in order to move only, and since moving proper is not his goal his interest in this area is completely different from that in the other areas. In the same way, we can study Society, Shells and Networks in a homogeneous part (of a region or a small village) and in a central area, etc.

In conclusion, I think I can say that, by relating the elements of the settlements to their structural parts, we begin to understand several special problems which exist—ranging from the psychology of Man to the construction of the Shells —and the special solutions required in each case. So the two-dimensional comparison of elements and structural parts is one of the steps towards the complete understanding of human settlements.

К

Networks

**in plants and animals the circulatory or nervous
systems and networks end towards one centre;**

**in human settlements there are two types of
circulatory systems: towards the centre and between
the parts**

a tree is an open circuit

the human nervous system is an
open circuit

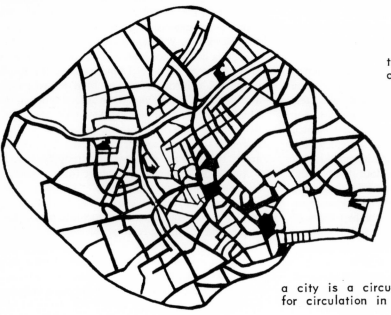

a city is a circuit allowing
for circulation in all directions

89

a guiding system of elements and parts

parts:	homogeneous	circulatory	nodal	special
Nature				
Man				
Society				
Shells				
Networks				

90

systems of the lowest order

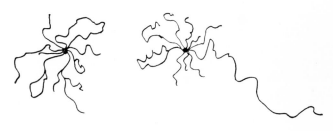

91

two level system of organisation

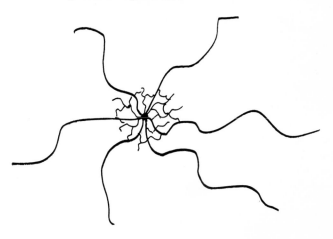

○ *Systems*

This first anatomical description shows that the human settlements form a continuum of interlocked systems of many orders, from the lowest, the single isolated man who has lost his connections with Society like Robinson Crusoe, or the single man who kept these connections like Thoreau, to the highest, the whole Ecumene, the inhabited Earth, or later perhaps the inhabited solar system and cosmos.

These systems are very similar to each other and can be presented by a centre and a network (fig. 90). If this network is not connected with any other network then the system is an isolated one which may well represent Robinson Crusoe's settlement or an isolated island or jungle settlement. If it is connected by a simple line then it can represent Thoreau's settlement or a mountain village with one road only connecting it with the world outside, or a remote island with one maritime line connecting it to the mainland.

As soon as we have more people or more settlements, even primitive ones, we have systems of several orders forming major systems in different combinations. We may, for example, have a city which is relatively isolated from others. Then it may well have two superimposed systems, the one serving its daily needs (vegetable production, walking in the fields, etc.) and the other connecting it with other systems (fig. 91). But we may have systems containing several levels of organisation (fig. 92), or systems with several levels of organisation and several sub-systems at the same level of organisation (fig. 93).

Settlements represent all sorts of combinations of systems of all orders and arrangements which can either be only hierarchical, or both hierarchical and parallel. Depending on the level of organisation the systems can either be classified by several orders, or as systems and sub-systems.

92

multi-level systems of many orders and levels of organisation

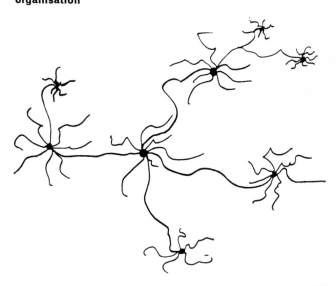

115

several systems at the same level

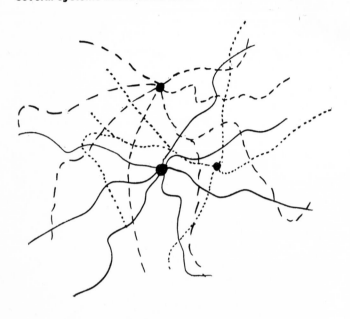

Rural settlements are systems of a lower order not only because of their small size but also because of their nature which requires a smaller number of functions and connections.

Urban settlements, on the contrary, are always systems of a higher order, and the larger they are, the higher their order. In this way we can tell how far their real body or area extends, since it comprises all settlements belonging to the sub-systems and depending on the central system. If the total area decreases in surface or importance, then the central settlement suffers. If the central settlement is deprived of its area it dies; if this happens in a war, it falls to its enemies. This is what happened to Constantinople, which was one of the three largest cities before the eighteenth century; it was gradually deprived of its whole empire. Thus its population which for many centuries had been of the order of 500,000, and at one time had reached the level of 900,000 if not a million, fell in 1453 to its lowest level of 50,000, and was conquered by the Turks. This meant that it became once again the capital of a great empire, its *real* area extended to Asia and Europe, and within one century, in 1550, its population rose to 500,000 once again (fig. 94).

○ *Measurements*

Science is based on facts which must be measured to be properly understood. We need measurements of two basic categories:
  ○ measurements of phenomena (functions, elements, etc.),
  ○ measurements of efficiency.

The first ones can be obtained in two equally indispensable ways, and can be very accurate and objective.

First of these is the natural measurement of each of the elements—Nature, Man, Society, Shells and Networks—in terms of its own scale. The second, which usually throws light on several of the phenomena of human settlements, is the ratio between the different elements.

For instance, if we are considering a house, we may only want to know how many people inhabit it to decide whether the floor space of the house or the area of the property is sufficient, etc. If, on the other hand, we are considering a public space, such a measurement may not be adequate, and we may have to resort to the more complicated measurement of man-hours per area. The latter can be an important measurement in the case of public parks, for example, where we wish to know the number of hours in a day, season or year, during which the park is visited. These then should be related also to climate, working hours, distance, etc. In this way we can estimate the total man-hours that can be spent in visiting the park and relate it to the surface of the park, both as an average for the whole period as well as an average for the peak visiting hours.

We can also measure, for example, built-up volume per unit of space, or income invested per unit of space. In this way, we can know not only that lower income groups invest less per unit of space, but that sometimes they invest only a minor percentage of their income, a fact even more indicative of the real problems faced by certain income groups. Following the ideas of Buckminster Fuller, we can also use the measurement of weight of construction per unit of space in an attempt to understand some of the real issues related to construction and to the necessity of a revolutionary approach to problems of mass construction for the great numbers of people who suffer from a lack of proper settlements.

This category of measurements does not need further explanation, since it is quite common; it only needs a systematic order which will help us to use the best type of measurement and to develop a system, which, once accepted, will facilitate the comparison of many examples and lead to better understanding. This book continuously gives examples of how such a system can be developed.

The second category, that of the measurements of efficiency, is very seldom attempted, and for this reason I selected the example of a system we used in the research project on the Human Community in the Athens Center of Ekistics and will present it in some detail. This project studies the problems related to the existence of a community on a human scale in the present-day metropolitan area of Athens.

The efficiency evaluation system presented below is meant only to be suggestive of the kind of system that is needed as part of Ekistic measurements. It is not a prescribed form, although it has been found useful in practice.

In several parts of this book, where I classify the knowledge

the Byzantine Empire at its maximum extent

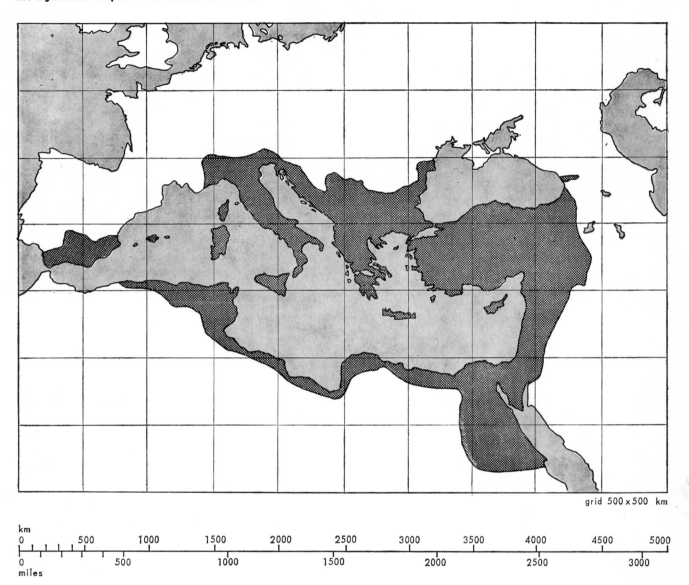

grid 500 x 500 km

km
0   500   1000   1500   2000   2500   3000   3500   4000   4500   5000

0   500   1000   1500   2000   2500   3000
miles

related to Ekistics (see Chapter Two: The Study of Human Settlements) and again when I speak of synthesis in a community (see Chapter Nine: Ekistic Synthesis), I have explained that a thorough study of an Ekistic unit requires a study not only of the whole, but also of various aspects of several of its parts. It requires the study of an Ekistic unit in relation to its region, as a whole and by elements, and then a study of the relevant factors and the role of the community. To study the efficiency of an urban community, I would try to take these different aspects separately and

give each of them a general rating of 100. Thus, the efficiency of the community as a whole has a rating of 100, as do the other aspects of the community: its elements, its role, its factors and its parts, all of which give us a total general rating of 500. If we then want to have this total equal to 100 or 1,000 we can change other ratings correspondingly.

When I speak of a general rating of 100 for every category of the community, this does not necessarily mean that these general ratings must have the same value in the final synthesis. Depending on the system we use, we can give each one of them a different value in the total rating of 1,000. How this will be done depends on the general approach we develop in every case concerning the importance of the different ways of looking at a community. For practical purposes, I consider it more useful to demonstrate the method by a general rating of 100 for every category. I will here attempt to analyse how this general rating can be constructed for two of the aspects of interest to us, that is the community as a whole and the community as seen from the aspect of its five elements.

There is no reason to maintain that the rating method I propose is better than any other. We are in too primitive a stage to be able to support such statements. The only thing I can say is that this rating is based on experience in dealing with several such cases in different parts of settlements and different sizes of Ekistic units in various parts of the world.

TABLE I

EFFICIENCY OF AN URBAN COMMUNITY

		General Rating
A. EXISTENCE AND ROLE OF A COMMUNITY		100
1. *Existence of community*		60
overall density	35	
shape	20	
cohesion (continuous texture)	5	
2. *Functions of community*		30
meaningful overall plan	10	
importance of central community functions	4	
form of central core	4	
accessibility of central core	2	
direction of the main arteries	4	
minor cores	3	
design of residential streets and squares	3	
3. *Relations with other communities*		10
distance from a community of higher order	2	
accessibility of the core of a higher rank community	2	
relations to other community cores of equal rank	1	
negative effects from other communities	5	

B. CENTRAL SERVICES		
1. *Central services of community with a positive effect*		100
residence	30	
commerce	5	
education and culture	5	
sports	5	
welfare	5	
recreation	5	
religion	5	
streets	5	

squares—parks	5	
drainage	5	
sewers	5	
water supply	5	
electricity	5	
telephone	5	
different	5	
2. *Functions with negative effects*		−50
physical formation	−10	
houses—abandoned	−10	
commerce	−10	
industry	−10	
transportation	−10	

I will begin with the study of the efficiency of the community as a whole, which could be described as efficiency based on the existence and role of the community. The total receives a general rating of 100, which is subdivided into three parts: the very existence of the community (general rating 60), the functions of the community (general rating 30) and relations with other communities (general rating 10).

In studying the existence of the community with a general rating of 60, I start with its overall density giving this a rating of 35. This is a most characteristic feature. Regardless of how rich, regardless of how well serviced a unit is, if it does not have the right density, it may not even be a true community. If the density is too low, the notion of community is weakened. On the other hand, if the density is too high, the community may suffer. It is very difficult to decide upon the right density, since it is related to locality, type of community, way of life, income, and so forth. I tend, though, to believe that there is an optimum density for every city and for every locality at every phase of their development. Recent studies show that the built-up area of Athens has practically always had a constant density. Figures taken over the last 3,000 years show that the average density of persons in the built-up area of the city has fluctuated between 160 and 180 persons per hectare (64–72 inh/acre). This figure has only changed during the last 100 years and more so during the last 50 years, when the expanding city of Athens spread over a much greater area and reached a population of 2,000,000 people. As a result the overall density became lower and was reduced to 71 persons per hectare (284 inh/acre) for the entire metropolitan area. However, the density within the limits of the municipality of Athens remains 172 persons per hectare (68·8 inh/acre), very close to the average of the last 3,000 years.

Taking this average as the optimum density for this city for residential purposes, we can work out a scale of density values. If double the optimum density has 50 per cent of the optimum value, and 50 per cent of the optimum density has again 50 per cent of the optimum value we can work out a scale showing degrees of desirable densities and giving these corresponding ratings. This is an area which itself should become the subject of a very important study. At present,

95

**rating of the shape of the communities considering
only the form and not the size of the community**

shape	special rating %	general rating
	100	20
	100	20
	90	18
	80	16
	70	14
	60	12
	50	10
	40	8
	30	6
	20	4
	10	2
	5	1

community. This is why shape should be rated as the second most important factor for the very existence of a community. Shape is rated with a special rating of 100 per cent (equals general rating of 20) if it is round or if it can be inscribed within an ellipse of which the two axes do not differ more than 1 : 1·5. If the shape is 1 : 2 we can decrease the efficiency of the community's rating by 10 per cent; if it is 1 : 3 by 20 per cent; 1 : 4 by 30 per cent. Further we can say that a community 1 : 20 has a value of only 5 per cent, 1 : 30 of 3 per cent and so on. Such elongated communities however scarcely exist within urban areas, though they would constitute a problem if we were rating rural communities (fig. 95). If the shape of a community is even more irregular, then it receives the rating of the community within which it can be inscribed, reduced in a way corresponding to its detailed irregularities.

Cohesion in the community structure receives a general rating of 5. Here the intention is to rate the continuous texture. This means that if we have a community with the proper density and the proper shape, but divided by ravines so deep that they cannot be easily crossed, or by small rivers, or by other natural or artificial barriers, if the ground is very broken or undulating, then the community loses in possibilities of intercommunication. The special rating of a community on the same horizontal level, or the same slope, provided that the grade is slight, is considered as equal to 100 per cent. For any increase in hindrances and decrease in cohesion and continuous texture, we should apply lower ratings. These ratings have significance within major urban areas where these hindrances are small, since had they been big, they would have constituted boundaries of communities. In the case of rural communities or that of urban ones in minor settlements, where a community may have to come into existence in spite of a great ravine running through it, other general ratings should be applied.

Then we come to the functions of the community, with a general rating of 30. The first characteristic is a meaningful overall plan (general rating 10) which guarantees the proper functioning of the community. If the community is in the form of a circle or an ellipse, then the core should be at the centre, and all streets should lead to it. This could be an ideal plan from the point of view of functioning of the community, though not of its total physical efficiency. In such cases the rating is the same, even if the ellipse is too elongated, for the weaknesses of an elongated ellipse have been taken into consideration in the rating of the shape. However, if the central part of the community is not in the gravitational centre of the ellipse, then the special rating is lower, perhaps of the order of 80 per cent. If the whole plan is a twisted one, rating is still lower.

The importance of the central community services has a general rating of 4. If the central community services play an important role in the existence of the community, then they become a very important factor. If they do not play the

we simply have to rely on general experience. If we want to be more specific, we can take several types of densities, find areas with corresponding densities, and analyse their efficiency from the economic, social and aesthetic point of view, so that changes in density can be measured and be given a specific value and rating.

Next, the shape of the community receives a general rating of 20. Regardless of how important or how right the density is, if the shape of the community is not a good one, the community feeling may be lost. For example, an ideal community should be round or slightly elliptical in form. This is due to the need the people feel to come together to one central area where they can find all the services they require. Therefore, from the point of view of structure of one isolated community, the ideal form is a circle—and this has been reflected in many considerations about ideal communities of the past.

Now if we take a very elongated community, let us say only one row of houses along a highway, it will form a very weak

96

rating of the overall plan of the community

special rating %	general rating	plan
100	10	
100	10	
80	8	
60	6	
40	4	
20	2	
0	0	

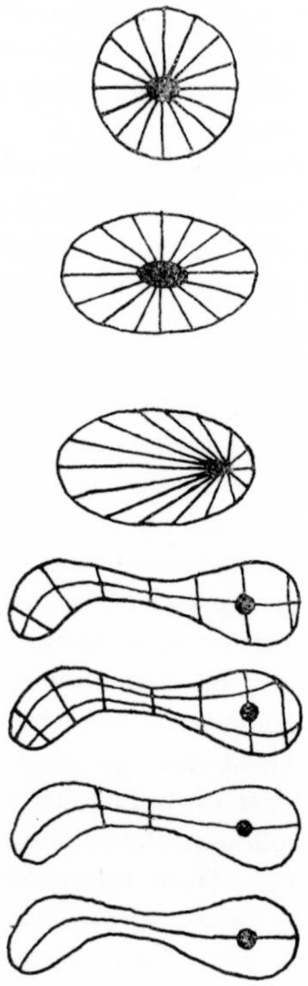

97

rating of the formation of the community's central core

special rating %	general rating	formation of central core
100	4	
50	2	
20	0.8	
5	0.2	
0	0	

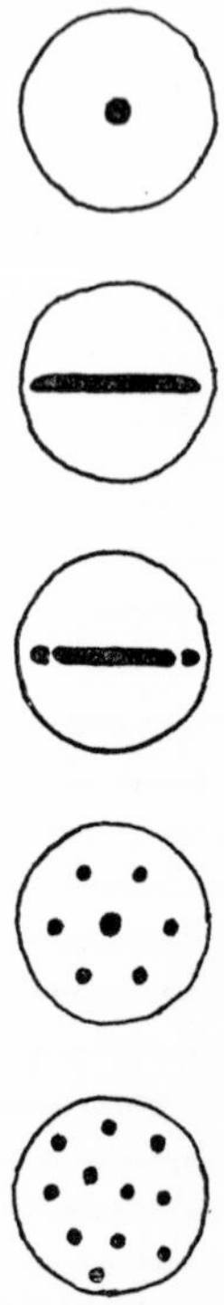

desired role, then they should get a lower rating. The judgment of the importance of the central services can be based on the best services in equivalent urban areas. If, for example, an entire urban area has ten shops per 1,000 inhabitants and our community has only eight, it may be that the special rating from the point of view of shops is 80 per cent. If every such community in the entire urban area has one church and our community has no church at all, the special rating from the point of view of church services is 0. The same ratings can be given for other types of central services, so that we may conclude that the special rating of our central services is 50 per cent in relation to the best communities in similar urban areas, which means a general rating of two (fig. 96).

The form of the central core has a general rating of four (special rating of 100 per cent). Parallel to the importance of the central services, we must consider the formation of the central core. If all central services are together in one central core, then—theoretically, and only from this point of view— the formation is optimum. Some services, like parks, need not necessarily be in the centre; they must, however, be in a good alternative location if the general rating is to remain at four (special rating 100 per cent). However, if the central services are scattered and not continuous, the rating should be much lower. If we have an elongated central core along the whole length of the community or a commercial street which collects all functions, then we have a continuous central core, which, however, does not have the proper shape since walking along it becomes tiresome, so the general rating should be two; if services are even more scattered, then the rating should be lower (fig. 97).

The accessibility of the central core (general rating of two) is also of great importance. If the central core is easily accessible from all parts of the community, it gives general satisfaction to the inhabitants. If, however, the central core is not easily accessible for all the inhabitants—if, for example, a third of the community is too distant, as compared with the others, because of the odd shape of the community or because of hindrances—then the rating should be much lower. Although this factor also appears in 'shape' and 'inter-

98

rating of minor cores in the community

special rating %	general rating	minor cores
100	3	
80	2.4	
60	1.8	
20	0.6	
0	0	

communication', it is so important that it has been given an additional rating.

The direction of the main arteries has a general rating of four. Apart from the overall plan and the importance of the central core, it is necessary for a community to have main arteries that give access to the outside world without disrupting its inter-communication, or the free access to its own central core. The existence of these arteries, their design, location and functioning within the community are very important.

Minor cores get a general rating of three. The existence of minor cores giving a certain character and cohesion to minor parts of the community is another important factor. A minor core may consist of a few shops, small restaurants, or even a small square or widening of the street, where people can meet, sit and talk, and children play. The existence of such minor cores in the right places, their formation and their role can be rated satisfactorily (special rating 100 per cent or general rating three) while their complete absence should be rated zero (fig. 98).

The design of residential streets and squares receives a total general rating of three. They are rated according to their location in relation to the collector roads, their size and relationship to the heights of buildings, and to their actual width. If all are satisfactory, the general rating is three. If only the location is satisfactory, but not the design or the width, the general rating should only be one, and so on. It should be made clear at this point that we are not referring to the road surface or sewers, etc., since these come under 'central functions'.

Relations with other communities have a total general rating of ten, sub-divided into the following categories, with rating from two to one. The distance from a community of an immediately higher order, receives a general rating of two. Here we have to take into consideration the average distance of cores of one type of community from the cores of the next highest rank and rate this distance as one. Fifty per cent of this distance will be reckoned as two; 200 per cent of this distance will be reckoned as 0·5; 300 per cent of this distance will be reckoned as 0·33, 500 per cent as 0, etc.

Apart from the distance, we must take into consideration the accessibility; the distance may be small but there may be no direct connection, or the connecting street may make a detour, there may or may not be a bus line, etc. The accessibility of the core of a higher rank community from the core of the one being studied receives a general rating of 2. Satisfactory accessibility, meaning a good connection with a paved street and a bus line, would be rated as 2. Good accessibility without a bus line would be rated 1, and so on. The distance from a community core of a community of an even higher class (i.e. class VI if we are studying a community class IV[8]), receives a general rating of 1·5. The same considerations obtain here, but the rating is less. The accessibility of the core of this higher ranking community receives a general rating of 1·5 on the basis of the same considerations made on a community of an immediately higher order. The distance from an even higher order community receives the rating of 1 on the basis of the same considerations, the rating being lower here since the distances are larger. The accessibility of a class VII community core receives a rating of 1. Relations to other community cores equal to the one we are studying, also receive a general rating of 1 for their accessibility to our community core.

The main tendency, if there is any, towards cohesion can be found in the class IV community. There, people tend to be well connected to the core of their own community and their community tends to be well connected with that of the class V community and this in turn, with the core of the class VI community, etc. Indeed there seems to be a natural tendency towards connections between different scales of community centre cores in a vertical or hierarchical fashion. It is not the same, however, for connections between communities of the same class. This does not seem to come about naturally. I have tried to solve this problem by creating connections mainly for pedestrians, as I did in the western Baghdad community development, one of the first major community groups I worked on (fig. 99).

There are cases where the other neighbourhood communities may have negative effects on our own community. For this we allow a general rating of minus 5, for a total for negative effects. If our own community has negative effects on others, we must also record it. There may be several reasons for a negative rating; for example, the noise of a neighbouring community's factories, or prevailing winds bringing in smoke from neighbouring communities; or there may be neighbouring communities which are decaying and depressed and which influence our community.

In most of the cases of negative influences, we should be prepared to subtract up to five points because of all these conditions. In very exceptional cases, however, we may have to subtract even more than the five points allocated. For example, if our community receives all the smoke and the noise of others (e.g. if it is surrounded by the industries of other communities) if it is also near a place where the garbage of other communities is dumped, and suffers from other poor conditions all around it, we may have to subtract even ten points. In this case, we would annul all points received because of positive relations with other communities. This, of course, would be a very exceptional case.

We must also study the central services of the community in the same way, giving them a total general rating of 100. These may be good (positive) or bad (negative). The general rating of 100 is sub-divided into two main parts, the first amounts to 60 and includes Residence (30), Commerce (5), Education and Culture (5), Sports (5), Welfare (5), Recreation (5) and Religion (5) and the second amounts to 40 and includes Streets (5), Squares and Parks (5), Drainage, Sewers, Water Supply, Electricity, Telephone and various other functions, each with a general rating of 5.

Residential areas in a community receive a general rating of 30. The overall condition of houses related to their income group is of the greatest importance. After all, in most climates people spend the greatest part of their life inside houses. Therefore, houses get a general rating of 30.

The function of commerce in a community receives a general rating of 5. Here we must consider the formation of the immediate environment and the shops themselves, that is, building, efficiency, appearance, etc. (not their location which has been taken care of earlier). If, for example, there are three shops and a small restaurant in a very small square, and all are clean, and if in front of them there is a sidewalk and a tree they could be rated with 5. If all these conditions are not present, the rating should be lower.

Education and culture, depending on the degree of satisfaction offered to the community, receive a general rating of 5 or less. Satisfactory schools in satisfactory surroundings, with a library, etc., should be given a total rating of 5. If there are only schools and no other cultural activities, I would give

them a rating of 4. If the schools are not satisfactory the rating should be less.

Sports facilities receive a general rating of 5. If all schools provide for all types of necessary sports the general rating of the community should be 3, because all school children will have access to sports facilities. If there are corresponding sports facilities for adults, the total rating can be 5. If schools have only 50 per cent of the necessary sports facilities, their rating is 1·5 making a total of 3·5.

Welfare functions also receive a general rating of 5. If a health clinic or first aid station and also a welfare centre are available, the general rating should be 5; otherwise, it should be reduced.

Indoor recreation receives a general rating of 5. The existence of satisfactory winter and open air cinemas, outdoor and indoor restaurants and coffee houses with music and dancing, should be rated with 5. If there are only cinemas, we should give 3 points. If there are only either indoor or open-air ones, the rating for Greece for example should be 1·5 since this is dependent on the climate.

Another service receiving a general rating of 5 is worship. The existence of one church or mosque or temple, depending on the belief of the inhabitants in a good location that is satisfactory for all the inhabitants should be rated with 5. If the inhabitants are not satisfied because the church is too small for the community, for example, the rating should be lower.

For the streets and their road surfaces, we give a general rating of 5. If streets are neither paved nor the sidewalks planted at all, the rating is 0. If there are paved sidewalks but the streets have holes, mud, etc., then the rating should be 1·5. If they are all completely paved and well taken care of in every way, the rating should be 5, even if the sidewalks are not planted. For instance a community may have streets which are not planted, but which are very well finished and fully satisfactory in other respects. However, if a residential street is wide, giving a feeling of emptiness and demanding the presence of some green, then even if completely paved it is not satisfactory and should be rated with only 3 points. The same conditions as above apply to squares and parks which also have a general rating of 5.

Drainage also receives a general rating of 5. If the community is not properly drained, if the water stagnates creating mud, etc., the rating should be lower. Sewage facilities for all houses and installations receive a general rating of 5; if there are fewer connections, there is a corresponding reduction. Water supplies also receive 5. If all houses have internal connections the rating is 5. If all houses are connected, but only in their yards, the rating should be 2. If this is only true for a percentage of them, the rating should drop lower. Electricity also receives a rating of 5 if all houses are supplied. The same considerations hold good for telephone communications and various other functions depending on prevailing conditions in the country.

We now come to the functions with a negative effect on the

99

human sector in western Baghdad

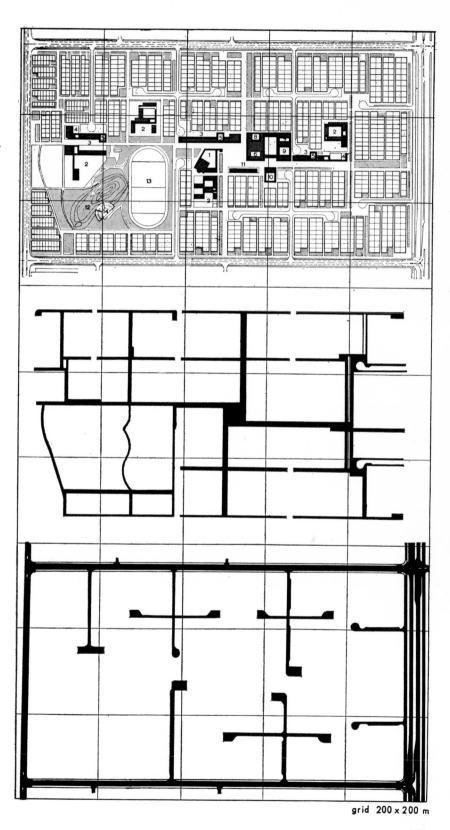

1 mosque
2 school
3 market
4 public baths
5 coffee houses
6 administration
7 red crescent
8 cultural centre
9 public health centre
10 police station
11 shops
12 public park
13 sports ground
14 open air theatres

general layout

pedestrian roads

vehicle roads

grid 200 x 200 m

community. Assigning general ratings to them is a difficult task. If the negative functions were equal to the positive ones, the community would cease to exist. Since such extreme cases can occur, leading to a depressed area and abandonment of the community, we must theoretically say that the total general rating of negative functions is minus 100. But in any community which manages to survive, all negative functions added together should not surpass minus 50, divided into five basic categories each rated with minus ten (−10).

Negative physical formation receives a general rating of minus ten (−10). If there is for example, a ravine, creating dangers for the inhabitants or steep slopes which are very abrupt, or a torrent, or other elements which force the inhabitants to avoid them, then 10 points should be subtracted from the community.

The negative effects of houses receive a general rating of minus ten (−10). We may for instance have negative effects from abandoned houses. This can occur in a decaying, declining community where the houses are being abandoned by the inhabitants either because population is declining or because the houses are very bad, turning into slums and thus constituting a negative factor for the whole neighbourhood.

A negative effect of commerce also receives a rating of minus ten (−10). Here we take into consideration commercial activities hurting the community; for example, shops dealing in dirty, smelly goods, or handicrafts whose operation is noisy. In this category we should also classify operations of ill repute, the existence, for example, of a red light district, areas where people use narcotics, etc. These are all negative elements for the community.

Industries with negative effects also receive a general rating of minus ten (−10). Any noisy industry, any area with abandoned workshops and materials, and generally everything else disrupting the normal functioning of a community due to industry, must be taken into consideration.

Finally, the negative functions of transportation receive a total general rating of minus ten (−10). Any line of transportation breaking the continuity of the community, or having a negative effect caused by noise, bad location, etc., should be taken into consideration as a negative function.

The great number of points that must be taken into consideration in the value definition of a community shows how difficult measurements can be. This was only an attempt, based on experience to classify my personal opinions about the importance of all points mentioned. The value of such an effort is to show what gradually must be done by Ekistics in an impersonal and hence scientific way, opening the road for many similar attempts and gradually leading to the scientific approach that we need.

It must be clear, after these examples, that both the general and special ratings of the items mentioned can have a universal as well as a local validity. All efforts, therefore, to develop a system for the measurement of the efficiency of a particular

Ekistic unit (in our case an urban community) should be considered as efforts towards the development of the proper methodology for general Ekistic ratings. Some day we may be able to have general ratings of both universal and local validity, the addition of which will give the final answer to our problem. As in many other cases in this study, these examples tend towards the development of a system and an approach, rather than give a rule which must be strictly applied.

Physiology

○ *The need for it*

I will start this section by quoting Claude Bernard in his 'leçons' on the phenomena of life, common to animals and plants. I am doing this because it shows a meaning for the study of both the human body and medicine and the related phenomena in the operation of societies. This is what he writes about anatomy and physiology:

'Descriptive anatomy is to physiology what geography is to history, and as it is not enough to know a country's topography for the understanding of its history, it is not enough to know the anatomy of organs for the understanding of their functions. An old surgeon, Méry, compared anatomists to those messengers who are to be found in great cities, and who know the layout of the streets, and the numbering of the buildings, but do not know what goes on inside. Indeed, in tissues, in organs, vital physico-chemical phenomena occur which mere anatomy cannot reveal'.[9]

The physiology of settlements studies their functions, supplementing descriptive anatomy which studies their structure. Physiology, as in medicine, has been the neglected part of the disciplines of human settlements since they were much more concerned with structure. Nevertheless, physiology is an indispensable part of the study of settlements; not only does it supplement structure and give a picture of the operation of the settlements, but it also helps us understand the *raisons d'être* of the different organs and parts and the whole cause-and-effect process.

The importance and meaning of the physiology of settlements has been so overlooked, that even phenomena of functions and operation of the settlement which belong to physiology, as do densities of all kinds, have been studied in a static manner and consequently have been, in many respects, misunderstood, since densities of people, functions, motorcars, and so forth, have a meaning only if approached in a dynamic manner.

Only the densities of motorcars, because of the critical condition of transportation today, have been studied in relation to their change; but even this study was carried out without taking into account the proper relation to the total settlement and its operation, and consequently, did not lead to an understanding of the total problem, and could not contribute to its solution.

This misunderstanding of the problem of densities has been the cause of very low densities in many settlements built during the last two generations, and of the aggravation of the situation in many of them. In the present general introduction to Ekistics I am limiting myself to the questions related to densities and am trying to show the importance and extent of this problem, since the whole question of the physiology for which there is little data available requires a special presentation.

∘ *Meaning of densities*

Densities of people are defined by the desire and need of the said people to be close together, in order to serve one another, and also to be apart in order not to hurt one another. These densities change continuously from day to night, by the hour and by the moment, and are expressed as densities of people and of Shells, and of the machines serving them. Their study as a part of the physiology of settlements is the most important study which needs to be carried out in this field.

Density is very important for Man from many points of view, biological, physiological, social, economic, and so forth, since it refers to his relationship with the space in which he lives; the possibility of his survival, his physical and mental health, his welfare and happiness, all depend on his relation to space.

It can be seen from the above reasons that density is a result of the interplay of so many forces that the ensuing picture is completely confusing. Moreover, many of these forces work in different directions. Some, such as urban economic forces, work towards higher densities only; some, the biological ones for instance, towards lower densities, and some, the social and aesthetic forces, towards optimum conditions which are threatened equally by both low and high densities.

In order to gain a better understanding of densities we can conduct our studies in an analytical way—constructing the models of what we need from the very foundations of the system of human settlements; also in an empirical way— learning from the great laboratory which has come to be on this Earth and has been operating for about one million years with Man acting as both guinea pig and research director.

In the end, the findings reached through both these methods will lead to the same conclusions, since the analytical method will have to use for its calculations units based on empirical experience (how much space, for example, is needed between two people conversing or working). The empirical method will use an analytical approach in order to discover ways of improving present unfavourable conditions, and methods for projecting future trends.

In order to facilitate these studies we have to understand that densities depend on many forces belonging in two basically different categories: the texture forces and the directional ones.

Texture forces define space relationships and distribute people in rather uniform ways over any type of area. They can be of an economic nature: hunters may need one square kilometre per person and this does not change regardless of how many there are, or people in an auditorium need one half square metre per person which again does not change with their numbers. If we give them less space the hunters will suffer economically and the audience psychologically.

Directional forces, on the contrary, draw people in certain directions, towards points, lines, areas or volumes and are independent of any satisfaction of needs related to texture forces. Each one of us, for example, would like, considering his shopping convenience only, to settle in a shopping centre, or for his employment convenience to settle next door to or on top of the factory he works in. Directional forces can be positive as well as negative; therefore a factory draws people towards it as a place of employment and drives people away from it in search of a more pleasant place of residence.

Any actual density today, with the exception of those populations still living under primitive conditions, is the result of a balance between all sorts of texture and directional forces and can be explained using a system based on a grid consisting of the causes of densities and their nature.

In order to succeed with such calculations we must be sure that we use the proper units of space as units of reference. Such statements as 'the centres of cities lose in density', are very general and do not lead to useful conclusions since we do not define the space-unit of reference. To do so we must be aware that there are two ways in which we can use units of space: as absolute values (metre, kilometre, etc.) and as relative values (centre, business district, periphery, etc.). In order to illuminate any problem of density, we have to use both types of measurement.

If we say that the average density per square kilometre in one settlement is higher than in another, we have to specify whether the first covers an area of ten sq. kms. and the second of one tenth of a sq. km. In this case, the density in the second one may be much higher than the first one by hectare.

If we say that the centre of one settlement has a higher density than the centre of another one, we have to specify not only what we mean by centre but also what its relationship is to the whole settlement. Because, if in the first case it represents one tenth of the area and 50 per cent of the total employment, and in the second, one twentieth of the area and 40 per cent of the employment, we will have to make adjustments for proper comparisons.

We do not know enough about densities. Perhaps we know something of how to deal with densities in those settlement types which have been tested out long enough during Man's

100

densities in the urban built-up area

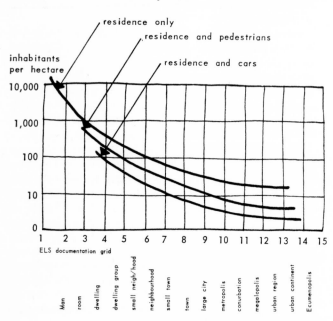

historical development, villages or small cities, for example. However, even in these cases, I doubt if we have anything more than empirical experience. In the case of big urban settlements, which have developed only during the last two centuries, and have created new extremes in densities, we know practically nothing. I will attempt to describe this phenomenon in a very general way in order to show how little we do know and how much we do not know even about the most basic phenomena.

Today, Man lives on the world's surface at an average density of 0·058 per hectare (0·024/acre); or over the land area of the Earth at an average density of 0·21 inhabitants per hectare (0·085/acre), or over the total inhabited areas of land at an average density of 0·74 per hectare (0·30/acre). This last density changes from country to country, from the highest of 2·0–4·0 inhabitants per hectare (0·8–1·6 inh/acre) in seven countries (Netherlands, Belgium, United Kingdom and Western Germany in Europe; Taiwan, Korea and Japan in the Far East) to the lowest of 0·003–0·007 inhabitants per hectare (0·0012–0·0028 inh/acre) in five countries (S.W. Africa, Mauritania and Libya in Africa; Mongolia in Asia; French Guiana in S. America). These contrasts show a ratio of 600 to 1.

Average gross densities of the built-up areas are, of course, much higher and range from over 400 inhabitants per hectare (160 inh/acre) in such cities as Moscow, to 12 inhabitants per hectare (4·8 inh/acre) in Los Angeles; that is, a ratio of 33 to 1. This means that there are cities which reach a density 100 times higher than the most densely inhabited countries.

However, there is no rational way of comparing these densities at present since both countries and cities of such high densities are not entirely dependent on their own space, but also depend on their relationship with the rest of the world. Both the countries and the cities in question are only areas of a higher concentration of activities which are spread over much wider areas.

Within the built-up parts of settlements, net residential densities may range from as high as 7,500 inhabitants per hectare (3,000 inh/acre), as in parts of Hong Kong, or some central parts of other cities to as low as one inhabitant per hectare (0·4 inh/acre) as in some garden-cities within major settlement areas; thus showing a ratio of 7,500 to 1.

Historically, we are able to observe the following trends: minor settlements of the past showed an average density of about 100 inhabitants per hectare (40 inh/acre) which increased to 200 inhabitants per hectare (80 inh/acre) in larger or more densely built cities, and even more, but perhaps not much beyond 300 (120), in some exceptional cases where defense or climate imposed such concentrations of population. These densities were quite suitable until the twentieth century, and they can be considered as representative of a natural settlement—with houses not exceeding two to four storeys and without means of mechanical transportation. These densities are the result of the interaction of natural, social and cultural forces and they represent the most that Man could achieve in a pre-industrial civilisation.

This is still the case in those parts of cities of the present which do not contain multi-storey buildings. Densities in such areas range up to a maximum of 200–300 inhabitants/ hectare (80–120 inh/acre). Beyond this limit the city requires multi-storey buildings. But even in the range of 300–400 inhabitants per hectare (120–160 inh/acre) the city can function only with great difficulty because of the existence of the automobile. These difficulties become greatly magnified where densities in some parts of the built-up area increase, as they do, up to 2,500 inhabitants per hectare (1,000 inh/ acre). These and other difficulties experienced at higher densities support a view that there is a natural density of 100–300 inhabitants per hectare (40–120 inh/acre) for urban settlements when we do not have multi-storey buildings and mechanical transportation.

The situation changed radically in the twentieth century, when buildings acquired dozens of storeys and transportation within settlements became mainly mechanical. Cities are exploding, and, contrary to what is commonly believed, the densities are dropping over the entire urban area. We are not however in a position to define these phenomena with exact data, although we can with certainty show that (fig. 100):
- density drops in larger Ekistic units more than in small ones;
- density drops in all settlements;
- this drop is much greater when cars enter the scene.

It is true that if we study the same area, within the same limits (as in the city of Athens) we may find that densities have remained stable or have increased only slightly over 3,000 years. But if we do not study the same area but the entire settlement, we find that in the middle of the twentieth century densities have dropped to half of what they were before. It is true also that if we study only the central urban area, residential densities may be low but densities of employment are very high.

With these remarks we bring to light the fact that densities are changing continuously throughout our contemporary urban settlements, just as these settlements are changing dynamically. In and around the central areas, when these are not limited only to the central business district (CBD), we find the highest densities and on the fringes of the entire area we have the lowest ones. Depending on how we define the different concentric bands of habitation within cities, we find several densities of residence.

If we study densities of cities by geographic regions, we find the highest average densities in Asia with over 100 inhabitants per hectare (40 inh/acre), the next highest in Europe, from 40 to 100 (16 to 40), or an average of 70 inhabitants per hectare (28 inh/acre) and the lowest in the U.S.A. with less than 50 inhabitants per hectare (20 inh/acre). To conclude from these figures that geography plays any role would be very dangerous. But we do have to recognise that the higher densities coincide with the lowest numbers of cars, and once again reach the conclusion that we know too little about densities to be able to draw any definite conclusions.

I do think, however, that we are now in a position to state that:

o densities in both rural and urban settlements have for thousands of years been fairly stable: around 100 inhabitants per hectare (40 in/acre) in the rural ones and around 150–200 inhabitants per hectare (20–80 inh/acre) in the urban ones, with variations from 70 to 200 (28 to 80) in the first case and from 100 to 300 (40 to 120) in the second;

o these densities are almost uniform among settlements;

o these densities have changed for the first time to any important degree, in the twentieth century, dropping to about half of what they were;

o this drop in overall density is accompanied by a loss of uniformity within settlements;

o in spite of the drop in their overall density, the normal functioning of urban settlements is no longer possible; which shows that Man, being faced with new conditions created by the new technology, has not been able to deal with densities in a reasonable way.

Man has learned empirically how to deal with densities under static conditions for thousands of years. Once these conditions have changed he does not know how to face his problem. We do not know enough about this phenomenon; we have not even been able to measure it properly and this

has been the cause of great confusion and of all sorts of irresponsible statements, as, for example, is the claim that we now live at higher densities.

We know even less about the real issues of densities: the satisfaction Man derives from different types and degrees of densities; the relations of man to man, or Man to his physical space, or the biological, economic, social, political, cultural, aesthetic and psychological consequence of density.

I will demonstrate by two examples the degree to which the problem is complicated and misunderstood, for it is both, even supposing we limit our view to a static one of residential settlements in their whole built-up area.

If we study densities in all types of settlements, taking into account the habitation densities in the entire settled area, we will see that density increases progressively from nomadic, to agricultural, to intensely cultivated, to urban-rural, and finally to urban settlements. This density can be followed up to the formation of urban settlements. For when a settlement begins to grow beyond this level, the density of habitation over its entire area begins to lose its significance since this area may coincidentally be small or large. What is really important for major urban settlements is not the area of their immediate surrounding, but the entire area under their influence, an indirect influence exercised through other settlements. The study, therefore, of the problem beyond the point of the formation of urban settlements, is much more complicated and has not yet been defined.

It is more meaningful to study densities within the nuclei of the settlements (fig. 101). To a point these follow the same trend as densities in the entire area of the settlements; that is, they increase from the nomadic to the urban-rural settlements, and then to the small cities. But we then note a drop of density in the larger city, a significant drop in the metropolis and an even more significant one in the megalopolis. We are not at all certain about the final density of the megalopolis; therefore, the curve from the metropolis to the megalopolis must be considered tentative. On this graph we note a change in the direction of the curve near the point of the small city which might seem a strange phenomenon concerning human settlements. But it is not really, since this turn of the curve is due to the fact that while in the categories of nomadic settlements up to the small city we are actually speaking about a change in function and a different way of life, from the small city to the megalopolis we are referring to changes of dimension within settlements of the same type. I will clarify this point. In nomadic settlements people live by the extensive exploitation of land; in villages this exploitation becomes more intense; in urban-rural areas it increases. In a small city there are even more instances of intense, even if indirect, exploitation of the land. If we were to continue to have small settlements with more intense land exploitation, the curve would climb still higher. But we do not. After the level of the small city, we begin to see different dimensions of urban settlements which, as already explained, all mean a lower

101

**settlements classified as to density within their
nuclei and population size**

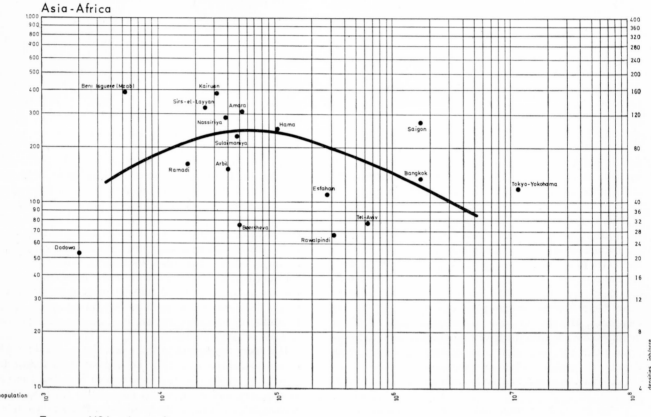

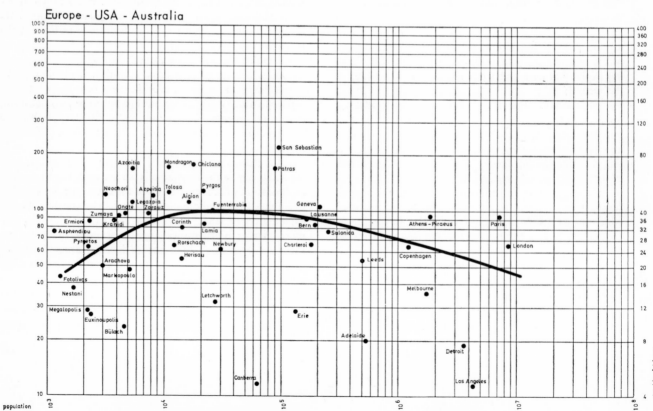

102

ratios of heights to lengths and surfaces of settlements

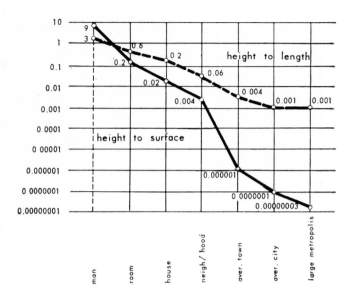

overall density. This point will be supported in another part of this study. In addition, we must remember that the large cities, the much larger metropolis and the megalopolis, are phenomena related to our era of development, where the human settlement has been taken over by many other inhabitants besides Man, that is, machines, cars, industry and many other functions. These two factors contribute to the drop in density.

However, if we consider smaller units of an urban character, either isolated in the countryside as, let us say, a big prison, or within the city itself, the density is far higher. We may easily have an urban institution with a density of many hundreds of inhabitants per hectare, or a hotel with thousands of people per hectare. It is, therefore, obvious that we are looking at two types of phenomena, whose overall attributes create a composite curve which appears to change direction; in fact there are *two* interlocking curves, which, in the case of smaller communities, are one and the same.

In connection with overall density, and after mentioning the fact that it drops in larger settlements, it is interesting to note that the usual statement, 'The larger the city the greater the height of its buildings', is quite misleading, for while the heights of buildings do rise in the larger settlements, the total surface of the city increases even more rapidly, and thus the ratio of maximum height to area drops in larger settlements. The truth of this can be seen in a simple illustration: in the smallest Ekistic unit—the room—we have an average height of 3 m. (10 ft.) with an average length and width of 4 to 4·5 m. (13 to 15 ft.) (i.e., a ratio of height to

length of 0·66 and a ratio of height to surface of 0·20); in a house these ratios drop. Assuming a typical length or width of a house of 12 m. (39 ft. 4 in.) and a surface of 150 m.² (1,600 ft.²), we see that the ratio of height to length is no longer 0·66, but 0·25, and of height to surface no longer 0·20 but 0·02. If we pursue these calculations, we will find that this ratio drops enormously in larger settlements (fig. 102). A study of these curves presents clearly one more reason why the density in larger settlements drops, since not only are additional networks like highways which consume urban land, and functions of a higher order added, but also the heights of the average building do not rise at the same rate at which their surface increases, or at least have not done so until now.

Study of densities

If we want to contribute to the solution of the problems created by changing densities—mostly by decreasing densities—within human settlements, in a world which is going to have a higher total density of inhabitants, we have to learn much more about this problem.

It is therefore my conclusion, after having been involved in practice for many years with this problem and after having carried out some research in it, that we must devote considerably more time and energy in a much more systematic manner in order to understand it completely and arrive at a solution. Such a conclusion may sound quite naive. Its value, however, lies in that it rejects most of the conclusions already reached by special studies on densities in settlements, it condemns most of the recommendations made for new settlements and dismisses many general statements as myths.

A better knowledge of our problem requires better study of all its aspects and their interrelationship. Such aspects being:
- nature of space (total space: Earth, country, natural region, etc.; developed space: with roads only, cultivation, facilities, etc.; built-up space);
- size of space (based on an Ekistic scale from room to Ecumenopolis);
- functions of space (residence, production, recreation, transportation);
- importance of space (physiological, psychological, economic, social, political, technological and cultural);
- space and time (space irrespective of time, space-time balance during 24 hours, space-time balance over a week, month, year, space-time balance over part of a lifetime and space-time balance over a whole lifetime).

The total human space in Nature is, for all practical purposes, equal to the habitable surface of the Earth (in Greek: Ecumeni). This limited space can be increased by the creation of new levels of space either in height or depth. From ancient times, especially since he moved into the cities, Man has created second and third levels of habitable space. In the

L

103

changing densities by increase of space

a. in the past:
increase of space by the addition ▨ of a second floor
meant reasonable density of traffic ▦

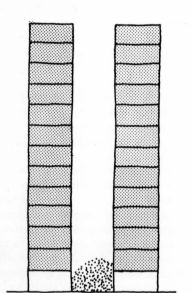

b. but at present:
we increase residential or office space many times without a corresponding increase of space meant for traffic

104

forces conditioning densities

causes of forces	nature of forces	
	texture	directional
biological		
physiological		
psychological		
economic		
social		
technological		
aesthetic		
etc		

105

forces conditioning densities by units of space

forces		Units of space					
causes	nature	1	2	3	4 a	b	c
biological	texture						
	directional						
physiological	texture						
	directional						
economic	—						
other causes	—						
	—						

twentieth century he has created many more levels; and, for the first time to an important degree, several levels of transportation.

The utilisation of additional levels in height is still sometimes considered a way of solving problems of high density at a low cost. But it is not! The moment we increase densities, we must create new corresponding levels of transportation. We have to learn a simple rule: that higher densities of residence, work, etc., require higher densities of transportation, in addition to higher densities for all sorts of utility networks. Unless we achieve this increase simultaneously, we are providing worse service for Man. If we increase the density of isolated areas of residence, work, etc., we finally end up with lower and not higher overall densities (as can be seen in most modern cities) as well as worse services for Man, as is all too evident in our transportation-time-consuming cities.

To face all these complicated problems, we need to carry out research on densities in the following fields:

- o the animal settlements;
- o historical development of human settlements;
- o existing human settlements;
- o degree of human satisfaction in human settlements;
- o mathematical models explaining densities, their laws and the problems created by them;
- o possible solutions of the problems of human settlements, such as relationship to physiology, psychology, cost, technology, culture, change, etc.

Nothing less than a research programme systematically covering all these fields can help us face the problems of densities in human settlements in a responsible way, by determining the different pressures being exercised upon Man and defining the policies which should be followed (fig. 103).

In order to study the densities we need a system of study, which has to be based on several grids like the ones in figs. 104 and 105. The horizontal of the grid of fig. 105 is based on the Ekistic Logarithmic Scale and expands on it. It starts with the completely enclosed space then it moves to the projection of this space on the surface of the Earth, to the plot or area which is necessary for the normal function of the previous space for its breathing, etc., to the space for parking, etc. Then it moves to community, city, metropolis, etc. In each one of these units it comprises changes of density created by pedestrians, machines and special functions.

The vertical of the grids presents other phenomena depending on whether we want to study the degree of density, causes of density, and so forth. On these tables we inscribe the different phenomena by curves. Fig. 106 shows how we can present densities by units of space and causes. The curves show several points of view. Fig. 107 shows space needed per person and fig. 108 shows densities by units of space and types of settlements. Measurements are made for every column of the table so that we can follow the increase of consumption of space or degree of density by its causes. On similar tables, we can inscribe cost related to densities, of traffic as well as problems of cost, and so forth and so on, and thus study interrelationships and develop policies and programmes.

106

densities by units of space and causes

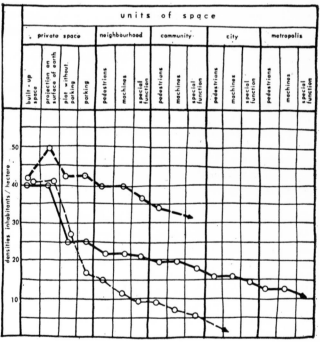

107

space needed per person by units of space and types of settlements

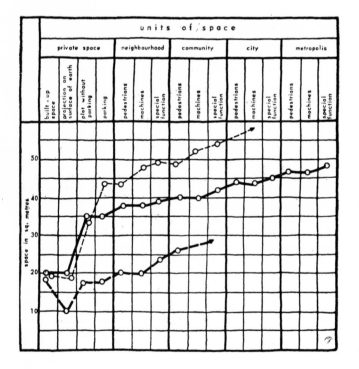

○———○ one storey house-no cars   ○— —○ two storey house-no cars

○— — —○ one storey house-cars

108

densities by units of space and types of settlements

○———○ one storey house-no cars   ○— —○ two storey house-no cars

○— — —○ one storey house-cars

EKISTIC SYSTEMS

Ekistic regions

We have seen that settlements consist of an area with a highly developed nucleus and a less developed hinterland. We have also noted that the latter is usually a homogeneous area covered by a network. We have thus arrived at the conception of a settlement consisting of two basic sections, the most characteristic of which is the nucleus.

Rural settlements depend on urban settlements for the supply of those goods necessary for their life and for goods and services they themselves do not produce. At the same time urban settlements not only supply urban goods and services to their own inhabitants, but also to other urban or rural settlements. Thus, besides single Ekistic units we also have Ekistic regions in which settlements are interrelated by the goods services that pass between them. Therefore, we cannot study settlements merely as isolated units but must see them within the framework of an Ekistic region.

What is the Ekistic region? The smallest region of any Ekistic unit is its own community, while the largest one is the entire habitable world, since there are lines of service and goods exchange connecting settlements everywhere. Every single village in China is connected with Peking, administratively at least. Every Moslem in the world, regardless of where he lives, is connected with Mecca, and not only when he turns towards it to pray. Students of the humanities are connected with Athens and the whole of Greece. How far then do Ekistic regions really extend? For every type of Ekistic study we must define the particular Ekistic regions it covers in order to have specific geographic boundaries of the subject matter.

Regions can be sub-divided in many ways, for example, into racial, national and geographic regions, regions formed by natural landscape or watersheds, and so forth. There are regions based on agriculture, industry, commerce, communications; there are also religious, social, administrative and cultural regions.

Which of these leads towards an Ekistic region, and what do we mean by an Ekistic region? Is it a region which has similar settlements? This is certainly not the case, for it would mean separating the agricultural from the urban settlements while recognising that the urban supply the agricultural, and vice versa. In the same way we cannot define Ekistic regions by selecting settlements of similar size, population or other characteristics.

If we superimpose all the types of regions mentioned above, we will find that the boundaries of many, or at least several of them, coincide to a great degree, leading to the conclusion that there is a type of region which has to some extent been expressed in various different ways, and which depends on a certain degree of geographic unity. These are regions surrounded by mountains, limited by seas, lakes or rivers,

132

109

determination of Ekistic regions
Thrace, Greece (1948)

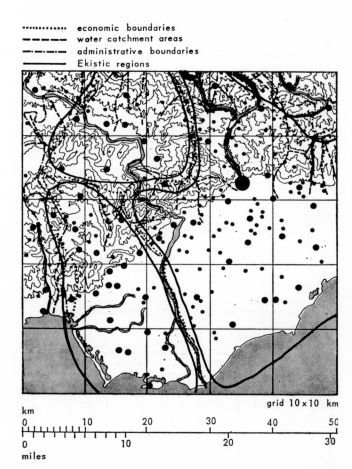

which over the years have developed a particular system of organised life within these natural boundaries expressed as a system of interrelated human settlements. Although this is probably not an ideal definition of an Ekistic region, I consider it a practical way of reaching a simple and approximate definition of the Ekistic region. An example of such a region in northern Greece was defined in 1945 by a team of the Ministry of Reconstruction (fig. 109).

This simple definition does not apply to one size of region alone. In a certain area we may have a valley surrounded by hills and open to the sea—a unified natural geographic region, the study of which would prove that the economic, the transportation and many other regions (and eventually the administrative ones) coincide with it. This valley, though, may be only part of an even larger geographic region which is defined by the sea surrounding a peninsula and higher mountains (fig. 110). This again may be part of a major geographic region beyond the mountains and eventually beyond the seas, connected with the islands; this would be a region of a higher order, which again could belong to one of an even higher order.

On the other hand, the basic region can be divided into smaller regions, since the initial valley can be sub-divided into three: the upper valley and two parts separated by minor hills and the river (fig. 109). These parts can again be separated into sub-regions (by water courses, etc.). From such a description it becomes apparent that one can distinguish a complete system of Ekistic regions beginning with the smallest ones and extending to continents and the whole Earth. The problem of defining the Ekistic region is not only a problem of definition, but also one of how many levels of regions should be defined. For this reason it is necessary to develop a theory of Ekistic regions which can serve as the basic foundation for the interpretation of regional Ekistic phenomena.

Hexagonal patterns

These thoughts arise from the work of the geographer Walter Christaller, who first explained the formation of space in southern Germany in his book, *Die Zentralen Orte in Süddeutschland* or *Central Place Theory*.[10] On the basis of his findings I will present a theory attempting to explain the systems of settlements which can be found in all parts of the world today. I could have called it his theory if it were not for the fact that I go into details, interpretations, generalisations and examples for the accuracy of which he cannot be held at all responsible.

We must first try to divide a uniform area of space into units of similar form and size, leaving no space between them. We may begin with circles, since communities are usually expressed in a circular form. We will soon find that this is unsuitable since space is wasted between the circles (fig. 111). If we experiment with other forms, we will find that a complete coverage of space by the same shape of unit can be accomplished only with triangles, squares or rectangles and hexagons. If we try it with any other polygons, octagons for example, we end up once again with wasted space between. A comparison of the three forms which satisfy our basic requirement (triangles, squares or rectangles and hexagons) shows that hexagons give the smallest average difference in distance of movements between the centre and the periphery.

In order, therefore, to have a uniform area of space sub-divided into similar and equal communities, we should use the hexagonal pattern. We will actually come to the same conclusion if we take circles as the basic form of a community and try to bring them closer together in order to cover the empty space between them. They will cut into each other until they form hexagons. So we reach the conclusion that it

110

determination of Ekistic regions
Thrace, Greece (1948)

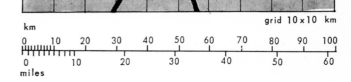

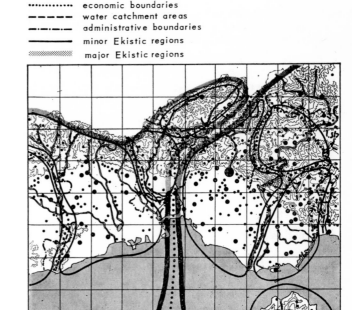

km
grid 10 x 10 km

is the hexagon which provides the best uniform division of space into units having the function closest to a circle. Nature has already offered similar solutions in both the inorganic world, with crystals, as well as the organic world, with the construction of beehives (figs. 112 and 113), or tissues, such as that of the compound eye of the bumble bee.

Such a pattern is the best solution for flat surfaces. But if the surfaces in question are curved (convex, concave, etc.) then they can be more easily covered by a mixed pattern consisting of both hexagons and pentagons. Such examples are given in nature by certain species of Radiolaria, by certain small viruses or by an insect's wing (fig. 114).

Let us now consider a uniform surface covered by hexagons. These hexagons represent small community units. In the centre are built-up nuclei, let us say, villages. How do these villages form systems of a higher order? Assuming that

133

creation of hexagonal patterns

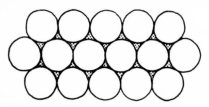

a. circles: lost areas between centres

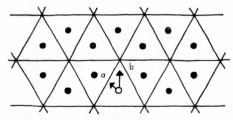

b. triangles: unequal distances from the centre

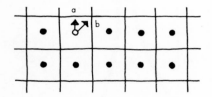

c. squares: unequal distances from the centre

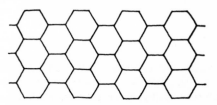

d. hexagons: a much better solution

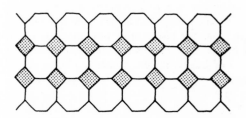

e. octagons: lost area between centres

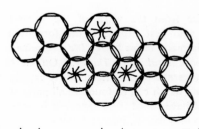

f. only hexagons lead to a satisfactory solution

in such a uniform area consisting of the same type of villages with an equal number of people and similar basic agricultural functions, it becomes necessary to create the first urban function, shops for instance, and that there should be one shop per village, it is clear that we can strengthen the basic hexagonal pattern simply by adding one additional function to each community nucleus. But if the shops cannot be distributed evenly because each shop cannot correspond to one village but to several, these shops will have to be located in those villages best able to serve the area around them. For the same reasons which led us to recognise the hexagon as the best form for the basic community, we find that the smallest unit beyond the fundamental 'A' community, which can be served by one central location, is community 'B' which serves itself, and six equal communities around it. This creates a star-shaped hexagon consisting of seven communities (fig. 115). Since the other communities will have to be served in a similar way, several 'B' centres will be created until the whole surface is covered by centres, whose number equals the total number of fundamental 'A'

communities divided by seven.

At this point I remind the reader that any two consecutive units in the Ekistic Logarithmic Scale (ELS) correspond in the ratio 1:7 which is one of the reasons for the selection of this scale.

In a similar way we find that the need for additional services of a higher order leads to the creation of a 'C' centre located in such a way as to serve seven 'B' areas (fig. 116). And seven 'C' areas create a 'D' area, and thus we develop several levels of fundamental or primary Ekistic systems (communities A), secondary ones (B), tertiary ones (C) and so on. We can now visualise a whole system in which the fundamental Ekistic units are the 'A' villages connected by streets with 'B' centres, which in turn are connected by more important roads with 'C' centres and these with 'D' centres, etc.

On the basis of such considerations, a whole Ekistic system can be developed consisting of:
  o the homogeneous parts;
  o the nodal points (the A, B, C, D settlements, etc.); and
  o the circulatory system consisting of the elementary

112

hexagonal patterns in nature

snowflake: its shape is due to the non-resistant aerial environment in which it develops and which allows it to grow outwards

114

patterns in nature

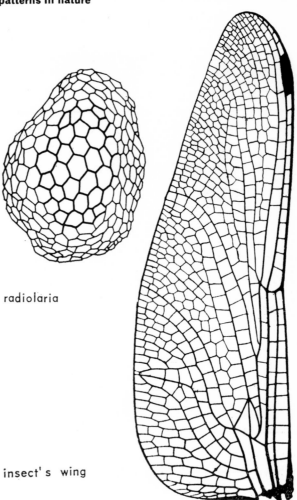

radiolaria

insect's wing

113

hexagonal patterns in nature

a three-storey wasps' nest

side view

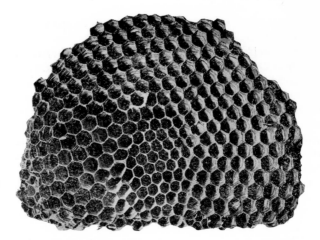

plan of second storey

115

creation of hexagonal patterns and systems

**communities class B and C in a uniform space
covered by hexagons class A**

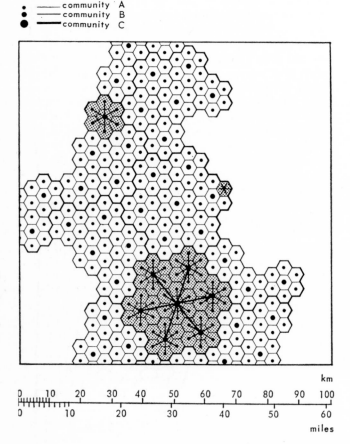

116

creation of hexagonal systems

**communities class A, B, C, D and their hierarchical
interconnections**

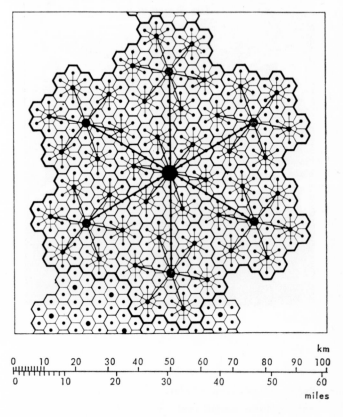

connections (A B), the secondary ones (B C), the tertiary ones (C D), etc. (fig. 116).

Such systems may grow in the same way until they cover the whole Earth with Ekistic regions of many levels (fig. 117). We have in this way reached the theoretical pattern of Ekistic regions of a different order as well as the theoretical pattern of the circulatory networks within them. These patterns presuppose the existence of a completely homogeneous terrain, a plain without any hills, mountains, rivers, lakes, seas or anything else. It is quite natural that these basic Ekistic regions and systems become altered in practice because of:

- ○ pre-existing geographic and topographic features or man-made elements like transportation lines, etc.;
- ○ subsequent Ekistic, economic or other activities created after the formation of an initial system;
- ○ changes of the importance of certain Ekistic centres such

as the expansion of the large centres and the incorporation of smaller settlements into such regions.

Let us first follow the changes in form caused by geographic and topographic patterns. If at a certain location the plain changes into a hillside, the sides of the hexagons touching this hillside will be shortened and compressed towards the centre, since we have assumed as one basic reason for the adoption of a hexagon the necessity for the periphery points to be as close as possible to the centre. Because of the upgrade, the travelling time or the travelling effort between the centre and periphery will tend to become longer and, therefore, in order to have approximately equal travelling time, there will be pressure from the hill on that side of the hexagon resulting in an irregular shape (irregular in a two-dimensional way but completely regular if we think of the time factor or of the travelling effort factor) (fig. 118).

117

Ekistic regions at different levels and scales

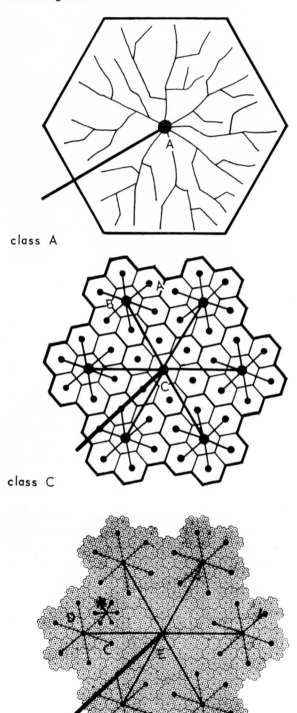

class A

class C

class E

Hillside communities of the same type as those of the plain (i.e., agricultural communities) and with the same quality of land are transformed into hexagons elongated along the axis of the hillside. In this way any hill or mountain leads to the transformation of a community.

If the hillside communities do not have the same economic functions as those of the plain (let us assume they are cattle-breeding communities), their dimensions will also be different. The inhabitants will not in this case have to move from the centre to the periphery and back every day for the cultivation of their fields. Cattle-breeders move around for days within their area; even if they have to return at night, they can cover much greater distances with their cattle than the farmer who must walk to work and back; thus we see communities of a different type taking shape on the hillside. The whole hillside may be covered by communities that are much larger because of their different functional purpose and probably elongated because of their location on a hillside (fig. 118). If there is joint exploitation of agricultural land, grazing land and forests located in the higher regions of the mountains—and this happens quite often in practice—communities will tend to be partly on the plain, and partly on the hillside, and therefore we will find some communities elongated in shape, extending from the plain to the top of a mountain (fig. 119).

If rather than a small hill next to the plain there is a big mountain with irregular curved slopes, then the system will not have to be a hexagonal one. On the contrary it will develop into a system of interlocked hexagons, pentagons and perhaps other types of surfaces as well, such as the natural patterns shown in fig. 114.

Other reasons for a variation in the hexagonal pattern could be the existence of a river or canal in the middle of the plain (fig. 120). Such an element cutting through the hexagonal pattern leads to the separation of some sections from their main bodies. It is natural that the nucleus, the built-up part of the settlement, should remain on one side, but then it will have to be smaller since its terrain will be smaller, unless there are bridges, in which case we may have a city on both sides. In the case of small settlements though, the cut-off parts of the hexagon are too small to form their own nucleus, and are usually absorbed and incorporated into neighbouring complete hexagons. In this way, a canal, for example, leads to a change in the shape of the hexagonal pattern. These changes will result in a change of location for the settlements if they have not already been built. If, however, the river is very small or often flooded, it may not offer any attraction, and the nucleus may either remain with its normal centre of gravity, or even be pushed away towards the other side of the community.

Similar phenomena can be observed along a coastal area when the plain is by the sea. There again the hexagons are cut and, if the remaining places are large, the hexagons retain their own nuclei, but if they are small the nuclei are either underdeveloped or absorbed by neighbouring ones. Again

137

118

**deformation of the pattern
owing to economic conditions**

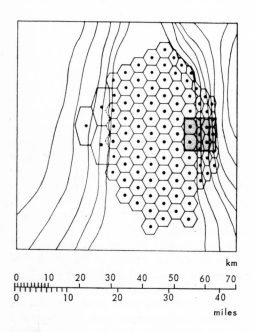
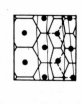

```
                                    km
0    10    20    30    40    50    60    70
|++++++++|    |    |    |    |    |    |
0         10        20        30        40
                                    miles
```

119

**deformation of the pattern
owing to geographic and economic conditions**

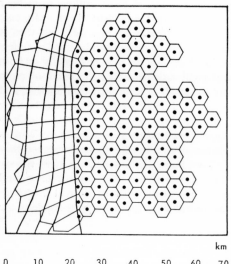

```
                              km
0    10    20    30    40    50    60    70
|++++++++|    |    |    |    |    |    |
0         10        20        30        40
                              miles
```

138

120

**deformation of the pattern
owing to the presence of a river or a canal**

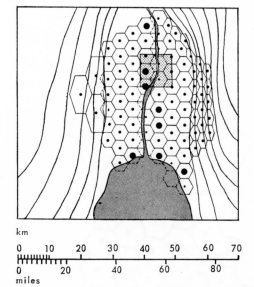

```
km
0    10    20    30    40    50    60    70
|++++++++|    |    |    |    |    |
0         20        40        60        80
miles
```

if they are attracted by the sea the nuclei are built on the shore. The attraction can be economic if, for example, the inhabitants engage in fishing, or transport their goods by sea, or climatic, if they seek the cool sea breeze. Otherwise, they will remain in the gravitational centres of the communities unless adverse conditions such as high seas and very strong winds exist on the shore, in which case they will be pushed inland.

If the element which changes the homogeneity of the region is man-made, it will have the same effects, depending on its importance. For example, a small road may not affect the hexagonal pattern at all as far as the boundaries of the hexagons are concerned. If the road is more important, it may attract the nuclei towards it, or at least half-way between its gravitational centre and the road. If the route is very important and cuts through the landscape, as does a limited access road or a railroad, making movement across it difficult, the effects will be the same as those of a large river or a wide canal.

Such a transformation may be caused by the railway. This is a transformation due to two factors; the line cutting through the area (as in the case of limited access roads), and the existence of stations on a railway line. While the railway line cutting through an area creates problems for minor communities, its various stations and stops draw new forces

121

**deformation of the pattern
owing to the presence of the railway line**

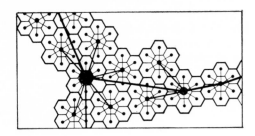

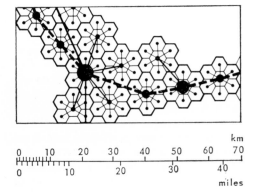

122

**deformation of the pattern
because of areas of special attraction**

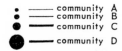

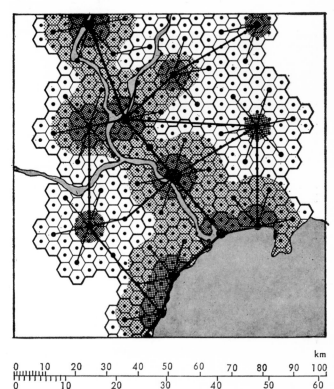

which accumulate around them (fig. 121). Much the same phenomenon occurs at the access points to a limited access highway, or around airports and sea ports.

It is quite natural that such geographic, topographic or man-made elements in the landscape should not only influence the primary Ekistic system, but also the secondary, tertiary, etc. How far they influence systems of a higher order depends on how important their features are. It is very probable, for example, that even a small hill will influence the secondary system and a navigable river will influence not only the secondary and tertiary, but probably further levels of Ekistic regions. Indeed a navigable river can attract all major centres along its banks. In such a case, while the lower level system may remain basically unhindered, the higher level system will be completely transformed since all major settlements will form an essentially linear pattern along the river. The same may happen near the sea, where all major Ekistic

centres may be located in the coastal area forming another linear pattern (fig. 122).

If new economic activities are added to an area, if, for instance, a factory 'f' is constructed in the midst of settlements 'A' (fig. 123), it may cause a decline of the nearest communities 'A' by its noise and air pollution. As a result of this decline, some centres 'B' may be strengthened by additional population caused by the additional labour force attracted to the area, as well as this decline of some settlements 'A'. Further, the lines connecting the 'B' settlements with 'f' will be strengthened, and a wider deformation of the transportation network will become apparent.

Another change in the shape of the transportation network may be due to the existence of a settlement of a higher order, a class 'E' settlement for instance. This settlement, having a nucleus with a diameter of 15 kilometres may absorb six class 'A' communities and the nuclei belonging to them, thus

123

**deformation of the pattern
caused by the establishment of a major factory**

community A
community B
community C
community D

f factory

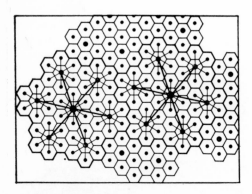

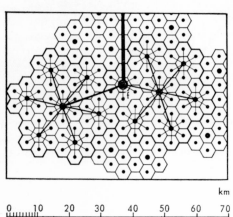

km

0 10 20 30 40 50 60 70

0 10 20 30 40

miles

124

**elimination of minor settlements
because of the expansion of a major one**

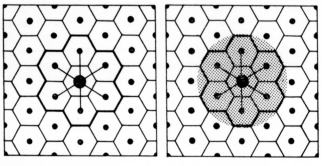

causing the elimination of six independent settlements, and effecting corresponding changes in the formation of the vicinity (fig. 124).

So if we look at an Ekistic system developed on the basis of this theory, we will see many variations of its basic geometric hexagonal conception caused by changes in form resulting from various forces.

If the systems spread very much and cover areas of the Earth which are, not only theoretically but also for all practical purposes, curved, then we should expect the hexagonal patterns to be replaced by systems composed of pentagons and hexagons. This would have happened had the whole surface of the Earth consisted of flat land without any seas or mountains. But since this is not the case and these two elements are so dominant the final pattern results from a combination of all patterns and the theoretical patterns.

Types of hexagonal systems

Several different types of Ekistic systems can exist in accordance with specific conditions. I will mention a few in order to illustrate that, apart from those due to structural reasons, major changes may be caused by even more basic factors.

First, there are regions which do not have enough inhabitants to populate the whole area with a system of fundamental communities. In this case communities do not touch each other. Some may be big and some small, but the region as a whole is not cohesive. This may be due to a primitive stage of development, or simply to the fact that although the inhabitants are highly developed, land is so ample that the region is underpopulated.

When the conditions are primitive, the pattern of settlements is very similar to that of expressions of animal life. The entire settled area, is physically expressed by the community's paths of movement which do not extend beyond it (fig. 125). Neighbouring communities are not physically connected. In the case of highly developed people who are not numerous enough to settle the whole area the picture is different; the communities, though physically separated, are inter-connected by a transportation system, making a complete though not cohesive Ekistic system.

We may also have some cohesive regions where the number of people is much greater than the normal Ekistic system can stand. In this case we find an overflow into areas of special attraction, coastal areas, urban areas, etc. When such major changes of density take place, the hexagonal pattern may change completely, since nuclei of settlements are no longer floating in an area of low density of investment—and resistance—but in an area where people and related investment have created a completely different basis for the major settlements and the nuclei.

In isolated areas we can have types of regions whose

140

125

Ekistic regions without cohesion

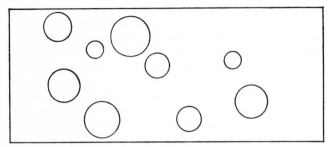

the fundamental communities do not touch each other

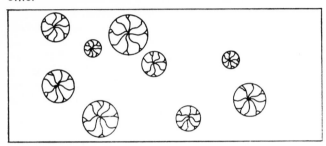

the paths are limited within the communities

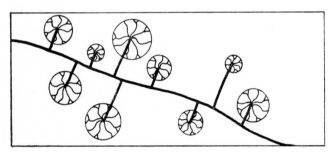

the communities can be interconnected into an Ekistic system but they still do not have direct cohesion

differences are solely due to their isolation (fig. 126). Let us assume we have an area surrounded by a desert which has developed normally; suddenly it is placed under the pressure of surrounding threats coming from the desert. This would mean that the settlements near the border line would be eliminated, or reduced to a minimum of inhabitants. The bulk of these people would be despatched to the major centres (B and C). We would have a movement of population; but the basic system would not be altered, the boundaries would remain the same, only the population would be much more dense near the centre of the threatened area. Hence the lack of security can be said to change an area's density pattern.

Lack of security may also completely change the pattern of

settlements within a certain region. In a location where the people once lived in the plains and used the mountains for grazing grounds, they may be forced to live on the mountains, still cultivating the plains during the day-time but retreating to the mountains at night; they might even be forced to abandon the plains completely (fig. 127). Similar patterns appear in all threatened regions.

Another area presenting different characteristics is an island. Here we see many typical characteristics due to conditions of economy and security. When there is a security problem (danger from the sea), the settlements tend to form near the centre of the island (fig. 128a). When there is no security problem, they expand over the island. However the attraction of the seashore is of great importance and transforms the pattern correspondingly. If the island is inhabited by farmers who export their products, there is a movement of many settlements towards the seaside, provided that sea transport to destination costs the same from all coastal areas (fig. 128b). If, however, the cheapest means of transport is by land to one port and from there to various destinations, there may be only one main port. The economics of transport decide in this case whether the pattern of settlements will be a variation of the hexagonal form (when only one port can be used for export), or if all settlements will be coast-oriented (when it is equally economical to send off the produce from many small ports).

The various types of Ekistic systems, combined with the causes which created them, show that all patterns have a relative rather than a permanent and constant value, since they depend on so many variables some of which remain the same (Nature, for example) while others (especially the economics and technology of transportation) change and may cause an alteration in the Ekistic system. Both Ekistic systems and the settlements forming them depend on a delicate balance of many forces, and a change in any one of them may result in structural changes in the whole system. These changes will be more or less apparent depending on their causes and the part of the region they affect. But one thing is certain: every important change of any nature in the region will have some impact on the structure and balance of the Ekistic system.

Dimensions of hexagonal patterns

The basic dimensions of Ekistic systems are dependent mainly on the dimensions of the fundamental community. If the area is homogeneous, it is relatively easy to calculate the basic dimensions of the system and to find the locations of the fundamental (class A) communities, on the basis of which the locations of communities of a higher order are decided. These dimensions depend basically on the economic functions of the community. They are influenced, however, by several other factors.

126

deformation of the pattern in isolated regions

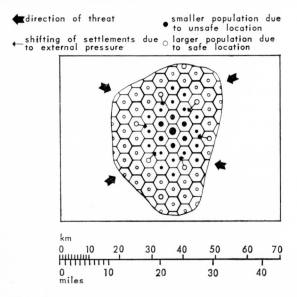

127

deformation of the pattern for reasons of safety

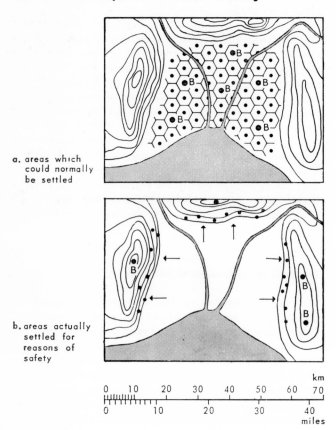

a. areas which could normally be settled

b. areas actually settled for reasons of safety

When a community is agricultural, the basic factor conditioning its dimensions is the maximum distance the inhabitants can travel from the nucleus to the most distant farm in the pursuit of their daily work. Experience has shown that it is usually up to half an hour one way, or a total of one hour's travelling time per day. In exceptional cases this reaches a maximum of two hours travelling time each day. Therefore, in communities where people walk to their fields or ride there on horse, mule, donkey or camel, the radius is about 2·5 kilometres (1·5 mi.) and the diameter about 5 kilometres (3 mi.). This is quite common in many countries of the world where agricultural production is based solely on human and animal labour.

When cultivation becomes mechanised and people drive to their fields, the dimensions of the community grow; but when this mechanisation is very extensive, it is usual for families to live on their farms and use their own mechanical means of transportation to serve their contacts with the community—market, education, pleasure, and so forth. In such cases and indeed in all cases where—for a variety of reasons—farming families live on their land, we may find communities of a larger diameter in which the nucleus of the community contains residences for a small number of inhabitants only while the remainder live on their farms. Such a community of people living on their farms with a service nucleus can reach a radius of 10 to 15 kilometres (6 to 9 mi.) or even more (fig. 129), since the size of the family farms changes to a very great degree (fig. 130).

As stated, the size of class 'B', 'C', etc., communities depends on the basic dimensions of the fundamental community and can be calculated accordingly. Experience has shown that market centres come into being at locations which permit people to leave their elementary communities at sunrise, finish their marketing business and return to their villages by sunset. This usually means three to four hours' travelling time each way; therefore, under primitive agricultural conditions, with farming and transportation based on human and animal labour, the market centres have a diameter of the order of 15 to 20 kilometres (9 to 12 mi.), equivalent to a three- to four-hour walk (i.e., class 'C'). But if transportation from elementary to major communities is made by car, the centres playing the greatest role become class 'D', since they are within easy driving distance. If the road network is very good and the transportation system well developed, even class 'E' centres can take over this role or, in exceptional cases where farmers own airplanes, centres of an even higher order (fig. 131).

From the above examples it is clear that several factors influence the dimensions of the Ekistic system. We will try to look into some of them. From the population point of view, the basic factor related to the dimensions of the system is the nature of the population as rural or urban. When it is rural, we often have the types of communities already described; even though the communities may have

128

deformation of the pattern of an island

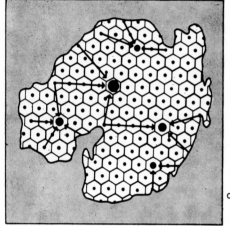

a . under bad
security
conditions

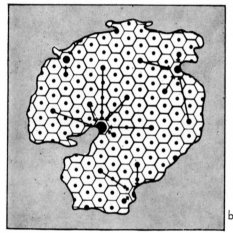

b . when the seas
are safe

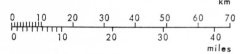

km
0 10 20 30 40 50 60 70

0 10 20 30 40
miles

129

physical dimensions of agricultural settlements

approximate area corresponding to 200 rural families

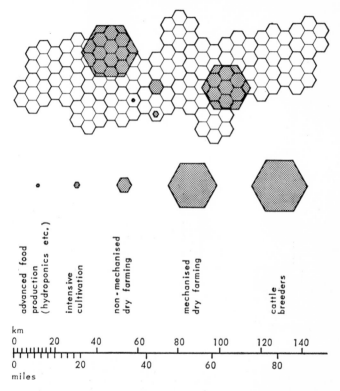

advanced food production (hydroponics etc.) · intensive cultivation · non-mechanised dry farming · mechanised dry farming · cattle breeders

km
0 20 40 60 80 100 120 140

0 20 40 60 80
miles

different dimensions if some special types of cultivation are practised. For example, an olive-growing community is larger than an arable farming one since olive trees require attention only during a short part of the year, and therefore the farmers need not commute daily. In this case the farmers usually live together in much larger settlements, and during the cultivation and harvest periods they either organise their transportation by mechanical means (the burden is small, taking into consideration the small number of trips necessary per year) or settle in temporary huts among the olive trees. Such a type of cultivation may lead to communities with a radius of 10 to 15 kilometres (6 to 9 mi.).

When, on the other hand, the community is on irrigated land, and the cultivation is intensive, the farms are much smaller, thus removing the necessity of walking up to half an hour a day. In this case, the inhabitants may form much smaller communities with a walking distance of no more than 500 metres (1,640 ft.), in which case, even if they do seek security, the people may still live on their farms. In such a case the nucleus of the community may be smaller than usual with residences mainly for those people connected with the services provided by the community, that is, connected with its central functions. It is interesting to note here that both oversized and undersized agricultural communities may

143

130

physical dimensions of agricultural settlements

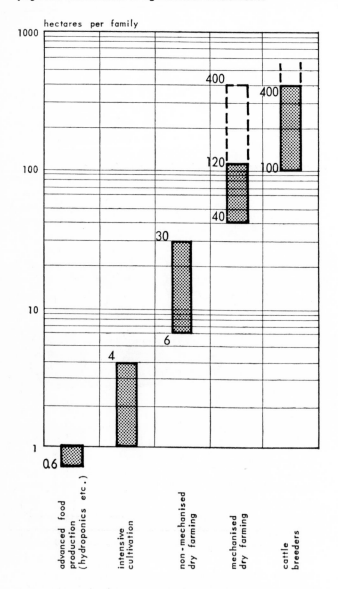

turn to irrigate his own land by opening his canals), and second because the distances cannot be covered easily on foot or, what is the opposite, because the farmer can, because of mechanisation, afford to commute easily to the central nucleus of his community in order to partake of its services.

Communication is not the only factor influencing the spacing of the fundamental communities. Social organisation plays a big role as well. In autocratic or feudal societies the seat of power, or that of the feudal lord, is of great importance. The entire system is influenced by it and there is a greater density of habitation close to it and a lesser density far away. But even in such cases we may find unreasonable patterns of distribution of human settlements, which may result from the landlord's desire to rotate the people on the farms in order to cultivate land according to a rotation system, or so as not to allow people to settle permanently and become attached to a specific section of his lands.

Another important factor in the formation of the pattern and the dimensions of the systems is the income level of the inhabitants. If the land yield is very low, only a small number of families can be supported. It would therefore be necessary for most of the people to walk longer, say one to two hours each way, which would mean enlarging the physical dimensions of the basic community so that its normal diameter of about five kilometres (3 mi.) might increase to ten or more (6 mi.). Such a situation becomes very demanding upon the inhabitants, since travelling time takes up such a large part of their day. When, however, a community is kept small and supports only a very small number of families, the number of the inhabitants cannot maintain the basic community facilities (such as a shop or one-class elementary school). In both cases it is difficult for communities to survive; sometimes they are deserted and the land lies fallow, or is turned into grazing ground when a different type of people, the cattle-breeders, take over. When this happens, the diameter of the community may increase a great deal since the new people do not have to cultivate the land and commute every day, but can simply walk with their herds.

Every type of community has minimum, maximum and optimum physical dimensions. The most important factor in determining them is that of time-distance, as I already explained. The minimum dimensions of the community depend also on the level of community organisation, as well as the standard of life regarded normal in the region and locality concerned. If people, for example, consider the existence of a school or a church as a necessary prerequisite for life in a village, then the village must be big enough to support such a school or church.

To the factors of Man, functions, transportation and economy which have been mentioned, we must add those of geography, administration and organisation of the economy. All of them taken together lead to the final definition of the structure and dimensions of the fundamental communities and the entire system.

lead to a settlement consisting of a small service nucleus, with residence on the farms for most of the farmers.

We have already seen that the physical dimensions of the fundamental communities can vary from a few hundred metres to 15 or more kilometres (from 100 feet to 10 or more miles) and that when the dimensions of the community approach either extreme, the tendency of the people is to live on their farms. In some cases this may occur, first because it is so easy to combine the security of proximity to the centre with living on the farm and seeing to the cultivation (on irrigated land the farmer may have to rise at night if it is his

131

organisation on the basis of the time distance factor

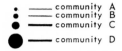

. ———— community A
: ———— community B
● ———— community C
⬤ ———— community D

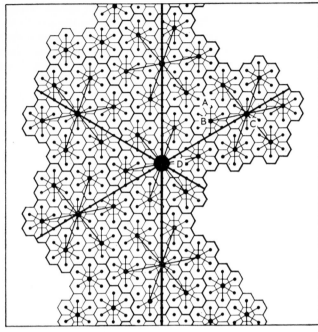

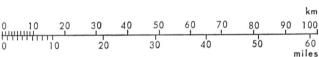

A   minor centres
B   minor centres as A but with a few central functions
A-B approximately 5 km covered on foot
C   important market centres
B-C approximately 15-20 km
D   major market centres
C-D approximately 40 km

Size of settlements

In the same way as we can calculate the geographic dimensions of settlements, we can gauge the size of their population, the volume of their production, their economic activity, and so forth. Take the example of a homogeneous area with a fundamental community (class 'A') of 200 families, or 1,000 people. Let us assume for reasons of simplicity that this community is able to support within it only one additional urban family, a merchant's family. If this

is the total amount of urban functions the community can support, then its population consists of 1,000 members of agricultural families plus five members of an urban family. The population of a class 'B' community will be of the order of 1,005, plus three more families of merchants to serve the seven communities (one class 'B' and six class 'A'), two families of teachers, and two families of administrators, which makes 35 additional members of urban families, or a total of 1,040. The population of a 'C' centre will be 1,040 plus the members of the urban families needed in order to serve 49 communities (one class 'C', six class 'B', 42 class 'A'); these members may number 200 to 300, which means that the centre may have a population of 1,300 inhabitants. A 'D' centre can have the population of 1,300, plus 2,000 or 3,000 serving the special functions of this centre.

The population of the different communities or centres increases in accordance with their centrality. The increase of population from one class to another is always larger in the higher classes for the simple reason that while a class 'A' community serves just one unit, a class 'B' serves seven, a class 'C' 49, a class 'D' seven times 49, a class 'E' 49 times 49, etc. The additional population could, therefore, be calculated in the following way: if seven units are added every time, and the second community has a difference of ten persons from the previous one, the difference later becomes 70 persons, 490 persons, etc. In practice, though, these differences are even larger, simply because at every community level there is a small residue of income which flows by necessity to the community of a higher order in exchange for the goods and services this community provides. If there is no such residue, there can be no communities of a higher order. If the residue is high, the differences between the different levels of communities are even larger. Theory and experience show that the curve of population increase, in centres of several levels, rises if technology and incomes are higher. This is the reason why in less developed countries the local centres of a higher order have not the same ratio of population to the centres of lower order as in high-income countries.

We must now consider that apart from the agricultural or fundamental income of the communities, whose residue is the cause of larger population in centres of a higher order, we also have secondary production in communities of a higher order (fig. 132). This creates a higher per capita income, and constitutes an additional reason for a rise of the population curve. We must also add the curve of tertiary production which rises even higher, and we can then see the reason why there must necessarily be a great difference in the population levels between centres of several categories.

Using the same method we can now estimate the incomes of every size community. We find that the income in a class 'A' community may be $101,000, assuming $500 per agricultural family per year, and $1,000 for the one urban family.

M

145

population by communities of several classes, incomes and technology

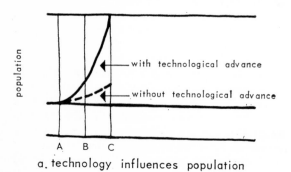

a. technology influences population

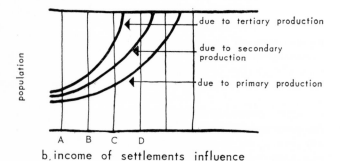

b. income of settlements influence the size of their population

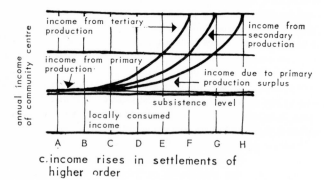

c. income rises in settlements of higher order

The income of a class 'B' community is $101,000 for the same unit as in the class 'A' community, plus $10,500 for the seven additional urban families (three merchants, two teachers, two administrators) which have a higher income ($1,500) than the agricultural families and even than the one small urban family of the class 'A' community. Thus the total income of the class 'B' community is $111,500. On the same basis we can estimate the income of a class 'C' community to be of the order of $200,000 and so on.

In all these calculations we must not forget that in every community of a higher order, not only does the income per urban family increase, but the rural family income as well, since once there is a market of urban dwellers who can afford to pay for products of more intensive cultivation (fruit, vegetables, etc.), several rural families shift from low to high intensity production, thus increasing their income.

We can see that the average incomes per settlement increase normally at a higher rate than the population, for in settlements of a higher order we have a larger income in addition to the larger population since the more elaborate services provided receive a higher remuneration.

Dynamic systems

We have already noted how a railway line or a highway may influence the Ekistic region by attracting several settlements to it, or towards it. Such transportation lines have gradually created a different type of Ekistic region in which the hexagonal pattern is broken by forces radiating out from several centres along the main axes of transportation. This is a recent phenomenon witnessed only during the last two centuries. For thousands of years humanity had settlements in which transportation always took place at the same speed (that of man, cart or horse), which was always about five kilometres per hour for men (3 m.p.h.) and about double that for carts. Certainly the horse could run at a much higher speed than Man but only for short distances and very seldom within the city itself. Messages could be transported this way, but not large numbers of people or goods. For the great majority of people and for all goods, the normal transportation speed was the same outside the settlements as within. As a result, movements in all directions were of equal importance, therefore communities tended to become circular and their patterns hexagonal.

The changes during the last 100 years have caused a variation in speeds ranging from five kilometres an hour for Man (3 m.p.h.), to a cruising speed of more than 800 kilometres an hour (500 m.p.h.) for a jet airplane, a ratio of one to 160 (fig. 133). Even if we count only the speed on the surface of the Earth, we still have a range from about five kilometres an hour to 200 kilometres an hour (3 m.p.h. to 120 m.p.h.), on highways and railways; or, if we do not want to take such an extreme case, from five kilometres to 100 kilometres an hour (3 m.p.h. to 60 m.p.h.), hence ratios from 1 : 40 to 1 : 20. This means that where transportation allows for such differences in speeds along certain routes, the basic form of a settlement is no longer circular but must follow the rule of equal time-distances, equal effort or equal cost-distances; this is a basic rule of contemporary human settlements.

Undeveloped rural areas with no such transportation lines, which still rely solely on animal transportation, retain the

133

comparative distances travelled in one hour by different means

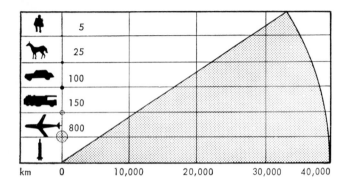

134

settlements and speeds of transportation

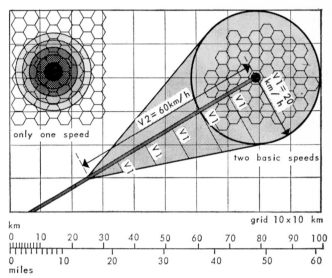

typical hexagonal pattern with no changes. Where there are other types of transportation, as is usually the case around major urban areas, we have a transformation of the hexagonal patterns through the forces operating on the basis of the rule of equal time-distances. If within an urban metropolitan area, where people move at an average speed of 20 kilometres per hour (12 m.p.h.), a major highway is opened connecting the countryside with the centre of the metropolitan area and allowing for an average speed of 60 kilometres per hour (40 m.p.h.), the form of the metropolitan area, probably expanding previously in concentric circles, will change, since, in the same amount of time on the highway, people can now travel three times the distance they previously travelled within the normal metropolitan area. This will lead to a new composite shape, the exact form of which depends on the ratios of the two or more speeds (fig. 134).

If a major metropolitan area has six such highway connections, it takes the shape of an asteroid (fig. 135). If along one of these axes there is, in addition to the highways, a high-speed railway which brings the people to point E not at the speed of 60 (40), but of 120 kilometres per hour (80 m.p.h.), then the asteroid changes its shape along one of its branches, since people can travel the distance from E to F at a higher speed and then move at the normal speed of 20 kilometres (12 m.p.h.) in every other direction. In this case the final form of the region will be determined by a

combination of three forces: railway, highway and the normal network (fig. 136).

If we now assume that there can be no further technological or economic progress and no possibility of acquiring more high-speed highways, but that the metropolitan area continues to grow, we will witness a new expansion tending to fill the gaps previously left between the branches of the asteroid, a movement gradually leading to an area of the previous type until a full circle is once again completed. This can happen in two ways, either by expansion along radii, or along radii and ring connections (fig. 137).

If, however, a series of new transportation lines allowing for an average speed of 200 kilometres per hour (120 m.p.h.) is constructed, the whole process of evolution will once again be repeated and the radius of the region will be doubled. If progress stops at that level, the results will be the same, and the dynamic Ekistic region, star-shaped in development, will once again start tending towards the circle. Such an evolution can take place in different ways and lead to different forms, depending on the creation of one or more means and lines of transportation. The forms of the dynamic regions can be of different categories:

- concentric, if all means of transportation develop in all directions simultaneously;
- pear-shaped, if a system of a higher speed develops in one preponderant direction;

147

135

composite growth
stimulated by two transportation networks

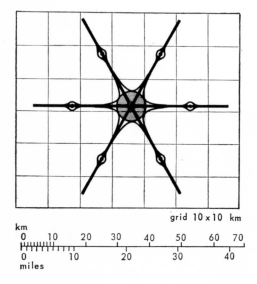

grid 10 x 10 km

137

dynamic growth
stimulated by a network of radial roads only

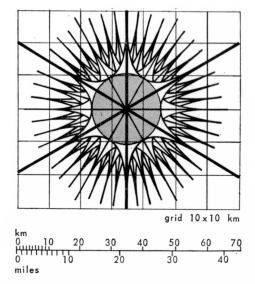

grid 10 x 10 km

136

composite growth
stimulated by three transportation networks

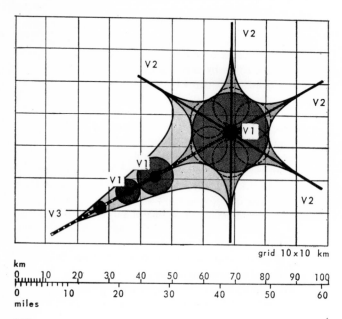

grid 10 x 10 km

○ star-shaped, if high-speed lines are developed in several directions simultaneously;
○ twin star-shaped, with areas of major growth along some of the radii of the stars, if there is a combination of several means of transportation.

Such developments, determined by different and changing systems of transportation, show that we are now witnessing on the one hand a combination of hexagonal patterns, where no differences in types of transportation exist, as in areas untouched by modern technology, and on the other dynamic Ekistic systems, resulting from modern technological advances in transportation.

The impact that modern technology can have on the Ekistic patterns can be seen on a macro-scale by the isochronic distances around major urban areas, as in the example of France (fig. 138) where the isochronic distances of 90 minutes connect Paris, in four out of the six directions around it, with nine urban areas to form one system. The case is similar in the southern coast of France, which, if we consider 90 minutes as an urban distance, already constitutes one continuous urban area.

In practice there are Ekistic systems throughout the world which are a combination of the two basic patterns of the hexagonal and the dynamic systems. This combination is determined by:

138
isochronic distances of urban extensions
France (1954)

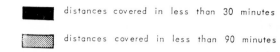

distances covered in less than 30 minutes

distances covered in less than 90 minutes

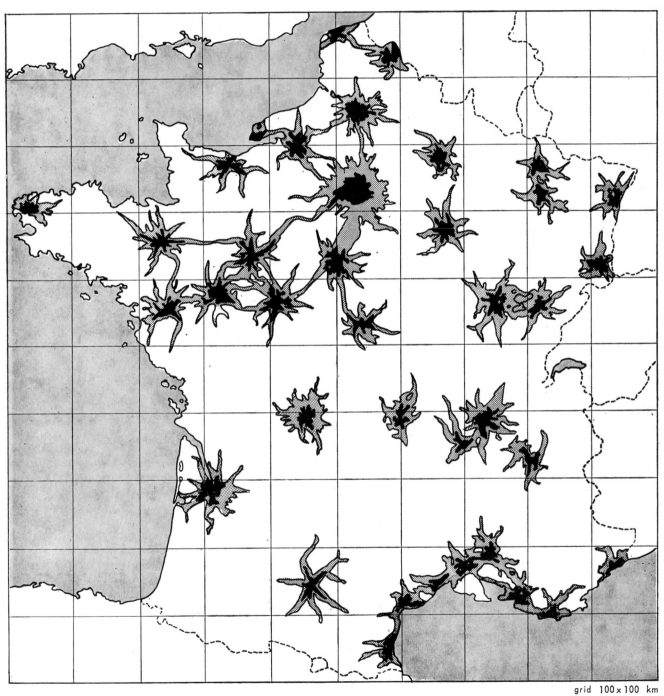

grid 100 x 100 km

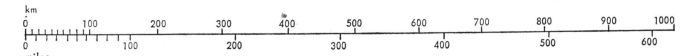

km
0   100   200   300   400   500   600   700   800   900   1000

0   100   200   300   400   500   600
miles

o historical force; in the past most of the systems were based on the hexagonal pattern, which is now changing to the dynamic pattern;

o evolutionary forces due to continuous technological and economic changes.

The combinations vary enormously since even in our era of technological change some areas by necessity rely on older systems of transportation for several levels of connections. This means that there are areas where, for example, although transportation within 'A' communities is mainly by foot, connections between 'A' communities and between 'A' and 'B' are by car on small roads allowing for a speed of 30 kilometres per hour, and connections between 'B' communities and between 'B' and 'C' are by car on roads allowing for speeds of 50 kilometres per hour, and so forth. The result is that even within these areas hexagonal patterns are still valid since the system of transportation is uniform for the same community level.

Therefore, we are already witnessing, and should be preparing ourselves for, the era of Ekistic systems which will be a combination of the two basic types of patterns— the hexagonal and the dynamic. This combination will allow for the survival of the system with certain adjustments. Even when the connections within every level of systems are the same, there will be some directions in which they will have a different importance. I take as an example a typical hexagonal pattern situated in a plain (fig. 139). As we can see, connections between 'A' and 'B' communities are the same. There are, however, some 'A' communities which are on a class 'C' highway. These will be influenced by this highway in a dynamic way. In a similar way all the highways leading to 'C' are not of the 'C' category; two belong to class 'D', since through the 'C' centre they lead to the 'D' centre. It is quite probable, therefore, that these lines will be of greater importance and therefore settlements 'C' on the line 'CD' will be influenced by these lines and develop in a different way, even if the transportation lines within these settlements are of a class equal to, or lower than, those provided by line 'C'.

All these transportation networks have been based on the assumption that there is only one hierarchical system of settlements. This was indeed the case in the past for most of the regions of the world, especially if they had passed through long periods with the same conditions. But this is no longer the case. Not only are the Networks changing dynamically, but it is quite possible that we may have several different hierarchical systems in the same area, as indicated in the section on descriptive anatomy (pp. 109–124). Hence, the situation can be an even more complex one, when in the same area we may have two or more interlocked hierarchical systems which are combinations of hexagonal and dynamic patterns (fig. 140). Such systems may tend to merge into one but such a thing cannot happen, since this merging pre-supposes a long period without any economic or technological changes; and at present we cannot foresee the possibility of such a period.

150

139

influence of the transportation network on the hexagonal pattern

community A
community B
community C
community D

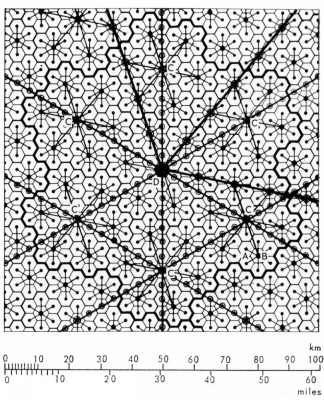

km
0   10   20   30   40   50   60   70   80   90   100

0   10   20   30   40   50   60
miles

To calculate the physical dimensions of dynamic systems or composite interlocked ones and the size of their settlements is not as easy as it is with hexagonal ones. It can be done, though, on the basis already described. The difficulty does not lie so much in the calculation of the forces within every settlement as in the calculation of the overall dynamic forces of the region which will influence the dynamically growing parts of the region to various degrees. This difficulty is mainly due to the fact that the region is part of another region, which in turn is part of another one, and all are parts of, or receive influence from, more and more regions to an increasing degree in a world which is gradually being integrated into one system. We cannot anticipate any alleviation of this difficulty. We need, therefore, to study all types of systems until we develop a theory of their growth and can foresee their evolution. This is difficult, but not impossible, now that we can use advanced methods of computation and simulation.

140

two interlocked hierarchical systems

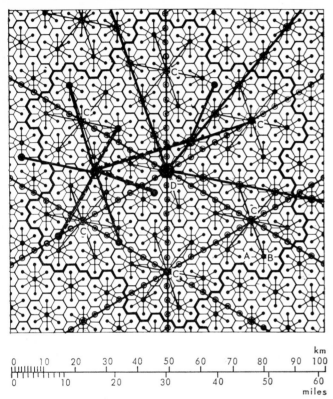

RURAL SETTLEMENTS

Types and numbers

The basic types of rural settlements are:
- nomadic, or temporary;
- semi-nomadic, or semi-permanent;
- one-family permanent, or farmsteads;
- composite permanent rural settlements or villages;
- the hybrid category of semi-agricultural, semi-urban settlements, rural-urban centres which are in some ways also looked upon as rural settlements.

Nomadic settlements are usually very small, seldom exceeding a hundred families or a few hundred inhabitants; in very exceptional cases they may be larger. The same is the case with semi-nomadic settlements; these may often be larger than nomadic settlements, but are generally smaller than villages.

Farmsteads are usually limited to one family even though some relatives and farm-hands may live on them, and they usually have fewer than ten inhabitants. The villages number from ten inhabitants up to a maximum average of about 2,000. There are exceptional cases, such as can be found in India, whose population reaches 10,000, but of them I have no personal experience. However, such villages usually have accumulated enough urban functions to merit classification in the hybrid category of rural-urban centres. For all practical purposes it can be said that the great majority of villages do not usually have more than 2,000 people.

In 1960 a little more than half of the population of the Earth—1,625,000,000 out of 2,960,000,000, or about 55 per cent—was living in rural areas. Of this, the nomadic population of the Earth is calculated to be of the order of 40,000,000 people living in temporary or semi-temporary settlements. The temporary settlements are mainly tents and huts, the difference between them being that the nomads take their tents with them, while huts are constructed of local materials and are abandoned when the nomads leave. A certain part of this nomadic population is semi-nomadic, moving from one camp to the other twice a year and very often returning to the same place for the summer or winter months. In such a case they have a semi-permanent settlement with semi-permanent structures, to which they return during the same season every year. These semi-permanent settlements either have a temporary kind of construction, in which case the whole settlement has the characteristics of a nomadic settlement; or they have permanent constructions, in which case the settlement bears the physical characteristics of a village, only in a more primitive form.

The greatest bulk of the rural population lives in permanent settlements, of which a small percentage are farmsteads. On the basis of the best available information (although we cannot be very certain about such phenomena when dealing with such small settlements), there are only about 4,000,000 farmsteads with a total population of about 20,000,000 people.

If we classify all permanent agricultural settlements from ten people to 2,000 people—where 1,560,000 people live—as villages we are comprising the largest percentage of the world's settlements. There are 8,137,800 such villages, with an average of 192 inhabitants per village. If we add the category of rural-urban centres with 2- to 5,000 people, the total number of settlements becomes 8,197,300 with a total population of 1,731,000,000 and an average size of 211 inhabitants.

Basic characteristics

The basic characteristics of rural settlements are:
- their inhabitants live by the cultivation of the Earth or the collection of its resources on land and sea and depend on Nature, and their whole life is based upon, and influenced by, this relationship;

151

141

rural settlement resembles a natural system
Zagliveri, Greece (1961)

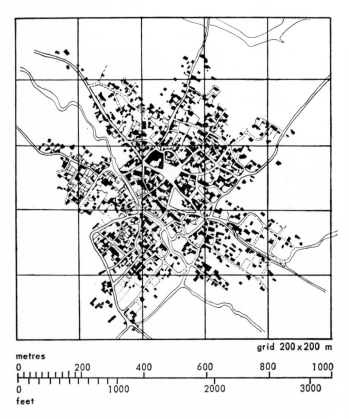

grid 200 x 200 m

metres
0 ___ 200 ___ 400 ___ 600 ___ 800 ___ 1000

0 ___ 1000 ___ 2000 ___ 3000
feet

o the settlements are small and inward looking, very seldom exceeding 2,000 inhabitants, with an average of no more than 300; therefore, most communities are not provided with such necessary services as an elementary school and a few basic shops, for these demand a community of close to 1,000 people (to justify a good elementary school of six grades with 120–150 students, for example);

o these settlements are very seldom planned—they have grown naturally, usually without any guidance or regulation;

o while nomadic and semi-nomadic settlements are amorphous, villages have a very characteristic form— they are simple, fundamental communities.

The entire rural settlement resembles a natural system, a plant or an organ, much more than densely built-up settlements, since its whole network leads towards one centre and does not have any ring connections (fig. 141). So an entire settlement resembles a wild shrub whose stalk (the main road) leads to the nucleus village which is in turn

connected with its foliage (the smaller units around it) through the branches (the small roads) (fig. 142).

The nucleus or built-up part of the community lies near its centre of gravity unless security reasons force it to be located off-centre as on a hill for example. Sanitation can also be a determining factor; so, if the community is marshy, or threatened by floods, the nucleus may be located on higher land. A scarcity of fertile land also may force the inhabitants to build on a barren hillside to conserve the better land for farming, or perhaps also on piles in the water to save the limited valley land for farming and grazing as is the case for the prehistoric lake dwellers of Switzerland.

A rural nucleus has a characteristic structure. Because Man depends on Nature, because he struggles all his life to get the maximum produce possible out of Nature in order to survive and develop himself, because he spends his whole life out in the open, the nuclei of most villages tend to take shape in such a way as to protect him from the elements of Nature. Everything contributes to the creation of conditions opposite from those Man has to deal with in the open country. Space is restricted, the streets are narrow and very seldom straight. Winds cannot easily race through the village, and there are few open perspectives to the countryside. Man tends to isolate himself from natural forces. Characteristic of the failure of contemporary Man to understand the real issues of rural settlements is the fact that most settlements planned by governments or landowners are based on a grid system that opens perspectives into the countryside, which is exactly what the inhabitants of the villages want to avoid. Needless to say, many of these planned villages are the picture of isolation and lack of cohesion when compared with any naturally developed village.

This shows how careful we should be in dealing with villages. We should not forget that the majority of people working with them on a governmental level are urban dwellers, and are apt to handle many problems of the village as problems of their own, that is, as urban problems.

I will mention an example. In an urban area we know that there is a direct relationship between the income of a family and its dwelling; it cannot be otherwise, since the family must pay for its dwelling. In rural areas, however, we very often find no such direct relationship; there are many families living in houses whose cost, taken at its original value, could never be justified by the family income. The explanation is often based on the fact that people in rural communities build their own houses, sometimes with the assistance of the whole community. The labour they invest (and sometimes the labour of their relatives or even the whole community) produces physical shells whose apparent cost cannot accurately be assessed in terms of money, but is certainly very significant. An urban house is usually built in a short period of time and then inhabited by a family which may or may not add additional structures to it. The basic nucleus of the rural house, however, may be originally built for one

142

patterns in nature

**a wild shrub resembling one part only of the networks
of human settlements**

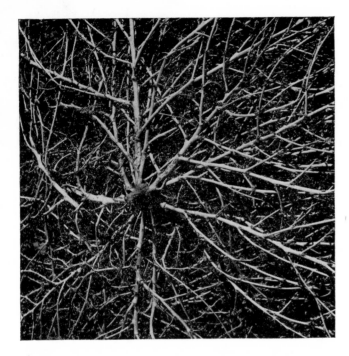

family, but have additions made over several generations. Thus, when stables, storerooms and additional living space have been added to the house, it appears to have a much greater value than is justified by the annual family income. This is the reason why destruction in the countryside may have a much more disastrous effect than in an urban area. When during World War II people who lost their houses in urban areas were given a house corresponding to their income group, they were satisfied with it. But when that happened in the countryside, the people were seldom satisfied because their income might have warranted a one- or two-room house, whereas, due to the investment made by past generations, the family was used to a house with many rooms and additional space for animals and produce.

The most characteristic element in the village itself, is its centre where all community functions are located. This is usually in the centre of gravity of the built-up area, and operates as the community centre for all the non-residential, non-agricultural functions. In major villages it is the shopping centre, the centre of production (where dyers dye their wool, weavers dry their produce, artisans work their clay) and the centre of all religious activities, with a temple, mosque or church. It is there that buildings housing administrative or social functions are built, and where all gatherings, be they commercial (open air markets), social (dancing, etc.), political or otherwise, take place. Even in small villages without any urban functions, the central square has great importance if, for nothing else, as a gathering place for the people.

Beyond this centre the functions are homogeneous; usually residences with the stables, storehouses and workshops of each family are connected with the countryside. Only in a few cases can the stables be found outside the village—this in hot climates, in villages with a long tradition and good community organisation which provide community responsibility for the protection of the cattle.

○ *Variations*

As is natural, rural communities present great variations in structure and form depending on variables such as the elements of Nature, Man, Society, Shells and Networks. The two basic categories of variables which must be discussed even in such a general outline, are economic and technological.

The economic basis of their society has influenced the formation of villages more than anything else. Villages with intensive production, such as fruit-growing, tend to have their houses in the orchards. Thus the shells spread out into the whole farming area; the nucleus proper remains very small. On the other hand, dry-farming communities and fishing villages, in areas developed traditionally, usually have compact nuclei within which practically all the shells of the community are situated (figs. 143 and 144).

The second variable is technology. Wherever modern methods have reached the rural community, they have had a great impact. When cultivation is carried out by tractor, the need arises for larger farms and better community organisation so that some type of organisation (government, co-operative or private) will handle tractors and mechanical equipment. The result is that Man changes his skills (in order to handle machines) and his attitude; he becomes much more developed technologically, and since cultivation of the same fields takes a shorter time, has more free time. When he is the owner of the land, this may mean greater leisure; but if he is not the owner, it may mean unemployment, a decrease in population or even the total abandonment of some villages.

It is quite characteristic that whenever the mechanisation of agricultural cultivation has taken place, either many people have left their farms and villages and moved into the big cities, thus causing a decrease in rural population and a change in the local balance between Man and Nature, or, if people have remained in the villages, there has been dissatisfaction caused by the displacement of Man by the machine. In such cases, the problems of the Shells were relatively minor since social and political issues were much more important; it was of little importance that the Shells were being partially abandoned and deteriorating. Many men in the villages are unemployed and desire an opportunity to move to major

Facts

143

rural settlement consisting of dispersed shells in a mountain village   Metsovo, Greece (1961)

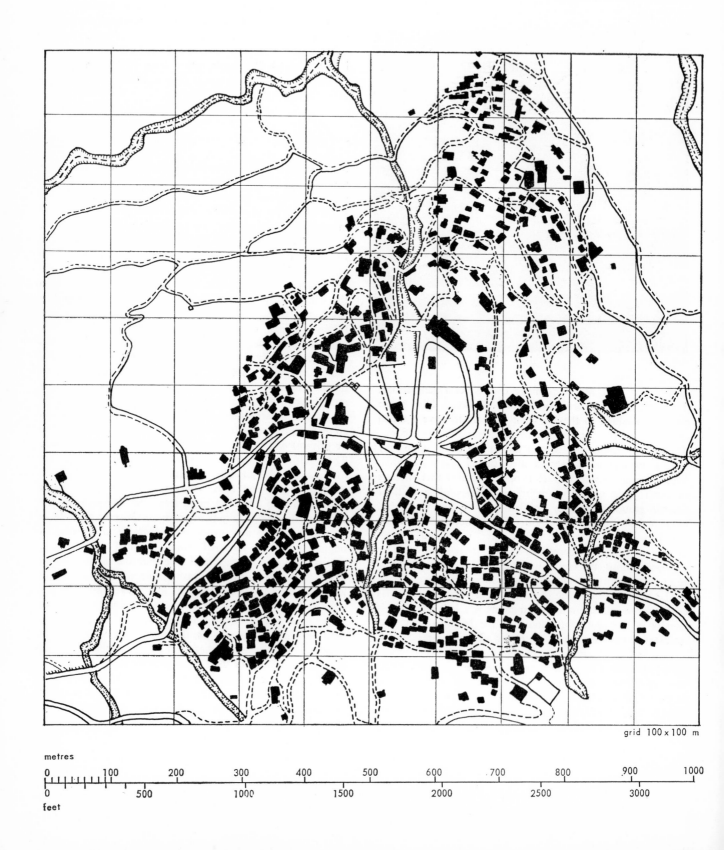

grid 100 x 100 m

metres

| 0 | 100 | 200 | 300 | 400 | 500 | 600 | 700 | 800 | 900 | 1000 |

| 0 | 500 | 1000 | 1500 | 2000 | 2500 | 3000 |

feet

144

fishing settlement consisting of compact shells in a coastal village   Myconos, Greece (1961)

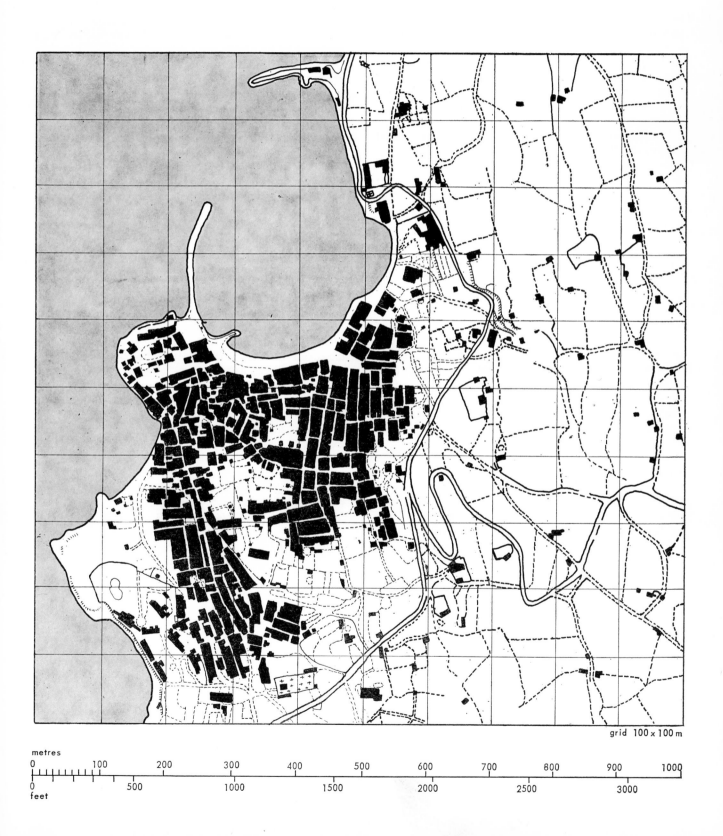

grid 100 x 100 m

metres
0   100   200   300   400   500   600   700   800   900   1000

0   500   1000   1500   2000   2500   3000
feet

centres; those profiting from the change, bigger landowners and the owners of tractors being rented to others, have no reason to live in the village. The new means of transportation, higher incomes and shorter periods of cultivation allow such people to live in nearby cities. Thus the decline of the fundamental rural communities, where those in control tend to be absentees and many of those who remain tend to be unemployed, is hastened.

This is mentioned as just one example of how modern technology upsets the balance which existed in the past; the effect on the settlements may result in a complete change of the Ekistic system, since the elementary communities are weakened and some class 'B', or perhaps class 'C', centres are strengthened. The latter tend to become much more urban than rural since it is there that the services for mechanical equipment (agents, workshops, etc., plus technical education institutions, as well as more important shopping centres) are usually situated. Thus, a changing technology in cultivation transforms not only the way of life and the very existence of the farmer, but also his agricultural society, and hence the settlements themselves.

URBAN SETTLEMENTS

Types and numbers

There are many types of urban settlements, and many ways of dividing them into categories—by size, by the economic basis of the settlement, by the average income of its inhabitants, by geographic or topographic location (on a plain or a hillside, for example), and so on. But among the most important classifications to be made today is the division into static and dynamic settlements. This coincides approximately with size, since almost all settlements with more than 100,000 people (numbering approximately 1,460 on the Earth), are dynamic while the majority of urban settlements with less than 100,000 people (numbering approximately 90,740), are more or less static. As has already been stated, the total number of the world's urban settlements is 92,200, with a total population of 1,335,000,000, or about 45 per cent of the world's population, which, in the year 1960, was 2,960,000,000.

When we speak of urban settlements, we are referring to those having predominantly urban characteristics. However, some settlements with a few thousand inhabitants (to be found especially among those in the bracket between 2,000 and 5,000) have both urban and rural characteristics; these, as has already been mentioned, are considered semi-rural or semi-urban settlements. This is why in the former classification the number of urban settlements appear smaller and the percentage of inhabitants reduced. In order to form a more accurate picture of the numbers and types of settlements by sizes and the corresponding urban population of the world, we can divide the settlements into categories of 2,000–5,000

people, 5,000–10,000 people, etc., until we reach a category of more than 20,000,000 people, which at present comprises the world's largest settlements, such as the megalopolis on the eastern seaboard of the United States (fig. 145). Officially, there are no 'settlements' in this category. In actual fact, however, there are several areas in which settlements have merged physically over even more extensive areas.

In the following I give the general information about all categories of sizes of urban settlements, together with one example of each category to allow the formation of an opinion about the general characteristics of this category. It can be easily understood that when I deal with categories having hundreds, thousands and even tens of thousands of completely different settlements, the selection of one representative type depends, at this stage of Ekistics, on the information available and the personal experience of the author.

At the end of this book there is a list of settlements giving their population size so that the reader will be able to find different examples and compare them to each other.

The first category of urban-rural centres, of between 2,000–5,000 people (fig. 146) contains 59,500 settlements with a total population of about 171,000,000. If we subtract these from the total 92,200 so-called urban settlements, the remaining number of purely urban settlements becomes 32,700 with 1,164,000,000 people (87·2 per cent of the total urban population or 39·3 per cent of the world population).

The second category of urban settlements, those of 5,000–10,000 inhabitants, contains 17,750 settlements with 121,000,000 people (figs. 147 and 148). If we again subtract these, we are left with 14,950 urban settlements with 1,043,000,000 people (78·1 per cent of the total urban population, or 35·2 per cent of the world population).

The third category consists of settlements with 10,000–20,000 people. There are 7,750 of them with a total population of 107,000,000 (figs. 149 and 150). When we subtract these, we have 7,200 urban settlements left, with 936,000,000 people (70 per cent of the total urban population, or 31·6 per cent of the world population).

The fourth category has settlements of 20,000–50,000 people. There are 4,145 such settlements with a total population of 126,000,000 (figs. 151 and 152). Subtracting these, we have 3,055 urban settlements left with 810,000,000 people (60·7 per cent of the total urban population, or 27·4 per cent of the world population).

The fifth category comprises settlements with 50,000–100,000 people. There are 1,595 of them with a total population of 108,000,000 (figs. 153 and 154). If we subtract these, there are 1,460 urban settlements left with 702,000,000 people (52·6 per cent of the total urban population, or 23·7 per cent of the world population).

Next come the settlements from 100,000 to over 10,000,000 people. The settlements of the sixth category have 100,000–200,000 people. There are 751 of them with a total population of 106,000,000 (figs. 155 and 156). If we subtract these, there are 709 urban settlements left with 596,000,000 people (44·6 per cent of the total urban population, or 20 per cent of the world population).

The settlements of the seventh category have 200,000–500,000 people. There are 426 of them with a total population of 130,000,000 (figs. 157 and 158). If we subtract these, there are 283 urban settlements left with 466,000,000 people (34·9 per cent of the total urban population, or 15·7 per cent of the world population).

The settlements of the eighth category have a population of 500,000–1,000,000. There are 142 of them with a total population of 96,000,000 (figs. 159 and 160). If we subtract these, there are 141 urban settlements left with 370,000,000 people (27·7 per cent of the total urban population, or 12·5 per cent of the world population).

The settlements of the ninth category have a population of 1,000,000–2,000,000. There are 86 of them with a total population of 125,000,000 (figs. 161 and 162). If we subtract these, there are 55 larger urban settlements left with 245,000,000 people (18·4 per cent of the total urban population, or 8·3 per cent of the world population).

The settlements of the tenth category have a population of 2,000,000–5,000,000. We are now in the realm of the great metropolis. There are 38 of them with a total population of 107,000,000 (figs. 163 and 164). If we subtract these, there are 17 larger urban settlements left with 138,000,000 people (10·3 per cent of the total urban population, or 4·7 per cent of the world population).

The eleventh category has settlements with a population of 5,000,000–10,000,000. There are 14 of them with a total population of 97,000,000 (figs. 165 and 166).

If we subtract these, we still have three larger urban settlements left with 41,000,000 people (3·1 per cent of the total urban population, or 1·4 per cent of the world population. This last and twelfth category of settlements comprises those with 10,000,000–20,000,000 people. These are New York, Tokyo-Yokohama and greater London (figs. 167 and 168).

Basic characteristics

○ *Nature*

The settings of urban settlements differ from those of rural settlements. The landscape is usually more expansive; and the settlements are usually located on plains, close to lakes, rivers or seas, and close to transportation routes. This is of particular importance for settlements with more than 20,000 people, and becomes an almost imperative prerequisite for settlements with 100,000 people and over. Small urban settlements, such as were created in the past for reasons of security, may be on hillsides, hilltops or mountains. But settlements built recently, or larger settlements of the past, need big plains and a proximity to major communication lines in order to survive.

A special study has been carried out at the Athens Center of Ekistics on the geographic location of all settlements with more than 200,000 people of which there are 640 with a total of 54,200,000 inhabitants. There are three major concentrations, one in the southern part of the northern half of the western hemisphere, one in north western Europe and one in southern Asia, with several more scattered around the world (fig. 169). The greatest numbers of them (587) can be found in the northern hemisphere in a location with an average latitude of 38°. There are only 53 in the southern hemisphere with an average latitude of 27° (fig. 170).

The greatest numbers of them can be found by rivers (224), next by seas (201), and inland (193), with only 24 by lakes. But if we consider their population, the greatest number of people are by the rivers (201,000,000), and seas (194,000,000), then inland (119,000,000), with only 26,000,000 by lakes. The largest settlements are by rivers (average population 1,901,000) and lakes (1,108,000), then come those by the sea (967,000), with the inland ones last (617,000) (fig. 171).

If we consider the altitude of these settlements we find the greatest number (574 out of 642) below 500 metres, with decreasing numbers in higher altitudes. The same is valid in the case of their population; 498,000,000 out of 542,000,000 people live below 500 metres with decreasing numbers in higher altitudes (fig. 172).

○ *Man and society*

Urban settlements differ radically from rural settlements, and partly because of this their inhabitants have different habits and characteristics. The greater the change of a settlement from rural to urban, and the greater the density and size of the urban settlement, the greater the difference in people. New dimensions and new characteristics in the urban pattern of life demand that men develop adaptive mechanisms in order to achieve and maintain adjustment to the new resources and conditions of the habitat. In the larger and more dense cities, there are differences in age and sex composition, in the occupational structure, in the division of labour and the social structure. This forces Man to develop different characteristics as an individual, as a group, as a unit and as a community. Man in the urban settlement is a member of a much larger community, a much larger Society, and his range of social interaction increases. Members of his family are affected by different social institutions which gradually take over certain family functions. Much greater educational opportunities are available, raising Man's expectations. His greater distance from Nature means that his former ties with Nature are weakened and his understanding of it diminished.

Apart from changes in the individual man, we witness changes in the patterns of family size, structure and life. The family tends to become smaller, while the percentage

urban settlements in the world (1960)

━━━━━ % of urban population existing in settlements above the size mentioned

━ ━ ━ % of world population existing in settlements above the size mentioned

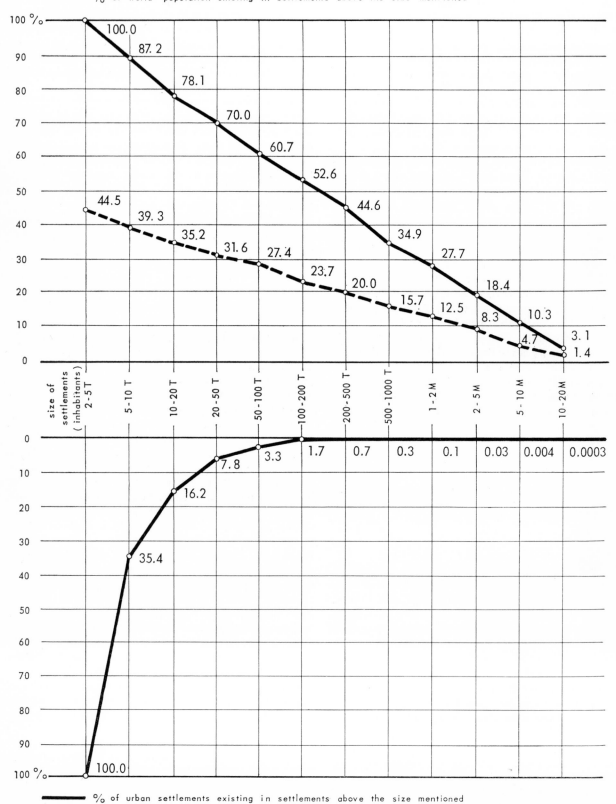

━━━━━ % of urban settlements existing in settlements above the size mentioned

146

urban-rural settlements   2,000-5,000 group   Kranidi, Greece (1961)

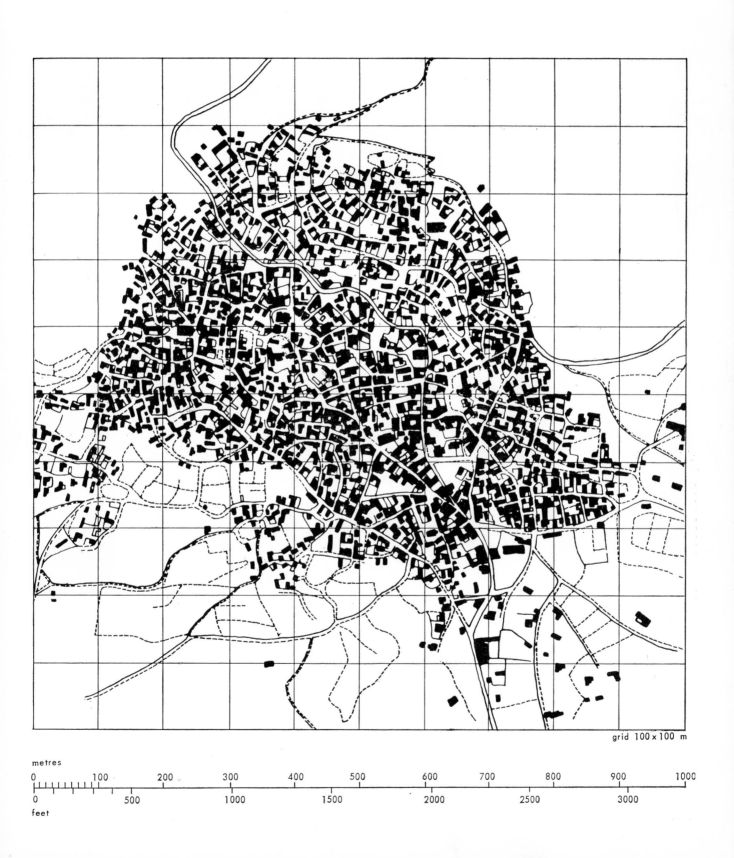

grid 100 x 100 m

metres

| 0 | 100 | 200 | 300 | 400 | 500 | 600 | 700 | 800 | 900 | 1000 |

| 0 | 500 | 1000 | 1500 | 2000 | 2500 | 3000 |

feet

urban settlements   5,000-10,000 group   central area   Koropi, Greece (1961)

grid 100 x 100 m

metres

| 0 | 100 | 200 | 300 | 400 | 500 | 600 | 700 | 800 | 900 | 1000 |

| 0 | 500 | 1000 | 1500 | 2000 | 2500 | 3000 |

feet

148
urban settlements   5,000-10,000 group   Koropi, Greece (1961)

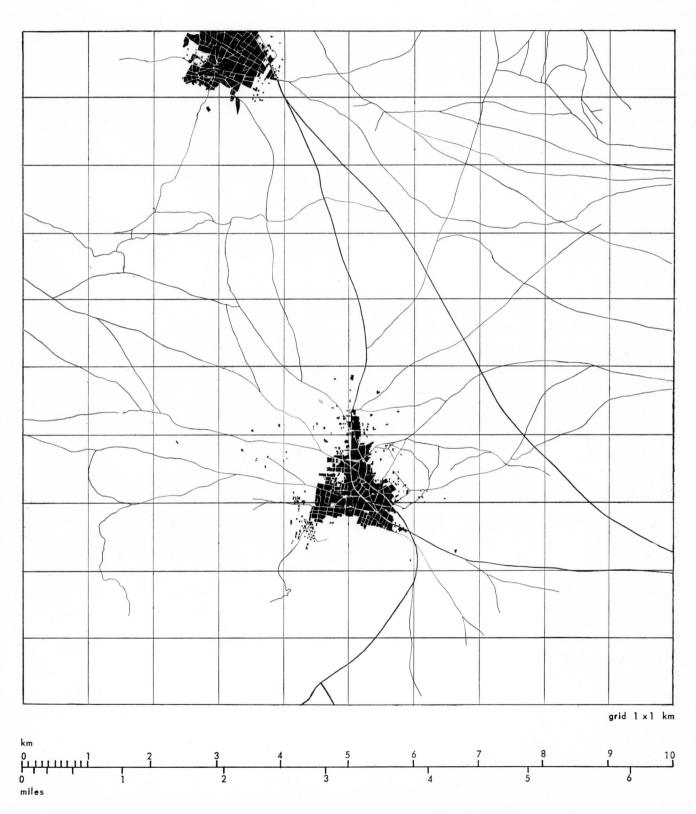

grid 1 x 1 km

km
0 — 1 — 2 — 3 — 4 — 5 — 6 — 7 — 8 — 9 — 10

0 — 1 — 2 — 3 — 4 — 5 — 6
miles

N

urban settlements   10,000-20,000 group   central area   Rethymno, Greece (1961)

grid 100 x 100 m

metres

0	100	200	300	400	500	600	700	800	900	1000

0	500	1000	1500	2000	2500	3000

feet

150

urban settlements**10,000-20,000 group****Rethymno, Greece (1961)**

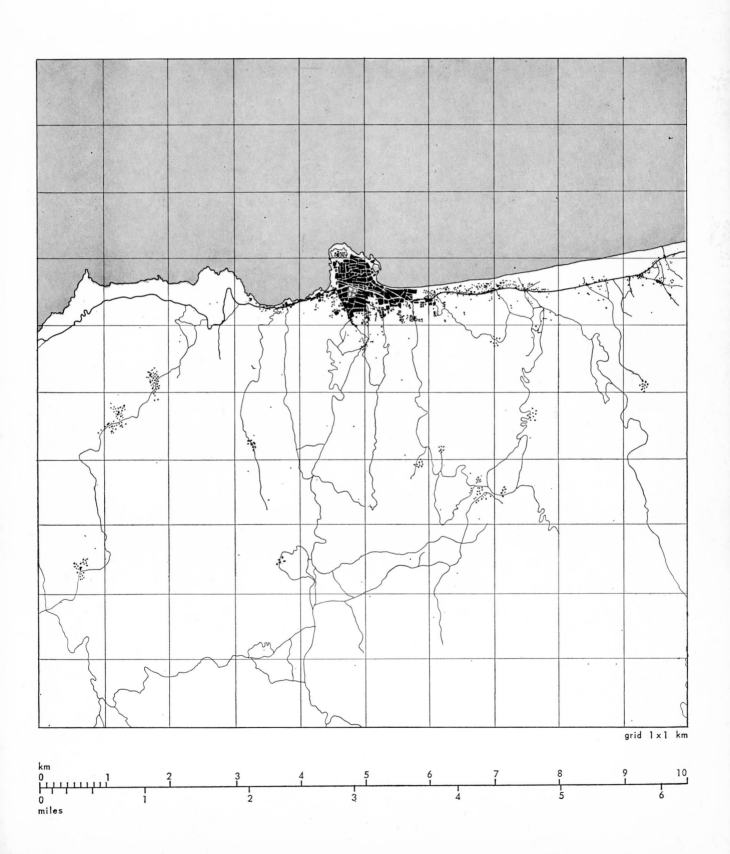

grid 1 x 1 km

km
0   1   2   3   4   5   6   7   8   9   10

0   1   2   3   4   5   6
miles

grid 1 00 x 100 m

metres

0	100	200	300	400	500	600	700	800	900	1000

0	500	1000	1500	2000	2500	3000

feet

152

urban settlements   20,000-50,000 group   Ioannina, Greece (1961)

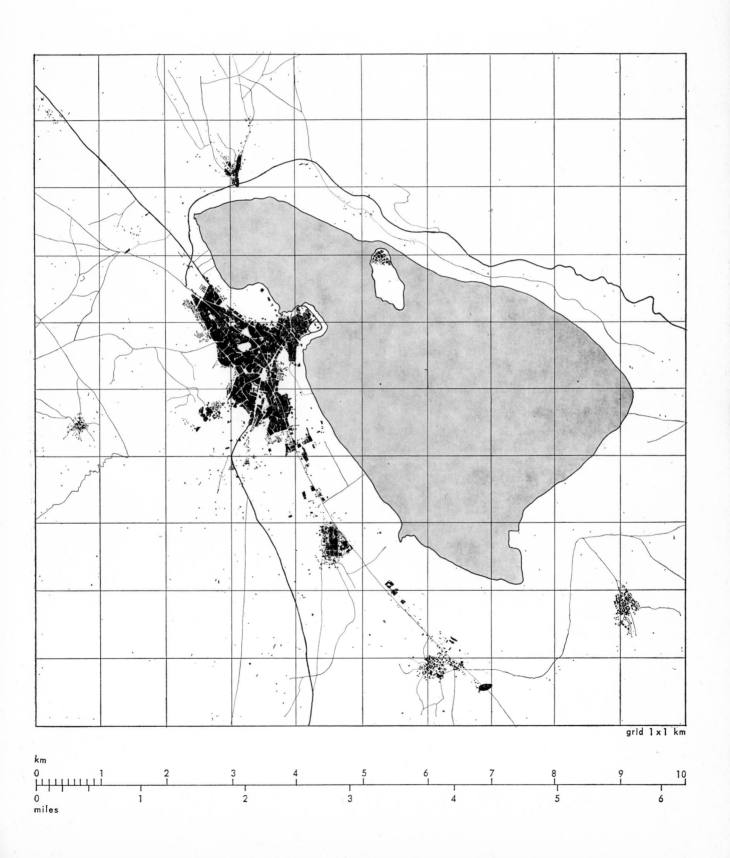

grid 1 x 1 km

km

0   1   2   3   4   5   6   7   8   9   10

0   1   2   3   4   5   6

miles

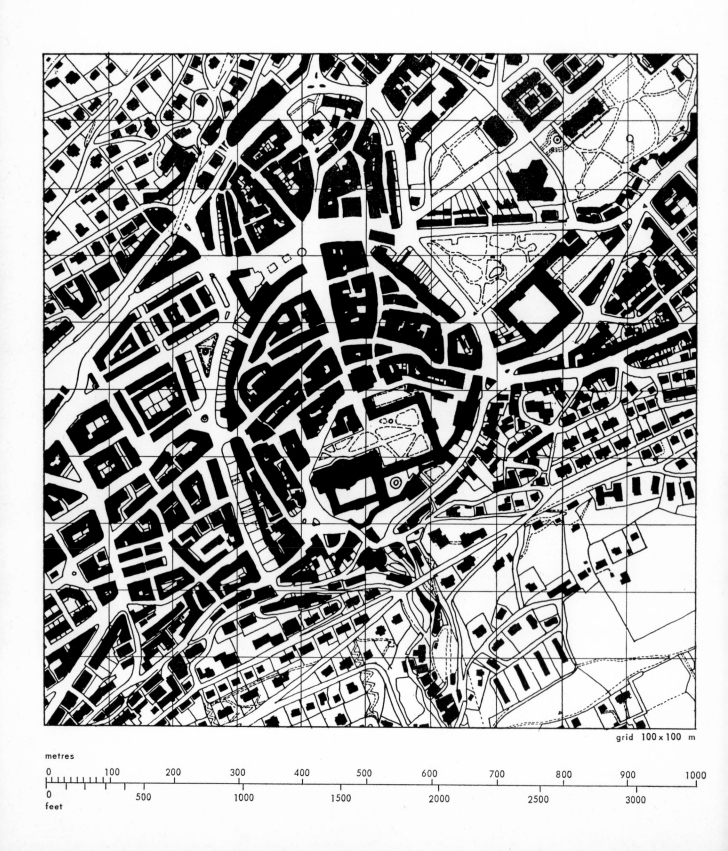

grid 100 x 100 m

metres

0   100   200   300   400   500   600   700   800   900   1000

0   500   1000   1500   2000   2500   3000

feet

154

urban settlements   50,000-100,000 group   St. Gall, Switzerland (1957)

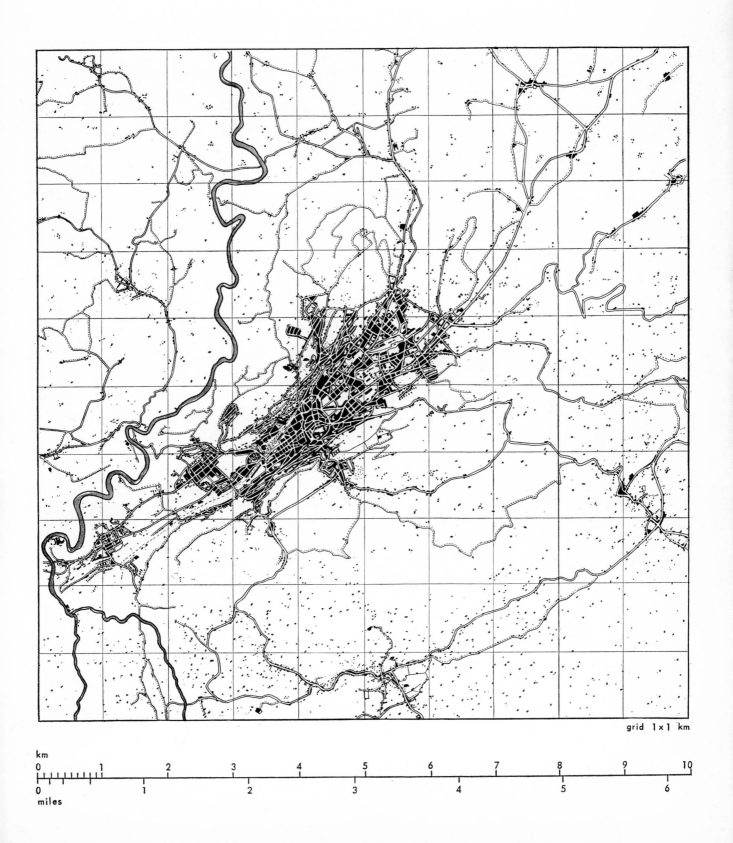

grid 1 x 1 km

km
0   1   2   3   4   5   6   7   8   9   10

0   1   2   3   4   5   6
miles

urban settlements 100,000-200,000 group central area Homs, Syria (1961)

grid 100 x 100 m

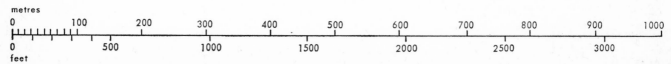

metres

0	100	200	300	400	500	600	700	800	900	1000

0	500	1000	1500	2000	2500	3000

feet

156

urban settlements   100,000-200,000 group   Homs, Syria (1961)

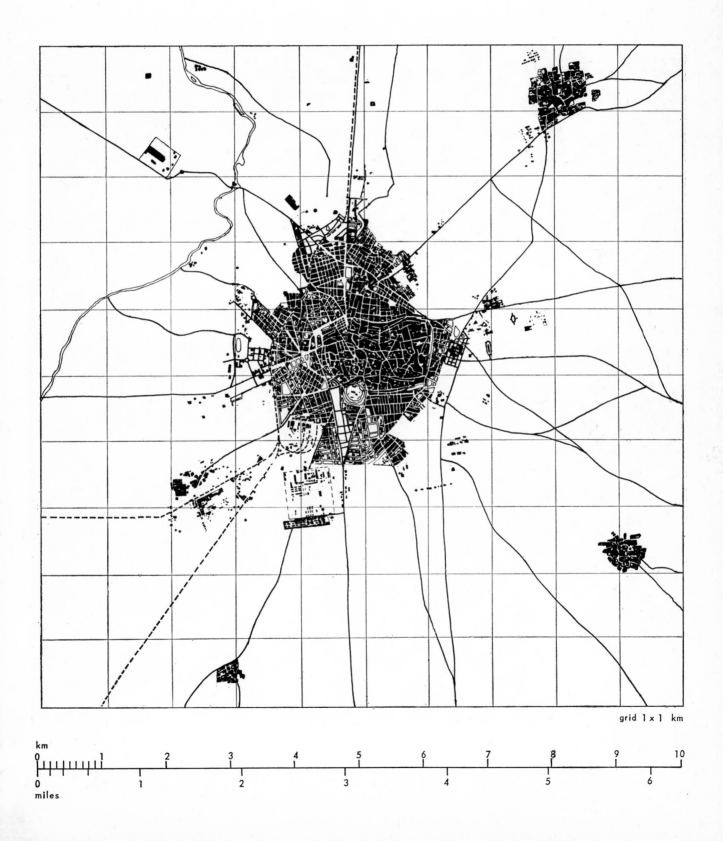

grid 1 x 1 km

km
0   1   2   3   4   5   6   7   8   9   10

0   1   2   3   4   5   6
miles

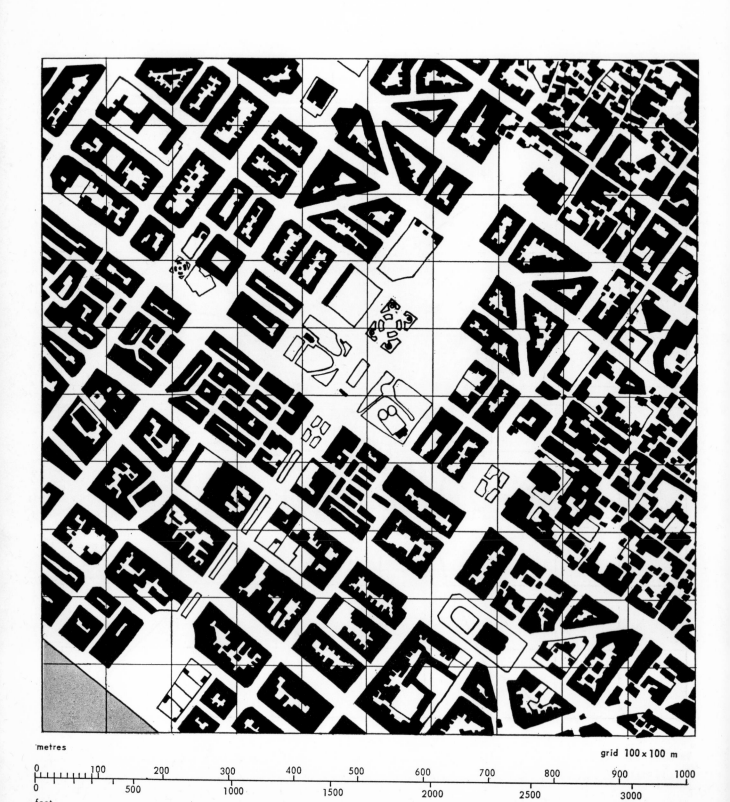

metres

grid 100 x 100 m

0	100	200	300	400	500	600	700	800	900	1000

0	500	1000	1500	2000	2500	3000

feet

158

urban settlements   200,000-500,000 group   Salonica, Greece (1961)

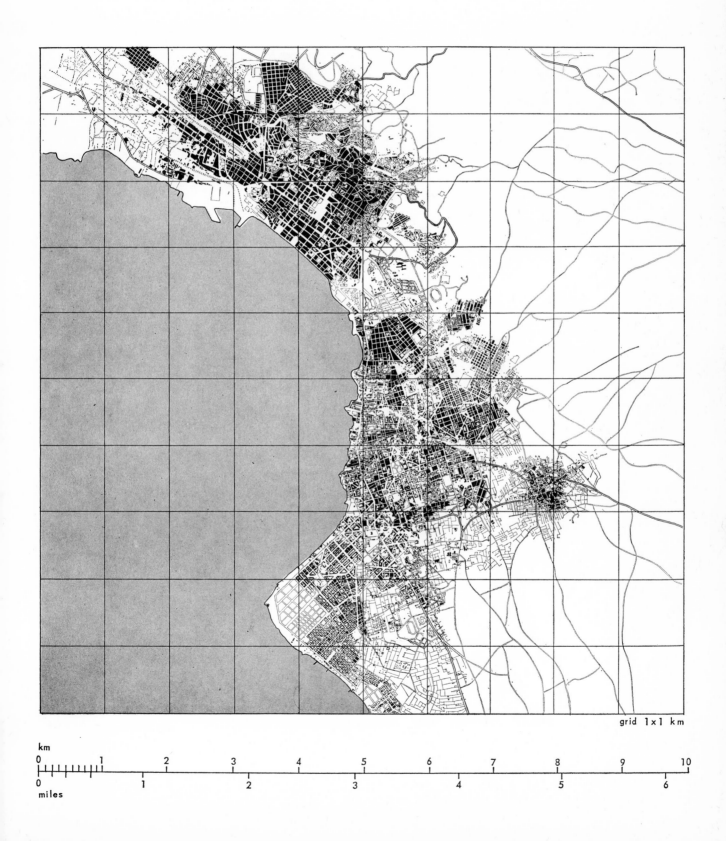

grid 1 x 1 km

km
0   1   2   3   4   5   6   7   8   9   10

0   1   2   3   4   5   6
miles

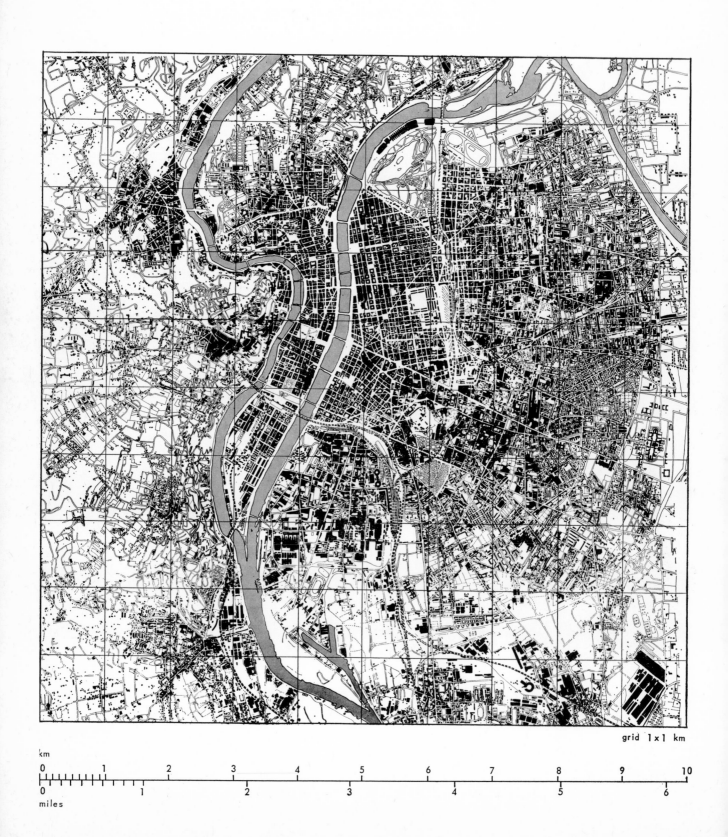

grid 1 x 1 km

km
0   1   2   3   4   5   6   7   8   9   10

0   1   2   3   4   5   6
miles

160

urban settlements   500,000-1,000,000 group   Lyon, France (1954)

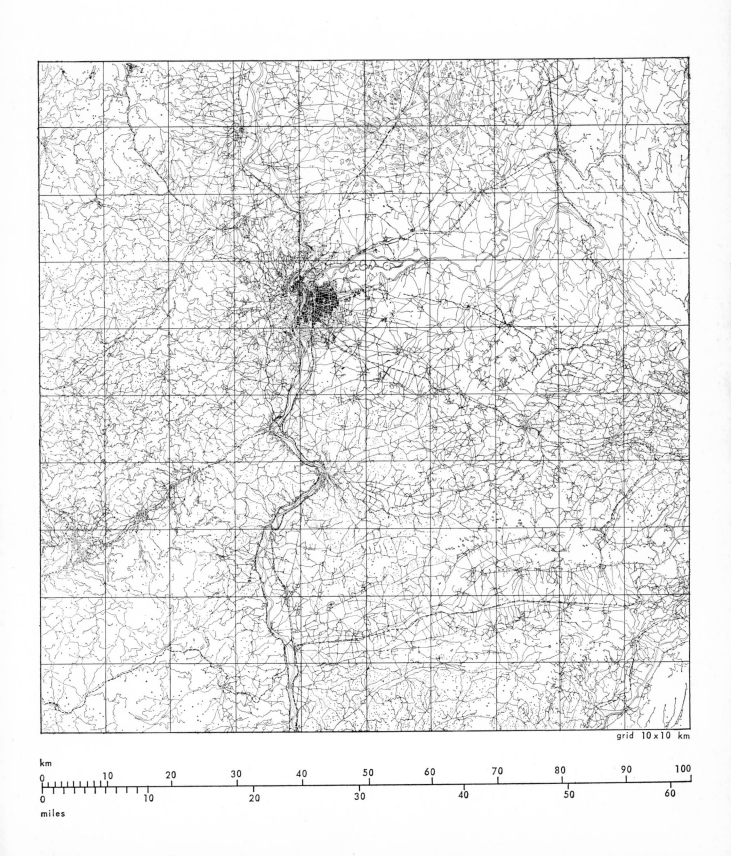

grid 10 x 10 km

km
0   10   20   30   40   50   60   70   80   90   100

0   10   20   30   40   50   60

miles

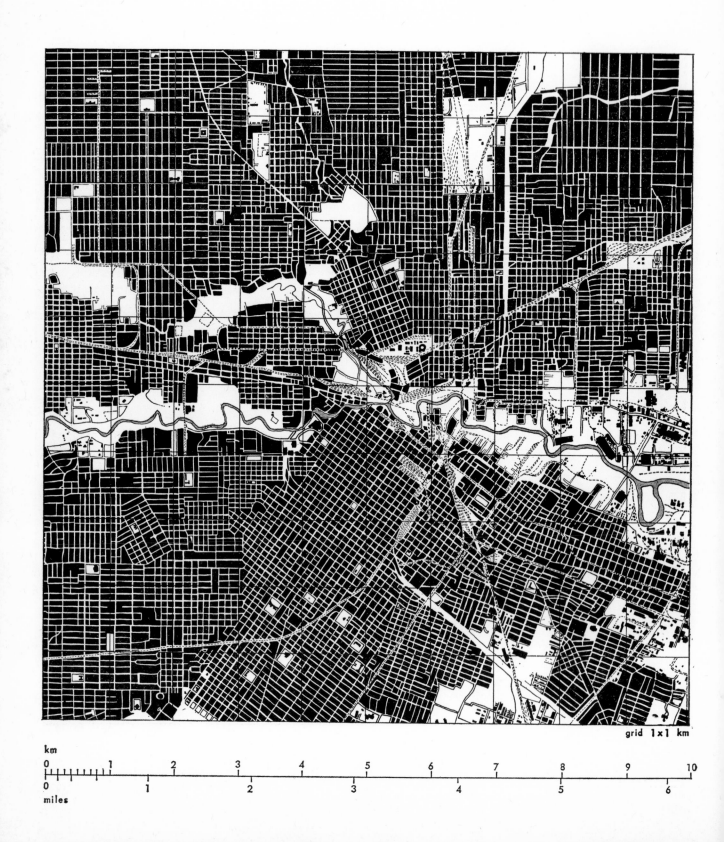

grid **1 x 1** km

km

0   1   2   3   4   5   6   7   8   9   10

0   1   2   3   4   5   6

miles

162

urban settlements   1,000,000-2,000,000 group   Houston, Texas, U.S.A. (1963)

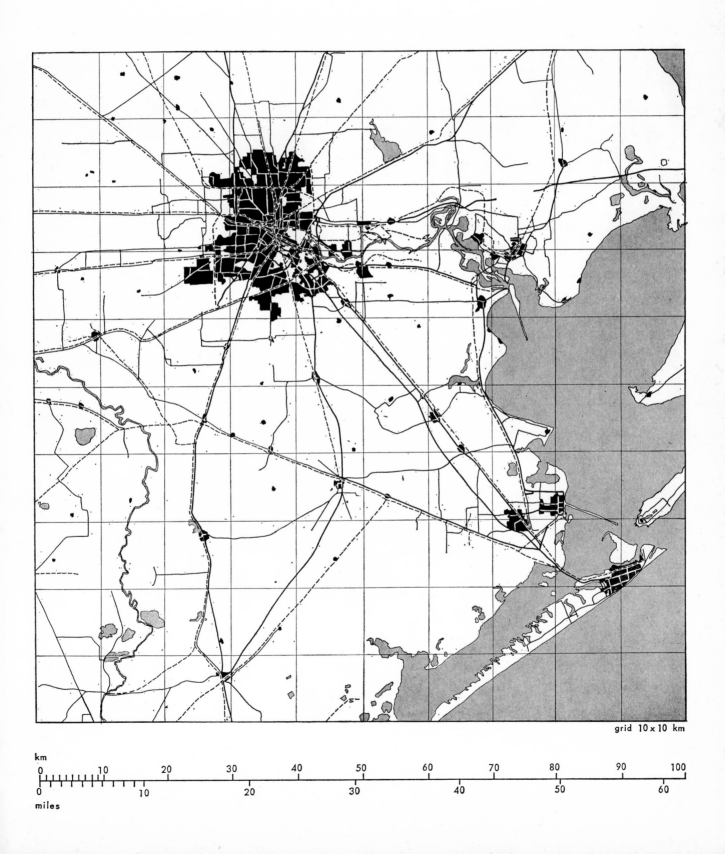

grid 10 x 10 km

km

0   10   20   30   40   50   60   70   80   90   100

0   10   20   30   40   50   60

miles

urban settlements   2,000,000-5,000,000 group   central area   Rio de Janeiro, Brazil (1964)

grid 1 x 1 km

km
0   1   2   3   4   5   6   7   8   9   10

0   1   2   3   4   5   6
miles

164

urban settlements   2,000,000-5,000,000 group   Rio de Janeiro, Brazil (1964)

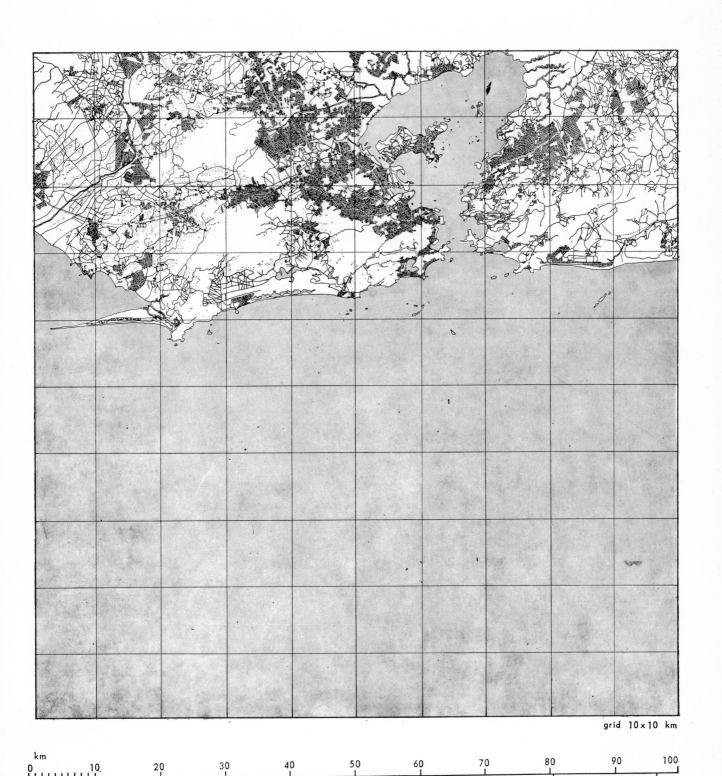

grid 10 x 10 km

km
0   10   20   30   40   50   60   70   80   90   100

0   10   20   30   40   50   60
miles

urban settlements   5,000,000-10,000,000 group   central area   Paris, France (1956)

grid 1 X 1 km

km

0   1   2   3   4   5   6   7   8   9   10

0   1   2   3   4   5   6

miles

166

urban settlements   5,000,000-10,000,000 group   Paris, France (1956)

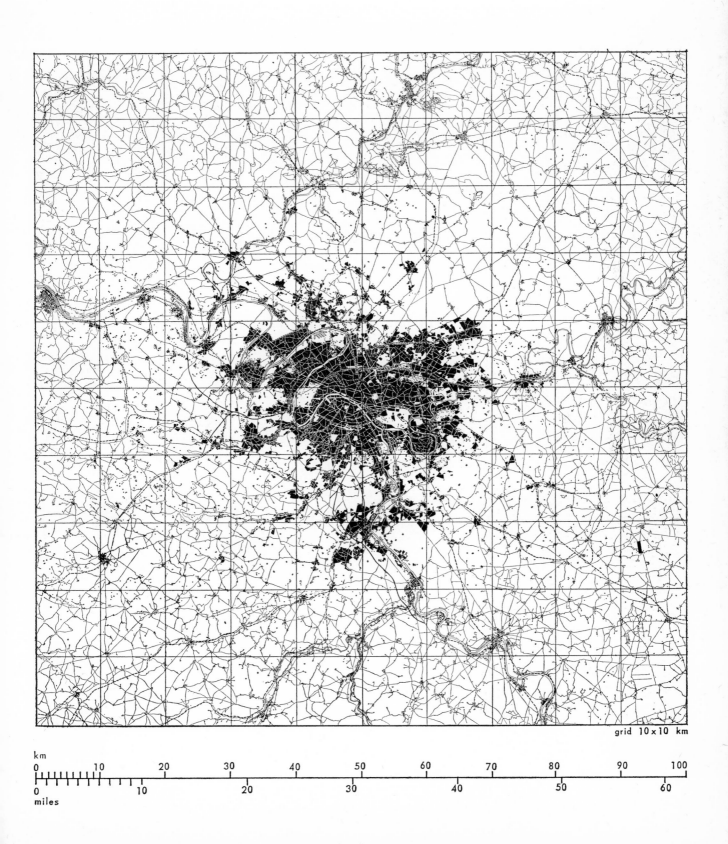

grid 10×10 km

km
0   10   20   30   40   50   60   70   80   90   100

0   10   20   30   40   50   60
miles

urban settlements   **10,000,000-20,000,000** group   **central area**   **Tokyo, Japan (1962)**

grid 1 x 1 km

km
0   1   2   3   4   5   6   7   8   9   10

0   1   2   3   4   5   6
miles

168

urban settlements   10,000,000-20,000,000 group   Tokyo-Yokohama, Japan (1962)

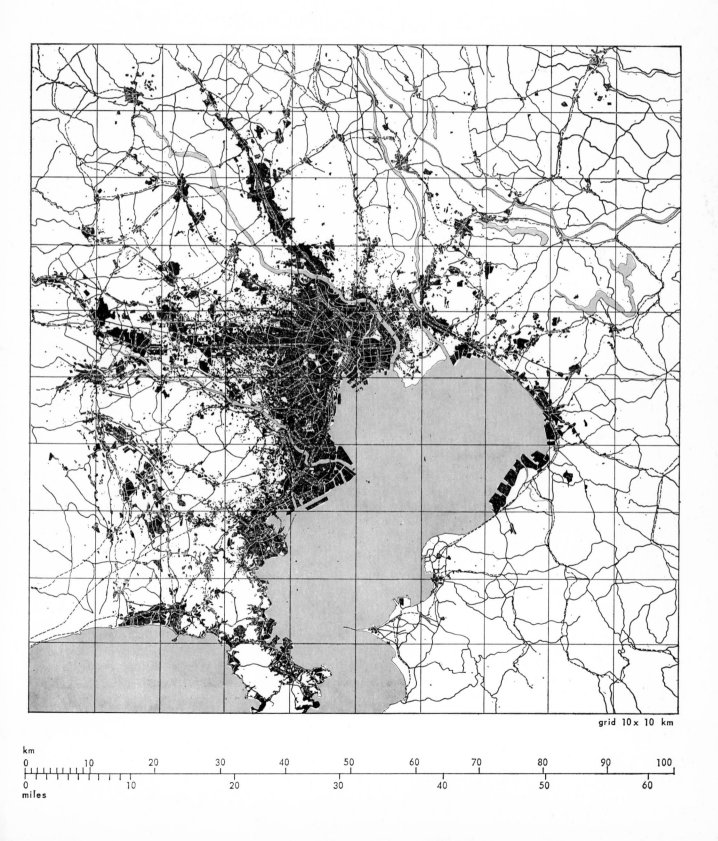

grid 10 x 10 km

km

0   10   20   30   40   50   60   70   80   90   100

0   10   20   30   40   50   60
miles

169

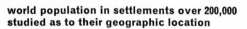

**world population in settlements over 200,000
studied as to their geographic location**

·	200	-	500 T
·	0.5	-	1 M
·	1	-	2 M
•	2	-	5 M
•	5	-	10 M
●	10	-	20 M

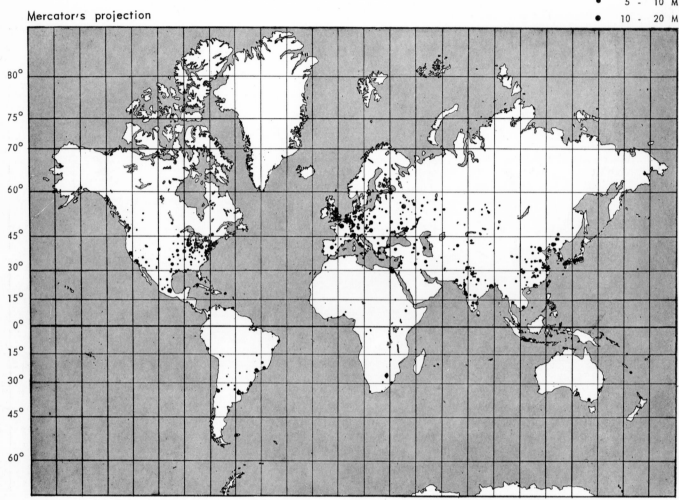

Mercator's projection

of nucleus-type family units increases with the growth of urban settlements. Because of the greater distances between people, the opportunities for members of a family to live close together, or even to see each other often, are decreased. The impact of the family on the children weakens. There is less parent-child interaction. Because of the greater opportunities offered by the total community and Society, and because the notion of the small urban community has usually been completely overlooked in the great urban areas, there is a weakening of the local community and a strengthening of communities based on professional, religious, social and other connections.

Social organisation as a whole in the great metropolitan areas leads to different, much more complicated patterns resulting from many new forces that do not follow any preconceived, well planned and rational pattern. This entitles us to say that social organisation, in spite of the greater opportunities modern Man has to face managerial and organisational problems of great magnitude, is not as efficient as in the rural communities, where, because of the small numbers of factor and forces, there is much greater cohesion in the population.

In the past there were specialised settlements such as military settlements, university towns, and so forth. Gradually,

170

**number and size of settlements over 200,000
studied as to their geographic location**

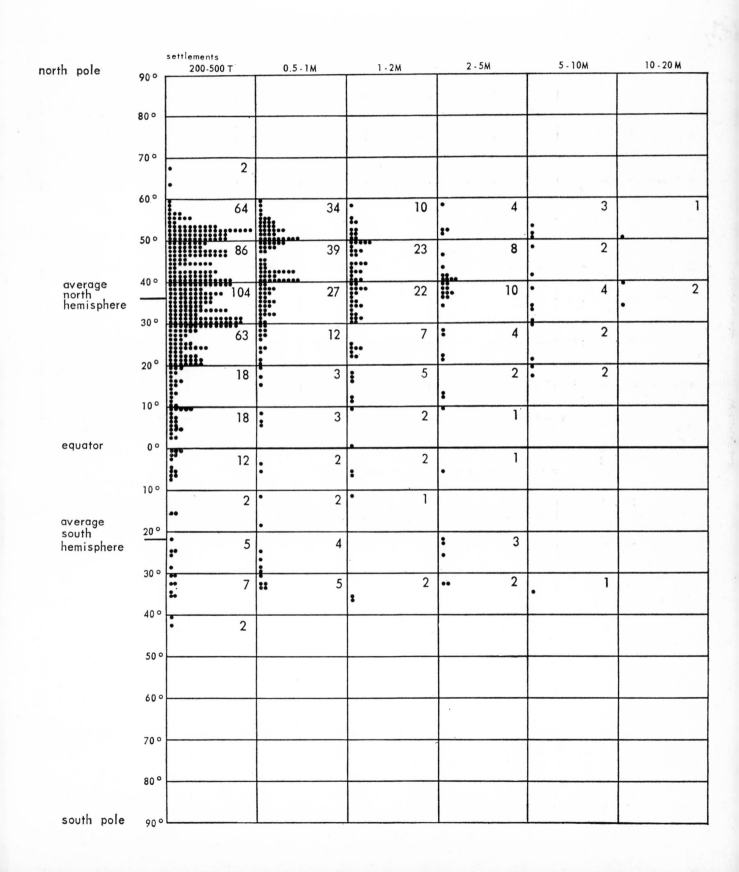

**world population of settlements over 200,000 studied
as to their geographic position**

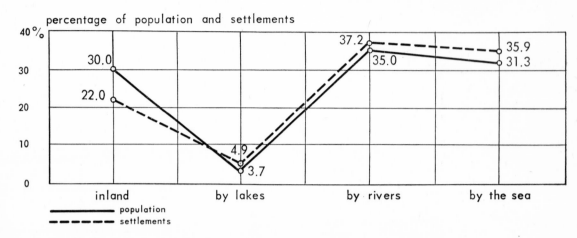

percentage of population and settlements

- population
- settlements

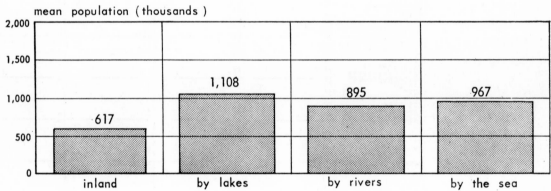

mean population (thousands)

a. population in thousands (total 542,080)

inland	36,398	31,822	26,517	7,170	17,343	—	119,250
by lakes	2,878	6,637	3,181	6,615	7,281	—	26,592
by rivers	43,311	21,866	40,110	40,277	45,610	10,680	201,854
by the sea	35,828	29,661	35,984	42,011	20,900	30,000	194,384

	200 - 500 T	0.5 - 1 M	1 - 2 M	2 - 5 M	5 - 10 M	10 - 20 M	sub total
by the sea	114	43	25	14	3	2	201
by rivers	140	33	29	15	7	1	224
by lakes	10	9	2	2	1	—	24
inland	122	47	18	3	3	—	193

b. number of settlements (642)

**world population in settlements over 200,000 studied
as to their altitude**

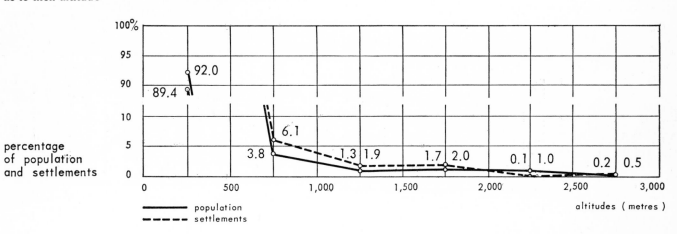

percentage
of population
and settlements

population
settlements

altitudes (metres)

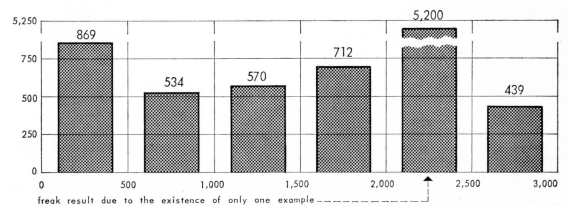

mean population
(thousands)

freak result due to the existence of only one example

a. population in thousands (total 542,080)

	200 - 500 T	0,5 - 1 M	1 - 2 M	2 - 5 M	5 - 10 M	10 - 20 M	sub total
2,500 - 3,000	757	560	—	—	—	—	1,317
2,000 - 2,500	—	—	—	—	5,200	—	5,200
1,500 - 2,000	2,478	2,612	2,040	2,130	—	—	9,260
1,000 - 1,500	2,884	2,017	1,940	—	—	—	6,841
500 - 1,000	5,711	4,209	6,755	4,160	—	—	20,835
0 - 500	106,585	80,588	95,057	89,783	85,934	40,680	498,627

altitudes in metres	200 - 500 T	0,5 - 1 M	1 - 2 M	2 - 5 M	5 - 10 M	10 - 20 M	sub total
0 - 500	343	118	66	31	13	3	574
500 - 1,000	25	7	5	2	—	—	39
1,000 - 1,500	8	3	1	—	—	—	12
1,500 - 2,000	7	3	2	1	—	—	13
2,000 - 2,500	—	—	—	—	1	—	1
2,500 - 3,000	2	1	—	—	—	—	3

b. number of settlements (642)

173

economic activities in human settlements

174

local and international characteristics of human settlements

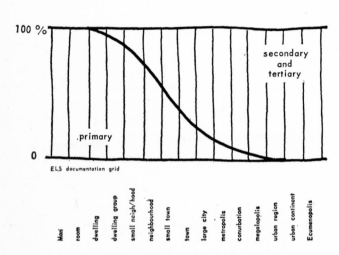

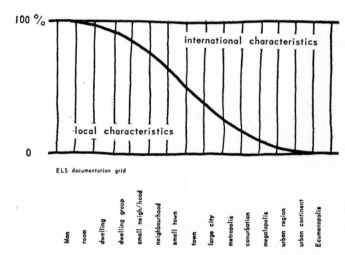

additional activities were attracted to them, so that today all major urban settlements tend to have all types of urban economic activities, even though some, especially for historical reasons, do have a preponderance of certain ones, such as industry, administration, education, religion or defence. The larger the settlement, the greater the probability that all economic activities will tend to be represented in a way corresponding to their average importance in all settlements. A typical distribution of activities in the average type of several categories of settlements can be seen in a tentative graph, in which we take the number of people employed by basic categories of functions as the most characteristic index for the type of economic activity involved (fig. 173).

○ *Shells*

The Shells of urban settlements have many common characteristics even though their size varies. The larger the settlement, the more international its characteristics; while the smaller it is, the more they are influenced by local factors. This is partly because many smaller settlements still bear the characteristics of local cultures of the past, and partly because the economic investment in most of them is lower than in larger settlements and this strengthens the forces of the locality rather than those leading toward international solutions. I shall mention two examples: there are fewer cars per capita in most minor settlements than in most major ones. This means that in small urban settlements there is proportionately more pedestrian traffic, which means that most

streets are more adjusted to the human scale. In the major settlements cars and public transport are used by the bulk of the people; therefore, the highways, parking areas and transportation lines are more adjusted to the requirements of the car, which are international in character. Lately people have started to walk more in the centres of some very big cities such as New York, but this is by no means the rule. For many settlements, railways, international seaports and airports contribute basic characteristics which have nothing to do with the local landscape or local culture. We can, therefore, say that the local characteristics which existed for historic reasons in the small cities of the past, or which exist today in some smaller cities, tend to disappear in major settlements (fig. 174), or in some of them appear in an altered form. The smaller settlements are influenced by local conditions and by the decisions of a few people; in the larger settlements forces of influence become not only more international, but also more impersonal, because the many centres of initiative for action gradually dissociate the creators of the initial settlement from the final form.

○ *Networks*

One of the most basic ways of describing the structure of settlements is related to their Networks and especially to the circulatory system—their lines of transportation and nodal points. Minor urban settlements like the village have one nodal point. This is usually a central open space which can have different forms, from very natural to strictly geometric ones.

When the population rises above a few thousand people, the one nodal point tends to be either elongated along a main axis, or split to form one or more additional nodal points. These are smaller than the central one and serve those areas of the urban settlement farthest from it. When such additional nodal points come into being, they diminish the importance of the central nodal point. If, for example, there were ten shops in the central nodal point for every thousand people in the town, and additional nodal points appear, the corresponding services in the centre may be reduced to seven or eight shops per thousand, while two, three or more shops per thousand are created in the new nodal points, making up the same total of ten shops per thousand. If, however, as is quite probable, the income of the settlement has risen, we may have an increase in the total facilities.

In larger settlements there are three or four levels of nodal points, and in the very large ones there may be as many as seven to eight levels, ranging from the very smallest to the largest and more central ones. The structure and importance of all nodal points varies according to their level, and the activities which they accommodate are different at different levels. This does not mean that the same activities may not exist at nodal points of different categories; but it does mean that their importance, their percentage of the total and their quality differ from one level to another; which in turn means that the total of nodal point activities differs between levels though it perhaps remains the same in most nodal points of the same level.

The nodal points are usually situated on the basic circulatory lines; therefore if we map the system of all nodal points and all basic circulatory lines, we will find that they coincide and form a pattern which becomes more dense towards the centre of the urban area (fig. 175).

In the larger urban settlements, as well as an increase of central nodal points, there is an increase of centres of special activities. These coincide in the smaller settlements with the basic nodal points. When the settlements start to grow, specialised activities develop near the nodal points. But when they grow more, the specialised activities gradually come to concentrate in areas farther from the centre, though still close to the basic circulatory system. In major settlements, however, they may move quite far from the basic circulatory system as well, especially if they have little to do with the mass transportation of goods or people—as does a specialised research centre, for example.

The micro-texture of urban settlements also differs according to their size as has already been noted. In many small urban settlements, for example, the whole texture consists of rather uniform, small units or blocks separated by streets of approximately equal width; such small cities have a more or less homogeneous texture in which the central square plus the major lines of circulation constitute the only big textural difference. In major settlements the texture is not so uniform. The transportation lines are wider, the railway

and other functions, such as production, education, and so forth, all require larger areas. Also, the larger the settlement, the greater the chances of its spreading not only in plains since a big city does not necessarily always find plains around it, but also in part over uneven terrain, or over non-uniform areas, for example, areas including rivers, lakes, hills and natural parks, which are difficult to build on, and all of which contribute to less uniformity of texture. History also adds to the lack of uniformity of texture, since most major urban areas have grown over long periods, during which different ideas and technologies imposed different structural solutions thus leading to a different texture. These differences can be seen by comparing two plans of a small city and a part of a major city as in the preceding plans 146 to 168, some of which are shown in the same scales of 100 metre grid to facilitate comparisons of texture.

If, however, a settlement has been planned from its beginning, we may still find that the texture is not uniform, even in the case of small cities. This can be seen easily in Renaissance cities and in some new cities of the nineteenth and twentieth centuries. This lack of uniformity of texture does not necessarily mean an absence of synthesis. In some cases it is justified, when, for instance, the lack of uniformity is caused by the creation of a better circulatory system, or by other services of traffic, or by factors contributing to the better appearance of the city. In some other cases, though, the lack of uniformity is not justified. In most cases it seems that, while it is reasonable to expect a uniformity of texture in small cities which have grown naturally, a lack of uniformity is very often necessary to a better synthesis; but of course it does not guarantee success. Quite often, especially when introduced without a system justified by organic reasons, it leads to failure. On the other hand, if a major city has been planned so as to be completely uniform, and if what is meant by uniformity is the consistent repetition of the basic unit of the city block with no differentiation between areas, functions and lines of circulation, then such a city may well be considered a failure.

In general we can say that the greater the size of the settlement, the greater the variations in all its elements: in Nature, Man, Society, Shells and Networks. This explains why we are now being faced with such difficult problems. Experience has shown that problems in major urban settlements do not increase at a rate equal to that of the population increase, but much more rapidly. This happens because:

- Nature is much less uniform over larger areas and very often consists of several types of landscape;
- people belong to more diversified social, professional, racial, religious and other groups;
- social problems increase enormously;
- economic activities and functions are varied;
- problems of the Shells are much more complicated.

In larger settlements there are many more combinations—more people of a greater variety with more social problems and functions spreading over more diverse types of landscape.

187

central functions and circulatory system   **population 2,000,000**   **Athens basin, Greece (1962)**

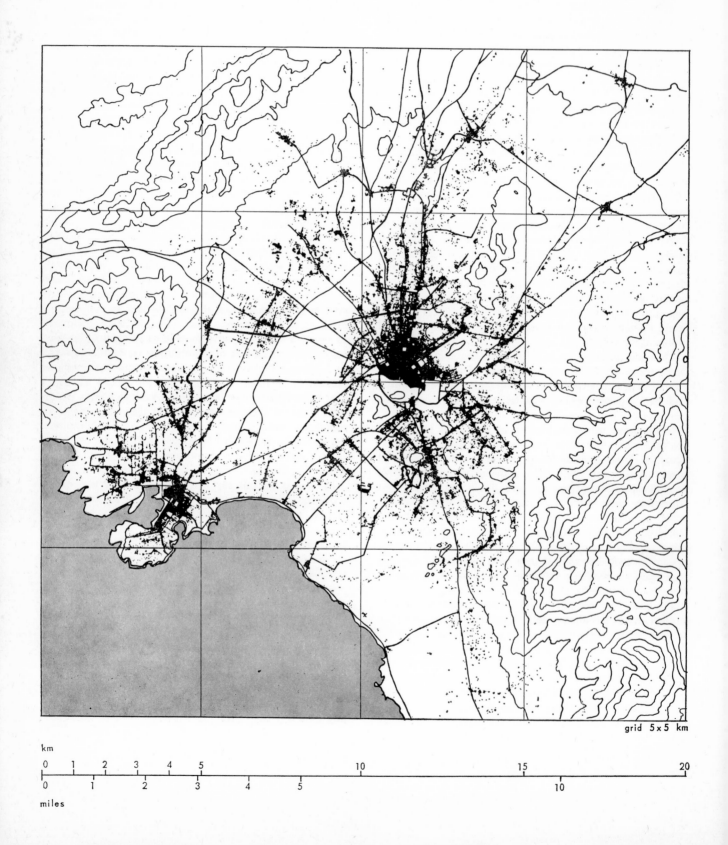

grid 5 x 5 km

km

0   1   2   3   4   5   10   15   20

0   1   2   3   4   5   10

miles

This helps us to realise how much more complicated the problem of the final structure is. I will try to illustrate this difficulty and the huge number of problems we are facing. Man's relation to Nature in the small town is quite simple. In the evenings or over the week-ends he can walk around his town and come into contact with its natural landscape. He will probably follow one or two roads in order to leave his town. In a city of 1,000,000 people, however, he is first of all deprived of the chance to walk out of the city into Nature. Thus his choice is, either not come into touch with Nature at all, or drive to it, ride a train, a bicycle or bus. His contact with Nature is becoming increasingly complicated.

One man living in a small settlement of a few thousand inhabitants has a maximum of personal relations among the total population. If he lives in a city of 1,000,000 people, his problems become, theoretically, problems of eventual contact with 1,000,000 people.

In most small towns, there is just one community centre and several residential neighbourhoods. If we assume that there are five neighbourhoods and our man lives in neighbourhood A, he has a problem of contact with the inhabitants of neighbourhoods B, C, D and E, that is a problem of four channels of relations and contacts with other groups. In the big city, though, we may have 500 or more communities of the size of a small town and over 2,000 units corresponding to neighbourhoods. Therefore, the problem for the same man becomes one of eventual contact with the inhabitants of 500 or more communities and over 2,500 neighbourhoods.

In the small town, the man has very few choices in the purchase of clothes, for instance, for there are very few clothing shops. In the big city there may be 1,500 clothing shops, with many variations in their location, prices and style, so that his possible choices are multiplied enormously.

The same is true of every other activity in the large city. The problem of where to send his children to school is another example. In a small town, he has probably no choice as there is only one school. But in the city of 1,000,000, he will find private, public and denominational schools, near or far, offering different types and costs of education. The choices are greatly increased, and much more complicated.

There is no question but that Man is offered a much greater variety of choices in the big city than in the small town. Where, normally, we should have expected that, since the big city has 500 times more people than the small town, a city man would have 500 times more choices in all his relationships with the city, we find in practice that things are not so at all. Because of the great variation of types, the people he can meet are multiplied by thousands and the resulting figure is again multiplied even further, since contacts in a city are not only between man and man, but also between man and community, and these people belong to different types of communities. We then have to consider the number of choices Man can make among the facilities provided by the city. In a city of 1,000,000 people, Man has an enormous number of choices to make in selecting his human, social, professional and service contacts. This creates many complications for him, not only in the choice of a single factor, like the location of his house, but also in the need for combinations of several factors. Let us take one simple example; his choice of a location for his residence. In a big city he may decide he wants his residence close to his place of work. If so, it may be far from employment opportunities for his wife, and from the college of his older children, but close to schools for his younger children. His residence may be well situated, or not, in relation to shopping centres, sports fields, parks, religious centres, etc.

If this is so complicated for just one man, we can now understand how much more complicated are the decisions that have to be taken for the entire community in relation to the policies to be followed regarding the use of natural, human and social resources, policies for the activities and functions to be developed, and finally the policies relating to the structure and form of the city. The problems in major cities are enormous as compared to those of the small cities, and this is why they have not been faced properly. We have not been prepared to face problems which are, not simply hundreds of times more complicated than in the small cities of the past, but thousands or millions of times more so. However, Man has not only failed to face the problems of the major urban areas which he was not accustomed to in the past, he has also failed to face the problems of recently created minor cities. One reason for this is, that more often than not, these new minor cities are not independent settlements, but parts of major urban areas, and thus they share many of its problems. The fact that most of us live in major settlements is another such factor. In them we are confused, we have lost our perspective, and are, consequently, unable to face and solve even the problems of minor urban settlements.

Static and dynamic settlements

The main characteristic of static settlements is that their predominant elements are in a relatively static balance in terms of dimensions; their population does not increase or decrease, no more land is necessary, the total built-up volume remains the same, and so forth. This is mainly due to the fact that within them there is no significant population or economic growth. At what degree of growth a settlement ceases to be static, we can not exactly say. Suppose we consider a settlement with a one-half per cent annual population growth and a one per cent annual per capita income growth. Even these slow rates of growth mean an increase of 1·5 per cent per year in the composite growth potential of the settlement, so that in one generation the potential will increase by 50 per cent, and before two generations (58–60 years) by 100 per cent. Such a change will mean that people, over a lifetime

189

of some 60 years will see their settlement doubling in importance. For them, therefore, even this low rate makes their settlement a dynamic one.

I do not believe it is possible to give an exact definition of static and dynamic settlements, since the notion of a static settlement is relative. On the basis of present experience, however, I am rather inclined to believe that if in one generation's time there is no apparent change or expansion in the micro-scale of the city (that is in its neighbourhoods and communities), then the settlement appears static. In actual figures this may well be a total growth in one generation of about 20 per cent for the entire potential of the city, which may be expressed as a 10 per cent growth in the existing texture and a 10 per cent expansion of it. This means an average of 0·6 per cent per year in the total growth potential of the population and economy, indicating not a population increase of 0·6 per cent, but a mixed increase of population and per capita income.

I would like to repeat that there can be no absolute criteria for a distinction between static and dynamic settlements, since every settlement is dynamic in some way (there is always a turnover of people) and every settlement is static for short periods of time. These are relative concepts. We must take into consideration the total forces developing within a settlement and the final expression of these forces by physical means. In doing so, we must keep in mind the fact that if a settlement is loosely built at a low density, it may increase considerably and still seem relatively static since the increase is being absorbed by the existing texture; while another settlement, already densely built and increasing at the same rate, may seem to be growing dynamically because the total increase is being expressed as a physical expansion of the existing texture. For all practical purposes, though, I think that if we want to express the difference between static and dynamic growth as we conceive it today (the concept may change a generation or even a decade from now), we can use, for normal cases, the figure of up to 0·6 per cent per year of composite growth as the limit of static settlements, of over 1·2 per cent of yearly growth of all the forces in the settlement taken together as the borderline of what could be considered dynamic settlements, and the settlements with a rate between 0·6 per cent and 1·2 per cent as mixed settlements.

Seen in a different way all settlements go through both static and dynamic phases. When the settlement first comes into being, it is dynamic, later it may become even more so, then the rate of growth may well slow down, and the settlement will turn into a static one. This situation may change once again and the settlement may pass through several static or dynamic phases.

Static settlements today include most of those with fewer than 100,000 inhabitants. If, however, such settlements are situated on major transportation lines, or near major centres of transportation such as a port or an airport, or near an expanding major settlement, they are probably dynamic

since even though they are small, their location makes them part of a major settled area.

It is difficult to generalise about all settlements with over 100,000 people, but I am inclined to believe that very few of them are static. To be static, such settlements must either be in a mountainous area, off the main lines of transportation, or be without ample water supply (power supply no longer presents a problem even at greater distances); unless, of course, their initial existence had been due to natural resources in the area which were exhausted before any new major functions or important investment could be created.

Dynamic settlements with fewer than 100,000 inhabitants, although small as a percentage of the total, can be calculated in the thousands, for the total number of urban settlements with fewer than 100,000 people is around 90,740. Also, many minor settlements which are static at present may gradually become dynamic if they come within the influence of forces creating dynamic growth (such as new resources or an expansion of the Ekistic systems). We have no exact statistics of the percentage of settlements with fewer than 100,000 people which may be or may become dynamic, or of the distribution of this percentage among different sizes of settlements or different types of countries. Even if there were such statistics, they would only be of relative importance, since the conditions which transform static settlements into dynamic ones are changing with the continuous changes in the Ekistic system. In theory, though, we may estimate the percentage of static and dynamic settlements in the following way.

o Since settlements with fewer than 100,000 people, according to the classification of settlements in Ekistic systems, are in class A, B, C and D we can estimate the number of these settlements in a given region. Therefore on a percentage basis in an area which has about 10,000 settlements of all classes from A to F, only seven are likely to belong to those which, because of their size, are dynamic. However, several of the smaller settlements are in the proximity of these seven or on major transportation lines (this can be calculated on the basis of the hexagonal pattern of Ekistic systems).

o On such a basis we can estimate the number of those settlements which we expect to grow at a higher rate, that is, become more dynamic: those situated close to settlements F and E, those situated on lines connecting the F settlements with F settlements of other regions, and connecting class E settlements with F settlements, and so forth. This calculation can take place on the basis of fig. 117.

Such a calculation would lead to a classification of relatively static and dynamic settlements. Where the borderlines should be drawn, as I have already explained, does not depend only on the relative location of the settlements, but also on the overall growth potential of the area. If this is very small, even settlements of class E and F may be static; while if the potential is great, perhaps all settlements of class **D** and several of classes C and B may be dynamic.

If such an estimate is drawn up only on the basis of the hexagonal pattern of settlements it cannot have great practical significance, since it presupposes equal conditions in the location of all settlements, that is, a uniform plain. But in practice we have to take into account the variety of geographic and topographic conditions and make our estimates in a more practical way. We can make some of the following considerations, for example: we can definitely say that the smaller the settlement, the greater the possibility of its being static; but this is only valid for older settlements which, if minor, are most probably in remote areas which will not be influenced by modern technology and the expanding system of settlements. But in the case of newer settlements we cannot be so sure; settlements situated at the crossroads of new highways, or on new canals or other lines of transportation, may indeed be small in size, but we must not forget that they came into being as a result of new forces being exercised in new locations; their present size, therefore, might well be incidental—the first phase in the development of ultimately major settlements—a development determined by the new conditions. Such considerations show how difficult it is to make any exact estimate when dealing with a changing pattern of Ekistic systems.

I will now give some general assumptions based on my experience without justifying them with exact figures. There are about 90,740 settlements in the world with 2,000–100,000 people. About two-thirds of them (some 59,500 settlements) belong to the category of 2,000–5,000 people. Out of these it is questionable if 10 per cent or 6,000 settlements are dynamic. We are left with the settlements with 5,000–10,000 people, totalling 31,240, out of which probably about 50 per cent are dynamic, which means 15,620 settlements. Then we have 1,460 urban settlements with more than 100,000 people each and a total population of 702,000,000 people, almost all of which are dynamic. Therefore, the total number of dynamic settlements on this Earth may be roughly 23,000, or about one-fourth the total number of urban settlements; but since these are the larger settlements, their population totals about 950,000,000 people or about 70 per cent of the total urban population of the Earth and about 30 per cent of the population of the Earth. This means that at present about one out of three living persons lives in a dynamic settlement.

So there are about 69,000 static urban settlements in the world, with a population of about 385,000,000 people or about 30 per cent of the urban population of the Earth, or about 13 per cent of the total urban and rural population. If we add to these people the 55 per cent who live in rural static settlements we see that two out of three living persons live in static settlements.

We need to understand these static settlements better. They are static because there is no considerable growth of their elements. Thus, the chances of the static settlements being balanced, or tending to a balance are relatively strong. Most of these static settlements are old, and they approximated their present dimensions before modern technology had affected them. Thus, having developed slowly and normally, they grew into well-balanced, well-built cities, as is the city of Venice, for example (fig. 176). When cities have been influenced by technology to a considerable degree, this will result in their dynamic growth, a growth which is, very probably, still in progress. Therefore, such settlements are not static, since experience and theory show that under normal conditions, once the process of growth starts, there is no reason for it to stop unless major changes take place, drawing the whole Ekistic system of which they are a part towards decline. Therefore, we can assume that it is very probable that static settlements are those which have not been affected by modern technology to any considerable degree. In other words, their rate of growth has been minor since the time they were well-balanced, which means that modern technology has only resulted in a few technological additions instead of a technological revolution.

If technology has only influenced static settlements as a minor addition to their previous elements, with no major impact on the number of people and the economy, then the changes probably consist of motor transport, and some more modern equipment added to the existing factories, workshops, shops, institutions and residences. But the introduced technological changes have not been enough to affect any major alteration in the form of the Shells, since we have assumed that they do not presuppose economic growth of any considerable degree. While the addition of new means of transportation (cars, buses, trucks or perhaps street-cars) would be noticeable in a city of below 100,000 people which had otherwise remained static, it is not very probable that these additions would make a major change in the functioning of a major settlement. The reason for this is that if the city has not been affected by modern technology sufficiently to raise incomes to a marked degree, not many people will be able to own cars and most will, even today, go to and from work and to most places of their daily needs on foot. Let us not forget that the average size of such cities below 100,000 people is 15,000 people, which probably means an average diameter of no more than three kilometres (two miles) and a maximum distance, even from the outlying residences to the centre, of a quarter of an hour. In all probability, therefore, the addition of a small number of cars, buses, trucks or even a street-car, will take place without affecting any major change in the city structure. The only apparent difference would be the existence of mechanical means of transportation in the streets, since they would displace the pedestrians and might have a disastrous effect on the narrow streets; they might also necessitate the transformation of several squares into parking lots. All this would result in depriving the inhabitants of the former quiet, and possibly some aesthetic values of their city.

Facts

176

well-balanced pattern of an old static settlement   Venice, Italy (1959)

grid 100 x 100 m

metres

| 0 | 100 | 200 | 300 | 400 | 500 | 600 | 700 | 800 | 900 | 1000 |

0   500   1000   1500   2000   2500   3000

feet

If, however, the static city is a relatively new one it is quite probable that its elements are not in balance whether it was originally built in the pre-technological era as a small city and remained static since, even during the technological era, or founded during the technological era and turned static later because the general evolution had bypassed the region. What is most probable is that the Shells are out of balance with the other forces, and that the resulting patterns are confused (fig. 177). This is what has happened in cities which started out with great expectations of growth that were later not realised. It is quite characteristic of cities in new countries, such as the U.S.A., Canada and Australia, where at a certain stage there was an expectation of rapid growth and ample land; this led people to build larger settlements than they needed. As a result, parts of some of these cities have remained undeveloped. Therefore, their texture shows completely unequal densities and use of plots, both in two and in three dimensions. The results are: uneconomic development, lack of social cohesion, absence of good administrative machinery (since the administration actually costs more than it should since it has to take care of more streets and services than are necessary), and finally an absence of beauty, since beauty cannot be attained without proper cohesion in the texture. Such cities often have wide streets in relation to their traffic, since they have over-estimated their needs, predicting growth which has not taken place; therefore, traffic under-employs the streets instead of over-employing them, which once again leads to a weak texture that is in many respects very unsatisfactory. On the other hand, their layout corresponds to a pedestrian era, therefore motorcar traffic is badly served.

Dynamic settlements

Dynamic settlements almost always contain elements which are out of balance, and are not even in a systematically changing balance. The situation is sometimes so bad that it is questionable whether it is possible for the elements to re-establish a balance. In many cities of the world, we can note from the way in which the officials of the cities handle their problems, and the way in which the population reacts to efforts being made to face them, that in the long run the balance will not be re-established, and that people are not tending towards re-establishing it. Indeed, as has already been explained, I do not believe that we can ever have a static balance in a dynamic settlement. However, we should have an overall dynamic balance, expressed by a continuous attempt to re-adjust all the elements in order to re-establish the general balance, as well as an actual balance at local levels.

We have defined dynamic settlements as those growing by more than 0·6–1·2 per cent a year in population and

economy, very often they grow much more rapidly; usually by more than 1·0 per cent in population and more than 1·0 per cent in annual per capita income, or by a total of 2·0 per cent. Many dynamic settlements are growing at an even higher rate than this; in fact, those urban areas of the world which have more than 100,000 people grow at an average rate of 4·3 per cent per year in population and more than 3 per cent per year in per capita income, which means a composite total growth of the order of more than 7·3 per cent a year.

This rate of growth is intensified even more in some categories of larger settlements. For example, the rate of annual population growth in settlements of between 1,000,000 and 2,000,000 people is 4·9 per cent per year. It is also probable that their per capita income rises at a high rate; therefore these settlements probably grow by more than 8 per cent per year. We cannot, however, continue such estimates for even larger settlements (in which the rate of growth probably increases), since the statistics on larger urban areas are very confused. The reason is that larger settlements in most parts of the world do not consist of only one administrative area. Therefore, statistics, which are usually based on one administrative area, do not correspond to the actual growing urban settlement, but only to parts of it represented by single administrative units.

It must be noted that I always speak of the actual urban settlements, that is, of the total area of each urban settlement, regardless of its administrative boundaries, which are very often completely misleading. Some of the dynamically growing settlements may increase their potential at an average rate of 10 to 12 per cent a year. The growth of these settlements is, therefore, physically demonstrated in many ways, since it usually results in a corresponding increase of life, of public space and growth of investment. So, if the annual increase is 3 per cent the total potential of these settlements in people and economy doubles in one generation's time, or even in only ten years if the annual increase goes up to 7–8 per cent, or in only 6–8 years if the rate is 10–12 per cent.

The total number of dynamic settlements, as I have already stated, is of the order of 23,000, with a population of about 950,000,000 people, or one-third of the total population of the Earth. So, dynamic urban settlements—the youngest of all categories of settlements—are already inhabited by 32 per cent of the population of the Earth, and this percentage is increasing continuously. On the other hand the static urban settlements, although many more in number, contain only 385,000,000 people, or 13 per cent of the world population, and this percentage is continuously decreasing. The average population of a dynamic settlement is 41,000 people, if we take all 23,000 such settlements into consideration, or 55,000 people if we exclude those of fewer than 5,000 people. This shows that dynamic settlements tend to be 2·5 to 3 times larger than the static ones.

the unbalanced pattern of a new static settlement   **Psychico, Greece (1961)**

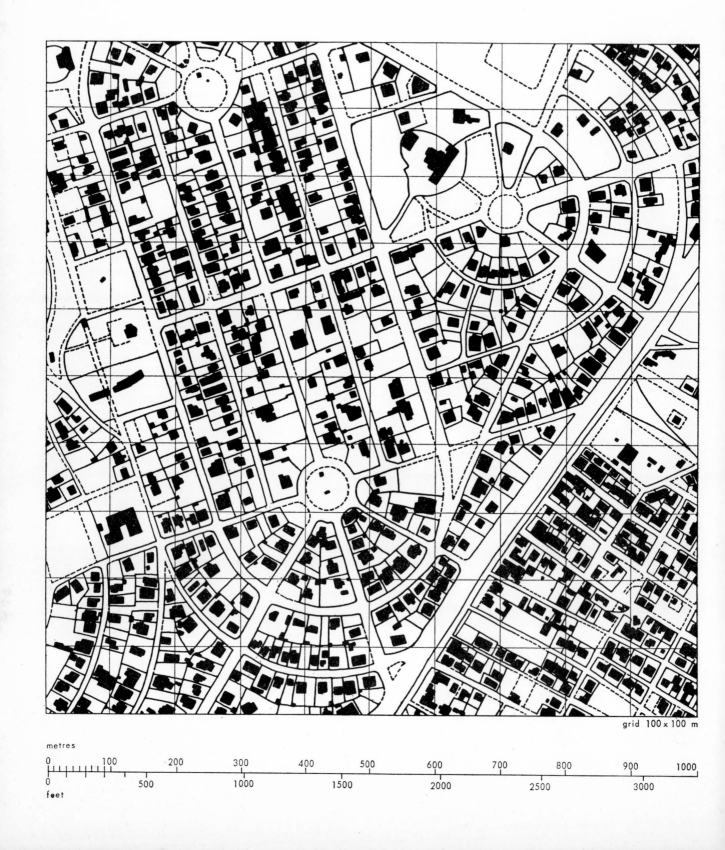

grid 100 x 100 m

metres

0   100   200   300   400   500   600   700   800   900   1000

0   500   1000   1500   2000   2500   3000

feet

TABLE 2

STATIC AND DYNAMIC URBAN SETTLEMENTS

Categories by size of population in thousands	Total number of settlements	Population in millions	Dynamic		Static	
			Settlements in units	Population in millions	Settlements in units	Population in millions
2–5	59,500	171	6,000	17	53,500	154
5–10	17,750	121	—	—	—	—
10–20	7,750	107	—	—	—	—
20–50	4,145	126	15,600	231	15,600	231
50–100	1,595	108	—	—	—	—
100–200	751	106	—	—	—	—
200–500	426	130	—	—	—	—
500–1,000	142	96	—	—	—	—
1,000–2,000	86	125	1,400	702	—	—
2,000–5,000	38	107	—	—	—	—
5,000–10,000	14	97	—	—	—	—
10,000 and over	3	41	—	—	—	—
	92,200	1,335	23,000	950	69,100	385

As stated already, the five elements in the dynamic settlements are almost inevitably out of balance. Men from the countryside swarm into them very often unprepared for the necessary adjustment. Also the older inhabitants of these settlements are often, due to natural disposition, tradition or training, unable or unwilling to adjust to its dynamic growth. Some of its social institutions are able to adjust to the dynamic change but many others cannot. One way of finding out whether Man and Society are adjusted or not to the dynamic growth of the city is to look at the streets of a major city and witness the numbers of people unable to comply immediately with the new traffic conditions and regulations imposed upon them. There are always those who need time for the readjustment. In the meantime there is a lack of balance.

The activities of the city change. Practically every one of them increases in dimension and intensity, while new ones are being added continuously. Man and Society are not prepared for all these new activities. They concentrate their attention either on the more profitable activities, such as private business, or on those requiring a lot of their attention, which may be unremunerative and difficult to implement. A characteristic example of this is the need to adjust to new administrative tasks. The very fact that the city has outgrown its administrative boundaries but that very few people are willing to face this problem, demonstrates how difficult it is for Man and Society to adjust to the new situation.

The growth of the settlements takes place with little respect for Nature: for its landscape, water, climate, and so forth. The loss of areas with beautiful landscapes, changes which are effected with no pre-arranged and well-conceived plan, air and water pollution, changes in the micro-climate, all are the characteristics of this phase of development.

Similar effects can be noticed in the Shells. Uncontrolled forces blow up the Shells in an unbalanced manner; urban expansion takes place in many unreasonable directions and distances, and with patterns that are unsuitable for the convenient overall expansion and welfare of the total settlement. Thus both the central city and its changing parts suffer from pressures caused by concentrations of high buildings, surgery (justified in the name of traffic), or slum clearance programmes, which contribute very little to the whole.

The intrusion of the machine, especially the car, has influenced development of this situation, since it is mainly the number of machines being thrown into the pre-existing texture of the city that has caused most of the trouble. The city itself cannot tolerate the advent of the machine and resists the intrusion with its very structure.

growth of the population of Athens, Greece

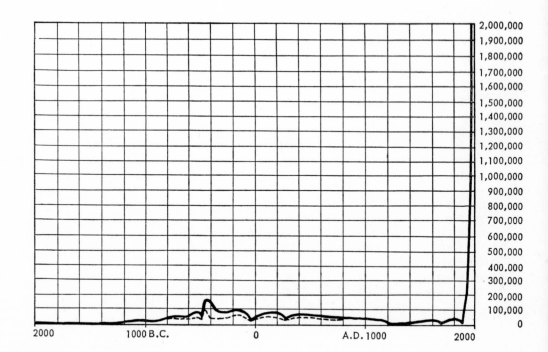

----- city of Athens

—— urban area (total)

Some examples may show the extent to which the elements in the city are out of balance. I will draw these from the population, traffic and the Shells, using a series of charts showing the growth of greater Athens. I am intentionally not speaking about the administrative city of Athens, as the urban settlement has outgrown by far not only the ancient city of Athens, which came into being thousands of years ago on its Acropolis in the middle of a valley, but also the modern administrative area. The population of Athens had always been that of a small city of the past, until a century ago when modern forces caused it to grow beyond that level and eventually reach the 2,100,000 level of today (fig. 178). The result was that a city, which until the sixth century B.C. was small, which turned into a larger twin city in the fifth century (fig. 179), which again was confined to the limits of a smaller city over long centuries (fig. 180), started growing physically by 1850, and finally developed into a Dynapolis. For the next 70 years this growth was slow and the city compact (fig. 181), but after that the population explosion, combined with the technological one, changed the city of Athens into a greater urban area, into a Dynametropolis (fig. 182).

When speaking of dynamic settlements I have used examples showing only the growth of the built-up area, which is what

we usually do when dealing with settlements. The fact is, however, that these built-up parts are only the most visible ones, with the total body of the settlement extending far beyond. It is when we manage to see the non-built-up parts as well, that we understand the dynamic nature of settlements, following the changes of the entire body and predicting the changes of the built-up part which follow the other in space and time.

One of the non-visible changes of the non-built-up part is the change of rural land into urban land, a procedure taking place when the landowner loses interest in cultivation because of the rise of land value; when this happens he eithers sell his land or holds on to it in anticipation of more profit.

In a recent study we have carried out for the Urban Detroit Developing Area, we have been able to follow these changes in the rural land for the period between 1900 and 1959. How the waves of urbanisation spread into the countryside, even before this phenomenon could be perceived, is shown in figure 183 which gives the percentage of land in farms. These five maps show how clearly that the dynamic city covers much greater areas than those of its physically developed nucleus and this is important evidence of the forces being radiated by such dynamic cities.

179

Ekistic evolution of greater Athens

- 7th century B.C.
- 5th century B.C.

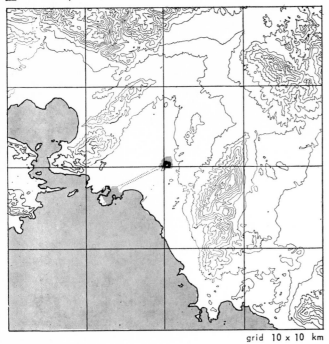

grid 10 x 10 km

180

Ekistic evolution of greater Athens

- first phase Turkish occupation 1456 - 1687
- second phase Turkish occupation 1687 - 1833

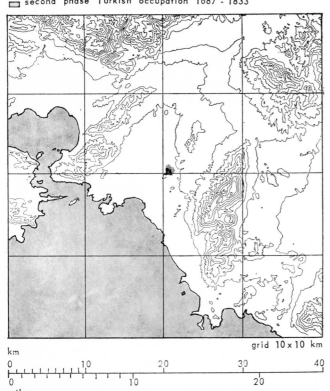

grid 10 x 10 km

km

0   10   20   30   40

0   10   20

miles

181

Ekistic evolution of greater Athens

- 1850
- 1900
- 1920

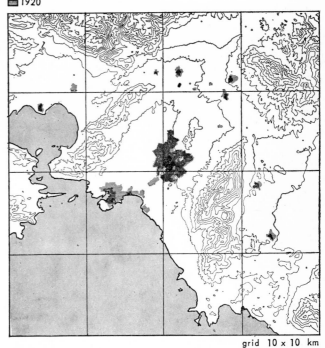

grid 10 x 10 km

182

Ekistic evolution of greater Athens

- 1940
- 1960
- 1963

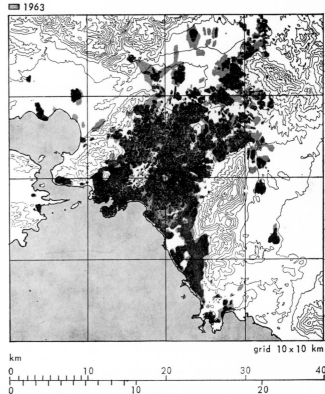

grid 10 x 10 km

km

0   10   20   30   40

0   10   20

miles

the waves of urbanisation spread into the countryside   percentage of farmland   Detroit, U.S.A.

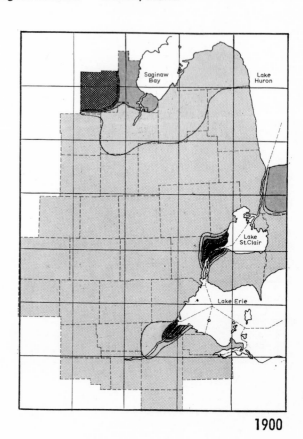

1900

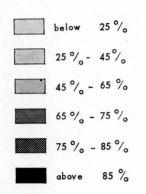

below   25 %

25 % - 45 %

45 % - 65 %

65 % - 75 %

75 % - 85 %

above   85 %

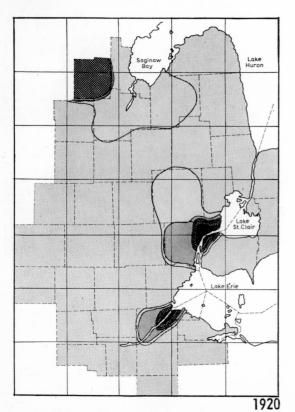

1920

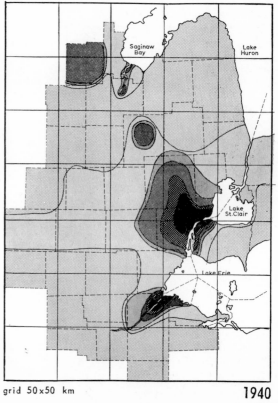

grid 50 x 50 km

1940

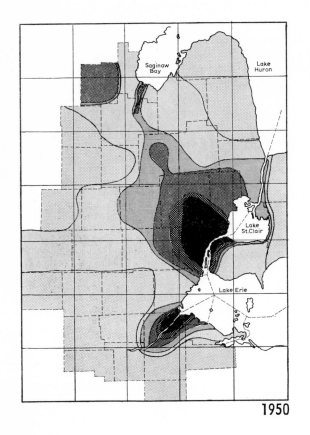

1950

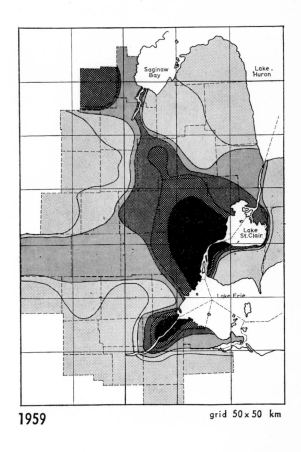

1959

grid 50 x 50 km

CHAPTER FOUR
EKISTIC EVOLUTION

EVOLUTION OF SPECIES

Process and phases

One of the gravest weaknesses in our knowledge of human settlements is the absence of a theory of evolution, in spite of the fact that we have known from the days of ancient Greece that 'we shall not obtain the best insight into things until we actually see them growing from the beginning' to remember the words of Aristotle.[11] From Darwin's time on there can be no excuse whatsoever for underestimating the great understanding of phenomena and situations that a correct theory of evolution can offer. I will try in this chapter to outline such a theory as regards human settlements.

The evolution of human settlements is a continuous process taking place at all levels of Ekistic units, from the smallest, the room, to the largest possible, the universal human settlement. During the process of evolution various species of human settlements have developed, ranging from the most primitive to the most complex. Human settlements, like plants and animals, are born, develop, decline and die. Like plants and animals they belong to different categories, different species, which either survive as such or die, or lead to the formation of new species; and most human settlements begin as very low forms and develop into higher ones, though unlike plants and animals, they can also—if planned by Man—start out as higher forms. Like plants and animals, they usually start out as single-nucleus settlements and may develop into multi-nuclei ones, but, once born, they can be developed into any of the primitive or more developed species; unlike plants and animals, their development is not necessarily limited by their 'genes'.

Settlements may have an initial structure which only allows for a certain degree of growth, but nothing excludes the possibility of an expansion and transformation of this structure which will allow them to surpass the initial structural limitations. Unlike plants and animals, human settlements have no pre-determined death, though there may sometimes exist initial conditions that pre-determine the death of one of their activities—as in the case of mining settlements which one might assume will face extinction when the mineral is exhausted. This is sometimes true; but there is nothing to prevent the settlement from developing other functions, so that by the time the mine is exhausted, the inhabitants (or a considerable percentage of them) are carrying out other activities, thus continuing the life of the settlement. Even if the settlement has reached an advanced state of decline—exhaustion of a mine without the creation of other activities—there is no reason why Man cannot develop, even at this point, activities which will allow the settlement to revive, eventually expand, and even become more successful than in its earlier stage.

In the light of what I have explained, the evolution of settlements until now can be divided into five major phases:
- the phase of primitive non-organised human settlements (This most probably started with the beginning of the evolution of Man.);
- the phase of primitive organised settlements (This is the period of villages—Eopolis—which has lasted about 10,000 years.);
- the phase of static urban settlements or cities (Polis—which has lasted about 5,000–6,000 years.);
- the phase of dynamic urban settlements (Dynapolis—which has lasted 200 years, and may last 400 years in all.);
- the phase of the universal city (Ecumenopolis—which is now beginning).

Primitive human settlements

Non-organised settlements

The period of non-organised settlements is a long period of the pre-history of Man, covering several hundreds of thousands of years. During this period Man began to modify Nature and to settle temporarily or permanently in different locations. Man, according to Ian McHarg, modified Nature in several ways. He probably began with fire, then went on to animal husbandry and the domestication of grazing animals; afterwards came deforestation and agriculture, and, with it, permanent human settlements.[12]

Man had settled first in natural shelters such as hollows in the ground, hollow trees or shallow caves, before he began to build his own primitive and unorganised habitat. After first exploiting natural formations and transforming them into dwellings, by various changes and additions, he began to create Shells independent of, and unrelated to, pre-existing natural forms. Many of the first man-made Shells were round cells—huts with a round ground-plan and a parabolic dome of straw, branches, clay or hides. Others may have started as rectangular huts built with timber and brush. When more of these Shells were built, they remained independent as structures, separated from each other by a small living space around them. Where compound walls existed around one or more dwellings, they also tended to be circular. Such primitive forms survive today in many nomadic societies, from the jungles of Africa to the Polar Zones.

If we look only at the physical structure of settlements, we will see some circular forms in space, sometimes of two sizes; huts and compound walls. However, if we also look at the ground around these structures—at the human settlement as a whole—we will see a great number of lines which are more dense and thick near these circular forms and which grow thinner at longer distances from them. These are the manifestations of the functions which are physically apparent because of the paths of Man which show the primitive Networks enabling the settlement to live, and which together with the Shells created by Man within Nature define the whole container of the human settlement (fig. 184).

Similar phenomena can be observed at the level of agricultural communities. The communities take up a smaller area where they are agricultural, and a larger one where they are hunting and cattle-breeding communities. Their nucleus under normal conditions is in the centre of gravity; or, if there is a security problem, in the safest place in their area, or even beyond their area of cultivation. There are no transportation and communication lines between the communities. Most communities do not touch each other, so as to avoid the clashes which would be inevitable were they too close together.

If we look at these primitive non-organised communities on a macro-scale, we discover that they consist of a nucleus, which is the built-up part of the human settlement, and several parts which lead out into the open, thinning out until they disappear—either because nobody goes beyond certain limits of the community or because these trips take place so seldom that they would not be placed on the same scale of densities. This is valid in minor settlements which may subsist on agriculture, or major ones which may exist on hunting and cattle-breeding, or even those living solely by hunting (fig. 185).

If we look at the micro-scale of these primitive, non-organised settlements, either at the scale of the one hut or of the earliest agricultural communities, we will notice that both have one common characteristic—a thickly built nucleus with a great density of human movement, with lines spreading all

184

primitive, non-organised huts

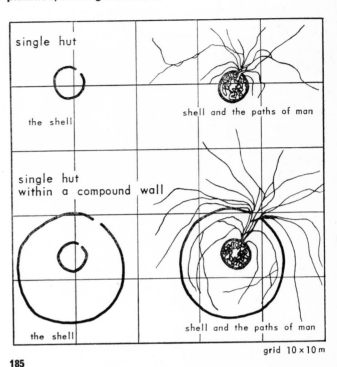

single hut

the shell

shell and the paths of man

single hut within a compound wall

the shell

shell and the paths of man

grid 10 × 10 m

185

primitive, non-organised communities
built-up nucleus and the paths of Man

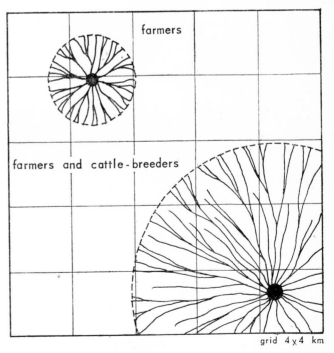

farmers

farmers and cattle-breeders

grid 4 × 4 km

201

186

primitive forms of life

marine diatom Arachnoidiscus ornatus magnified approximately 165 times

187

synthesis of circular forms

baked clay vase from Syros

around it and thinning out until they disappear completely. The one difference is that in the one-hut scale these lines start from the same point, while in the compound settlement they may start from several points in the area of the nucleus, the several gates of the village. There are no physical lines connecting this primitive settlement with others; there are no networks between settlements. If we now look at other primitive forms of life, we will find that they are quite similar to the primitive expressions of non-organised human settlements. One example of this is the marine diatom (fig. 186); but many other such primitive organisms have the same morphology and the same general characteristics as primitive human settlements.

In this phase of evolution there is no necessity for networks connecting all cells—their connections, if any, are achieved by diffusion between them. Once again we have a parallel with animal evolution. According to Sir Julian Huxley:

'When the animal is small, no transport is necessary to get the food or water or oxygen to the cells from the original absorptive surface; all goes well by diffusion alone. But bulk brings difficulties here too. The flatness of the larger flatworms is partly due to the need for having every cell near enough to the surface to be able to get oxygen by diffusion. The elaborate branching of their intestines and all other internal organs is needed to ensure that no cell shall be more than a microscopic distance away from a source of digested food.'[13]

○ *Organised settlements*

When Man, some ten to twelve thousand years ago, began to enter the era of organised agriculture, his settlements also began to show some characteristics of organisation. This did not happen easily or quickly. It required the acquisition of experience in organising the relationship between Man and Man, Man and Nature, and finally in expressing these relationships through more cohesive forms of settlements. This certainly took time. We do not know exactly at which point in time, but sometime in the beginning of this period, Man began to live at higher densities and he recognised that the forms of human settlements he had been creating up to then—either at the level of the lowest Ekistic unit or of a higher one, the community—were not such as would allow people to live close together in the best and most reasonable manner.

It is probable that he discovered that round forms gave him no opportunity for cohesive structure. This discovery he probably made in the attempt to expand his own room, that is, to relate his initial one-room dwelling with more living space, or to organise the relationship of his community with other communities. It may have led him to placing many round forms side by side, as we can see in some circular clay models (fig. 187); this was certainly not a satisfactory solution, either from the point of view of the use of space or from the

188

towards a synthesis of houses and plots

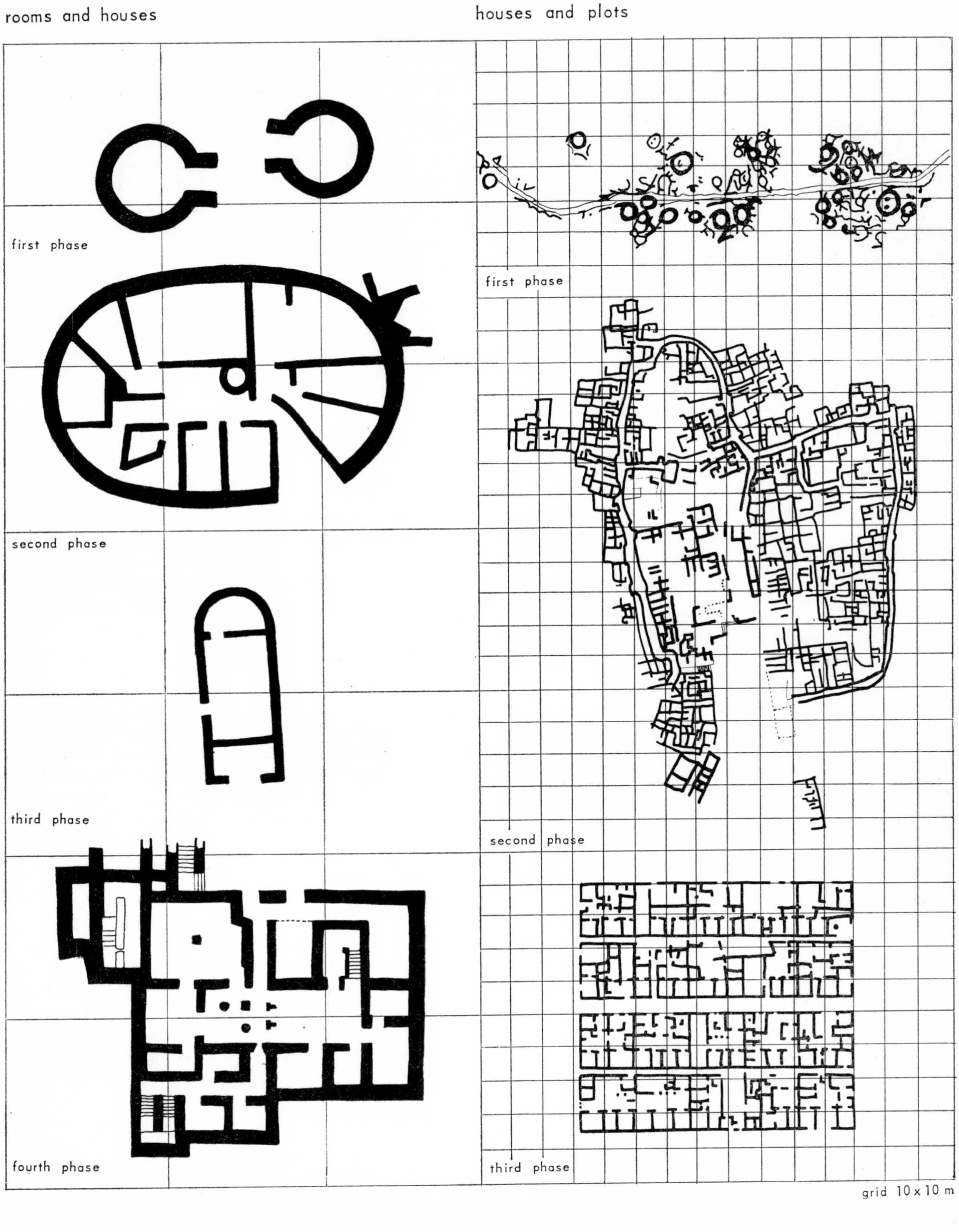
rooms and houses
houses and plots
first phase
second phase
third phase
fourth phase
first phase
second phase
third phase
grid 10 x 10 m

point of view of construction. This probably led him to the idea of elongating the circular cells to form elliptical ones, even though this could not provide for a major enlargement of space; so at some point he probably came to the conclusion that he should adopt rectilinear forms, which allowed for the possibility of placing many rooms next to one another with no loss of space either within or between them (fig. 188). This required a different type of roof construction from round buildings.

The change-over from circular to rectilinear forms also took place in the formation of the built-up nuclei of settlements by the synthesis of houses and plots. The latter, from irregular forms with space lost between them, developed gradually into more regular shapes with no space lost between them, to rectilinear forms with parallel boundaries (fig. 188).

When evolution reaches the stage at which a rectilinear pattern develops into a regular grid-iron one, Man has made his greatest discovery in the synthesis of human settlements. Whereas in the past his system had been a primitive one leading like a system of roofs towards one centre which could be controlled by one source of power (political, social, religious, etc.), with this later development he is giving himself the maximum of reasonable choices (fig. 189).

In the same period Man probably recognised that isolated circular forms could not lead to a synthesis on the community level either. When the first communities, that is the whole settlements, moved closer together, there were clashes over the disputed areas, while at the same time there could exist open unoccupied spaces in areas close by, such as those between the circles formed by these communities. Such experience gradually led to the recognition, perhaps even subconscious, that a continuous system required rectilinear and not circular boundaries and that the hexagon rather than the circle was the pattern which could lead to the normal co-existence of as many communities as possible in the same space. This certainly coincided with the increase of population, which was a result of the systematic cultivation of land, and with the desire of many people to settle on the land which yielded more. Thus, circular communities were gradually transformed into hexagonal ones (fig. 190).

In Nature we can see a great variety of cases where cells coming close together lose their circular form and tend to be hexagonal. In some cases we can see the circles clashing, as in the case of a Volvox colony, then proceeding into synthesis, as in a cross-section of the tubules of the Boletus in higher fungi, and finally forming a homogeneous pattern, as seen in the hollyhock (fig. 191). As an extension of these textures in more developed forms of life, there are the honeycombs or the eye of the bumble-bee, which have already been mentioned.

Beyond this phase of evolution we find a distinction in the direction followed in the creation of tissues and structures of Nature in plants, animals or crystals, and also in the tissues and structure of human settlements. In Nature evolution works towards a compression of circles and the gradual

204

189

the primitive and the grid-iron pattern

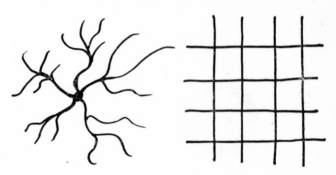

one choice and one point of control versus a maximum of choices

190

towards a synthesis of whole settlements

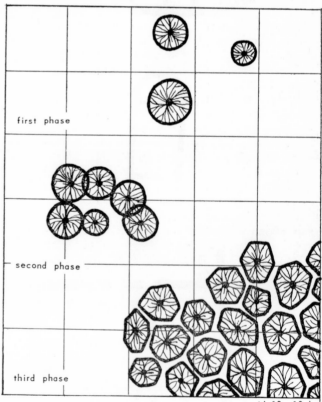

first phase

second phase

third phase

grid ·10 x 10 km

formation of polygonic systems, the clearest form of which is the hexagon. In the evolution of human settlements we see two courses:

- o on the micro-scale, where Man must divide the land, construct one or more Shells (rooms and houses), and circulate within a built-up area (neighbourhood), the solution leads to a synthesis at a right angle;
- o on the macro-scale, where Man must own and use space but not build it, and circulate within it, although to a much lesser degree than before (usually no more than one movement to and fro every day), Man continues to follow the course of Nature towards hexagonal patterns.

So we see that at this phase Man accepts the fact that he must follow two patterns in relation to the human settlement: the right-angle synthesis for the creation of his Shells on a micro-scale, and the hexagonal pattern for the organisation of his entire settlement on the middle- and macro-scales (fig. 192).

On the basis of this data we can now understand that the first phase of a synthesis in space is the placing of many similar individual phenomena (cells, rooms, communities, etc.) side by side, without making any changes in their original shape.

The second phase begins when Nature or Man understand that such a procedure leads to an unreasonable synthesis and begin to change the biological individuals. During this era of the development of the human settlements the patterns or regional distribution of the settlements differ depending on the phase of evolution and the prevailing conditions of safety. During the period of unsafe conditions, the villages or the built-up nuclei of settlements can be found on the hills and mountains, while the plains may not be inhabited at all, although they may be cultivated or used for grazing purposes (fig. 193). When conditions are safe on the other hand, and the population still small, the villages can be found in the plains, near the rivers and near the sea (fig. 194).

Finally, when the population becomes dense, new patterns develop, and the villages come to cover the entire plain on the basis of the small hexagonal pattern and the hills and the mountains on a larger hexagonal pattern (fig. 195).

In the time of unsafe conditions, the population of an area of 10,000 sq. km., would only be a few thousands; in the era of safe conditions before the development of land cultivation, the population might be larger, but would still be smaller than that of the era of large population and full exploitation of the land, when it would reach five hundred thousand or even one million.

Static urban settlements

At some point 5,000 or 6,000 years ago, in some villages in key locations where the paths of men met in periods of safety, or, when there was no safety, in locations which could

191

utilisation of space in nature

the full use of space leads from the circle to the hexagon

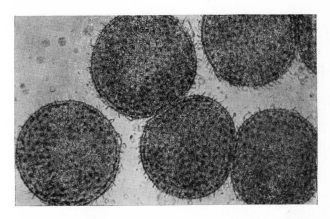

a. hollyhock (Althaea rosa) pollen grains

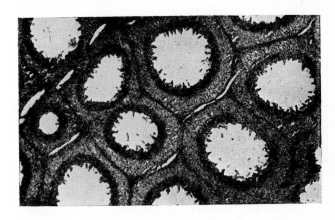

b. higher fungi — cross-section of the tubules of a species of Boletus.

c. honeycomb section

in Nature   in human settlements

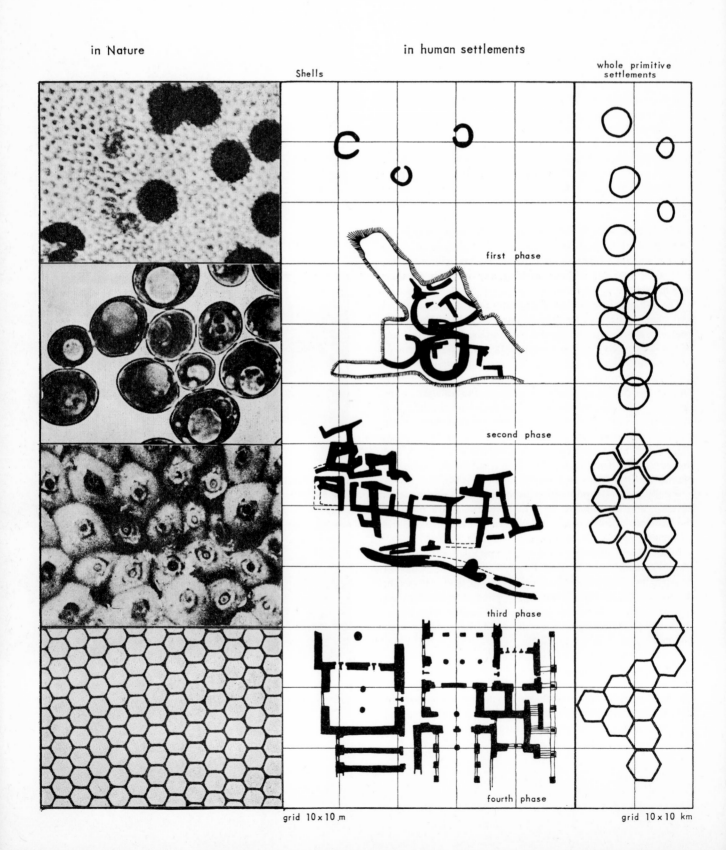

Shells

whole primitive
settlements

first phase

second phase

third phase

fourth phase

grid 10 x 10 m   grid 10 x 10 km

193

villages under unsafe conditions

primitive, organised life (early phase)

194

villages under safe conditions

primitive, organised life (early phase)

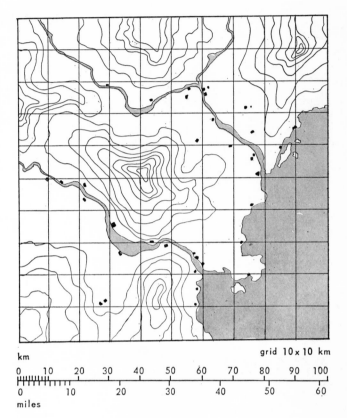

be easily defended, the first urban settlements appeared as small cities in a plain or as fortresses on hills and mountains. Much later cities of the plains tended to coincide more with free institutions, while fortresses became the strongholds for dictatorships and the feudal system; but this pattern was not invariable. Some cities became the seats of feudal lords and some fortresses were built by communities on the basis of different social patterns. Man entered a new phase of his history, that of urban life. He became a trader and manufacturer, and at the same time developed abilities in administration and organisation, as well as in the promotion of civilisation and culture.

On the micro-scale Man recognised that the principle of rectilinear right-angle synthesis, although not necessary for the creation of an organised village, was imperative for the organisation of his city, not only in the two dimensions of the land surface, but also in the third dimension of height. The rectilinear right-angle synthesis allowed Man to build compact cities in three dimensions as soon as he acquired

the ability of placing one floor on top of the other, that is, soon after he learned how to build strong horizontal roofs.

As his settlements grew in size, Man came to realise that the principle of the single-nucleus was not always valid in the internal organisation of the total Shells of the community. He saw that when his settlement grew, the single nodal point, which was adequate for the village and for small cities, no longer sufficed. The first thing to happen was the expansion of the nucleus in one or more directions; it was no longer limited to the settlement's centre of gravity (fig. 196). This was what happened in the small settlement of Priene, in ancient Greece, where the central nucleus expanded in two ways: first in a linear form along a main street which contained shops that would normally be clustered in the central agora, and secondly through the decentralisation of some functions, such as temples (fig. 196c). In larger cities additional nodal points and central places gradually came into being within the Shells of the settlement—a phenomenon which is unique to human settlements. It cannot be observed in plants or

207

Facts

195

villages under safe conditions

primitive, organised life (full development)

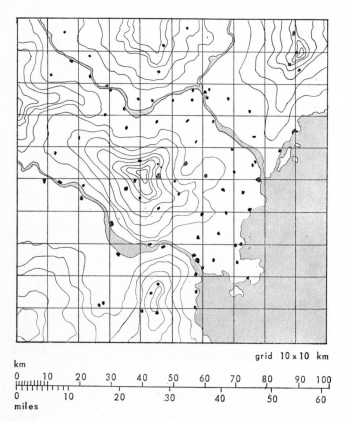

grid 10 x 10 km

km

| 0 | 10 | 20 | 30 | 40 | 50 | 60 | 70 | 80 | 90 | 100 |

0   10   20   .30   40   50   60

miles

form of an addition of whole communities to be gradually filled with houses. The initiative for such action cannot rest with the single citizen, but only with the community as a whole as we see in examples from ancient Athens (fig. 197) and Europe of the recent era. Therefore, only when there was a need for a considerable expansion of the city, were new walls built at greater distances, which allowed for the creation of new communities between the old and new walls.

At the regional scale we find that the cities occupied the key locations; they were situated in the gravitational centres of the larger inhabited areas, and were surrounded by a small or large number of villages which more or less followed the hexagonal pattern. In cities or castles the highest density could be found within the walls. Close to them were densely built settlements quite large and important as compared to the other settlements of the entire area, since the city or castle was the heart and centre of defence of the whole system. It provided better protection for those who had settled near It. Further out, the settlements were smaller and poorer, and the entire pattern thinned out until near the boundaries of the feudal area there might be regions with no settlement at all —a no-man's-land which extended as far as the first settlements of the next feudal lord's area (fig. 198). In the case of cities the pattern did not need to weaken away from the centre; it could be quite normal regardless of the distance from the city.

Even though the era of static urban settlements was practically over by the seventeenth century, our descriptions and thoughts were still based on static settlements. It took us three centuries to recognise the birth and development of the dynamic settlements (fig. 199).

Dynamic urban settlements

The phase of dynamic urban settlements started in the seventeenth century and became apparent only a century later; in all probability, it will last for another 100 or 200 years until we reach the next phase—that of the universal settlement. In the dynamic urban phase settlements in space are characterised by continuous growth. Hence, all their problems are continuously intensified and new ones continuously created (fig. 200).

One of the new problems being created in this phase is that settlements, which up to now had occupied very small areas, are now coming to occupy very much larger ones, and, in so doing, are destroying Nature in many respects, eliminating fields and forests, levelling hills, either in the process of constructing the Shells or in the pursuit of building materials such as stone or timber. Water is beginning to be polluted not only inside the settlement, as might have happened before, but also outside it, and not only in springs but also in big rivers and lakes. Air is beginning to be contaminated, not only in a small part of the city, as might have happened previously, for short periods of time, but all over the city and

animals, for even though they may have a decentralised specialised function or a linear extension of a central function, they do not ever have a repetition of a central function at a different point in the organism. As far as I know, the cases in animals with more than one heart or brain fulfilling the same functions in other parts of the organism are limited to some very special cases such as the brontosaurus which had two brains but has not survived, and the hag fish with four hearts.

Most cities had a very definite form imposed by the limits set by the defensive walls surrounding them. When the city expanded, it did so in a definite form. Very often the expansion took place in one direction, in an organised way, as in the case of Athens in the first century A.D. at the time of Hadrian. At that time the city did not expand in a disorganised way creating thin layers of accretion all around it. The city was a cohesive human community and it could only expand by adding new sections similar to the whole, that is, by human communities. The fact that each expansion and addition had to be protected, promoted the cause of organised developments, which, to some extent, explains why this expansion took the

208

196

formation of the city   evolution of the core

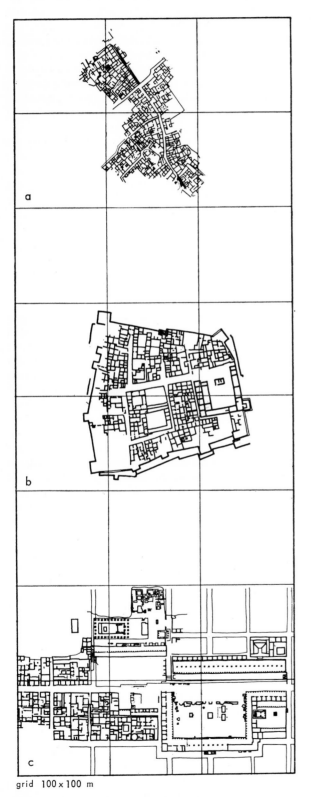

a

b

c

grid   100 x 100 m

Q

197

expansion of the static city   ancient Athens

☐ existing city in 5th century B.C.

▨ expansion under Hadrian A. D. 120 - 130

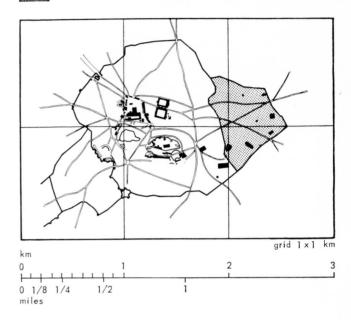

grid 1 x 1 km

km
0   1   2   3

0 1/8 1/4   1/2   1
miles

198

the feudal settlements   castles

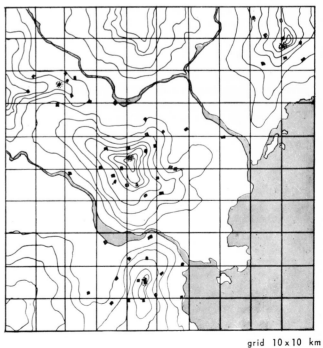

grid 10 x 10 km

km
0   10   20   30   40   50   60   70   80   90 100

0   10   20   30   40   50   60
miles

199

beginning of the urban era   cities (polis)

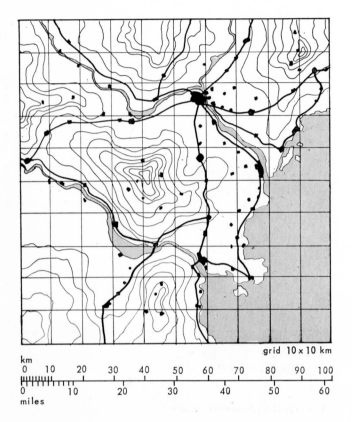

grid 10 x 10 km

km
0   10   20   30   40   50   60   70   80   90   100

0   10   20   30   40   50   60
miles

even in wide areas beyond it. Hence, whereas in the past settlements were well adjusted to the landscape, today they are quite maladjusted and have even become a threat to Nature. Professor McHarg says:

'With the emergence of the nineteenth century industrial city, there arose an agent certainly of comparable consequence, perhaps even of greater consequence, even more destructive of the physical environment and the balances of ecological communities in which man exists, than any of the prior human processes'.

and later:

'The large modern metropolis may be 30 miles in diameter. Much, if not all, of the land which it covers is sterilised. The micro-organisms in the soil no longer exist; the original animal inhabitants have largely been banished. Only a few members of the plant kingdom represent the original members of the initial ecology. The rivers are foul; the atmosphere is polluted; the original configuration of the land is only rarely in evidence; climate and micro-climate have retrogressed so that the external micro-climate is more violent than was the

case before the establishment of the city. Atmospheric pollution may be so severe as to account for 4,000 deaths in a single week of intense "fog", as was the case in London. Floods alternate with drought. Hydrocarbons, lead, carcenogenic agents, carbon dioxide, carbon monoxide concentrations, deteriorating conditions of atmospheric electricity—all of these represent retrogressive processes introduced and supported by man. The epidemiologist speaks of neuroses, lung cancer, heart and renal disease, ulcers, the stress diseases, as the badges of urban conditions. There has also arisen the spectre of the effects of density and social pressure upon the incidence of disease and upon reproduction. The modern city contains other life-inhibiting aspects whose effects are present but which are difficult to measure: disorder, squalor, ugliness, noise'.[14]

These urban settlements, in spite of the fact that they are spoiling Nature around them and hence provoking the protest of their inhabitants, continue to expand because of the action of all those suffering and protesting people. In expanding, the urban settlements become first metropolises, then, when they are larger, conurbations, and, very recently, the very large ones, megalopolises. Regardless of what specific name it is that we give these settlements, the names correspond to their dimensions, or to their structure; 'conurbation', for example, implies a new settlement created out of the merging of many others. In all our definitions of dynamic settlements based on form, structure and size, we have been overlooking one characteristic that completely differentiates them from previous types of urban settlements. These new urban settlements are growing continuously. They are dynamic settlements, created as a result of an industrial technological revolution, multiplying in number and form, and now being created at an even higher rate. The evils described in them are the evils of yesterday which are being multiplied today in a very dangerous manner. This is what makes the dynamic settlements completely different from any other category of settlements and a real threat to humanity itself.

Man is lost within his settlements. He has lost his balance with Nature and is losing his balance with himself and with Society, but he is not yet completely aware of this. Only a few people are finally beginning to be aware of the new problems. I will try to show how dangerous Man's position is in dynamic settlements by a simple graph, even though it has not been possible to obtain very accurate data for it. At the beginning of the Industrial Revolution an average western urban dweller spent his day in three basic ways: sleeping and resting for probably one-third of the day; working and learning for probably another third; and devoting the remaining third to recreation, relaxation and thought, mostly during the quiet hours of the afternoon and evening. This pattern changed, when a fourth major factor was introduced into his life. Today the citizen of a dynamic settlement spends probably the same amount of time sleeping and resting as before and he probably spends the same amount of time working

200

evolution of a Dynapolis   **London, England**

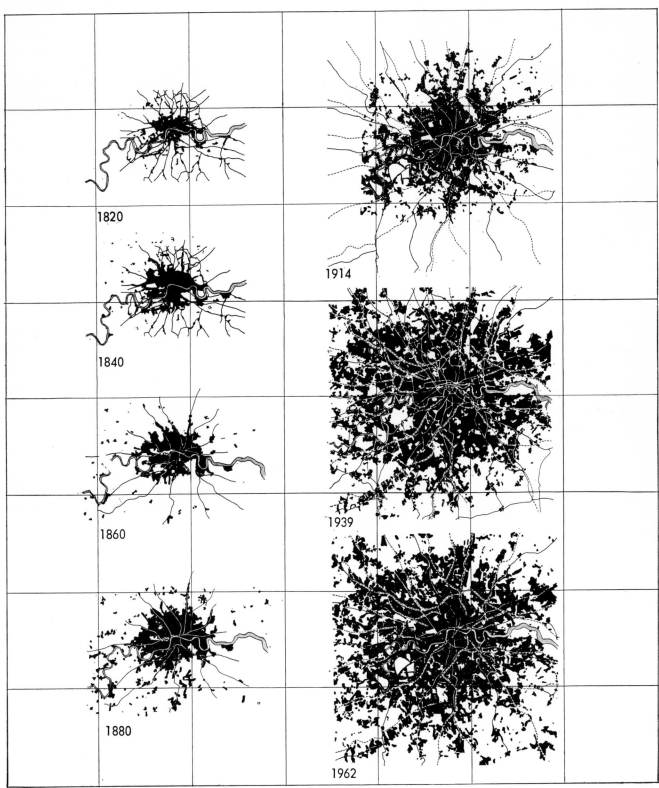

1820

1840

1860

1880

1914

1939

1962

grid   20 x 20   km

201

the use of time in a 24 hour week day by an average urban dweller

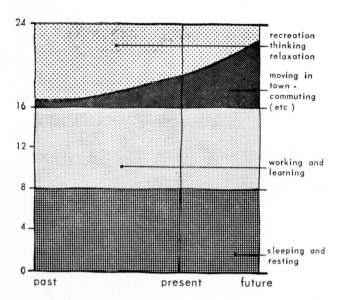

and learning, although a greater proportion of it has probably shifted to learning, since working hours have decreased and learning hours increased. But the remaining third of his time is no longer spent only for recreation, relaxation and thought. An increasing part of it, perhaps, one-third of that remaining time (one-ninth or one-tenth of the day), is being spent on transportation within the settlement. Where transportation once was a problem of the rural dweller, who sometimes had to spend an hour or more commuting to his field, his suffering seems small in comparison to that of the urban dweller today. By spending as much as two hours, or one-twelfth of his time, commuting between residence and work, residence and leisure, residence and education, Man is not only wasting the most precious time of his day—that left to him for living as a human being—but he is also spending this time in a miserable way, a way requiring his full attention and causing enormous strain; the result is that he also spoils a part of the hours dedicated to working and learning (think of the coffee a man needs when he reaches his office early in the morning in the urban area) as well as his recreation, relaxation and thinking time. And what is happening today will be even worse tomorrow, since we are living in dynamic settlements (fig. 201).

If we want to understand better how important this time is, we should not calculate it as a percentage of the total hours in a day, since a large number of them, two-thirds usually, is already committed to resting, sleeping and producing. What Man is actually left with is a third of his time, eight hours which he can call his own, and to spend

two hours of it commuting means losing 25 per cent of his free time. Seen in this way, any loss of time in commuting emerges in its real dimensions, and should be recognised as a definite danger for Man.

Activities within these dynamically growing settlements are much more complicated not only because of their size, but also because they are changing from year to year, practically from day to day, thus creating additional difficulties for Man who has to adjust himself to their great numbers and categories, and to the fast rate of their change.

Because of all the previously mentioned complications, the Shells of the settlement face an enormous variety of problems. Some of these will be discussed in greater detail in the following section, but it will be interesting to look into some general—if only external—characteristics of the evolution of settlements within a certain landscape. For this purpose I have selected several characteristics already used for the presentation of the overall pattern of development.

Let us begin with the first dynamic urban settlement—the early Dynapolis. This is the phase when small independent human settlements with independent administrative units are beginning to grow beyond their initial boundaries. From the economic point of view this development is related to industrialisation, and from the technological point of view to the railroad era, which first made commuting from distant points possible. For some countries, like England, this means the second half of the eighteenth century. For other countries it may only come in the second half of the twentieth century—the post-war period. By now, almost all countries (some with the achievement of their independence), have entered the phase of the first dynamic urban settlements, or the phase of the early Dynapolis. The city is breaking its walls and spreading into the countryside in a disorganised manner (fig. 202).

A few decades later, or, in some countries, only a few years later, early Dynapolis developed into the Dynapolis itself, which development coincided with further considerable industrial growth, and, in many cases, with the period when the railroad began to play an important part in suburban connections. In this phase the settlement expands in all directions, instead of spreading only along the railway lines creating new islands of dependent settlements around the railway stations, as during the phase of the early Dynapolis. During this era the phenomenon of the early Dynapolis spreads to include other centres which had formerly been minor urban or even rural centres. The Dynapolis radiates its influence affecting all settlements around it, and creating new islands of dynamic settlements which in turn radiate their influence to others. By the time the first city has become a fully-fledged Dynapolis, a dynamic evolution has started for many other settlements in the region (fig. 203).

The next phase is that of the metropolis, which usually incorporates several other urban and rural settlements of the surrounding area. This happens because the city has turned into a Dynapolis, which is the reason why no modern metro-

202

early Dynapolis

**expansion of the static city occurs when it becomes
the centre of larger political units**

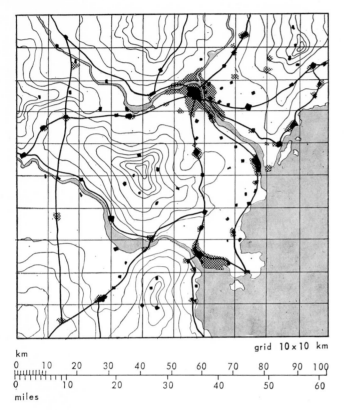

grid 10 x 10 km

km
0   10   20   30   40   50   60   70   80   90   100
miles
0   10   20   30   40   50   60

203

Dynapolis

expansion in the industrial and automobile era

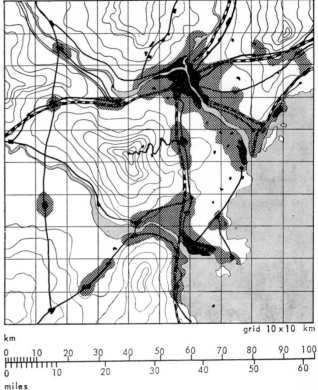

grid 10 x 10 km

km
0   10   20   30   40   50   60   70   80   90   100
miles
0   10   20   30   40   50   60

polis can again become a static city. The only metropolises which can be called static belong to previous eras, when cities sometimes did grow into larger units which, after a certain stage, could perhaps be called metropolises. This was, to a certain extent, true of ancient Rome in its last phases and of Byzantine Constantinople.

The few metropolises we know of from the past became static following a period of dynamic growth, then declined and died. Humanity was not prepared to deal with such complicated organisms. Indeed these two big metropolises of the ancient Western world—Rome and Constantinople—disintegrated to such a degree that the mobs in the streets became uncontrollable and sometimes succeeded in imposing their will on the government. From the economic, social, administrative or technological point of view, the fate of the historical metropolises has been dynamic growth, a static phase, and then death. Therefore, if we are to base our experience on the history of cities, we must recognise the fact that a static phase for a metropolis is the prelude of its decline and death. In such a case we should say rather that a dynamic

metropolis, after losing its momentum for growth, becomes negatively dynamic, taking its course towards decline and death, even though this transition may mean a short static phase in its life.

Present-day metropolises are all dynamic cities and have grown continuously after having reached the phase of the metropolis. London, with one million people at the beginning of the nineteenth century, was the first modern city to reach that size. It has continued to grow and now has more than ten million people in its area. It was a metropolis then and is a metropolis now. Or we should say rather that it is now a Dynametropolis, continuing its course towards becoming a megalopolis (fig. 204).

I know of no contemporary metropolis which is static, though there may be some which are not expanding now as much as they did in the past. This means that we should always call a metropolis a Dynametropolis to express the common characteristics it has with the Dynapolis, despite their difference in size. In practice there is no need to use the more systematic term *Dynametropolis*, but we should not forget

213

204

Dynametropolis

expansion in the industrial and automobile era

205

Dynamegalopolis within a very large political unit

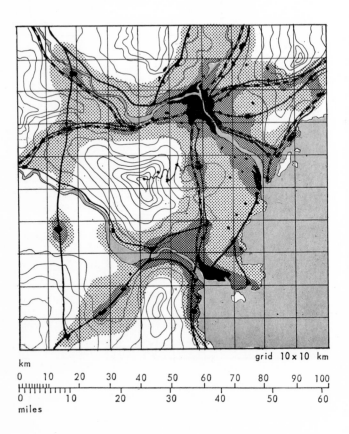

grid 10 x 10 km

km

0   10   20   30   40   50   60   70   80   90   100

0   10   20   30   40   50   60

miles

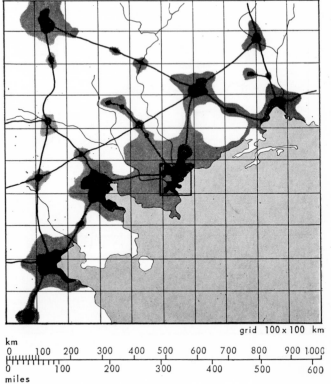

grid 100 x 100 km

km

0   100   200   300   400   500   600   700   800   900 1.000

0   100   200   300   400   500   600

miles

that every metropolis today is in fact a dynamic settlement. Today the creation of a typical modern metropolis does not coincide any more with the railroad era, as was the case with London and later with Paris, but with the automobile era, which is conducive to easier growth in all directions.

If we try to calculate the number of metropolises attributed to the effect of the railway and to the effect of the automobile, we will find the latter to be much greater, out of all proportion to the number of the former. We need only remember that many countries had no railway networks at all, or no real railways big enough to have an impact on their economy and physical structure, while today there is no country without automobiles. If we take any country, even a highly developed one, and compare its railway networks with the highway networks, we shall realise why a greater number of dynamic cities and metropolises owe their dynamic character to the automobile than to the railroad.

When a metropolis grows beyond certain limits, it absorbs all settlements close to it. These may be small or large, rural or urban. A broader urban organism is then formed which

extends far beyond the built-up parts of the metropolis itself. London today, two centuries after it became a metropolis of one million people, has a population of more than ten million and is still growing. If in the same area as a metropolis we have another major expanding settlement, as well as a number of small ones, the whole area tends to become one major Dynametropolis including many types of dynamic settlements growing in various ways and at different rates in several directions. An area of this sort develops a complicated, confused pattern, with several circulatory networks, several networks of facilities, and several types of land use, confused with each other and sometimes even working against each other. Unless the government takes action and buys land, thus acquiring control of large tracts, the whole area will tend to become impossibly confused, natural resources will be spoiled and gradually lost, and the pattern of habitation will lead to worse living conditions for Man.

Such an area on a large scale including more than one metropolis and many other urban settlements, has been called the megalopolis, and, following Jean Gottmann's

214

excellent analysis of the best known megalopolis in the world—the eastern coast of the United States—it has recently become recognised as a new form of settlement. This is a development of the twentieth century, for never before have we known of a megalopolis.[15]

We certainly have no reason to believe that any static megalopolis could possibly exist. We cannot refer to history, as we did for the metropolis, since there was no such thing as a megalopolis in the past. But for the same reasons that we cannot expect a metropolis to be static, we certainly cannot expect a megalopolis to be static. If it became static, it would mean that many of the characteristics of the civilisation which created the megalopolis have ceased to exist, hence drawing the megalopolis towards decline. By declining it remains a dynamic settlement, only in the negative sense. As things stand at present, we can only have a Dynamegalopolis, although for all practical purposes we may use the simpler term 'megalopolis', bearing in mind that by it we always mean a dynamic urban settlement of major dimensions. There are several areas now tending towards becoming a megalopolis. I have already mentioned the eastern coast of the U.S.A. from Boston to Washington D.C., an area six hundred miles long, with a surface of 53,576 sq. miles (138,762 km²). Other areas which show definite characteristics of a megalopolis are the Greater London area, the Great Lakes area of the U.S.A. and Canada, the central urban areas of the Netherlands and Belgium, the main region of the Rhine River, the Tokyo-Osaka region, the eastern coast of China, and to a minor degree, the extended areas of Paris, Los Angeles (or the southern Californian megalopolis), Moscow, etc.

A megalopolis has the same external characteristics as the metropolis, the only difference being that every phenomenon appears on a much larger scale. It is characteristic that although I could show all phenomena of the development of human settlements up to the metropolis on a 100 km² scale, I now have to change the scale to 1,000 km² in order to present the phenomena of the megalopolis (fig. 205).

Universal human settlement: Ecumenopolis

Regardless of whether dynamic settlements are simple (Dynapolises), or composite (metropolises and megalopolises), they have been growing continuously during the last centuries and this is apparent everywhere at present. It has even been intensified in speed and significance. Where is this leading us? Is this growth going to be checked or reduced? Is it going to continue, and if so, will it lead to a phase in which the whole Earth will be covered by one human settlement? These are questions which we must investigate so as to be able to foresee the next phase in the evolution of human settlements.

We must begin by investigating the major problem concerning humanity today: the population explosion, which will definitely be the most decisive factor in the next phase of human settlements. Every problem related to settlements in recent years has had its root in the population explosion. How long is this explosion going to continue? Where is it leading? Trends so far show that the rates of growth are increasing and even accelerating (fig. 206). Before answering any other question, we must look at the problem of how large a population can possibly survive.

In the opinion of population experts, it is quite probable that the population of the Earth—now 3.3 billion—will be somewhere between 6.5 and 7 billion at around the end of this century. According to one estimate, by A.D. 2100 it will be about 25 billion, and then it will begin to stabilise. There is a considerable probability, however, that the rate of increase might be even faster, in which case the population will reach the figure of 25 billion long before A.D. 2100. It is just possible that this will happen a century from now, let us say around A.D. 2060, so that the population might reach a 50 billion plateau before the end of the next century (fig. 207).

Richard L. Meier speaks of 30 to 80 billion people as the limit,[16] and the studies of the Athens Technological Institute indicate 40 to 60 billion.[17] Some estimates even place the world's population at 100 billion or more by the end of the century. It seems, however, that it is neither too optimistic nor too pessimistic to assume that a levelling off will take place at some point between 20 and 50 billion, and that this is likely to happen in the second part of the twenty-first century. Limitations of water and energy as well as food, which are likely to be the most serious restraints on such a population explosion, seem to be compatible with those estimates of a stabilisation level.

We should note that even under the most conservative estimates, and even if effective policies of birth control are implemented, the population of the Earth will be more than 12 billion a hundred years from now. Since it is not very likely that such policies will be implemented immediately and everywhere, humanity may well reach a minimum of 20 to 30 billion people a century from now, and 50 to 60 billion people before the end of the next century. It is therefore reasonable to assume for all practical purposes that sometime between 2060 and 2100 the population of the Earth will be around 35 billion people and it may stabilise itself at that level.

Several diagrams of population growth trends show rates of increase reaching their maximum half a century from now, and then decreasing till, towards the end of the next century, they become negligible. This would mean that the population of the Earth, after going through an even greater explosion than the present one, would probably be stabilised at a level of several billion people. If this is so, we may expect another phase of equilibrium between the population and the total resources of the Earth, an equilibrium that would tend to be maintained. Any major evolution in human knowledge, or

**annual population growth rates by settlement sizes
expressed in number of inhabitants**

━━━━━ assumption : 20 billion Ecumenopolis in A.D. 2060

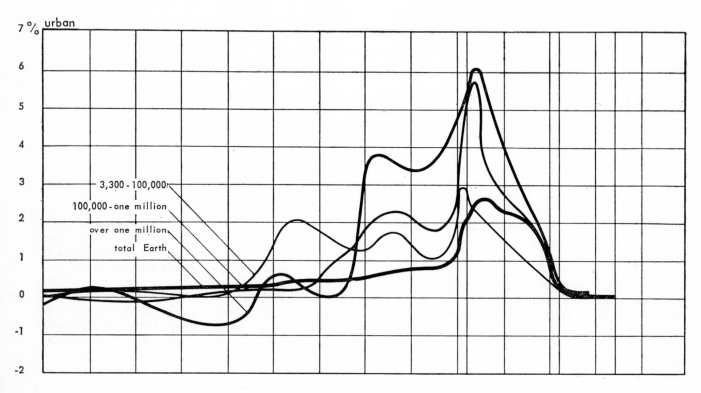

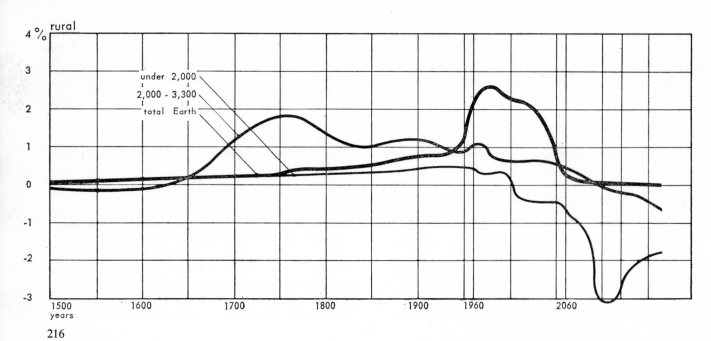

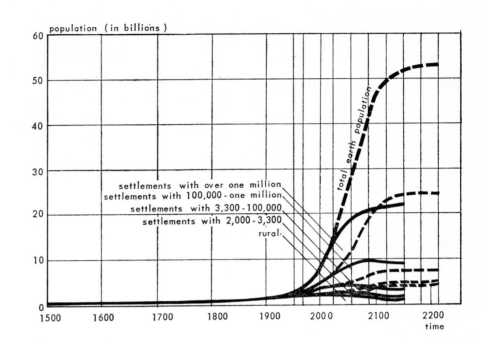

total Earth population and settlement sizes expressed in number of inhabitants

population (in billions)

settlements with over one million
settlements with 100,000 - one million
settlements with 3,300 - 100,000
settlements with 2,000 - 3,300
rural

total earth population

assumption : 50 billion
Ecumenopolis in A.D. 2120
assumption : 20 billion
Ecumenopolis in A.D. 2060

time

in the relationships with other inhabited worlds, might once again upset this equilibrium, but such an eventuality cannot be foreseen today.

The growth of the total world population has been moving at an increasing rate, especially from 1650 onwards. This rate suddenly accelerated in the twentieth century, and its peak may come somewhere near the end of the first half of the twenty-first century. The growth of the rural population, which rose slowly for several hundred years, has levelled off and has been declining since the first part of the twentieth century. As a result, the growth of the city population has been rising at a much higher rate and will reach a maximum rate of over five per cent a year around the turn of the century.

From these curves it is apparent that the increase in urban population will be vastly greater than that of the rural population, which means an even greater shift of the world population into urban areas. Projecting these trends, we can foresee that the present ratio, which is 45 per cent urban and 55 per cent rural the world over, will likely change to a ratio of 95.0 per cent and 5.0 per cent respectively, a hundred years from now. On the same basis, we can forecast that at the end of the next century, 98 per cent of the population will be living in urban settlements, and 2 per cent will be living in minor settlements oriented towards agricultural production. The latter, however, will also have many of the characteristics

of the urban population, since production will be completely mechanised and even the agricultural settlements will actually be overhauling bases for mechanical equipment.

We must now think of the impact of the predicted population growth on human settlements. We know that since we have acquired mechanical means of transportation, the ratio of the built-up or settled area to the urban population has been increasing at a much faster rate than the growth of that population. All signs indicate that this will continue for many decades. If so, the total area of the settlements of the future will be much more than ten times larger than the present area (i.e. enlarged by the same coefficient as the population) and maybe thirty, forty or even fifty times as large.

If this happens—and we have no reason to suppose that it will not—it will mean that the trend leading from connected cities to metropolises and metropolises to megalopolises will continue. Thus, it is quite probable that all settlements will become interconnected to form a continuous system covering the inhabitable Earth. We call this continuous settlement the Universal City, or *Ecumenopolis*.

After reaching the conclusion that we are tending towards the creation of a universal settlement or Ecumenopolis, we must understand this new type of settlement as clearly as we can. As we have seen, humanity took many thousands of years to move into the era of large dynamic urban settlements.

The correct study of such an evolution, may enable us to predict the formation of the Ecumenopolis.

When trying to visualise the Ecumenopolis, we should not consider that we are only dealing with a settlement of the future, since even though it will be completed in the future, we are already witnessing its birth in several parts of the world. The growing dynamic megalopolis is but a characteristic area of concentration of urban functions, whose expansion will cover larger areas to be eventually connected with the areas of other megalopolises, thus heading towards the Ecumenic or universal city.

So we can speak about the Ecumenopolis which, excluding major disaster such as world nuclear war or a great reduction of the world population caused by an unexpected disease, will inevitably take shape. Certainly if effective birth control policies were adopted world-wide the universal settlement might never be completed in all its branches. If however, we assume that a major war will be avoided, and that birth control policies will be implemented only at a gradual rate, then we can be fairly certain that the world will witness the formation of the Ecumenopolis. Therefore, since the Ecumenopolis is already beginning to take shape, and since the trends it will follow are similar to those which led to the formation of the metropolis and the megalopolis, we should attempt to visualise this greatest of all human cities.

If we try to visualise Ecumenopolis on the same scale as our previous diagrams, we will find it to consist of a continuous urban system interspersed with smaller or larger areas for cultivation. The picture has been reversed. While in the past settlements were isolated spots within the countryside, in the future the open areas will be isolated within an urban system. These open areas, however (some of which will serve solely for cultivation and some, such as parks and green areas, will maintain their natural vegetation), will be much larger than were the earlier urban settlements.

We are entering a new phase of urban settlements, the phase of the one large urban settlement which will establish an ecological equilibrium with the rest of the world. The shape of Ecumenopolis will be conditioned by the formation of the ground (mainly on the plains), by water resources (its basic parts will be where ample water resources exist) and by climate. Beyond its limits there will be very small settlements, some urban and some rural, surviving in the remote mountain or desert areas much as remote rural settlements and even nomadic settlements survive in the present era of dynamic cities. Because there will no longer be emigration into this ecumenic settlement but only migration between its parts, and because there will be no population increase, since we have assumed a levelling off of the population curve, the total ecumenic settlement will be static. So the next one-hundred to two-hundred years may well be the last years of dynamic settlements. Indeed the rate of urban expansion may even start to decrease within the next fifty to one-hundred years, and its total expansion may be completed by the end of the twenty-first century. From then on we shall be in a

218

208

Ecumenopolis as a dying city

the centres receive higher pressures, but they cannot expand any more along the white arrows

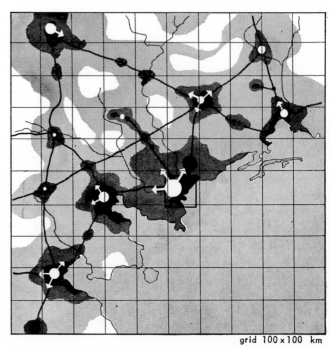

grid 100 × 100 km

km
0   100   200   300   400   500   600   700   800   900   1000

0   100   200   300   400   500   600
miles

period of amelioration and continuous renewal of existing settlements.

Though there is not enough data to justify these conclusions in detail, they are as a whole logical enough; and we cannot afford to wait a few generations to be convinced of the truth of each prediction. Indeed, we cannot even afford to remain inactive until all studies on Dynapolis, Dynametropolis and megalopolis are completed. This work will take decades, and by then it will be too late to start, for we will be in the midst of the problems of the Ecumenopolis.

I repeat, the Ecumenopolis is already beginning to take shape and if we do not intervene actively, it may take shape as a city bearing in its very roots the elements of death. It will inevitably expand over the Earth, it will cover greater areas, and these areas will exercise enormous pressures on the existing nuclei of cities. Because of these pressures, existing cities which will still constitute the basic nuclei of the multi-nuclei Ecumenopolis, may die a slow death. So Ecumenopolis may be born as a dying city, since the slow death of its many centres will affect the total body (fig. 208). But this death is not inevitable. Some methods by which it can be avoided will appear in the following chapters. In all probability humanity will act in time to avoid this fate. After all, even this book is inspired by the faith that a solution can be found, and represents one of the actions being taken in search of it.

Time dimension

Such a review of the history of human settlements in an attempt to present a theory of their evolution raises the question of the fourth dimension as an important factor in the life and study of human settlements. This is particularly the case during the present phase of dynamic settlements. It is, therefore, useful to explore the problems related to the time dimension in order to understand the situation better.

First there is the problem of time as a practical dimension. In this regard we may draw a parallel with the pictorial arts. Painting is two-dimensional and sculpture three-dimensional. Both can theoretically exist outside of time; theoretically they both exist in an infinitesimal fraction of time. Architecture cannot exist without the time dimension, as architectural space is an expression of Ekistic space on its micro-scale. Such space does not exist unless it can be inhabited, unless people can move in it. In order to understand, to sense architectural and Ekistic space, people need time. The larger the space, the more time required for its understanding. We cannot circumvent this issue by saying that with mechanical means we can now cross space at a much higher speed. If we do so, we are minimising the importance of its physical dimensions: if we pass over the Acropolis of Athens in a jet, the Acropolis of Athens no longer exists as far as our senses are concerned. The Acropolis was built for Man to walk on, and it must be seen within this frame, Man's time dimension. The important conclusion we must draw is that in the synthesis of architectural and Ekistic space time is an indispensable dimension that was taken into consideration in its creation, and we should therefore come into contact with each space on the same time scale. We cannot imagine visiting the Piazza de la Signoria in Florence by bus. Regardless of whether buses are allowed to shatter its scale, we must visit it on foot. In the same way we cannot walk on a 100 mile-an-hour highway, it would be comparable to seeing a film in slow motion. Not only would our life be threatened by cars, but we would be out of our scale. We would be confused by the image of swiftly moving cars and bored to death by the slowly moving image of the landscape, which in the better-designed highways exists only for the driver going at a normal car speed.

A second question is related to the first, but goes beyond practical questions of time into a purely aesthetic interpretation of architectural synthesis. This question asks why cities and parts of cities built over many periods are more lively than cities, or parts of cities, completed in a single period. Why is the Roman forum harder, less plastic, than the Greek agora? Why are even such important squares as the Piazza di Campidoglio in Rome, designed and built by Michelangelo, much harder as an expression than other piazzas of the Renaissance which grew by phases and which were created by more than one architect, such as the Piazza di San Marco in Venice?

When we view such architectural space and do not find it as naturally attractive as that which has grown gradually, are we not being bothered by the fact that behind it all is one person, one strong will which created the space in question? Is it possible that one spirit, one will, creating such a space, loses in the synthesis the ability to incorporate the notion of time so physically or metaphysically indispensable to Man? Can this be an explanation for the fact that such a synthesis is not as satisfactory as the other? Is it necessary for Man to see his Ekistic space reveal itself gradually? And is this a natural characteristic of Man, or is it an acquired one, due to the fact that Man has always lived in habitats which have been developed gradually by collective human forces; are we, therefore, perhaps subconsciously, rejecting the idea of a synthesis inspired and realised at one stroke? These questions boil down to one basic one: is the time factor indispensable to an Ekistic synthesis, not only because Ekistic space is four-dimensional, but also because Man needs to feel it as four-dimensional? And regardless of the answer, is the Man of the future going to feel the same about these questions as the Man of the present and past? I do not know the answer. I can only draw our attention to these facts, as I have done once before in my book *Architecture in Transition*.[18]

When speaking of time, we must also face the question of the length of the life of human settlements. If we consider them a species which are born, develop, decline and die, how long does this process take? I must give an answer which shows that, unlike plants and animals, human settlements have no pre-determined life. Their elements, however, may have a pre-determined life. A house has a certain life-span which can be prolonged or shortened depending on its maintenance, as is the case with plants and animals; but this cannot go beyond certain limits unless maintenance is interpreted to mean a gradual replacement of all its parts, in which case it can theoretically live forever. This, however, is not the normal provision for a house or a building. On the other hand, it is normal for composite human settlements, villages, cities, Dynapolises, etc., which consist of many elements with different life-spans, to undergo continuous maintenance and continuous renewal. Therefore, they can theoretically live forever, or at least as long as it is considered useful for them to be maintained.

So, unlike plants and animals, human settlements can live forever if Man wills it. This has not happened up to now mainly because the continuously changing structure of the economy and the changing social and political situation in the world have been forcing the Ekistic systems and human settlements to change their location, role, shape and size, and in the process many have been eliminated, or when they have remained, their Shells have been eliminated and rebuilt. There are thousands of settlements, some well known and some unknown, which have lived for many centuries and which have probably been practically the same for long periods in history, although some elements of the Shells may have changed.

In practice, the life of human settlements seems to depend on the conditions of their creation and the length of time during which conditions related to their creation can remain the same. It is not possible to generalise on what this has meant until now in actual terms of years, although we can estimate that it has meant a life-span of a few decades for temporary settlements, centuries for permanent ones, and millennia for a very few. This is valid only as a statement of what has happened until now, but it is based on such a short span of the total time of evolution (ten to twelve thousand years maximum for small rural settlements and no more than six thousand years for urban ones) that it is not possible for us to take it as an indispensable rule for the future. We should not forget that:

- the life span of some settlements is long for the period of our experience—we have not had enough time to witness any phases of succession of one settlement by another in order to be able to draw conclusions about the evolution of all types of settlements;
- we are still near the beginning of the history of dynamic settlements which may prove of revolutionary importance for many problems related to human settlements as well as to their life span.

At this point we must repeat: the first phase of primitive non-organised human settlements lasted for an unknown period of time, of the order of several hundreds of thousands of years at a maximum and several tens of thousands of years at a minimum. The second period of primitive organised settlements lasted for 10,000–12,000 years. The third period of static cities lasted 5,000–6,000 years. The fourth period, that of dynamic cities, has lasted only two centuries, and may last a maximum of four centuries, while we do not know anything about the fifth period. It is interesting, however, to note that the time-spans of the first four categories become progressively shorter. What does this mean? Might it not mean that we are heading towards a period of maturity, during which, perhaps after passing through another class of settlements, we may find ourselves in a phase of stable conditions? Does this not point to the Ecumenopolis towards which we are heading?

Also if we count the different categories of settlements, we find that the primitive organised ones are still the great majority; the urban static ones are few, and the dynamic ones even fewer. This is another hint of where the trends lead: first to an even smaller number of larger settlements, and finally to a single one (fig. 209). However, if we look at the corresponding graph showing the numbers of their inhabitants, we will see the increasing role of the population in the larger settlements, and finally the emerging Ecumenopolis, which, together with its branches, probably will absorb the majority of the population of the Earth.

I would like to close this topic of the possible life span of human settlements by referring to a story I heard from the nomads in the deserts of the Middle East. Once upon a time a saint came to this Earth and found himself in the middle of a big desert. He saw a caravan coming towards him; he waited, and stopped its leader, asking him how long the desert had been there. The leader, without thinking, said that his father, grandfather, great grandfather and all his ancestors had crossed this desert, guiding the camel caravans. 'So', he said, 'this desert had always been there'. The saint came back to exactly the same location a thousand years later and found himself at the crossroads of a big city. He stopped a passer-by and asked him how long this city had been at this location. The man answered that he himself, his father, his grandfather and all his ancestors had been born and were active as merchants right in that city. 'So', he said, 'this city had always been there', and he left in a hurry. Finally, a thousand years later, the saint returned to exactly the same location and found himself in the middle of a thick forest. He saw a woodcutter passing by, stopped him, and upon asking how long the forest had been there, received the same answer: the woodcutter and his father, his grandfather, and all his ancestors had been woodcutters in that same forest, so, the forest had always been there; then the woodcutter went on his way.

This story impressed me the first time I heard it as being very illuminating—a wise story. What it means for me is that, although Man considers all natural elements eternal and settlements as a permanent part of Nature, in fact both Nature in its expressions on the skin of this Earth, and the settlements, are changing. On the human scale they seem eternal; on the eternal scale they seem ephemeral. There is a second conclusion, though, which is also quite important. The story implies that there is a change of major features, including the settlements, every thousand years. This is not bad for a story, since, although we have no exact calculations, it is quite probable that the average settlement has had a life lasting perhaps a thousand years. And, as a final conclusion: settlements have come and gone for the last few thousand years; and their evolution has not lasted long enough to allow us to draw general conclusions about their life-span. But we can probably come to the conclusion that we are heading towards a new era of human settlements which may well be quite different from that of the past. Some day, some centuries from now, people looking back may consider the whole evolution with which we are so concerned merely a preface to the large human settlement covering the entire Earth. We may well be living in a period the whole importance of which is to prepare Man to live in the universal settlement to come.

total population of the Earth by categories of human settlements

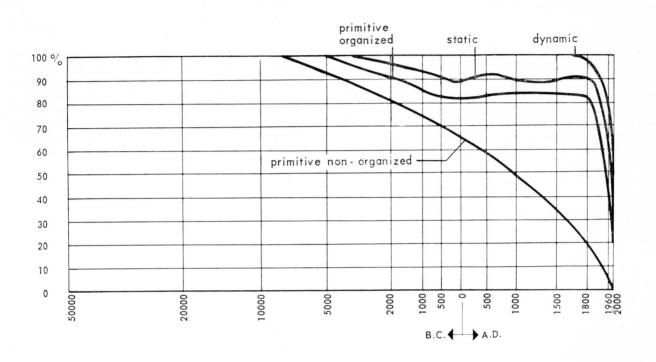

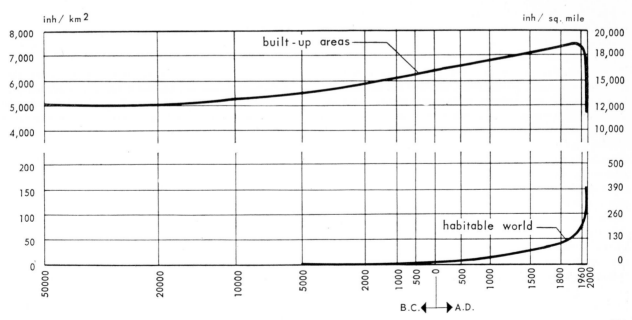

DEVELOPMENT AND EVOLUTION OF SYSTEMS

Systems of the past

○ *Process of initial settlement*

Following what I said on the present conditions of systems in Ekistic Analysis (Chapter Three) and the formation of Ekistic systems, I will give some more examples leading to a better understanding of the problems of Ekistic systems and regions of the past, an understanding vital to the study of the Nature and problems of the dynamic regions we are beginning to be faced with today.

We usually have two types of movements of people leading to the formation of new settlements. The one is a natural movement from the mountains to the plains, and the sea, from rural settlements to urban ones, from smaller urban settlements to major ones, in exactly the same way as water flows from high to low ground, from small rivers into big ones. This is the natural movement leading to civilisation through a normal process in which Nature recedes and Man takes over. The other movement is the opposite one; it can be observed in times of decreasing security when people retreat to minor settlements in the mountains, or move into rural territory, the cultivation of which has been abandoned or never previously undertaken. This type of movement requires a pressing situation in order to take place and great skill to be successful.

When settlers first enter a new region, they always try to select the most favourable area for their first installation. This is the first phase in the creation of an Ekistic system. When the settlers were hunters, they would select a central area of hunting grounds as well-protected as possible. When they were farmers, they would select a central area of the best fields, again as well-protected as possible. When they were tradesmen, they would select an area favourable to trade. When conditions were not safe and the deciding factor was security, each group would select the safest locality closest to the one which would have been selected under normal conditions.

This suggests that there were two poles of interest for settlers: the most favourable area for the normal functioning of the settlement and the most favourable area from the point of view of security. On the basis of the first criterion, an evaluation of every locality would show that there are localities satisfying this criterion fully, and others satisfying it to a lesser degree. The same would be the case on the basis of the second criterion, that of security. If conditions were completely unsafe, the combination would be one leading to maximum security, even if that meant little realisation of the first condition of function. When conditions were completely safe, the criterion of safety would be overlooked and action

would be taken on the basis of the first criterion. And when conditions were relatively safe, a combination of the two criteria would lead to the selection of the locality. Several cases illustrate this pattern. A characteristic example is the West African coast, where European traders settled to organise the slave trade and later to exploit the mines and the natural wealth of the area. The criterion for the selection of an area in the first case was easy access from the sea to a hinterland with inhabitants who could be obtained fairly easily. If the place became unsafe, a fortress was built; when natural resources, and not the slave trade, were of greater importance, settlements were built as close as possible to their sources.

The success of the initial settlement was determined by many factors and especially by the degree of resistance of the surrounding area to the new settlement. This is why the success of settlements built on islands was more attainable than that of those neighbouring a wide hinterland from which all sorts of threats could develop. This explains perhaps why the island of Aegina just 29 km. (18 miles) off the coast of Athens could develop into a strong city-state many years before Athens (fig. 210), and also the fact that Crete—and of course we are now speaking of a different scale—could develop a civilisation before the continental part of Greece and, as a matter of fact, Europe (fig. 211).

Initial settlement was followed by a second wave of settlers. Those who were friendly with the previous settlers and interested in the same functions settled in the second best location, usually close to the first. If the function was urban, the second wave could be added to the first within the same urban settlement. But if the settlement was rural, a new rural community came into being next to the first one, which meant that although their external surfaces were in direct contact, the nucleus of the new community was at a distance from the original one equal to the diameter of the normal agricultural community. If the new settlers were hostile to the original ones, they would settle at a distant location, regardless of whether or not it was the second best from the point of view of the functions they were interested in. Otherwise, the only alternative would be to fight for the best location.

These processes led to several types of Ekistic systems. The first was based on one central settlement from which several other settlements spread out. When the pattern was rural, it meant a continuous system of rural settlements gradually covering the entire plain (fig. 212). When the entire pattern was urban, this meant first the creation of an initial small urban settlement, then its growth and development, and finally the creation of other urban settlements at distances imposed by their functions and their relations to the initial one (fig. 213).

This was what happened when colonisation was organised and carried out on the basis of a pre-conceived plan. When the ancient Greek cities of the sixth century B.C. decided to create a new colony, they would conceive of it as an urban settlement which was in many ways a small replica of the

210

the city state on an island develops before the mainland

Aegina and Athens

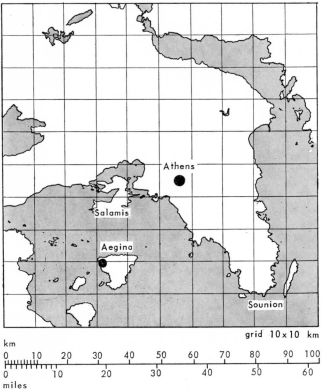

grid 10 x 10 km

km
0   10   20   30   40   50   60   70   80   90   100

0   10   20   30   40   50   60
miles

211

the island of Crete develops a civilisation earlier than Greece

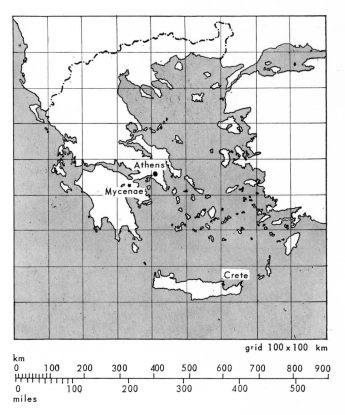

grid 100 x 100 km

km
0   100   200   300   400   500   600   700   800   900

0   100   200   300   400   500
miles

mother-city or, as the Greeks called it, the 'metropolis'. In a way this was similar to the process of growth of a live cell—it divides itself into two cells which develop independently.

In the next phase the settlement tended to expand over the entire region. This could only happen when the region was homogeneous. Then, the pattern would be a regular one. In the case of rural settlements, it would be a normal rural hexagonal pattern, while in the case of urban settlements it would be an urban hexagonal pattern or a mixed one.

If the second settlement was created by people unfriendly to those of the original one, there would be a distance between them. If the distance was large, there would be no conflict of vital space between the settlements, and both could survive. However, when both grew, a clash would be inevitable, leading either to war and the submission of one settlement, or to a collaboration and the formation of a broader system. Very often the systems passed through both stages. This process has taken place both in rural and urban settlements.

The formation of such systems and patterns has up to now been explained on the basis of the assumption of normal

homogeneous conditions in the whole area. When conditions are heterogeneous—which in rural areas means the existence of both fertile and infertile soil, or areas suitable for cultivation and others suitable for cattle-breeding or other functions—the patterns are not as regular as have been shown, but the process of development of the regional settlement is the same. When the conditions are unsafe, again the patterns developed are not regular, but the process does not change. We have taken into consideration variations due to the basic functions of rural or urban settlements, to the existing security conditions, and to the broader existing conditions of Nature, Man, Society, Shells and Networks. We can now see that Ekistic systems can develop in new areas in accordance with many patterns depending on many combinations of the above variables. In order to understand the development in new areas, we must understand that in all these cases the process remains the same. In practice the situation is even more complicated, since there are more factors and more variations of these factors to be taken into consideration. For example, the assumption of the existence of wholly urban settlements is an oversimplification,

223

212

formation of rural Ekistic systems

213

formation of urban Ekistic systems

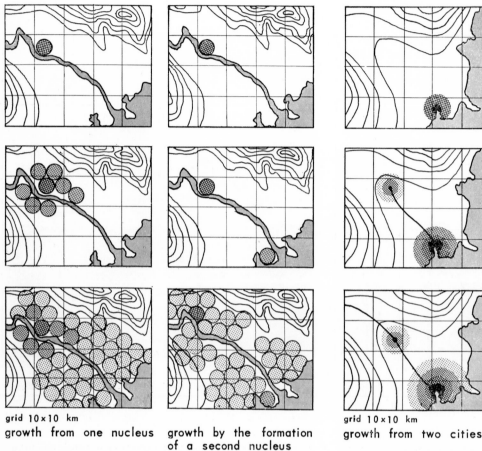

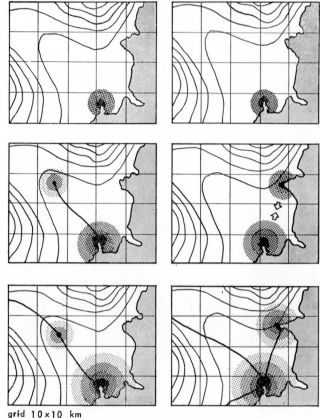

grid 10 x 10 km

growth from one nucleus   growth by the formation
of a second nucleus

grid 10 x 10 km

growth from two cities

since rural and urban elements may co-exist, which is very often the case in the second stage of development. Then there are settlements of special functions, such as transportation, or military centres, or educational, cultural and other settlements, intermixed with the previous types. Regardless of how many factors and how many variables we have, it is important to know what the process is, for it is only on this basis that we can hope to understand the evolution of an area in the first stages of settlement.

In this whole process, I do not believe there is a conscious creation of regional systems on the basis of any well-conceived theory and pattern. While the individual action of each person or even group of persons forming one community is in every instance conscious and justified (since otherwise the new settlement would not survive), the overall pattern is not the result of conscious action on the part of the community.

This does not mean that we have never had systems of

settlements developed on the basis of a deliberately conceived pattern. We cannot say, for example, that the colonisation of many parts of the Mediterranean coast by the ancient Greeks or that of several areas in the Middle East by Alexander the Great, or of several new provinces by the Roman Empire, did not take place on the basis of conscious plans of greater or lesser importance, some covering small, others large areas.

To these examples we should add more recent ones, such as the colonisation of the American West, which followed a pattern imposed by geographic, economic and political conditions, but which was not based on any broader pre-conceived plan. In a different category, we can mention the colonisation of broader areas by the great Moguls in India and Pakistan, not only by way of the towns they created, but with the transportation stations they founded along their roads as well. The colonisation of the Indian peninsula by the British can be classified in a similar category, since most of the new settlements they created were an expansion of the

224

existing transportation networks. No important settlements were created by the deliberate action of British invading forces. All large and successful settlements are expansions resulting from the growth of old ones, like so many of the cantonment towns and, more characteristically, the city of New Delhi. On the other hand, some new settlements have been created, by invading forces on new land never before settled, which were failures in spite of their very important architectural form. The most characteristic example in this category is the administrative city of Fatehpur-Sikri in India, whose abandoned, majestic and impressive ruins are a monument both to architectural imagination and to the ignorance of Ekistic rules concerning the importance of selecting a location in relation to an Ekistic system and to water resources.

There were also periods during which new settlements in rural areas were formed either by the expansion of a nation to include previously non-inhabited areas, or by the conquest of land previously covered by water, or a desert being irrigated for the first time. In such cases the rural settlements were quite often created on the basis of a system of simple rules, such as that of one market town to serve a certain number of villages, and one village to serve a defined area.

But although the authorities fixed the number of locations for urban settlements and the locations for rural settlements, there was no overall pattern determining the exact location of these settlements on the land. This is why we do not find normal relationships such as we can find in areas developed in a natural way. And this is why such areas do not function as well as those which have developed naturally. More often the shapes are rectangular, especially when the authority in charge of the settlement distributed the land on the basis of a grid-iron system (which may make little sense in most of the cases of a regional pattern), or where the prevailing consideration was the formation of an irrigation system. While it is certainly natural for a good irrigation system to influence the overall Ekistic pattern, it is not natural to have a pattern developed solely on the basis of it. This has happened in several cases where the decision was made by experts who understood only the problem of irrigation, and not the overall problem of human settlements.

○ *Planned settlements*

As far as we know, in almost all the previously mentioned cases, physical planning, when it existed, was limited to town and city plans; and even these plans were not always man-made. Very often the settlers, especially in rural settlements, were led to create the nucleus of their settlement alone, the interest of the authority settling them being limited to the distribution of the farming land, and not to the selection of the nucleus or the location of the built-up settlement, or to its formation. The only case we know of in which physical planning went beyond the creation of one urban settlement was

214

Athens and its port Piraeus were connected by long walls in the fifth century B.C.

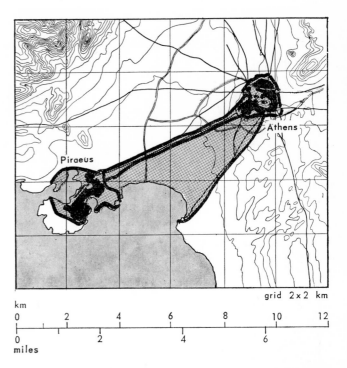

in ancient cities like Athens and Megara for reasons of defence. Athens was connected with its own harbour city, Piraeus, in 478 B.C., by long walls; in this way, the connection of the two settlements—the one as a central location in the land and the other covering a central location by the sea—was expressed physically. This physical connection lasted about 74 years, for in the year 404 B.C., the end of the Peloponnesian war, these Long Walls were destroyed following the defeat of Athens; so the best physical expression of a regional plan ceased to exist (fig. 214).

○ *Changing systems*

Throughout human history, because of changes in Man, Society, or economic activity, the patterns of Ekistic systems have changed. One change occurred in Europe during the transition from feudalism to national states; another when the national states developed an industrial economy. These changes can help us understand the Ekistic structure of many regions in Europe, and to some extent in Africa and Asia as well, since parts of these continents are now undergoing similar changes to those Europe experienced a few centuries ago. The basic characteristic of a feudal Ekistic system was great density at the centre of every feudal region, then

R

old and new patterns of regional distribution of settlements

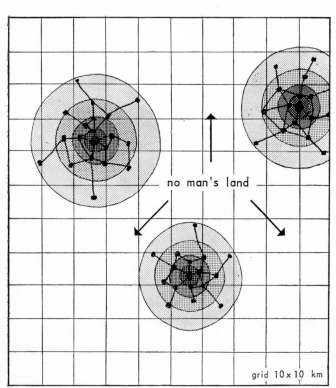

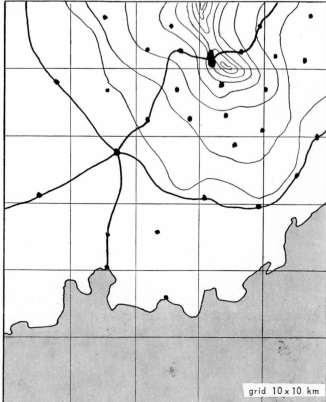

pattern of isolated states

in more primitive patterns the castle or city is in a relatively more secure position

progressively lower densities until near the borderline of the region, a no man's land was reached leading to another feudal region. These feudal regions formed isolated states (fig. 215).

From feudalism, European Man moved to the nation states, each of which incorporated many feudal domains. This meant that conditions of security were spread over wider areas and the density of settlement tended to become more equal in all its parts. This sometimes meant the abandonment, or at least the decline, of certain old feudal settlements which were no longer in positions of importance on the new systems (fig. 216). When European development proceeded to the phase of industrial technology, settlements began to grow rapidly either close to the existing central locations or close to new central locations, often causing the previous central locations to decline. The enlargement of a network of highways or railways has often meant the transference of a regional centre and a decline of the old ones.

Some changes can affect a whole region and completely upset the original patterns of its settlements. This has happened in areas which changed from a nomadic to an

industrial economy (as has happened in several new countries), or in areas where the security conditions have been completely altered. In some Greek islands, for example, the whole pattern of settlements was based on the fact that for many centuries, there was no security in the surrounding sea; therefore, the whole system of settlements had to depend on fortresses on the coastal area or, if this was not practicable, the settlements grew on locations far from the sea. In the latter case, the main settlement or settlements could be found at the farthest distance from the sea and the minor ones closer to the sea, but never on the actual coastal area, always a certain distance from it. Even when the people were cultivating a valley opening out to the sea, their settlements were built a certain distance inland, since they needed a breathing space in which to organise their defence when pirates or enemies landed on the coast (fig. 217).

A movement from the plains to the mountains, which is another such reversal of the more natural movement from mountains to the sea, takes place not only because of human enemies but also because of mosquitoes carrying malaria. Under this threat the settlements in plains are abandoned

216

old and new patterns of regional distribution of settlements

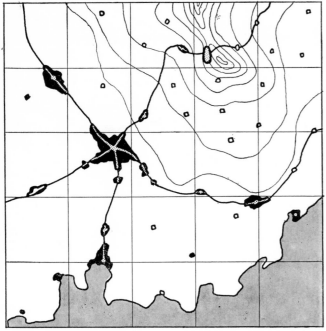

a. in more recent patterns new major cities are created and the older ones decline

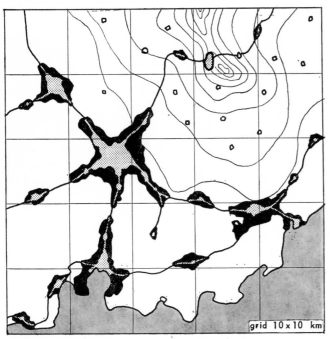

grid 10 x 10 km

b. the expanding major settlements incorporate the older ones

and replaced by those on the mountains (fig. 218).

Similar conditions existed in many areas of the world being threatened by alien armies. In such cases, the people of the plains went to the mountains leaving only small (if any) settlements in the plains. When security was re-established, the pattern changed once again. The main settlements of the islands descended to the sea; the inland settlements descended to the plains, and only minor ones were left on the mountains. These transfers did not take place overnight, but very slowly due to the great investment each settlement carries, an investment in economic, cultural, historic and sentimental terms that creates in the population an inertia, a reluctance to make a change.

Once a settlement has been created, people have invested so much in it that a very strong counter-attraction would be necessary to make them abandon their ties with the existing settlements. Experience has shown that major changes tend to take place in regional Ekistic patterns in the first generation after the cause of the change, and that this change is usually completed in a maximum of three generations, though sometimes, it is completed within one generation. The speed depends on the rate at which investment of new effort can take place so that the abandonment of the old investment can be justified. And the period of change during which the pattern shows the greatest difference from the past is the generation after the new pattern has been created, since this coincides with the period when the new generation, which has no strong ties with the old settlements, takes over the decision-making.

New forces

Recent years, first in the more developed countries and now in every country in the world, have witnessed a major change in the forces shaping Ekistic systems. We have entered the era of dynamic systems (Chapter Three) while still operating in the era of static hexagonal patterns.

There are three major forces which by attraction are shaping the new dynamic systems and forming new dynamic regions. These are:
- major Ekistic centres,
- modern circulatory systems,
- pleasant areas, such as coastal ones (fig. 219).

The major Ekistic centres' forces of attraction are apparent everywhere. Whether they are new centres, corresponding to the requirements of the new era, or old ones, adjusted to the requirements of the new era, they attract a great volume of activities and people to and around them. This can be seen in the physical expansion of the whole settled area and the built-up area, but it extends far beyond areas in which we can see the results as a physical expression. The built-up area is only the nucleus of a much broader urban area—the vital space of the urban settlement which may contain within it

227

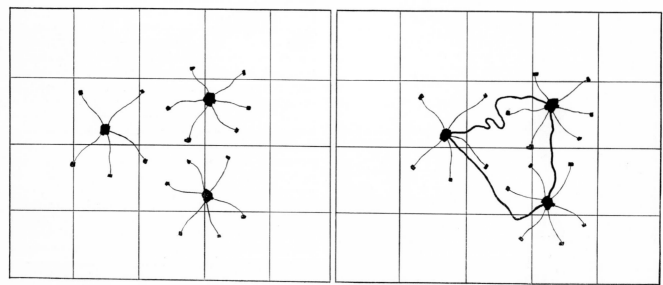

no interconnection

primitive interconnection

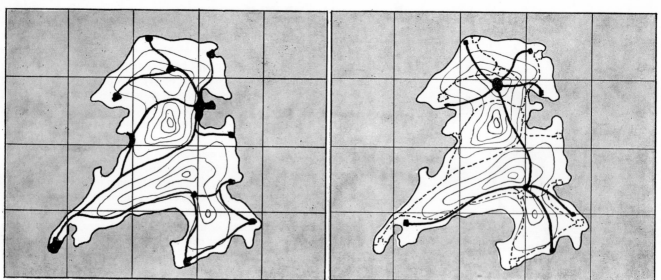

grid 10 x 10 km

the need for defence arising from the change from safe conditions on the seas
to unsafe ones results in the change of the ekistic pattern on an island

228

218

(below) regional Ekistic patterns

219

(right) forces shaping Ecumenopolis

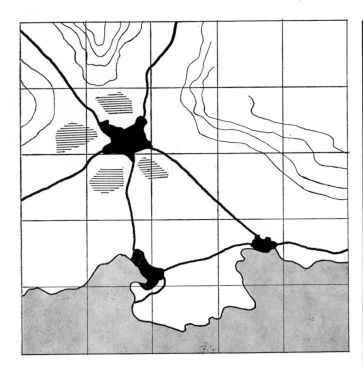

initial pattern with major urban centres

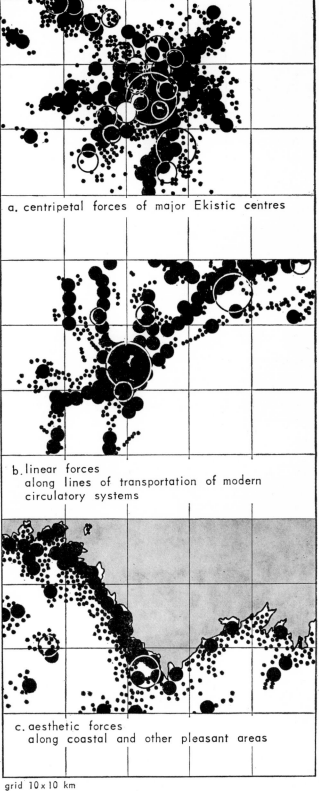

a. centripetal forces of major Ekistic centres

b. linear forces
along lines of transportation of modern
circulatory systems

c. aesthetic forces
along coastal and other pleasant areas

grid 10 x 10 km

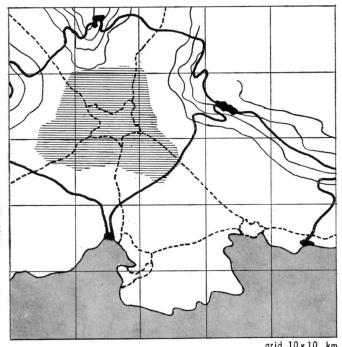

grid 10 x 10 km

eradication of the area after the spread of malaria

Facts

220

**influence of Athens on several zones from the inner
one to the whole of Greece in 1960**

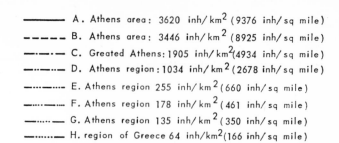

● urban centres

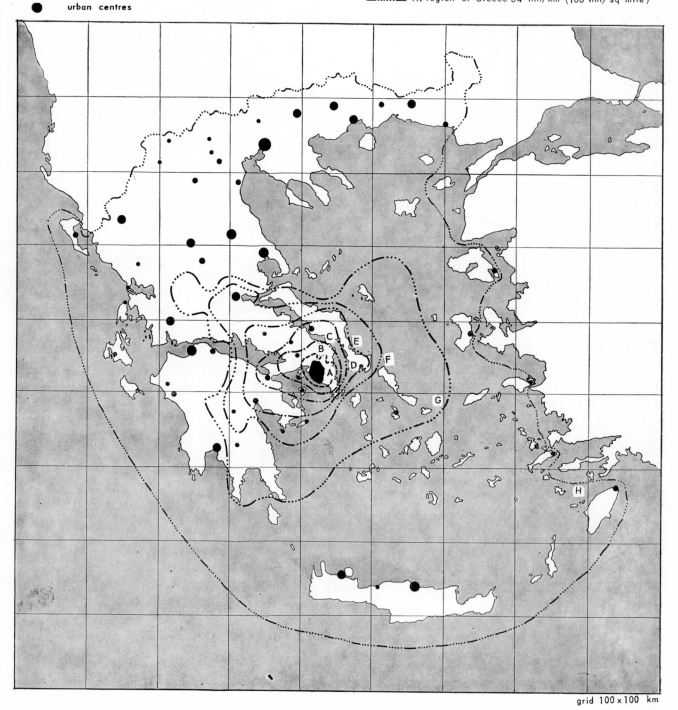

grid 100×100 km

km

0   100   200   300   400   500   600   700   800   900

0   100   200   300   400   500

miles

221

attraction by major Ekistic regions and coastal areas in the U.S.A.

percent of rural non-farm population in rural territory by county

(according to J. Gottmann)

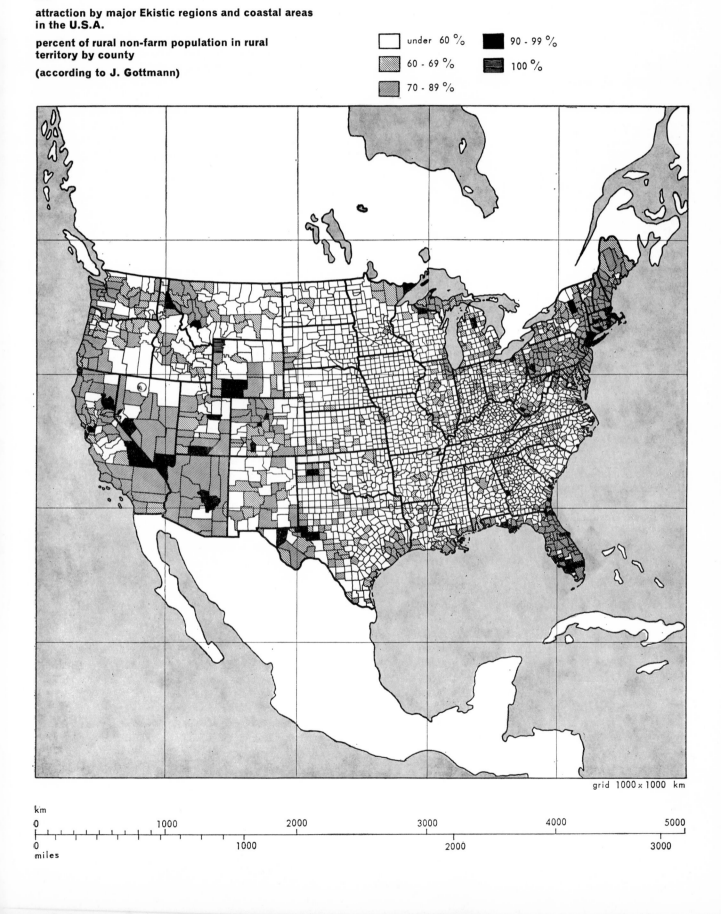

	under 60 %		90 - 99 %
	60 - 69 %		100 %
	70 - 89 %		

grid 1000 x 1000 km

km
0   1000   2000   3000   4000   5000

0   1000   2000   3000
miles

222

**growth of Standard Metropolitan Statistical Areas
(S.M.S.A.) in the U.S.A.**

population in millions
and number of S.M.S.A.

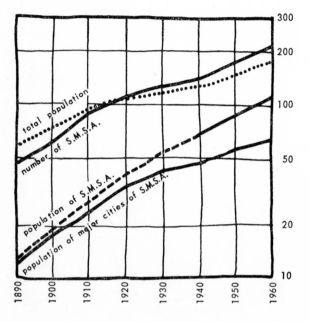

than is indicated by urban population statistics—and it is also quite clear where this is leading.

The second force (attraction to circulatory networks) has always been in operation. The greatest density of human settlement could always be found near these networks. This was not so apparent in the past, because transportation lines were not so strongly differentiated, and even the major inland ones were of minor importance, but also because security conditions did not allow a physical linear spread but only concentrations along main lines of transportation. Thus the physical expression of the settlements along them was not so strong, though the coastal and river zones, which provided the best and cheapest transportation always attracted important urban settlements.

But with the railroad and the highway eras, the importance of land transportation networks increased enormously, and their attraction became very apparent. Hence, an important principle in the creation of human settlements—that the circulatory networks attract the built-up areas—is for the first time expressed so strongly, not only within the settlements themselves and within a small distance from them, but also in very wide areas, in regions and sometimes in whole countries.

Such forces lead to ribbon development if the transportation lines are at a considerable distance apart, or to continuous areas of development if the transportation lines are close together, irrespective of the scale at which we are studying the phenomena. If we are considering a small settlement and the roads all around it with a few houses, we see it in the cases of the few houses. If we are speaking of a major settlement, the highways around it and the additional settlements around them, it is again true on that scale. Therefore, fig. 223 which presents this phenomenon does not need a scale; it could represent tens or thousands of square kilometres.

The third force (the aesthetic one causing an attraction by pleasant areas for enjoyment and living) can be observed in coastal areas alongside seas and lakes, quite often in areas overlooking rivers, sometimes in areas related to especially beautiful landscapes or important for historic, cultural, climatic and other reasons. Of all these, the strongest force is the attraction of the sea coast, a phenomenon we are already witnessing in many parts of the world; on a minor scale this attraction results in one line of houses, on a major one in the formation of many settlements as has been the case in southern France (fig. 224).

All these forces have some positive and some negative effects on the movement and relocation of the population. Here the meaning of positive forces is not in any way qualitative, but merely quantitative. The fact that problems are created in areas that have a total positive attraction for new inhabitants and new settlements should not mislead us into believing that the attraction itself is bad. It is much better to have people coming together—let us not forget that this, after all, is the meaning of civilisation—trying to solve their problems of

many other settlements with different functions. In a rural settlement, all related phenomena can be recognised in the nucleus and in the vital space surrounding it on a small scale, but in major urban areas, the relationship between the nucleus and its vital space is confused by the existence of many other settlements. We must, therefore, be careful in defining the impact of the forces of attraction by major Ekistic centres on the whole pattern of settlements. This can be understood when we study the spread of urban densities over a wide area. We will see that the major centres create the greatest increase in density around them. Such is the case in fig. 220 which shows the influence of Athens on several zones from the inner one to the whole of Greece.

This can also be seen on the map of the United States showing 'urbanisation' as a percentage of the rural, non-farm population living in rural areas.[19] On this map, we actually see not only results of the first force, but also the third force (attraction to pleasant areas) which draws the population towards almost all coastal areas (fig. 221). The corresponding graphs (fig. 222) show how the growth of the Standard Metropolitan Statistical Area (the SMSA) is much more important than the growth of major American cities, and how their numbers increase in relation to the total and their own population. It is clear that these areas attract more people

223

attraction by transportation lines

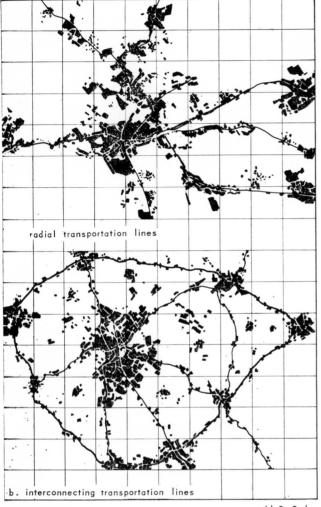

radial transportation lines

·b. interconnecting transportation lines

grid 2 x 2 km

o the population of rural areas increases by a much smaller percentage, or even sometimes decreases.

On the basis of these considerations and the criteria derived from the impact of the new forces on the evolution of the Ekistic systems, we can divide settlements into three basic categories:

o developing settlements, where the positive results of the new forces are apparent;

o static settlements, upon which the new forces have had little or no impact, but which have not suffered negative results; and

o declining settlements, which suffer from the negative results of development. Here the activities decrease, the entire community declines and the people leave.

The nature of the settlements classified on the basis of the previous criteria can be recognised even by their Shells. In some settlements we see great activity in the creation of new Shells—houses, buildings and facilities. In others we see many abandoned houses, lack of maintenance, etc. The physical decline of a settlement does not follow immediately upon its economic decline or its decrease of population. In fact, there are settlements which, even though losing in importance and being abandoned by some of their people, continue to be maintained because of their cultural, aesthetic or historical value. In other cases there may be misleading phenomena, such as remodelling financed by an income earned elsewhere and being sent back home to members of the family who still live in the old settlements. But this procedure cannot last very long unless the old settlements are able to attract new activities. If, for example, the value of the Shells of a settlement is considerable, the Shells may be revived by new inhabitants who move in or just pay short visits. But unless something like this does happen, the settlement is doomed to decline.

There are several degrees of decline in settlements. If for example a new transportation network in a certain area enables people to reach the major urban settlements more easily, there may be no decline in the smallest rural settlements, while there may be a decline in its small urban settlements. Such a situation may mean the decline of B and C centres and the development of D centres. If the decline is general, and spreads over the countryside, it will also affect settlements the main function of which may be to supply and serve the rural settlements of the Ekistic system.

Naturally, static settlements, present fewer problems than the other two. Since they have little change in population or physical size and no major changes in their activities, the rate of growth of new phenomena is very slow and can be easily dealt with. But in declining settlements a disaster is possible when decline is taking place at a relatively high speed or at a suddenly accelerated speed, since this speed may create an atmosphere of despair and a desire for immediate abandonment not justified by the facts. Therefore, declining settlements must have our careful attention, as they present serious problems both for the individuals involved and for the Society.

cohabitation, than to have them fleeing from the areas in which they have settled.

Negative or centrifugal effects are apparent in areas which:
o are at the greatest distance from major centres,
o are at the greatest distance from transportation networks,
o are at the great distance from pleasant areas, or are themselves not at all attractive.

As a result of these forces the total picture, by categories of settlements and types of areas appears as follows (fig. 225):
o the population of the big cities increases by percentages which are often above 4 per cent annually;
o the population of minor cities increases but at a lower rate;
o the population of average countries increases by about 2 per cent annually;

attraction by the sea

**Southern France from Nice in the west to Menton in
the east (1958)**

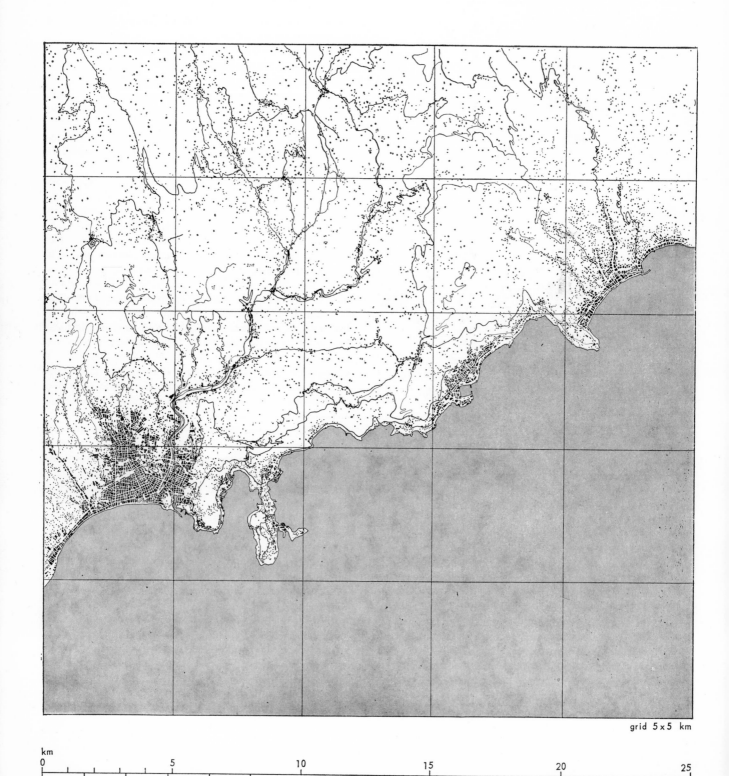

grid 5 x 5 km

km
0   5   10   15   20   25

0   5   10   15
miles

225

rate of increase of population

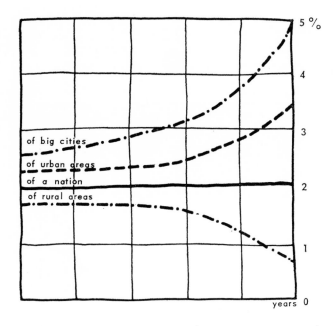

of big cities

of urban areas

of a nation

of rural areas

5 %

4

3

2

1

years 0

typical indicative example of contemporary trends which are the result of a changing economy

But of all three categories, the one presenting the gravest problems is that of the developing settlements, for despite the very different psychology of their inhabitants and the fact that everybody is optimistically looking forward to a better future, there may exist more urgent problems for much greater numbers of people. Actually, in declining settlements, some services provided by the Shells and functions may even improve; for example, where there may not have been enough schools for all the inhabitants, there may come to be even more classrooms than are necessary. On the contrary, in a developing settlement there may be no classrooms at all for the new inhabitants, and a big gap between the influx of new children and the supply of educational facilities for them.

We can understand the meaning of declining settlements through an explanation of the phenomena taking place within them. Man and Society are facing big problems, but Nature is being threatened only by the abandonment of a certain part of the cultivation, meaning a return to the natural patterns of plant and animal life, which in the long run is not bad at all. In declining settlements, the decay of the Shells is in fact unimportant as compared to the decline apparent in Man, Society and their activities in the area.

We can perhaps add that there are no major Ekistic problems in the static settlements; where they are concerned there is time for proper action because they are not suffering either from positive or negative pressures. Depending on the type of country and the phase it is going through, we will have to concentrate either on the developing settlements, which present most of the Ekistic problems, or on the declining ones which may need special care.

Dynamic systems

It is quite apparent that today we are witnessing the transformation of the rather static hexagonal pattern into the dynamic pattern of Ekistic regions. Since we are now in the middle of this change, what we have are composite patterns of:

- the older static hexagonal patterns which will remain so, for reasons already explained, over comparatively wide areas of many regions;
- the new dynamic patterns, resulting from the three new forces which will be intensified in the future;
- mixtures of the two.

With the second and third of the above patterns constantly changing, it is quite clear that no dynamic Ekistic system can be considered as being about to reach a final static stage. Continuous changes are taking place on all levels of the system, from the lowest to the highest.

This can be presented in four diagrams. The first one shows the traditional forces which are still leading to hexagonal patterns (fig. 226). In the second, a basic change has been brought about by a rapid transit line connecting the central settlement E with the large port of the area, and an electric railway line connecting centres D2 and D3 with E, centres with only one stop in between (fig. 227). In the third diagram, the impact of the rapid transit line and the electric railway has been even stronger, while an additional line connecting the rapid transit with the Ekistic centre D1 has caused the first changes in its area (fig. 228). In the fourth diagram, we see the results and the impact of the intensification of the existing connections and some new minor ones, plus the results of the first regional circular route connecting D1, D2, D3, D4 (fig. 229).

By this point the settled area has changed completely in relation to what it was when influenced only by the hexagonal pattern, and it is apparent that all sorts of new forces will keep the pattern continuously changing. Superficially, this pattern will appear more and more irregular, though to anyone following the changes, they will appear organic and natural. This means that although settlements in this phase may have come to exist as a result of apparent and rational cause and effect, they have not taken on rational forms, since there is no overall system towards which all these causes and effects lead. This paradox can be explained by the fact that while decisions taken for parts of the settlements may be rational if only a few facts have been taken into consideration (which is usually the case), they are irrational

evolution of dynamic Ekistic systems

first phase: primary settlements

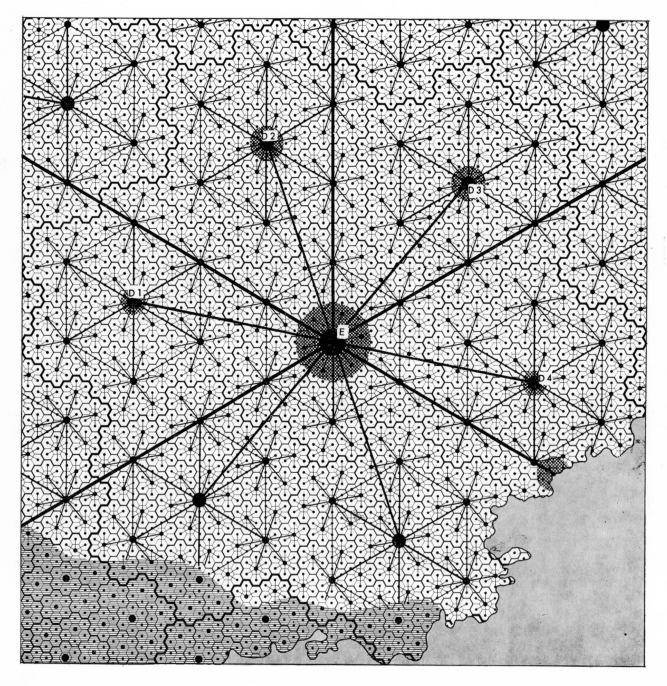

227

evolution of dynamic Ekistic systems

second phase: some central settlements are interconnected

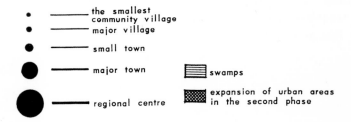

the smallest community village
major village
small town
major town
regional centre
swamps
expansion of urban areas in the second phase

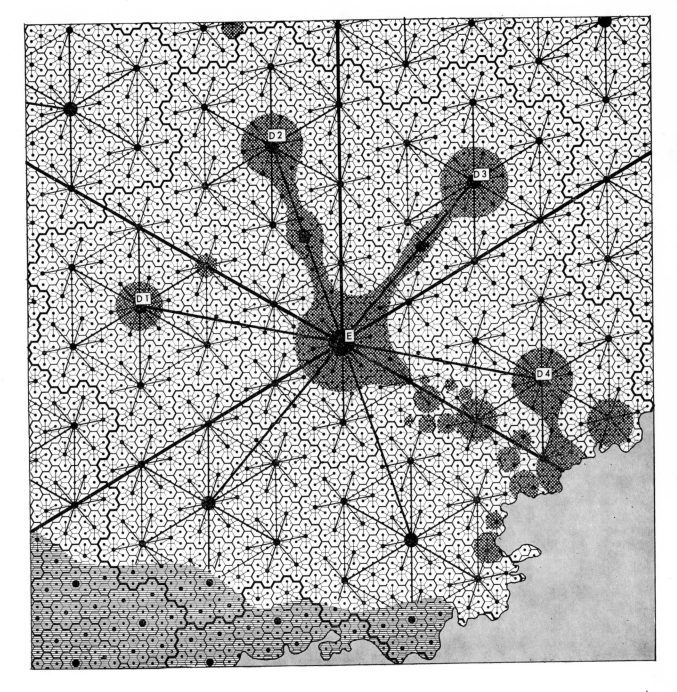

km

100   200

0

0   100

miles

evolution of dynamic Ekistic systems

third phase: more settlements are interconnected

- the smallest community village
- major village
- small town
- major town
- regional centre
- swamps
- expansion of urban areas in the second phase
- expansion of urban areas in the third phase

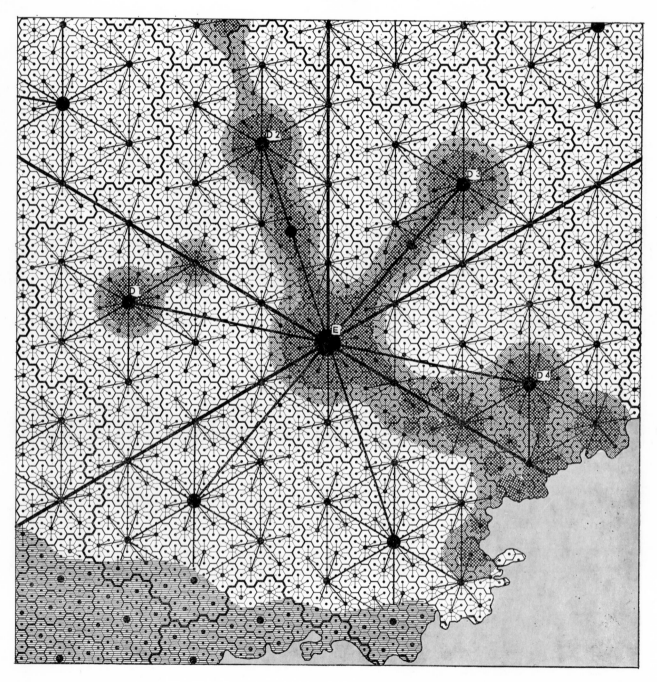

km

| 0 | 100 | 200 |

| 0 | 100 |

miles

229

evolution of dynamic Ekistic systems

**fourth phase: all major central settlements
form one urban system**

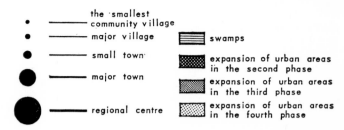

the smallest community village

major village

small town

major town

regional centre

swamps

expansion of urban areas in the second phase

expansion of urban areas in the third phase

expansion of urban areas in the fourth phase

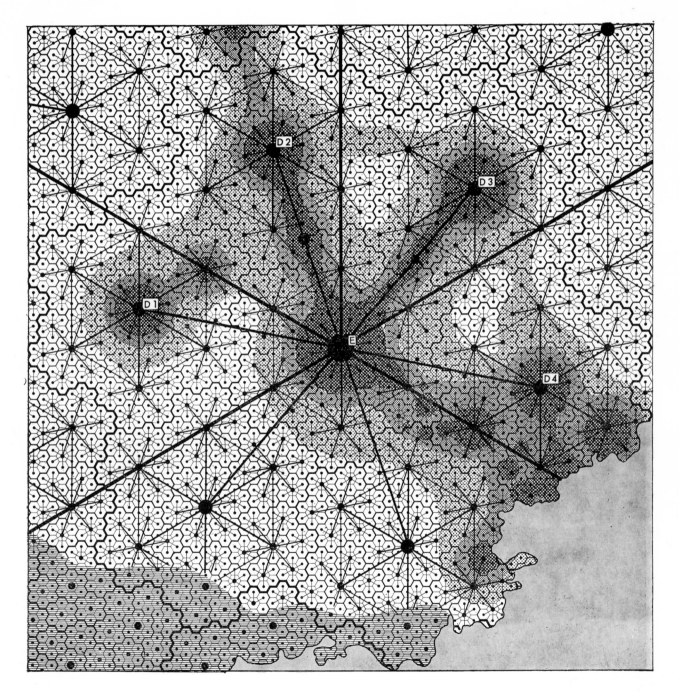

km

0   100   200

0   100

miles

**traffic patterns change from inter-city to radial and
circular routes**

**Eastern Megalopolis of the United States
(according to J. Gottmann)**

――――――― main linear routes

▬▬▬▬▬ new circular boulevards

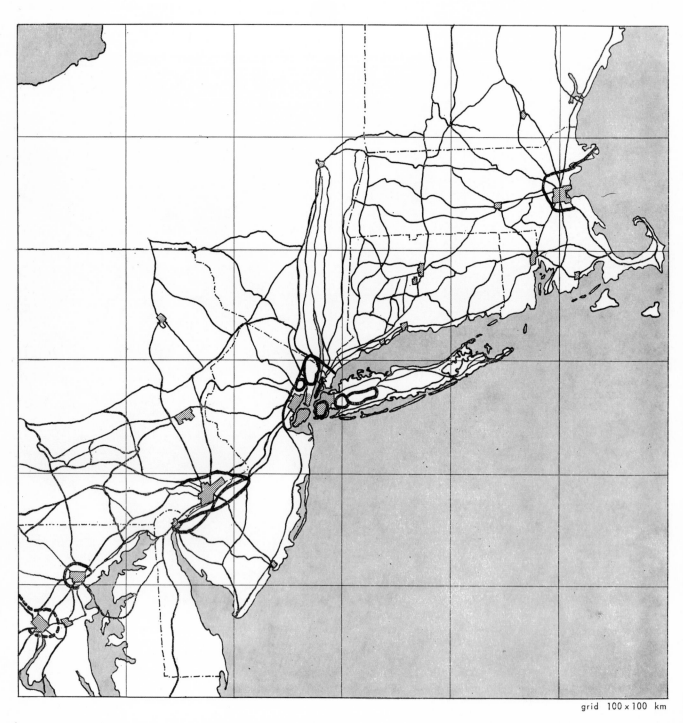

grid 100 × 100 km

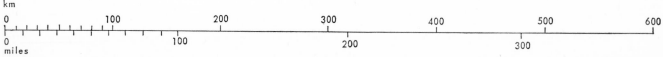

231

densities of population reveal that the Great Lakes Megalopolis is beginning to be formed

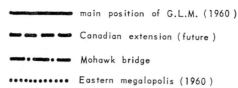

━━━━━━ main position of G.L.M. (1960)

━ ━ ━ ━ Canadian extension (future)

━·━·━·━ Mohawk bridge

•••••••••• Eastern megalopolis (1960)

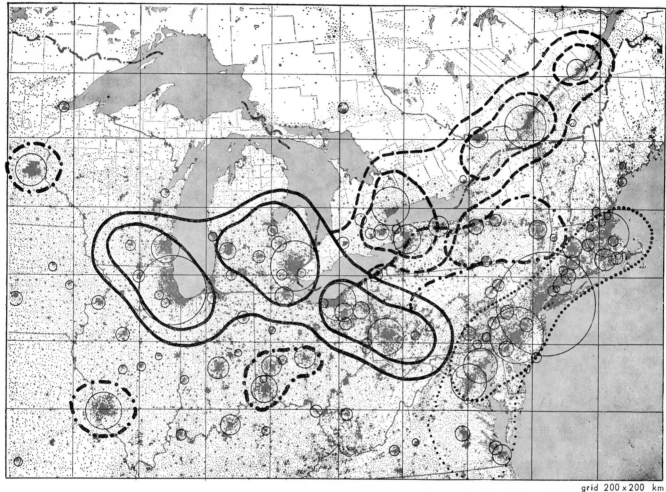

grid 200 x 200 km

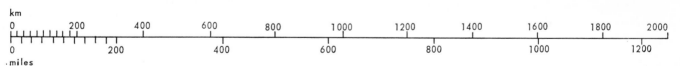

when we consider the total settlements, the total forces influencing their development, and the total resulting structures and forms.

For example, in an urban region such as the one described, the initial static settlements change into dynamic ones that usually grow first in concentric circles and then along the main lines of transportation. Because, however, the total Ekistic system contains many such dynamically expanding centres and many lines of transportation of varying importance developing at different rates, the whole—even though composed of clearly defined geometrical patterns which started from a rational hexagonal pattern—appears, and in some respects is, irrational. This is apparent from the fact that most of the centres within the dynamically expanding settlements can no longer be properly served—and this is particularly true of the central area of the whole system.

s

growth of an organism means change of form

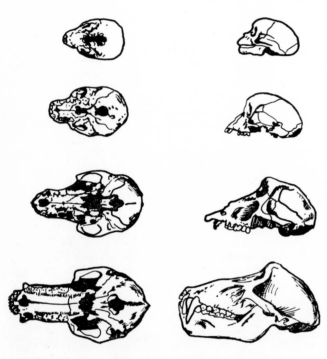

differential growth of the skull of the baboon as seen from the under surface and inside view: 1, 2, and 3 are from newborn, juvenile, and adult females, and 4 from an adult male

Such situations, which now exist in regions of up to 300 km. (187 mi.) in length, are eventually going to be true of much larger regions covering as much as 800–1,000 km. (496–620 mi.) and later even more. This is already happening in the megalopolis of the eastern coast of the United States between Boston and Washington due to many causes such as the transportation network consisting of the radial concentric and circular routes already described by Jean Gottmann[20] (fig. 230).

We have similar cases in other areas of the world as well. A characteristic example is the potential megalopolis of the Great Lakes which is beginning to take shape between the United States and Canada, surrounding the Great Lakes, as a recently initiated study reveals (fig. 231).

During this dynamic evolution of Ekistic systems, there are two major Ekistic problems in the areas of growth of settlements by expansion, and within the existing settlements. The first are problems of growth, while the second are problems of transformation. These categories of problems will be examined separately in the next two chapters.

GROWTH OF SETTLEMENTS

Uncontrolled and confused

The development of settlements takes place by growth and transformation; the first causes the second and therefore I will start with it. There is considerable confusion regarding the process of growth, its significance and the implications it has for the life of the settlements. This is true also if we are speaking about the growth of living organisms. Characteristically a leading biologist, Sir Peter Medawar, wrote in 1954 that:

' "Growth" is a word of notorious imprecision, but it stoutly defies semantical reform. It may mean increase of length, area, weight or volume; it may mean the act or accomplished fact of reproduction, i.e. increase of number; or it may simply mean development—the adverb is not well chosen—with all that development implies of increasing complexity and elaboration.'[21]

Growth means change of size and, by necessity, it means change of form as well. This change of form is quite natural; we cannot enlarge a house without changing its form, nor a road, nor a city. The same thing happens in Nature even though the cells in living organisms are much more flexible than the walls of a house or of a street. We cannot, after all, expect the water supply pipes to change their diameter as arteries do in mammals, at least not yet. Even in Nature growth necessitates a change of form, especially when this means changing a part which consists of bones and organs, as is the case with the skull of a mammal, as demonstrated by Sir Solly Zuckerman and used by Sir Peter Medawar in his articles on 'Pattern of Organic Growth and Transformation' (fig. 232).

I am once again using examples from the world of Nature, and trying to learn from biology. This is not because I believe that analogies can always be found. In most cases they cannot and I am in agreement once again with Sir Peter Medawar when he states that:

'. . . that growth of organisms can be likened to, for example, the growth of houses is not acceptable even in the roughest first approximation. The two processes have nothing in common at all'.[22]

I am using these examples in order to draw useful lessons from sciences which are much more developed than Ekistics, and to fill some of the great gaps which have been left in the systematic knowledge of human settlements. And I do not mean to say that there cannot be *some* analogies between human settlements and natural organisms when we select the right case at the right scale; what I mean is that analogies do not necessarily need to exist between phenomena in order to be useful—it is enough if they exist between approaches, so they can help us to develop a new current approach.

233

the city and the metropolis

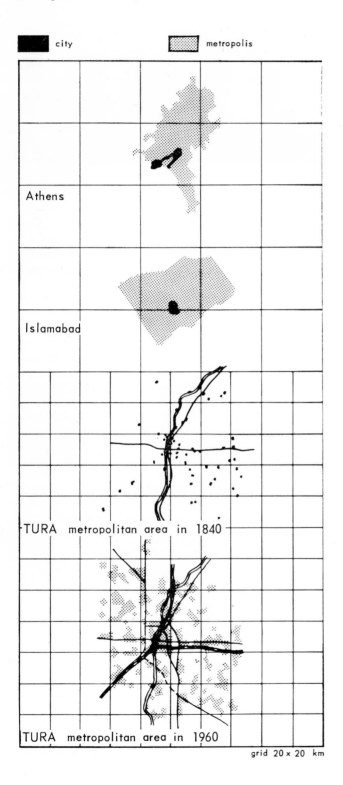

city ▮   metropolis ▨

Athens

Islamabad

TURA metropolitan area in 1840

TURA metropolitan area in 1960

grid 20 x 20 km

As we are dealing with growth, I will also go into some special problems of form—since the two cannot be separated—even though I will deal more extensively with the subject when I discuss transformations. Actually three basic changes can be observed in growing settlements: expansion in surface, expansion in height and transformation. The growth of a settlement can be more easily understood through the study of changes in the container, in Nature, the Shells and the Networks—especially Shells since they are the most visible of all. By the following observations on the growth of the container we can understand the phenomena also as related to the content, Man and Society, as well as the total balance between content and container.

The scale of the problem of the expansion of settlements can be seen by looking at one very old, and one very new city. The old city is Athens. The area of ancient Athens, which for thousands of years had been sufficient, and sometimes even more than sufficient, for the city which is called the cradle of Western civilisation, was less than one-fortieth of the area of the modern metropolis of Athens (fig. 233).

The other example is a very new city, the new capital of Pakistan, Islamabad, now being built five miles from the old city of Rawalpindi; the new capital now looks very small indeed as compared to the area being planned as its eventual normal metropolitan built-up area. The scale of this city, which is comparable to the basic settlement of the past whose size and image we are still accustomed to, when seen in conjunction with the scale of the future metropolis, is an example of the size of the problem of its physical dimensions and an indication of the vastness of the several other kinds of problems it is facing[23] (fig. 233).

I will also present a third example showing the region and metropolitan area of TURA (Typical Urban Renewal Area). TURA is a model city constructed for the study of problems of urban renewal in the United States and is quite typical of the average metropolitan area there. The two drawings of figure 233 show how the initial city of TURA in 1840, a small black spot near a river with some even smaller settlements in the surrounding area, has turned into a large metropolitan area, which appears completely uncontrolled and confusing.

Many major contemporary settlements, whose expansion is due to dynamic growth, show several common characteristics over the last hundred years:

o they have covered from ten to over forty times their previously built-up area;

o there has been no effective control or plan for their overall growth;

o as a result the size and form of the present settlement is very confusing.

This confused situation is being expressed not only in the overall structure of the human settlement but in its details as well. For example, in the past there was a hierarchy in the height of the buildings of any normal city. Houses were small, community buildings were larger, the city hall was even larger,

in the past   and now

while the church, temple or mosque represented the tallest physical element in the community structure. Now the monumental symbolic buildings of the past, instead of forming the apex of the city, are very often set in holes left in the urban structure, holes which remind us that changes have taken place (fig. 234). But these changes, although very natural, have not led to better city structure, a better settlement, or at least to a settlement which could preserve the values of the past.

The situation in all urban areas which have grown dynamically during the last century is such that after looking at them we can believe that growth today is leading to uncontrolled sizes and uncontrolled and confused structures and forms. The fact that growth in the past did proceed in a regular manner is no consolation for what is happening today; the realisation only leads to the rather pessimistic conclusion that we have lost the ability of achieving what in ancient days appeared simple and natural.

Natural and predictable

In spite of the confusing picture presented by dynamically growing cities, their growth has not been unnatural: Man has always been behind it. Even though his action has not followed a conscious plan, Man has done everything with some specific purpose in mind, based on what he believed to be reasonable. The whole has failed, but this does not mean that his separate actions were not consciously directed towards the fulfilment of a need. This is why we can say that the growth was predictable, once we understand the laws that guided it.

A city in a uniform surrounding grows by concentric circles around the nucleus of the static city. If the surrounding is not uniform, the city grows more along the lines of more favourable conditions and may tend to grow into star-like shapes; this can be observed in many cities around the world (fig. 235); it is shown graphically in a series of sketches (fig. 236). If the conditions of the surroundings tend towards

equalisation, the dynamic growth of the city will eventually be led once again towards a circular shape. If the conditions change and are not uniform, the city may once again tend towards a star-shape (fig. 237), which might be geometric, or irregular, depending on the existing conditions in the particular location.

On the basis of these diagrams we can explain why we have witnessed concentric growth by rings, or irregular star-like growth. We saw earlier that if all the physical conditions around the settlement are the same and all pressures equal, and the settlement grows with the same system of transportation, and the same type of activities and buildings, its growth would take place in regular concentric circles. As soon as some conditions of the surroundings cease to be equal—let us say that there are hills in some areas and valleys in others—the settlement in question follows the valleys and avoids the hills, thus ending up with a star-like formation. The same thing will happen if the transportation network is not equal in all directions (if for example, some highways allow traffic at higher speeds in some directions); this will once again lead to a star formation. Such examples indicate that the overall development has always been a natural process, one that could be explained on the basis of existing conditions.

We must now look into the possibility of predicting growth. If growth is controlled by the physical formation of the surrounding landscape, we can certainly predict what will happen in the long run, even if mistakes are made for short periods and over minor areas. For example, even though it is unreasonable to build on hillsides if water cannot be supplied at a reasonable price, we very often witness the creation of slum areas on such hillsides. When the community and the people later realise how unreasonable it was to build up there, there is a tendency to move to a lower area, if the values invested in the old location are not very high. This course of events is both time-consuming and expensive, but in the long run the right course is followed. The situation is more difficult to predict when Nature does not impose any

235

urban growth

**the initial radial development tends towards
a circle**

Limassol, Cyprus

1885

1958

1965

municipal boundaries 1923
municipal boundaries 1946

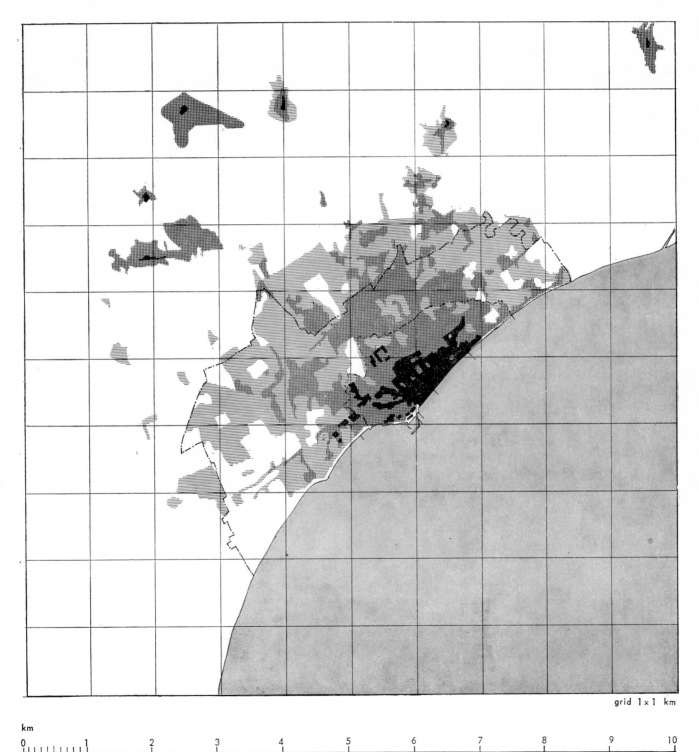

grid 1 x 1 km

km
0   1   2   3   4   5   6   7   8   9   10

0   1   2   3   4   5   6
miles

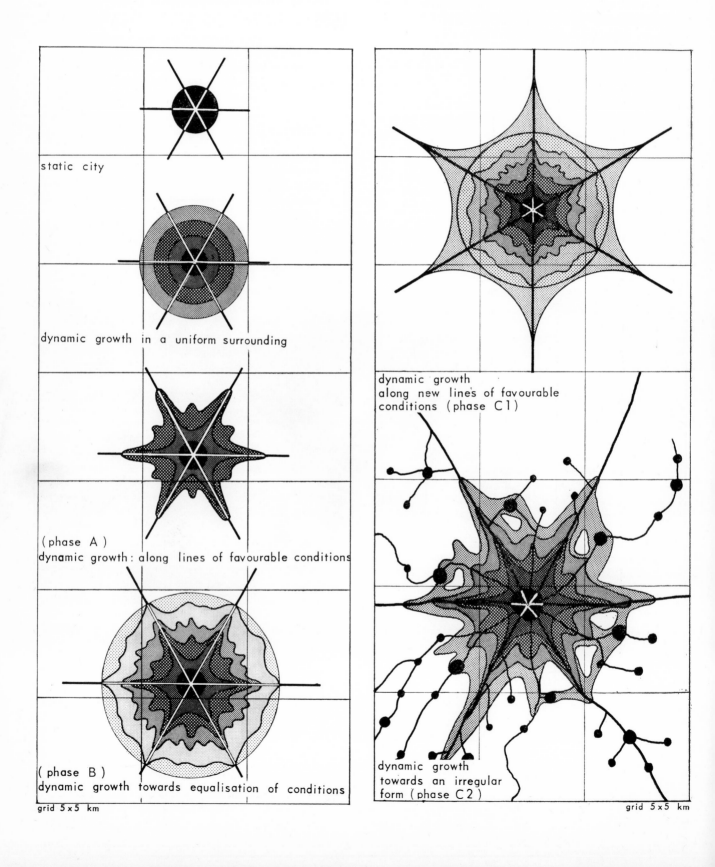

static city

dynamic growth in a uniform surrounding

(phase A)
dynamic growth: along lines of favourable conditions

(phase B)
dynamic growth towards equalisation of conditions

dynamic growth
along new lines of favourable
conditions (phase C1)

dynamic growth
towards an irregular
form (phase C2)

grid 5 x 5 km

grid 5 x 5 km

basic lines of growth. A distinction can then be made between those actions undertaken by government authority, and by private individuals. It is not difficult for the government to predict some of its future actions (if it is properly organised) for it is responsible for long term investments and therefore it must not only predict, but also direct certain actions. The situation is less clear-cut in cases where the initiative is being undertaken by private developers; but since it is the government which has the power to plan and to construct most public works, or at least to guide and to approve the public works programmes being undertaken by private individuals, it can be argued that the minimum the government should do is to understand what is happening and to foresee what will happen, even when it does not have power to interfere with everything that is being undertaken by private individuals.

However, with very few exceptions (to be mentioned later), governments have not been planning on the proper scale, and, what is worse, in most cases people have believed that the growth they observe is unpredictable. This confusion is so great that many areas of the world are still living under the influence of myths. One of these myths, which is completely unreasonable, is that the solution can be found in the building of satellite towns.

This myth runs: our cities are becoming unbearable for life, Man and Society, and are not carrying out their proper economic activities. They are spoiling the natural landscape and becoming hideous in themselves. Let us avoid them, let us go out into the open beautiful countryside and build small cities where people can be safe from the evils of the growing metropolitan areas. Hence, many people move out.

The result is that, a few years or decades later, since we are no longer in a period of static cities but one of dynamic settlements, the central settlement catches up with the satellites. This means that everybody who had hoped to live in an isolated satellite is sooner or later swallowed up by the city. Thus the creation of the satellites has only confused the situation, for such detached settlements cannot be well incorporated into the total Ekistic body, partly because up to the last minute everybody has believed that the satellite provided an escape from the facts of life.

The second effect new satellites have is that instead of relieving the central city from pressures, they increase these pressures (fig. 238), because every addition of population in a satellite means that additional services of a higher order have to be provided by the central city, inasmuch as everybody expects to have these services (education, welfare, hospitals, etc.) regardless of how far from the centre he may be.

I have often heard people say that such services can be provided within the satellites. This is wrong, and it is confusing. The satellite can only provide services corresponding to its order of magnitude. If it is a community of 10,000 people, it can only support schools for the children of 10,000 inhabitants. Under present conditions it cannot support a technical school, a college, a concert hall or a major hospital. The satellite has to turn to a settlement of a higher order for services of a higher order and in this way it increases the pressures on the city.

Satellites have the following characteristics:

- they provide a temporary escape from the pressures of the big city and create a community on a minor scale which may provide some proper services within it—their maximum contribution is the creation of better conditions of life within this small community;
- but as for services of a higher order, or professional and social contacts, those provided are shown to be insufficient;
- in search of these services and contacts satellites increase the pressures on the centre of the cities from which they have escaped;
- they contribute to the confusion of the situation by creating the belief that they can remain outside the Ekistic body;
- finally, when the expanding central settlement catches up with them, they cease to provide even the proper services for their original community, since at this point it is suffering from the pressures of the urban tissue expanding around it.

What has just been demonstrated in the case of a city growing within uniform surroundings is also valid for a metropolitan area. Here again it is only a matter of time before recently built satellites or other older cities within the metropolitan area become absorbed by the expanding settlement (fig. 239).

After World War II in England, the concept 'satellite' was replaced by 'new town', the basic difference being that the new towns were at greater distances from the central settlements, and were larger than the satellites of the past generation. But what was considered large during the former period of the satellites, may be small by today's standards, both as regards population of the settlement and distance from the centre. But these new towns will create new lines of communication and become new centres of attraction. Because of this, new activities will be attracted towards them and their transportation and communications networks, and this will contribute to an early growth of that part of the country and its connection with the major expanding settlements.

On the other hand, these new towns will still need services of a higher order, which must be provided by the existing central towns, the centres of which will suffer from pressure, even though, because the distances between the new towns and the towns themselves are both greater, this pressure will be less than if the towns had been small satellites closer to the centres. With the creation of the new towns the problems are certainly decreasing, but not enough to provide a permanent solution and the full relief of the total Ekistic body. And what we still do not know is whether people are

247

238

(left) urban growth

satellites in a metropolitan area are finally swallowed up by the dynamically growing city

239

(below) urban growth

satellites in a metropolitan area growing from a non-uniform to a uniform entity

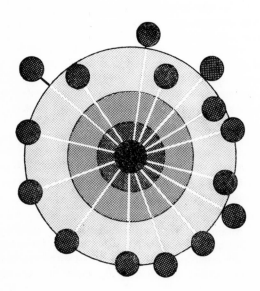

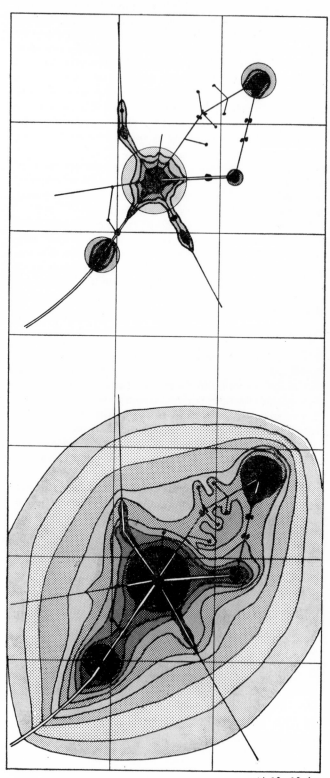

grid 10 x 10 km

happier in satellite towns than they were in the great metropolitan areas.

Another myth is the myth of densities. High densities, this myth asserts, are disastrous since they cause damage to public health, transportation, and so forth. This very vague statement, in most cases, leads to the wrong solutions. We certainly cannot say that in a big block of high-cost flats, or in a large hotel, where the highest densities in the world can be found, conditions are necessarily bad either from the point of view of public health or from the point of view of traffic and transportation. It is not high density in itself that causes harm, but the conditions under which it is brought about. If we plan for high densities, taking into consideration all the problems created by living at high densities, we can avoid the weaknesses and exploit the advantages of this form of living. But even this statement may be misleading since we have not yet defined high densities. The notion of which density is high varies greatly from country to country, from city to city, and even from one part of a city to another. We can say that we have no proof that living at high densities is worse than living at low densities, but that it is necessary in each case to select the proper density in relation to the functions of the settlement and the means available for the solution of its problems.

A similar assertion is that the solution of many problems is in building multi-storey apartments. This once again is generally erroneous, for in many cases multi-storey buildings cannot, for economic reasons, be built or maintained at present-day costs. Even when we can afford to build them, it is not at all certain they will provide better living for all types of residents, such as families with children, while they may provide a very good solution for specific types of families and specific types of functions.

We can close this discussion with the statement that even though the growth taking place today is natural—since it corresponds to actual needs of Man—and is in many ways predictable, it is not leading to the best solutions because:

  ○ decisions are being taken on problems of the parts, and not on the combined interests of the parts and the whole;
  ○ there are many misconceptions about what is right and what is wrong.

Growth and disease

The dynamic expansion of settlements in surface and in height causes great changes and creates both great profits and great losses because of the changes which are continuously taking place on the periphery, and within the urban structure. These profits and losses can be of economic, social, political, technological or cultural importance. They are very often much larger than they should be and are not distributed reasonably. The profits mainly go to those individuals who own undeveloped land or who take the initiative for its development, or to those whose property lies on key locations within the expanding settlement. At the same time, other people, whose property does not lie at the best locations lose greatly. Meanwhile the city and the government, which finally cover the expenditure of change by assisting the suffering areas, always lose in the process.

Let us look into the case of those who suffer losses in the process of city expansion. Those people are either in no position to use the expansion for their own good, even though their property is in areas of expansion, or else their property is in the areas of negative transformation formed by the expansion taking place elsewhere.

In the first group are individuals who are unable to develop their own land, even though they may own large tracts of it, or owners of small places whose role has been completely changed, because of the expansion of the city, without their being able either to readjust themselves to the expansion, or to profit from it. Even though the losses in this category are great, the losses in the second category of people within the areas of transformation are much greater. In this group, we must count not only single individuals, but also whole communities being upset by many new projects such as new highways, which may cut through them and completely upset their economic and community life. The downtown area, for example, may lose a big part of its business, while other communities, properties and individuals may suddenly lose the profitable balance they formerly enjoyed without being able to do anything about it.

We can now risk a generalisation about the significance of dynamic growth for those involved in a dynamically growing area. Because of uncontrolled and confusing growth the distribution of profits and losses is unequal. Profits are limited to the few individuals whose property happens to be located in areas of rising importance, or those who were able to foresee these locations, or those who influence development to favour their locations. Dynamic growth may cause losses which will have to be borne by the total community plus many other private individuals and businesses with no direct connection with growth and change.

This kind of expansion of settlements does not make sense. In the process the whole settlement suffers: Nature, Man, Society, Shells and Networks do not derive any benefit from the growth of the settlement. The total structure suffers and pays for the losses, while only a few people—deliberately or by chance—are able to gain great profit from it. Such growth is not normal, it is a growth that may have a disastrous influence on the economic, social and political stability of the settlement.

As an example I will mention the severe problems caused by abnormal growth leading to the formation of slum areas. Such areas attract the economically weakest groups. Once these groups are confined within slum areas they contribute to their further decline. Problems of physical deterioration are followed by problems of social deterioration and ultimately to political trouble. Abnormal growth leads to disease!

Planning for growth

As I have already said, the fact that we are now dealing with dynamic settlements has not been fully realised, and most planning of urban settlements is still based on past notions of static cities. There are only a few exceptions to this that I know of—where a conscious effort has been made to avoid the conventional solution to urban growth and to search for new solutions. Two such efforts are in Copenhagen and in Washington D.C. The first has already been tested in practice, while we must wait to see how the second will be implemented and where it will lead.

In addition, I have been personally responsible for the development and implementation of several dynamic settlements during the last 15 years. I am presenting these ideas of mine after having developed a theory for urban growth; I will demonstrate how I had the occasion to implement it. At present I will limit myself to examples of efforts carried out by others which I consider of a major importance.

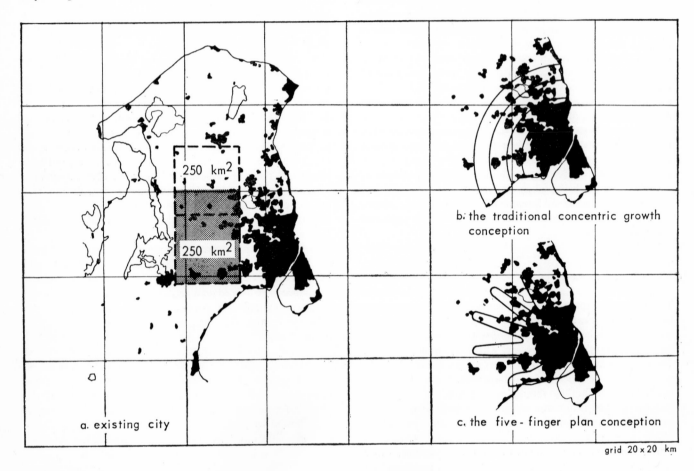

a. existing city

b. the traditional concentric growth conception

c. the five-finger plan conception

grid 20 x 20 km

o *Copenhagen*

Copenhagen is a densely built city of the past in the process of becoming a city of the twentieth century. It has the advantage of a carefully studied master plan, the 'five-finger' plan, which has now guided its development for over a decade. Published in 1947, and enforced by an Act in 1949, this plan has formed the basis of Copenhagen's growth.

The 'five-finger' plan became well known because of the courage underlying its conception: the courage to break the walls of the old city, not in order to create a city which would be similar in conception to the old one, except for the fact that rings would replace the walls, but to create a city growing only along the main transportation lines in a star-like fashion.

Figures 240b, c show what could have been expected had the Copenhagen plan conformed to the plans of almost all the other cities being prepared at that period. Instead, Copenhagen's plan opened a new path for the planned

growth of cities. Eleven years after the publication of the 'five-finger' plan and only nine years after the 1949 Act was passed, it was felt that it was necessary for the whole metropolitan region to be conceived afresh. The work started then was published in a series of documents in 1961. On the basis of this study, the situation in Copenhagen was presented as follows:

The population of Copenhagen, then 1,500,000, will increase to 2,500,000 by the year 2000, which means an increase of 66 per cent in about 40 years. The population of the country, which was then 4.5 million, will be 6 million by the year 2000, an increase of 33 per cent during the same period. The total urban population, which was 3 million, will be 5 million by the year 2000, an increase of 66 per cent.

The conclusion was quite obvious: the total growth of the local population in the next 40 years would occur in urban areas, while the rural population would remain at the present 1.5 million mark. Out of the total urban population increase of 2 million people, 1 million would go into Copenhagen. If this does happen, Copenhagen will be relatively lucky, for in other places, given similar trends, we could expect a much higher percentage to go into the largest urban area in the country. We should keep in mind, however, that this is an optimistic proposal, and it is possible that the increase in the Copenhagen area will be greater than in the other urban areas of the country, so that the population of Copenhagen may well be doubled by the year 2000.

According to these assumptions, about 50 per cent of the total national expansion in industry and commerce will go into Copenhagen. Again we have to keep in mind that this is probably the minimum possible increase. On the basis of the assumption of a population of 2.5 million people, houses and flats in the Copenhagen area will increase from 0.5 million to 1 million, an increase of 100 per cent, which is perhaps a bit low for a population increase of 66 per cent.

On the basis of the official plan, the land requirements per capita, which is now 300–350 square metres (1600–1850 sq. ft.), may become 400 square metres (2100 sq. ft.) in the year 2000. This prediction, made on the basis of examples of other cities which have grown under the influence of the automobile, may be on the low side. Our experience is that the per capita consumption of land increases at a much higher rate in an era of developing motor transport. This slower increase in Copenhagen may be possible because of constraints imposed by scarcity of land. Yet, unless special measures are taken against the waste of land, which is a normal phenomenon in growing metropolitan areas, the land requirements per capita might well go beyond 400 square metres (2100 sq. ft.).

These considerations are based on the prediction that the 200,000 automobiles registered today will reach the one million mark, an increase of 400 per cent. The built-up area itself is expected to increase by 200 per cent. How these predictions affect the Copenhagen area is shown in fig. 240a, where two squares show the land requirements in the whole metropolitan region up to 1980, and from 1980 to the year 2000. The shaded area shows land requirements up to 1980, together with a reserve area of 100 sq. km. (38.6 sq. mi.).

The new proposals substantially change the five-finger conception into a one major finger conception, as shown in fig. 241. This is based on the idea of reliance on a high speed mass transport system. It is in substance an adjustment to the technological progress of the initial five-finger projection. Both plans are based on the idea that urban growth follows the lines of the most easily organised transportation. In detail, this one-finger expansion assumes the form of a high-density residential development, especially around the proposed new centres, residential development of a more open character in most of the area, and industrial zones. The whole area will have half a million inhabitants with two sub-centres, each of which will serve a quarter of a million people.

The conception of a one-finger expansion, instead of the former five-finger one, is mainly a result of a traffic study

241

Copenhagen

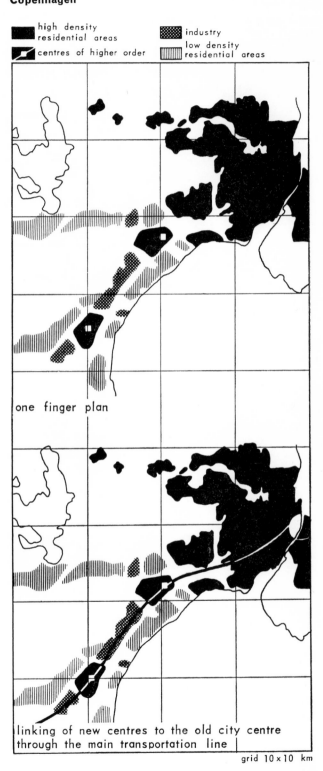

high density residential areas

centres of higher order

industry

low density residential areas

one finger plan

linking of new centres to the old city centre through the main transportation line

grid 10 x 10 km

251

Copenhagen

five-finger plan, main transportation network

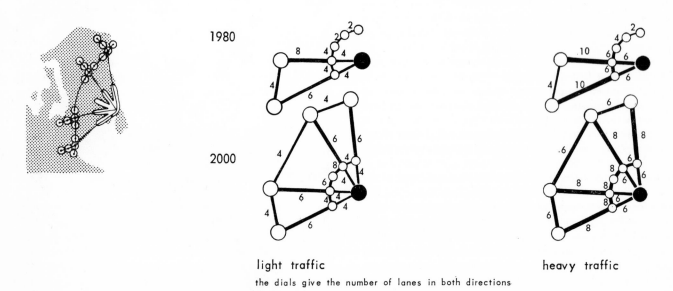

1980

2000

light traffic

heavy traffic

the dials give the number of lanes in both directions

one-finger plan, main transportation network

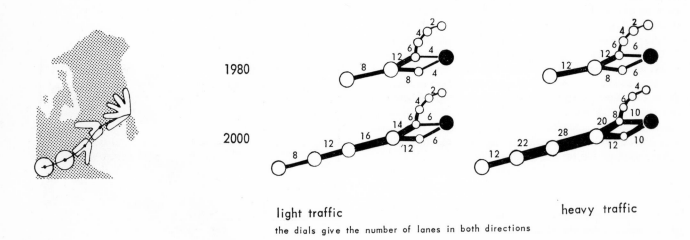

1980

2000

light traffic

heavy traffic

the dials give the number of lanes in both directions

which is shown in fig. 242 in which several possibilities were compared. The first possibility could be termed a solution of satellite sub-centres at major distances from Copenhagen, while the second involves a linear development solution of several centres along one main axis.

Copenhagen was the first major city to look clearly into the future, recognise the need for a different, more imaginative type of growth, and then have the courage to plan for it.

Even so, however, Copenhagen had to repeat this action within 11 years. The fact that such a forward-looking city had to revise the basis of its plans after only a decade shows that the real problem was not so much related to the form of the city, as to its nature. To allow Copenhagen to grow in concentric circles would probably have been wrong; it had to grow in a different way. Hence the five-finger plan was conceived; but it was once again a static plan, as if the

252

problem were a matter only of form, and therefore could not be successful. So the process had to be repeated later and a new plan conceived to replace the initial plan.

The degree to which the first plan was implemented can be seen in fig. 240, which compares the initial conception with the actual growth, and shows how difficult it is to influence metropolitan growth even when you have an imaginative plan, if it does not happen to be the right one. It also shows some of the weaknesses of this plan, weaknesses which still exist in the second plan. Both plans, though they are creative and far-seeing, overlook certain points: any problem of dynamic settlement expansion creates two main areas of difficulties, one being the area of external expansion, and the other the central area. While both plans take the areas of expansion into consideration, they do not take care of the central area of the city, since both permit additional pressures to be exercised on it.

Another point they do not take into consideration is the force of the attraction of coastal areas. The impact of this force can already be seen in fig. 240. Despite the fact that the fingers conceived in 1947 as directions of expansion did not include the northern coast at all and the southern one only partially, the greatest linear expansion of the city has taken place along these coasts.

After a short visit to Copenhagen in 1963 I attempted to show how such a situation could be dealt with in a different way, in answer to the request of the Danish magazine *Arkitekten*. The basic idea was that the city cannot grow normally if its heart cannot develop correspondingly; the physical proposal that followed is shown in fig. 241.

○ *Washington D.C.*

Another big city to break through the concentric conceptions of the past was Washington D.C. Here again a star-like conception was developed. This time the star spreads all around the city, which is natural, since Washington is in the middle of a plain, while Copenhagen is near the sea.

The plan which was proposed for Washington in 1958 is shown in fig. 243. Its advantages are the same as Copenhagen's plans, so are its weaknesses. Washington also gives no answer to the problem of pressure on the central area, and shows no special concern for the possibility of a natural expansion along the Potomac river. Though Washington has no coastal area, it has the Potomac which, although not as magnetic as a sea coast, attracts population both as a line of easy and cheap transportation (this fact has been completely overlooked) and as an area of natural beauty, leisure and sports.

If we look at Washington's new plan, having in mind the analysis of the forms of city expansion of the preceding chapter, we will see that there is no reason to believe that the next phase of Washington's star-shaped expansion will not be concentric development as in fig. 236. It is quite probable

243

Washington D.C.

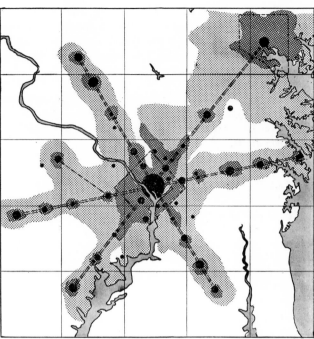

a   year 2000 plan
proposed by the National Capital
Planning Commission

grid 10 x 10 km

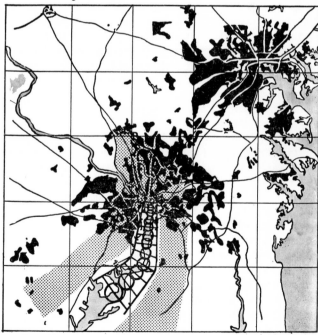

b   the future extension
proposed by the author

grid 10 x 10 km

that even if the proposed plan is implemented, it will not solve the real problems of the area.

Against these proposals I had the occasion, following a visit to Washington and a request by the Washington Redevelopment Land Agency in 1958, to develop a proposal for a dynamic expansion of Washington D.C.—not along the lines of transportation which were already overburdened by the regional traffic but along the Potomac (fig. 243b). This proposal may now have to be adjusted to new conditions created since (fig. 244), but it still has to be based on the creation of the main axis of growth where there are no pressures from regional forces and where the largest natural highway exists.

TRANSFORMATION OF SETTLEMENTS

A confused situation

During the development of settlements, transformation or change of form accompanies growth. While changes of size and form during the expansive period may be very great—when, for example, a city of one million begins to grow by 40,000 people a year instead of the 1000 of the beginning of its life—usually the rate of change, in both size and form gradually slows down with time.

This is a natural phenomenon and it is a general rule for many types of organisms, as D'Arcy Thompson pointed out in his discussion, previously quoted, of the development of animals. The difference between animals and settlements lies in the fact that while for the former there is no possibility of a reversal of this rule, for the latter many changes are possible, if Society undergoes major changes or takes basically different decisions. These rules are not reversible for animal organisms but correspond only to average normal solutions for human settlements.

Settlements reach a stage—as animals and plants do—at which even though there is a continuous change of their elements (Nature, Man, Society, Shells and Networks) the form of the settlement remains constant unless Man interferes consciously to change it. The analogy is only partially true, since while in the case of animals the form, after a certain stage, remains permanent for the whole body, in the case of settlements this is true for their older parts only and perhaps only for two of their dimensions. The analogy is also not valid from the point of view of satisfactory operation of the organism—since in animals the organism continues to operate satisfactorily after permanence of form has been reached, while in settlements this generally is not so. The central part may become permanent, but if the settlement continues to grow its operation will become more and more unsatisfactory.

The change in form creates many difficult problems. If the overall picture of expanding settlements can be called uncon-

254

244

Washington D.C.

proposal for dynamic growth based on an expanding centre

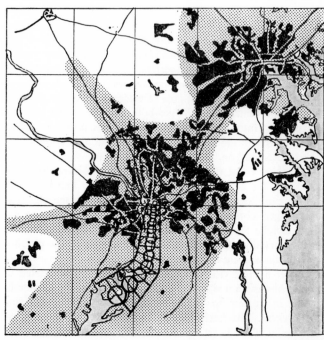

grid 10 x 10 km.

245

growth of settlements

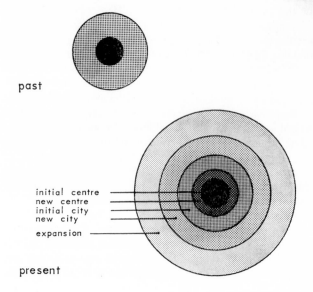

past

initial centre
new centre
initial city
new city
expansion

present

gross residential densities of settlements

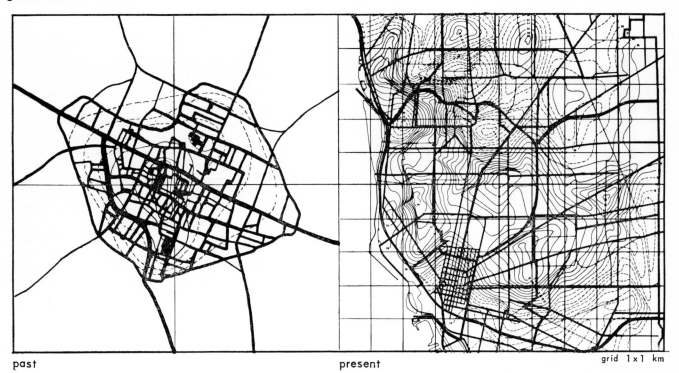

past   present   grid 1 x 1 km

————— above city average
‐ ‐ ‐ ‐ ‐ below city average
contour lines present two
persons per gross acre

trolled and confusing, the situation within the expanding settlements is even worse. There everything is chaotic. Even though many functions—such as proper underground networks or a modern traffic control system—may be highly organised, confusion reigns in the interrelationship of Man, Society, Shells and Networks. Confusion also reigns in the community and among the officials, who do not know what to do, since their actions often work against the goals they are trying to attain. And the area of the most extreme confusion is the central part of expanding settlements.

The reasons for this are quite natural:

- the original centre has had to stand very great pressures, for which it had not been prepared;
- the centre has spread into areas which formerly had other uses—mainly residential—thus creating a new problem zone;
- the whole of the older city has become relatively central, and even those parts that have not yet been taken over by the expanding centre are already beginning to feel the pressures of this expansion.

In all these areas there is continuous change caused by the expanding city, a change the inhabitants, and very often the administrators of these areas, do not know how to cope with. Even when they do know, they are unable to implement solutions, since they have no control over the causes of the problems which are found in the expansion of the settlements, over which they usually have no administrative control. The result is a city growing and being transformed on the basis of no plan preconceived by Man (fig. 245).

As a result of these pressures and changes, the formation of the city, which in the past always had higher densities of residence in the centre, is now changing, and there is a recession in the centre (fig. 246). It is not only the density of population which is being reduced; the central shopping areas are losing their importance as well. Some say that the people prefer regional shopping centres, implying that the centre should be abandoned if people themselves do not like it. I cannot accept this theory at all, and I do not believe that it has proved to be true. It is like saying that because somebody suffers from heart trouble, he no longer wants to climb stairs, and so we should consider this normal and abstain from any effort to ameliorate his health condition or to build upper

247

TURA centre, U.S.A.

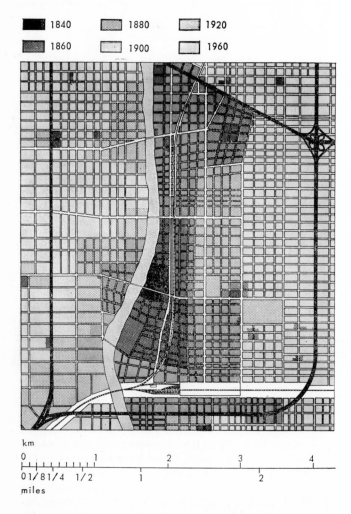

■ 1840 ▨ 1880 ▨ 1920
▨ 1860 ▨ 1900 □ 1960

km
0 ————————— 1 ———— 2 ———— 3 ———— 4
0 1/8 1/4 1/2 —— 1 ———— 2
miles

floors. The fact that many activities are fleeing from the central area does not mean that the central area should lose its importance at all. Certainly the dynamic growth of a settlement does necessarily mean that many additional nodal points, or points of central functions will be required. It can also mean that the central functions will change into functions of a higher order. But there is no validity in the statement that in this phase of change the centre will lose its importance as the real heart of the growing settlement. We could only maintain this if, after furnishing the main centre with as good possibilities of access (parking, etc.) as the outlying centre, we still witnessed a reduction in its central functions; but up to now no city has offered such possibilities to its central business centre, so we still have to try and see, in spite of the confusion of the situation, how we can revive the centres of settlements and

re-establish them as the most important areas in the whole region. As for the overall confusion of the situation, our first task is to try to understand it.

Central areas

In order to understand the magnitude of the confusion in the centre of the growing city in the process of becoming a Dynapolis, let us follow the evolution of the centre of TURA city, which, as we have seen, passed through many phases of growth until the need for surgery became apparent.

What in 1960 was considered to be the central area of TURA, had not even been built in 1840. The whole city then had been less than one-tenth of the present centre. By 1860 some of the parts of the present centre were still open fields, and this held true even in 1880. It was only in 1900 that more than 50 per cent of the present centre had become a built-up area, and only in 1920 was the present centre completely built-up. Between 1920 and 1960 it became a smaller and smaller part of the total metropolitan area of TURA, and by 1960, it had to suffer from surgery which cut through areas that had been created only 40 to 60 years earlier (fig. 247).

How confused the activities in the centres of such areas are, can be demonstrated by the example of Athens, where public services, government and administration, educational and cultural institutions are mixed with commerce and all the other central functions of a metropolitan area of 2 million people (fig. 248). A simple example suffices to show how unreasonable it is to allow this to happen. Let us look at the widths of the streets and the volume of their traffic (fig. 249). If we draw in a schematic way the widths of major streets of a metropolitan area with a very old centre, we will find that the central area has the narrowest streets of all, and that they grow progressively wider as we move further from the centre. If we now superimpose traffic volume on this pattern of street widths, we will find that the highest volume of traffic can be found in the areas with the narrowest streets. This alone is enough to demonstrate the irrationality of what is happening in the central areas of metropolitan cities. We will also find other inconsistencies. Not only do we find narrow streets where wide streets are needed to accommodate heavy traffic, we also find that instead of extensive parking facilities for public buildings we have very small parking areas. Though large plots are needed for both public and private functions only very small irregular plots are available. Instead of freedom for new designs we have no room in which to move, and where we most need freedom for expropriation, we have the largest investment and the highest prices (fig. 250).

The result is that the central area does not correspond as structure and form to the existing needs and does not function properly; both people and several functions abandon it, and—as we have already mentioned—the conclusion is drawn

256

248

central area of Athens, Greece

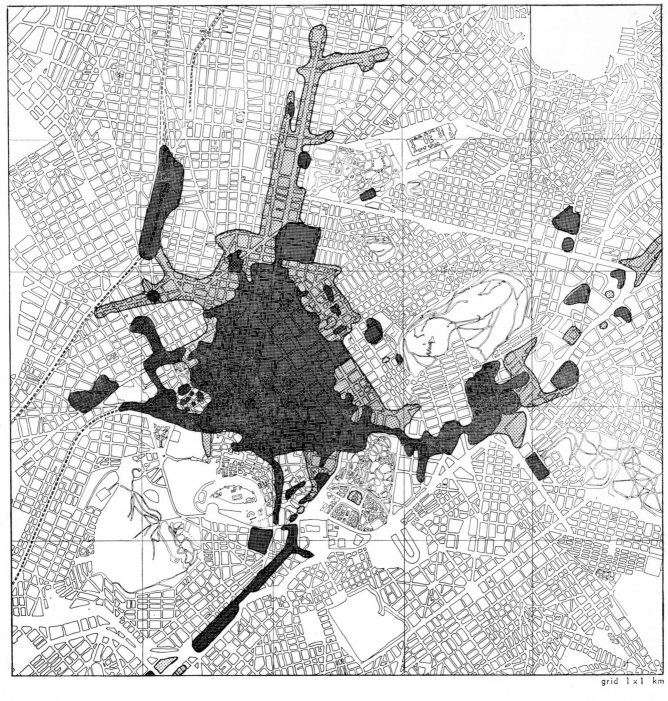

central area and central functions in 1940

expansion of central area and functions 1940 - 1964

grid 1 x 1 km

km

0   1   2   3   4   5

0   1/8   1/4   1/2   1   2   3

miles

T

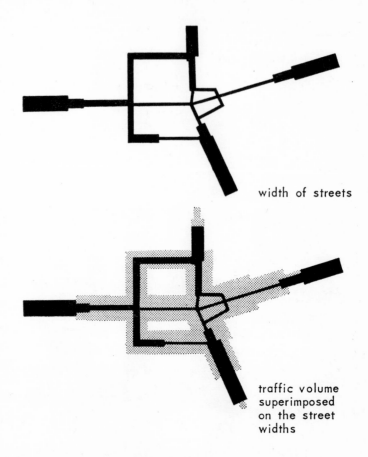

width of streets

traffic volume
superimposed
on the street
widths

that central areas are disliked by people, and should not be revived. In this way we are abandoning the patient who is suffering from heart disease while continuing to add fat all around his body and thus exerting even more pressure on his heart muscles.

Whole settlements

This critical situation is not limited only to the central areas. In varying degrees it appears in all parts of the existing settlement, some areas of which suffer from great pressures, others from depressions in their neighbourhood, and so on. This can be demonstrated by an electromagnetic model in which we compare the conditions of certain activities in TURA at two points in time, 1920 and 1945 (fig. 251). We can see the significance of such changes within the total urban body, in a series of drawings showing changes in the urban structure and form caused by urban growth (fig. 252), changes due to special developments (fig. 253) and changes due to irregular growth in height (fig. 254). We can then see the

result of all this: an abnormal pattern in the distribution of elements (fig. 255); a pattern physically expressed by the wholly irregular combination of a variety of functions, varying heights of buildings, mixed social groups, etc.

I believe we can identify three major areas of change:

o in all nodal points, both the main centre of the city and centres of parts of the city;

o along all circulatory lines, the impact of which is sometimes beneficial for the surrounding area and sometimes not, depending on what type of circulatory line it is, what the degree of its importance is, and what kind of traffic it has, as well as what type of area surrounds it;

o those surrounding very specialised activities, which, again, may or may not have a beneficial effect on the surrounding area.

If we map these areas of change, we can define the locations where dynamic changes in a certain urban area are likely to take place (fig. 256). The closer the Shells are to the main lines and nodal points of greater importance, the greater the changes they will have to meet.

250

in the growing city

we need:

wide streets for
heavy traffic

but we have:

narrow streets

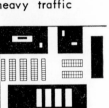

big parking plots for
public buildings

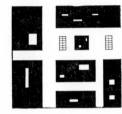

very small parking
facilities

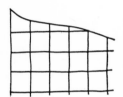

large plots for public
and private functions

very small
irregular plots

freedom for
new designs

no room to move

freedom for
expropriation

the largest investment
and the highest prices

251

**TURA: electromagnetic model showing densities
of general activities**

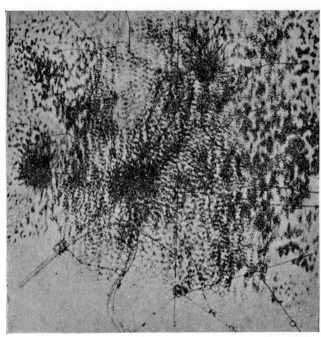

1920

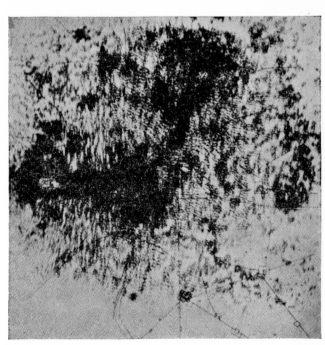

1945

259

changes of urban structure and form
microscopic view

changes of urban structure and form
microscopic view

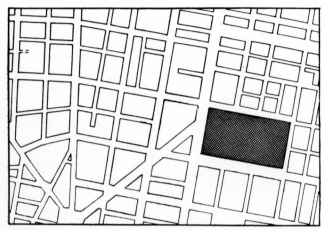

in a residential area not far from
the town centre a large market is built

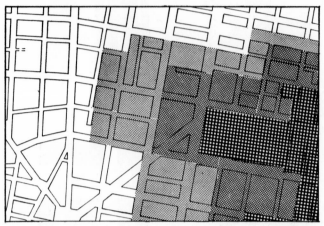

normal residential area not far from the town centre
the residential area is changing as the central area
expands

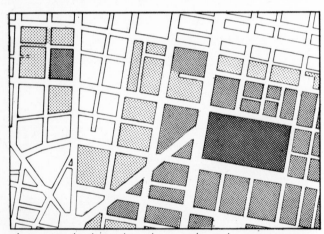

shops are built within the residential area as an
extension of the market with warehouses next to
them - the first inhabitants move out

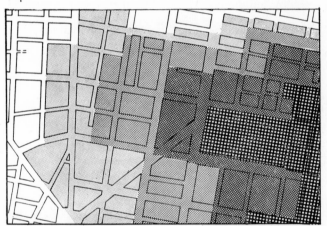

changes are spreading as the central area
continues to expand

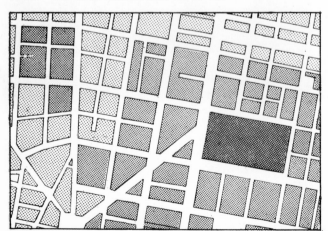

more inhabitants have moved out and new, lower
income groups are moving in
the original character of the area is entirely changed

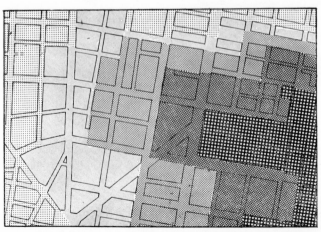

ultimately the whole area is changed to a greater
or lesser degree

254

changes of urban structure and form

buildings of ever increasing height

 1 - 2 floors

 3 - 4 floors

 5 floors and over

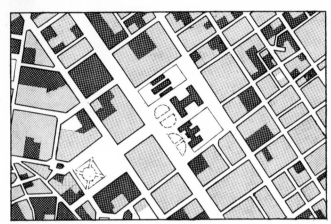

first phase

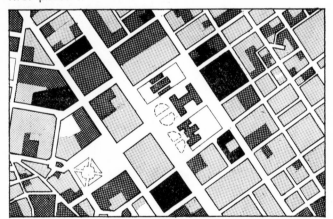

second phase

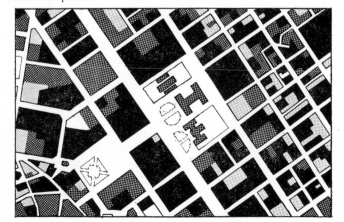

third phase

255

changes of urban structure

changing pattern of income groups

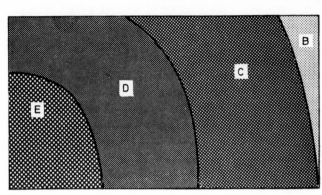

a. early phase highest - income group next to the business centre E

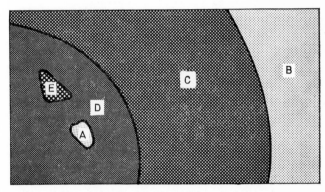

b. business spreads into the high - income area the first slums (A) appear as areas are taken over by lowest - income groups

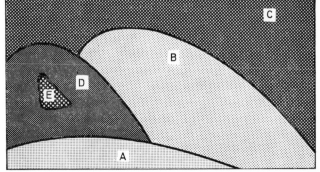

c. the unplanned continuation of change means a continuing deterioration of several areas and a consequent uncontrolled redistribution of social and economic groups

256

changes of urban structure

areas of positive and negative influence

257

the fate of a cell 'C'

first phase: a farm in 1840

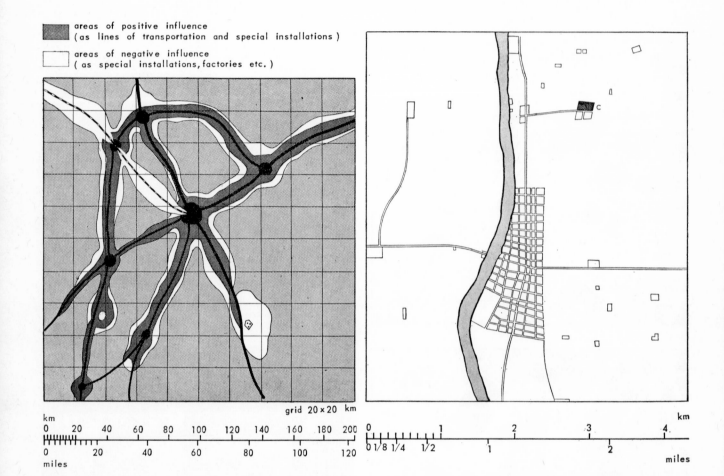

areas of positive influence
(as lines of transportation and special installations)

areas of negative influence
(as special installations, factories etc.)

grid 20 x 20 km

km
0   20   40   60   80   100   120   140   160   180   200

0   20   40   60   80   100   120
miles

km
0   1   2   3   4

0 1/8 1/4   1/2   1   2

miles

Such changes affect every small cell of the city as the history of a cell in TURA will show from the period of 1840 to 1960. It started as a farm (fig. 257) and turned into a residential neighbourhood of a small settlement within only two years, then became a centre of activities for an expanding urban community (fig. 258). Its deterioration started because of pressures from a nearby centre. Then it became a part of the central area of the city (fig. 259), although its character soon changed because of a nearby highway; finally (fig. 260) it became the junction of two highways. Thus, in 120 years it has suffered six basic transformations, or one every 20 years. This means that in the last 40 years, during which one city-planner was active, this cell suffered three changes. Had the planner, at the beginning of his career, planned for the first change, in the middle of his career he would have had to

change his plans completely, and the new plans would once again have ceased to be valid by the end of his career. A grim outlook for the cell of the city and for its planner.

The types of problems which parts of the city suffer from are not the same everywhere. In some cases they mean the elimination of the values of the past. This is particularly true of good sections of old cities which had a certain human scale or certain values which have been eliminated by new functions and their demands. This is the problem of many existing monuments where there is a necessity for a synthesis between them and their scale of the past.

Another example of how far changes affect the micro-scale of the city can be demonstrated by the history of a square in Athens during the last 40 years (fig. 261). In 1920 it was a square planted with pine trees, where children played, and

262

258

(right) the fate of a cell 'C'

second phase: centre of activities of an expanding urban residential area in 1880

259

(below left) the fate of a cell 'C'

third phase: absorbed by the central area of TURA in 1920

260

(below right) the fate of a cell 'C'

fourth phase: expropriated for a clover leaf for access to highways H1 and H2 in 1960

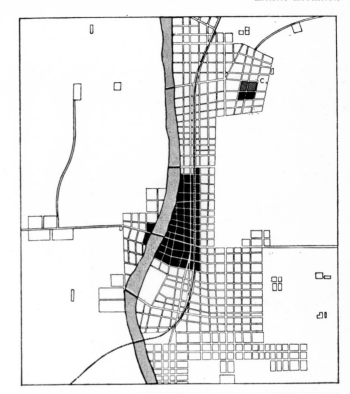

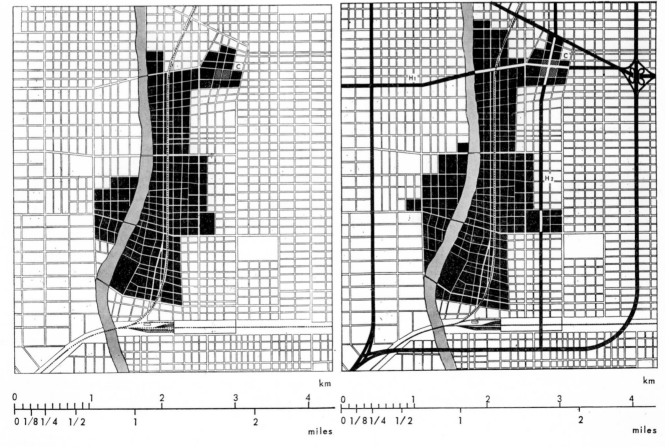

twenty years ago

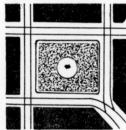

forty years ago

ten years ago

thirty years ago

and now

which grown-ups used as a park. Thirty years ago the streets all around it were widened, and a monument placed in its centre; but people could still visit the square and enjoy its facilities. Twenty years ago the square was remodelled into a roundabout and the statue in the middle began to look like a traffic policeman. Ten years ago it was turned into a bus station and one-way high speed traffic moved around it.

Recently the high volume of traffic required a complete remodelling of the square: another bus station was created and the statue was transferred to a corner, from which it could follow the traffic and contemplate urban evolution. In the meantime, the buildings of the square which had one and two stories in 1920, have been demolished to give place to eight and nine storey buildings.

CHAPTER FIVE
EKISTIC PATHOLOGY

DEFINITION AND SUBJECT

Pathology and diseases

Our dynamically growing settlements have problems of health; they are suffering because of their growth. This suffering may be just growing pains, or it may be more than that, a real disease; they may be suffering from a typical functional or structural disease. We have realised that settlements do suffer in many respects, and we are taking measures to relieve them of their ills; but I do not believe that we have ever made a systematic study of their ills, and that is the cause of the confusion surrounding so many matters concerning settlements.

I think that there is a need for a systematic study of the ills and diseases of settlements, a need for an Ekistic pathology. For this term I turn once again to medicine. I have already made myself clear as to how far we are allowed to go in borrowing from the other sciences. Like human organisms, settlements suffer from many diseases which have to be studied through pathology; this is as far as the analogy can take us. Unlike those of human bodies, the growing pains of settlements may constitute a fatal disease. The pathology of settlements, unlike that of human bodies, may in certain cases reach the conclusion that it is necessary not to relieve the ills but to make alterations in the patient.

Ekistic pathology has to study the diseases of settlements, the functional and structural changes resulting from them, the deviations from normal conditions, which may be either physiological or anatomical ones that constitute or characterise a disease and finally, the causes of such diseases or abnormal changes of settlements.

In order to succeed in this study we must start by defining normal conditions, those existing in a healthy settlement. This is the most difficult part of our undertaking, since such a definition depends on many objective and subjective factors. When we say, for example, that a street is congested by cars, we can show that this is so and we can measure its intensity; but when we say that it takes people a long time to drive home, we can measure the phenomenon, but will probably

not agree on whether the time is in fact long. People may by this time have become used to long commuting hours and may not react unfavourably to them. After all, if the average citizen could consciously define normal conditions, he would be in a position to recognise deviations from them immediately, and settlements perhaps would not reach such critical conditions.

For a definition of health, I turn to René Dubos who, speaking of Man, says, 'Health is the expression of the extent to which the individual and the social body maintain in readiness the resources required to meet the exigencies of the future',[24] and 'health depends upon fitness to the environment; it involves a state of adaptiveness'.[25] I think that by using this definition, we can say that healthy or normal conditions exist in a settlement if it is operating in accordance with the standards set consciously for it by its inhabitants, and if it maintains in readiness the resources necessary to meet the exigencies of the future. We can also state, I think, that the health of settlements is determined by their ability to meet the requirements set by their inhabitants and the environment.

It becomes apparent that the definitions used by medicine to define healthy and normal conditions for Man, are not adequate where human settlements are concerned. But they may constitute part of the complete definition that we need. Unlike human organisms settlements are not genetically conditioned by Nature, they are created by Man. Here again we find that difference between biological individuals like organisms and settlements which are biological individuals of a higher order. Their normal conditions do not depend only upon fitness and adaptability, but also upon the standards or norms set by Man; they have to represent the attainment of goals set by Man and not by Nature and they can be altered to accommodate the requirements.

Causes of diseases

There are many causes of diseases of settlements, as can be expected when we remember that they consist of five elements and many organs and parts, every one of which can be affected either separately or in connection with others.

There are four basic causes of disease:

- aging,
- abnormal growth,
- changing functions and norms,
- wrong action.

Aging is the cause of many diseases as it is in biological individuals of a lower order. Unlike the diseases of these other biological individuals though, the aging of settlements need not be fatal, since their life-span is not pre-conditioned in any way—only the life-span of some of their elements and parts is. There is no reason why human settlements should not be eternal or at least live to be thousands of years old. Modern Man would have been very comfortable in Crete had he been allowed to reside in the palace of Minos, without it being necessary to make any changes. I believe even further that living in that palace during the summer would have been much more satisfactory than in any other house or building in Crete of today.

Abnormal growth is the cause of many diseases and can be defined as growth beyond the limits for which the settlements have been built. The diseases it causes are not incurable, but they are nevertheless very grave. Unlike human organisms, settlements have not been genetically conceived for growth; a street cannot widen by itself as an artery does and a central square cannot grow, as even the brain does within the confines of the skull. Man, however, usually builds settlements with some margins for increased performance, and these margins constitute the limits of normal growth; once the settlement grows beyond them diseases begin to appear.

Unlike in human organisms—where abnormal growth can be observed very seldom—in settlements this phenomenon has been cropping up continuously during the last two centuries; the underlying cause is of great concern to us. The population is growing, the economy expanding, the surface increasing, the densities becoming either too high or too low, the traffic very problematical. In the present era abnormal growth has become the normal case for large settlements, but in the way in which the situation is being handled at present, it still constitutes a grave disease, since settlements have not become adapted to growth.

Changing functions and norms are the other grave cause of diseases of settlements. One of the most apparent of these diseases is the use being made of street networks, originally meant for Man, by motorcars which differ in nature, size, speed and requirements. No reasonable mechanical engineer would construct two bands moving any kind of products in directions crossing each other at the same level, and try to control their movement by red lights. Yet this is exactly what we are doing in our cities. The function has changed, but the structure has remained the same.

What is really happening is that in the beginning certain initial functions—in our example people walking—are accommodated by certain structures, in this case narrow straight streets in a grid-iron system. Then the functions change—motorcars are introduced into the system and the disease begins, since the structure cannot be adjusted. In Nature, in such cases, the unfit organisms die while the fittest survive, leading to evolution. In settlements we let the disease continue or try to cure it with half measures. We cannot sit around waiting for the fittest to survive while continuing to live in unfit settlements with the consolation that time will take care of them. Their lives are long and ours are short.

But norms may also change; what had been satisfactory for the past generation may not be so any more. The settlement may remain the same; its structure and function may not have changed; but Man is demanding more from it—for him the settlement is below normal as the new function cannot be served by the old structure.

The last cause of disease is the wrong action taken by Man when dealing with other diseases or when creating new settlements, organs or parts of them. This cause has been entering the picture lately much more often than it used to, since Man is more confused now than he has been at any time on the subject of his settlements.

VARIATIONS OF DISEASES

Diseases and individuals

The four basic causes of disease may have their impact on a settlement either separately or in different combinations. There are no two similar settlements and since the causes of disease influence each settlement in different combinations and in different degrees, we can repeat, and apply to settlements, what medicine learned long ago: that diseases do not exist in the abstract, but only in individual patients. Seen in this way every disease in every settlement is a case by itself and depends on the conditions of the locality at a given time.

The study of such diseases shows that apart from their individuality they have some universal characteristics and some general variations. These are in accordance with certain general conditions, such as geographic location or phase of development. There are also however some misconceptions about the variations of the diseases, and for this reason I will deal in this section with both real and fictitious variations.

To do this I am forced to rely on my experience only since these questions have never been dealt with systematically. Since no measurements of the abnormal conditions have been made, I will speak in general terms about diseases of settlements in which the inhabitants themselves have spoken about problems, or in which the experienced observer can recognise definite deviations from what experience has shown to be the normal conditions.

Universal settlements and diseases

There are types of settlements which can be found in many parts of the world, and diseases of the same universal nature. These are the most important categories of the problems we have to deal with. Any review of the present problems and diseases of human settlements presents a grim picture. The failure of humanity to face them during the last two centuries is quite evident. Indeed, humanity has failed even to realise their existence, much less develop a system of handling this difficult and complicated situation.

We are not yet conscious of where the evolution of human settlements is taking us, even though we think we know where we will be tomorrow. As long as we do not know this how can we be certain what 'normal' means and how can settlements be made fit to face the conditions of the future? I do not believe that we can be sure whether or not the present-day settlement types—village, city, Dynapolis and Dynametropolis—will survive. Are they perhaps merely a modest introduction to the only settlement that will ultimately remain on the Earth: a universal, polymorphous, multi-nucleated human settlement? Perhaps the settlement types we know are simply the experiments necessary to the eventual evolution of this universal settlement.

Vast changes are taking place at such a high speed that we do not realise them. We see the results, and because of the enormity of the problems they imply, we retreat from facing them. We can be sure of only one thing: the problems and diseases of human settlements which are so large and complicated, cannot be well understood in the absence of a general theory.

Variations due to civilisations

Differences between cultures and civilisations, expressed in human settlements, are determined by various historical, racial, geographic and climatic factors which have exerted an influence over each nation and have led to the formation of local cultures. These are expressed by differences in the pattern of life and of settlements, in the concept of normality and therefore also in the concept of diseases.

However, it is highly probable that before cities were built, when mankind lived in villages, there were no differences among settlements in different parts of the world. All were of a primitive character and, most likely, all had the same general characteristics. It may be that the differences between settlements became apparent with the birth of local civilisations. So, we may roughly say that, before the creation of the early cities, 5,000–6,000 years ago, human settlements everywhere were more or less similar; or, at any rate, that there was nothing besides the speed of evolution leading to different kinds of settlements. Their diseases must have been the same as well.

Then local civilisations began, and, within these, when the settlements and buildings outgrew the primitive stage, a differentiation between settlements was revealed, in the form of local solutions and local architectural systems, as well as in local problems and diseases (fig. 262). These local systems gradually prevailed in the most developed and civilised parts of the world, since their creation was caused by a process of civilisation. Conversely, primitive expressions, mainly in villages and remote towns that had not been affected by advanced civilisations, were governed by similar rules and bore the same primitive characteristics.

With the advent of modern technology certain integrating forces were set in motion, and once again there was a movement towards the creation of uniform expressions throughout the world. These forces have been mainly scientific and technological. So, whereas a primitive villager's house is influenced solely by local forces such as climate, workmen, materials and traditions, a railway station or a harbour is built for trains or ships common to all parts of the world, and an airport is built for similar airplanes manufactured in a limited number of places in the world. Local expressions, which were so important until the seventeenth century, competed with new machine forces which moved towards universality. In the past, prior to the rise of civilisations, the forces of integration were solely represented by local, natural elements; later local civilisations differentiated the expressions. Today, universal forces are beginning to exert integrating influences that tend to suppress local expression.

These integrating phenomena have been intensified in the twentieth century, to the extent that there is danger of the extinction of local expressions. Since we do not know if the universal forms resulting from the forces of world technology will develop into settlements that are in all respects superior to those of local expression, it behoves us to protect existing local differences. Until we know which of the elements of Ecumenopolis should be based on ecumenic culture, we should do our best to preserve as many as possible of the existing settlements which embody local cultures and well-established values.

Thus, what have often appeared to be great differences between an Eastern and a Western civilisation, are in fact differences between local and ecumenic civilisations. Does this mean that there are no problems especially affecting the Eastern countries? The major problems affect both East and West, since they are of universal nature. But, the Eastern countries are entering modern technological development at a later time, which means that several problems are much more critical there than in the West.

In the West technological development started two or three centuries ago and local expressions have been gradually diminishing ever since. In most of the East, the advent of modern science and technology has taken place suddenly, threatening local expressions with complete suppression. The West at least has had some time in which to try to find an

267

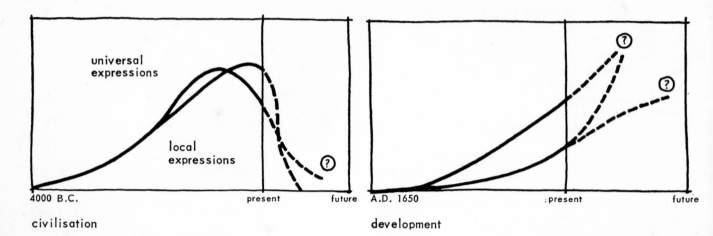

civilisation   development

the different curves indicate that several civilisations followed their own roads

equilibrium between local and universal expression. For the East, this is a much more difficult task, since it is at present absorbing a mature technology so intensely that it is destroying local expression long before it can create the necessary balance between the local and the universal. This is why settlements of the East are wearing out more rapidly and more dangerously than those of the West.

For the future, the dangers of rapid technological development in the West are that, being the pioneer, it cannot be shown examples of the new problems confronting it. When large new motorways destroy the pattern of a well-established American city there is no precedent from which to learn how to handle this menace. The dangers for the East lie in the fact that the immediate absorption of the technological progress achieved in the West is effected without allowing the time necessary for its assimilation. As a result, it is possible that settlements in the East may be led to extinction faster than in the West, though by the same diseases unless they are able to benefit rapidly from the experiences of the West.

Thus, speaking about different civilisations and their influence upon settlements, we may say that:

o Different civilisations have led to different problems, diseases and solutions in human settlements. Before local civilisations exerted their influence, diseases, problems and solutions were basically universal.

o Local civilisations have recently been evincing a tendency to become ecumenic or universal. But the time and degree of this change vary.

o There is a great danger for mankind that local cultures may be lost before they can be replaced by a universal culture of a higher quality.

o In the West, this danger is primarily caused by the fact that it has no experience from which to learn.

o In the East, this danger is caused by the fast rate at which it is absorbing Western technology, allowing no time for assimilation.

o The need to preserve local cultures before they are engulfed by the forthcoming world culture is universal.

Variations due to other factors

Civilisations are not the only factors which influence the creation of special types of settlements, and their problems and diseases. There are many more factors which differ depending on region, country and locality, on geographic, climatic, economic, social, political, technological and aesthetic forces. If we overlook these and concentrate only on the universal problem, we are running the risk of making a mistake in the diagnosis of the disease and eliminating cultural differences and local factors, which must be respected as much as the universal ones. We shall then witness the destruction of many solutions and values which generations of nations and cultures have worked hard to develop. We do not have the right to overlook these values, at least not until we have created others of equal, if not greater importance.

Many different problems have local importance. There are problems of developed and undeveloped areas, problems of built-up jungles as well as tropical jungles. All areas have certain common universal characteristics, as well as many specific local characteristics, apart from problems of different cultures and civilisations. To exemplify the kind of problems we face, I will discuss one which usually creates confusion—that of the differences of settlements, problems and diseases between Eastern and Western nations.

It is difficult to speak about East and West. Our conceptions are so general that each of us attributes a different value to them. These conceptions are geographic, cultural and political. Perspectives change in relation to our position and so, inevitably, we tend to give different interpretations of the same phenomena because of the angle from which we observe them. We may be looking at them too closely or from too great a distance (fig. 263). This is valid for both space and time; making it possible for us to overlook either the universal aspects or the local ones.

We are obliged to adopt some boundary between East and West, and the simplest is the geographic one. As a matter of rough approximation, we will accept a dividing line between East and West that places Europe, America and Oceania on one side, and Asia on the other.

It is much more difficult to place Africa, for if we speak of civilisations which have adopted Western technology part of Africa may be said to comply. But if we speak in terms of the degree of economic development, the whole of Africa is less developed than any other continent, and consequently the whole ought to be classified as a less developed region. So we must consider Africa as part of an intermediate area. Geographically, Africa would belong to the West, since the dividing line runs through the Aegean and the Red Sea; whereas if we were to place it according to its degree of economic development, it would belong to the East; but even so, what about South Africa, and what about the white population of the remaining continent?

In viewing the East and the West in this manner, we see that they have many points of similarity, but also many differences. Their differences may be classified into two categories:

o those due to differences of civilisations,
o those due to differences in degrees and phases of economic development.

One might wonder why we do not mention differences of climate, topography, etc., as well. Usually, the tendency is to associate the East with tropical climate and the West with a colder climate. Yet this is not correct, since many cold climates exist in Asia, both in the mountains of the south, as well as in the north, while numerous areas of the West have tropical climates. It would have been much more correct to associate climate with north and south than with east and west, but even this would have required qualifications about hemispheres, latitudes, etc. Consequently, the conception of climate should not affect our minds as a principal factor of difference between East and West. On the contrary, we might say that the range of different climates common to both East and West is rather an integrating element.

It appears that the differences between settlements of the East and those of the West are caused not by geography and

263

settlements and their diseases can be seen from different distances and then the conclusions are different

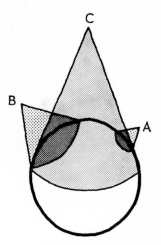

climate, but by the fact that their phase of economic development of settlements is different and so are their civilisations; that is, the conditions of evolution have varied in different parts of the world, and technical evolution has taken place at a different rate in different civilisations. We must therefore distinguish between countries with different degrees of development.

At this point it might be useful to consider whether the terms 'developed' and 'underdeveloped' are applicable to settlements in the same way as they are to countries. The truth of the matter is that in some respects developed countries do not have better settlements than underdeveloped ones. From a technological and economic standpoint, more developed settlements can be found in developed countries; on the other hand it is not at all certain that the large cities of developed countries give more hope for better living than the smaller settlements of underdeveloped countries which are in many ways similar to the small settlements of the past.

We are therefore faced with a very intricate problem. We have both good and bad old settlements in developed and underdeveloped countries. There are technologically deficient settlements as well as technologically developed ones. If, however, we consider the overall results achieved in present-day large cities of developed countries as far as the way of living is concerned, we must be highly reserved in saying that the developed countries have better settlements than the less developed ones; technological development does not necessarily produce better settlements. If we handle this query carefully and critically we will recognise our inability to judge even the settlements we are now building as compared to the settlements of the past. It is with this doubt in mind that we should approach the subject of the overall result achieved in human settlements.

CLASSIFICATION OF DISEASES

Several classifications

There are many possible classifications of diseases which make sense, depending on the case and the purpose of the study. They can be divided into two basic categories—those dealing with the general characteristics of the disease (cause, structural or functional nature, etc.) and those dealing with the location of the disease (in relation to the elements or the Ekistic units, or organs or parts of them which have been affected).

A classification by causes follows the four basic causes (aging, abnormal growth, changing functions and norms, and wrong action) and can proceed to their subdivisions as related to the degree of the disease. This allows comparisons between diseases resulting from the same cause or between their subdivisions as related to subdivisions of the causes. Abnormal growth of a settlement may be caused by the abnormal growth of its population, area, buildings, etc.

Classification by structural or functional diseases can be of great importance for the prescription of therapy. If a disease is structural, for example, if a section of a settlement has been built on too steep a gradient, or a crossroads has been badly designed, the only remedy would involve a structural alteration. If the disease is functional, for example, if a road is overcongested with people or motorcars, the remedy can be functional, a diversion of people or cars to another road. If the disease is both structural and functional, which is very often the case, then structural changes are imperative.

Classification by elements is very important since it locates the disease and relates it more easily to its causes. A disease may affect only one element or more, or all of them. This depends on the extent of the infection, since in the long run, if the disease is not cured when it appears in the first element, it is bound to influence the whole settlement.

A disease may well start by affecting only one element. Let us say the buildings of the area are aging and turning into slums. Very soon this area will be abandoned by its original inhabitants and begin to attract the settlement's weakest economic and social groups; as a result of this not only the buildings but the Networks, the parks, etc., will deteriorate. The whole settlement will eventually be affected.

The spread of the disease into the system and the infection of one element by another is so powerful that after a while not even the initial infection and cause is recognisable, and there is a great confusion of causes and effects.

The classifications by units and organs can be equally important, as the disease is completely different at each level and scale. We may have a disease of the circulatory system but this could be caused either by the inefficiency of the small residential roads which have no room for parking and, therefore, force the function of parking onto major arteries

264

basic classification of diseases

by causes	by aspects	by elements					total
		Nature	Man	Society	Shells	Networks	
aging	structure						
	function						
	structure and function						
abnormal growth	structure						
	function						
	structure and function						
changing function and norms	structure						
	function						
	structure and function						
false action	structure						
	function						
	structure and function						

thus choking their own traffic, or it may be a disease of the major arteries themselves, which being insufficient for their own traffic, cause its diversion into minor residential streets.

Basic classification

In order to face the problems of different diseases we need a system of classification which can help us to order and understand them. Such a classification has to be based on causes and elements, and can be presented in a two-dimensional diagram. So as to be more complete it can incorporate classification by structural and functional diseases (fig. 264). Further elaboration will lead to location of the areas affected; consequently elements will have to be subdivided by Ekistic units.

SOME BASIC DISEASES

Disorderly new patterns

Many settlements created during the last generations do not have the orderly patterns of structure, and consequently of function and life, which are necessary for normal healthy conditions. Since this necessity is disputed by some 'free thinkers' who believe that order is not necessary and that our settlements can be left to develop in a disorderly manner, I have to go back to their history to prove my point, which is that disorder in human settlements constitutes a disease.

In the beginning mankind created rooms which were circular. Then, when one room ceased to suffice, several rooms were built side by side. But they could not be connected to form an orderly and meaningful system. Man kept on trying, and finally succeeded in constructing an orderly house by changing the form of the rooms and making them into squares or oblongs. The house had a certain size and a certain order. When it grew beyond its normal size and turned into a school or a hospital, the order changed as well. There is a proper pattern for every size. The same thing happened with the villages which, at the beginning, did not have a specific size and order. Man gradually learned that they were necessary and he created them. This progress was even more pronounced in the cities which finally reached the point of having both definite sizes, and order.

Now, after thousands of years, both size and order have been lost because of new requirements. We must face the fact that our settlements cannot be successful until they once again have proper size and order.

If we turn to Nature and the different kinds of biological individuals it has created, ranging from lower order cells to higher order organisms such as plants and animals, we will find that they all have a definite size and order. Such also has been the case with all successful settlements of the past; and we, therefore, are entitled to consider our present-day settlements, lacking size and order, as deficient and ailing, and their disease a very grave one.

Disorderly changes

This is a very basic disease which, when manifest in a reasonably small scale at a slow tempo is quite harmless; but when it covers large areas and develops quickly it can be disastrous. It has already hit several cities, especially in the United States, and has led to the adoption of special measures known as 'urban renewal'. The causes are very seldom limited to the aging of the settlement concerned. Very often the causes are many, and they include age, abnormal growth, faulty action, etc. They all result in disorderly transformations of the settlement. Because of the importance of both disease and therapy I deal with them at some length.

Aging and an evolution of functions in the central areas of settlements, and attempts at renewal and remodelling in the effort to take care of the increasing demands, follow alternate phases (fig. 265). As long as the growth of the city is slow, the growth of the centre presents no special problems. The centre can stand the gradual addition of some new activities which are absorbed by existing margins, while small additional pressure can be dealt with by relatively simple measures, such as traffic regulations. However, the time comes when the growth of traffic in the centre surpasses the maximum capacity of the container. Consequently a new highway will probably be opened to permit a better evolution

265

phases of growth of a settlement's centre

relationship between growth of traffic and functions

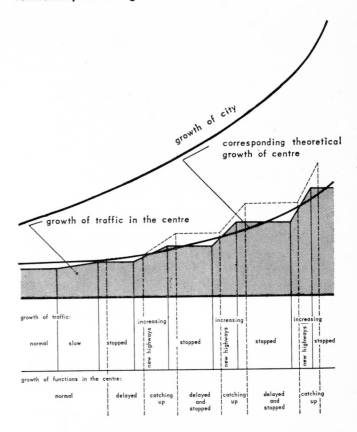

of the centre. But as traffic increases it may go beyond what the improved centre can stand. As a result there will be a discontinuation of the growth of the centre, since it will no longer have the possibility to develop (fig. 266). Perhaps new highways will be opened, and as a result traffic will once again be free to develop, and the centre will grow until its traffic once again increases beyond the capacity of the central area, which means a levelling of traffic and of the centre's development. Then, through new highways and new surgical action, traffic will again catch up, then the centre will catch up, and so on. In this way we have alternating periods of growth and delayed growth, before and during the surgical operations. Such action, however, can only lead to the eventual death of the centre, a death through repeated surgery (fig. 267). An example of this gradual elimination of the centre can be found in Los Angeles, where two thirds of the downtown area is devoted to traffic, freeways, streets and parking (fig. 268).

The situation is equally difficult when we consider urban renewal (fig. 269). In a dynamically growing settlement, the

266

(below) death of a settlement's centre by surgery

267

(right) urban renewal by surgery
Downtown Detroit, U.S.A. (1961)

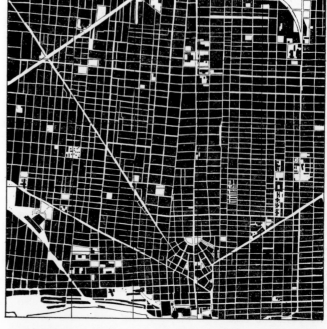

a. before

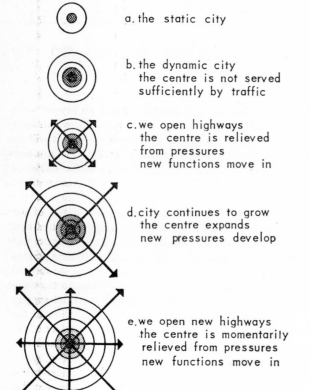

a. the static city

b. the dynamic city
   the centre is not served
   sufficiently by traffic

c. we open highways
   the centre is relieved
   from pressures
   new functions move in

d. city continues to grow
   the centre expands
   new pressures develop

e. we open new highways
   the centre is momentarily
   relieved from pressures
   new functions move in

km
0   1   2   3   4   5

grid 1 x 1 km

0 1/8 1/4 1/2   1   2   3
miles

b. after the work started

two-thirds of downtown Los Angeles is devoted to freeways, streets and parking

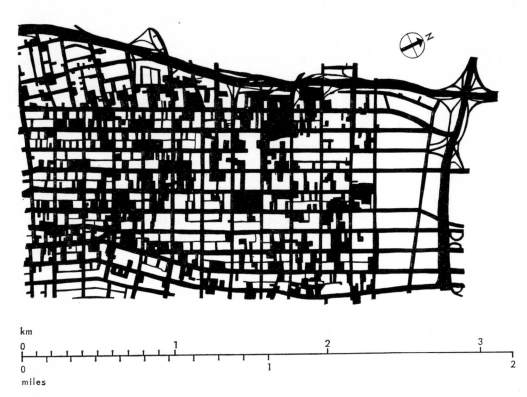

km

0   1   2   3

0   1   2

miles

central area A, and perhaps a ring B surrounding it, is blighted; efforts at improvement are made and these areas are remodelled or completely rebuilt. By the time this process has been completed, a new ring C has been blighted due to the continuous growth of the city. This area is then taken over by some low-income groups which are interested in being near the centre. Thus, the settlement moves in a vicious circle.

An interesting problem of densities arises here concerning the people who discover that they can settle at a low cost in these depressed areas. If areas A and B are rebuilt with the same density of residences and activities as before, they immediately become congested and all new growth is forced to move into ring C. When we try to relieve existing pressures by rebuilding A and B at lower densities, ring C will inevitably suffer greater and perhaps unbearable pressures. If, on the other hand, we rebuild areas A and B at a higher density than before, we shall be adding new problems to this area, as a direct consequence of its increased density.

Such examples show that urban renewal has now in many cases become a necessity, and that we must go about its implementation in a very systematic way. Urban renewal by

the method of replacing each building as it becomes obsolete, the method in use for thousand of years, is no longer satisfactory in areas which suffer from very great pressures, because economic and technological developments have resulted in a much faster rate of change in the patterns of life and those of the corresponding buildings and facilities. Therefore, we are being forced to start thinking of renewal over extensive areas as a public responsibility.

It is time to ask ourselves why government sponsored urban renewal has only now become indispensable, when urban areas have been developing for more than 5,000 years. The answer is simple. There is no need for large scale urban renewal when cities remain small, or change at a normal rate. The need is created only in dynamically growing settlements. In the past, if dynamic growth did take place, it was early in the life of the settlement when its structure was flexible and could respond to the requirements of the settlement's growth. After all, there were few cities with hundreds of thousands of inhabitants, and even fewer which reached the million mark. Some of these cities may have required renewal, but we know of no effort made on a

U

Facts

269

the vicious circle of a growing settlement

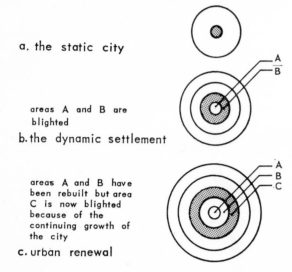

a. the static city

areas A and B are
blighted

b. the dynamic settlement

areas A and B have
been rebuilt but area
C is now blighted
because of the
continuing growth of
the city

c. urban renewal

270

evolution of cities by stages

**total Ekistic wealth by periods of creation and parts
which need renewal**

parts which need renewal

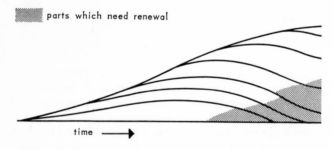

time ⟶

in the past

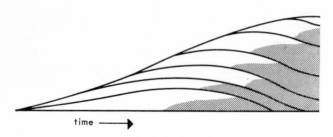

time ⟶

at present

274

large planned scale; with the possible exception of ancient Rome, which was perhaps burned by Nero so that it could be rebuilt on a major scale. This is not an example we can be certain of, or one which should be counted as a precedent. Beyond it, we know only of minor efforts such as the remodelling of Constantinople on a small scale, and that of Paris when the big boulevards were created. Planned urban renewal with the meaning we give it today has only become important since the advent of the era of dynamically growing cities. Its implementation should have been started sooner than it was: the delay has been caused by the fact that we did not recognise the new evolution and the changing nature of our growing cities soon enough (fig. 270).

We are now entering a new era of large-scale urban renewal, with no experience and no preparation. It is a problem which is manifest everywhere, in every major dynamic city regardless of its nature, as well as in many minor ones.

The problem of urban renewal is a gigantic one, but we are just becoming conscious of its great importance. It is being discussed only in those countries where the problem is most acute, such as the United States, England, the Netherlands and Scandinavia. It seems that an understanding of such a problem becomes possible only when it reaches a critical stage. However, it is important that it be understood not only when the need for the solution is so urgent as to be inescapable, but as early as possible. It must be understood as a problem which must always be dealt with, even when it appears to be on a very small scale.

Public health measures have to be taken not only during periods of epidemics but also during normal times, so that the onset of epidemics can be avoided.

There are two reasons why planned urban renewal has become not only necessary, but indispensable:

○ many urban areas have outlived the period of their usefulness, and
○ their owners and inhabitants do not have the ability or the power to re-build them in order to make them useful for themselves and the city.

Why have such areas outlived the period of their usefulness? We can give four reasons:

○ the age of their buildings and construction;
○ the unsuitable location which has made the buildings—even when still useful in themselves—lose their importance;
○ or a combination of these two;
○ changes in the structure of the city area in which they are located, causing changes of use, of type of inhabitants, etc.; such changes result from rapid and uncontrolled urbanisation.

We must now ask ourselves why a planned urban renewal effort has become indispensable in these areas, and why the natural urban renewal effort on the part of private owners who in the past, as a matter of course, replaced their buildings when the time was ripe, can no longer serve us. The first

271

the need for planned urban renewal

		non-useful buildings because of		
	useful buildings	age	location	location and age
				changes of structure of the city
owner able to rebuild	1	3	5	7
owners unable to rebuild because of changes of structure of the city	2	4	6	8

and most important reason is the rapidly changing structure of the city, such as:

o different land uses: e.g., a residential area in the process of turning into a commercial one;

o much higher densities of the same land use: e.g., a residential area of single-family houses may turn into an area of multi-storey apartment blocks with corresponding parking places, garages, etc.;

o different economic or technological conditions: these may demand changes beyond the capabilities of the owners or inhabitants of the area involved.

The second reason is that at times an entire area must be demolished. This usually happens with a uniform area, which has been built at one time, frequently by a single developer or owner, and is now owned by numerous people. Although the initiative for its development probably came from one man, the initiative for its renewal is now a matter involving many. In such cases it is often difficult for the individuals themselves to initiate renewal measures, since they are not at all confident that the others will follow them.

These problems are intensified when the area is large. The cases in which a present-day developer has taken the responsibility of buying larger areas and renewing them on a comprehensive plan (such as Rockefeller Center in New York and some large developments in other American cities), are too few and on too small a scale to allow us to expect such a

system to operate widely in the absence of a governmental policy which will make it more feasible. Such private initiative means buying land and buildings that belong to many owners, and unless government is in control of land values, or aids in the acquisition of land in other ways, this becomes increasingly difficult. People who are themselves unable to carry out the desired renewal do not yield easily to requests to sell their property at a reasonable price.

A diagram may help to explain why there are areas which cannot undergo natural urban renewal (fig. 271). One direction of our diagram represents the buildings, divided into useful and useless ones. The other direction represents the owners who are able to rebuild and those who are not able to do so. It is apparent that the first square of the diagram presents no problem as the owners are able to rebuild and the buildings are useful. In the second square we have useful buildings whose owners are not able to rebuild. As long as the buildings are useful, however, they constitute no problem for the city. In squares 3, 5 and 7, there are useless buildings whose owners are able to rebuild (regardless of whether the buildings are no longer useful because of age or location or both). We have no problem here either. It is only in squares 4, 6 and 8, where the buildings are not useful and the owners are unable to rebuild, that problems arise. There are also likely to be cases of useful buildings, which may have to be demolished because they happen to be in areas which must be completely remodelled. Their numbers, though, are not likely to affect the appearance of our chart in any significant way.

Some buildings become useless simply because of their age. In such cases a problem arises when the owners are unable to rebuild. Other buildings become useless because of their location, or because of a combination of age and location. In these cases it may be changes in the structure of the city which have changed the location to such an extent that the buildings have been rendered useless, or which have affected the owners so that they are unable to undertake renewal.

There are still areas where owners have the means and can undertake renewal, either by the creation of larger buildings or buildings of different uses. This is normally the case when an area is developing slowly. This gives the owners time to recognise a general trend and to finance the renewal of their own property, or, if they cannot do this, to sell their property to somebody else who can undertake the renewal. In cases, however, where a large area is declining, a single owner (or even a small group of property owners) financially able to undertake renewal, cannot be expected to make an effort to build better buildings, since if too great a percentage of the surroundings is dilapidated, the few better buildings will not be able to improve the quality of the area, enough to arrest its decline, and will consequently be doomed to failure.

The situation is made even more difficult by the fact that when the owners or occupants are financially unable to undertake renewal themselves, they usually resist others

272

buildings rising high meant hostility between inhabitants

a. Mani - Greece

b. San Gimignano - Italy

c. Svanetia - Caucasus

273

direct contacts between people

- - - in present-day multi-storeyed buildings

——— in settlements of the past

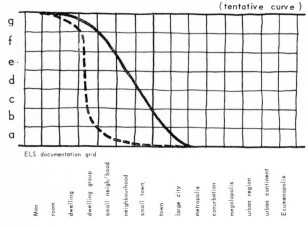

initiating it, since they know or suspect that they will not be able to own or occupy the new buildings. This is especially true in slum areas, especially when the buildings are already amortised and maintenance is minimal. In such cases, when there is no proper government action, all rents paid are, except for taxes, clear profit.

There is undoubtedly a need for planned urban renewal undertaken by the community; it is inevitable and overdue in many dynamic settlements around the world. In spite of a recognition of this need, the lack of a general theory of human settlements has prevented major efforts from being successful. No overall effort for the urban renewal of an entire urban area has yet been undertaken and conceived on the basis of a well-thought-out system of policies, programmes and action. There have been several projects covering parts of cities, some unconvincing as regards their efficacy, and some showing influences of a basic conception of what urban renewal should achieve. The most successful and consistent conception I know of is for downtown Philadelphia. There a systematic effort has been made to develop a conception of the centre of the city, with its traffic systems at several levels, and its shopping, parking and other functions so well balanced that the remodelling of its centre can take care of its problems for quite a number of years. What even this well-conceived urban renewal plan cannot achieve, is the solution of the problems of pressures which will be exercised on Philadelphia because of developments in the whole region, over which the city of Philadelphia, even with the best of intentions, can have no control (fig. 475).

A great problem has arisen and is awaiting its solution: the problem of planned urban renewal through which the complete transformation of dynamic settlements should be effected. This is the task ahead for every one of us.[26]

Abnormal three-dimensional growth

As I have already dealt with several cases of abnormal growth of whole settlements when describing their anatomy and their evolution and growth, I will concentrate here on a very special—and so far overlooked—disease of growth, the one affecting the settlements in their micro-scale.

Man has always built settlements of such forms and dimensions, as facilitated the contacts between people at the same level—the street level. People could see each other, talk to each other, become friends or enemies—they could communicate. When their buildings first rose in height they had only two or three floors, seldom more, they housed either one family or so few families that a social unit could be formed within each building.

In the past when buildings rose to greater heights it was mostly for reasons of defence in towers and castles. When several such solutions could be found in the same settlement they were indicative of hostility between families, or other units of the society. Such was the case in the Italian village of San Gimignano, or the Greek villages of the Mani, or the fortified villages of Svanetia in the western Caucasus (fig. 272).

During the last generations we have been building multi-storeyed buildings without having defence as our aim, but nevertheless achieving the same end. People have been alienated. This alienation can be explained: people can come together easily when we place them at the same level— head facing head and feet facing feet. Today, in many Ekistic units this type of encounter is no longer possible and people are being deprived of the opportunity to meet each other. If we try to compare tentatively the opportunities of natural, direct contacts within every Ekistic unit of the past and in the multi-storey buildings of today we will recognise the extent of our failure (fig. 273). This is certainly a very basic disease which is expressed in sub-normal social contacts, and is rooted in mistaken structural concepts.

CHAPTER SIX

EKISTIC DIAGNOSIS

NEED FOR DIAGNOSIS

Medicine or creation

If I am asked where the greatest weakness of professionals dealing with settlements lies, I have to answer: in the lack of a desire for a proper understanding of the situation they have to deal with; in the absence of a proper diagnosis. When I demand a diagnosis I am told that the people who build the settlements are not physicians but creators, so the question of whether this is true arises immediately. Is Ekistics an act of medicine or one of creation?

The truth is that it is both. The situations we have to deal with in settlements require medical treatment—otherwise there would be no necessity for action or interference. Even where we are called in to build a new city, a new neighbourhood, a complex of buildings or a single house we find ourselves up against a situation needing medical treatment since we must supply a part that is missing from the vast system of settlements which serve human needs, whether that part is a complex of Shells and Networks, or a single shell. If we manage to see the human settlements in their proper perspective as a system of elements serving Man, then we will understand that both an ailing part of a settlement and a missing one are cases requiring our understanding and intervention. In this sense we act as physicians.

On the other hand, once we have to act there is nothing compelling us to re-establish the pre-existing normal situation, which is what medicine has to do in most cases, since it has neither the power nor the freedom to affect structural changes. Pursuing this process of re-establishment may be one way of acting, but there are many cases where there is every reason why our intervention should lead to new solutions; after all we are often called in to add new settlements, or their parts, serving new needs. So our task is the creation of new settlements.

Ekistics, therefore, in its prescriptive aspect, being a process of treatment and of healing, must necessarily include the act of diagnosis in order to be fully developed. Without it the possibility of proper understanding of any disease, problem or situation, becomes impossible and Ekistic action and creation loses its foundations.

Definition and purpose

Ekistic diagnosis is the act, and perhaps the art, of identification of a diseased or abnormal condition and of the cause for it, after careful investigation of its signs, symptoms and history. It is also the study of the causes and the nature of diseases and problems; and finally it is the conclusion which is the outcome of this whole process of understanding the situation. From this definition it is clear that a proper diagnosis has to answer the questions what is happening, why it is happening and how it is happening. Since the ultimate goal of diagnosis is the treatment and the therapy of the disease, the diagnosis has, as its purpose, to describe its findings in a way leading to proper conclusions about therapy or action. Diagnosis has to relate the general experience and knowledge of human settlements and their diseases, with the knowledge concerning the specific settlement under consideration.

'Diagnosis always relates more to the patient than to the disease, either to *his* disease or *the* disease in general', as Karl Menninger very clearly put it when referring to mental patients. 'The need to particularise regarding the affliction of the individual patient is paralleled by a need to generalise, from the afflictions of this and other patients, regarding pathology and illness in the abstract. Such abstractions make up the substance of medical science'.[27] Menninger is speaking about medicine; I have only to extend these statements to include Ekistic diagnosis.

Quite apart from the fact that diagnosis enriches our general experience of the disease and the problems of settlements, it is of direct importance for the settlement concerned, and in this respect it is unique and is valid only when applied to it, since the settlement itself is unique, both genetically and by its evolution. A diagnosis is necessary when a disease or an 'abnormal' condition has been apprehended by those directly concerned, by those indirectly suffering or concerned, or by outsiders who are called in for other reasons—to plan the expansion of a settlement, for example, or to design a new building; they may discover that the existing settlement is suffering and that diagnosis and action are necessary on a broader scale.

Such a definition of disease or abnormal conditions brings to the surface once again the question of criteria, which alone

278

can define what is normal and what is not. But such criteria are not a matter of science alone, they involve desires, the setting of goals and prescriptions. I will deal with these in the chapter on Ekistic synthesis.

METHOD FOR DIAGNOSIS

Hypothesis and verification

Any diagnosis should be founded on a method beginning with a hypothesis. This is valid in medicine, and it is valid in Ekistics in the same way. It is a basic scientific method which runs as follows:
- making a hypothesis,
- testing for verification,
- re-shaping the hypothesis,
- testing it again until we have its verification or rejection.

Our mind operates during these phases by isolation of phenomena and elimination of those which are of no importance or of secondary importance, until it can reach the point of isolating those which advance it towards the final conclusion and diagnosis.

There is nothing wrong with starting with a hypothesis, provided that we do not turn it into a belief before showing its general validity. In many cases it is inconceivable to do anything before formulating a hypothesis, for otherwise it would be impossible to proceed, since the amount of data that will have to be studied is so enormous.

To illustrate this point I will start from the opposite end and assume that there are no indications about the disease: that the subject is so vast that nobody knows it well enough to describe the pains or ills that go with it; or let us assume that there are so many ailments in so many elements, units and locations, that a general study of the subject is imperative. In such a case we could start from one hypothesis and concentrate on one direction right from the beginning. We would have to start with a wide field of many alternatives. If so our best method would be to proceed in forming a hypothesis about important factors, then isolate them and find ways of eliminating those which make less sense. In this way we would help ourselves to concentrate on one or a few reasonable hypotheses until we would be led to one solution. This method will be presented at length in the chapter on Ekistic synthesis.

No progress is possible unless we are able to make a hypothesis; and progress is easier if experience and intuition help us to select the proper hypothesis or one close to it. In certain periods, it was thought that formulating a hypothesis was not scientific—in medicine it was considered magical or mystical—but now it is recognised as the normal process for any scientific enquiry; progress is not possible unless we have the courage and the ability to make a hypothesis.

The validity of this process is recognised in many fields and characteristically Sir Peter Medawar writes about medicine:

'It is right to point out, because of the irritating *mystique* that has grown up around it, that clinical diagnosis illustrates the act of hypothesis formation in an uncomplicated and fairly lucid way. The clinician seeks an hypothesis that will account for his patient's illness. There is no time in the course of his investigation during which some hypothesis is not in the background of his mind, and during its early stages there may be many. If his mind ends up blank after examination, that is not because no hypothesis sought admittance, but because all that did so had to be turned away. The experienced clinician is very well aware of the intuitive nature of the act of mind by which he hits on an hypothesis, but he sometimes fails to realise that this is the commonplace of scientific discovery'.[28]

Process of diagnosis

From what has already been said about hypothesis it is clear that diagnosis has to proceed in three basic stages.
- First: hypothesis, or recognition of a situation, a problem, an illness.
- Second: collection of data and facts.
- Third: final diagnosis.

I will follow these three stages in some greater detail. The need for the hypothesis has already been explained; its successful application is a matter of intuition and experience, and since I cannot add anything on the nature of intuition, but only accept what science accepts and what I feel about it, I would like to insist on the point of experience. The greater it is, the greater the chance of making the right hypothesis. I do not know how to recommend intensification of intuition, but I am completely in favour of the greatest possible experience in the largest number of cases. Nobody can have enough experience where difficult cases are concerned—there is an imperative need for involvement in as many cases as possible; and by this I do not mean simply knowledge of, but real actual involvement in. This is why I favour centres, institutes, offices which can deal with many cases, as, for example, big hospitals do.

Collection of data is a very important stage, the one that requires the longest and greatest effort. It requires a system, a systematic mind and patience. It does not provide the solution, but no solution can be successful unless work at this stage has been carried out properly.

Collection of data has to cover the four following sectors:
- history of the settlement,
- history of the disease,
- physical examination,
- psychological examination.

Without proper study of these sectors an understanding of

279

the problems and the disease is impossible. A proper study demands that we cover the following aspects:

o location of the problems,
o external relationships,
o internal relationships (five elements),
o change in time.

The chapters on Ekistic analysis, evolution and pathology provide enough examples and methods to cover these aspects of our problem and therefore I will mention only one example in order to cover mainly the point of internal relationships which is usually the most complicated one.

Let us take the Greek island of Hydra which is at a distance of 40 miles from Piraeus, the port of Athens in the Aegean Sea. It has become very fashionable, attracts many people and it is apparent that it needs care and protection. A careful study proves that it receives much greater pressures from outside; its external relationships have changed. Instead of one shipload a day it receives ten. Instead of holidaying Greeks only, it receives many different nationalities. Internally the Shells are the same and so is Nature and they both attract the tourists, but this is where the problem starts; the tourists want to buy souvenirs so several new shops have opened; the tourists need much more water and electric light, so the Networks have been developed. The first motorcars have started to appear. What is worse is that Society has been changed, and because of that Man himself is changing. Is Hydra the same as it was? It is not. For a new inhabitant it may not be suffering, but be excellent in every way; but for an old one it is very very ill. Here we see that an examination

by elements leads to different conclusions and that what we need to formulate the proper opinions are the proper criteria.

In order to collect data properly and accurately we now have several methods and instruments. We can make tests and carry out experiments, and process the resulting data through computers. But, above all, we must visit, see, hear, smell, touch the settlement ourselves, and this means come into proper contact with all its elements, contact by walking, driving, flying (for all scales), by sitting leisurely and by feeling. Without this personal direct contact, understanding is not possible. There are no diseases but only patients, and we have to come into contact with them, we have to touch them.

The last stage is the final diagnosis. It is not the longest but it is the most difficult one. Here we have to achieve a synthesis of all facts and data. We usually work in the following way:

o connect data and facts into a meaningful complete whole—too heavy traffic means circulatory problems;
o compare the implications of our conclusions with other data and facts—a circulatory problem means improper residential densities in the areas affected;
o select the hypothesis for which all known data and facts provide complete confirmation—if other developments along our artery are normal, perhaps the traffic is not heavy and the cause of the disease should be different.

Such a process will lead to the final diagnosis, provided it is followed in a systematic way, so that no gaps are left in the fabric of assumptions and their verification procedure.

BOOK THREE

THEORY

'The observation of objects constitutes only a lower form of science, the descriptive form. Descriptive science classifies phenomena. But the unchanging relations between variable quantities—that is, the natural laws— only appear when science becomes more abstract. It is because physics and chemistry are abstract and quantitative that they had such great and rapid success. Although they do not pretend to unveil the ultimate nature of things, they give us the power to predict future events, and often to determine at will their occurrence.'

ALEXIS CARREL   *Man, the Unknown*

Theory is based on facts—only then can it have value—but it is not facts, it is their interpretation and interconnection into laws which lead to a system of thought. To form a theory we must use abstractions with all their advantages and disadvantages. I tried to present here only abstract examples which by necessity are very close to facts. This book contains three chapters:

CHAPTER SEVEN: TOWARDS AN EKISTIC THEORY

CHAPTER EIGHT: BASIC EKISTIC THEORY

CHAPTER NINE: EKISTIC SYNTHESIS

CHAPTER SEVEN

TOWARDS AN EKISTIC THEORY

NEED FOR A THEORY

We cannot limit ourselves to facts, regardless of how many they are and how well they have been collected. Facts alone do not lead anywhere; they are indispensable, in the same way as the foundations of a building are indispensable even though it is the building we need; in the same way as the stones forming a wall are indispensable even though it is the wall we need. In order to reach the final product we need to order our facts in a meaningful way, so that we can build a wall and understand it. We need a theory relating the facts to each other; when we have such a theory, then we have science.

Such a theory does not need 'to unveil the ultimate nature of things' if it helps us build a meaningful whole out of scattered knowledge and in this way understand our subject better; if it helps us to predict its course, and when necessary, to guide it. We need a theory that can connect the facts to form hypotheses, principles and laws, and all of them to form a comprehensive whole which can help and guide us to progress. It does not have to be *the* theory, just one theory which can light our way until we can make the next step and develop a better one. Such a theory has to be based on the observation of phenomena, which lead to the formation of hypotheses which will have to be tested and tried until we arrive at an acceptable theory verified by all our tests and experiments and based on all the facts that we have assembled.

In Ekistics, as in so many other sciences, we can proceed by the inductive method. I believe that many of the grave mistakes which are now being made in architecture and planning are being made by people who thought (or as a matter of fact who did not think but who acted as if they did) that they could proceed deductively. We have to collect and observe as many cases as possible; only then can we induce the laws that govern these phenomena. We can only learn about settlements from the settlements themselves.

To achieve this is difficult since we have not yet organised a system of knowledge, we have not accepted common measurements and scales, we do not agree on classifications of settlements and phenomena and we do not have laboratories or hospitals where many cases are available to us. But this is no reason why we should excuse ourselves from trying to learn about settlements by observing them and inducing their laws.

We do not need to observe just the successful settlements—as town-planning handbooks do—or just the modern villas and sky-scrapers thought by architectural magazines to be the most beautiful or 'exciting', modern and 'unusual' ones; we need to observe all settlements old or new, small or large, good or bad (thus avoiding the danger of subjective eliminations); only then can we be sure that we will find the proper principles and laws to be able to formulate a theory and a science.

It may be asked whether we are not acting scientifically today, and if not how we should proceed. I will try to explain this process as I understand it. In dealing with human settlements, we are still acting on the basis of belief and experience—personal or general. Normally, general experience is better. However, there is no reason to believe that what is often called common experience is objective and scientific and not merely the result of some older ideas surviving by inertia, or a total of the incorrect ideas one community has copied from others. Belief and experience are both inefficient and insufficient to enable us to grasp the real issues in human settlements.

It is sometimes said, for example, that the city is the root of the evils of our present condition. But what does this mean? Even if the city were the root of these evils—which is questionable—what do we mean by 'city', and what aspects of it are 'evil'? Is it the size, the shape, the form, the Society living in it, Man who has created it, its economic activities or the way in which they operate? There is no satisfactory answer. It can only be said that probably several of the city's elements and expressions may be indispensable for purposes not necessarily directly related to human settlements. The great size of cities, which to many appears to be the root of the evil, offers many advantages which are unobtainable in smaller settlements. The fact that a large city provides a major centre with a major market for goods and ideas cannot be overlooked when we reflect that a greater variety of exchange leads to a greater variety of choice and to higher intellectual and material goals.

An attempt at a systematic interpretation of these phenomena shows that some of the elements and expressions seem to be inevitable and indispensable, while others may not be. For example, the form of the present metropolis is not necessarily the one best suited to the purposes for which the metropolis was created. Thus in the study of human settlements we should:

○ clarify the different phenomena and separate what is essential and indispensable from what is non-essential and can be altered—we must acquire the ability of isolating phenomena in different scales (For example, we might come to the conclusion that the size must increase at a certain rate in order to be beneficial, but that forms of cities and shapes of buildings should be changed in different ways.);

○ classify all phenomena according to their value and importance to the successful operation of human settlements;

○ find out how, by controlling several variables, we can eliminate expressions of elements, organs or parts which do not contribute to the successful operation of settlements (For example, we might create better living conditions in a settlement by re-forming its Shells.);

○ ascertain how we can achieve the optimum combination of favourable and unfavourable elements.

Without such an understanding of the real issues of human settlements, we are bound to fail in the interpretation of their phenomena. This can be disastrous when acting to enlarge or modify our settlements. Any action undertaken without the proper conception and understanding of what the settlements are and how we should deal with them, can only be successful and beneficial by accident. It is more likely to work against, than to work for the attainment of our goals. The phenomena of human settlements are too complicated to be faced without an overall theory which can incorporate their conception and interpretation. This is gradually being understood by those seriously concerned with the problem, whether their special interests are related to the physical aspect of settlements, or to social or economic activities. I think it typical that Leonard Duhl, who is a member of the Space Cadet Group in the U.S.A., a private group which is concerned with Man and human settlements, leaves no doubt about the position of the psychologist and some other social scientists when he says:

'Action programs concerned with specific areas executed without a comprehensive theoretical base may be wasteful and even misleading. All groups concerned with the well-being of man, who at the same time either consider themselves scientists or are responsible for the administration of a scientific program, should allocate energy and manpower to the development of such theories.'[1]

The need for a theory of human settlements as the basis for action is indispensable in order to help us:

○ properly understand the phenomena of human settlements and consequently develop the descriptive science of Ekistics;

○ take action in every field of human settlements and thus develop a prescriptive science of Ekistics, a policy, a technology and an art for their formation.

It may be argued that such a body of knowledge would be better acquired by concentrating separately on each one of the elements—Nature, Man, Society, Shells and Networks. I believe that such an approach to the solution of the problems of human settlements would be completely wrong. In a way, this is what is happening today. There are attempts in each of the fields concerned with each of these elements, at forming theories related to each. These theories are not always of equal value; and even if one of them has great value it is not sufficient to guide the development of entire human settlements. The failure to merge theories into a system has contributed to two situations:

○ It has led to the development of a separate approach for every element and the real issue of interest has been treated by these fields only as a side issue. For example, physical geography, concerned with Nature, has not concentrated on relating Nature to human settlements as a whole.

○ The disciplines concerned with these elements have tended to develop particular approaches towards the entire human settlement. For example, the approach of the anthropologist is different from that of the planner, which in turn differs from that of the engineer, the architect, etc.

It is exactly this which must be avoided in the future. What we need—and this is the only way of achieving the best results—is a unified approach to the entire problem of human settlements. Only a balanced knowledge of all elements and their interaction in the formation of settlements can lead to a successful theory. Only then can we branch out into more specific fields.

If we look at a diagram showing the five Ekistic elements as spheres and their interrelationships as straight lines connecting them (fig. 274), we can say that Ekistics is concerned with all these lines of interrelationships and especially with the total system of these straight lines, while the spheres are the subject of the study of other disciplines contributing to Ekistics.

Once we have a theory of Ekistics, we can proceed with much greater confidence to develop a theory of Ekistics and economics, Ekistics and sociology, Ekistics and anthropology, geography, planning, engineering, architecture, administration, etc. But in order to be successful, such a theory must be part of a broader theory of human and natural phenomena, and must be well coordinated with related theories.

It could be argued perhaps that at the start such a theory must be called a series of hypotheses, for the usual procedure in scientific method is to start with a hypothesis and gradually build up a theory by testing and verifying a sequence of hypotheses. I consider that we no longer need to go through this procedure for the whole theory because:

○ even though we have not had an Ekistic theory up to now, we have had Ekistic phenomena for thousands of years; and the total accumulated experience is wide

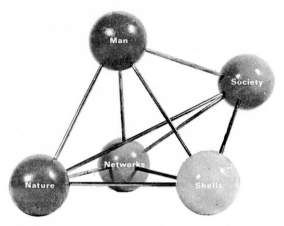

is not concerned with the study of the elements by themselves but with their interrelationship

the subjective. It is imperative that the body of knowledge to be built up be completely objective and as free as possible from subjective interpretation. This does not dispute the need for strong personal opinions on how to interpret and solve many of the problems of human settlements. To deny this would mean denying the essence of freedom and creative action and the contribution of individual thoughts and ideas. My point is that in order to allow proper freedom of thought and personal creation, we must first understand exactly what the problem is. A great artist only expresses himself in a subjective way after careful study of his subject; he is led to subjective expression through objective study. If this is true of art, which is after all a personal expression, it should be much more true of human settlements, which are not phenomena of personal expression, but which express the needs of a whole Society, formed by the action of the community. Therefore the experts who advise on the problems of settlements should have mastered a wide field of knowledge based on objective facts and leading to a creative expression growing from reason and imagination.

A sound Ekistic theory should assist all who are involved in the intepretation and creation of human settlements. It should be equally helpful to the anthropologist, the scientist, the architect, the humanist, the technologist, the mason, the builder and the artist. It must, therefore, take their experience and knowledge into consideration, but cannot be based on any partial theory related to special aspects of human settlements. There is always a danger that such a theory, concentrating on only one element, will not touch on the heart of the matter, that its lack of focus will mislead it into partial and personal interpretations. So an Ekistic theory must be based on:

o existing settlements;
o extinct settlements known through history or from their ruins (as additional elements of study the settlements of the past can help to shape many parts of the theory, especially those related to the evolution of human settlements and to settlements of minor sizes);
o critical interpretation of the phenomenona of these settlements;
o theoretical models, the validity and importance of which should be checked with existing settlements;
o tests and experiments to be carried out in existing settlements, the conclusions of which can be fed back in order to check the theory.

Since it will take time to draw conclusions from the experiments and tests of theoretical models with existing settlements, the theory, at its inception, will necessarily be based mainly on knowledge of existing and extinct settlements and its critical interpretation. The importance of experimentation and theoretical models however, should not be minimised. Although a total reliance on these methods would undoubtedly mislead us at the start, gradually, with increasing experience, we will be able to rely on them more and more.

enough to allow us to check on hypotheses and to have an opinion about their validity;
o the phenomena of human settlements are so broad and multiple that the total field of knowledge forms a theory incorporating a number of different principles, laws and hypotheses, and their number will probably increase with time. Thus if some of the hypotheses are proved wrong, there will be no difficulty in changing the larger theoretical concept. I do not believe that such a necessity is very probable for the theory I have tried to outline, but the possibility of some of our principles and laws being inaccurate should always be foreseen, and the theory of Ekistics, like any other theory, will adapt and evolve in the light of experience;
o because of the dangers, even limited ones, of developing an invalid theory, our effort at the beginning should be restricted to very general principles and laws; since it will be based on general, universal phenomena, observed over long periods of time and in a great number of cases.

On the basis of such considerations I proceed to the formulation of an outline of a theory of Ekistics in two stages, trying to formulate some principles and laws first (in the present chapter) and then to connect them in one basic theory in the next chapter.

FORMULATION OF A THEORY

How do we build up a body of knowledge to form the principles, the laws and theory of human settlements? One thing is certain: we should separate the objective from

A basic question to be answered in relation to the formation of a theory of Ekistics concerns the interrelationship of the different elements of human settlements and their importance in the interpretation of existing Ekistic phenomena as well as the creation of new settlements. In very simple terms this question could be presented as follows: which of the elements should be the basis of our observations and the measure of the others, and which should be adjusted to the others? Should the Shells be matched to the needs of Man, or should Man be adjusted to the requirements of the Shells? Should the Shells be adjusted to Nature, or Nature adjusted to the requirements of the Shells?

There is a tendency—usually unconscious but sometimes conscious—to give a rather one-sided answer to such a question. Many people creating settlements today would answer that the Shells should be adjusted to Man. But I do not believe those people fully understand the implications of such a statement, for in practice many architectural and engineering solutions are adjusted only indirectly to the expressed needs of Man, and in fact, impose on him Shells for which he has expressed no desire.

There is much talk about the need to adjust architecture and buildings to Man, because, the argument goes, we pay more respect to architectural forms and structural regulations than to the unexpressed desires of Man. What we should really find out is what Man needs and what can serve him best. We should not always regard the prevailing as important and try to perpetuate the existing situation because it requires the least intellectual effort. On the other hand, we should not overlook the fact that a great part of the settlements we will have to deal with throughout our lifetime already exist and, even if we believe that they are unsatisfactory, we cannot change them overnight. So even though it is necessary to find out the real needs of Man, we cannot easily implement solutions which will meet all his requirements. There are also people, especially medical doctors and social scientists who are prepared to give greater importance than is necessary to the opposite statement—that Man should adjust to his habitat for his own happiness. While this is true for the immediate future (because unless Man can adjust to his surroundings, he will be unhappy) there is no need at all for Man to retain his habitat just as he has inherited it, because this may not serve his needs best, and because he is in a position gradually to change it.

In building up a body of knowledge on human settlements we cannot regard any principle derived from existing human settlements as the sole criterion of the phenomena we are trying to interpret, describe and understand. Personally, I believe that, to some extent, each of the positions mentioned above is valid. Man by necessity adjusts to his natural environment and has to respect its basic characteristics; he cannot disregard the formation of the ground and the natural landscape. On the other hand, he can respect these characteristics only to the degree that they are related to the forces

he is developing and to the degree that he cannot change them for his benefit. For example, a nomadic settlement's adjustment to Nature is practically 100 per cent, since nomads interfere with Nature only by utilising grazing grounds. Farmers, however, interfere with Nature by cultivating a certain part of it, by opening paths, by building various small Shells. And urban dwellers interfere even more drastically by transforming the Earth's surface into a man-made landscape. The real issue is to what extent due respect is given to Nature at every level. Man is adjusted to Nature, but Nature must also be adjusted to Man. When it is, the ensuing balance will mean a healthy settlement. To pretend that full respect for Nature would supply the answer, or that full respect for Man only is the answer, implies disregard of the real issues. As an example, the first case would mean that where swamps are found, they must be respected and Man must live in them. In the second it would mean that any form of Nature and pattern of life found in an area may be upset for Man's sake. This means that if Man does not want to climb, we are entitled to level off any landscape utilised for human settlements. This is unrealistic from both the financial and technological points of view; also it means working against Nature, which has already had a pattern of life developed on it. In the long run these two views, the latter of which is often supported by those responsible for development—some building contractors for instance—only lead to disaster for Man himself: in the end all wrong solutions for the total settlement work against Man, its founder.

Much the same can be said about the relationship between the other elements, such as that of Man to the Shells. The Shells have to be adjusted to Man. But there are certain characteristics of the Shells today, such as their large dimensions and new traffic requirements, which create new conditions for Man; in these respects Man must become adjusted to the Shells. When one floor is placed on top of another and people are obliged to climb stairs, we cannot say that we are adjusting the Shells to Man. In this case, we are adjusting Man to the Shells. When one must take an elevator and be closed in a box for several seconds or minutes in order to climb to the top of a multi-storey building, again it is Man who is adjusted to the requirements of the Shells. The final question in all these cases is: what is the best balance between Man and Shells in a changing settlement? We know by now that it is not simply a matter of adjusting the Shells to Man or Man to the Shells, but of attaining the best balance between all the elements and then between the elements and the entire settlement. This is the basic criterion which should guide us in formulating our theory.

The present body of knowledge of human settlements is based mainly on the past natural development of human settlements. By this I mean development which was never abstractly conceived and implemented in order to be tested in actual life. Development can be called natural when it is based on the desire of Man to serve those of his needs he considers intrinsic through the most direct means. When he wanted a shell over his head, he selected a cave. When he thought that he could build a shell he tried a beehive dome, which was the only way he could then cover the small space needed for his hut. Gradually he attempted to transform this through other types of construction. In every case he sought a desirable accommodation, conditioned by his conception of what could be done; he always tried to build the possible. From time to time he probably attempted the impossible as well, and failed. History does not record the failure of Man in building his settlement, except in a very few instances when great monarchs tried wild schemes which failed but still exist because of their great investment in stone and brick. These failures, however, strengthen my point that the main line of development leading to our present-day settlements was natural.

Most of the principles and laws of human settlements which can be developed today could well be called the natural laws of human settlements, and they will continue to be valid unless some day it is proved that with abstract methods we can evolve other laws that are more beneficial to Man. When this happens, they can be added to the Ekistic theory. Personally, I have great doubts as to whether abstract laws will ever upset the validity of natural laws. Through abstract methods we may reach new types of solutions, but this will not affect the natural principles and laws of Ekistics, if they have been properly conceived.

PRINCIPLES AND LAWS

Facts are connected in meaningful ways in order to lead to conclusions of more general significance and with validity for a certain number of cases having common characteristics. These meaningful ways have been given different names, depending on the schools of thought which introduced them, on the acceptance of their findings, the chronological order of the reasoning, etc. Such are the postulates, the 'common notions' of Euclid, the axioms of Aristotle. Several of them have been called principles and laws but there is no general agreement as to which one is which, and when a principle turns into a law. I will not enter into these discussions and I will deal with only three terms, *hypothesis*, *principle* and *law*.

Hypothesis is, chronologically, the first consideration in a meaningful process of inducing general conclusions from specific facts. At the beginning it does not provide sufficient evidence and remains therefore a tentative explanation. A hypothesis is tested in several ways, especially by experiments. If it passes the test successfully and if it fits into a broader system of ideas, it becomes a valid hypothesis and may be accepted as a principle or law. A *principle* or *law* follows a hypothesis. They are accepted hypotheses since it has been found or proved that the statements which they contain remain unvariable under the same conditions.

I do not believe that at this early stage of our effort to formulate a theory of Ekistics we need to enter into a discussion of the differences between all these statements (this may or may not become necessary at a later stage) and therefore I limit myself to the use of the term *hypothesis* to mean statements which need to be validated and *principle* or *law* for those statements which I believe have been validated, either by 'common sense' which after all is the basis of science, or by special explanations which appear in this study.

Efforts have been made at times in the past to state laws about settlements but they were never systematic and seldom accurate. When I was a student I learned that 'all major cities grow towards the west' which was definitely inaccurate, although it could be reasonably accurate for some north-western European industrial cities where industry was based on coal and therefore the best neighbourhoods, in their attempt to avoid the smoke, moved west, away from the prevailing winds. It is now commonplace that a city should grow in the direction of the areas of greatest attraction and minimum resistance and these can be found at any point of the horizon.

The principles and laws needed as a foundation must have an indisputable validity, since they will form the central body of our theory. They should, therefore, be based on as much experience and as many examples as possible. Thus, these principles should:

o have a general validity regardless of the period of human settlements under study;
o not refer to phenomena drawn from only one category of settlements.

They should cover as wide a spectrum as possible and should not be limited to a single period or to one species. Laws about villages will by necessity have a much greater validity than those concerning dynamic settlements. We cannot express opinions about the laws of the megalopolis, since it is only now beginning to take shape. Neither the natural evolution of human settlements nor experimentation can help us today with the megalopolis. We will need time to formulate its laws and we must devise as many models as possible to help us do so. At present we must simply observe and record the data of these new phenomena and proceed carefully on the basis of what we know and what we can demonstrate (fig. 275).

If we are to formulate laws about human settlements we have to ask ourselves what their nature will be. We have to decide what kind of laws we are talking about. Which, out of the multitude of phenomena, are we going to select in order to express the common characteristics of settlements. I think that what we should expect of all laws is that they be:

o true,
o helpful,
o general, and
o simple.

287

It is obvious why they have to be true and it is understandable that they have to be helpful; any effort to develop a law correlating the age of the citizens with the age of the city, for example, would be pointless, if it existed at all. For similar reasons laws have to be general; we could not possibly be interested in a theory about the existence of a law relating the orientation of the settlements of Java with their size. And they must also be simple, since we cannot expect to develop laws with many terms at such an early stage of our endeavour. When we have a satisfactory system of laws then we can proceed to more detailed and more complicated ones. Even so these laws will have to be true and helpful.

We can have many kinds of laws; they can be divided into laws of elements (connecting two of them at least), or laws of the whole settlement, relating it perhaps with some of its elements.

The first laws that we can develop seem to be causal laws, as, for example 'lines of transportation attract other functions, such as houses and buildings'. We have the cause—the road and its function of transportation; and the effect—the attraction of other functions. If we look at any map of a region in the macro-scale we will recognise the truth of this law. It would, however, be wrong to assume from such statements that the Ekistic theory can be a theory of causality.

Causal laws have to be exact and valid always. 'Every line of transportation attracts other functions', is not exact and not always valid. If the line has just been built, then there has been no time for the attraction of any function. We must qualify the law adding 'after a reasonable period of time'. Moreover, it does not attract functions if they are not related to the transportation line. A railway does not attract the farmhouses, they are primarily attracted by the best farmland and only to a secondary degree by a transportation line.

On the other hand, if we look at the micro-scale of a settlement we will notice that pedestrian paths may not attract other functions, if they are not meant to. As a conclusion we can say that settlements as large units and in a macro-scale seem to follow a deterministic type of law of cause and effect; but this does not *always* happen, and not at all scales. To make this statement true we must know all the factors influencing the location of functions attracted by lines of transportation, and discover their influence on these functions; only then can we formulate a law of cause and effect that is always valid.

Since such a procedure is not possible we are forced to say that large units usually do follow laws of cause and effect, but that we are unable to determine their totality to such a degree of accuracy as will allow us to formulate these laws in a scientific way.

In practice we have many causes and forces to deal with. In such cases we are much closer to the laws of chance and effect. Our previous law will come close to reality if formulated as follows: 'most lines of transportation attract other functions which are related to them'. In this way we are avoiding grave mistakes—such as taking the statement to mean that tunnels, for example, or transatlantic cables, attract any functions and we are qualifying the functions as 'related'. This law can be elaborated even further: 'most lines of transportation on the surface of land attract other functions which are functionally related to them'. This, in practice, is a law of chance and effect.

Thus, we reach the conclusion that the Ekistic laws are much closer to the laws that modern science in general is following. From the days (in 1927) when Heisenberg introduced in physics the principle of uncertainty, to the theory of games developed by von Neumann, to the theory of statistical differences, modern science is moving on a more realistic road, describing phenomena as they are regardless of how probabilistic this description may be.

If we now think of individuals who are one of the elements of settlements, and their movements, it will be obvious that we can foresee their actions only on the basis of the laws of chances, and if we try to predict their actions only statistical laws can help us.

Whether we start from settlements in a macro-scale or in a micro-scale we will find that their laws are statistical laws. They are laws of approximations, with greater validity for greater numbers of phenomena. It is easier to foresee statistically the movement of people in major arteries of a metropolis than their stroll in one of its small parks. In this respect, the validity of our predictions increases in the larger Ekistic units (fig. 276) unlike the validity of our laws about settlements (fig. 275) which were based on the knowledge which we have about them.

On the basis of these considerations I proceed to the formulation of Ekistic laws based on our experience and divided into three groups. The first group refers to the life cycle of human settlements, regarding them as species which are born, develop and die. The second group refers to the internal balance of human settlements and the third to their location, structure and form.

I have numbered these laws not because I consider that this is necessarily their order—although a reasonable ordering has been attempted—but mainly in order to introduce a proper system of reference.

LAWS OF DEVELOPMENT

Creation

Law 1. A human settlement is created in order to satisfy certain needs expressed by different forces, needs of both its own inhabitants and of others.

If a certain group of people needs to produce food for its own survival, it is attracted by an economic force to an area where food can be produced; there it settles, serving its needs

275

**validity and development of Ekistic laws in relation
to the available historical number of examples**

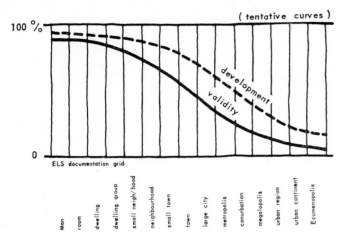

276

**validity of predictions about basic Ekistic phenomena
in relation to the size of the unit**

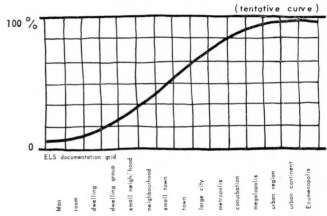

in the best way. The need is for food, and the force connects the producer with the locality of production.

However, there may be an area of many villages which need a market or administrative centre to serve them all. As a result, a corresponding urban settlement will be created in the area best serving all the villages. The need is the provision of services to others, and the force is an economic one connecting those providing services with the best locality for this purpose.

Law 2. Following the creation and operation of a settlement new functions are added which had not been foreseen, and consequently the settlement has to satisfy the initial as well as the additional needs. The more it grows the more important these additional needs may become.

Even though a settlement may be created as a marketing centre for the villages of the area, it may develop industry, administration, cultural institutions and other functions, which, once created, are not at all lacking in importance as compared to the original ones, since the settlement has to satisfy all the needs of its inhabitants and of those others served by its inhabitants. At first these needs are structural ones being added to the initial functions by the structure. With the passing of time they become functional needs themselves and lead to the creation of other structural needs.

Law 3. The ultimate goal of a human settlement is to satisfy the needs of its inhabitants, and of the others it serves—particularly those needs leading to happiness and safety.

So we come back to Aristotle. Twenty-four centuries of human experience have brought us to the same old truth. The *ultimate goal* is happiness; and happiness cannot exist

unless it is coupled with safety, for otherwise it is deprived of the fourth dimension of time: the concept of future happiness and consequently the feeling of happiness itself is lost.

Law 4. The satisfaction of the inhabitants cannot be ensured unless all their needs—economic, social, political, technological and cultural—are largely satisfied. There is a unity of purpose in the creation of a settlement; it cannot fulfil Law 1 if it covers only a few of Man's needs (fig. 277).

When one category of these needs is not satisfied, there cannot be full satisfaction, and the system is an unstable one tending towards destruction.

The balanced satisfaction of human needs is not only indispensable for the existence and survival of the settlement; it is also necessary for the satisfaction of its inhabitants in their everyday life. Consciously or unconsciously, people are dissatisfied when one aspect of their needs is not covered. Let us assume that in a mud-brick village somebody manages to build a marble house. Such an act will upset the pattern of the village from every point of view. Economically, it will be an unwise action because the economy of the village cannot stand a house so different. Socially, it will create trouble, for one person will be trying to live at a much higher level than the others. It will also have internal political repercussions. Technologically, if such a house is built by the villagers, it will be of poorer construction than the mud-brick houses since these people know how to build the latter but not the former. Finally, there will be no aesthetic adjustment to the requirements of marble, no proper expression of marble construction (no builder adjusts to a new material overnight), and the house itself will disrupt the aesthetic unity which had prevailed in the village.

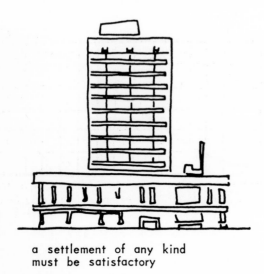

a settlement of any kind
must be satisfactory

economically

socially

politically

technically

culturally - aesthetically

The claim that economic criteria are the only ones of importance in Society cannot be supported where human settlements are concerned, unless one manages to express in economic terms all values of interest to the settlement and to all its elements. This means, for example, being able to express the practical and aesthetic values of the settlement's landscape as well as Man's connection to the landscape in economic terms. The same holds true of a work of art, or of the aesthetics of a street.

I spoke of unity of purpose, and gave it the meaning of unity between the settlement's elements. But this is not the only meaning and the only expression of unity in settlements. We must think also of the unity throughout the space covered by human settlements, from the smallest to the largest unit. In the building of a settlement a unity of purpose can be found in the serving of all its elements and in the serving of all its units, large or small, throughout terrestrial space. When we are building a house or a room, or merely putting one stone on top of another, we are only soldiers in a great army of builders. We must bring Man and his environment into balance, a balance we have lost in our age. We must understand this basic unity of purpose, and thus relate the house to the town and the town to the countryside. Within this framework we must build roads and villages, and in turn relate these to the central town and the towns further out, ending up with a conceptually comprehensive Ekistic system

covering the whole Earth. The reason I use the word 'conceptually' is that many times a pattern will express itself without a specific project, for quite often there is no need for one.

Law 5. Human settlements are created by their inhabitants and their existence depends on them.

This principle raises several questions. First it may be asked why the settlement is created by the inhabitants themselves. Do we not know of cases where the settlement has been created by external action, such as the decision of a ruler, or an industry, or a central government? This is true. Although the great majority of settlements are created by their own inhabitants, there are some which are created through external decisions and actions. If this action ultimately corresponds to the will and ability of those who will inhabit the settlement, it will be successful and will survive. If the opposite is true, there is no hope for the survival of the settlement, unless it is turned into a prison in which the people are forced to remain. Such a thing might happen, but it will not represent the typical case of a human settlement. It is an extreme case of an external force imposing itself on the inhabitants of the settlement not limited to problems of the settlement, but extended to the conditions of their freedom and way of life.

**the development of human settlements is a
continuous process**

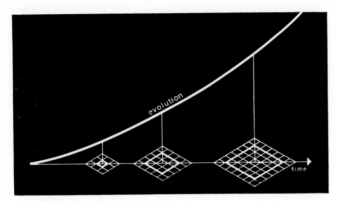

leading to growth

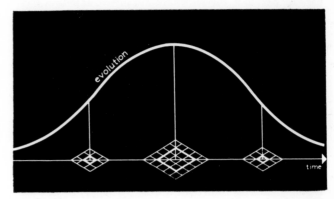

or decline

A question may be asked concerning the initiative the technicians involved in the creation of the settlement can have. Regardless of the authority which undertakes the creation of the settlement, how about the action of those who must plan, design, finance and build it? Our principle still holds valid, for if the technicians through their action express the deeper will—conscious or unconscious—of the inhabitants, their decision will be respected and carried out, not only during the phase of creation, but also later during the evolution of the settlement. If the experts do not create a settlement which can satisfy the basic needs of the inhabitants, the settlement will either be abandoned or altered—the latter if the difference between what the experts have done and what the inhabitants need is related to structure or form of the settlement involved. Only when the experts have the full backing of the community can the settlement have a normal period of gestation and a normal birth for only then will it have those strong chacteristics which aid it in its early life.

Law 6. A human settlement is created only when it is needed, and lives only as long as it is needed, that is only as long as there are needs expressed by forces strong enough to justify its existence.

When cattle-breeders are obliged to stay on a mountain for a short period, they build their huts with branches or, if there are no available materials for their shells, they pitch tents. When farmers have to cultivate new land a long distance from their villages, they must build their own shells, be they temporary or permanent. An urban settlement which serves a port or an industry is born and grows together with the port or industry, and the same happens with a settlement at an important crossroads in the country.

The moment of birth is determined by the needs created in a certain location. If these are not sufficient to justify its

creation, the settlement will not come into existence. This means that there may be a need for the creation of a new market centre to serve several villages. The economic force, however, which is exercised on a new central location may be very weak because of the distances involved. In such a case a new settlement cannot be created even though there is a need for it. The economic forces are not strong enough to counterbalance the needs of such a new settlement, that is, the income is not high enough to justify a sufficient number of inhabitants.

Development

Law 7. The development and renewal of human settlements is a continuous process. If it stops, conditions leading to death are created; but how long the actual death will take depends on many factors.

A settlement is a living organism and must develop continuously (fig. 278). This development is related to all its elements: Nature, within which it is created, changes. Man and Society develop, and the Shells and Networks change correspondingly. Even if there is no change in appearance, the moments which are added to the life of the people, the movements they make within the settlement, the leaves which grow or those which fall, the changing quality of the texture of houses under the sun or rain—are all changes of the entire settlement. Man, Society, Shells and Networks age—therefore, in a living organism they must be replaced; otherwise, they will recede, and only Nature will gain, recovering the ground lost through the creation of the settlement.

Law 8. The potentiality of a human settlement depends primarily on its location and the whole Ekistic system of which it is a part. These same factors condition the type and size of the settlement at every period of its life.

If a settlement has been created because there was a natural harbour next to it, this settlement will survive as long as there is no larger port near enough to take over the role of the first harbour. If the settlement has been created at a crossroads, it will survive in the same form and size only if the converging roads are not transferred and a new, more important cross-roads created. If the settlement has been created as a commercial centre, it will survive until some nearby commercial centre takes over the market it has been serving.

As with all living organisms, the capacity of a settlement for survival depends mainly on its ability to meet competition with similar species, a competition for survival in the same space. If it is a cattle-breeding settlement, and the grazing ground all around is turned into farming land, the cattle-breeding settlement will cease to exist; its Shells may be either eliminated or transformed. If it is a farming settlement producing vegetables and fruit for a nearby city and this city ceases to exist, the settlement cannot survive; it will probably have to grow and market other products which can be transported over longer distances to other cities, which means a different role and probably a reduction of its population. If it is an agricultural settlement within a non-mechanised farming area, it will soon be absorbed by the other settlements which will be economically stronger and will manage to buy up its lands. In each case the survival of the settlement depends on its relationship with the surrounding area and the Ekistic system.

Law 9. The total investment of economic, social, cultural, and other values in a settlement depends at every period of its life on the potential of the settlement itself, and on the broader role it can play in its system, since both condition inside and outside investment.

Normally, a settlement which is built to provide shelter for farmers and their families should correspond to the investment proportionate to their total income. The total value of investment should be in balance with the other needs of the inhabitants, such as for food, clothing, education, entertainment, etc. It is possible, though, that a government interested in cultivating an abandoned or new area and drawing farmers into it, may offer them more extensive facilities than those normally corresponding to their income. In such a case the additional expenditure will be borne by a wider area, eventually by the entire country (or even by other countries). This will be undertaken because of the broader benefits a wider area will gain from such additional investment. In this case, the Ekistic system is supporting a weak settlement for the benefit of the whole system.

The same is valid for other types of human settlements. The economy and total potential condition the value of investment. This is especially true when a settlement is

completely isolated and has grown by itself. However, when it belongs to a system covering a broader area, region, nation or the whole Earth—as is usually the case—certain external forces, depending on its role in the broader area, are added to its own forces and potential. A national government may well create army settlements near it for defence purposes, better administrative centres in order to compete with neighbouring areas, or institutional welfare settlements for the rehabilitation of depressed areas.

However, over longer periods and in a wider Ekistic area the first part of Law 8 which states that the total investment depends on the potential of the settlement itself, is valid. Even though for a few settlements, and over a short period of time, investments can be larger than the potential, this is impossible for most settlements over longer periods because the total balance of economic forces would be lost. So, we are led to a broader definition of the same principle: the total investment of values of all kinds in Ekistic regions depends on their own potential. Variations of this basic law will exist only in a rather limited time and area.

When settlements are born and grow without planned action, there is a continuous adjustment of the effort made for additional investment to the needs and potentialities created. In general, there is a relative similarity between the curves of demand and needs, and the curves of the supply of facilities. In these settlements, demand precedes supply. If this lasts over a long period, however, it is probable that supply will catch up and may even precede demand, in which case, if it precedes it beyond a certain limit, it will slow down, waiting for a new growth of demand (fig. 279a).

When settlements are born or grow on the basis of planned action, it is easier to make mistakes in the estimates, and there may be over-investment or under-investment at first. Such action can have a great impact on the life and development of a settlement. Over-investment may have a negative effect because it will mean small results in relation to expectations. This may well mean disappointment among the people who created the settlement and might lead to its abandonment or to a reduction of the necessary effort for its maintenance and functioning. Under-investment, on the other hand, may slow down the normal flow or normal increase of the population (fig. 279b).

Law 9a. Investment in each part of a settlement depends on the forces being exercised on it.

If the forces are only dependent on pedestrian movements then the investment will be in shops and other facilities of interest to pedestrians; if they are dependent only on trucks then we should expect storehouses. If they are forces of cars at very high speeds passing through a non-access highway then there may be no investment on the side of the highway.

Law 10. The values created within a settlement, in addition to the initial needs leading to its creation, act as a secondary

279

relationship between demand and supply in natural human settlements

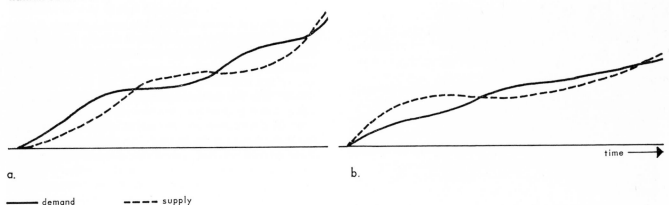

a.

b.

time ———→

——— demand   - - - - supply

force contributing to its speedier development; or, in case of depression, they slow down or even arrest and reverse its decline.

It is quite possible that a settlement created as a harbour town cannot survive when the harbour suffers from nearby competition. If important factories have also been created within the harbour town, let us say during the period when boats were made of timber, this settlement may not be able to survive as a harbour in the era of steel ships; on the other hand, it may well survive as an industrial settlement, based on the timber industries which had been established in it. In such a case, it may lose the percentage of its activities and inhabitants corresponding to the purely commercial activities of the harbour. But if the competing harbour is within commuting distance and the initial settlement has developed important residential facilities, the latter may also survive as a residential suburb of the new harbour settlement. Or perhaps, if the residences and workshops created during the period of timber boats have historic or cultural-artistic value, the initial harbour town might become a tourist or cultural centre.

On the other hand, even if the settlement does not face a decline because of the elimination of some of the causes which created it, but has a normal period of life ahead of it, because of the primary reasons of its development, the fact that it has created additional factories, residences and other functions of some value will attract even more people and thus encourage its further development (fig. 280).

If the initial settlement is agricultural and the primary causes of its creation change—let us say that a large urban settlement is created close-by which grows and takes over the farms of the agricultural settlement—the values already invested in it may determine whether it can survive and in what form it can do so. If its farms have not been irrigated and the land value rises, they will easily become building

plots. If on the other hand, its land has been irrigated and intensively cultivated, its transformation into building plots will be delayed and the settlement may even be able to survive as a truck gardening island within a metropolitan area.

If the investment in the built-up part of the village is small in comparison with the urban investment taking place around it, when the farms are turned into building plots, the Shells of the village will be easily eliminated and replaced; but if the value of the village Shells is great, either from the economic or cultural point of view, it may not be eliminated, but be incorporated into the metropolitan area (fig. 281).

Law 11. In a growing system of settlements the chances are that the largest settlements will grow faster than the others.

This is a basic law of dynamic systems; because of the reasons already mentioned in the evolution of settlements (Chapter Four) the larger ones attract greater and more functions and grow more than the others.

Law 12. The per capita cost of a settlement increases (other conditions, such as income, being equal) in proportion to the services provided by it and the number of its inhabitants.

In order to show the validity of this law, both parts of it must be explained. I will begin with the first. In order to understand the truth of this statement, we must consider how equal types of services could be provided within several different settlements. If the settlements are of the same size, but the services are increasing in one of them, it is quite natural that these services will become a very heavy burden for the same number of people. If, for example, one out of a number of equal settlements builds a large hospital which serves the inhabitants of only that particular settlement, the burden may become too heavy for these inhabitants, because

impact of a new centre on an existing settlement

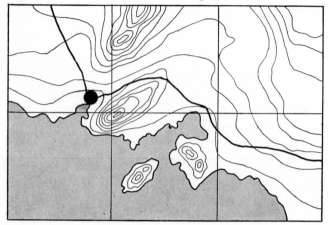

the existing settlement

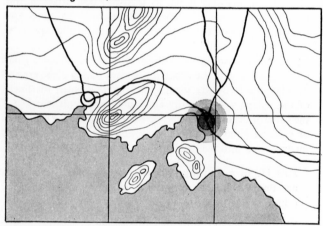

one possibility : the new centre causes the decline of the old settlement

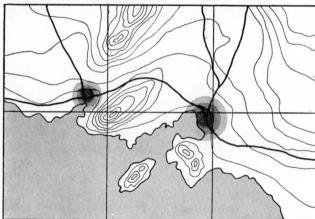

grid 20 x 20 km

another possibility: the existing settlement survives and grows together with the new one

294

had it been bearable, it is probable that similar hospitals would have been created in all settlements of a similar size. This is why where a service of a higher order is necessary, the majority of people must live close enough to it to be willing to split the cost among them. This is most economic if other people come into the same settlement because if they live in different settlements, the cost of the total settlement will be higher per capita. A greater number of people will bear the cost of the hospital; but because of the longer distances between them and the institution, the total cost is going to be higher than it is when everyone lives close to it.

We must now show why the cost of a settlement increases also in proportion to the number of its inhabitants regardless of the services provided. Let us take a simple example of a water supply network. If this network supplies a certain number of gallons of water per capita to a settlement of 1,000 inhabitants, it needs only narrow pipes. But if this settlement has 10,000 inhabitants, not only would the narrow pipes of the distribution network be needed to supply all of them with the same amount of water per capita per day, but some mains would also be necessary to bring the water for the distribution network into the communities of 1,000 inhabitants. This water main is an additional cost which must be borne by all the inhabitants. For them, the per capita cost for the supply of water increases because they inhabit a major settlement, although the quality of the services provided is exactly the same. In this case, it is not the facilities provided which increase a settlement's cost, but the number of people they serve.

Law 13. Time is a factor necessary for the development of settlements. As such it is inherent in settlements and is physically expressed in them.

The fact that settlements develop in time compels them to respect certain rules. When, for example, the central square of an old city was originally given certain dimensions, it was not done with the initial number of inhabitants, which could be very small, in mind but the number which the original inhabitants thought that their city would eventually attract. This was quite easily expressed in static settlements, for the element of time in development did not influence them to a very considerable degree. It becomes a much more critical and important problem, however, in dynamically growing settlements. In some of their elements the time factor has been taken into consideration, as when a certain width has been given to highways to permit them to bear heavier traffic in the future. But this is valid only up to a certain point beyond which the calculation does not allow for more traffic; therefore, a conflict is created between the highway's design and the demand for higher traffic capacity. The conflict is even more considerable in terms of the shape of cities still considered static without recognition of the fact that they are actually growing dynamically and that the whole city must expand at a high speed. The fact that this basic principle has

281

elimination of an agricultural settlement by the expanding city

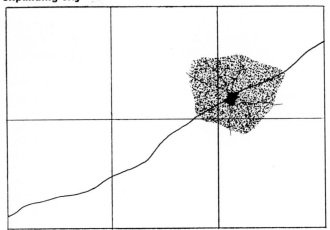

1st phase : the agricultural settlement

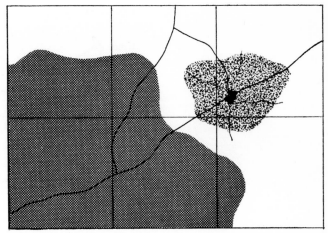

2nd phase : the expanding city gets closer

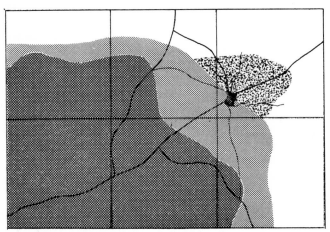

3rd phase : alternative a : the city absorbs a part of the agricultural land

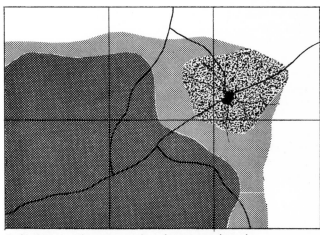

3rd phase : alternative b : the agricultural settlement resists because of intensive cultivation

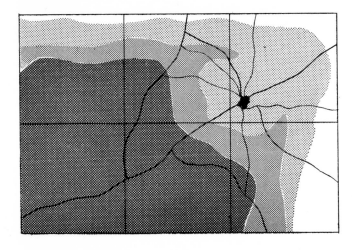

4th phase further stage of alternative b : the urban investment overruns the intensive cultivation turning the farms into urban plots

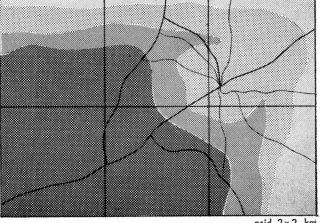

grid 2 x 2 km

5th phase : the agricultural settlement is completely eliminated by the advancing city

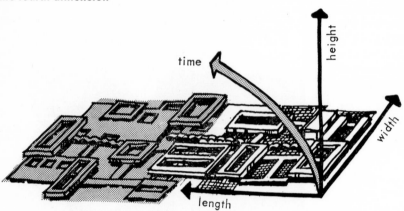

been overlooked in the present-day cities means that they suffer from the pressure of the three dimensions expanding in time with no space to cover their additional requirements. The Shells are too static to serve the needs of a dynamically growing organism. The 'snail' is growing too quickly in its static shell, an event of tragic significance for dynamic human settlements (fig. 282).

Law 14. Time is not only necessary for the development of settlements, but also for their existence. Therefore, time, along with the three physical dimensions, becomes a fourth dimension, indispensable to the settlement.

The fact that we walk in a street gives it dimensions proportionate not only to the three physical dimensions of Man, but also to the fourth. If Man could run as fast as a horse, the streets would always have had to be wider and their crossroads and turnings completely different; and if Man crossed the streets at the speed of a bullet, the streets would have had to be straight and the crossings on different levels.

The same holds true for the expressions given to the architectural details of the Shells. For example, because Man walks in the streets of a village, the walls, the doors and windows of the houses are appropriately painted and decorated. When Man moves at the speed of a car, there is no need for the kind of external street decoration which has been in use for thousands of years. The architecture of the settlement where Man moves at his own speed is different from the architecture on a highway. This is another expression of the fourth dimension of time as a factor used by Man in human settlements.

Extinction

Law 15. The gradual death of a settlement begins when the settlement no longer serves and satisfies some of the basic needs of its inhabitants or of Society in general.

A settlement connected with a port begins to die as soon as the port loses some of its traffic; a portion of its population can no longer survive and decides to move, taking certain values with it. In such a case men are the first to move to a different location, and then the values created by them, if they can be transferred, follow. A work of art can be easily transported, while a building, especially one having no artistic value, will be demolished if the site is needed for another purpose, and abandoned if it is not. Even local traditions may be transferred, though they will change during such a transfer; but such things as the trees in the central square of a village, the elements of Nature under which such cultural values and traditions have been created, will necessarily remain in the same location.

Law 16. In the death process of all or part of a settlement, no investment is eliminated unless its value has been amortised from the economic and cultural points of view, either because of changes within it, or because of changes in the system to which it belongs.

Under normal conditions no investment is eliminated unless its value has been amortised from every point of view. But there may be cases where this is not valid, due perhaps to the decline of the entire system to which this settlement belongs. In such a case the decline of the system or a part of it, may mean the decline of a settlement before its values have been amortised. If, for example, a new city has been created as a market centre for a rural area and needs 30 to 40 years for its amortisation, it will not decline before that period. If, however, the whole rural area is abandoned for some reason, then the city which had been its market centre cannot survive on its own and will decline despite the fact that the investment in it has not been amortised. The case of the need for urban renewal in many cities is a similar one. In the past, a house was not demolished unless it was fully amortised. Today many houses may have to be eliminated even though they are not amortised, if the whole area in which they belong has declined for some social, political or other reason.

Law 17. In the death process of a settlement its elements do not die simultaneously. The same holds true for the values that it represents. As a consequence, the settlement as a whole has much greater chances of surviving and developing through renewal even if some of its elements are dying.

The five elements of a settlement last and live for different lengths of time (fig. 283). This means that if one element dies, the others may cause a regeneration giving the settlement the power to continue living. This is made even stronger by the fact that every element does not consist of one unit only, but of many; consequently, the death of a few houses, or inhabitants, or trees, is not felt by the settlement as a whole since other houses, inhabitants and trees continue to live.

The same principle holds true for the different aspects of life represented by a settlement, i.e., economic, social, political, and so on. All these aspects can be satisfied for periods of different length. A settlement may be amortised from the economic point of view in fifty years, and from the social point of view it may be able to survive for one or two centuries, while from the cultural-aesthetic point of view it may survive for even longer (fig. 283). Thus several aspects with a longer survival value carry the ones with shorter survival values over longer periods and the settlement continues to exist beyond initial expectations.

Law 18. During the process of death, inertia caused by existing forces plays a very important role in slowing down the process.

When the reasons for the employment of people in a city cease to exist, some of the younger people tend to abandon it. Yet the fact that a lot has been invested in good housing and other facilities may keep many people there for a much longer period. A man could move into other settlements to look for new employment, and his family be left behind to make use of a comfortable house and good community facilities until he has been successful enough in the new settlement to provide his family with corresponding facilities. So, the Shells of the community act as a very strong force of inertia. This may even have the effect of reviving a declining

283

life expectancy of settlements

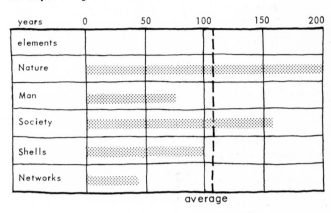

a. in relation to its elements

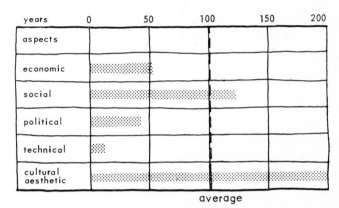

b. in relation to several aspects of life

settlement, since, during the period when the forces of inertia are operating, new functions may be added to the settlement and a part of its population may be attracted back, allowing the settlement to survive the crisis and live again (Law 17).

The settlement may also develop forces of inertia because of the Shells' capacity to survive for some time even if they are abandoned. While first the productive and then the non-productive forces of the population may abandon it, the Shells of a settlement which have not been demolished have the capacity to survive for several years, perhaps several decades. During such a period the fortunes of the settlement may change once again and new forces may flow in.

So, the forces of inertia slow down the decline of a settlement and delay its death, first because only one part of the population leaves while another part stays behind for quite a long period; and second because even when the entire population abandons the settlement it still retains the values of the Shells, and even dead, the Shells develop forces of inertia.

The value of the Shells determines the strength of the

inertia. If the settlement is temporary, with Shells consisting of tents, the forces of inertia will be nil, since when nomads decide to move to a different location, they take their tents with them. If the Shells are permanent, but of low value, not only absolutely but in relation to the income of the people as well (since perhaps they have had no time to invest enough in accordance with their income) the settlement will be easily abandoned. If, on the other hand, the people, although of a low income level, have remained in the same location for centuries, not only individually but as a community, and the investment is high, the forces of inertia will be much stronger. In such cases, it is very difficult to disassociate the existence of the settlement from the values invested in it, for the latter exercise a very strong force of inertia over their population. Such forces make settlements last not only for decades and generations, but also for centuries although perhaps with fewer inhabitants and functions, and a smaller capacity.

Law 19. The death process of a settlement is complete when every reason for its life has ceased to exist, or when the facilities it provided have been made available in a location which can be approached more easily, or which can provide them to a higher degree.

This means that in spite of the forces of inertia a time will come when the settlement can no longer provide enough for its inhabitants, at least not as much as a new settlement nearby provides, and this induces even the people who were kept behind by forces of inertia to abandon the Shells, which then die.

As long as the Shells have a relatively high value, the forces of inertia are strong and people develop a certain resistance to movement. But when investment in the new settlement and opportunities for life are of higher value than the total of opportunities provided by the old settlement, the latter can no longer survive and is abandoned. In very exceptional cases such settlements are maintained as dead Shells, not by the communities, but by the broader areas interested in them, especially if they have great historical or cultural value; an example of this type of settlement is Williamsburg in the U.S.A. However, in such cases they are given additional life and very often are completely revived and become settlements of even greater importance than before, just because of the values invested. In these cases the Shells have survived and have caused the creation of a new type of life within them. If the settlement had been completely abandoned and no interest had been shown in it, its death would have been final.

Before closing this section containing the first basic laws I would like to point out that these laws are valid only if Man and Society do not take action to reverse them. When I say, for example, that settlements die under certain conditions, this means that Man and Society have not reacted to the ongoing forces in order to save the settlements. This, we should not forget, constitutes the basic difference between the laws of organisms in nature (animals and plants) and laws of settlement where the thoughtful decision of Man can change the course of their development in a revolutionary way.

The course of the life of settlements can be conditioned by their laws if Man does not consciously intervene. This leads us to the last law of this section.

Law 20. The creation, development and death of settlements follow certain laws unless Man decides to reverse their course.

The question whether he is able or wants to is one depending to a great extent on the laws themselves.

LAWS OF INTERNAL BALANCE

Law 21. The elements in each part of a settlement tend toward balance.

If one of the elements gets out of balance, within reasonable limits, the settlement tends to re-establish this balance. If this can be done in time, the settlement is normal again. If the loss of balance is so extensive that the settlement cannot re-establish it within a reasonable time, the results may be disastrous. When, for example, the population of a settlement grows very quickly and there is not enough shelter for everybody, this leads to the creation of more shelters; should this happen within a reasonable period of time, the settlement will move ahead normally. But should the gap between demand and supply for more shelter be too great, the settlement will definitely begin to suffer, perhaps producing many undesirable effects.

When balance is reached the settlement is satisfactory and orderly. Balance should exist at all times. But overall balance is not enough; it should prevail in each part of the settlement, in each Ekistic unit. If it is limited to the general framework only, the units of a lower order will be in need of redevelopment and renewal.

Law 22. The balance among the elements of a settlement is dynamic.

Since we have noted in Law 7 that the development of a settlement is continuous, we cannot expect the elements to remain in constant static balance. As each of them changes, and in accordance with Law 21 tends to regain balance, we can also expect the balance to change and become dynamic. A population increase means an increased demand for housing, educational institutions, facilities, social institutions and functions; higher incomes mean more complicated functions, and greater investment in the Shells.

Law 23. The balance of the elements is expressed in a different way in each phase of the creation and evolution of a settlement.

In the first phase of creation there is a different balance between Nature, which is the controlling element, and Man, who constitutes the one element added from the outside. The balance in the first phase is dynamic, with Nature playing the greater role. Man must begin to understand Nature, transform and control it. In the next phase Man manages to impose small, probably temporary, Shells on the landscape. He then expands these Shells. It is quite clear from these examples that a different type of balance exists in each phase of creation.

Law 24. The balance between the elements is expressed in a different way in each section and at each scale of a settlement.

This dynamic balance is reminiscent of the Heraclitan philosophy of constant change. We can therefore say that settlements continuously find themselves in a Heraclitan state, while they are tending towards an Aristotelian one.

This balance is expressed in one way in a room, where Man alone is the controlling factor and the Shells are the only other major one. It is different on a highway where the function of traffic is preponderant, where Man is an element under the control of another element, the car, and where Nature is practically altogether absent. On a larger scale, in a whole community, on the other hand, Nature—expressed first by the landscape and then by the climate—plays a much greater role; and on the metropolitan scale the landscape may become the most important factor, influencing even the form of the settlement.

In the past, human settlements were built on the human scale only. Their only inhabitant was Man (and domestic animals) moving at his own speed. Recently, and especially since the beginning of the twentieth century, first the car, and then the airplane and rocket, have entered the life of Man, imposing new scales and new problems. The car in particular, existing in cities made for Man, ruins their texture, cannot itself move freely, and creates many problems for Man. For this reason, one scale for every kind of inhabitant is the only natural solution for settlements (fig. 284). Man used to have full control; the car has displaced him in various scales and has taken control. What is wrong is that Man is still interfering with the scale of the car, while at the same time he has not succeeded in saving his own scale outside his buildings.

This is the reason why scale is of major importance where human settlements are concerned, and why in Ekistics forms have no importance at all unless they are specific expressions on a specific scale. I will mention one example (fig. 285a). If we take some Ekistic units—houses with their plots—and distribute them along a minor road, their inhabitants will be connected with each other by small lines which are either vertical to or parallel to the small road crossing the settlement; they all form a small community. If we now widen the road and turn it into a highway, and leave the houses as they were (fig. 285b), a community will no longer exist, since people

284

many masters and many scales

but balance must be established in every scale

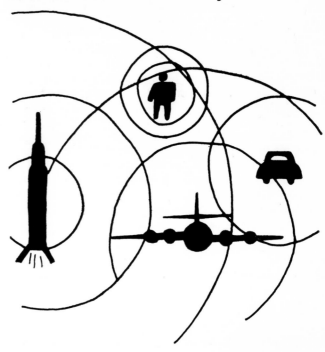

will no longer be connected to each other across the highway, which due to its width and traffic has ceased to connect and acts as a dividing element. This is why the first so-called 'linear city' of Madrid by Soria y Mata, 1882, could not have succeeded; the design of its elements was completely out of scale. The great width of its main street and its street-car-line destroyed the unity of the small community with one- and two-storey houses. Cohesion was impossible.

In order to re-establish cohesion between these houses, we should consider two rows of them with a small street in between as one Ekistic unit, and should then build the highway outside this unit in order to allow it to retain its scale (fig. 285c). In this way, more Ekistic units could be created around the highway and a larger Ekistic unit would emerge (fig. 285d). These minor Ekistic units could then be enlarged without touching the highway, which will form the spine of the greater community (fig. 285e). The result would be the same as with the first houses along the small road, the difference being that instead of houses we would have cohesive communities which are small units connected to a major community by a major highway. Synthesis in space is expressed in different ways in accordance with the scale of the Ekistic unit.

Law 25. The most important balance of all the elements in space is that of the human scale, which is fully controlled by Man through his body and senses.

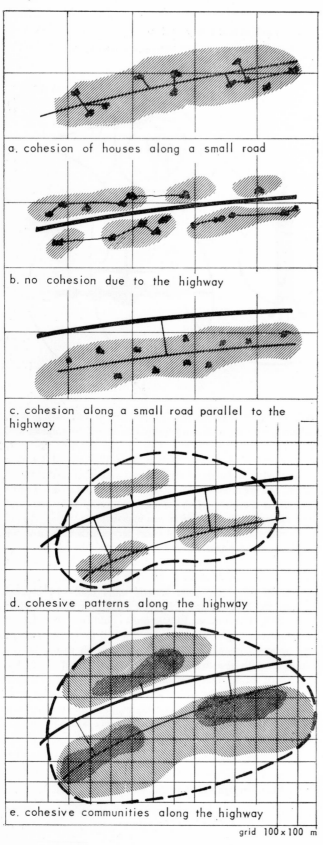

a. cohesion of houses along a small road

b. no cohesion due to the highway

c. cohesion along a small road parallel to the highway

d. cohesive patterns along the highway

e. cohesive communities along the highway

grid 100 x 100 m

285
(left) creation of ribbon development

286
(below) the human bubble
as defined by the body of Man

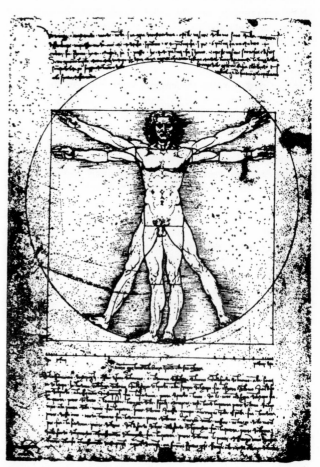

drawing by Leonardo da Vinci

The human scale begins with the space required by Man in his movements, which for all practical purposes is in the shape of a bubble with a diameter equal to Man's maximum dimensions when he stands with his arms extended horizontally. The drawing of Leonardo da Vinci, although drawn for another purpose, is the best representation of the average dimensions of this bubble (fig. 286). Naturally, its size changes from man to man, and even for the same man, since his position in space, his movements and his speed change, and the bubble changes accordingly. When he is sleeping, for example, the bubble is elongated and flat at the bottom. When he is walking, the bubble is an elongated spheroid which is rather elliptical on a horizontal plane with the longer axis parallel to the direction of his movement. When he is running, this spheroid is even more elongated (fig. 287).

The complete study of the human scale cannot be limited to the static human bubble as represented by Leonardo da Vinci. We must look at it in two ways. First, Man does not consist of a body alone; the complete Man has body, senses, mind and soul. The real human bubble consists of many bubbles radiating in different ways around Man as shown tentatively in fig. 288.

Second, Man does not stand still. This is why Leonardo's drawing alone is misleading and we have to show it side by side with the moving man, who not by his dimensions alone but by his movement as well defines the human scale (fig. 289).

When we understand the single human bubble and the scale it imposes properly we can proceed to combine many of them in different ways, depending on the conditions and the forces which are being exercised on them (fig. 290).

This human bubble is the smallest unit we deal with in Ekistics. Its normal dimensions in a horizontal projection are between two and three square metres (21–32 sq. ft.) depending on the size and the position of Man. The next unit is the room; then come the house, the dwelling, the group of dwellings, the small neighbourhood. These units increase up to a certain size, beyond which we begin to lose the notion of the human scale. The limit is, as practice has shown, a unit corresponding to the ancient cities and to the urban distances Man likes to walk today. Both lead us to believe that such a unit has a radius of no more than a ten minute walk, which means a maximum diameter of 2 kms, or an average of 1,500 metres or just less than a mile. This distance coincides with the distance from which one is able to see a building of importance, which may be located at the centre of a community. This is the distance over which Man can easily have a visual aesthetic grasp, the area which he can easily comprehend with his own senses. It is up to this scale that Man is in full control, a control which decreases from the smallest Ekistic unit, the room, to the larger one of the community (one mile long). His control decreases at a higher rate beyond this limit.

287

single human bubbles
as defined by the body of Man

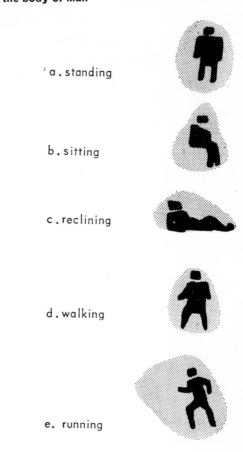

a. standing

b. sitting

c. reclining

d. walking

e. running

LAWS OF PHYSICAL CHARACTERISTICS

Location

Law 26. The geographic location of a settlement depends on the needs it must serve for itself and for the Ekistic system to which it belongs.

A settlement whose role is to be a transportation centre must be located in an area which all kinds of transportation networks can cross; near the sea or on a plain with as much open land as possible. But the geographic location does not depend solely on the natural formation of the area. It also depends on the formation of the Ekistic system. A settlement which is to be a main transportation centre must not only be located in the proper natural setting, but also in a key position in relation to the whole system of settlements. For example, if all settlements are coastal, the transportation centre should be near the coastal region's centre of gravity, and not near that

301

288

the total system of human bubbles
as defined by total Man

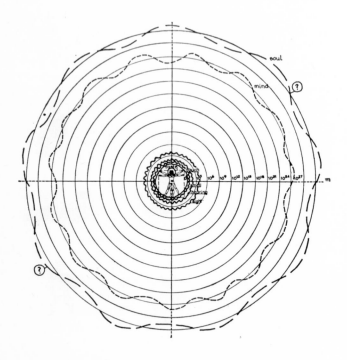

289

the human bubble
as defined by the body of Man

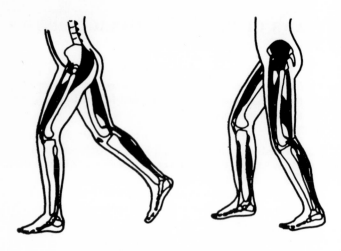

towards a study of the dynamic
human bubble based on Man's
movements

302

of the inland plain, where only small and unimportant settlements are located.

Law 27. The topographic location of a settlement depends on its needs and its physical size. If a settlement must cover the need for a port, it will be drawn by an economic force to a natural harbour.

If the size of the settlement which is to become a port town is very small, it can be located on a hill near the port. But, if the settlement is large, only a plain near the harbour will give it a chance for proper development. The dimensions of the settlement determine the selection of the topographic site.

Size

Law 28. The population size of a settlement depends on its role in servicing certain needs for its inhabitants and for its Ekistic system.

Needs and the forces which express these needs determine the size of a settlement. In our era a settlement is no longer an independent organism separated from others. At the beginning of Man's history there used to be relatively independent settlements, self-sufficient and located at great distances from other settlements. This type has by now been practically eliminated, or is in the process of being so. Today the size of a settlement depends on its geographic and topographic location, which conditions its Ekistic location (i.e. its location within a broader system), which in turn conditions its role as a part of it. Any attempt to understand the size or any other basic phenomenon of a settlement by disassociating it from the system of which it is a part will be misleading. The belief that the size of settlement D can be disassociated from its whole system is erroneous, for it is quite clear that the population of D depends on its role in the entire Ekistic system (fig. 291). The same is true of any small settlement A1. Its general role is that of a class A community, and consequently its population is conditioned by this class A location. In addition to this, its specific location in the proximity of D, in spite of the fact that its primitive function was the same as A2, leads to a greater population than A2. A1 has been brought into closer contact with a major settlement, from which it absorbs the capacity of new functions, which leads to a different population size.

We do not know much about what happened in the past and whether there were any conscious attempts to limit the size of settlements, or of cities in particular. We have reasons to believe that the size was limited in most cases by the population itself. The very fact that in many cities people built walls and managed to live within them over long periods of time implies that the population size of the settlement was confined by the limitation of its physical size through walls. Because of all the existing conditions in our era of dynamic settlements, we know of many efforts made either in theory or in practice to limit the dimensions of settlements. We

290
combined human bubbles

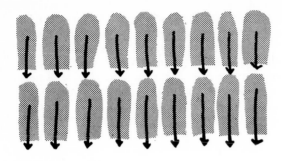

order imposed by a spectacle

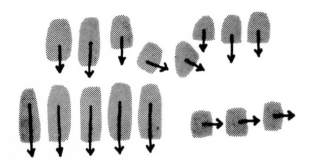

disorder when the spectacle is over
the bubbles shrink

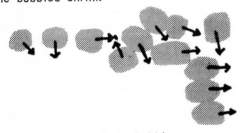

further shrinking of the bubbles

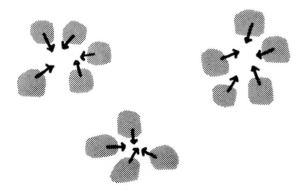

a new order created.

know equally well that these efforts are doomed if they overlook the fact that the settlement can and must grow in accordance with the requirements of its Ekistic role. If its functions in their evolution do not require a larger population, then the population is limited to what was originally thought possible. If, however, the functions in their evolution require a larger population, there is no reason to believe that any human force can set a limit to the size. No political or social system of the present era has proved to be stronger than the force of economic activities and the Ekistic system, which in the final analysis defines the population size of every settlement.

Law 29. The physical size of a settlement depends on its population, its needs, its role within the Ekistic system and its topographic location.

Whereas the population size depends on the functions of the settlement and its Ekistic role, the physical size is influenced by various factors. The size of the population is the first and deciding factor, but the functions of a settlement and its Ekistic role can play a very important role as well. If we have two settlements of 1,000 inhabitants each, one urban and the other agricultural, their physical size will differ immensely, since the urban settlement will need much less space than the rural one. The latter might be relatively small, if the farmers live by intensive farming, or very large if they live by extensive farming or cattle-breeding and need grazing grounds. This is valid both for the total settled part, i.e. the entire community area, and the nucleus or built-up part. A farming community of 1,000 people with a very large area can have a built-up part as small as an urban community, or perhaps even smaller if the whole community lives on dry-farming and there are no cattle to be housed in the built-up part. On the other hand a farming community where the cultivation is intensive, may have its houses built on the farms, making the built-up area much larger than that of the dry-farming community (fig. 292).

The physical size also depends on the topographic location and many local factors—from climatic to cultural—linked with it. A windy location may force a settlement, be it urban or rural, to be very densely built in order to mitigate the heavy winds (fig. 293). On the contrary, if it is a very hot area and the winds are an important factor for a better micro-climate and better living conditions, we may then witness a completely different community structure tending towards a much less dense pattern in order to allow for ventilation (fig. 294).

Functions

Law 30. The functions depend on the geographic and topographic location, the population size and the Ekistic role of the settlement.

The geographic location determines the general functions of a settlement, such as its function as an agricultural or

population size of settlement D is a result of its connections within a whole system

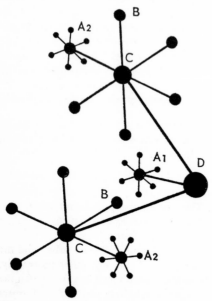

292

physical size of settlements of 100 inhabitants

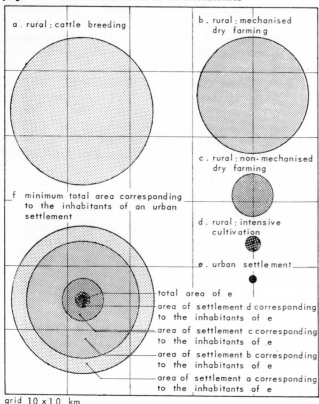

grid 10 x 10 km

304

industrial centre, while the topographic location conditions these functions more specifically. If the geographic location allows for agricultural production in general, it is the topography which finally conditions the produce of the area.

It may be asked whether the population size determines the functions, or vice versa. It is quite clear that on the contrary it is the functions which basically determine the population size. However, once a certain size of population prevails, the settlement by itself acquires additional functions because of that size. For example, a small industrial centre is created because of the required function of serving a big new industry in a large agricultural region. The city acquires a population of 10,000. Because of this population it now plays the role of a small urban centre serving the surrounding area, for unlike the villages which existed previously, it has certain facilities which can serve the whole surrounding area much better. Such additional functions, conditioned by the population size, draw additional population, and so on.

Finally, the Ekistic role conditions specific functions. If an urban settlement has certain functions, let us say if it acts as a commercial and administrative centre, its Ekistic role as a class D or E centre conditions its specific functions.

Law 31. The role of a settlement in the Ekistic system depends on its functions, its geographic location and its population size.

Basically, the Ekistic role depends on the geographic location, since it is this which conditions the basic class of the settlement. However, the role also depends on the functions. In the same geographic location an additional function which may have been added to the settlement because of special local conditions or a decision concerning the role of the settlement (such as turning it into a military, administrative or educational centre) also conditions the Ekistic role. Finally, the population size which has been reached because of the functions of the settlement adds to its Ekistic role by changing and reclassifying the settlement within the whole system, if new functions have increased the population. A class C settlement, for example, can play a class D Ekistic role if the functions established because of government decision add a population which may change the Ekistic role and increase its importance.

Law 32. The functions and Ekistic role of a settlement are interdependent with geographic and topographic location, population and physical size.

Although basically several of the physical and functional characteristics of a settlement determine the others, in the final analysis they are interdependent. For example, the population size may depend on the functions, Ekistic role and physical size, but the latter also depend on the former. In these relationships greater value may be attributed to one factor or group of factors than to another; this is why in some of the previous laws, emphasis has been placed in only

293
climate effects upon the physical layout in a coastal area
Paros, Greece (1961)

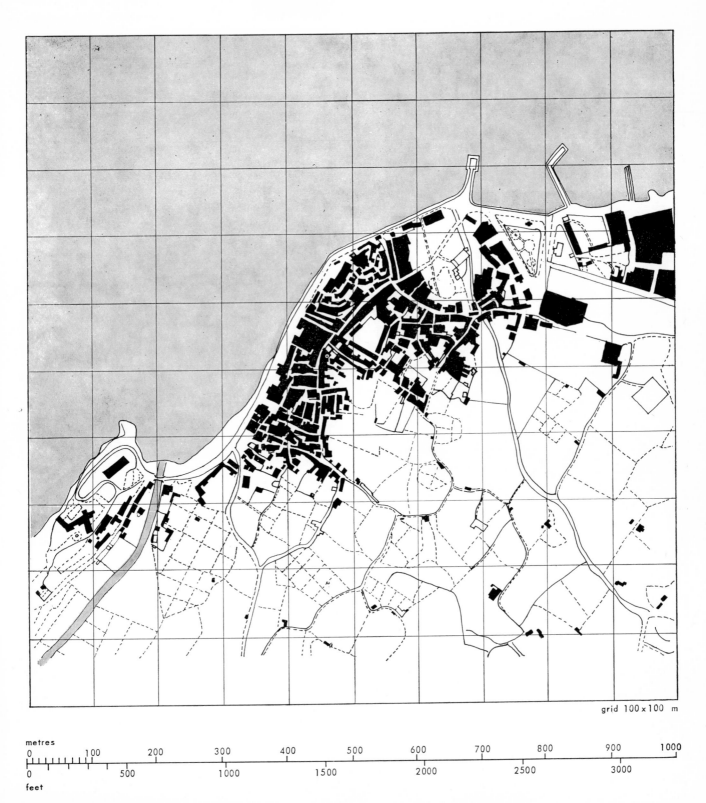

grid 100 x 100 m

metres
0   100   200   300   400   500   600   700   800   900   1000

0   500   1000   1500   2000   2500   3000

feet

x

climate effects upon the physical layout in a tropical area
Somanya, Ghana (1961)

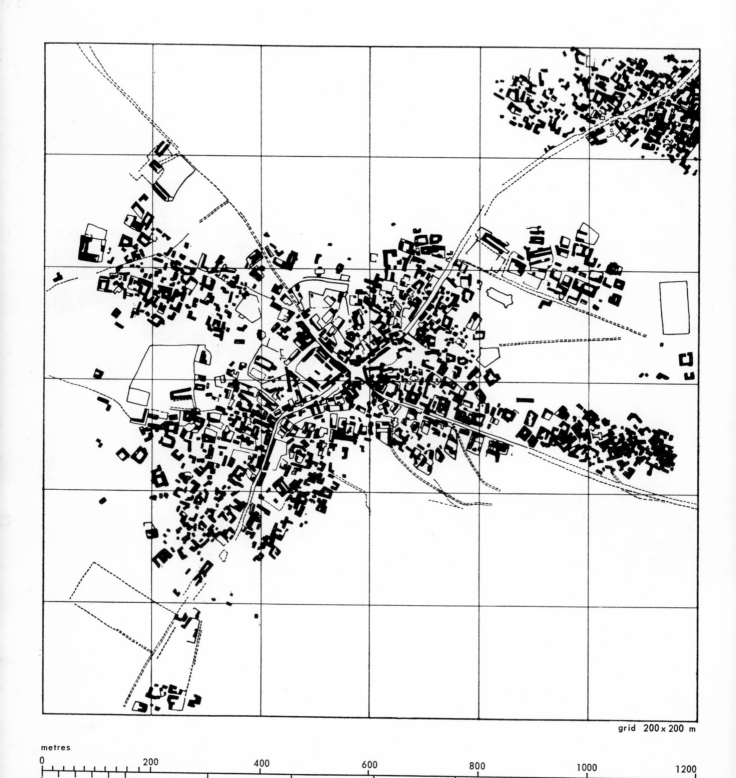

grid 200 x 200 m

metres

0		200		400		600		800		1000		1200

0		500		1000		1500		2000		2500		3000		3500	

feet

one direction. However, there is no relationship between these physical factors and functions which is not reversible. The relationship is merely more basic in one direction than in the other.

Because of these relationships, each of the six factors already mentioned in Laws 26 to 31—that is, geographic location, topographic location, population size, physical size, functions and Ekistic role—forms a circle within which all possible connections are justified to different degrees. There are no missing links between the circles; some of them are simply stronger than others. The radiation to and from every one of these circles represents one of the previous six laws while the total stands for the law of interdependence (fig. 295).

Structure

Law 33. The basic cell of human settlements is an Ekistic unit which is the physical expression of a community. This unit should function without being fragmented in any way, for if it is, the settlement will not perform its role properly.

People tend to live in communities of common economic, social, cultural, religious, political and other interests. In human settlements this fact is also expressed in a physical way, by the Shells of the settlement. For example, one basic characteristic connecting all the elements of a community (a shopping centre serving the whole community), should be enough to discourage the splitting of the community into two parts by a canal, if there are no bridges, or by a highway or railway, if there are to be no proper connections above or below it, etc. Should such a split occur, the uniformity and the continuity of the community's texture will cease to exist, in this respect the community will stop functioning as a whole, and the settlement will be deprived of its most basic characteristic—the existence of properly functioning Ekistic units.

In order to function properly, a settlement must have specific social dimensions which are expressed in the form of communities. These may be on a minor or major scale, but on every level they must be complete in order to function properly. Any part of a human settlement should consist of an appropriate number of communities. If we expect an independent Ekistic unit to function properly, it should be a community of such size as to guarantee its survival.

Law 34. All communities, and therefore, all Ekistic units tend to be connected to each other in a hierarchical manner. Every community of a higher order serves a certain number of communities of a lower order, and the same is true of specific functions within Ekistic units.

A small city may well be the centre of an area of five or six smaller cities and 30 to 50 rural settlements. And it may also be one of the five to eight cities of a similar size which are served by a city of an even higher order. The same holds

interdependence of factors and functions

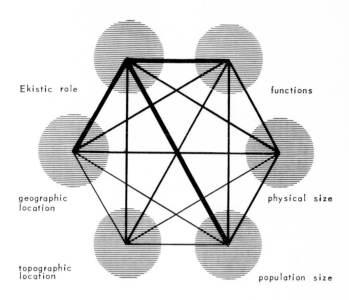

Ekistic role functions

geographic location physical size

topographic location population size

true for all specific functions within the city. If a city is a commercial centre, it serves the commercial centres of the smaller cities and the rural settlements in its area, while it in its turn is served by a commercial centre of a higher order in the Ekistic area to which it belongs (fig. 296).

Law 35. The fact that all communities tend to be connected in a hierarchical manner does not mean that this connection is an exclusive one. Many other connections at the same level or at different ones are equally possible, but for organisational purposes the connections are hierarchical.

The settlements do not create one-way connections between communities, on the contrary they tend to create many types of connections in all directions; therefore, the possibilities of multiple and not only hierarchical connections are open (fig. 296). It is natural, however, that any organised activity should follow a pattern of hierarchical connections; a merchant with a shop in a community class III, for example, does not buy from the wholesale merchant of class IX, but from the distributor of class V or VI. The administration of municipal services follows the same pattern. This pattern is also followed by any citizen connected with any function, unless he is dissatisfied with the services close to him or unless a service of a higher order is closer to him than one of a lower order. If he wants to buy bread he normally goes to centres class III or IV, but if a supermarket class V happens to be

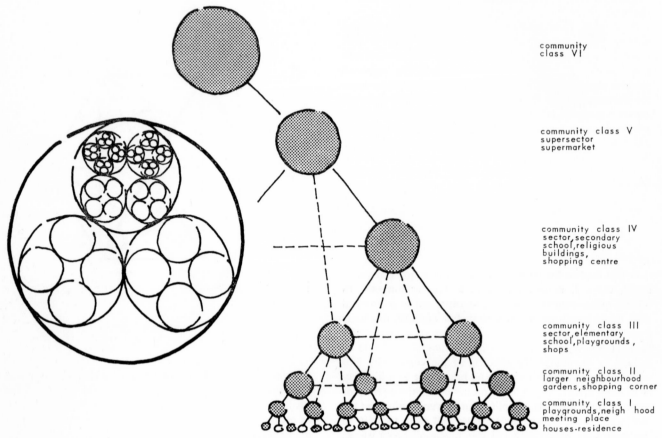

community
class VI

community class V
supersector
supermarket

community class IV
sector, secondary
school, religious
buildings,
shopping centre

community class III
sector, elementary
school, playgrounds,
shops

community class II
larger neighbourhood
gardens, shopping corner

community class I
playgrounds, neigh hood
meeting place
houses-residence

the continuous lines represent the hierarchical structure, the dotted ones represent the possibility of other connections also

closer to him he might satisfy a need of a lower order in a centre of a higher one.

Law 36. The existence or creation of communities and functions of a higher order does not necessarily mean the elimination of those of a lower one.

The need for a large shopping centre does not mean the elimination of all corner-shops. The same holds true for an urban supermarket and a 'regional supermarket'. Every commercial centre has a function of a different class, magnitude and structure. The corner-shop serves needs which cannot be served by a supermarket situated at a great distance from homes. This law has been overlooked by many people. The fact that we need corner-shops and small units has led them to believe that supermarkets are inhuman. They are as mistaken as those people, who, when the supermarkets first appeared, thought that we should eliminate all services of a lower order because we no longer needed functions or

communities or Ekistic units of this type. Practice has shown that both points of view are equally wrong, since there is a hierarchy of functions and communities, and the hierarchical system must function as a whole if the settlement is to function satisfactorily.

This law mentions the existence and creation of communities of a higher order. While it is clear how widely valid this is in existing communities, it is not always true in practice, since the creation of communities of different orders often leads to the elimination of communities of a lower order; especially if their existence depends on the same authority which decided on the creation of a community of a higher order. Sometimes attempts have been made by the local people to ameliorate the situation by creating, sometimes in spite of the decision of the planning authority, the missing communities of a lower order. This has happened with several new schemes where only a supermarket has been planned and no other shopping facilities have been allowed at lower levels.

In such cases people have often remodelled houses in order to provide the missing minor shopping centres, or even created temporary markets on street corners.

Law 37. The type of services and the satisfaction provided by every Ekistic unit, community and function of a higher order to those of a lower order depend on time-distance and cost-distance.

The fact that a hierarchical structure of Ekistic units, communities and functions is needed does not mean that the services provided are the same on every level, for the type of services depends on the level of the Ekistic units and communities. The type of services alone is not enough to measure the satisfaction afforded to the inhabitants. In order to measure the satisfaction one must measure the time-distance and cost-distance, which play an equally important role. An Ekistic unit and a community may well provide services of a higher order, services desired by the inhabitants of Ekistic units and communities of a lower order; let us say that it provides a theatre where the lower units have only a cinema. If, however, this theatre is located at a distance of 100 km. from the lower communities, they will visit it infrequently. The satisfaction being offered is weakened by the time-distance especially, and eventually much more so by the cost-distance if there is no public transportation.

Law 38. The overall physical texture of a human settlement depends on its basic Ekistic unit, that is, its Ekistic modulus.

The Ekistic modulus can be as small as a house, or the size of a block, or even the sector of a major community unit between highways, etc. This modulus depends on the size of the Ekistic units and defines its scale. If the Ekistic unit is a house and the modulus the room, and if the rooms are large, the scale of the house is large. If the Ekistic unit is a small city, its modulus is the city block; and if the block is large the scale of the city's texture is large. As a city grows to a large size the original size of its blocks (i.e. its street networks) becomes too small a modulus: they become out of scale. Then there is a necessity for a larger modulus which can be made of groups of blocks—or super-blocks separating pedestrian and vehicular traffic—such as the half mile square blocks in some city plans; or the community unit itself may become much more cohesive, as in the case of the sectors of the metropolitan area of the city of Islamabad.

Law 39. The texture of a human settlement changes as its dimensions change.

For a small city the house or even the housing group or city block may be a good modulus for the entire texture; but for a major city it is too small a unit. The texture of larger human settlements should change when the population of a settlement grows from say 100,000 to one million, since the settlement is unable to operate efficiently with a texture of small blocks. During this expansion major arteries must have made their

297

centripetal forces

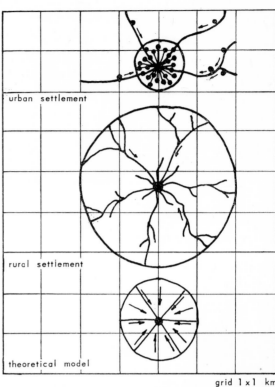

grid 1 x 1 km

appearance, either as railways or highways. The texture of the human settlement has probably been re-shaped during its growth. If this has not occurred, it is because of the settlement's inertia; while its inability to change its built-up structure results in its texture being no longer appropriate. The settlement has failed to adjust to the new requirements and consequently it is suffering.

In this respect we can compare Tokyo and London where the old texture of the city has been preserved (figs. 167 and 77), to Paris where the texture was changed in the time of Baron Haussmann (fig. 165), and to an American city, like Detroit, where the texture was again changed with the opening of freeways (fig. 267).

Form

Law 40. The main force which shapes human settlements physically is the tendency towards a close interrelationship of all its parts.

Since all parts endeavour to congregate as close as possible, they tend to form a circle with a centre which exercises a centripetal force. As new parts are added, they come to the

309

298

equal effort principle

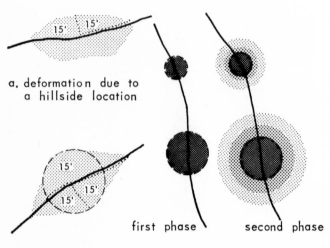

a. deformation due to
   a hillside location

first phase   second phase

b. deformation due   c. deformation due
   to a highway   to a railway line

centre in order to be as close as possible to all others. When new parts can no longer be added in the centre they come as close to it as possible. It is only when they cannot be effectively incorporated in the centre of the built-up area, that they are arranged on the periphery.

Because of this law and because of the centripetal force, small settlements have a very cohesive shape, always tending towards a circle. Without such a force, their parts would be unconnected and would practically 'float' at will. On the basis of this principle, houses not connected with production or any function connected with Nature also tend to be as close to each other as possible. The degree to which this is possible is defined by the space needed around them (fig. 297).

Since within a settlement the parts are not of equal dimensions and importance, they tend to arrange themselves so that those more closely connected are brought even closer, while those less immediately connected to each other move even farther apart. In a village, the peasants' houses are close to its centre. Since these occupy a small space, they can be densely built; they contain the families of people who have many reasons to be close together in order to use common facilities, etc. Dry-farming areas on the other hand, which only certain members of the family occupy for a certain number of hours a day, need not be as close to each other and are usually arranged in the periphery of the settlement. Such a structure is physically expressed as a settlement consisting of two parts: the nucleus or built-up part with a network of streets quite close to each other allowing for small plots and small houses,

with the remaining part of the settlement containing the farms served by streets at a much larger distance apart corresponding to the considerably larger size of the farms in relation to the building plots within the built-up nucleus. Theoretically, were this force the only one shaping the settlement, we should be led to the formation of nuclei or built-up parts consisting of one central square and radial streets leading towards it (fig. 297).

The centripetal force does not seem to work in very small settlements. When there are only a few houses—say, ten or 20 —a centripetal force is not always in operation. It seems that because the distances are too small and because it does not matter whether people walk two minutes instead of one, their need to congregate in one centre does not work in the same way. There can also be another explanation for this phenomenon. Such very small settlements have no focal point and are not big enough to have developed a central square or central functions; therefore, in the absence of a centre there is no centripetal force. The fact is that centripetal forces only appear to begin operating in settlements with a few score houses. A parallel could be drawn with the capillary forces in very narrow tubes, where, instead of having the surface of a liquid at a horizontal level, we see it taking a convex or a concave form. As in many natural phenomena, general principles are no longer valid on a micro-scale, the same stands true for settlements.

Law 41. A centripetal force leads to forms of settlements conditioned by curves of equal effort, which ideally appear as concentric circles.

This effort may be expressed physically as the effort required to walk a long distance across a plain versus the effort required to climb a hill, or in the time required to cover these distances, or in the money needed when one must pay in order to move within the settlement. Whether the prevailing curves are of effort, time or money, depends on the values of these elements in every specific case. If, for example, the settlement is small and people do not own mechanical means of transportation, the only important characteristic is human effort, which is the deciding factor. In such a case a settlement on a hillside will tend to have its larger dimensions along the contour lines rather than at right angles, since moving horizontally is easier than going up or downhill (fig. 298).

If the settlement is large and the inhabitants are wealthy enough to own cars, the prevailing characteristic will be time. Thus, a settlement which has a network of streets allowing for the same speed throughout tends to be circular. If, however, one highway crosses the settlement, and the speed on it is twice as much as that within the normal road network, the settlement will tend to take a form corresponding to a combination of the time required for movement both within the normal network and on the highway (fig. 298).

If the settlement is such that some people move on foot, some by private car and others by mass transportation, the money factor tends to prevail and the settlement will usually take a form corresponding to the amount the inhabitants can spend on transportation. This may lead to much more complicated forms, since the movement of one part of the population may be determined on the basis of the human effort required, another on the time required and a third on the basis of money needed. But if, in addition to means of transportation by road, the city has a railway passing through it which stops only at certain distant points easily accessible by train, the fares may be quite expensive for everybody, so that the train will be used only by a certain number of inhabitants. This may lead to a still more complicated form of a series of built-up parts around the station, which can later merge into one (fig. 298).

Law 42. Linear forces lead to the formation of linear parts of settlements; under certain conditions, this may lead to a linear form of the entire settlement for a certain length only, and after a certain period of time.

If instead of having railways (which create settlements around their stations) we have highways (which facilitate traffic along them while access to them is not completely limited as with railways), then the settlement tends to become linear (fig. 299). If the highway has limited access, then we may have a tendency for the creation of a linear settlement on the one side. The width and distribution of land uses along the highway always tend to be the same.

Law 43. Undetermined forces, usually caused by the form of the landscape, lead to the formation of settlements of an undetermined form.

These settlements may take shape on the banks of a river or by a lake or by the seashore with a beautiful view or even by a narrow valley. They may resemble linear ones or they may well be of a completely undetermined form. Their width and distribution of land uses may also not be the same.

Law 44. The form of a settlement is determined by a combination of the central, linear and undetermined forces in adjustment to the landscape and in accordance with its positive and negative characteristics.

An elongated valley will by necessity have an elongated settlement, for its development along the main axis of the valley is easier than at a right angle (fig. 300). A landscape which is divided by rivers will lead the settlement to a form adjusted to the shapes of the land left intact. It is not easy to cross a river many times or to build a settlement on a delta. Thus, a settlement which grows in a valley near a river is built mainly where the river is most easy to cross. Its later expansion will follow forms that avoid the necessity of building on the swamps of a delta or of making many river crossings.

There are also positive aspects of the impact of the landscape on the form of the settlement. If, for example, a settlement is

299

linear settlements

theoretical pattern

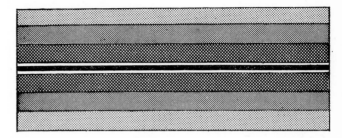

built near a bay, it is quite natural for parts of it to be influenced by the positive aspects of a coastal area which attracts both residents and industry. This may occur even if there is no economic motive for the sake of better contact between Man and Nature. If the inhabitants are fishermen they want to be as close as possible to the beach where they can pull their fishing boats out of the water whenever the weather is bad. In this case, the element of Nature acts not only as an element of production, but also as a line of transportation. But even when this factor does not exist, in order to take full advantage of the beauty provided by the sea, or the sea breeze, the settlement will become adjusted to the form of the landscape; this may well result in a crescent-shaped form. In such a case, the focal point of the settlement, the centre itself will also be elongated.

Law 45. A settlement grows in the areas of the greatest attraction and least resistance.

Laws 43 and 44 lead to the conclusion that settlements and their overall functions develop along their main lines of transportation, conditioned by other elements, such as Nature, the type of Society, special functions, the types of transportation used, the cost of movement, etc. These laws also lead to the statement that the growth of settlements takes place on the basis of the curves of equal effort, equal time, equal money, etc., or a combination of these, as adjusted to the actual landscape. In addition to them, Law 45 clarifies that not only attraction but also the least resistance influences the growth of settlements.

Law 46. A factor with a direct impact on the form of a settlement is the need for security which may at times be even more important than the main centripetal force.

The form conditioned by the need for security depends on the kind of potential danger. In the past, the need for security influenced settlements in the same way as centripetal forces did. The danger coming from outside exercised pressures on the settlement leading it to a circular form which offered the minimum length of walls to be defended with the maximum enclosed surface (fig. 301a).

300

forms of settlements

determined by the landscape

301

forms of settlements

determined by the need for security

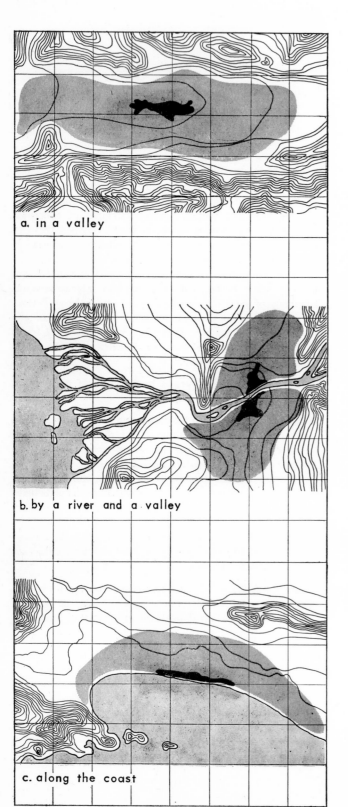

a. in a valley

b. by a river and a valley

c. along the coast

grid 1 x 1 km

grid 500 x 500 m

a. attack by land leads to a compact walled city

grid 5 x 5 km

b. attack by air breaks the city into pieces

grid 50 x 50 km

c. nuclear attack leads to the conception of a system of settlements

Then, airplanes threatened the settlement and therefore the opposite form was necessary for defence against an air attack. It was no longer necessary to present the minimum length of periphery line for defence; on the contrary it became necessary to be spread away from the centre, which might be hit, in order to present the enemy with a maximum surface. In this case, security comes into conflict with the settlement's natural centripetal forces (fig. 301b).

The fear of an attack by an even larger force from the air—nuclear weapons—may force settlements to be even farther apart, since the vulnerable area will be much larger and entire major settlements could be eliminated during an attack. Security, therefore, develops centrifugal forces which may spread the settlement over larger areas, with a number of very small parts and many others which may become linear. Thus, from the point of view of security, modern weapons are leading us towards new types of settlements which look much more like systems of nodal points and transportation lines than the compact built-up areas that prevailed in the past. A system which depends on many nodal points and circulatory lines becomes more important than the one-nucleus compact settlement since only such a system can survive, even if its central nucleus is completely destroyed (fig. 301c).

Law 47. Another force which exercises an influence on the form of a settlement is the tendency towards an orderly pattern.

For example, if the settlement is small, the centripetal forces may themselves define the final shape (fig. 302a). But should the settlement grow large enough, it will become apparent that the centripetal forces lead to an unmanageable form (as in fig. 302b) because the blocks will be very small in the centre and very large in the outlying area or if we want equal blocks, the street pattern will not make sense. In any case the form of the plots does not help the construction of rectilinear buildings. If we respect only the principle of order as derived from the desire of people to build their houses in rectangular space, which requires rectangular plots, this will lead to a grid-iron system for the road network (fig. 302c).

So, we are led to the conclusion that a settlement should be formed like a wheel on the basis of the centripetal principle, and like a grid-iron on the basis of the desire and tendency for absolute order. These two patterns contradict each other. We cannot combine a centripetal with a grid-iron pattern. Neither the desire for maximum cohesion nor for maximum order has any meaning or leads anywhere if deprived of the comprehensive view of how best to serve the total problem of the settlement. Only those forms of settlements make sense which can on every specific occasion merge reasonably the basic principles of settlements for cohesion and an orderly pattern. How this is done depends on each specific case and is the subject matter of a chapter on the morphology of settlements.

302

tendency to achieve an orderly pattern

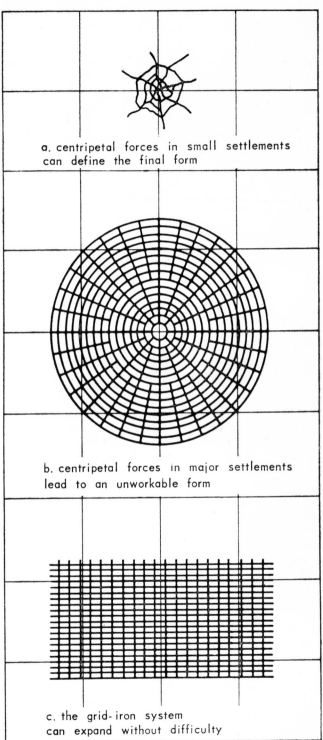

a. centripetal forces in small settlements can define the final form

b. centripetal forces in major settlements lead to an unworkable form

c. the grid-iron system can expand without difficulty

grid 1 x 1 km

313

303

forces influencing the form of Ekistic units

percentage of forces belonging to every unit of the Ekistic scale

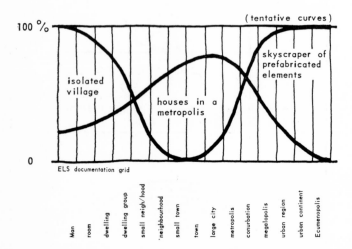

Law 48. The final form of the settlement depends on the total sum of the forces already mentioned as well as others such as tradition and cultural factors, which play a greater role in the lower units. The final form is a result of the interplay of these primary, secondary and tertiary forces.

How these forces interact, which one is stronger and which weaker, is not an easy question to answer, since their interplay changes on the basis of many variables. Location, as we have seen, differs in importance according to the size of the settlement. The basic structure of a settlement depends not only on its size, but also on its type of traffic. Traffic not only depends on the number of people, or on economic activity, but also on the means of transportation. It is reasonable to try to acquire gradually a better understanding of the interplay between some of these forces which will lead us to the formulation of rules. In this sense, it is useful even at this point to explore some of the related laws.

Law 49. The form of the settlement is satisfactory only if all the forces of varying importance within it can be brought into balance physically.

We have already seen that all the elements of a settlement tend to be in balance (Law 21). This must also be expressed in a physical way, otherwise the form of the settlement will be unsatisfactory. The elements and the forces are diverse and play a different role in the varied types of Ekistic units and at the various levels of the Ekistic scale.

There are forces which influence only the smallest Ekistic scales. For example, the preference of one individual or one family for a certain type of house is a force of only local

importance. The architecture of this house is a combination of the force of the smallest Ekistic unit—that is, the preference of the inhabitant—with the forces of the community in which he lives—the forces of a major Ekistic unit. Man alone cannot decide on the architecture of his house; he must respect the regulations, and in a certain way also the common desire of the community for a house acceptable to most of its members. For example, even if there are no regulations prohibiting it, it is difficult to accept a house painted black. The community would most probably protest and force the owner to change the colour to a more acceptable one.

All forces are broken up and act at different levels. For example, the house is much more influenced by the forces of the immediate neighbourhood than by those of the major community or the major city. In accordance with this rule, however, we will find that there are forces influencing this house which are derived from the city, the region, the nation, and finally even the whole world. Forces such as industrialisation, building materials, the behaviour of concrete and the rules conditioning it, are of international importance; whereas decorations, which may be created even with the same concrete, are very local in content.

Thus, the sum total of the forces influencing a settlement on every level is equal to that of the forces derived from Ekistic units on all levels (fig. 303). The curve showing this may vary in steepness due to forces derived from the smaller units or from forces derived from the higher unit.

Law 50. The right form for a human settlement is that which best expresses all the static positions and dynamic movements of Man, animals and machines within its space.

Man sits, stands, walks and runs in a city; so do animals serving his purposes, as well as machines. The form of the city should respect and express all these positions and movements within the settlement, for otherwise the form will not correspond to the main content of the city, that is, Man as well as the animals and machines. In the same way in which Marshall McLuhan states that 'only phonetic writing has the power to translate man from the tribal to the civilized sphere, to give him an eye for an ear',[2] only the proper expression of all needs can satisfy us aesthetically. I will mention one example: a central square serves the functions of people who stand, walk and circulate in it. It is stable and static and the people in it move slowly. So, the perspective of the roads leading to it should not be open, since this will transmit the image of through movement, which is contrary to the function of stability in the square (fig. 304a). The perspective leading to such a square should be closed, only then will it truly express the real needs of the square and those who use it (fig. 304b).

Law 51. The right form is that which expresses the importance, class and, consequently, the relative scale of every Ekistic unit with the proper basic moduli and their subdivision.

304

conception of space

in relation to the human and mechanical scales

a. this space conveys the notion of movement
   it is weaker for the human scale than for
   the mechanical one

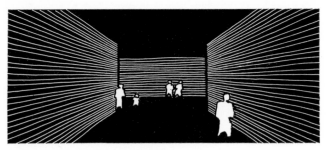

b. this space conveys a static notion
   it is correct for the human scale and false
   for the mechanical one

In a small city, let us say ancient Greek Miletus, the traditional city-block is its proper modulus (fig. 305a). The same is valid for most other small cities or villages. When the city is larger, a normal city-block, as the only modulus of its texture, leads to an overall form which is deprived of scale and character (fig. 305b). Such an overall form needs divisions of a higher order; the block may remain as one of their sub-divisions (fig. 305c).

Law 52. The densities in a settlement or in any of its parts depend on the forces which are exercised upon it.

Traffic density depends on the forces which bring traffic into a certain area. Population density during office hours depends on the forces which create a need for office functions in this particular area. The same is true of residential or of any other type of density.

Law 53. In human settlements formed by a normal process the pattern of densities changes in a rational and continuous way according to the level of the Ekistic unit and the functions served.

305

the proper structure of a settlement has to express its scale by the proper modulus

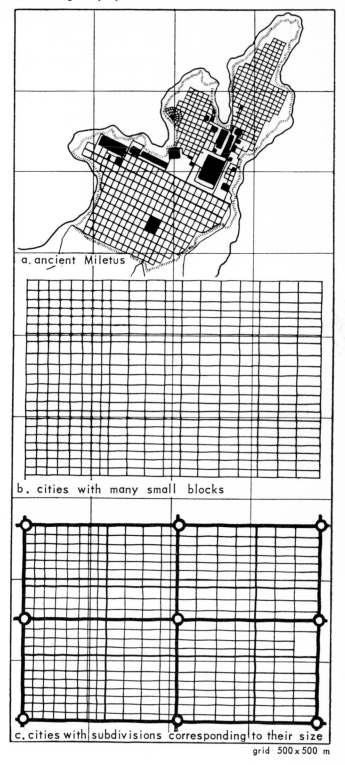

a. ancient Miletus

b. cities with many small blocks

c. cities with subdivisions corresponding to their size

grid 500 x 500 m

Such a principle means that there are no unreasonable transfers from very low to very high densities. There is a rational pattern for changing densities following the pattern of the hierarchical community structure. This principle is valid when the development of the settlement has taken place slowly over the years, either without conscious planning by Society, which imposes regulations, or with an intervention which respects the natural structure of the entire settlement.

According to this principle it is impossible in any Ekistic space which has been developed normally, especially at a normal speed, to have an area with a density of habitation, functions, investment and settlement not adjusted to the whole. If in the texture of the settlement there is any waste space, it will tend to be taken over by functions which will fill this area at the required density of people, functions and investment. If this does not happen, it will usually be due to man-made conditions of legal, administrative or economic significance. Human settlements cannot bear vacuums or a weakening of their texture in any section. If a vacuum remains, the settlement tends to fill it with functions, the densities of which are conditioned by those of the surrounding area.

Law 54. The satisfaction derived from the services provided by the Ekistic unit to the inhabitants greatly depends on the proper density of the settlement.

A settlement may have a great number of inhabitants, but the services provided to them may be on a very low scale, should the density of their habitation be very low, and the distances between people and between the people and central functions be large. On the other hand, an area with a smaller number of inhabitants who have settled in the right density is able to provide them with more satisfactory services.

The principles of the relationship of satisfaction derived from services to densities is derived from Law 37, since time- and cost-distances increase with lower densities, the services provided at lower densities decrease in importance. Densities can be expressed in different ways, such as in the physical proximity of the people who have settled, the physical proximity of the functions and the elements of the Shells, the degree of investment which has taken place over the whole area, etc. All these types of densities are of a similar nature, and they tend to increase or decrease simultaneously, although these changes are effected by different coefficients.

CHAPTER EIGHT
BASIC EKISTIC THEORY

CONSIDERATIONS ON THE THEORY

We need an Ekistic theory that will explain Ekistic phenomena. Until now we have described the phenomena in different ways and dimensions and have arrived at several laws based on our observations. To say that this was purely a description of facts concluding in a series of laws would be wrong; the fact that only certain phenomena of the many related to settlements have been selected, and that certain laws have been arrived at and presented in a certain order presupposes some overall conception of human settlements, some theory about them. But this theory although necessarily implied at times has not, so far, been formulated.

I think that the time is ripe for the laws and the underlying ideas to be connected to form a theory, in the same way in which facts and data were connected to form laws in the previous chapter. This is, I think, the normal process of thought: we begin by observing facts, then we connect them to form laws, and gradually we come to connect these laws to form a whole system—a theory. These mental processes run parallel perhaps, but their expression becomes apparent in these three stages.

We need a total Ekistic theory into which all phenomena can merge and by which all phenomena can be explained. This can be achieved in the future. For the time being I think that I can present a basic Ekistic theory which can gradually grow into a total one. It may be argued that we are not completely prepared for it; nevertheless I think that we must develop it. If we do not, there is a great danger that the entire Ekistic knowledge and action will not be understood, and consequently will not serve Man and his needs. There is even a danger that, due to the lack of a basic Ekistic theory, the partial efforts which are developing very specific methodologies, such as traffic and economic models, may not work towards but against the creation of satisfactory human settlements.

On the contrary, if the basic Ekistic theory which we can now develop is headed in the right direction—and I think we are beginning to know enough to achieve this—we will receive great benefits by connecting all the pieces of our knowledge to form a complete system. Even if the theory is not correct, its presentation will allow others to criticise it, and in doing so lead to the formation of a more accurate one. We should not forget that great progress has been achieved in many fields even on the basis of theories which were later proved to be wrong, and which were superseded by new ones, which in turn were again superseded by others, thus leading step by step to continuous progress. Hans Selye is right when he asserts that 'Our facts must be correct. Our theories need not be if they help us to discover important new facts'.[3]

In this part of my book I have attempted to develop such a theory by selecting the most important aspects of the preceding chapters. For this reason I repeat a few of the phenomena and laws which have been previously presented at greater length. Concentrating on the essentials of our knowledge and trying to interconnect them to form an entire system of ideas explaining all its components, even those which have not been taken into consideration in its formation but which are a part of the same phenomena, is the only way to present a basic theory. This is exactly what we have not done for human settlements. This is what is missing.

In formulating this basic Ekistic theory I will try to make it as simple as possible so that it can be easily understood. Therefore, I will not use all the laws already presented; they all form a part of this theory, but here I will limit myself to those statements which are indispensable to the formulation of the whole system of thought. I will follow the classical process of ordering the statements, beginning with ones that are simpler, basic and primary, and continuing to those which follow logically, which entail them and are explained by them.

In order to achieve this I will not think of our 'suffering cities', or 'exploding metropolis', or the 'racial problems'. These are diseases which should not distract our attention from our basic subject which is the settlements of mankind. Only if we look at the whole picture of this Earth with all its settlements, can we recognise the substance of their nature and evolution, and define their normal conditions. When we achieve this, we will be able to recognise the abnormal cases, the deviations, the diseases and conceive their therapy. It is time that we stopped concentrating on the 'suffering city' and turned to the healthy ones; looking on their diseases only as deviations from normality.

NATURE AND GOALS OF SETTLEMENTS

Human settlements consist of five basic elements, Nature, Man, Society, Shells and Networks, which together form a system. Their goal is to make Man happy and safe.

If these statements are true, and my whole effort has been based on this assumption, how can we connect them in a reasonable way? If human happiness and safety is our only goal, have the other elements no value at all? Hardly. Even though it is Man who is our ultimate goal, since he needs both Nature and Society in order to survive, these two elements necessarily constitute secondary concerns; we must care for their preservation and safety. And since Man and Society created for themselves the need for Shells and Networks, these should constitute our tertiary goals; we must care for their development, maintenance and operation.

In this way our pentagon of five elements can turn into a pentagon of Ekistic goals (fig. 306) where every element corresponds with a goal of a certain order.

Since our primary goal is Man himself, we have to face the question of how to translate into practice the fact that even though Man is singular, he is plural as well; our concern is for the individual, for the one man, but we have many of these men. The answer is that Man as an individual is our main goal and concern. In practice this means that we must do the maximum we can for the individual. Where he is alone, this effort will not meet with any competition. Where there are many we must once again do the maximum we can for the benefit of every single man. In this way the primary goal of a settlement is to maximise the services to Man whether alone or in a group.

This means that in a private room our only concern will be its inhabitant, but in the living room of a family our concern will be the satisfaction of all members of the family as individuals, and, in a more composite settlement, the satisfaction of all the inhabitants as individuals. The goal of the settlement is to maximise the satisfaction and safety it provides for all its citizens, to create the best frame for each man living there.

Such a goal, however, may be of theoretical value only. It may require two rooms or one very large room for each inhabitant, and this may be impossible in practice. The goal of a settlement, therefore, has to be modified in order to cover both the desirable and the possible. The goal of a settlement is to maximise the satisfaction and safety of all its citizens by defining the best that can be conceived, and by coming as close to it as is feasible.

It becomes clear that in order to attain such a goal we must be able to define very clearly the desirable goals first, and only then the possible ones. Without the former we cannot define the latter—and if we try to do so we will fail.

Up to this point I have based my definitions of goals on the

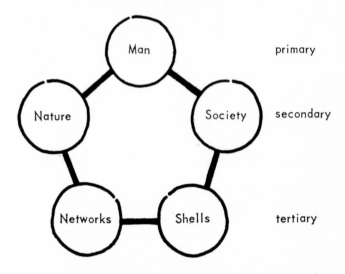

satisfaction of Man. What do we mean by Man's satisfaction? I believe we mean the satisfaction of human needs. So we are left with the basic unknown of human needs, which we must now try to define.

HUMAN NEEDS

Meaning of needs

In trying to define human needs we are up against the most difficult of our problems and we are running the risk of not being able to give an answer that psychologists and psychiatrists would accept as 'scientific'. I am aware of this danger; I am aware also of the fact that since this is a problem concerning directly and exclusively only one of our elements —Man, it is not necessarily a problem for Ekistics. So I could turn to the disciplines concerned with Man, to anthropology, medicine, psychology and psychiatry for an answer to this problem. I could turn to a total discipline covering the whole knowledge about Man, the Science of Man as suggested by Alexis Carrel, which on the basis of my Greek tradition I can tentatively name, *Anthropics*.[4]

But transferring the responsibility for the problem would not help Ekistics, which needs an answer now in order to proceed to the development of its own theory. For this reason I am proceeding with the attempt to tentatively define human needs on the basis of what I have been able to learn from the disciplines which are much more directly concerned with this question, even though I know that my definition will not be final in any way. Humanity has, after all, left us a great laboratory in which Man has been developing ways of satisfying his needs. The study of this laboratory gives me reason to believe that my effort is not far removed from reality, at any rate not the reality which is represented by Man's endeavours and achievements. What I am trying to do therefore, is initiate an empirical approach to the question of human needs.

One thing I consider as certain is that not only the average man, but also the scientist and the philosopher speak continuously in both their everyday life and their scientific or philosophic endeavours of human *wants, aspirations* and *needs*. I could also state with certainty that everybody has a subjective meaning for his own needs or for the needs of mankind and that there is no accepted system of values which allows us to measure, to compare, and to judge these needs. In addition to all these difficulties I could add that needs vary enormously with time, locality, conditions, etc., and that even for the same person they change continuously.

In spite of this we know that there are certain minimum needs which do not change and these are the very basic ones, such as the need for a certain number of calories per day, the need for certain cubic metres of oxygen per hour and the need for certain kilos of water per day. I could also add that there are minimum spatial needs for Man; he needs space in which to stand, to sit, to move, to stretch his legs; unless he has this minimum space his satisfaction and maybe even his survival are endangered.

There are also other needs which cannot be defined as clearly, or perhaps at all. If we ask ourselves which road a certain person is going to take, in order to go from point A to point B, so as to allow adequate space for this movement, we can answer only with probabilities; if we are asked which dress a lady will select first out of a collection, or which flower she will pick first in a garden we cannot give an answer even if we do happen to know the taste of this lady.

We recognise, therefore, that there are needs about which we can speak with certainty and needs about which we cannot express an opinion at all. In such cases we usually speak of a 'reasonable' need or a need that 'makes sense' and here comes the expert, Dr. Karl Menninger, to state that this is not scientific since:

'We are only saying that the steps in our explanation follow logically upon one another. If a mouse "wants" a grain of wheat we think it is logical that he translate this want into muscular contractions of his legs so controlled that they take him in the direction of the grain of wheat. We also assume that this attraction which the grain of wheat has for the mouse is something different from the attraction which a magnet has for a bar of iron, or vice versa. But when we try to say just wherein lies the difference we have to use words which according to strict scientific usage are not permissible. We have to speak of purpose, or wish, or goal, or intention and we have to distinguish between conscious and unconscious wish and intent'.[5]

After these explanations I think that I am under the obligation to proceed with my empirical approach to this problem of human needs with complete recognition that I am not answering the deeper questions that underly this important question, especially where human behaviour and motivation are concerned. I am obliged to proceed, however, since human settlements are built every day to serve basic human 'needs' and there is no reason why we should not define the definable because we are afraid of the undefinable.

In my effort to define the needs, I emphasise that I deal not with each single person, each individual, but with the average person. If I want to deal with the individual then the only way to define his needs is through him, to talk with him and help *him* define his needs which I, as an expert, have to serve. The same is true of any group of people, small or large. Once our question is related to real people then the definitions have to be made only by them or through them. This is the only practical and democratic way.

The first category of needs is the one I call *objective measurable needs*: so many calories, so much water and oxygen, so much land for the production of so much wheat or rice, and so much space for sleeping, sitting in a classroom, and so on. These needs, with slight variations, can be defined and measured. The needs of one person multiplied by the number of persons define the needs of the group.

The second category of needs is the one I call *subjective needs*. They involve such questions as: which road is everybody going to follow to the beach or the forest, which beach or forest is preferable for everyone, or which type of city, village or house. We cannot answer in any uniform way, we cannot even say 'the most reasonable one' because science does not accept the fact that Man always behaves reasonably. Here, however, we have two ways of easing the problem.

First, human settlements are not defined by the clock-mechanism of the law of cause and effect but by the statistical laws of effect and chance. We cannot define which beach or forest any one person is going to select; but we can decide which one most of the people or a certain percentage of them will prefer. This means that the larger the group of people we are dealing with, the greater our chance to define its needs with accuracy.

The second is due to the fact that the larger the type of needs we talk about, the greater the chances for a reasonable, as opposed to an emotional, definition of them. An individual can afford to dream of a villa on Mount Everest and even build it in a location which will be completely unreasonable even for him; the distance and inaccessibility will allow him to visit it but very seldom. A city cannot afford to build a summer resort for its school children in an inaccessible locality. The process of decision and the cost of such a project greatly decreases the possibility of its realisation. I believe that the same is also true of expressions of art which do not entail any major cost. An individual may wish to have in his home a type of painting which may not be accepted by any other living

307

definition of human needs

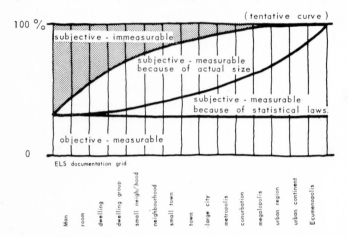

his action, Man is motivated by his needs. As long as they exist, there will be settlements regardless of whether parts of their elements are developed or even partially or totally eliminated within a certain locality. If Man survives, even though his crops have been burned and his village destroyed, he will build another village. Even if all the inhabitants of a certain city have been killed and the city completely destroyed, this city will be re-built and re-populated if the surrounding area needs a city to operate the port which feeds the hinterland.

Out of all the needs of Man those of greater importance for human settlements are the spatial ones. These are the forces which create human settlements. As long as they continue to exist there will be settlements. These needs can be understood through the functions they create: the need for food and clothing creates the function of gathering or production of foodstuff; the need for movement, the function of transportation; and the need for shelter, that of housing.

The satisfaction of needs and the operation of functions depends on the existing conditions (natural, human, etc.), and the possibilities they present. The relationship of needs and functions to conditions and possibilities is not a uni-directional but a two-directional one. Together they form an interdependent system, which when expressed in space, forms human settlements. Thus human settlements are conditioned by a two-dimensional system of needs and possibilities or functions and conditions in which there is no way of defining which starts first since the system exists and operates as an entity (fig. 308).

I shall use some examples to illustrate this interdependence of needs and conditions, functions and possibilities. Agricultural production is a specific function which depends on the existence of good soil, of a proper climate, of sufficient land and of other factors. Easy accessibility is an indispensable condition for the creation of a big market-settlement—it would have no meaning, however, if there were not enough people settled all around it, or if it were exposed to dangers that would make people avoid it.

person; such a painting cannot be hung in the lobby of the City Hall.

In conclusion I think that I can present the totality of the needs in a diagram (fig. 307) which shows that the larger the Ekistic unit we are dealing with, the greater is our chance of defining the totality of needs. Let us, for example, remember that the chances are very small that translatantic connections will be defined against economic considerations—except in single cases with some influence of political considerations and treaties—and that the position of the telecommunications satellite cannot be any but the most reasonable one. On the other hand many minor roads have been designed to cover only some special personal needs instead of the totality of needs.

In such a way we have an empirical rule which helps us to proceed with the definition of needs—in the case of the personal, emotional, subjective ones, by interviews with those concerned, and in the case of the impersonal, objective ones, by actual measurements for larger Ekistic units.

Needs and conditions

Human settlements are created because of Man's desire to satisfy his needs by settling in a certain locality for as long as is possible and necessary. In this way he tries to satisfy his needs for survival by collecting or producing food, creating breeding conditions for himself and protecting himself from danger.

The locality in which Man settles, the space that he occupies, has many different qualities and forms. In order to achieve the best possible satisfaction of his needs, Man shapes a very thin layer of the crust of the Earth, changing the flora and the fauna and creating human settlements. In

Nature and classification of needs and conditions

Needs are imposed by Nature or created by Man either for his satisfaction as an individual, in which case they are physiological needs, or as a member of a group, in which case they are social ones; they can, therefore, be divided into individual and social needs. Needs can be primary, as is, for example, survival, leading to the need of a minimum amount of food; or secondary and tertiary, as is the need for the production and preservation of food. They can be related to the satisfaction of Man's physical, sensual, intellectual, psychological or social needs or even to his need for safety. It may be asked what the intellectual spatial needs of Man are. One answer would be: the freedom to have different kinds of space from the smallest to the largest, as well as to know that

320

one is free to move in them if one so desires. These can be classified as primary spaces, coinciding with the space that Man's senses perceive and his body needs to collect his food, and secondary spaces when he learns that there is more space beyond what is indispensable to him. They develop together with his knowledge and thinking. In our days the point has been reached at which Man is considering the need to expand his space out into the cosmos.

Needs can only be referred to an individual or to a group. A group may, for example, settle close by a port in order to operate it; this group needs shelter which leads to housing; its permanent settlement attracts others to serve those who operate the port and in this way a composite settlement and composite needs are created. One way to show Man's needs is in a two-dimensional system, on one axis of which we have the basic categories of individual and social needs, while on the other their nature as primary, secondary, tertiary, etc. (fig. 309).

Human needs can be classified in many ways depending on the point of view which is of interest to us. Two ways have already been discussed; they were related to the basic nature of needs in relation to the individual or social group and to their order of creation as needs of primary or secondary importance, etc.

Another classification is based on the type of relationship between Man and space. We have natural relationships—hearing an orchestra play in a concert hall for example; or artificial relationships—hearing an orchestra on radio or television. So needs can, in this way, be divided into natural and artificial ones based on the technical extensions of Man's senses.

Needs can also be classified according to the disciplines which deal with them, as biological needs (breathing of air), economic ones (cost of air-purification in a factory with contaminated air), social ones (contacting other people or staying away from them for security reasons), political ones (proper organisation of political and administrative units in space), technological ones (the technology of air-purification) or cultural and aesthetic ones (selection of a beautiful area for residence). Each one of these groups of needs can again be re-classified in different ways; we can have the economic needs related to primary production (cultivation of food), secondary production (processing of food), transportation and trade, services, residence, etc.

On the basis of such classifications we can build two- or three-dimensional systems which will help us study and understand Man's various needs, and consequently lead us to a way of measuring them. Such is the two-dimensional system relating the disciplines concerned with the different needs and their economic importance (fig. 310).

In the same way in which we have classified needs, we can also classify the conditions which exist—or which are created after the process of settlement has begun—and which influence the needs, sometimes changing them and leading to the final

308

needs and conditions creating human settlements

309

nature of needs creating human settlements and an orderly pattern for their measurement

balance between needs and conditions. Such a classification is, for example, one based on the natural physical conditions—the ones imposed by geography, topography or climate, and the social ones—the existence of an inhabited area exercising positive (market) or negative (lack of security) influences.

These conditions have already been included in our

Theory

310

needs classified in accordance with disciplines and economic importance

disciplines	economic		importance		
	production.	secondary production	transportation and trade	services	residence
physiology:					
economic					
social sciences					
political sciences					
technical disciplines					
cultural aesthetic disciplines					
etc.					

311

space needed for an automobile in different Ekistic units

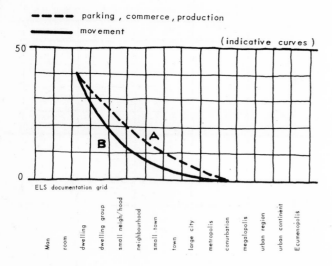

tabulation, since, for example, when we speak of secondary and tertiary needs (fig. 309); the very fact that the needs are secondary means that they are so as a result of the influence of some external factors upon the primary needs—that is, of some external conditions.

This is also the case with primary needs; they have already received the influence of conditions. When we say that Man needs a certain number of calories per day, this may be the result, among other things, of the fact that he lives in a cold climate and consequently needs more calories than he would if he lived in the tropical areas. Conditions can, in the same way as needs, be classified into two- or three-dimensional systems.

SPATIAL HUMAN NEEDS

Needs of the individual

We have already seen that Man expands into space in different ways, because of the bubble needed to surround his body, and because of consecutive concentric bubbles formed by his senses, his mind and his soul (fig. 310). But these bubbles show how far Man, with his organs, is able to reach in a natural way. The question now is how much space Man actually needs.

In several instances I have already referred to the types of space that Man needs: at times a spherical bubble, or an elongated one, a small or a large one, etc. It becomes clear that Man needs many types and sizes of space at different times under different circumstances and conditions.

The space that he needs may form either a direct or an indirect relationship with him. When he needs space to stand in, this is a direct need; when he needs space to cultivate his wheat, it can be either a direct or indirect relationship, since he may either cultivate his farm on which he lives in order to grow the wheat he needs in order to survive, in which case the relationship is direct, or he may receive wheat from hundreds of miles away, in which case a part of a distant farm will correspond to him and his survival.

In times past the Man-space relationship was commonly a direct one; but this gradually has changed. Today, with a few exceptions to be found among people living under primitive conditions, the Man-space relationship is both a direct and indirect one. We all need space in which to stand, breathe and move, but the space which provides us with goods is very distant. We receive automobiles from Detroit made with steel from Detroit, derived from iron ore from Michigan. We receive tweeds from Scotland made with wool from Australia. In a way we have a space of a few square centimetres in the Scottish mill, and many square metres of farm land in Australia being exploited for us. One day up in the tea plantations of Sylhet in East Pakistan I felt at home. I touched the tea bushes which had supplied me with tea, via London, all my life. I felt as if I were the owner of a small tea bush there, and of a few square centimetres in a huge storehouse on the Thames.

When we are dealing with the small space around us we are concerned only with the direct relationship between Man and space; but if we are concerned with broader regions and major settlements then we must define both the direct and the indirect spatial needs of Man in a systematic manner. I will take a simple example of how these needs develop. For my car, I need garage space and a driveway leading to it; all this may total 40 sq. metres (440 sq. ft.). To park in town I need a parking lot for several hours a day, and this will be about 15 sq. metres (160 sq. ft.). I also need a repair station, a big dealer in my town from whom I will buy my car in the first place, a factory to manufacture it, and so on. All this means that I need space of different sizes in different Ekistic units; this space is represented by curve A (fig. 311). If I also consider the space I occupy with my moving car as a fraction of the time I occupy it, then I need more space—this is represented by curve B.

A systematic study of all the space needed and the meaning of it would require the definition of types of needs in relation to Man and space in which these are directly or indirectly expressed.

The types of needs can be classified first as biological, physiological or sensory and subdivided in relation to the aspects of the whole human being that they refer to—that is body, senses, mind or soul. If we present these two ways in a two-dimensional table we can define the combinations which are of importance (fig. 312). On such a table we can also define the space which Man needs exclusively, and that which he can share with others. The need for space to stand in is an exclusive one, nobody else can occupy the same space at the same time; but the space he needs between him and a painting is not an exclusive one since his sight will not be hindered if other people look at this painting from the same distance.

We can also present the space where these types of needs are carried out on a map in accordance with the previous classification. The surface, or volume of space needed can be represented in two ways, both of which are important. The first is the total area needed for every function in every location. Men playing football need an area of 7,350 sq. metres (79,000 sq. ft.), the size of an ordinary football field. Since this field, however, is shared by two teams consisting of 22 players, one man only needs 1/22 of this area, that is 334 sq. metres (3,590 sq. ft.). If the teams change three times a day, he actually occupies 1/66 or 111 sq. metres (1,197 sq. ft.). The first measurement gives absolute figures and the second social ones. The total needs on a city plan can be shown as in fig. 313.

Finally we can combine the findings of these previous tabulations and show the total space needed by Man, by type of need and locality, expressed in terms of Ekistic units (fig. 313). On the basis of such considerations and calculations we can come to a very meaningful expression of the spatial needs of Man. We can say, for example, that he needs A space (expressed in surface as projected on the ground, in volume and form) in Ekistic unit 1 of which $\frac{A}{X}$ exclusively, $\frac{A}{Y}$ for a certain length of time, etc.; B in Ekistic unit 2 and so on.

312

total space needed by Man by type of needs

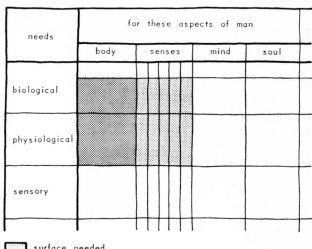

surface needed
exclusive need of space by one individual
(indicative presentation)

313

space needed by Man for direct use, by locality
example of a man moving in the city of Athens

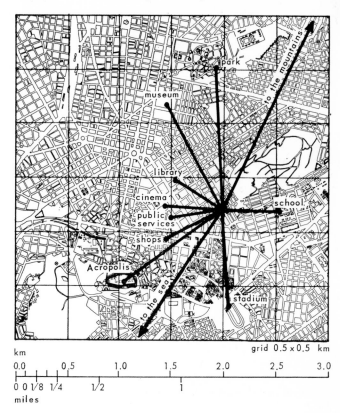

total space needed by Man by type of need and locality

(indicative)

needs		Man	room	dwelling	dwelling group	small neigh/hood	neighbourhood	small town	town	large city	metropolis	conurbation	megalopolis	urban region	urban continent	Ecumenopolis
biological	body															
	senses															
	mind															
	soul															
physiological	body															
	senses															
	mind															
	soul															
sensory	body															
	senses															
	mind															
	soul															
total	body															
	senses															
	mind															
	soul															

In this way we will find how much space Man actually occupies in his settlement, and in the same way we can define how much he needs, where and for how long.

We can now think of formulas and equations representing Man's optimum use of space during his life in his settlements. Is it better for him to use space $A_1 + B_1 + C_1 + D_1 + E_1$ etc. at a total cost X_1 or space $A_1 + B_2 + C_2 + D_1 + E_2$ at a cost X_2? We can even go further and calculate the space-time coefficient and measure whether it is better to spend $A_1t_1 + A_2t_2 + B_1t_3 + B_1t_4 + C_1t_5 + C_1t_6$ etc., or $A_1t_1 + A_2t_2 + B_1t_5 + C_1t_3 + C_1t_4$ etc. In this case the optimum use of space is based on the best use of time in space, and if this leads to the division of the total space needed into space by Ekistic units, we will gradually be in a position to recognise the best use of space by Man (fig. 314).

Needs of groups

To speak about the needs of social groups after this elaboration on the needs of the individual may seem superfluous to the reader; it might be assumed that a multiplication of the units found by the numbers contained in the group will provide the answer. But this is not true at all. When speaking of the needs of an individual we assumed him to be isolated in space, but when he is a member of a group he does not simply have his own needs, he also has relations with others which have a direct influence on his needs. Robinson Crusoe at first had only one concern—to provide for himself; but when he was joined by his man Friday he had to consider the relationship between them as well.

Relations with others can be of positive or negative nature; the need to come closer to his wife decreases the size of the intimate bubble of a man but the presence of an outsider or enemy increases all dimensions.

With these remarks we touch on the most important aspect of the formation of human settlements—the effect they have on the relationships between people. Unless the settlement is meant for one person, the question of interrelationships is the most crucial of Ekistic questions.

Composite human settlements become cohesive because of Man's desire and need to be closer to others, to provide and to receive services. On the other hand people cannot come too close together, because of the annoyance they would cause each other, and because they might actually hurt each other.

Because of these two opposing forces people tend to come together or be apart at different times, and in different ways, so that both their urge for closeness and for distance can be satisfied in a balanced way. Because of these forces we can imagine the human settlements as systems allowing their molecules a continuous flow between points of concentration and isolation, as systems alternately contracting and shrinking or expanding by places (fig. 315). The life of the people is a continuous interplay between points of condensation and diffusion, a continuous succession of being together and apart.

This synthesis of opposites can be achieved in two ways:
o first, by keeping people at continuously different distances for minutes, hours, days, weeks, sometimes months and years so that the sum-total of their relative positions satisfies both opposing needs;
o second, by physically isolating people through Shells of different kinds so they can live and work at short distances from each other without doing any harm.

In this respect, the task of the human settlement is:
o to keep people as isolated as possible with as short distances as possible between them;
o to give people the chance for the greatest choice of interactions with other people and localities.

a group of people, a system which contracts and expands continuously

shown here in three examples of the same space at different hours

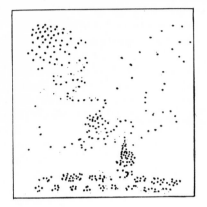

To achieve this we cannot be satisfied with the formulas expressing the total spatial needs of the isolated man as formulated previously; we need a formula which expresses the total relationship of Man with his settlement, consisting of the five elements, a formula giving the maximum choices for space and connections with the minimum effort and in the minimum time. Once this is achieved, we will have the human settlement which maximises the advantages of people coming together and minimises the harm; in which every citizen can have both the highest degree of contacts and of isolation.

In order to proceed towards such achievements we must analyse both the forces that bring people together and those which keep them apart. Man, in his relationship to the world, acts in three ways—as Receiver, Processer and Transmitter; whether he is dealing with food, information or sentiments, he fulfils these three functions. If we analyse them properly we will arrive at the forces which connect him with his environment, and also the forces that shape him.

If an individual receives and transmits only to one person, he must be very close to this person; if this happens with several people, then he is the centre of a system; if his relations are limited only to his neighbours, he might get lost among the many. In each case it is imperative for us to understand the type of system that relates him to the other members of the group, since this system needs to be expressed by the settlement (fig. 316).

However, people are not only attracted to each other, they can also be aggressive in their relations. The nature of Man includes biologically determined aggressiveness. Man, is like a hedgehog, Karl Menninger once said[6]; he wants to come closer to others when the temperature drops but his spines

do not allow him to do so. On this occasion Dr. Menninger drew a sketch which I think very useful for us to remember (fig. 317) since it shows not only the separate unities of people, as we usually draw them, but also one of their characteristics, their spines.

It now becomes clear that people are drawn together or pushed apart by certain forces which determine their distances. Such distances exist between animals also, and Edward T. Hall classified them very systematically in his book *The Hidden Dimension*. He says that when individuals of different species meet we can recognise one flight-distance and one critical distance between them.[7] Is this not true perhaps between primitive people as well, and, even in our days, between people with great hostility?

On the other hand he points out that in 'interactions between members of the same species' we can recognise one personal and one social distance.[8] Speaking of people and especially 'The American non-contact group, and possibly for others as well', he observes four distances—the intimate, the casual-personal, the social consultative and the public, and he gives complete definitions and measurements of them.[9]

We are now, I think, in a position to conclude that there is a certain distance between people which is felt as normal under given conditions of culture and purpose of meeting. When this distance increases then the interaction between people (the forces connecting them) weakens and beyond a certain limit distance ceases to make any difference. When, however, the normal distance decreases, the forces connecting these people increase enormously until the point when they come so close that they either have to enter into intimate relations, or break away. There is a parallelism of this relationship between

316

system of connections relating the individual to others

a. only to one person

b. to many persons from a central location

c. only to his neighbours

317

group of people like hedgehogs in a cold room (Sketch by Karl Menninger)

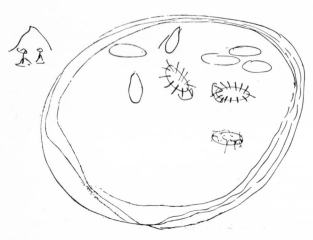

318

attraction and repulsion between atoms in a molecular structure

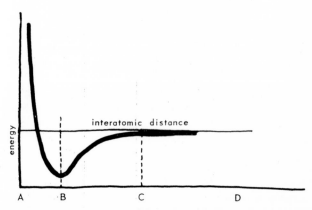

is this also valid between people?

people with the interatomic forms of molecular structures which operate in the following way: for a given pair of atoms, they are forces of attraction when these atoms are far apart and of repulsion when they are close,[10] as shown in fig. 318. I am not in a position to say at this point how accurate this parallelism is—I have only the impression that it is valid to a great extent and can be useful for our further research.

What is interesting to note in what I said about the forces of attraction and repulsion is that the rule is not always 'The closer the better', but on the contrary 'The closer to an optimum distance, the better'. It is of the greatest importance that we remember this since it is valid not only between people but also between people and localities accommodating functions. No one wants to reside on a highway—only at a reasonable distance from it; no one wants to have his factory or office either next to his home, or too far from it—always at a reasonable distance depending on walking or driving habits. This distance may well be equal to zero for some people, either because they are compelled to economise in money or effort, or because they like it that way; but the general rule is that such a distance is necessary.

FORCES SHAPING SETTLEMENTS

Categories of forces

Our purpose is eventually to express those human needs pertaining to settlements as 'forces' and hopefully to find a way to order or perhaps even measure these forces. However, only spatial human needs and conditions can be expressed as spatial forces. General forces which cannot usually be expressed as spatial ones, may be either economic, social, political or cultural. An entire population may demand or resist changes in settlements. The same can be true of special groups of people, such as political parties, which cannot be identified with any one part of space. In such cases, although we may be able to quantify the progressive or conservative forces, considering them seriously in our total Ekistic programme, we may well be unable to express them as spatial ones. A population demanding better architecture constitutes a great force, but not a spatial one.

There are cases, however, in which even these general forces can be expressed as spatial ones. This may happen in two cases. The first is when these groups are concerned with a problem that has a spatial expression, in which case we can add the support or resistance of these forces to the sum-total of the other forces forming our total programme. The second case appears when, even though their views have no spatial expression, these groups can be identified as residents of one locality. In this case, these forces may help us to understand and eventually solve problems of this locality by adding them to or subtracting them from the sum-total of its forces.

Spatial forces are the ones which have the greatest influence on the formation of human settlements operating everywhere, from the smallest Ekistic unit of one room, to the largest, the Ecumenopolis. We must think of them as the muscles which move the entire body, sometimes visible, as when expressed in the movement of people and cars, and sometimes invisible, as are for example, the negative forces created by the proximity of a factory. These forces are the muscles covered by the Shells or hidden within the Networks of human settlements, as the snail is covered by its shell and as the muscles of the human body are covered by the skin.

If we want to study any human settlement, we must understand the forces operating within it. If they move out, then the Shells are left empty and die. If they are transferred or changed in any way, they may create grave problems. As a whole they are represented by the functions of a settlement and they can be understood by its physical formation, but only if the forces form the functions and the functions lead to a physical formation of Shells and Networks without any mistake or inconsistency. If, however, they change, and because of the pre-existence of functions and structure they do not correspond properly to them, we might become confused. It is better, therefore, to study the spatial forces by themselves even if we are to take the functions and structure of the settlement as indications of their existence.

We can say that the relationship between spatial forces, and the functions and structure of settlements is the following:

- *forces* of all kinds lead to the formation of human settlements;
- the spatial forces are the ones which give a physical meaning and a form to *functions*;
- functions lead to the *structure* of settlements by shaping Shells and Networks;

- the structure of settlements leads to its *form*;
- *texture* and *density* are the result of the operation of spatial forces within structure and form.

A systematic study of spatial forces requires the knowledge of their nature, direction, intensity and quality, as well as of the ways in which they are brought together, influence each other, and form systems of forces.

All spatial forces can be divided, depending on whether they have a certain direction or not, into two basic kinds, directional and non-directional ones. We very often recognise the first ones and use them as such, but not so the second kind; these we fail to recognise as a force, and this quite often leads to misunderstandings about the sum-total of spatial forces. These non-directional forces are the ones referred to in the section dealing with spatial human needs; they too are divided into two kinds—the *physiological* spatial forces, expressed by the space needed by an individual for his normal functioning, and the *texture* forces, expressed between individuals as connecting or repelling forces conditioning the patterns, the form and their distances in space.

On the basis of these considerations we have three categories of spatial forces:

- physiological ⎫
- texture   ⎬ non-directional
- directional   ⎭

The physiological spatial forces are non-directional. The air that we need to breathe has to be of a certain volume but not necessarily distributed equally around our head; the garden needed to surround a house does not need to have a pre-defined space, and the area of fields necessary for a village can have any shape provided that a certain number of hectares correspond to each family; also the area served by a port can have any form provided it can absorb enough merchandise to allow the port to operate profitably. There is no one specific form or direction for these spatial forces.

The texture forces are non-directional ones; they keep all elements or parts of them in certain patterns at a certain distance from each other. People sitting in a room, houses built in a garden-city, automobiles on a highway, cities of equal order spread on an open plain, form patterns defined by the physiological and the texture forces. When we said that the human bubbles of people watching a spectacle become elongated (fig. 290 of Chapter Seven) or that the circular communities become hexagonal (fig. 190 of Chapter Four), we took into consideration the fact that both the physiological and the texture forces came to a balance. This is shown in fig. 319 where people, and houses are shown at certain distances defined by the operation of physiological and texture forces.

We may have forces attracting every person who wants to hear an orator to a certain point. These are centripetal forces but this does not mean that all persons in the audience will be close to the speaker or even equally close to him. When people stand, they need a certain space; when they are sitting they need much more. Unlike directional forces, physiological

327

319

texture forces

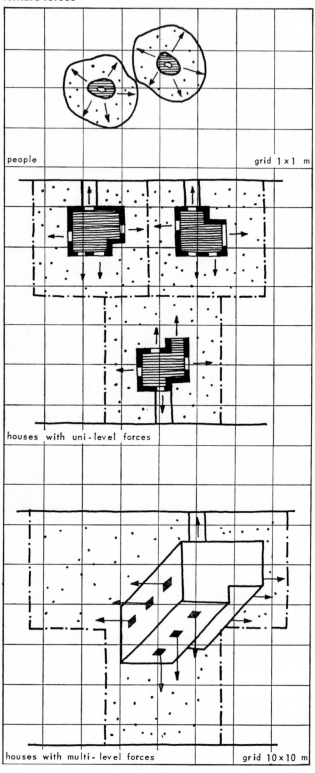

people   grid 1 x 1 m

houses with uni - level forces

houses with multi - level forces   grid 10 x 10 m

and texture forces do not tend towards or away from certain spaces; their tendency is to occupy space. Unlike directional forces they do not have any direction, but they tend to expand enough to guarantee to each of their elements (persons, cars, houses, factories, etc.) space ranging from a certain minimum to a certain maximum. Beyond these points the texture breaks because there is a limit to compression and expansion. If we want to avoid the breaking of the texture, we will be led from uni-level to multi-level solutions.

People, however, do not need only a physiological space and proper relationships with the others. They also need to be as close as possible to the localities of their interest which attract them with directional forces. Directional forces can be divided into several kinds depending on their focus; this focus can be a point (a crossroads or a water tower or centre of a market), or a line (a highway or a coastal line), or a surface (a plain attracting agricultural production), or perhaps a volume (a cathedral which can be seen from the whole surrounding area) (fig. 320). The basic kinds are the following:

- central forces are the ones which have a focal point— they can be positive or negative, centripetal or centrifugal;
- linear forces are the ones with a line as a focus—they can be geometric (a highway) or non-geometric (a coastal line); they can be positive or negative, coming together or breaking apart;
- surface forces are the ones with a surface as a focal point—these forces, like rain, are equally or at random diffused over the whole surface; had it been otherwise, they would have generated central or linear forces— depending on the surface, they can be either geometric or non-geometric;
- volume forces which, however, are very rare since up to now we have moved mostly on one surface, have an entire volume as a focus—a volume which can be connected with the three-dimensional space around it.

All these forces can be positive or negative, centripetal or centrifugal, creating areas of compression or rarefaction and causing many Ekistic problems, as, for example, in the central areas of overcongested cities. Consequently, in such areas we have witnessed the emergence of compression and rarefaction forces of people or functions which cannot all be where directional forces lead them which are the by-product of primary forces and usually operate at a right-angle to the primary ones which created them. These are closely connected with texture forces but do not necessarily coincide with them; they may well be added to them.

Synthesis of forces

Only when Ekistic units find themselves isolated in space, may they be under the influence of the single category of physiological spatial forces. As soon as we have a combination of two Ekistic units (people, houses, villages, cities) texture forces are created, and as soon as a group is formed it also creates directional forces of some kind.

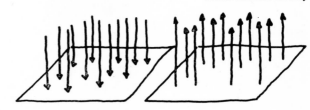

d. surface diffused geometric

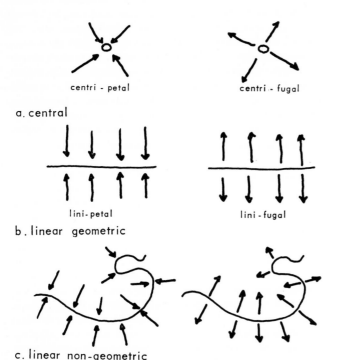

centri - petal   centri - fugal

a. central

lini-petal   lini-fugal

b. linear geometric

c. linear non-geometric

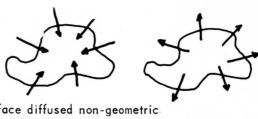

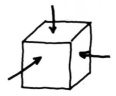 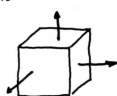

e. surface diffused non-geometric

f. volume geometric

g. volume non-geometric

Because of directional forces many units and functions compete for the same locality and place. Because of physiological and texture forces, they cannot occupy the same space and competition starts. The strongest units, the fittest eventually obtain the best locality and place. The others obtain places depending on the forces and their nature and ability to compete. This is a struggle for space which in critical cases might mean a struggle for existence.

Because of the interplay of all three categories of forces we have a synthesis of them which may mean major changes in the arrangements of the physiological spaces, as when we are dealing with farming areas corresponding to certain farmers (fig. 321), or when we are dealing with minor modifications of the human bubbles caused by the attraction of a public orator (fig. 322).

Intensity and quality of forces

Once we can proceed to the synthesis of all forces we have to be able to measure their intensity so as to be able to understand their relative values. We may have a central force equal to 100 and other radial or linear forces equal to 10, in which

case it is clear that the settlement will be influenced mainly by the central force (fig. 323).

It is possible, however, that the physiological and texture forces may be so great as to require so large an area for their expansion that the settlement is forced to spread over uneven land, entering valleys where the linear forces will be intensified due to new negative forces being exercised by the form of the landscape (fig. 323). It is quite clear that the intensity of the forces is as important as their direction, and that together they form a system which is of considerable importance to human settlements.

Today the measurement of forces is systematically undertaken only in a few instances, in vehicular traffic, for example, and even there only for the forces generated along main transportation routes. These studies are of the greatest importance for the transportation system of a given settlement, even for the recognition of the traffic problems of a new one. However, since such studies do not take the texture forces of the settlements into consideration, they tend to overlook the overall picture and usually do not lead to the solution of the overall problems. Systematic measurement of forces is also

321

synthesis of spatial forces causing great changes of form

a - four farmers need four equal physiological areas

b - if they form a family their physiological areas are united and unified

c - if they come close they are unified

d - when attraction of a city starts

e - they may move to it in which case their area changes shape

undertaken in some cases of economic analysis of settlements; but since it is limited to the economic criterion, it, also, cannot have the importance needed by the settlements as a whole.

It can perhaps be said that measurement, related to densities of settlements constitutes an effort related to texture forces. Even if this is so, these efforts are very superficial and based only on a few empirical considerations. If we want to understand and make full use of the forces influencing settlements it is necessary to develop a system of measurements which will take into consideration all essential forces playing a role within them.

This is not an easy task. If we only think, for example, of the unit Man and the different forces that attract him, we will understand how complicated this problem is, since Man can be seen in four different ways, as body, senses, mind and soul, and each of these can be attracted in different directions by forces of different intensities. In spite of these difficulties, the task of measuring the spatial forces is so important for settlements that it has to be attempted.

Apart from direction and intensity, forces have other characteristics that can be brought together under the title of quality. Such are the secondary characteristics related to their

direction which can be, as already mentioned, positive or negative, attractive or repellent. Other characteristics are related to the time during which these forces are exercised. They may be seasonal or periodical; in this sense they may be regular or irregular.

A different way of looking at these forces is to consider whether they are pleasant or unpleasant. People may be attracted every weekday morning to the central business district of a city, but this may be so unpleasant that they would never go there unless they had to. In a different city, the attraction of business may not be as strong while the beauty of the city's centre may be such as to attract these same people plus others much more often. In this case, the psychological satisfaction becomes an important factor and is finally expressed with a new force of high intensity. Tourism is a result of this force. In conclusion it can be mentioned that forces have certain qualities that can be expressed by direction and intensity and, hopefully, measured accordingly.

Force-mobile

The sum-total of all the forces shaping a settlement, having taken into consideration direction, intensity and quality, composes a force-structure of the settlement which we shall call a *force-mobile*, since neither the direction, the intensity or the quality of the forces remains stable. The mobility of forces is also true of single elements of the system. Take rain as an example; when it falls, it is a surface-diffused force, after that it becomes a system of linear forces on the streets, merging into a strong linear force, the river, running through the city and finally it extends beyond the settlement, reaching the sea. The traffic system in a city is a similar case. At rush hours most of the cars move on a few highways within specific areas generating linear forces. At night, on the contrary, most of the problems created are due to texture forces—parking requirements. The system changes continuously.

What is important is that we find a method allowing for all forces to be taken into consideration, so that we can follow their changes and form an opinion about the whole structure of forces or the force-mobile. Such a method would be based on a series of tables such as fig. 324 presenting the sum-total of forces at any given moment for any given settlement or part of it.

After defining the forces attracting or repelling the elements of a settlement towards certain points we can measure the forces connecting them; in this way we will have the actual force-mobile in operation (fig. 325a). If we elaborate on this force-mobile in detail we can perhaps include all important forces in our settlement (fig. 325b). Because of the fact that in larger Ekistic units the probabilities of more accurate predictions increase (see Chapter Seven, fig. 276), it is natural to assume at this point that the wider the area of study the better we can work with force-mobiles.

322

synthesis of spatial forces

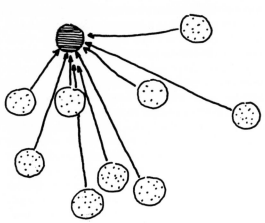

a. an orator attracts an audience -
his positive forces are in operation towards one point

b. these positive forces do not result in the
accumulation of the audience

c. nor in a tight squeeze of one man to another and
to the orator

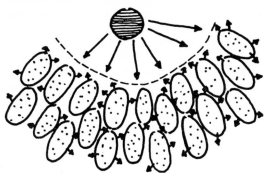

d. but as the texture forces are in operation they establish
a balance with the directional forces
orator and audience are in equilibrium

323

intensity of forces

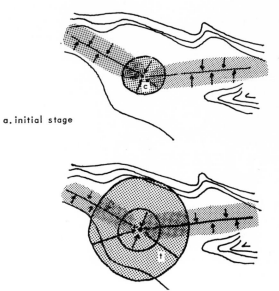

a. initial stage

b. area defined by additional physiological and texture forces

c central forces
l linear forces
t texture forces

c. area defined by the previous forces and by conditions creating
negative forces

324

spatial forces within a force-mobile

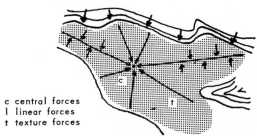

cause of forces		categories of forces										
		directional							texture		physiological	
	central	linear		surface		volume			people	houses		etc.
		geom.	non geom.	geom.	non geom.	geom.	non geom.					
conditions	geography											
	topography											
	climate											
	economic											
	social											
	political											
	technology											
	cultural											
	etc.											

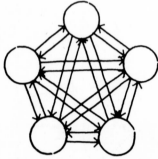

a. schematic presentation of equal circles and equal attractions

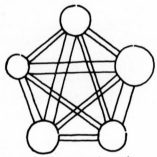

b. the surface of the circles shows their total force of attraction and the width of the corridors the importance of the connections

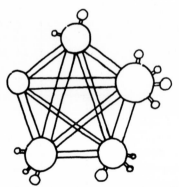

c. additional circles represent minor forces exercised only through the major circles

Individual and group force-mobiles

Force-mobiles which condition human settlements can be seen also as individual and group force-mobiles which correspond to every person or group for each of his interests, or composite ones for all of their interests within a settlement. In this section I will present such an individual force-mobile and explain how it operates in order to deal also with the aspect of the criteria we must establish in order to compare the different forces.

At the beginning settlements had to satisfy two fundamental needs: the ones related to economy (especially the need for food and shelter), and the ones related to safety. The need for survival was so pressing that other criteria were, by necessity, suppressed either completely, or for most of the time and most of the decisions. For example, how could people satisfy an aesthetic criterion by living in an area with the best view, if there was no security for them in it? Other criteria acquired importance only when economic and safety conditions allowed it. Wealthy people could live in beautiful areas even if it was very expensive, and strong landlords could live in isolated localities if they could pay the cost of their protection. History has shown that other criteria—both good and bad— became important after the first two needs were satisfied.

Today humanity has entered—probably for the first time— an era during which a very great and continuously increasing number of people have satisfied their basic economic needs and sometimes, as far as the individuals are concerned for their daily life, their need for safety as well. This situation has increased the importance of other needs and other criteria. In the past, people, when selecting their residence within a city, thought in economic terms of how close to the centre they could be. Such a thought included the notion of time— how quickly they could get there—but there was no difference between the two since economic distance and time distance were the same when people had no other choice but to walk to the centre.

Today, with the many choices for transportation, the economic criterion (the distance from the centre) is different from the time criterion (the time it will take to reach it) and from the combined one (the time and the cost). The situation is the same with regard to another criterion which in many cases was suppressed completely in the past—the criterion of psychological satisfaction (the comfort and the pleasure involved). A decision to be taken today is more complicated since it must satisfy not one or two but several criteria. An individual or group taking a decision related to the use of space is influenced, in varying degrees, by the different criteria; he is, consciously or subconsciously, aware of their different values and grades each according to the satisfaction he receives from it on the basis of one of his criteria. The sum-total of all points, each one multiplied by its relative value, leads to a final estimate of total value which guides a decision.

326

individual force-mobile

selection of location of residence

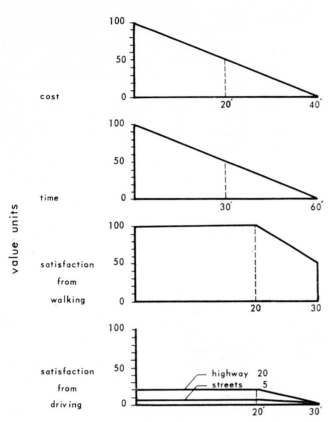

		cost	time	satisfaction	total
1		100	75	100	275
2		100	65	100	265
3	walking	100	50	75	225
3	driving	75	90	5	170
4	walking	100	50	75	225
4	driving	50	90	5	145
5		75	85	3	163
6		50	75	3	128
7		25	70	2	97
8		100	75	100	275
9		100	65	100	265
10	walking	100	50	75	225
10	driving	75	90	5	170
11	walking	100	50	75	170
11	driving	50	90	20	160
12		50	95	20	165
13		–	–	–	–
14		–	–	–	–
15		–	–	–	–

On the basis of these considerations I can proceed with the example of an individual force-mobile and express it in terms of a man's need for the proper location of his home. The selection of his residence works approximately as follows: due to a feeling of lack of security within his city, he wants to live in an area where only people of his income group reside (fig. 326). He can afford to spend up to 40 currency units a day for his round-trip to and from the centre of the city, and is in any case prepared to spend 20 currency units if it means a pleasant neighbourhood. He thinks that spending nothing is worth 100 value units and that spending 40 currency units is worth zero to him. In terms of time he thinks that one hour spent commuting is the limit, and he rates it as zero value unit; spending zero time is worth 100 value units. In terms of psychological satisfaction he gives 100 value units for walking up to 20 minutes and 50 for walking 30 minutes, 20 for driving on the highways and only five for driving through streets.

If we make the necessary calculations we find that areas such as numbers 13, 14, 15 are excluded for specific reasons;

the other areas receive different ratings. Finally this individual must make his selection among areas 1, 2, 8, 9 as those most likely to give him the satisfaction he wants. If he cannot find a proper residence in those areas, then he has to move into those with the next lowest rating, and so on.

By such an analysis of the individual force-mobiles we can arrive at some conclusions concerning the decisions of persons or groups which are based on their personal or group criteria of cost, time, psychology and safety, or on an even greater number of criteria which may exist or will be developed in the future (fig. 327).

In the same way we can proceed to develop group force-mobiles. If instead of considering only one person as we have done so far we consider a family of five persons and the five sets of forces and decisions which can influence each member of the family in relation to the most commonplace activities (residence, employment, shopping, education, entertainment), we will see how complicated the entire picture becomes.

If we multiply these personal and family alternatives by the number of members of a group and then combine them

327

individual force-mobile

selection of location of residence

AB areas of accepted income groups
CD areas of accepted cost for commuting
E areas of accepted time for walking
F areas of accepted time for driving

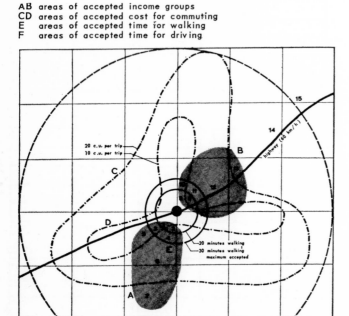

grid 5 x 5 km

328

forces, structure and form

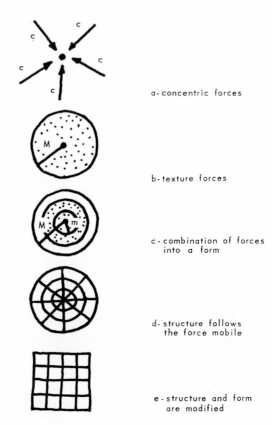

a - concentric forces

b - texture forces

c - combination of forces into a form

d - structure follows the force mobile

e - structure and form are modified

with all the business, administration and other decisions to be taken in order to allow a settlement to operate, we will arrive at an impossible figure which can confuse the best minds in the world. The situation, however, is not as bad as it appears, since there is no necessity for any settlement to solve all the problems of all its citizens; its role is to create such conditions as will permit people to solve their own individual problems in the best possible way.

The goal for the community is to create the right framework for the best solution of all of its citizens' problems related to spatial needs. In order to attain this, it must understand how its people can best be satisfied. This happiness and safety of the citizenry, which appears in such a vague expression, can become very specific in Ekistics which deals with human settlements, that is with the spatial needs of Man, if we have the ability to analyse Man's needs and express them in specific terms with as many measurements as possible. This is the only sound way of preparing an Ekistic programme and achieving its realisation, while keeping in mind the goals of the individual and Society: happiness and security.

STRUCTURE AND FORM

From force-mobiles to structure and form

If we have built our force-mobile properly, we can proceed to analyse the structure of the settlement since the force-mobile is the essential part of this analysis. A properly built force-mobile is one which incorporates all forces, those created by Man (physiological, texture and directional forces) and those created by the existing conditions which have to be translated into corresponding forces.

There are cases when the force-mobile of the given forces is not enough to define the structure. This happens when the conditions do not create enough commitments (in a flat plain for example), and when there are not enough forces (for example a highway, a mine, a big factory, etc.) created by Man prior to the settlement. In such cases even the basic structure may not be given by the force-mobile, and it will have to be conceived by those creating the settlement who have to complement the existing and necessary force-mobile. The more we move into Ekistic units of lower order the more true this becomes.

The most intricate aspect of this process is the definition of the relationship of the different kinds of forces. This definition depends on many factors—on the economy, the social structure, the political conditions, the technological and cultural levels, etc. We can define these relationships only on the basis of the criteria or values accepted by the inhabitants themselves. When we know the criteria, we can develop out of the force-structure a model which will be the value model leading to the definition of structure and form.

The way in which we move from forces to structure and form can be seen by the following example. If, in a plain, we have only concentric directional forces, we can expect a circular form. Since the texture forces existing in settlements do not contribute to the form but to the density and size, concentric forms would lead to a settlement consisting of only one point (fig. 328a). Physiological and texture forces alone tend to cover a circle with the maximum diameter permitted by their texture (fig. 328b). Texture forces exist together with concentric forces focusing on the centre with a minimum radius 'm' or a maximum one 'M' (fig. 328c). How large the final diameter will be depends on the ratio of the concentric forces 'c' to the texture forces 't'. Since there are no other commitments created by the force-mobile, Man is free to order the inner structure of this settlement, provided it serves its basic force-mobile and helps people go towards the centre. In such cases the solutions can either copy the force-mobile (fig. 328d) or modify it, and probably also modify the form, since there are no major commitments created by it (fig. 328e).

In order to take into consideration the correct sequence of phases we can use a two-dimensional tabulation with the order of spatial needs, functions, structure, form, texture and density in one dimension. In the other one we can insert the nature of all needs (classified by disciplines as in fig. 310 or economic importance, or their order as in fig. 309), or the aspects of Man (fig. 329).

Basic structures and forms

A few examples can demonstrate how different structures and forms are created by different force structures. I start with the simplest of structures, the ones created by only one set of basic and primary forces. The diffused functions tend to cover a circular space in a uniform way without creating any points of greater importance; such areas are the nomadic and the purely agricultural ones. However, if such an area spreads and comes to contain more than a few hundred people, and if the Society has achieved even a low degree of organisation, then the necessity for some common services becomes apparent and a central area is created in the centre of the circle. Even diffused forces alone tend, after a certain

329

sequence of phases for Ekistic synthesis

aspects of man	phases					
	spatial needs	func-tions	struc-ture	form	tex-ture	den-sity
body						
senses						
mind						
soul						
total						

330

forms due to diffused forces

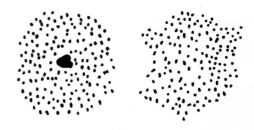

point, to create central structures and forms (fig. 330).

If the central forces alone are in operation and if there is no impact of any other forces, they tend to the circular structure and form of a settlement (fig. 331a). Linear forces tend to form linear settlements as long as the latter are small and do not need any common services (fig. 331b). When they become larger, they may easily lead to non-linear forms. This may happen if there is no space for linear expansion, or if the linear functions along one line meet another line with other linear functions. Then we witness the creation of a central point which may easily attract another linear force. Linear forces lead to linear forms only in limited areas; beyond them they lead to a combination of linear and central forms.

The natural forces (geographic, topographic or climatic) do not lead to any specific form since their value can be positive or negative and vary enormously in importance and intensity by location (fig. 331c). A geographic force may attract the entire settlement into a valley near the sea; a topographic one may stop it from spreading near the delta of the river; a climatic one may attract it to a hillside so it will have the

335

forms due to central forces

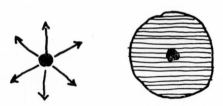

a. forms due to central forces

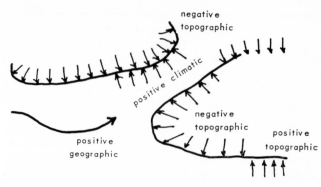

c. natural forces

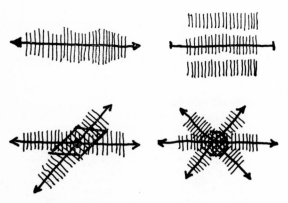

b. forms due to linear forces

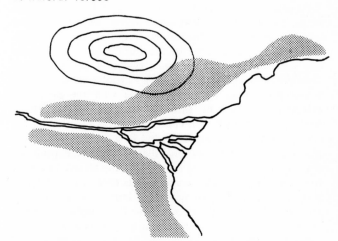

d. and forms resulting from them

benefit of a cool southeast wind, and an aesthetic reason may attract people to the northern shore of the sea offering the most beautiful surroundings.

The forces exercised by the region around the settlement may be of a positive or negative nature, and may be expressed either as diffused, central or linear ones (fig. 332a). Security conditions can create or eliminate a human settlement. They can also influence its location, its form, its density and many other characteristics. They can lead towards a strengthening of central structures and forms—as in the past when an attack was possible only from a short range, or a weakening of them—especially when the attack could come from the air in which case a system of centres and linear connections makes more sense than one centre (fig. 332b).

Man-made values also act as positive or negative forces in the formation of settlements; they can attract or repel parts of or the entire settlement with varying intensity in a way similar to that of natural forces, and like them they may not lead to any specific form (fig. 332c).

A study of all the previous structures and forms of organised settlements leads to the conclusion that they fall into three basic categories depending on their essential

structure, as follows (fig. 333):
- circular (one point for a centre);
- geometric linear (one geometric linear axis);
- non-geometric linear (one non-geometric linear axis).

Basic circular forms alone have been possible only in settlements of the past when:
- the landscape was completely neutral within the small area of the settlement and its vicinity;
- the road system was completely unimportant as a force because of no investment or minimum investment in it as compared to the city;
- no other man-made values existed in the vicinity;
- security conditions led to central forms.

Basic geometric linear forms alone have been possible only in very small settlements when:
- the landscape imposes them;
- the Networks and, more specifically, the road networks do not affect them since they are not close to a cross-roads;
- no other man-made values lead to the formation of any points of major importance;
- security conditions do not influence them.

332

forms due to regional forces

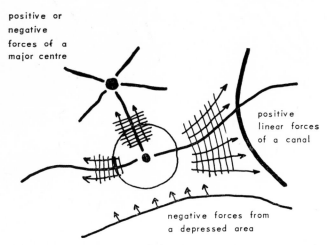

positive or
negative
forces of a
major centre

positive
linear forces
of a canal

negative forces from
a depressed area

a. forms due to regional forces

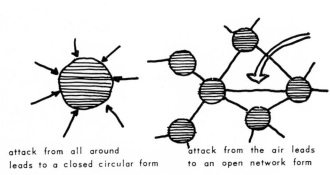

attack from all around
leads to a closed circular form

attack from the air leads
to an open network form

b. forms due to security forces

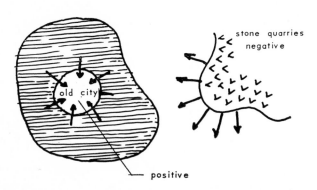

stone quarries
negative

old city

positive

c. forms due to man-made forces

z

333

three basic forms of organised settlements

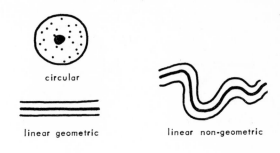

circular

linear geometric

linear non-geometric

Basic non-geometric linear forms alone have been possible only in very small settlements when:

   o the landscape imposes them;

   o the Networks do not impose any determined pattern;

   o no other man-made values impose any determined pattern;

   o security conditions do not impose any determined pattern.

These basic structures and forms of settlements can have several expressions, from very regular to very irregular ones. This is true both of the structure, because it can be transformed into several patterns of regular or irregular streets, and of the form which may well be circular or linear but expressed by very irregular patterns (fig. 334).

The three basic forms or their variations can vary even further depending on conditions of either their own locality, or the force-mobile which influences them from outside. These variations can be either natural and informal or consciously conceived by Man and formal. In both cases, although in the second one this becomes more apparent, they are reminiscent of the transformations we encounter in the animal world—for example the case of carapaces of crabs studied by Sir Peter Medawar, in *The Uniqueness of the Individual*[11] (fig. 335).

Composite structures and forms

Basic structures and forms exist only in very small organised settlements of up to a few thousand people and in exceptional cases up to a few tens of thousands. Many settlements, however, of this category of sizes, and all larger settlements have neither only a basic structure nor only a basic form—they have composite ones.

Composite structures and forms are derived from the basic ones through different combinations of forces. First, we can have structures and forms brought about by a combination of the basic ones by twos (fig. 336). In practice this is possible only for small settlements and only in extreme cases. Then we

337

Theory

334

structure and forms

as variations of the three basic ones

basic circular

irregular structure
regular form

regular structure
irregular form

irregular structure
irregular form

geometric linear

irregular structure
regular form

regular structure
irregular form

irregular structure
irregular form

non-geometric
linear

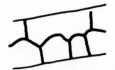

irregular structure
regular form

regular structure
irregular form

irregular structure
irregular form

335

patterns of organic growth and their formation

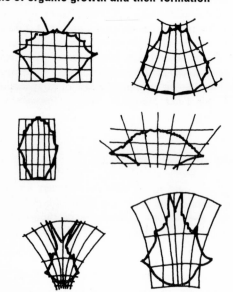

the carapaces of crabs of six different but related genera, showing how
particular differences of form may be expressed as the outcome of a
general process of spatial transformation

336

composite structures and forms

**created by combinations of the three basic ones
by two**

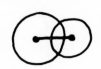

a. circular and circular

b. circular and geometric lineas

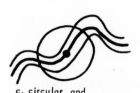

c. circular and
non-geometric linear

d. geometric linear
and geometric linear

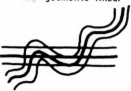

e. geometric linear
and non-geometric linear

f. non-geometric linear
and non-geometric linear

can have composite structures and forms created by a combination of all three basic types (fig. 337). In actual life this is the normal case for major settlements since in such a case all three basic types enter the picture.

Variations of these combinations can be numerous if we think that these combinations can be due to one part of the settlement belonging to each type (one central, one geometric linear, one non-geometric linear), or two or more or any other combinations of parts of several types. These variations are multiplied even further when we think of the great numbers of their irregular expressions and all their possible combinations.

Thinking in these terms, we can understand how complicated the structure and form of a settlement can be and why major settlements can be analysed only with great difficulty, and consequently, why people are confused. As an example of the great confusion, I can mention that seldom do we understand the basic characteristics of even small settlements. A grid-iron pattern of streets may keep us from understanding that a settlement is linear in substance, as in Priene (fig. 337), or central, as in a Roman town. However, if we think of how these towns would expand, we will understand that in the first case the forces are linear while in the second they are central. The grid-iron pattern of streets conceals two basically different types of structures.

In speaking of these composite forms, I have shown the combination of the directional forces only. In practice, however, the structure and form result from a combination of directional and texture forces. How this combination leads to the final form has been demonstrated in the simplest case of all, i.e., in the basic concentric and texture forces (fig. 328), when I spoke of how forces lead to texture and form (pages 326–8).

Texture forces exist in every settlement with no exceptions. So in every case of combination of directional forces, we must add the texture forces in order to have the overall picture of structure and form. This makes the variations even more complicated and more difficult to understand.

How these combinations work can be demonstrated in a composite form consisting of circular and linear geometric forms (fig. 338). The circular form results from a combination of central and texture forces, as already explained in fig. 328. The geometric linear form is again caused by a combination of linear and texture forces. Together they form the composite form (fig. 338) which is the product of the juxtaposition of both. Moreover, they begin to act on each other with the result that the areas influenced by both forces are strengthened while the ones influenced by only one are weakened. As a result of these changes, although the settlement in the final form has the same population as the first, it is different.

It becomes apparent that if we want to find the final structure and form of a settlement, we must analyse all the essential forces, both directional and texture, playing a role in its formation, and understand their combination.

337

composite structures and forms

created by the combination of the three basic ones

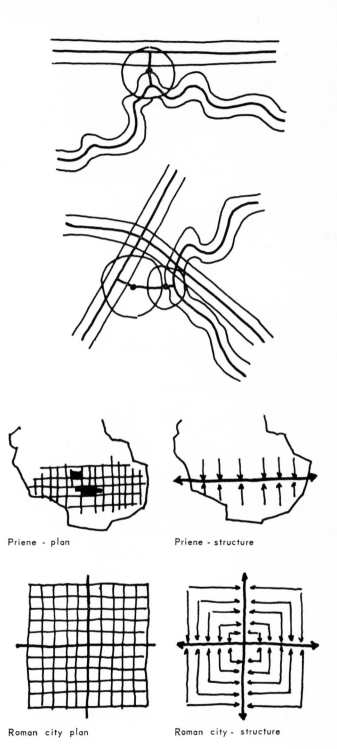

Priene - plan

Priene - structure

Roman city plan

Roman city - structure

338

composite structures and forms
created by directional and texture forces

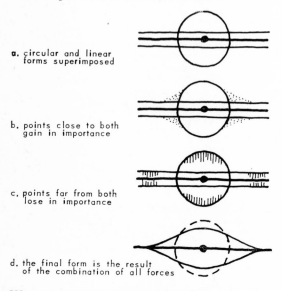

a. circular and linear
forms superimposed

b. points close to both
gain in importance

c. points far from both
lose in importance

d. the final form is the result
of the combination of all forces

339

composite structures and forms
created by all forces in Athens

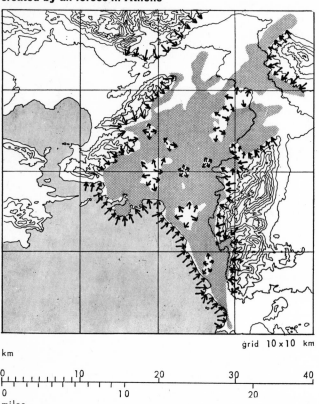

grid 10 x 10 km

km

0   10   20   30   40

0   10   20
miles

In practice we have a great number of directional and texture forces which combined give a final texture and form to the physiological forces contained by the settlement. How this works in a major settlement is shown by the example of Athens, Greece (fig. 339).

Some special cases

Every variation in structure and form presents its problems and can have its own solutions. Regardless of how complicated the structure and form are, there is a solution if we can recognise the basic structures and forms composing it, and when we are not misled by the appearance of the plan. Problems of structure and form are immensely intensified in dynamic settlements as all structural weaknesses become much more apparent during growth.

In the light of this analysis, we can understand each type of settlement, the problems caused by its growth and the solutions capable of eliminating these problems. I have demonstrated how this can be achieved in several types of settlements by first showing their static structure and form, then the problem areas—the ones suffering from pressure—in the dynamic phase, and finally the ideal form eliminating these areas (fig. 340). In this way we shall be led to the formulation of several ideal solutions, one for each type of structure and form. Details of these cases are given in Chapter Nine.

TEXTURE AND DENSITY

From structure and form we move to texture and density. This is only a way of imposing order on the study of our subject by going from major to minor characteristics; because, in practice, texture and density participate from the beginning in the process of creation, and play a role equal in importance to that of the other characteristics of settlements. In practice we have a continuous interplay of the three types of forces with structure and form on the one hand and with texture and density on the other. In the same way in which texture forces influence the directional forces in the creation of the structure and form of the settlement, the directional forces influence the texture ones and contribute to the definition of the density.

Texture forces and the final texture of the settlement vary in every type of activity between certain minima and maxima. Directional forces in every part of the settlement condition the pressures that will be exercised on the texture and also determine whether the latter will go beyond what it can stand, thus creating problems of texture and density.

Texture and density are of great importance for the life of the people in settlements as they are mostly felt by the people in their micro-space (house, street, neighbourhood-commun-

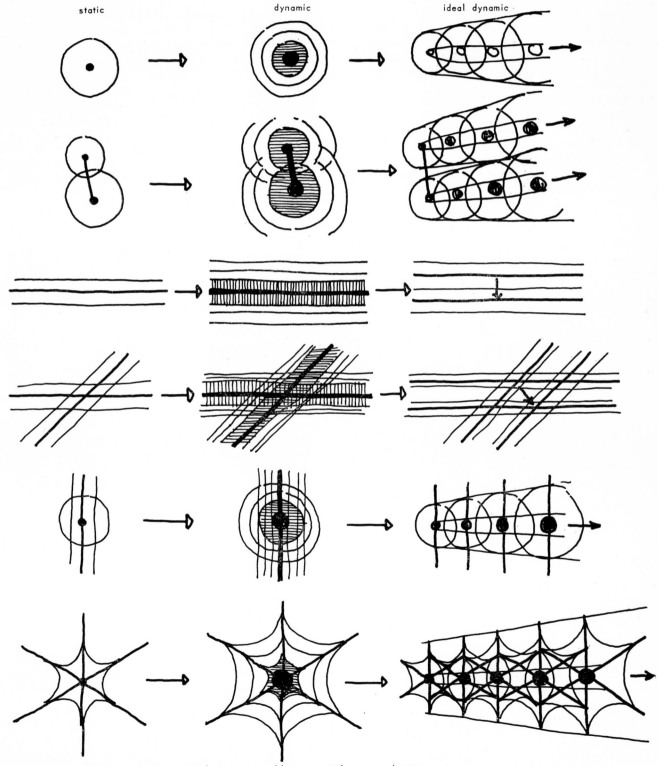

static   dynamic   ideal dynamic

growing centre becomes a problem area with impact also on
the whole structure and form

ity, factory or office). If these are not satisfactory, no matter how well the overall organism operates, people will be unhappy. On the contrary, if there is proper texture and density, Man, who spends most of his time in the micro-space, will be satisfied. The difficulty lies in the fact that it is very hard for a settlement to have a satisfactory texture and density in parts suffering from many pressures of many forces. Here lies a problem and a challenge.

One of these interrelationships of various kinds of forces, the study of texture and density, becomes very important since:

o under normal evolutionary conditions they reveal the forces (direction, intensity, quality) of every part of the settlement;
o they condition many aspects of satisfactory life, from the economic to the aesthetic.

However, texture and density acquire an even greater importance because of the elimination or change of the force of security. In the past, because of the intensity and direction of this force, settlements had a tendency to be very densely built. Very often the physiological and texture forces were squeezed to their optimum minimum and sometimes even beyond it. The habits of Man himself were conditioned by the lack of safety, and his conception of the desired texture was probably strongly influenced by it. Under present conditions Man begins to feel free to live in different densities and textures.

So we may witness the emergence of a different conception of densities which will be influenced by a different force-structure in the future. As a result, in the future we will not have the clear-cut definition of the past in built and non-built-up areas; but an enormous variety of areas from very high to very low densities. Due to this phenomenon, densities may become the only criterion of the degree of urbanisation of any area. In the future we may not have specific settlements but many settled areas to be known and classified by 1,000, 100, 1, 0.1, or even 0.0001 persons residing per hectare or 5,000, 300, or 10 persons working per hectare, etc.

The proper study of structure and density should not be limited to the existing phenomena, but also to their causes, as we will soon need to know what densities are satisfactory for Man. Conditions change, and it is time for us to learn what the real physiological and social conditions are which make Man happy in relation to the space he occupies. To achieve this we must understand the positive and negative forces that relate Man to the space surrounding him, expressing them, if possible, in proper measurements. The problem of texture and density which has been faced empirically in the past—and in most of the cases probably in a satisfactory way—must now become the subject of a scientific enquiry. There is no more time for us to face it empirically only, since the situation may get out of hand.

CHAPTER NINE
EKISTIC SYNTHESIS

CONSIDERATIONS ON SYNTHESIS

Meaning of synthesis

As opposed to everything said until now, which was based on the knowledge and analysis of facts, their interpretation and their interconnection to form laws and theories, and based on the description of existing human settlements, Ekistic synthesis is a prescriptive act requiring a completely different attitude.

In the present chapter, I will also change my attitude; instead of only describing the phenomena on the basis of a system of ideas, instead of drawing conclusions or reasonable theories about their interrelationships and their formation, I will accept these as given and proceed to develop an approach that can help us to build settlements. When the moment of action arrives, our best hypothesis must be transformed into a law upon which we will base our synthesis.

In this chapter, I will talk about Ekistic synthesis. In synthesis a great part is played by intuition as well as knowledge and a system. I cannot speak about intuition, but I can speak about my knowledge of synthesis, and the systems I use in my own practice.

Before leaving this point I would like to express myself once again in terms of the Ekistic Logarithmic Scale, which as the reader knows, is an indispensable scale for the study and presentation of our phenomena. If I had to clarify to what extent intuition and to what extent conscious action are parts of the synthetic process I would say that I do not know. I do know, however, that where the smaller Ekistic units are concerned intuition is much more important than it is in the large ones (fig. 341). When we have to connect two cities situated at a distance of 200 kilometres from each other, we do not need intuition; we need a knowledge of geographic and topographic formations and the technology of means of transportation in order to provide a solution. When, however, we are trying to conceive a house in an open landscape, or the location and, what is more important, the form of a monument, then intuition plays a very important role; so does creative ability.

Ekistic synthesis can be carried out and presented, either in the abstract or as applied to specific cases. In this chapter I will do both. First I will present Ekistic synthesis in one aspect of two groups of settlements—in the morphology of static and dynamic settlements. In the process I will present examples from the history of settlements showing where Ekistic morphological synthesis has led; then I will select abstract morphological cases and try to create a new synthesis corresponding to new conditions. I will then select one specific example and deal with the methods which can help us take on actual situations.

By using these two ways of presentation I am trying to help the reader test the theories already developed, since the use of abstract and specific models will bring his knowledge closer to the actual phenomena that we face in practice.

Natural and planned synthesis

For thousands of years human settlements developed in a natural way under the impact of a few small forces. Man was subconsciously implementing the hexagonal pattern in the distribution of villages and market-towns, and building radial villages and cities without any considerable effort. When these very natural solutions ceased to answer all his needs for order, Man switched consciously to the grid-iron pattern of streets which he gradually came to consider as a natural one.

With few exceptions, the entire process of evolution of settlements was a natural one which did not create any exceptional problems. Primary relationships of settlements with central forces could only lead to the hexagonal pattern which was so natural and so subconscious that it took Man several thousand years to discover that he was implementing it. Today, it is losing its importance in many cases of major settlements since the forces have ceased to be primary.

Today the great changes taking place in dynamic settlements result from the fact that, in addition to the primary forces, we now have to deal with forces of higher orders. A settlement attracts so many additional forces that its class changes and its problems become much more complicated. Where the central forces used to keep a balance in an Ekistic

343

341

intuition in Ekistic synthesis

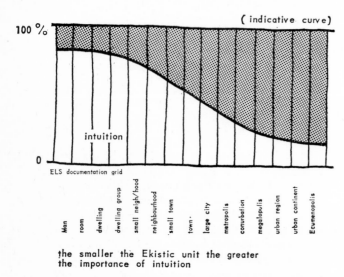

the smaller the Ekistic unit the greater
the importance of intuition

system, their combination with linear ones is now turning the circular form into a star-shape, which in its turn attracts other functions gradually leading to a naturally grown but very complicated structure and form.

Simple rules that were valid in the settlements of the past are no longer so. In the past we could say that a house close to the centre of a city was more satisfactory than a distant one since it meant a saving of time and greater safety. This is no longer the case since there are many locations in the city providing for greater safety at a distance from the centre and others which may be more time saving even though they might be situated at greater distances. Such rules are valid only within small units. Dynamic or even static but very large settlements can no longer grow in a natural way without the conscious intervention of Man; only with this intervention can grave problems be avoided. Today what we need is a planned synthesis.

Ability for synthesis

The ability for synthesis is a point which is very often overlooked in all efforts for the creation of human settlements and in the training of the experts concerned. This is not only characteristic of Ekistics—it happens in many fields of human knowledge and creation. We do not pay enough attention to the selection and training of the people who can achieve a synthesis of the many aspects of one problem or many aspects of several problems.

Knowledge of Man has suffered and is still suffering from the same problem. I will quote Alexis Carrel, who was one

of the first to draw our attention to this problem and the necessity to face it in order to acquire the right knowledge. I subscribe to what he says. I should add, however, that he is speaking mainly of a synthesis of knowledge of *existing* phenomena, while we in Ekistics need to proceed to a synthesis in order to *create* a new situation. In this respect we can express ourselves in favour of synthesis much more emphatically.

In his classic book, *Man the Unknown*, Alexis Carrel states that,

'Presidents of universities and their advisers do not realize that synthetic minds are as indispensable as analytic ones. If the superiority of this kind of intellect were recognized, and its development encouraged, specialists would cease to be dangerous. For the significance of the parts in the organization of the whole could then be correctly estimated'.[12]

He continues,

'At the present time our knowledge of man can only progress by attracting a powerful intellectual élite. Great mental capacities should be required from the young men who desire to devote themselves to biology. It seems that the increased number of scientific workers, their being split up into groups whose studies are limited to a small subject, and overspecialization have brought about a shrinking of intelligence. There is no doubt that the quality of any human group decreases when the number of individuals composing this group increases beyond certain limits. The Supreme Court of the United States consists of nine men whose professional value and character are truly eminent. But if it were composed of nine hundred jurists instead of nine, the public would immediately lose, and rightly, its respect for the highest court of this country'.[13]

If I asked myself now how I would describe the qualifications necessary for those who are to undertake the difficult task of synthesis in the total knowledge of human settlements in order to create new situations either in existing settlements or in new ones, I would answer: *knowledge, beliefs, experience* and *creative will*. Weakness in any one of these directions would make the task of synthesis impossible.

We need *knowledge* of facts and the ability to collect them; we need to understand the development and evolution of our settlement and to observe and carry out a diagnosis of its situation and disease.

But this is not enough, in order to locate our case in the whole spectrum of problems and compare it and understand its relationships with similar ones, we need conceptions, convictions and *beliefs* of laws and theories. Nothing less than a total theory of settlement can help us to understand relationships and priorities in this field.

In addition we need a vast *experience* which alone would allow us to select the phenomena having any practical importance for our action, and to develop criteria on the basis of which to formulate judgements of political, cultural and ethical importance.

Finally, we need the *creative will*. This is not a matter of knowledge or experience or feeling and intuition concerning a situation. The 'feeling' and 'thinking man' has in this case to be the 'willing' or the 'complete man' of Plato. Only with creative will can we take decisions and act *in time*, regardless of how sparse the available data.

This creative will is indispensable for the experts who are going to build human settlements; this, and the *inner order* which alone can help them to find some meaning in the superficially chaotic situation that major human settlements present since:

And Kung said, and wrote on the bo leaves:
'If a man have not order within him
He cannot spread order about him;
And if a man have not order within him
His family will not act with due order
And if the prince have not order within him
He cannot put order in his dominions'.

(Ezra Pound, *Canto XIII*)[14]

MORPHOLOGY OF STATIC SETTLEMENTS

Cells of human settlements

Static settlements of the past, which means almost all the settlements of the world, with very few exceptions, until the eighteenth century, had been developing in such a way as to justify our considering them the cells of the whole world of human settlements. This name is justified, not because static settlements *are* cells since they differ from them in many ways, but because they have some similarities which can help us understand our phenomena.

Interestingly enough these similarities are expressed at two levels of static settlements, first in the settlement as a *whole*, and then in its *nucleus* or built-up part. If we look at the whole settlement we will recognise how it consists of:

○ the uniform open area or the main part of the settlement, which corresponds to the body of the cell or the cytoplasm;
○ its periphery, where the boundaries dividing it from other settlements lie, which corresponds to the cell membrane even though that is physically expressed which is not the case in settlements; and
○ its nucleus, or the built-up part, which corresponds to the nucleus of the cell, since both are more densely built and both are the control centres of life within their organism.

The similarities, however, exist even if we do not take the whole settlement but only its nucleus, which has the additional

342

natural settlement tending to be radial
Leipsig, Germany (1954)

■ 1935
▨ 1954

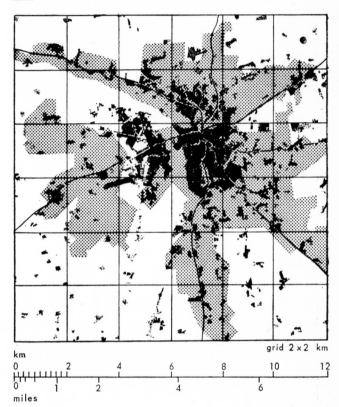

grid 2 x 2 km

km
0   2   4   6   8   10   12

miles
0   1   2   4   6

characteristic that it resembles the cell physically as well, especially when the cell is flattened. This nucleus in its turn consists of:

○ the uniform built-up area now corresponding to the cytoplasm;
○ its periphery, which in the past was very often expressed by the walls of the cities and which now corresponds physically to the cell membrane; and
○ the central area, which corresponds to the nucleus of the cell both being again more densely built and both being the control centres of life, growth and development in their areas.

The careful parallel study of settlements and cells reveals other similarities as well, only some of which have been indicated in the chapters on Ekistic analysis, development and evolution. These similarities induce me to accept the parallelism between settlements and cells, and draw useful lessons from it, while being aware all the time that any parallelism beyond the points of similarities is not only

natural settlement characteristic of informality
Tübingen, Germany (thirteenth century A.D.)

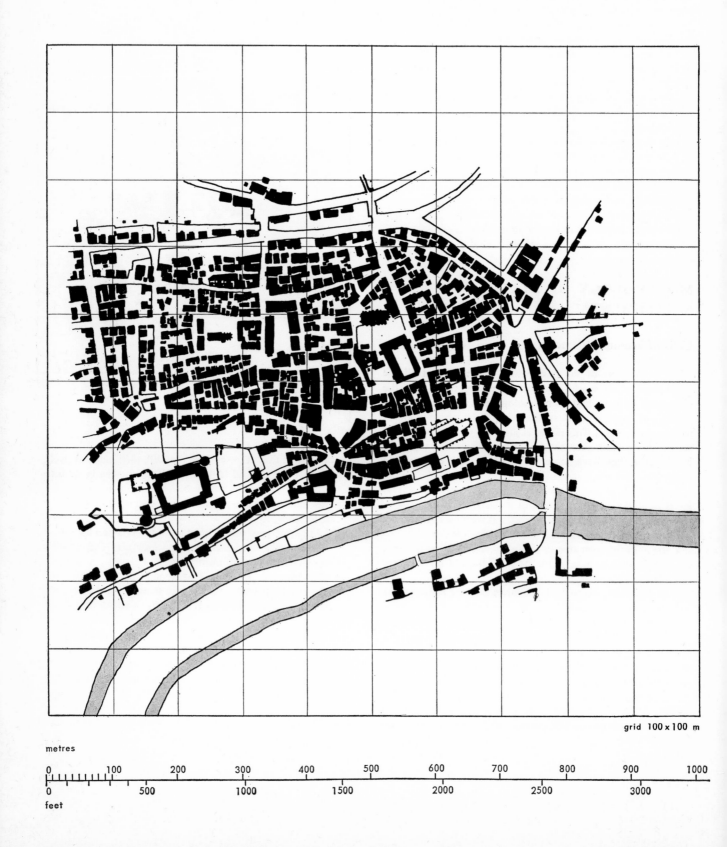

grid 100 x 100 m

metres

| 0 | 100 | 200 | 300 | 400 | 500 | 600 | 700 | 800 | 900 | 1000 |

| 0 | 500 | 1000 | 1500 | 2000 | 2500 | 3000 |

feet

meaningless but also completely unjustified and logically dangerous.

I do not believe it is very probable for the time being that humanity will build many new independent static settlements like cells; the understanding however of this phenomenon is of great importance for the rules of synthesis in dynamic settlements. This is why I dwell on the morphology of the static settlements and their similarities with cells.

Natural and planned

There are many ways in which we can divide the settlements in several morphological categories. One is based on whether they have grown naturally or whether they have been planned. Static settlements quite often retain the same characteristics, while dynamic ones, even if initiated as planned settlements, soon develop into very complicated organisms whose planned and unplanned parts form a new type of settlement, a mixed settlement from the point of view of its method of creation.

There are two basic characteristics of 'natural' settlements. The first is that they grow without a plan, slowly more often than not, and often tend to be radial, since all the people are interested in coming closer to the central nucleus from which the settlement started and where the most important functions are still located (fig. 342). The second characteristic of 'natural' settlements is their informality. Because they have grown without a plan, they very seldom have geometrically defined characteristics such as straight roads, rectangular squares, plots of similar size, etc. (fig. 343). Their general plan may be an approximate mixture of radial and grid-iron forms. In spite of the lack of such characteristics, however, they have a distinct character.

As opposed to natural settlements, planned ones almost always have an initial formality in their design. This is expressed by geometric forms of private and public space, by equal or similar constituent parts such as plots, squares, buildings, streets, etc. (fig. 344).

Radial and Hippodamian

Whereas all natural settlements tend to be radial, most planned ones fall into two basic categories or combinations of the two. These are radial settlements and grid-iron or Hippodamian settlements.

Radial settlements may not always be formal, but because of the very conception of their basic characteristic they are inflexible and they always appear very alike and quite formal (fig. 345). This formality increases when the size of the settlement does, since it necessarily becomes more apparent (fig. 346).

Unlike the radial settlements, the Hippodamian ones, which are derived from the principle of the repetition of similar and equal elements (houses, buildings, plots, etc.) can be much

344

planned settlement Zamosc, Poland (A.D. 1538)

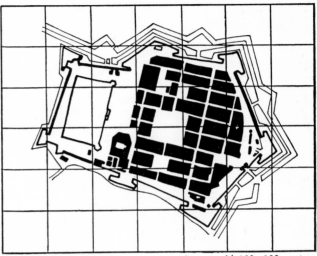

approximate grid 100 x 100 metres

345

radial plan in a small settlement
Palma Nuova, Italy (A.D. 1593)

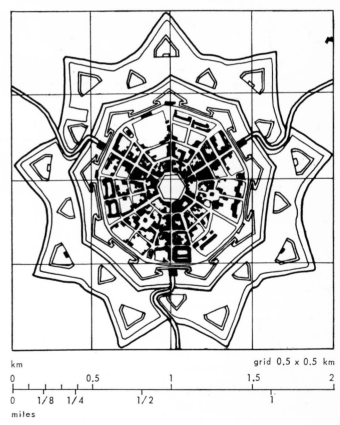

km

0   0.5   1   1.5   2

grid 0.5 x 0.5 km

0   1/8   1/4   1/2   1

miles

347

Theory

346

radial plan in a major settlement becomes quite formal   **Karlsruhe, Germany (A.D. 1834)**

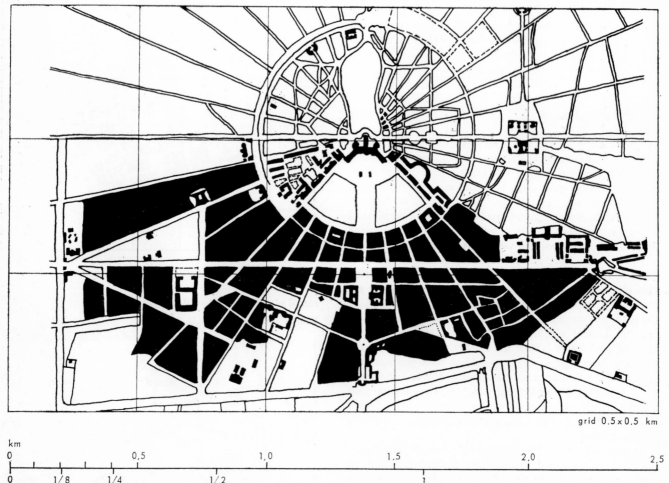

grid 0.5 x 0.5 km

more flexible, whether relatively formal or relatively simple in their construction. It is very interesting to note how adjusted the Hippodamian system is to the morphology of the landscape; a characteristic example is Miletus, which is divided into three major parts (fig. 347)—each one was probably intended for one of the three groups of citizens into which Hippodamus divided his cities. We tend to believe this is true also because the blocks, and probably the plots and houses, in each of these three parts of the city were of different sizes, probably corresponding to the different groups of citizens and the different types of accommodation.

Simple and monumental

While natural settlements are never monumental and are always simple, planned settlements tend to acquire monu-

mental characteristics. An illuminating example of this tendency is that of the Roman colonial cities which, even though sometimes very small, always had a character of monumentality because of their conception, which was based on the 'cardus' and 'decumanus', the two main streets which led to the main gates and divided the city into four equal sectors and which, of themselves, had a monumental character (fig. 348) in the initial phase which did not change in spite of the non-planned additions.

Beginning with the Roman colonial cities, we can find a great variation of monumental cities, of which the one in the largest scale is probably the city of Peking (fig. 349), with a most monumentally conceived overall plan. More characteristic perhaps are the efforts at monumental expression in sections of western cities; for example, in that part of Paris from the Tuileries to the Arc de Triomphe (fig. 350).

348

347
Hippodamian plan in a Greek settlement
Miletus, Ionia (fourth century B.C.)

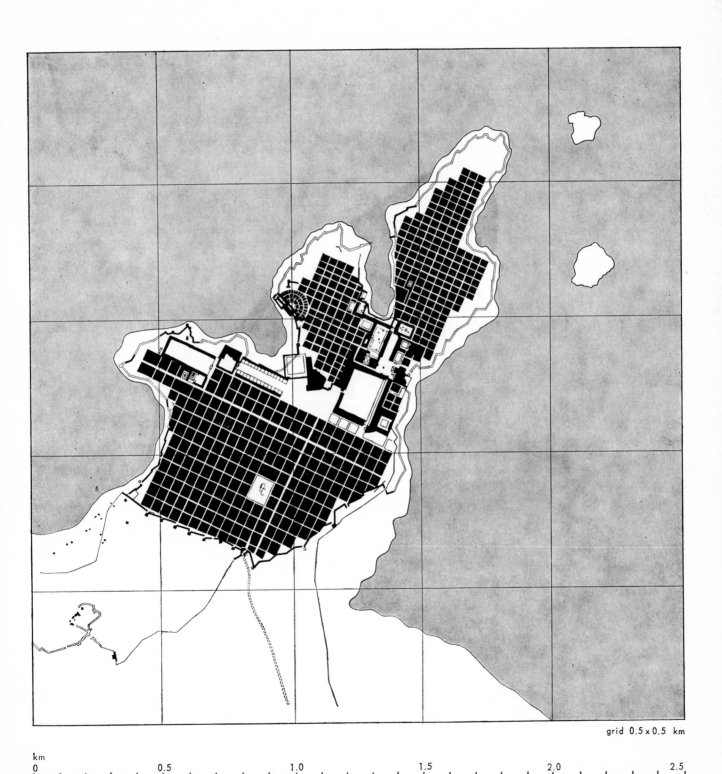

grid 0.5 x 0.5 km

km
0   0.5   1.0   1.5   2.0   2.5

0   1/8   1/4   1/2   1   1 1/2
miles

**monumental synthesis of the initial plan of a Roman
settlement and non-planned additions**

Timgad, Algeria (first-third century A.D.)

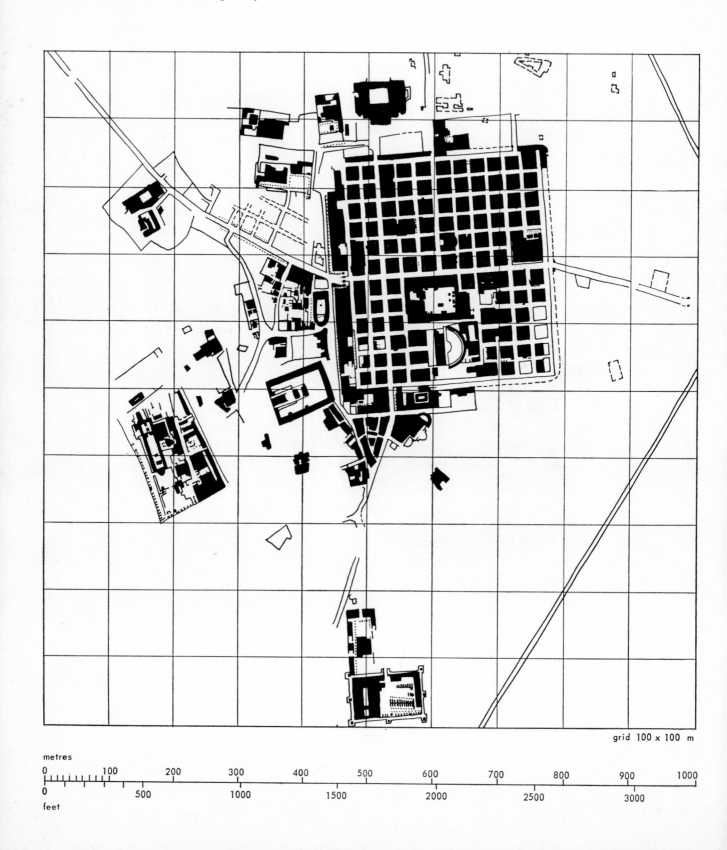

grid 100 x 100 m

metres

| 0 | 100 | 200 | 300 | 400 | 500 | 600 | 700 | 800 | 900 | 1000 |

| 0 | 500 | 1000 | 1500 | 2000 | 2500 | 3000 |

feet

349

monumental synthesis of the initial plan in a grand scale
Peking, China (A.D. 1409)

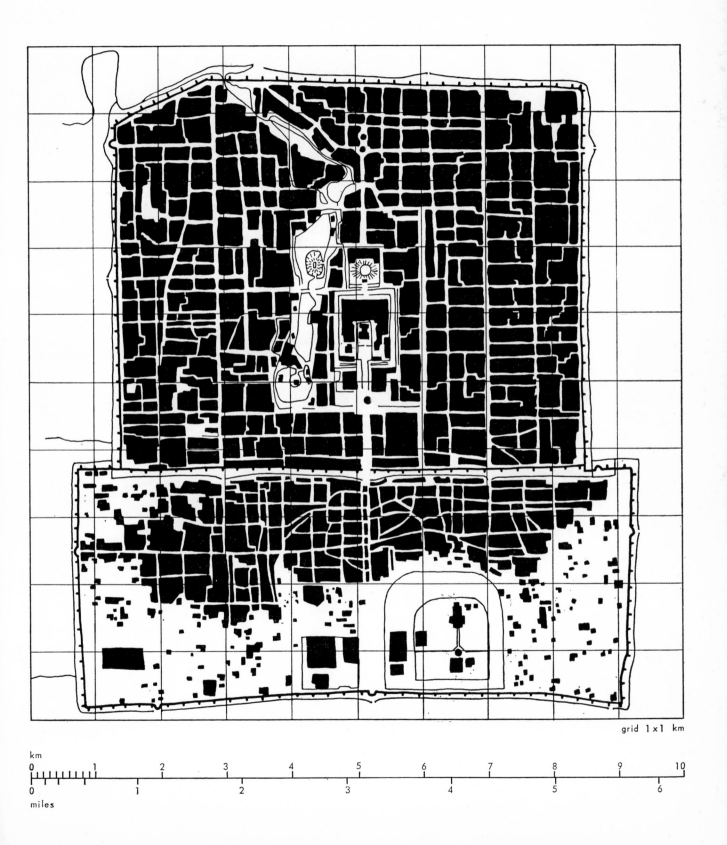

grid 1 x 1 km

km
0 1 2 3 4 5 6 7 8 9 10

0 1 2 3 4 5 6
miles

monumental city of western Europe
Paris, France (nineteenth century)

grid 1 x 1 km

km

0   1   2   3   4

0   1   2

miles

351

ideal cities of the Renaissance in western Europe

plans by Filarete and Scamozzi have been published without scale but are presented here with a tentative scale for purposes of comparison

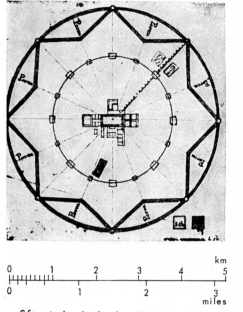

a. Sforzinda Italy by Filarete A.D. 1460

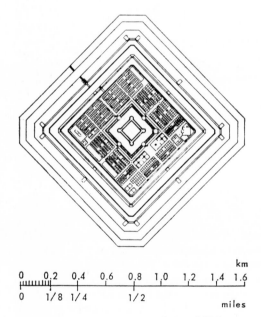

b. ideal city by Durer A.D. 1527

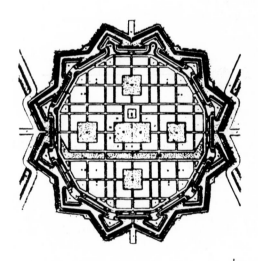

c. ideal city by Scamozzi A.D. 1615

Ideal and utopian

Once Man tended to conceive and build planned cities, it was natural for him to try and create ideal cities and then to move towards utopian conceptions. There is a great variety of ideal cities, most of which have the characteristics of being static and represent the idea of the isolated cell very strongly. Many were designed at the time of the Renaissance. These were inspired by the desire for the best defence or the best type of civil organisation. Such examples are Sforzinda in Italy by Filarete (fig. 351a) and proposals conceived by Dürer (fig. 351b) and Scamozzi (fig. 351c). We do not have

AI

353

utopian city: Atlantis

**plans have been published without scale but are
presented here with a tentative scale for purposes
of comparison**

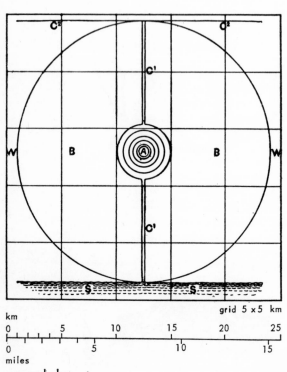

grid 5 x 5 km

```
km
0        5      10      15      20      25
⊢────────┬───────┬───────┬───────┬───────┤
0              5            10           15
miles
```

general layout
A   acropolis
BB outer city
W   main city-wall (50 stades from outer water-belt) (117C,D)
C¹ canal (50 stades), 115 D
C² main canal round plain (118 C,D)
S   sea

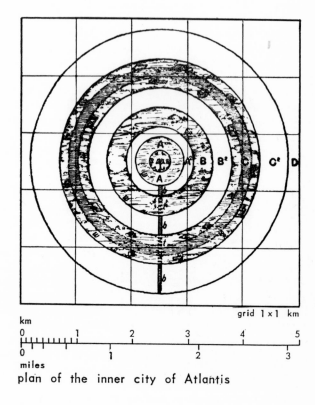

grid 1 x 1 km

```
km
0        1       2       3       4       5
⊢────────┬───────┬───────┬───────┬───────┤
0              1            2            3
miles
```

plan of the inner city of Atlantis

many physical plans of utopian conceptions since most were only described and not actually designed. One of the few that gives enough details to make a design possible is that of the utopian city of Atlantis conceived by Plato in the 5th century B.C. (fig. 352).[15]

MORPHOLOGY OF DYNAMIC SETTLEMENTS

Search for ideal solutions

Unlike the static settlements which have been developing for thousands of years and have gradually tended towards forms both formal and informal corresponding to their needs, the dynamic settlements have developed only recently and have not yet reached any clear form. The proposals for morphological solutions to problems of contemporary settlements which have been made during the last decades refer to rather small settlements, while those few referring to large ones—with Le Corbusier's Radiant City as the most characteristic example—do not face the morphological problems of the dynamic settlements. We need, therefore, to think about this problem now and work towards ideal solutions for dynamic settlements.

One of the characteristics of our era is its fear of the concept of the ideal. This results from the confusion prevalent in many intellectual fields; it can be explained, but it cannot be justified if we are to create the proper framework for Man's life. On the contrary, the search for the ideal is our greatest obligation. This implies neither the discovery of the ideal solution nor its implementation, should it ever be found. Both these problems are related to major philosophical questions concerning our life, which I do not intend to touch upon here. What I do intend, since I consider it an obligation, is to insist upon the necessity to seek ideal solutions.

Only by searching for the ideal can we hope to face the real issues. As long as we start off with the narrow-minded view that the ideal is neither necessary nor attainable, we are compromised right from the beginning; and there is no limit to how low this can lead us. If we make concessions with our concept of the ideal, we will also do the same with our concept of planning for the future needs of a developing settlement. If we compromise on the one-hundred- or twenty-year conception, we will also compromise on our immediate needs. On the contrary, only if we search for the ideal do we have a chance of finding the best solution.

The fact that we will try to find and continually re-define the best solution in accordance with the changing conditions, factors, data and knowledge available, does not mean that we will necessarily succeed. Even if we do set such an ideal goal, by the time we can attain it our concept of the ideal will have already changed. However, it is very important that we have an ideal so that we know where we are leading our settlements, even if we may have to re-examine our views on the way and establish new goals. Whether or not we attain these objectives is of no importance. It is the effort to attain them—either in conception or in practice that will have justified our action, the effort that guarantees the best possible results throughout our struggle.

However, it is not easy to search for ideal solutions. I have already spoken about the many complicated problems related to so many elements, factors and points of view. I will try to exemplify this search for ideal solutions with some examples concerning structure and form taken from the important problems of dynamic settlements. I have selected them because they can be visually presented in a simple way and can throw light on other problems which, although perhaps no more complicated, cannot be so easily presented. The search for such ideal solutions for the structure and form of a settlement should broaden our thinking about ideal solutions for all aspects of settlements and their dynamic balance.

In the following sections I will deal with problems of dynamic settlements as an example of the application of better analytical and theoretical methods to the problems of human settlements.

The research work which has been carried out is based on the principle of isolation of some basic aspects of our phenomena, an isolation which leads by abstraction to the answer of some basic questions. In this respect the examples, both imaginary and real, worked out in this section, are all abstract conceptions of some basic characteristics of structure

and form and they should be viewed as such—as answers to certain problems on the basis only of essential characteristics of their situations.

Need of static cells

One of the major problems dynamically growing settlements face is a continuous change of functions, dimensions, structure, texture and density. Nothing remains static; everything gets broken and very often must be changed. There is virtually no place in the dynamic settlements of the present where Man and Society can be satisfied in a balanced surrounding, where Man's functions may find the necessary expressions, where Nature is respected, and where the Shells can be properly expressed by artful forms. These major problems of dynamically growing settlements result from the fact that practically every one of its cells is influenced by dynamic forces and is changing continuously.

A study of growing organisms in Nature will show that in most of them the cells remain the same size regardless of the growth of the organism. The cells are the same whether a person is young or old, or whether a tree is at the beginning or the prime of its life. Here we can draw an important conclusion: the search for ideal solutions has to be geared towards static cells and the dynamic growth of the organism.

A study of these problems indicates that as long as all forces are operating within the cells, they will grow. If we have a small village and several country roads leading into it, any additional functions on the country road will mean additions to the heart of the village and to its periphery (fig. 353a). If we consider the village as a basic cell in human settlements, we will see that when a certain development begins, the nucleus of the village cannot remain static (fig. 353b). Thus if we want to save the village from the additional pressure leading to its growth and transformation, we must divert the roads in such a way that the village will remain intact as a cell while the new functions being added by the incoming roads are transferred to a new centre around which they will grow (fig. 353c). We can thus save the nucleus of a cell by creating a new and different one next to it.

The same is valid in a neighbourhood or a market within a city, a city within a metropolitan area, or in general in any Ekistic unit within space. It holds true for small shells or large groups of them. A simple primary school may be quite a small shell, but if we make it into a centre for all educational activities and bring people from distant areas to it, it must necessarily grow and break into the texture of the surrounding buildings. This can happen also in the central business area of a metropolitan region. Such an area is not a single shell, but a whole organism, yet its growth is going to create the same problems as would that of a single shell of changes and transformations in its vicinity. As long as these cells or organisms are located centrally to their function or at the

Theory

353

impact of new functions upon the cell

354

impact of a highway upon cells

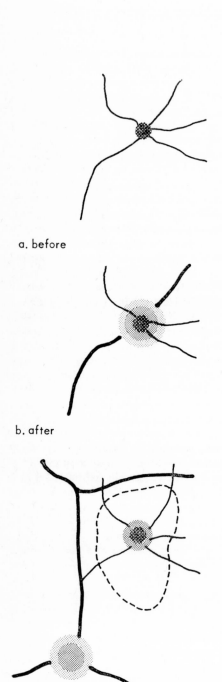

a. before

b. after

c. new solution

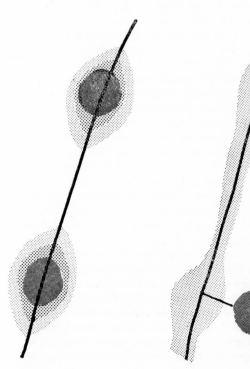

a. dynamic forces, such as
a highway, passing through
the cells result in their
dynamic growth

b. if the dynamic forces
by-pass the cells the
result will be static cells
within a dynamic settlement

crossroads of their main networks of communication, they cannot remain static. We can only keep cells, or parts of human settlements static if we avoid attracting new functions which otherwise would come into them (fig. 354a), and create all major communication and transportation networks outside them (fig. 354b). This also holds true for new settlements such as a community within an urban area (fig. 355a), or a city within a broader area (fig. 355b), or even a metropolitan section within a megalopolitan area, provided that we can isolate them physically from the surrounding areas so that they will not receive new pressures.

It could perhaps be remarked that by taking the main transport and communication networks out of the community and even out of the city, we are creating solutions contrary to normal evolution. For example, in mammals the main arteries of blood circulation are located closer to the centre of the body. However, it would be misleading to think that, once taken out of the community or out of the city, the main communication and transportation networks become external

356

to the whole organism. This could be true in the past but is no longer so, for when we remove these networks from a community they still remain part of a city; and if we take them out of a city, they still lie within the Dynapolis or Dynametropolis. By removing the main circulation networks from within the cells, we can help the latter to remain static and consequently much more directly related to the growth of natural phenomena. Such static cells are no longer subject to continuous internal changes. They provide Man and Society with time in which to relate themselves to Nature and to changing functions. Growth is thus guided towards a repetition of such static cells, as in most cases in Nature, and to the development of specialised cells (specialised Ekistic units) for specialised functions.

In relation to these remarks we can also remember how Man enters the basic units that he creates in his settlements and how he circulates in them. These are two different things which in contemporary settlements have been confused. We enter from outside and we circulate inside (fig. 356). We cannot mix the two as we now do.

In practice what we have said about the new type of static cells can be expressed at several levels, the first of which is the room. The natural way of expanding the activities of a room is to add more rooms of a similar or relative size. This is what both primitive and civilised Man have done. The same can be noted in all types of communities. Research tends to show that the most characteristic small community corresponding to human dimensions is that of communities class IV having about 2,000 families (with a minimum of 500 and a maximum of 3,000). The block used to be the basic unit, the modulus in the old city (fig. 357). Now a new one must be found. The community class IV surrounded by major traffic routes can become the basic modulus of major urban areas, replacing the block which, because of the new scale and dimensions of the city and the new type of traffic, can no longer remain the basic modulus. These moduli are combined in several ways in order to build major urban tissues. If the old city was fairly large, there were major roads at a certain distance apart between the moduli which created areas with dimensions not very different from what we now call an urban sector. The dimensions of the major units of the old city, or the basic units of the present one, tend to correspond to a human scale within which people can walk. This means a width of up to one mile, in which access to the central area of the sector as well as to all its facilities is easy for the pedestrian. So the structure of dynamically growing urban areas now is best based on sectors connected to form supersectors, which again lead to major divisions of the city, depending on how large the urban area is (fig. 358).

It is necessary at this point to discuss the shape of the sector. The basic analysis of forms proved that it should be rectilinear and rectangular. What then should be the ratio of its sides, should it be rectangular or oblong? The answer to this question is given by the functions that it performs and

355

creation of static cells in new settlements

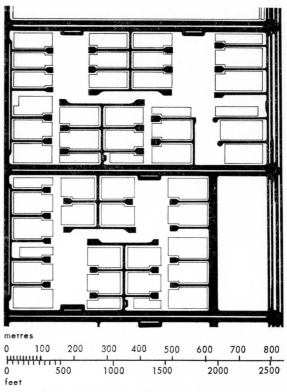

a. small communities within a city

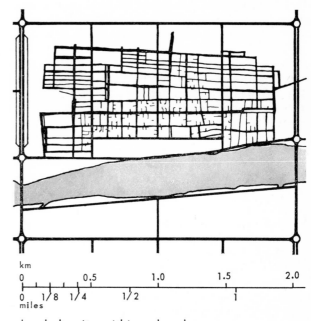

b. whole city within a broader area

357

**entrance to Ekistic units and circulation within them
are two different functions**

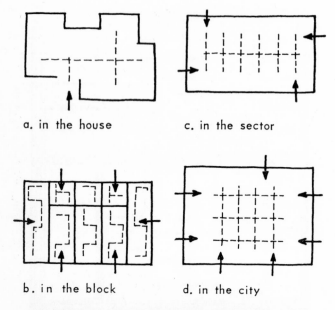

a. in the house   c. in the sector

b. in the block   d. in the city

its size. The city blocks have usually, throughout human history, been elongated (fig. 359a). The reason is that there is always one preferable orientation of plots and the block is elongated in order to form more of these plots.

When we move to the sector, we no longer have the same considerations. Now the form depends on its central functions. If it is a small sector, then central functions develop along one main commercial street—which means that it is reasonable for the sector to be an elongated one (fig. 359b). If the sector is larger though and if it is reasonably planned, then its central area will not need to lie along one road, it might easily be square or oblong, in which case the whole sector might tend towards a square (fig. 359c).

In order to make the new sectors function properly as the basic cells of a dynamic city, which can themselves remain static, we must achieve the following as shown in a new community class V of Islamabad (Pakistan) containing four communities class IV (fig. 360):

○ isolate them from through traffic as much as possible in order to allow functions within them to develop as they did in the old city—in a quiet, rather static way, independently of the functions on the other side of the highways surrounding them (fig. 361);

○ create as much cohesion within the sector as possible and serve as many needs inside it as possible without attracting outside population into it, thus eliminating the need for many of its functions to spill over its border line (fig. 362).
This can be done by:

○ not allowing through car traffic—in this way the major

connecting force within the sector will once again become that of the pedestrian, who is more sector oriented, whereas the machines are more connected with forces outside the sector;

○ creating as many facilities as possible at crucial locations of the sector in order to orient people towards them;

○ creating facilities and functions with isolating qualities along the border line of the sector in order to isolate it from outside influences, noises, etc; and creating obstacles for external influences and functions which may try to infiltrate the sector. This can be done by the creation of schools, sports grounds and parks around the border line of the sector, as well as by the creation of car parking areas, garages and light industries (fig. 363).

In this way we have defined the human community, which is a community class IV and V, as an independent sector in the sense of independence for services of corresponding classes. The question now arises how to define the supersectors or communities of a higher order. There are several ways in which to proceed. The simplest one is to accept the validity of the organisational principle that one centre can serve only a definite number of minor ones, perhaps 4 to 8, and decide to form communities of a higher order by merging 4 to 8 communities of a lower order into one larger one. This principle will lead to similar conclusions as the principle of hexagonal spatial organisation, which shows that one unit of a higher order serves 6 to 7 units of a lower order, depending on whether we consider this same unit one of both lower and higher orders. On the basis of this principle, we can build a system of communities of all orders.

Another approach is to measure the population or the area corresponding to facilities and centres of a higher order. If we assume that a community class IV has 10,000 people and one high school, we can then find that a professional school or a junior college corresponds to a population of 50,000 and take this population to be the unit for a community class V where a full college, corresponding to 200,000 people may serve as a basis for a community class VI, a university corresponding to 1,000,000 people for a community class VII and so on. The same applies for commercial centres, administrative units, services, etc. A combination of them would be the safest way of proceeding along this line of thought.

A similar approach is the one using cost-distance or time-distance as the factor defining the boundaries of communities of certain classes. In this respect it is interesting to note that, even as the human community in the past and the present seems to have been conditioned by the ten-minute walking distance, several new studies prove that the ten-minute travel time distance is an important factor in the definition of important relationships in land-use patterns. Such examples are given by the study of the travel time factors in the Baltimore-Washington area (fig. 364) and are gradually appearing in the studies of other cities.

basic units within larger settlements

grid 500 × 500 m

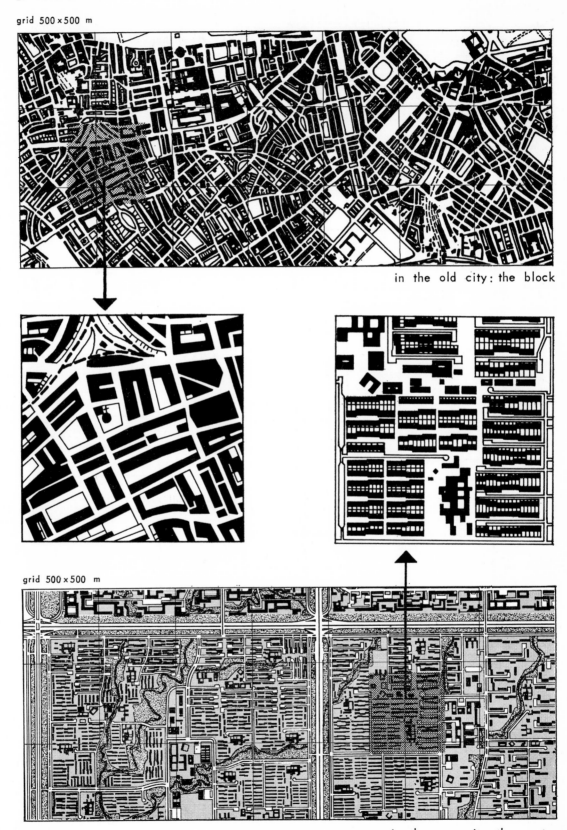

in the old city: the block

grid 500 × 500 m

in the new city: the sector

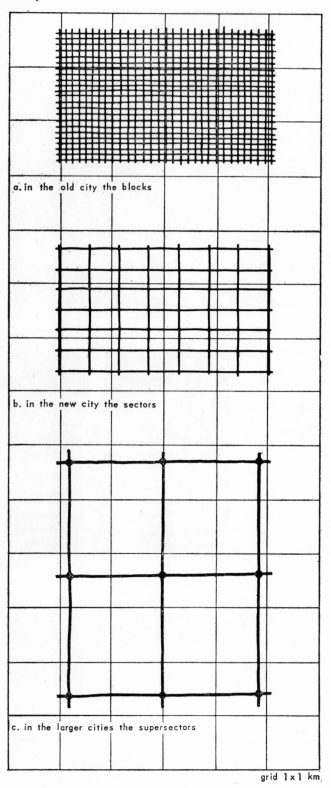

a. in the old city the blocks

b. in the new city the sectors

c. in the larger cities the supersectors

grid 1 x 1 km

358

(left) basic units within settlements

359

(below) shape of sectors

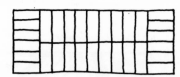

a. the block is influenced by the prevailing orientation of the plots

b. a small sector is influenced by its central functions

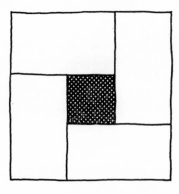

c. a larger sector is again influenced by its central functions

360
the static sector
the complete sector in a community class V
Islamabad, Pakistan (1960)

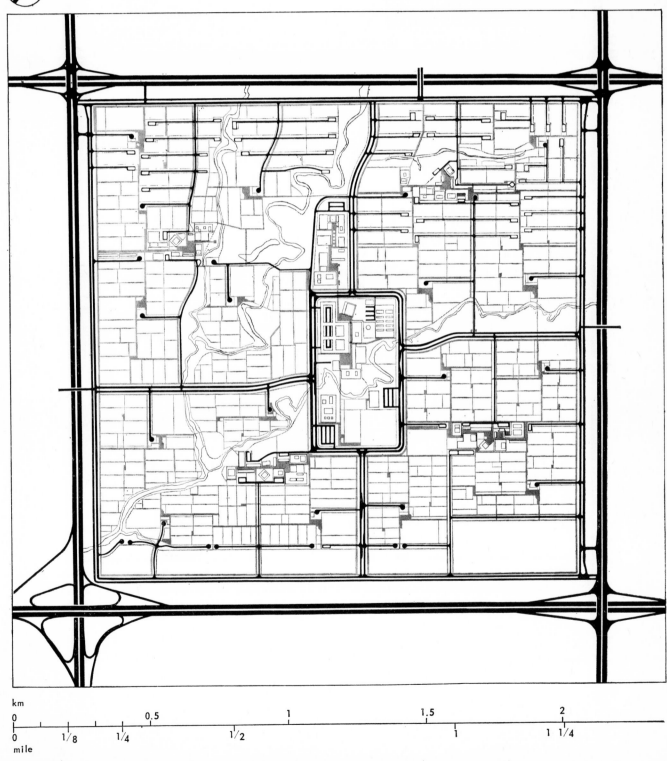

km
0   0.5   1   1.5   2

0   1/8   1/4   1/2   1   1 1/4
mile

Theory

361

the static sector

network of motor roads

**a community class V surrounded by highways
and without through traffic in minor units**

Islamabad, Pakistan (1960)

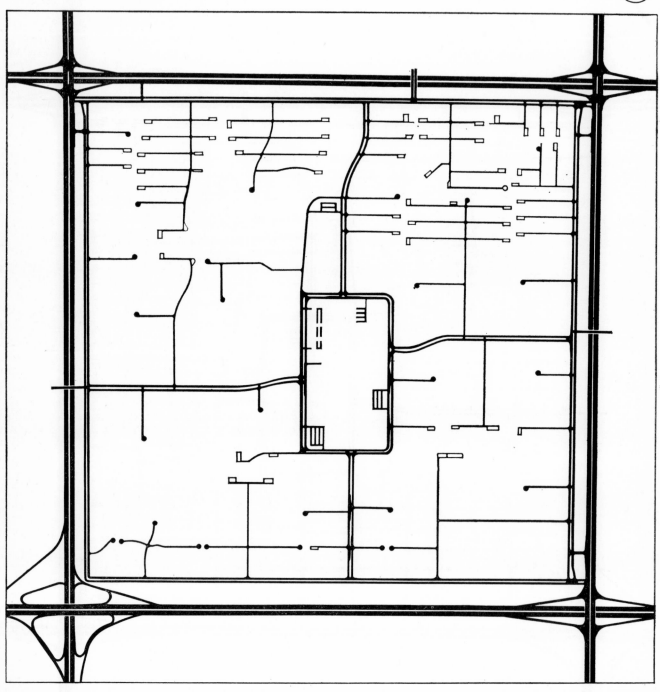

362

the static sector

pedestrian streets in a community class V

**internal cohesion due to the pedestrian circulation
and the placing of the central functions**

Islamabad, Pakistan (1960)

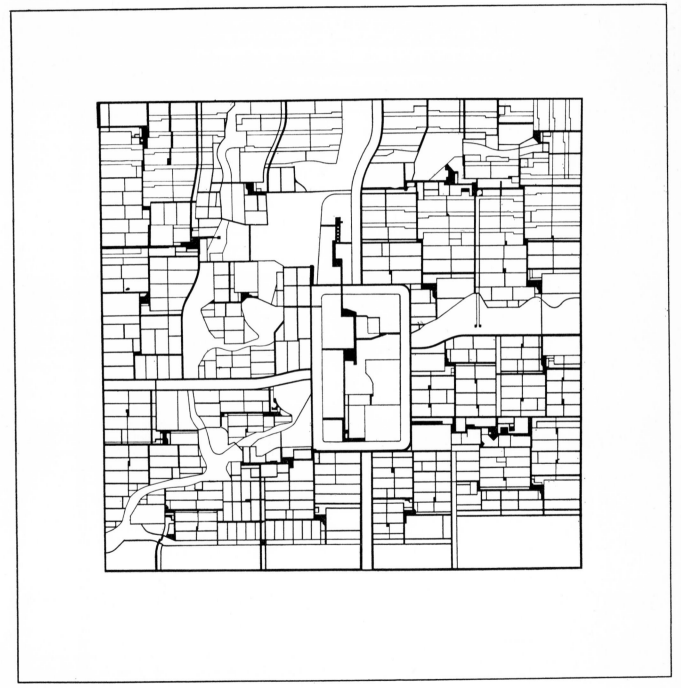

363

different zones of a major sector

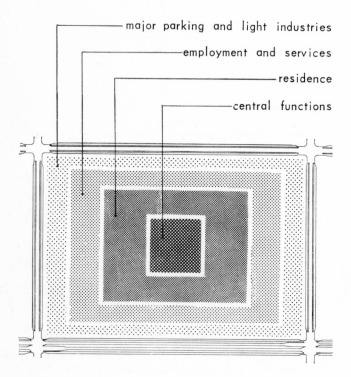

major parking and light industries

employment and services

residence

central functions

364

travel time factors
Baltimore - Washington area

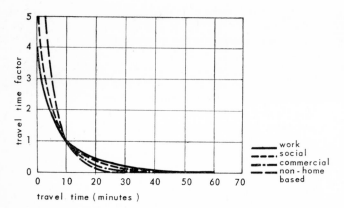

travel time factor

travel time (minutes)

work
social
commercial
non - home
based

Ideal Dynapolis

If we start building urban areas with static cells, it will be because of the need to create human conditions providing as much security against constant change as possible. However, this is not realistic when applied to the overall organism, since our urban areas must grow dynamically. The question is how to achieve this for certain sizes of Ekistic units only. This will be examined in the three examples of the Dynapolis, the Dynametropolis and the Dynamegalopolis. In order to face this problem we must strive towards ideal concepts and solutions in the sense that I have already explained by isolating the basic phenomena of structure and form.

We begin with Dynapolis, that is, the dynamically growing city, whose dimensions can range from the small ones of the past to the large ones of the present, provided the city has not become a multi-nuclei metropolis. A basic difference between the city (polis) and the metropolis is not only one of dimensions, which are larger in the metropolis; but also lies in the fact that the city has one major nucleus and some subordinate ones while the metropolis has several other nuclei which, although less important than the central one, have a certain independence because of historical and other factors. I will examine here the one-nucleus urban area, the city (polis), and its ideal form when it becomes dynamic—the Dynapolis.

A really static city (fig. 365a) presents no problem of dynamic growth. But when the city starts growing, it undergoes an undesirable transformation. Its periphery grows relatively normally although with great difficulties when the expansion is too great; but, right from the beginning, its centre is forced to grow like a cancerous growth, eating into those cells of the city which are close to it, transforming them from residential to commercial areas, changing their functions, contents, structure, etc. This is the main problem of a city turning into a Dynapolis, and this process becomes intensified as the city continues to grow (fig. 365b).

The only way to solve the problems of a Dynapolis is to conceive a pattern which will permit its natural growth, especially that of its centre, without allowing the new additions to destroy the existing pattern. The dynamic city must possess an expanding central part arranged in such a way so as to be able to expand without invading the other parts of the city. Perhaps people will answer, 'a solution has already been found, in height'. But this would be wrong, because height can never hold the entire volume necessary to the expanding functions, for not all buildings can continuously grow in height, and many of the functions cannot afford the high rents of higher and consequently newer buildings. In addition to this, expansion only in height increases the Shells of the city centre but not the arteries within it, which need much greater widths in order to serve the increased activities in the new buildings. The result is that the centre suffocates.

An analysis of the possible forms a city centre may assume, points to a solution which will permit free expansion along a

365

from the static city to the ideal Dynapolis

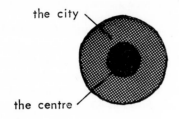

a. the static city of the past

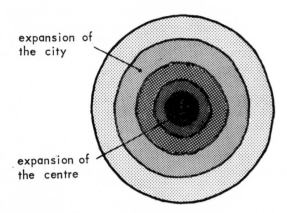

b. the static city which now grows into a Dynapolis

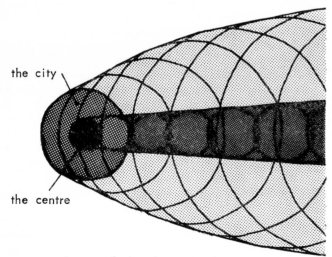

c. proper evolution of the dynamic city
the ideal Dynapolis is a parabolic settlement
with uni - directional growth.

365

from the static city to the ideal Dynapolis

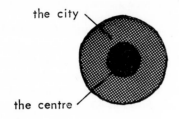

a. the static city of the past

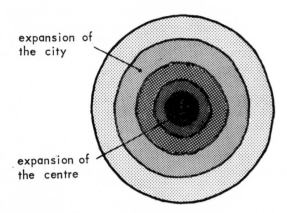

b. the static city which now grows into a Dynapolis

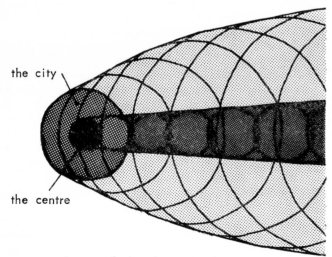

c. proper evolution of the dynamic city
the ideal Dynapolis is a parabolic settlement
with uni - directional growth.

predetermined axis. This axis will consist of the original central core of the city and its new development on both sides of, and along, a central core. Such a city will follow one physical direction; its expansion will be mainly uni-directional. In fig. 365c every circle represents a certain moment in time. For every circle of the city we have a new circle for its centre. Some people have called this type of development linear. But this city lacks a major characteristic of linear development which means expansion in two opposite directions. This is contrary to the very concept of the ideal Dynapolis. The ideal Dynapolis is *uni-directional*, for, if it were two-directional, there would be increasing pressure on the old centre, which would have to remain in its original location, and all new pressures would necessarily accumulate in the older part of the city.

If we try to translate the previous schematic city into concrete geometrical shapes which can be implemented, we will find that circular shapes will have to be transformed into squares and rectangles in accordance with the principle of rectilinear grid-iron patterns. This is due to the fact that an ideal city should be built on the basis of a rectangular grid network of roads. The diagonal roads that some cities have at times adopted are rapidly moving out of the picture since they have never been able to function as initially conceived. The so-called 'diagonals' date back two centuries, and were built for the purpose of military control of the city (later revived by Haussmann), or for saving transport time in an era when the horse-driven cart was the main means of transportation; this has been the case in Washington. None of the above conditions exists any longer and, as we are moving towards rational developmental thinking, we are coming to realise that the only road arrangement allowing a city free and consistent development is a major rectangular grid network of roads. Consequently, our previous schematic presentation of the city assumes the shape shown in fig. 366a.

When this scheme is analysed, a certain irrationality will be observed. Areas close to the central parts are not susceptible to development because of the considerable dynamism with which the city is expanding in only one direction. This refers to the areas around the oldest part of the city and those around its subsequent centres of expansion. So, our scheme as it stands, may not be ideal in practice under all conditions. The instance in which such a scheme could be ideal would be when the intrusion of the fourth dimension became so absolutely critical that all previous investment in the existing city could be disregarded and people could amortise the city of the past generation, or the past decade, in order to move into the city of the next generation. This, however, is quite unfeasible for economic reasons, as well as for reasons of speed of growth. It is never going to happen. In view of this, we have to make plans that will balance the design of the quickly expanding Dynapolis with the necessity of using the maximum of the investment that has already been made within our cities.

ideal Dynapolis

possible evolution of the parabola

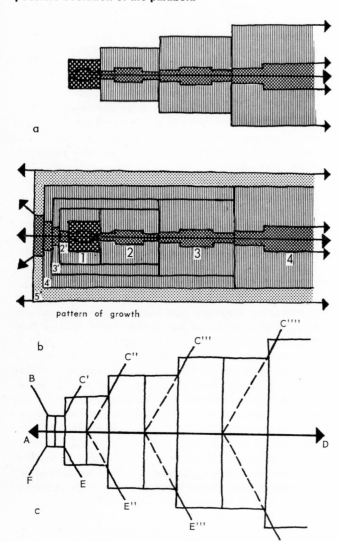

a

pattern of growth

b

c

realised and what the expansion in the main direction will be as compared to the expansion in the other three.

The exact form will therefore depend on:

o the speed of population growth,
o the speed of economic growth,
o the relationship between these two,
o the controls exercised on the city's growth.

Since there are many retarding forces of inertia within a city influencing its economy (mainly long periods of time necessary for the amortisation of invested wealth), it is much more probable that the cities of the future will acquire the type of development shown in fig. 336b at least in the fore-seeable future.

For our ideal city of the future, therefore, we will accept a centre growing along a predetermined axis. Let the centre of the original city be called Centre 1, the one of the first development Centre 2, the centre of the second development Centre 3, and so forth (fig. 366c). As we examine Centre 1, we find that it would not be adequate to serve the new ad-ditions to the city north, south and west of it. For that reason additional centres must be created. These (let us call them 2′, 3′, 4′, 5′) should be wider than Centres 2, 3, 4 and 5, since they must serve not only the new parts north and south of them, but also large parts of the city developing north and south of Centre 1 (note: the use of the terms 'north', 'south', etc. has nothing to do with the actual direction of expansion of the Dynapolis; it is due to the orientation of our diagrams, where the north is always at the top of the page).

The ideal Dynapolis is therefore conceived as a city built and developing at varying rates along a system of perpendicu-lar axes. This development, however, must become an integral part of the overall area around the city and, from a planning point of view, of the entire country's overall development, which is physically based on a system of hexagons. The hexagonal system is beyond doubt the best and most economic pattern for the organisation of space and the interrelation of settlements. This is why, in the overall development scheme of the Dynapolis, we must take into consideration the development of the proper highway pattern around it.

Figure 366 shows an A–D axis along which the main development of the city of the future is taking place. At the initial stage this axis is connected with the area around it through axes A, B, C, D, E and F. The major expansion is taking place mainly along the D axis. The first phase of expansion will mean a transfer of axes C and E to the new positions of C′ and E′. A second expansion again effects a movement of these axes to new positions C″ and E″.

Such a pattern of expansion indicates that highways A and D must not suffer any major relocation, since they are on the main axis of development. Highways B and F may remain stationary outside the city. Within the city, however, due to expansion, the relocation of highways B and F is imperative and inevitable. Their parts within the city must

Such considerations lead to the ideal scheme which shows a city moving and developing dynamically on one direction, while also expanding in the other three directions and gradually incorporating all the previous parts of the city (fig. 366b). The difference between this scheme and the previous one lies in the fact that the rectangle expands mainly in one chosen direction at a great speed, while also expanding at much lower speeds in the other three. So the ideal Dyna-polis, besides its uni-directional movement can also have well-balanced development all around it.

In practice the rate of population and economic growth will determine whether a proper Dynapolis can ever be

367

ideal Dynapolis

the role of texture forces

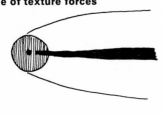

a

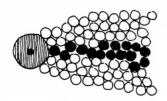

b

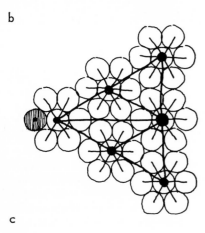

c

if the units defined by texture
forces are large then the overall
slope changes correspondingly.

either be rebuilt, or permanently closed to through traffic. Highways C and E will have to be transferred to new positions during every step in the growth of the Dynapolis, to C′ and E′, C″ and E″, etc. The parts of the highways to be incorporated into the city will have to be closed in every case and either be rebuilt, which will be very difficult or, what is more probable, be used as internal roads of a lower category. The main traffic will follow the north-south system of roads within the city.

Such a pattern of expansion indicates that the sides of the basic sectors of the city and the direction of the different axes assume an angular pattern with 30° and 60° angles. This again means that if we want to keep the city divided into sectors of similar shapes, we must provide for an expansion

that follows the rules imposed by the hexagonal pattern or the triangles mentioned above.

In such a case we have a pattern for the growth of the city by stages which can follow a geometrical rule. This rule may have different expressions. If, for example, we want equidistant main streets, we will have a certain type of city. But, if we want the distances between streets to be greater in the newer parts of the city, then the pattern will change again.

We have defined the three basic rules about the form of the Dynapolis:

- one main direction of development and one main axis;
- development of a system of axes at a right angle to the main one;
- a pattern of highways based on different expressions of the hexagonal pattern (but never of hexagons or diagonals placed upon the basic system of axes within the city).

The next step is the clarification of the modulus which we will use for the final definition of the texture of Dynapolis, which again will define the details of its form. An example can be seen in the gradual change of the modulus of growth which conditions the texture forces. If the modulus is almost non-existent in relation to the size of the city, then growth is continuous (fig. 367a); if the modulus is larger, then the growth follows the pattern imposed by the texture (fig. 367b, c).

If the Dynapolis is quite large and covers an area formed by several communities class IV or V then within it we will have transformations in structure which are worth noticing. When the settlements are hexagonal and their nuclei small, then their centres are not linear but central squares (fig. 368a). If the hexagonal settlements are completely built-up areas and connected to a system of a higher order, then the resulting centre will be unreasonable (fig. 368b). Because of this the synthesis tends to transform the hexagons into elongated ones first (fig. 368c) and then oblongs with parallel centres which are connected at right angles with the centre of a higher order (fig. 368d). If we have many such centres we have a new axis of major importance (fig. 368e); depending on the overall structure we may even have other types of formations as in fig. 368f. The final synthesis depends on the internal and external structural forces being exercised on our system.

The modulus of the ideal Dynapolis has to be the sector, which will approach the size of dozens of blocks of the past. Such a sector must correspond to the number of families served by one or more types of central functions. This number can correspond to a certain number of elementary or secondary schools, or to shopping centres, community centres, churches, etc., depending on the culture and the economic level of the area.

The sector should remain the basic unit in the structure of the Dynapolis. If the city is going to be small, it can have sectors of one class repeated in a similar way forming a uniform pattern, as in the new city of Marsa el Brega in Libya (fig. 369). If the city is large, or when it grows large, these sectors will be united to form a major or supersector,

internal transformations of structures in a growing Dynapolis

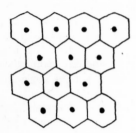

a . initial hexagons

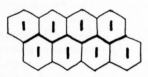

b . built - up hexagons developing elongated centre

c . hexagons also turn into elongated ones

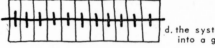

d . the system is transformed into a grid - iron

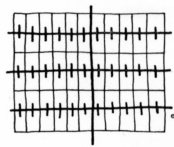

e . creation of a system of higher order

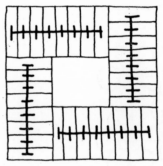

f . creation of a different system of higher order

which will, in its turn, become the modulus that can be repeated to form the city. If the city is even larger, the supersectors will be united into even larger sectors, which will become the major divisions of the city. Such a division of the Dynapolis allows for its natural growth from a city of blocks, to a city of sectors, supersectors, etc., such as the city of Islamabad in Pakistan, first planned in 1960 (fig. 370).

Such a division of the Dynapolis into sectors of different sizes should not be external only. On the contrary, in order to have meaning these sectors should correspond to real functions and follow their hierarchy. If one elementary school is needed for a sector, a supersector should correspond to a high school or a vocational school, and a major division to a more specialised educational institution. If a sector has a small shopping centre, the supersector may have the supermarket; and when a sector has a small community centre, the supersector will furnish the movie theatres of the area. In the Dynapolis all functions, buildings, roads, facilities, etc., will be designed and built according to their hierarchical importance.

The structure of the city must correspond to the hierarchy of its functions, while its main axes—the only ones passing through the whole length or width of the city—should define its major divisions, for otherwise there will be confusion and

chaos. Here I should point out that the axes passing through the whole city should define the sectors of the highest order which divide the city. This can work for cities with up to two or three million people. But if such cities happen to be larger and cover an area of, let us say, a length and width of 30 or 40 miles, then it is quite probable that their major sectors will be around five miles long in both directions, and the city may tend to have 25 such sectors as its first sub-divisions. This dimension may be prohibitive from the traffic point of view, since experience with the present types of communications shows that the axes passing through the whole city should in general be placed not more than two to four miles from the centre of the city; the closer they are the better. We have to bear in mind that this rule—that the major through axes should surround only the major sectors of any urban area—needs careful interpretation when applied to very large urban areas, because in such cases they may have to pass through or under them.

Such an analysis of the ideal Dynapolis proves that we can find ways of satisfactorily facing the problems of dynamically growing cities. If it is argued that this is pure theory, I would answer that several times in the past these principles have been implemented, and indeed very successfully, as the examples of ancient Cyrene (fig. 371) representing small

369

Dynapolis in practice
Marsa el Brega, Libya
first planned in 1962

Ekistic Synthesis

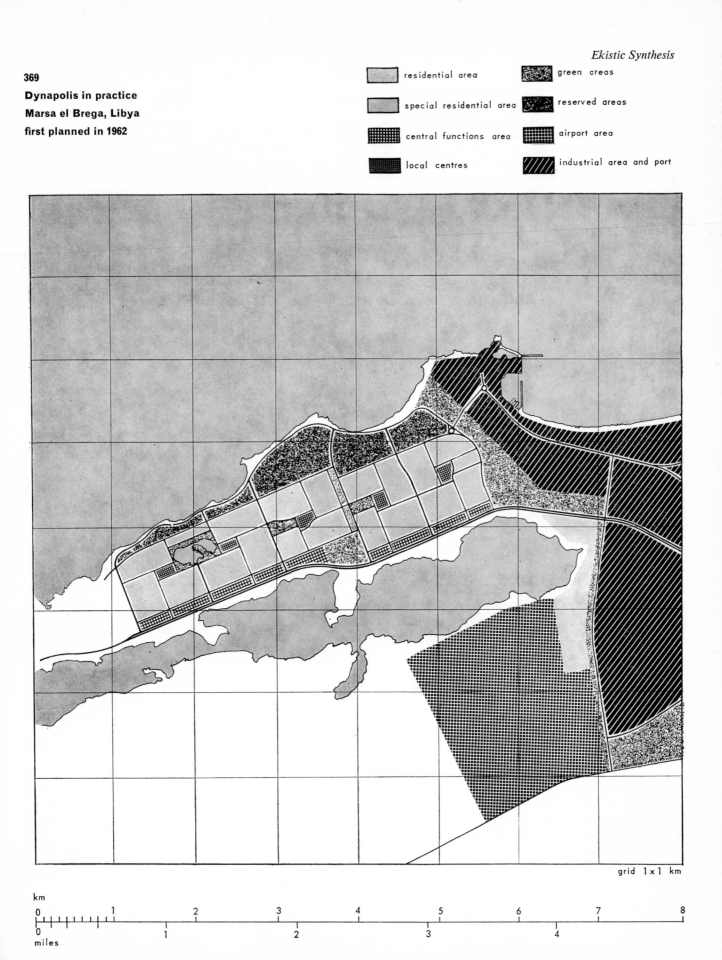

- residential area
- special residential area
- central functions area
- local centres
- green areas
- reserved areas
- airport area
- industrial area and port

grid 1 x 1 km

km
0   1   2   3   4   5   6   7   8

0   1   2   3   4
miles

BI

Dynapolis in practice   **first sectors of Islamabad,**

Pakistan   **first planned in 1960**

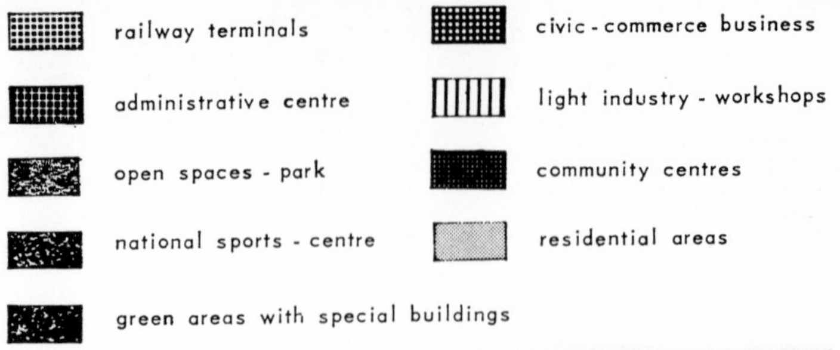

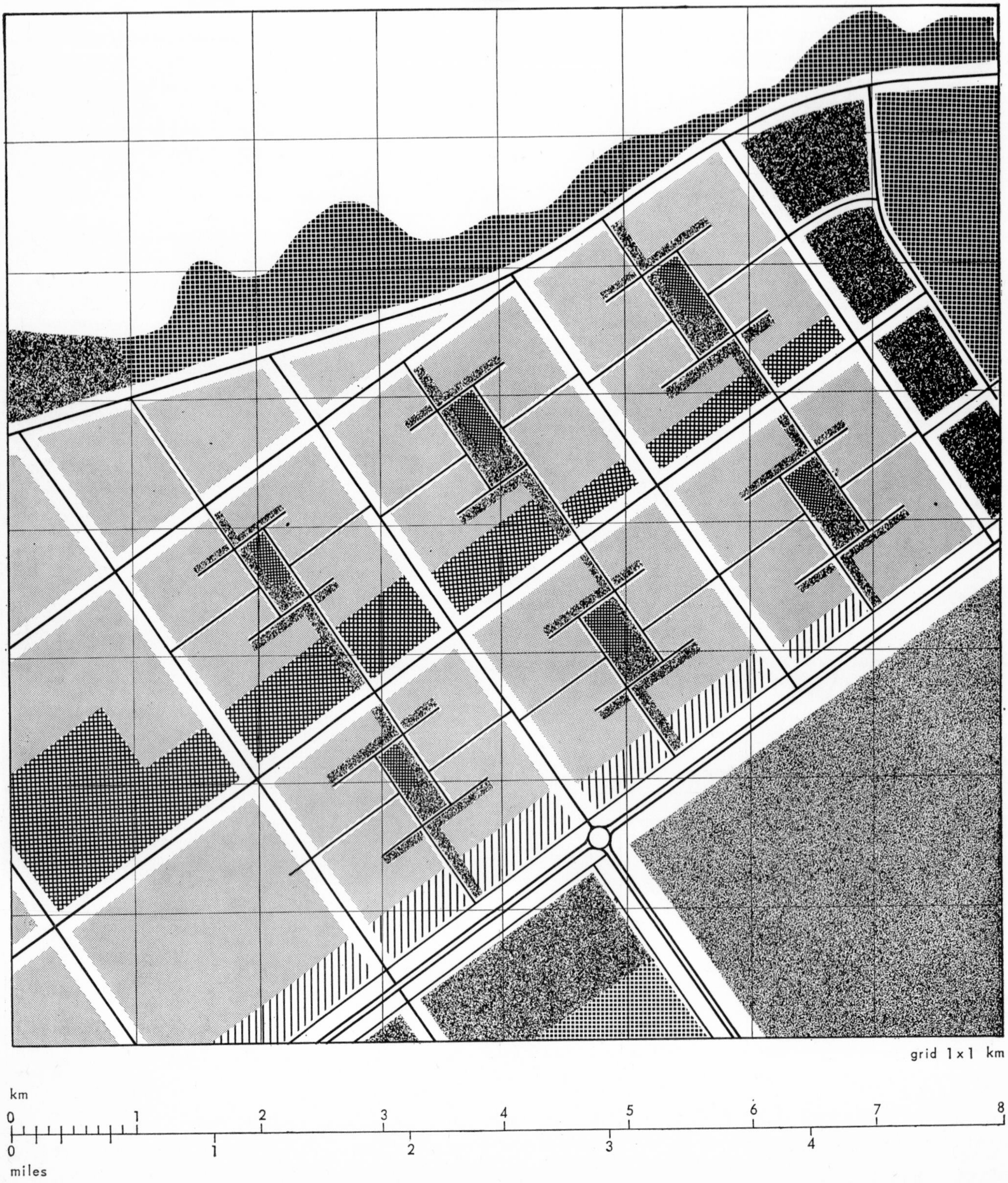

▦ railway terminals	▦ civic - commerce business
▦ administrative centre	‖‖ light industry - workshops
▦ open spaces - park	▦ community centres
▦ national sports - centre	▦ residential areas
▦ green areas with special buildings	

grid 1 x 1 km

km
0   1   2   3   4   5   6   7   8

miles
0   1   2   3   4

371

ancient Cyrene growing dynamically

■■■ acropolis
■■■ Greek town
▨▨▨ Roman town

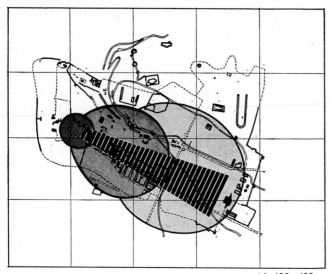

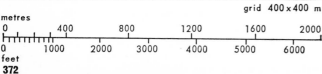

grid 400×400 m

metres
0   400   800   1200   1600   2000

0   1000   2000   3000   4000   5000   6000
feet

372

Paris centre growing dynamically

■■ middle ages   ┉┉ 1180
■■ 12th cent.   ─·─ 1370
▨▨ 16th cent.   ─── 1789
▨▨ 17th cent.
▨▨ 18th cent.

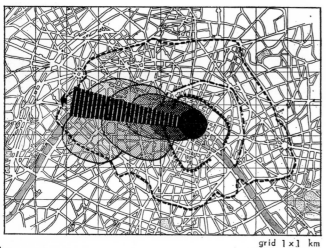

grid 1×1 km

km
0 1 2 3 4 5 6 7 8 9 10

0   1   2   3   4   5   6
miles

cities, and nineteenth century Paris (fig. 372) representing a much larger one prove. In these cases the cities probably developed gradually in a natural way, although it is quite possible that this natural development was understood as a need and therefore assisted by acts of planning.

In addition to these historical examples, we can learn from other organisms or works of art how we can lead an organism towards growth without destroying it. As an example I shall mention how from living organisms we can learn that a prolonged infancy may endow the organism with a greater ability to undergo changes. This may explain why old static cities can expand dynamically and still retain their values, while new ones may lose them completely when they suffer from new pressures before having settled into a balanced form. From composite steel cables we learn that we must have wires of a smaller diameter in the core than in the periphery; this is a good indicative example of why it is more natural to have minor moduli in the central areas of a Dynapolis than in the periphery (fig. 373).

Ideal Dynametropolis

The problems leading to the formation of an ideal Dynapolis also necessitate the formation of the ideal Dynametropolis. Here, in distinction to the polis (city), there is almost always a multi-nuclear centre. One centre is usually larger than the others, but they have some degree of independence, even when they exist within the same continuous built-up area, as is very often the case.

Because of the large dimensions of the area of a metropolis, and because of its multi-nuclear character—which makes it difficult for us to realise that it is fundamentally one area and one organism—its problems are not so apparent as those of a one-nucleus city, which has a continuous urban texture and whose growth is quite apparent. In a metropolitan area there may be additions of new nuclei which are organic parts of this metropolitan area, but which may be distinct built-up areas. The fact that they are separate urban areas does not mean that they do not create problems for the whole metropolis. These crop up at the expanding fringes, where the textures of old and new settlements sometimes become mixed and confused, and at the centre of the metropolis, where pressure increases enormously as other cities are added on the periphery. These problems cause the dynamic metropolis as a whole to suffer more than the dynamic city. The pressures exercised by the growth of a dynamic metropolis may affect only its central nucleus, or all the other nuclei as well, depending on their nature and on the formation of the whole area.

In order to relieve the pressures on a metropolis, the structures and forms of an ideal Dynametropolis must be conceived. This time I am speaking of 'structures' and 'forms' and not of 'structure' and 'form'. Because of the very essence

371

373

thinner strands of wire in the core of a composite steel cable

374

towards an ideal Dynametropolis growth against a solid front

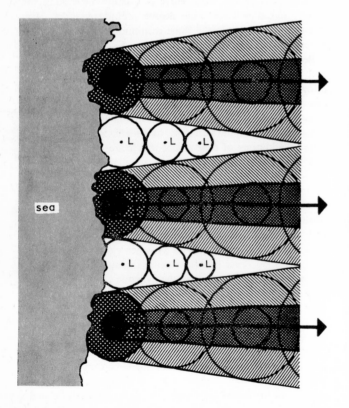

of a Dynametropolis which consists of several centres that eventually grow in several directions, the ideal solution is—even theoretically—not one, but as many forms as there are combinations of the different urban areas and their nuclei forming the Dynametropolis. I will mention two examples of how the ideal Dynametropolis can be conceived in two specific cases.

The first example is one of the simplest cases: a Dynametropolis which is, in some way, limited in space. This happens when the metropolis is not free to spread in all directions but grows against a solid front, perhaps the sea or a very large river—a situation that increases the number of alternatives and makes the system more complicated. Such a case may have several centres along this solid front developing separately in a somewhat parallel way. Later they may merge. This ideal Dynametropolis consists of a repetition of Dynapolises parallel to each other, with some gaps in between the parabolic designs and some overlaps. The ideal Dynametropolis gradually merges these parabolic Dynapolises to form one urban area with several nuclei and centres developed in a parallel manner—at a right angle to the solid front, either with rectilinear adjustments of the parabolic forms (as has already been shown with the Dynapolis) or with additional minor centres (L) between the parabolic Dynapolises (fig. 374).

The second example is that of a Dynametropolis which is free in space and develops in a star-shape by absorbing the centres of a minor order which exist on the axes leading out from the centre. Such a Dynametropolis can very easily be choked to death, since its growth continues to exercise pressure upon its centre. In addition to that, this Dynametropolis suffers because of the great weaknesses in the connection of those parts growing along several axes in the outlying areas. If these parts are directly connected, the Dynametropolis will gradually turn into a circular concentric city and will inherit all its weaknesses. It is quite clear that the best solution is not to be found in such a way (fig. 375a).

We must search for solutions of a different kind, which will first of all save the centre of the Dynametropolis, which suffers more than any of its other parts. The concept of a growing centre along one of the existing axes (fig. 375b) will gradually lead us to a Dynametropolis, the new centre of which will remove the increasing pressure and will mean the creation of several centres around it (fig. 375c). In this case, the old metropolis will suffer only from minor pressures since it will be the centre of only its own population plus some small additions which will not overcharge the existing heart but will allow it to function and gradually readjust itself to the increasing demands. This increase in demands will be under control, and the growth of the metropolis will be guided. These figures show that the new centre is created on an axis which already plays a certain role; we have superimposed the functions of a new centre upon the existing functions of a lower order.

375
(left) towards an ideal Dynametropolis
different types of growth

376
(below) towards an ideal Dynametropolis
growth by the creation of a new centre in an open area

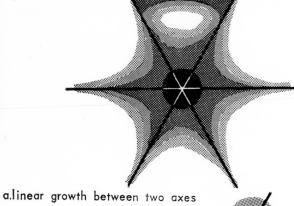

a.linear growth between two axes

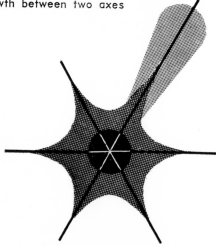

b.growth on an existing axis

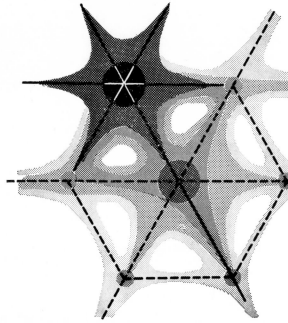

c.growth by the creation of a new centre
on an existing axis

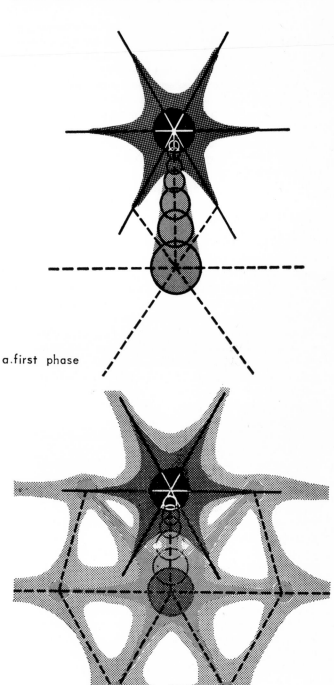

a.first phase

b.second phase

It is preferable to proceed with the creation of a growing centre for the metropolis in an open area between the existing transportation networks (fig. 376a). In this case, the centre will start functioning without difficulties, will be modelled on the basis of future demands and will be able to withstand the pressure of a Dynametropolis which has the following characteristics (fig. 376b):

- ∘ a new centre able to withstand pressure of a much higher order than the existing one;
- ∘ this centre facilitates the creation of several others around it, which are initially of a minor order and will gradually assume equal status with the initial metropolis;
- ∘ the original metropolis must withstand only a very small part of the pressure which would otherwise have been exercised on it, and it can thus survive, remodel itself, and serve its own population in the best possible manner.

If we now want to see this Dynametropolis growing in space and time as the ideal Dynapolis we will reach a more complex form based on the same idea of a continuous parabolic growth (fig. 377).

Ideal Dynamegalopolis

The Dynamegalopolis has the same problems as the Dynapolis and Dynametropolis, but on a different scale; the urban area grows beyond control and by doing so it:

- ∘ devours land indispensable for the proper balance between Man and Nature—necessary for health, food, water catchment, aesthetic satisfaction, etc.;
- ∘ creates an organism which cannot function because all its centres are being gradually choked to death (fig. 208).

In order to avoid these problems, an ideal Dynamegalopolis must be conceived afresh. As in the case of the ideal metropolis, there can be no single answer to such a difficult problem. Every megalopolis is different—therefore, there can be many ideal megalopolises. I will mention just one, based on the example we have investigated in several parts of this book (fig. 378).

The centres of such areas are being choked to death and there can be no hope if more pressure is exerted on them. In the case of the Dynapolis such a disaster was avoided by the conception of an expanding centre and in the Dynametropolis by the creation of a new one which could be the expansion of the old one. Such solutions show us where to look for the answer to the problem of the Dynamegalopolis. More so than in the case of the Dynametropolis, the only hope lies in the creation of a new system of centres and transportation and communication networks which will withstand all the pressure until such time as the Ecumenopolis is created in a static form and Dynamegalopolis becomes a part of it. Until then, the process leading to an ideal Dynamegalopolis will be the creation of new systems with centres and transportation networks of a higher order, which will allow the

377

towards an ideal Dynametropolis

growth in several stages by the creation of new centres

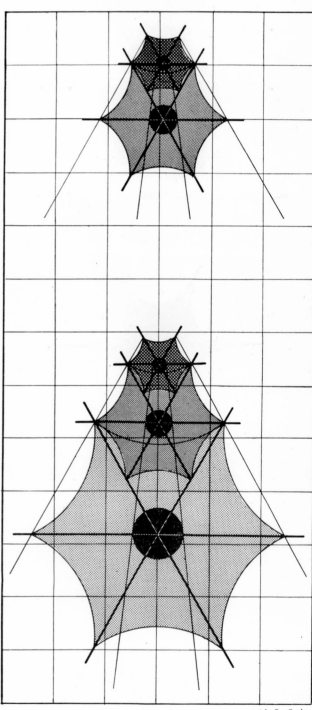

grid 5 x 5 km

378

ideal Dynamegalopolis

growth by new centres (first phase)

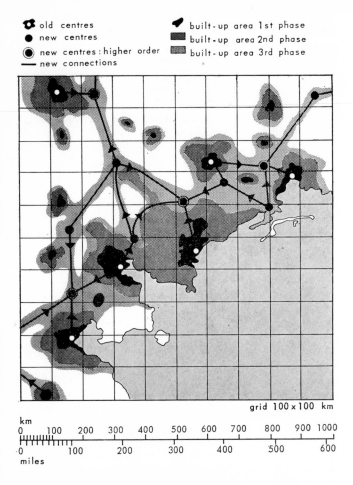

- old centres
- new centres
- new centres : higher order
- new connections

built-up area 1st phase
built-up area 2nd phase
built-up area 3rd phase

grid 100 x 100 km

km
0   100   200   300   400   500   600   700   800   900 1000

·0   100   200   300   400   500   600
miles

existing built-up areas to remain as static as possible, or at
least to have as little additional pressure as possible.

The principle of the decentralisation of functions of a lower
order cannot help us attain this goal, as the policy of satellites for the city, and the policy of 'new cities' for the metropolis
and megalopolis, have proved in England. As long as we
continue with these policies, we will, on the one hand,
decentralise many people and deprive them of the facilities
of existing centres, while on the other, we will not avoid
exerting more pressure on the existing structure of the
megalopolises. So, their major problem will not be solved;
on the contrary, these policies may lead to their death. It is
quite clear that the policy of decentralisation does not serve
the inhabitants, but works against evolution—which requires
centralisation—and does not help us avoid disaster in the
existing centre, where pressures are continuously increasing.

The solution is not decentralisation, but *new centralisation*.

We must create a system of centres of a higher order and
a corresponding circulatory network which will take over the
pressures and functions of a higher order. In this way the
existing urban areas will continue to have the same type and
intensity of problems which can in this way gradually be
coped with. Otherwise the increasing pressures will never
allow us to deal with the present problems, much less with
those to come.

Such an ideal conception of the megalopolis is shown in
fig. 379 which provides for a completely new system of centres
and corresponding functions, a system in which:

- the existing urban areas will become relatively self-
  contained for services of their order and will gain
  cohesion and be relieved of pressures because the new
  centres will attract certain functions of a higher order
  near them, which will then be subtracted from the older
  ones;
- the new centre of a higher order will absorb some
  pressure from the older ones instead of exerting more
  pressure on them;
- the new areas to be created will become like the old ones—
  relatively isolated, self-contained, and will thus be
  deprived of new unexpected pressures; from the beginning they will be planned—in dimensions, shape and
  structure—to fulfil their role, in the class of functions
  for which they have been conceived.

If we create the proper network in the ideal Dynamegalopolis, we will not simply remove pressure from the centre—a
lower degree of urbanisation within the same area also will
be achieved, which means that smaller areas will be built up
in the same total area. As long as new centres and transportation lines are not created, everybody will tend to come closer
to the existing ones and consequently the pressure on them
will be great, the built-up areas will be continuous and large,
and the inhabitants will be at greater distances from Nature.
On the contrary, if we take the initiative for new centres in
the countryside, these will draw people away from the older
urban area. This will have the following advantages:

- the new areas we will have selected will be less indispensable for agricultural production or for leisure;
- they will be at greater distances from the existing urban
  areas; so more areas closer to them will be left free, and
  a better balance between built-up locations and free
  nature will be achieved.

In this way the ideal megalopolis will lead to the elimination
of the two great dangers prevalent in the Dynamegalopolis,
which expands without any conception of its ideal form:
the strangulation of the centres, and the loss of precious land
—in other words the destruction of both the heart and the
body of the human settlements forming the Dynamegalopolis.

It could be argued at this point that in order to achieve this
the Dynamegalopolis would have to expand over larger areas
thus depriving people of the facilities being offered by the

379

ideal Dynamegalopolis

growth by new centres (second phase)

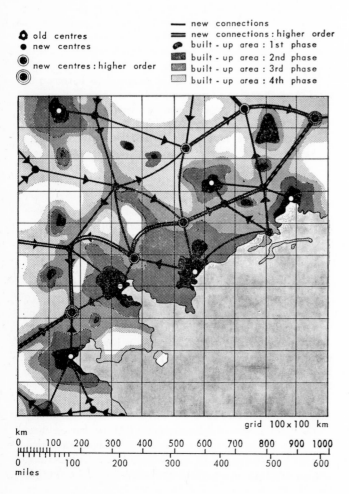

⬠ old centres
● new centres

◉ new centres: higher order
◎

— new connections
═ new connections: higher order
▣ built - up area: 1st phase
▦ built - up area: 2nd phase
▨ built - up area: 3rd phase
▢ built - up area: 4th phase

grid 100 x 100 km

km
0   100 200 300 400 500 600 700 800 900 1000

0   100   200   300   400   500   600
miles

time, or because future developments proved that growth is continuing at a higher rate or over a longer period than had been foreseen. The answer is that inherent in the idea of Dynamegalopolis is the notion of another system outside the first one which will absorb the pressure of an even higher order that will be created. Should we have even more people and pressure than had been predicted, we will need a larger area to bring our Dynamegalopolis in contact with other Dynamegalopolises—centres of an even higher order.

Thus, the technique of building systems of a higher order outside the existing dynamic urban areas will allow the Dynamegalopolis to grow in an ideal way. Such a method will gradually lead towards the Ecumenopolis which, being static, will not present any more problems of a similar nature. If ever it does then again the solution will lie in the creation of another system of an even higher order wherever it is needed.

Ecumenopolis

Dynamic settlements will continue growing up to a certain time according to the law of continuous compound growth, as we see in Nature and in the evolution taking place in many organisms. Then the growth will slow down for many reasons mostly related to densities affecting biological, physiological, psychological, personal and social factors. This is inevitable; it is as true of small organisms as it is of bacteria.

In this way the growing Dynamegalopolis gradually leads to Ecumenopolis, which will be relatively static as was the polis. During the phase of the Ecumenopolis humanity will once again reach a period of relatively static balance between all the elements of the settlements (Nature, Man, Society, Shells and Networks). In the past, this happened in isolated communities; a small island settlement would reach a point of balance and remain static. But in a certain way, this happened also on a greater scale, and more frequently in the ancient Greek city-states, which brought all their forces into balance and had a fixed population, since any overflow led to the creation of colonies in several parts of the Mediterranean and the Black Sea. Such a policy, which seems first to have been inspired by the oracle, or the wise men of Delphi, led to the solution of many problems of ancient Greece; the city-states avoided more disastrous wars by remaining quite static on the mainland and expanding in other areas during certain periods.

The fact that we are looking forward to a time when all the elements in our settlements will be in relative balance does not mean that the Ecumenopolis is going to be static in substance. It will be static in relation to the Dynapolis, Dynametropolis and Dynamegalopolis, from whose merging it will have been born. In the Ecumenopolis life will continue normally. It may even reach great heights of culture and civilisation. Conditions will change but because of the much lower growth in population, any great expansion of

centres of a higher order. This is not so. People are being deprived of facilities today when we do not plan for proper growth and the transportation networks created do not shorten time distances. People are not interested in physical distances, but in time- and cost- distances. These can be reduced only if we build the proper overall transportation network on the basis of the correct principles, regardless of the fact that some major lines of transportation will be longer than others. It does not matter if we go 20 miles further from an existing centre if, instead of driving 40 miles at an average of 40 miles an hour—an hour's drive—we cover 60 miles at an average of 90 miles an hour, which means 40 minutes' travelling time at the same cost.

We can now ask ourselves what will happen if for some reason even this new system becomes inadequate, either because it relieved pressure for only a certain period of

380

Ecumenopolis at the end of the twenty-first century

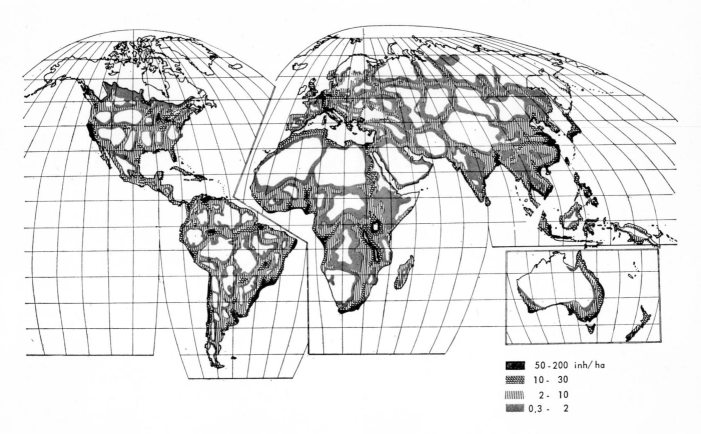

▓▓	50 - 200 inh/ ha
▒▒	10 - 30
‖‖‖	2 - 10
▬▬	0,3 - 2

Ecumenopolis will cease. This means that since its population and built-up areas will remain relatively static and constant, the Ecumenopolis will reach a phase during which it will undergo remodelling, but not basic changes.

Such considerations lead to the conclusion that the procedure for the creation of the ideal Ecumenopolis is divided into two phases:

o the building of ideal Dynapolises, Dynametropolises and Dynamegalopolises which will gradually form the permanent frame of the Ecumenopolis;

o the continuous improvement of this frame.

This means that the construction of the ideal Ecumenopolis has already begun, and we must see to it that its basic frame is as sound as possible because, although there will be a constant effort for its amelioration later, its basic characteristics cannot be altered easily. In this respect the ideal Ecumenopolis coincides with the conception of the ideal Dynapolis, Dynametropolis and Dynamegalopolis. This coincidence is evident during the first stage of the Ecumenopolis' creation. The second phase consists of its gradual remodelling until it becomes more satisfactory than it is in the dynamic phase of its creation when balance between the

elements will be striven for but will be difficult to achieve. By then the great problem existing today—the complete lack of balance between the expanding urban areas and their Shells—will no longer be so acute; the Shells will have caught up with the requirements of Man, Society and Networks; and if Man is going to survive within Ecumenopolis, it will be in proper balance with Nature, which Man will respect.

Ecumenopolis, when finally formed is going to look somewhat as in fig. 380 (after studies by the Athens Center of Ekistics for the end of the twenty-first century). By then it will have a population of the order of 20 to 30 billion people and it will operate as one organism. It may be of interest to note here that Professor J. Z. Young in his book *Doubt and Certainty in Science* and Sir Julian Huxley in his *Evolution in Action*, point out that the number of cells in the thinking organs of the human body (the cerebral cortex of our brain) is of the order of 20 billion and 'their organization is of a scarcely conceivable complexity'.[16] Is it not of interest for us to know that Ecumenopolis is going to have as many individual brains as the human brain has cells? And how about the complexity of the total human Society?

The anxiety manifested by those people who are beginning

377

Ecumenopolis in practice

Athens metropolitan area, Greece

master plan for the year 2060

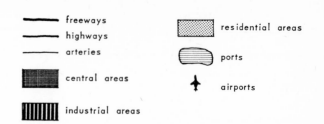

freeways
highways
arteries
central areas
industrial areas

residential areas
ports
airports

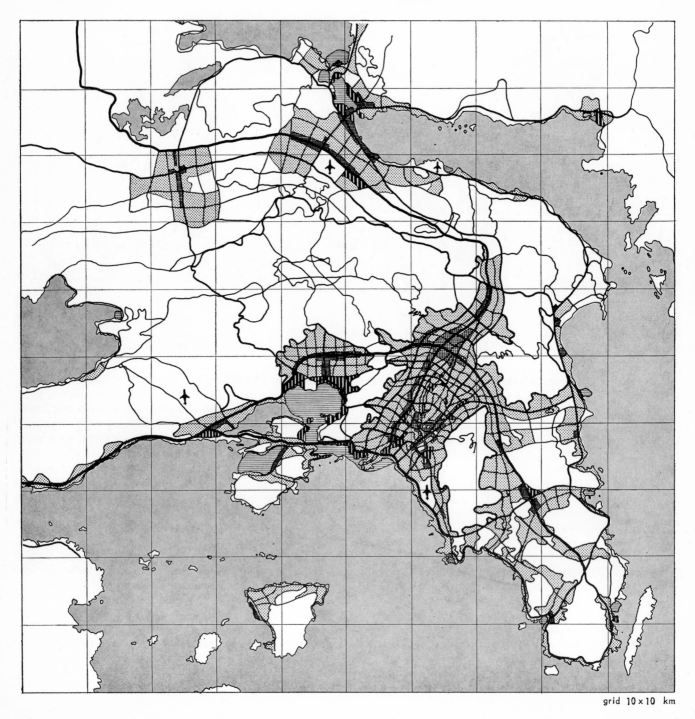

grid 10 × 10 km

km
0   10   20   30   40   50   60   70   80   90   100

0   10   20   30   40   50   60
miles

382

Ecumenopolis in practice

**Rio de Janeiro metropolitan area,
Brazil   master plan for year 2000**

heavy industry

central areas, institutions

green areas

existing city

civic, commercial, business

light and service industry

non-noxious industry

residential

recreation

port

airport

military area

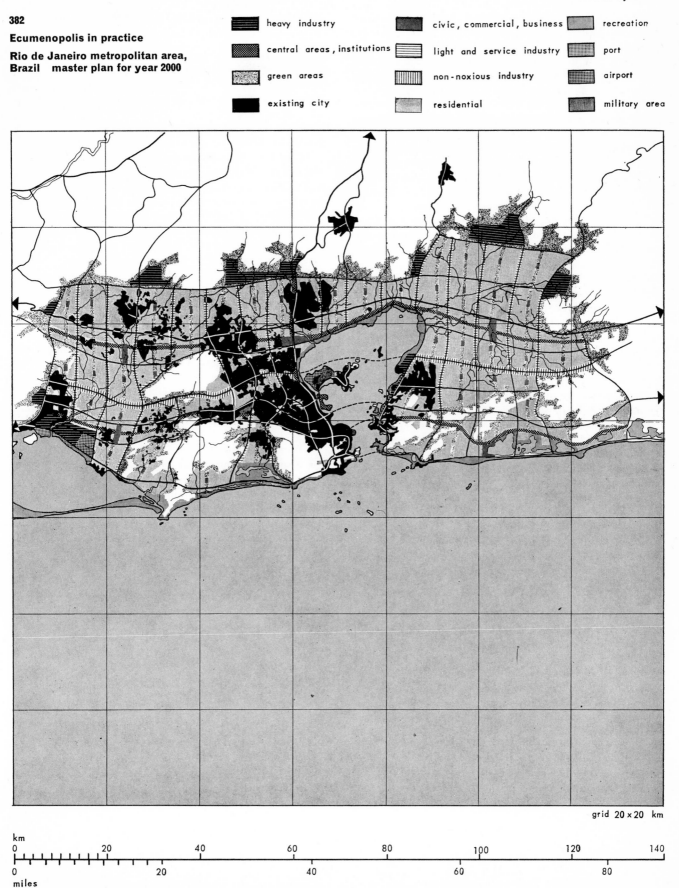

grid 20 x 20 km

km
0   20   40   60   80   100   120   140

0   20   40   60   80
miles

to understand the tragic antithesis between expanding functions and resisting Shells and Networks, is going to come to an end. The challenge at present is to build ideal urban areas, not only in terms of their own needs, but also with regard to the major areas of which they are going to become a part in the generations to come, until humanity reaches the stage of Ecumenopolis a few generations from now. By then humanity will not be concerned with the re-establishment of balance, but with the quality of human settlements. Because of the alleviation of immediate pressure on increased facilities, humanity will have ample time to think about its way of life and how to express this in human settlements. Here philosophers can precede builders in thought and thus influence their activity.

At this point, it may well be argued that while these ideas about the future can be quite important, they have no meaning today since the era of the Ecumenopolis is far off, and we cannot conceive the problems it is going to create, especially since it will gradually turn into a static settlement. The point about the era of creation of the Ecumenopolis being far off has already been explored; I have explained that the Ecumenopolis has already begun to take shape. The point about the lack of conception—since it will be turned into a static settlement—is also being faced in some way today, since some parts of the expanding tissue of human settlements are becoming static. If only we open our eyes, we will discover that these are mainly the parts which are expanding so as to completely fill the natural landscapes in which they are built. This happened in the past with small cities and harbours when the era of large ships dawned; the cities were not able to expand and the harbours could not be enlarged. If we study such cases as the El Sueda (in the Red Sea near Port Sudan), we can certainly learn some useful lessons. However, we have contemporary examples to draw upon. The city of Athens, for example, which now has approximately 2.5 million people and is heading towards many more, is located in a valley which will be completely filled before the end of this century. We are therefore already able to conceive the city of Athens turning into a static urban area although the broader urban tissue will be expanding beyond the mountains into a larger organism. If we limit our observations to the valley of Athens, we can then understand the type of Ecumenopolis we will face on a much larger scale (fig. 381). A similar example on a larger scale can be seen in the area of Rio de Janeiro in Brazil, where because of the expected growth of the population by the end of this century, a much larger valley will be covered by 20 million people or more (fig. 382). A careful study of such cases not only will help us solve the problems of these specific urban areas, but also help us experiment on the formation of the Ecumenopolis during its phases of dynamic growth and static form.

PREPARATION FOR SYNTHESIS

Considerations on synthesis

The process of our actions for synthesis is the same regardless of whether we are dealing with simple or with complicated problems. It is the process of intellectual action leading to a conception of how we are to face any Ekistic situation.

In the past, because the problems were much simpler in size and rate of change, this process for synthesis was natural, and in many cases it passed unnoticed. We cannot afford to let it remain so anymore; the problems are too complex to be even understood without a proper system, let alone be solved without a proper synthesis. We now have the obligation to conceive the system that we have always used subconsciously, or to create a new one.

This system will necessarily have to be based on the following:
○ our knowledge and experience;
○ the conscious or sub-conscious process leading to connections between the parts of a situation;
○ all the additional knowledge and experience we can acquire concerning our specific case;
○ a methodical approach.

In order to re-establish or establish such a system we have to plan our action in an orderly way. To do so we must define the following, and in this order of priority:
○ goals,
○ frame of time and space,
○ assumptions and criteria,
○ method of interconnections and comparisons.

This is the order which I will follow in order to present the preparation for synthesis as an introduction to the method of synthesis which follows in the next section. Although I have not consciously been following this order and this method since the beginning of my career, I believe now that I have always been going about things in this way, maybe subconsciously, while gradually developing it into a conscious method. I can even add, I believe, that this is the way in which we all think when we want to achieve a proper synthesis, even though we very seldom realise it.

Goals

No synthesis can be achieved if we do not have a goal. Programming, planning or designing for any settlement without a goal is meaningless; the same is true for any part of a settlement.

The goals have to be set by those concerned; but they have to be accepted by the Ekistician as reasonable ones from the aspect of feasibility, reason and ethics. In this respect the

Ekistician is responsible for the goals. But very often he has to achieve much more. Those concerned do not seem to realise the necessity for goals, or, if they do they cannot define them. Then the expert has the great responsibility of assisting the process of goal-setting, since without achieving the definition and acceptance of goals he cannot undertake any meaningful action of synthesis.

Frame of time and space

After setting our goals, we must define the frame of time and space within which we will operate. We usually fail in this by making them too narrow, while they have to be as wide as possible.

Widening the framework of time means being able to understand our problems as far back in the past as possible and project it as far ahead into the future as possible. To limit ourselves to the requirements of the present is as misleading as believing that we can save a person suffering from pain with a morphine injection without considering what will happen after its effect is over, and without understanding what caused the pain, and without realising that it is impossible to keep him alive in this way for very long. We must recognise the necessity for a study of the whole organism of human settlements over as wide a time framework as possible in order to best serve its future.

The same applies to problems of space. All problems of human settlements seem to occupy a distinct and limited space. People do speak of a village, a city, a metropolis, but if we try to confine our study of settlements to these areas, we will certainly fail. Let us take the example of the city. A city is not an isolated community; it is the nucleus and heart of a wider urban and rural area which may contain many villages as well as many other cities and functions. If we confine our study to the problem of the city (and by this we mean usually only the built-up area under a single administration) we will go wrong. In order to be able to see its real problems and devise their solutions, we must understand the whole organism of which the city is a part. The city consists not only of the built-up area, but also of its whole vital space. And this vital space not only includes the environs up to the area of the next settlements but spreads beyond this into a whole system of which the city is one part within a certain level of functions.

The same is also true of any part of the city. In order to understand it, we must understand the whole city. And this again is true of any community or neighbourhood, and, at the other end of the Ekistic scale, of any region comprising many cities and many urban and rural settlements. We shall not be able to understand any Ekistic unit unless we see the larger area within which it is situated and the role it plays in the overall system of the human settlements surrounding it. We must realise this in order to be guided in widening the framework of our observations.

Widening the frame of space is necessary, but it also makes our task much more difficult. This is not a reason for letting our frame shrink since that would be disastrous, but it is a reason which should make us aware of the difficulties, and help us face the problem within the broader frame.

The process of learning a better method for synthesis has suffered enormously in the era of the expansion of settlements and the complication of the elements, functions and factors within them. The process was much simpler when settlements were small. This is why most villages make sense as a conception. When they are not satisfactory, it is not due to a lack of ability for synthesis, but to the conditions under which they were created, the functions which they had to carry out and their level of income and education. When conditions were better, Man, even in urban settlements, could achieve much better results; this is why most of the ancient, medieval and Renaissance cities are so satisfactory as human settlements, so much so that they are still almost the only types of settlements we admire. Because of the small dimensions of the problems and the limited number of variables, Man was able to conceive these settlements as rational wholes and unconsciously or consciously develop them to a very satisfactory degree. This is why there were people like Hippodamus in ancient Greece, who could conceive and direct the creation of settlements with no hesitation as regards dealing with all the forces within time.

Such considerations lead to the conclusion that we can learn a better method and process for synthesis if we manage to isolate settlements, or sections of them so that the number of variables and their variations will be decreased. These are better cases to experiment with; if successful, we can then add variables and increase the rate of variations. This would be a great step forward, but it should be achieved without any unreasonable separation of a settlement or a part of a settlement from the Ekistic system and the wide frame within which it belongs. If the separation is injudicious, we are defeating our purpose by not complying with the basic rule of the study and understanding of settlements.

Is there any way of attaining our goal of reducing the inconveniences created by a wider frame without abandoning it? I think such a situation can be found when a settlement is cut off from its surroundings in a very clear and definite way by the natural morphology of the landscape. This is the method which I recommended by the introduction of the static cells in our synthesis. This also as I have already mentioned, happened in some small cities of the past and is beginning to be in prospect for some major cities of the present, such as Athens and Rio de Janeiro. Our progress will be easier if we select such cases for the study of our methodology, rather than settlements which can expand without limit in all directions; for with the former there is a simplification of our subject through the limitation of its natural expansion, which is, of course, one of the great variables influencing settlements. I had the occasion to work on both these cases—Athens and Rio—and they are the

systems of settlements in practice

the region of Guipuzcoa, Spain (1964)

proposed roads

area of dense development
(industry, residence, tourism)

area of medium density
(green area, outskirts, one-storey buildings)

touristic area
(touristic development)

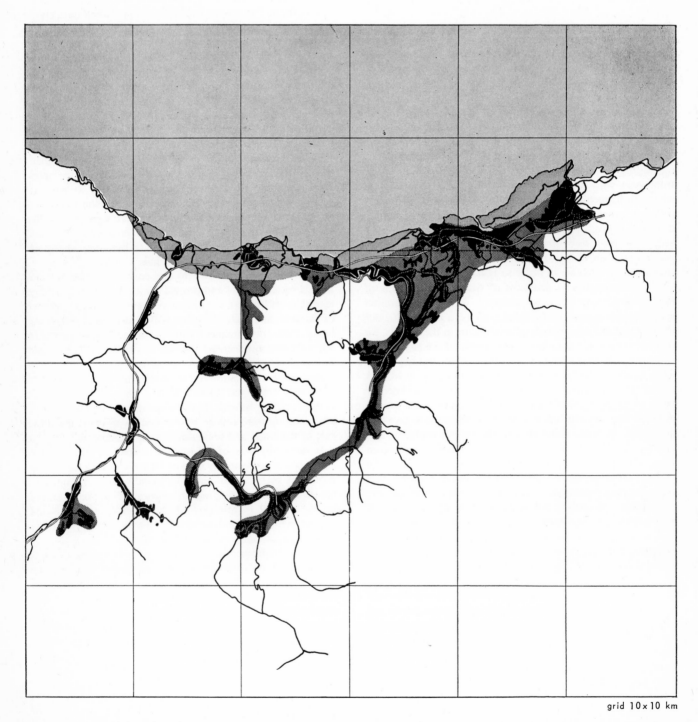

grid 10 x 10 km

km
0   10   20   30   40   50   60

0   10   20   30
miles

types of examples I recommend for the development of a methodology.

Another case from which I have learned a lot is that of regional development in the province of Guipuzcoa in northern Spain. There, because of the very considerable limitations of the landscape—the whole province consists of narrow valleys with steep hills and mountains on all sides—it was relatively easy for us to define the maximum area which could be reasonably taken over by a settlement. Once this area was relatively fixed, the settlement was deprived of any further expansion. Thus, the whole structure of the future pattern of human settlements in Guipuzcoa was simplified, and I think, has led to a more rational plan (fig. 383). In such cases we can turn the disadvantage of a difficult landscape into the advantage of the definition of the container in advance which will then help us to define the content as well. The relationship of container to content can be calculated on the basis of the physiological and texture forces which can be included in a certain space under the pressure of economic and safety forces.

In order fully to exploit this possibility of reduced Ekistic units within broader frames, we must also see whether we cannot isolate minor parts which could be good examples for the development of a methodology for minor Ekistic units. This is happening today in many of the major urban areas, which are being cut in reasonable or unreasonable ways by highways and divided into sectors separated from each other by major obstacles. In these cases it makes sense to try to develop a process for synthesis in the minor parts of the Ekistic unit scale, especially if they approximate minor types of communities such as class IV (the human community). I think, therefore, that we should select such areas as our moduli in carrying out efforts for the development of a better synthesis.

Assumptions and criteria

As soon as we have set goals and created the frame of time and space, we can begin to make assumptions about what needs to be done and how, and then compare them with certain criteria in order to discover whether they lead towards the attainment of our goals, and whether they can be implemented. It is of the greatest importance for our process that we define the proper assumptions and the proper criteria, otherwise the product of the mill through which we pass our alternative thoughts cannot be the proper one.

The selection of assumptions and criteria takes place continuously in each one of us for any of our actions. When an individual selects the location of his home, he has consciously or subconsciously made certain assumptions and selected the criteria which are important for him; they will be mostly economic, if he has a very low income, or aesthetic and social, if he has a high income, etc. However, this ability of the individual to select and compare criteria and then proceed to a synthesis is not shared by the community.

384

concern and criteria in relation to Ekistic units

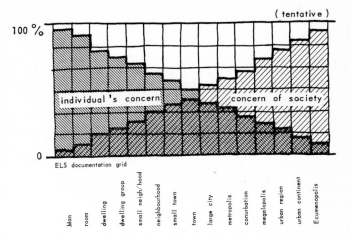

What we need in Ekistics is the ability to compute the total of our personal criteria regarding the city as an entity which can satisfy the entire community in its common needs, its parts in their own needs, and the individuals in their own individual needs.

At this point we must be aware of the fact that the concerns of the individual—and his criteria—do not develop parallel to those of the community. His main concern is usually for himself, and his concern diminishes from the neighbourhood to the community, the city, the metropolis, etc. On the contrary the concern of the broader society is, or should be, strong where the larger units are concerned, and diminished for the individual cases (fig. 384).

If we cannot find any solution on the basis of the assumptions made and the criteria set we still have to do something. We have to re-examine assumptions and criteria and finally consider whether we should not change our goals, whether we should and can adapt ourselves and even change our nature. René Dubos warns that 'a gift for adaption is now the key to survival',[17] and this is even more true for human settlements since it is in them that Man has to live.

Interconnection of parts

When goals, frames of time and space, assumptions and criteria have been agreed on we have reached the point at which we must consider how we can interconnect all parts, factors, elements and units related to a human settlement in such a way so as not to overlook any one of them. Whether we attach great or small—or any—importance to them is not the question at this point—it is part of the process of the system we are following. The question is, how can we be certain that we have not overlooked anything of importance

A. Ekistic units

1   2   3   4   5

B. elements

Nature   Man   Society   Shells   Networks   etc

C. functions

residence   commerce   industry   administration   defence   etc

D. factors

money   labour force   building materials   urban land   plans   etc

E. Ekistic units of higher order

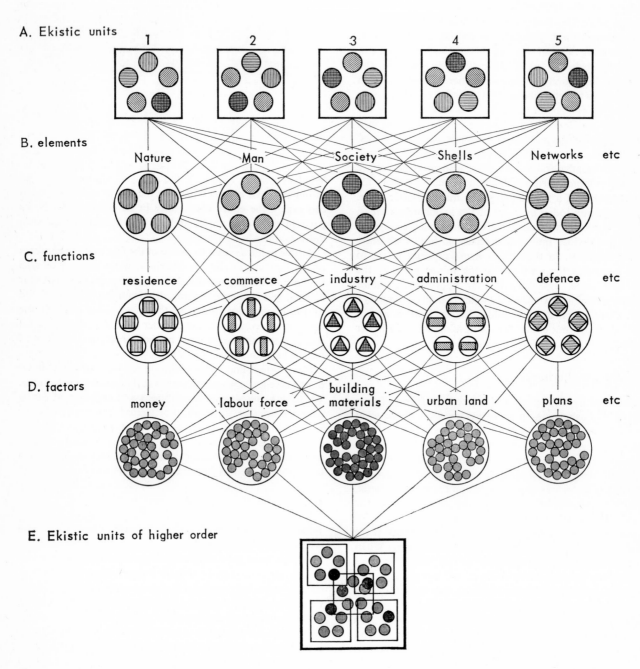

for our synthesis and how can we interconnect all parts to form a systematic whole?

This I will try to explain with the help of one diagram as in fig. 385. On the basis of this diagram, our study must be started and completed by the full recognition of the fact that a synthesis is based on Ekistic units. We should never forget that these are the basic units of any Ekistic study. They are the real human settlements regardless of size— whether they are houses, neighbourhoods, villages, cities, communities or major regions.

The diagram does not show the order of magnitude of Ekistic units. It merely shows the process of study from Ekistic units of one order to those of a different order. Let us assume that we are dealing with a city which is divided into communities. In such a case we have to proceed towards synthesis from the community level to the city level, and vice-versa. We must start from both ends, going from the parts to the whole and from the whole to the parts. The omission of either approach will lead to failure. By not employing the approach going from the whole to the parts, we will have a very weak overall conception, while a lack of the opposite approach may well lead to the non-recognition of the real texture of the fabric we are trying to build, and consequently to a failure to understand the scale of the synthesis.

In order to approach our problem by the previous diagram, we must be well acquainted with the elements leading to the synthesis of the whole. We spoke of the communities of a city as its elements, but we must realise that they form an entity, and that their parts—which may be neighbourhoods— must also be understood. This approach leads to the conclusion that the concepts of 'whole' and 'part' are very relative. For the purpose of a systematic approach we may call the city a whole, and its basic communities its parts; but if we are to understand the parts well, we must remember that every one of them is an entity with parts of its own which must also be comprehended.

Our conclusion is clear: the proper approach towards synthesis must fully recognise the whole as a composition of its parts, and the parts as the particles forming the whole. Ours is a process of moving from units of a lower order to those of a higher order, and vice-versa; in other words, conceiving, planning and building a human settlement as an independent unit or as a part of a broader one.

If this process is understood as reversible, we can proceed to grasp the notion of Ekistic units. To do so we must move to the second level of our synthesis, that is, to the elements of human settlements. It is not enough to regard Ekistic units, regardless of their size, as indivisible. We must realise that they consist of elements which have to be viewed as such. Since the beginning and the end of our effort is the Ekistic unit itself, we must remember that this unit can never be successful unless there is proper balance between its elements.

In order to attain this goal, we must study every element

separately and then see how they are all combined within the units. The units must be viewed not by size but by elements. We must move from those to the complete unit, and from the unit to its elements.

We begin with the study of specific elements. First comes Nature, which must be properly understood. But to study only one Ekistic unit is not enough. The study of a river as it crosses a city has no meaning unless we can study it in relation to a broader region. This means that we should take all the elements of Nature out of the Ekistic units and interconnect them in order to select those of its problems which are related to our settlements. In this way the overall picture of Nature in human settlements will be under study.

The same holds true for Man. He can be found in every Ekistic unit, and we should try to bring him into balance with the other elements; but Man and his problems must be conceived both as part of every Ekistic unit and as an independent subject matter. Studying Man in one settlement alone is not enough. If he is unemployed there, he may have employment opportunities in the next settlement. We must therefore take Man out of all Ekistic units and study him as a phenomenon related to a broader area. Only then can we conceive his problems and formulate reasonable policies concerning his role in the human settlements of our era. The same process will be applied to Society, Shells and the Networks of the community.

On the third level we must isolate the functions in order to study them separately. The function of residence influences every element we have studied on the second level, which in turn exists within every Ekistic unit at the first level. Now we must take the functions one by one. This will mean taking the function of residence out of all the elements and out of all Ekistic units and developing an understanding, a conception, a policy and a programme for the whole system of residence in our settlement. We must do the same with all other functions in human settlements—commerce, industry, administration, etc. All of them should be studied separately if we are to formulate proper conceptions of each of them.

We then move to the fourth level, that of factors. There is the money factor in every function—labour force, building materials, urban land factors, etc. In order to understand all these, we must do the same as we did for the functions and elements, that is, be able to isolate them from their applications to settlements and study them separately. The problem of urban land within all Ekistic units, since it is related to all elements and functions, must be conceived and an overall picture of the problems and solutions should be formulated.

We can then move to the fifth level, where a synthesis of all Ekistic units of a lower or higher order must be achieved. For example, first we must find out how to incorporate the policies conceived for the elements, the functions and the factors within our policies and programmes for human settlements. This may not be possible, which would mean that somewhere a mistake has been made, and must be discovered.

The whole pattern would have to be re-examined to see whether the conception of units or of elements or of one of the elements was in error.

The same should be done for activities and factors. Policies, programmes and plans should be checked until we have understood the Ekistic unit as an entity and within the wider framework of time and space. This process must continue until we are certain that we have correct conceptions, policies, programmes and plans for all our units, elements, activities and factors.

METHOD FOR SYNTHESIS

The I.D.E.A. and C.I.D. methods

After defining the frame which prepares the stage of synthesis we have to establish the process by which we will proceed from one stage to another in order to:
- cover the whole area in the proper time period;
- cover all aspects of our problem at the right time and at the right scale and details;
- create as tightly knit a system of answers to our problems as possible.

To achieve this we have developed the Isolation of Dimensions and Elimination of Alternatives (I.D.E.A.) Method, combined with the Continuously Increasing Dimensionality (C.I.D.) Method. This method had been under development for years, but was presented for the first time in 1966 when it was implemented in the study of the Developing Urban Detroit Area (UDA).

Before starting an analysis of the Method it is useful to point out that if the subject is small we may be able to cover it mainly by the isolation of several phenomena and the comparison of all possible alternatives. If the numbers of alternatives is large—which is the usual case—then a systematic approach for the gradual elimination of alternatives should be employed.

In order to make the I.D.E.A.-C.I.D. Method more easily understood I will present it not as a theoretical case, but as it was actually implemented in the Detroit project.

From the beginning of this study in 1964 it was recognised that the UDA suffered from the usual problems of having been studied in small pieces and for short periods of time; therefore only on the basis of the extrapolation of existing present trends. The only remedy for such a situation was to study the area on a scale large enough to include dynamic changes in the foreseeable future, in terms of both space and time. A preliminary study of how far the Urban Detroit Area could extend had indicated that it could cover a surface of 23,000 sq. miles, 200 miles from north to south and 150 miles from east to west, including 37 counties (25 in Michigan, nine in Ohio and three in Canada) (fig. 386).

Beyond these limits the UDA could not expand as such since it would enter the urban areas of Chicago to the west and Cleveland-Pittsburgh to the east.

The Urban Detroit Area has to be studied over several decades, since major projects sponsored by the Government or private industry are usually conceived many years before their implementation, and only prior physical planning can help towards their being conceived and implemented without the usual clashes between partial private plans which have been conceived early and general public plans which follow them at a time when commitments have already been undertaken by many decision-makers of urban development.

In order to attain the goals of this study we realised that we must proceed to the systematic conception of possible alternatives, then to their systematic evaluation and the elimination of those which were less satisfactory, and finally to the selection of the most suitable. To reach this end we had to *isolate* several phenomena in order of importance, at the phase and scale at which the examination was being made, and proceed by *eliminating* those solutions which were the weakest in relation to the phenomena selected. This method is the Isolation of Dimensions and Elimination of Alternatives Method or, the I.D.E.A. Method.

The application of this method makes it imperative that one start with phenomena of the greatest importance, and these are the ones which influence developments at the macro-scale. This requires, therefore, continuous increase of the scale so that greater numbers of parameters or dimensions can enter into every successive step, and phenomena of a lower order can gradually be taken into consideration. This is the Continuously Increasing Dimensionality Method or, the C.I.D. Method.

The method for synthesis is based on the simultaneous application of both methods of Isolation of Dimensions and Elimination of Alternatives and Continuously Increasing Dimensionality (I.D.E.A.-C.I.D. Method), and the study is organised by steps in each of which we isolate phenomena and eliminate alternatives at the proper scale.

Each step is divided into two movements, as follows:
Movement 1:
    Assumptions about the phenomena to be isolated which define the alternatives, that is the *input* into our system.
Movement 2:
    Criteria on the basis of which the alternatives that do not comply, or do not comply as well, with our goals can be eliminated, which leads to the output of the step.
The final output of every step becomes the input of the next one. The selection of phenomena, criteria and scales for every step is based on experience about their importance.

In the Detroit report we applied this method in eight steps and 16 movements, progressing from a theoretical number of tens of millions of alternatives to some tens, a few and finally

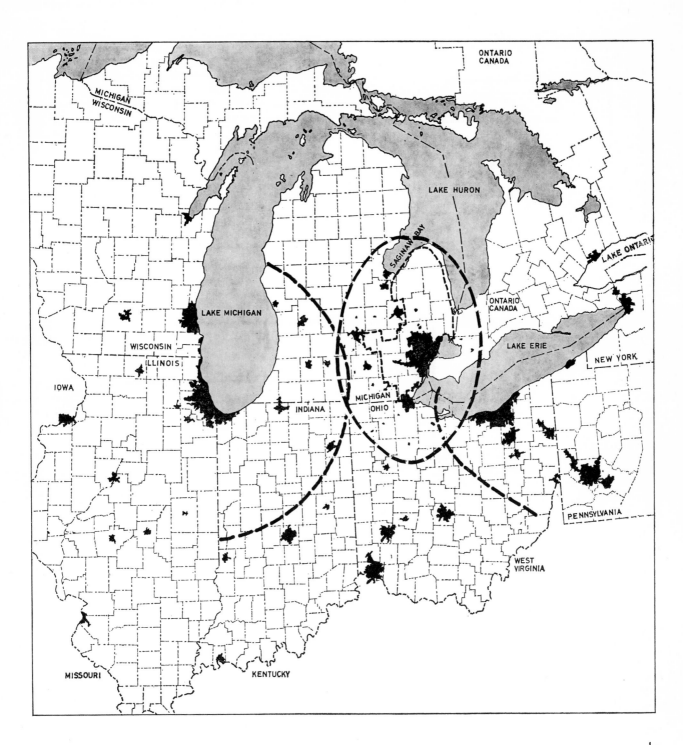

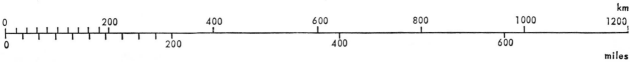

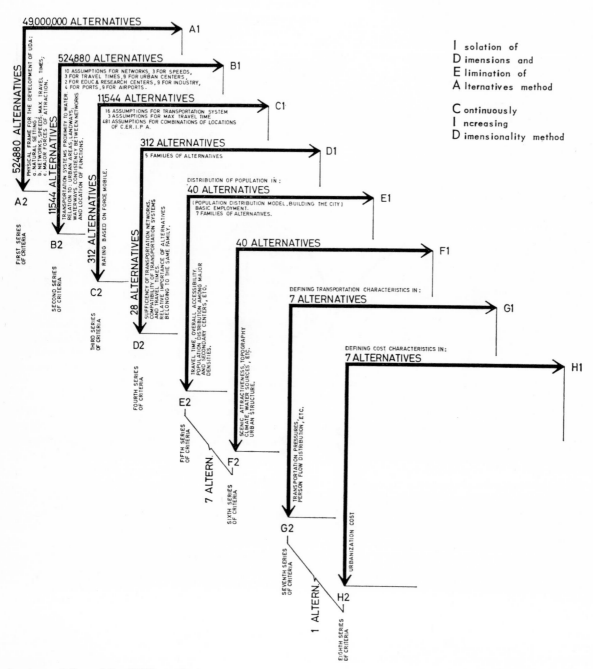

49.000.000 ALTERNATIVES → A1

524880 ALTERNATIVES → B1

10 ASSUMPTIONS FOR NETWORKS, 3 FOR SPEEDS,
3 FOR TRAVEL TIMES, 9 FOR URBAN CENTERS,
2 FOR EDUC & RESEARCH CENTERS, 9 FOR INDUSTRY,
4 FOR PORTS, 9 FOR AIRPORTS.

11544 ALTERNATIVES → C1

16 ASSUMPTIONS FOR TRANSPORTATION SYSTEM
3 ASSUMPTIONS FOR MAX TRAVEL TIME
481 ASSUMPTIONS FOR COMBINATIONS OF LOCATIONS
OF C.ER.I.P.A.

312 ALTERNATIVES → D1

5 FAMILIES OF ALTERNATIVES

DISTRIBUTION OF POPULATION IN:
40 ALTERNATIVES → E1

(POPULATION DISTRIBUTION MODEL, BUILDING THE CITY)
BASIC EMPLOYMENT.
7 FAMILIES OF ALTERNATIVES.

40 ALTERNATIVES → F1

DEFINING TRANSPORTATION CHARACTERISTICS IN:
7 ALTERNATIVES → G1

DEFINING COST CHARACTERISTICS IN:
7 ALTERNATIVES → H1

524880 ALTERNATIVES
A2

PHYSICAL FRAME FOR THE DEVELOPMENT OF UDA:
a. NATURAL SETTING;
b. NETWORKS, SPEEDS, MAX TRAVEL TIMES;
c. MAJOR FORCES OF ATTRACTION.

FIRST SERIES OF CRITERIA

11544 ALTERNATIVES
B2

TRANSPORTATION SYSTEMS PROXIMITY TO WATER
RELATION TO: URBAN AREAS, LANDWAYS,
WATERWAYS, CONSISTENCY BETWEEN NETWORKS
AND LOCATION OF FUNCTIONS.

SECOND SERIES OF CRITERIA

312 ALTERNATIVES
C2

RATING BASED ON FORCE MOBILE.

THIRD SERIES OF CRITERIA

28 ALTERNATIVES
D2

SUFFICIENCY OF TRANSPORTATION NETWORKS,
COMPATIBILITY OF TRANSPORTATION SYSTEMS
AND TRAVEL TIMES.
RELATIVE IMPORTANCE OF ALTERNATIVES
BELONGING TO THE SAME FAMILY.

FOURTH SERIES OF CRITERIA

E2

TRAVEL TIME, OVERALL ACCESSIBILITY,
POPULATION DISTRIBUTION AMONG MAJOR
AND SECONDARY CENTERS, ETC.

FIFTH SERIES OF CRITERIA

7 ALTERN.

F2

SCENIC ATTRACTIVENESS, TOPOGRAPHY
CLIMATE, WATER SOURCES, ETC.
URBAN STRUCTURE.

SIXTH SERIES OF CRITERIA

G2

TRANSPORTATION PRESSURES,
PERSON FLOW DISTRIBUTION, ETC.

SEVENTH SERIES OF CRITERIA

1 ALTERN.

H2

URBANIZATION COST

EIGHTH SERIES OF CRITERIA

I solation of
D imensions and
E limination of
A lternatives method

C ontinuously
I ncreasing
D imensionality method

**implementation of the IDEA method
in the Urban Detroit Area**

388

comparisons between several alternatives of
dynamic growth

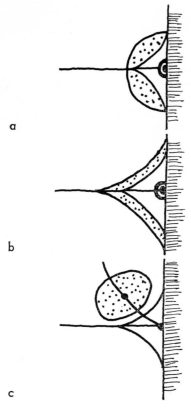

a

b

c

one (fig. 387). Necessarily, since many assumptions had to be made about probable conditions and solutions based on desirable goals, the implementation of this whole system has no finality at all. Decisions can only be taken by the population of the UDA; or in some cases by the administrations of the counties concerned, but the whole system does not need to change. If we feed in a new assumption at a certain step we will simply find some more corresponding alternatives and we will proceed with them. Because of similar considerations the last steps are even more indicative of how a final solution can be selected since, before this takes place, many decisions have to be made about basic assumptions of this study, such as the future lines of transportation of a high order, the creation of a new Urban Centre of a high order to relieve the pressures on the city of Detroit and allow it to develop properly, etc.

Simulation models

In order to facilitate the application of the I.D.E.A.-C.I.D., or in simpler terms, the I.D.E.A. Method, we need a number of models which allow for the simulation of situations under

certain conditions, and the comparison and evaluation of several alternatives based on the assumptions made. Such models are sometimes very simple (as the models for the rating of basic functions in relation to other functions and localities) and can be studied on the basis of simple calculations; or are so complicated that they require the use of computers, such as the accessibility and comparison models which compare alternatives under varying local conditions.

All these models can be elaborated in very great detail and fed into computers. This is not necessary, however. On the contrary, in this early phase it was thought much more practical to proceed using alternately simple and detailed elaborated models in accordance with the actual needs and possibilities of each case, in each separate step. In any case we must be aware that every step of our work needs different types of models depending on the scale and dimensions we are using and the Ekistic unit we are dealing with. I find, for example, that it is almost ridiculous to use transportation models in too small communities where the traffic volume is very small.

The models used in this study are the following:
- a. Projections of urbanisation trends based on the change of land use from agricultural to urban.
- b. Projections of general growth trends.
- c. Projections of densities of habitation (residential densities).
- d. Projections of population distribution based on established trends.
- e. Force-mobile model.
- f. Population distribution model (several variations of the parameters entering were attempted—use of computer).
- g. Comparison models (of the various alternatives with local conditions—use of computer).
- h. Transportation models (use of computer).
- i. Cost models.
- j. Human community models.

In addition there is a necessity for the use of abstract models which can illustrate the impact of new forces on the existing structure and form. These can be very simple initially and become more elaborate in the more advanced phases. If, for example, we want to study the possible expansions of the settlement, assuming several alternatives for the location of the new central forces, we proceed as follows. We build tentative models showing several possibilities, such as the related problems for the centre, the arterial system, etc. (fig. 388) and conclude by the selection of the most reasonable alternatives which then have to be calculated carefully and compared with corresponding mathematical models.

Present and new trends

The next question that arises is how we can conceive future alternatives which can be compared in the different steps determined by the models to be used. The usual mistake is one of relying only on an extrapolation of existing trends. Because of forces inherent in all settlements, there is a certain course of development which is followed by the city itself. Unless major changes take place, this course is not expected to alter, and can be foreseen within reasonable limits of approximation.

Because of this, the conventional method of foreseeing and planning for the future is based on the extrapolation of present trends in an attempt to determine where the present course is leading. If this is done for such problems as transportation, it will result in the planning of new arteries to take care of the existing trends as they develop. Because of this approach, the new action taken in major cities tends to serve existing trends, and by doing so intensifies and stabilises them. Even if there was a natural tendency to change the present trends in some section of the city (because, for example, of the construction of a major factory in a different location) the opening of new arteries in accordance with the existing trends keeps development closer to the projected lines than it would have been otherwise.

It is quite clear that such a course leads to impossible situations. It would have been all right if existing trends were to lead to a better city, in which case it would have been reasonable to extrapolate existing trends. This, however, is not the case at all. On the contrary, experience has shown that existing trends create a snowballing process around existing centres of activities, existing axes of transportation, etc., and lead to congestion and paralysis.

We should use this method of extrapolation of present trends into the future as carefully as we can, not in order to show where we must go, but to find out *where we are going* now and what such trends will lead to. If the present trends are leading towards impossible situations, we must discover these situations, determine the dangers created for the city and the problems it will have to face in the future.

On the basis of these considerations we proceeded for the UDA to extrapolate the city's growth through expansion to the year 2000 by five different techniques. To do this we adapted existing models to the requirements of this study and developed new ones. The five techniques are as follows:

° *Projections based on urbanisation trends:* In order to define these trends we based our observations on the change in land-use from agricultural to urban, for which very good statistics were available. This was done because the change in land-use between the years 1900 and 1960, for which we have data every 10 years, allows us to derive an equation for the change which we subsequently applied to the whole study area as fig. 389 shows.

° *Projections based on general growth trends:* The trends in the participation of each county in the total population of UDA observed from 1930 to 1964 were projected in order to estimate future population distributions by county.

° *Projections based on residential densities:* By extrapolating

the trends in density changes observed from 1940 to 1960 in a way that takes into consideration the observed facts that lower densities near urban centres tend to increase at a higher rate than high densities, as well as the effect of saturation limits, we obtained a picture of the future size and shape of the city in the form of iso-density contours (fig. 390).

○ *Projections based on established trends:* Trends in the change of more composite phenomena were studied, such as facilities, transportation, densities in relation to local factors and saturation levels, etc. On this basis, ratings were given to the various localities in relation to their overall growth potential, and, assuming again that present trends will continue, the future distribution of population in the UDA was estimated by the extrapolation of these trends.

○ *Projections by the population distribution model based on the concept of accessibility:* A computerised mathematical model using the concept of accessibility was developed for the distribution of population in the study area. We are not yet sure how well this model corresponds to the phenomena themselves, especially as regards their details, but the use of several types of accessibility models shows that in the projection of the basic phenomena about wider areas, we get a good simulation of reality (fig. 391).

Some of these methods lead to conclusions which are comparable. Thus, by comparing and combining the projections obtained by these techniques we came to conclusions about which parts of the projections are more valid.

A study of the results of these projections about the urban area to be created by the year 2000 if present trends continue, shows that Detroit which in 1960 had a population of 3,540,000 within its urbanised area, will have about 8,000,000 people in the year 2000. It is easily concluded that as the city of Detroit already has very great problems and difficulties in its central area it would be unreasonable to expect it to cope with future pressures exerted by 4,460,000 more people (an increase of 126 per cent), which implies an even greater percentage increase in the number of cars, the movements of people and goods, etc.

The analysis of the continuation of the present course leads to the conclusion that it is most necessary to change it. This is theoretically justified for all such urban areas, and specifically demonstrated for Detroit. In order to achieve this, goals must be set which can lead to a solution of the problems which make the present course unacceptable. These goals will have to be set further in the future and will define the desires for a better urban area which will avoid the weaknesses of the present and also the future towards which we are being led by present trends. As these goals will be set for a later date, in this case for the year 2000, it will be necessary to connect the situation defined by the future goals to the existing situation, in order to estimate how we can proceed from one to the other. We

389

Detroit area project

expansion of area having more than 75% non-farm land from 1900 to 1959

projections to years 1970, 1980 and 2000

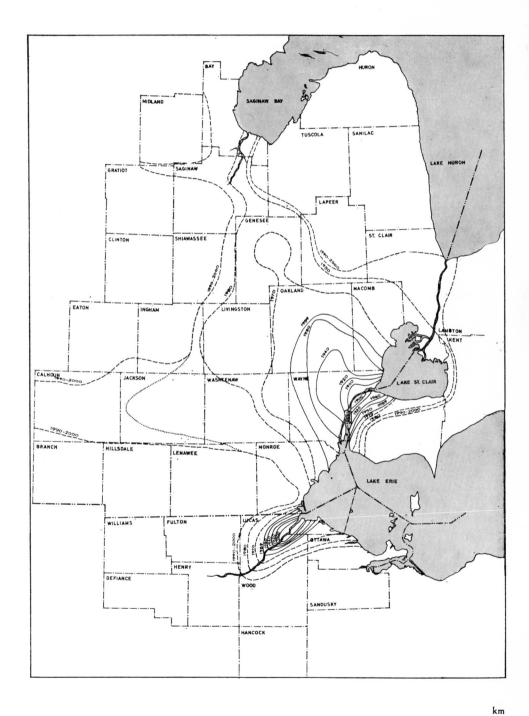

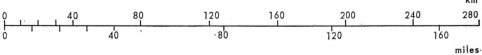

Detroit area project

estimated isodensity contours for year 2000
corresponding to a total population in **U.D.A.** of
13,500,000 inhabitants

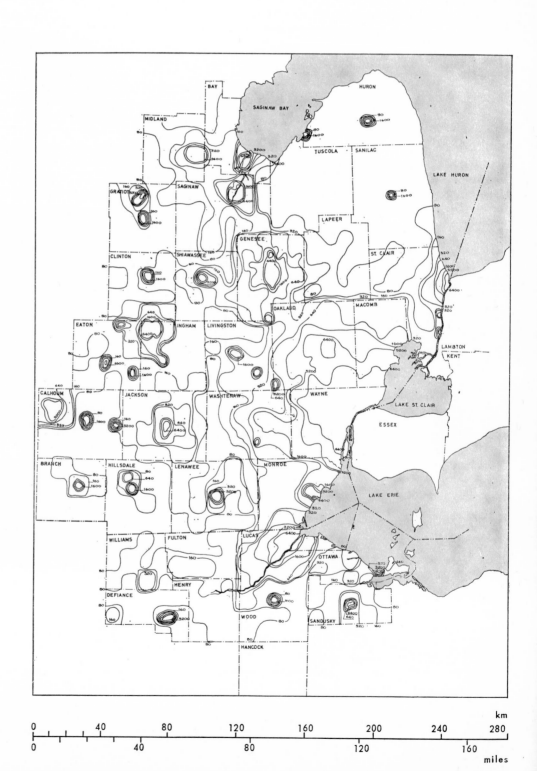

km

| 0 | 40 | 80 | 120 | 160 | 200 | 240 | 280 |

0   40   80   120   160

miles

391

Detroit area project

population distribution by accessibility model for the year 2000
single centre in **Detroit** – radial configuration of the higher order transportation networks—
speeds 100 and 250 m.p.h. – maximum travel time 30 minutes

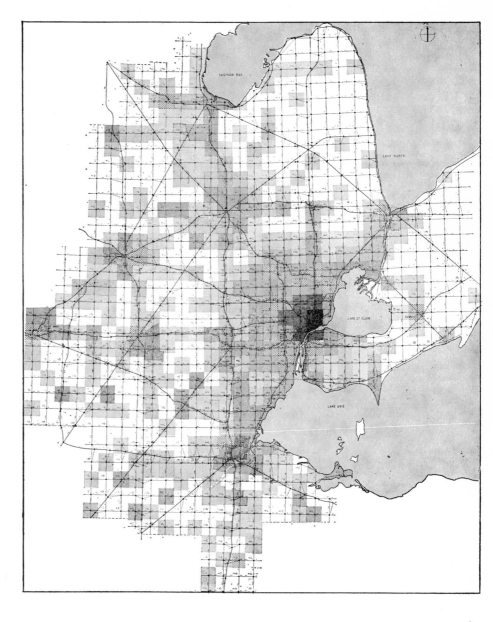

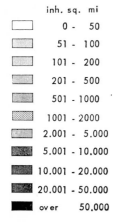

inh. sq. mi

	0 - 50
	51 - 100
	101 - 200
	201 - 500
	501 - 1000
	1001 - 2000
	2.001 - 5.000
	5.001 - 10.000
	10.001 - 20.000
	20.001 - 50.000
	over 50.000

matrix of alternatives for the Urban Detroit Area

step A1: input

PARAMETERS OF PEOPLE		PARAMETERS OF FUNCTIONS																													
		URBAN CENTRES					MAJOR EDUCATIONAL AND RESEARCH CENTRES					INDUSTRIAL POLES					PORTS					AIRPORTS					OTHER FUNCTIONS				
		1	2	3	4	5	1	2	3	4	5	1	2	3	4	5	1	2	3	4	5	1	2	3	4	5	1	2	3	4	5
POPULATION	1																														
	2																														
	3																														
	4																														
	5																														
DENSITIES	1																														
	2																														
	3																														
	4																														
	5																														
TRANSPORTATION NETWORKS	1																														
	2																														
	3																														
	4																														
	5																														
SPEEDS OF TRANSPORTATION	1																														
	2																														
	3																														
	4																														
	5																														
MAX. TRAVEL TIME	1																														
	2																														
	3																														
	4																														
	5																														

This matrix which includes eleven types of parameters with 5 assumptions for each parameter leads to the conclusion that there are 49 million possible alternatives.

may, for example, desire a situation which is reasonable but not feasible for the target period of the study, or which may be unreasonable for any period.

We proceed by foreseeing alternatives and applying the Isolation of Dimensions and Elimination of Alternatives Method. We start with the question of how many alternatives there are about the future. If we consider that we want to base our alternatives on some basic assumptions about major urban centres, major industrial concentrations, major educational and research centres, major ports and airports and other important functions, as well as on different assumptions about population, densities of residence and work, transportation networks, speeds of transportation, maximum travel time and some other parameters, we shall have to estimate the number of alternatives that these basic assumptions create. If we present this in a theoretical matrix of possible alternatives, we will find that even if we accept ten alternatives for every one of the factors mentioned, we will be heading towards a total number of alternative combinations of the order of billions.

Implementation of the method

For practical purposes the process of evaluation and elimination started with an initial number of 49 million alternatives. This was a theoretical number corresponding to five assumptions for each basic parameter of the urban system (fig. 392).

393

matrix of alternatives for the Urban Detroit Area

step A: output and step B: input

524,880 alternatives

PARAMETERS OF PEOPLE		PARAMETERS OF FUNCTIONS																														
		URBAN CENTRES									EDUC. AND RESEARCH CENTRES		INDUSTRIAL POLES									PORTS				AIRPORTS							
		I	II	III	IV	V	VI	VII	VIII	IX	o	n	I	II	III	IV	V	VI	VII	VIII	IX	I	VII	VIII	IX	I	II	III	IV	V	VI	VII	VIII	IX
TRANSPORTATION NETWORKS	N_{o1}																																		
	N_{o2}																																		
	N_{o3}																																		
	N_{o4}																																		
	N_{o5}																																		
	N_{n1}																																		
	N_{n2}																																		
	N_{n3}																																		
	N_{n4}																																		
	N_{n5}																																		
SETS OF TRANSPORTATION SPEEDS	S_L																																		
	S_M																																		
	S_H																																		
MAX. TRAVEL TIME	45'																																		
	30'																																		
	20'																																		

Following considerations made in step A we reach an output of eight types of parameters (with two to nine assumptions for each parameter) which lead to a total of 524,880 alternatives.

In step A an effort was made to go from the theoretical thesis of five assumptions for each basic parameter to more meaningful ones. For example, as far as major functions are concerned, the consideration of the main transportation networks in the physical space of UDA led to the determination of the more important nodal points for their location. The number of assumptions referring to location of major functions was adjusted accordingly.

As far as parameters referring to people and their movements are concerned, a medium projection (equal to 15 million people by the year 2000), has been accepted for population; the study of the most probable patterns of communication networks, in combination with various sets of speeds, led to the acceptance of eight transportation net-

works; three variations of maximum travel time have been considered. Finally, densities have not been included in the parameters of the problem, because it was thought advisable to let the total human settlement acquire shape and texture corresponding to the assumptions made about functions and other parameters. Thus only a ceiling for densities is specified, leaving the decisions about them for future phases. The above assumptions and eliminations led to an output of 524,800 alternatives.

In step B the transportation networks were considered and those failing to satisfy a logical functional hierarchy were eliminated (fig. 393). The nodal points selected in step A for the location of major functions were further evaluated and the weakest among them were eliminated. The consistency

matrix of alternatives for the Urban Detroit Area
step B: output and step C: input
11,544 alternatives

This shows only the lefthand side of the total matrix consisting of 481 columns with all combinations of major locations.

PARAMETERS OF PEOPLE			PRESENT TRENDS MAJOR FUNCTIONS AT PRESENT LOCATIONS C_0 ER_0 I_0 P_0 A_0 0	Serial Number	PARAMETERS OF PEOPLE			MAJOR FUNCTIONS AT PRESENT LOCATIONS C_0 ER_0 I_0 P_0 A_0 0'	NEW ALTERNATIVES — MAJOR FUNCTIONS AT NEW LOCATIONS (C_0, ER_0, I_0 P_0/P_1/P_2/P_4, I_1, I_2; columns 1–37)
N_o1	S_L	mtt 45'		1	N_n1	S_L	mtt 45'		
		mtt 30'		2			mtt 30'		
		mtt 20'		3			mtt 20'		
	S_H	mtt 45'		4		S_H	mtt 45'		
		mtt 30'		5			mtt 30'		
		mtt '20'		6			mtt 20'		
N_o2	S_L	mtt 45'		7	N_n2	S_L	mtt 45'		
		mtt 30'		8			mtt 30'		
		mtt 20'		9			mtt 20'		
	S_H	mtt 45'		10		S_H	mtt 45'		
		mtt 30'		11			mtt 30'		
		mtt 20'		12			mtt 20'		
N_o3	S_L	mtt 45'		13	N_n3	S_L	mtt 45'		
		mtt 30'		14			mtt 30'		
		mtt 20'		15			mtt 20'		
	S_H	mtt 45'		16		S_H	mtt 45'		
		mtt 30'		17			mtt 30'		
		mtt 20'		18			mtt 20'		
N_o5	S_L	mtt 45'		19	N_n5	S_L	mtt 45'		
		mtt 30'		20			mtt 30'		
		mtt 20'		21			mtt 20'		
	S_H	mtt 45'		22		S_H	mtt 45'		
		mtt 30'		23			mtt 30'		
		mtt 20'		24			mtt 20'		

Following considerations made in step B we again reach an output of eight types of parameters but with a smaller number of values assumed for each parameter (two to eight) which lead to a total of 11,544 alternatives.

In the matrix C_0, C_1, C_2, C_3, indicate the location of the major urban centre C at the nodal points 0, 1, 2, 3, respectively. The same method of notation is used for the alternate locations of the remaining major functions as well. Example: P_2 denotes the location of the major port P at the nodal point 2.

between assumptions referring to Networks and assumptions referring to locations of major functions was critically examined and the inconsistent combinations, i.e. Networks with radial configuration coupled to locations of major functions determined from transportation lines of grid-iron configuration, were rejected. As a result, the number of alternatives was reduced to 11,544, which is the output of step B.

In step C the force-mobiles corresponding to the 11,544 alternatives were evaluated on the basis of a simple model used for the rating of groupings of major functions (fig. 394). This led to the selection of the 312 alternatives corresponding to the most reasonable force-mobiles.

In step D the surviving transportation networks were further evaluated and the weakest of them were eliminated because they were not considered sufficient for the proper servicing of the region. The compatability of assumptions referring to maximum travel times with the assumed transportation systems were critically examined and the weakest combinations, as for example, high sets of speeds coupled to high travel times, were eliminated. Finally, families of alternatives with the same configuration of Networks and the same locations of major functions were considered, and the highest ranking group from each family as obtained from the force-mobile model was retained. The output of step D was 28 alternatives.

In steps E and F a new dimension was introduced, i.e. the basic employment and its spatial distribution over the

395

**Detroit area project population distribution by
accessibility model for the year 2000**

**twin centres in Port Huron Area – grid-iron
configuration of the higher order transportation
networks – speeds 60 and 100 m.p.h. – maximum travel
time 45 minutes**

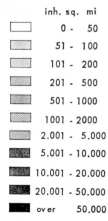

inh. sq. mi
0 - 50
51 - 100
101 - 200
201 - 500
501 - 1000
1001 - 2000
2.001 - 5.000
5.001 - 10.000
10.001 - 20.000
20.001 - 50.000
over 50,000

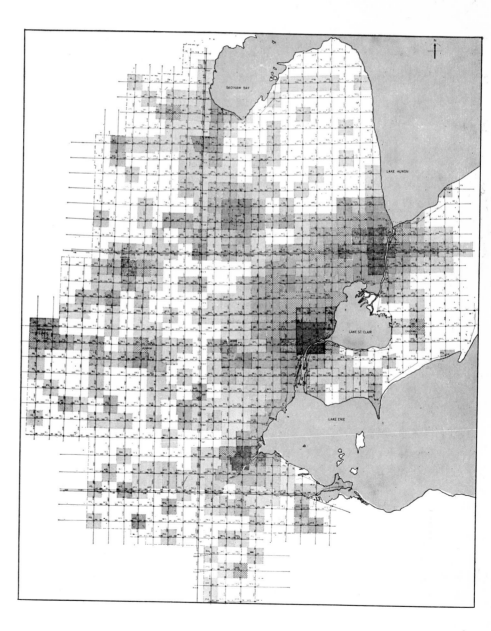

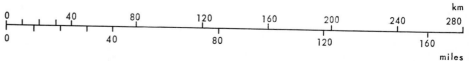

Theory

396

**Detroit area project population distribution by
accessibility model for the year 2000**

**twin centre in Toledo Area – grid-iron configuration
of the higher order transportation networks – speeds
100 and 250 m.p.h. – maximum travel time
30 minutes**

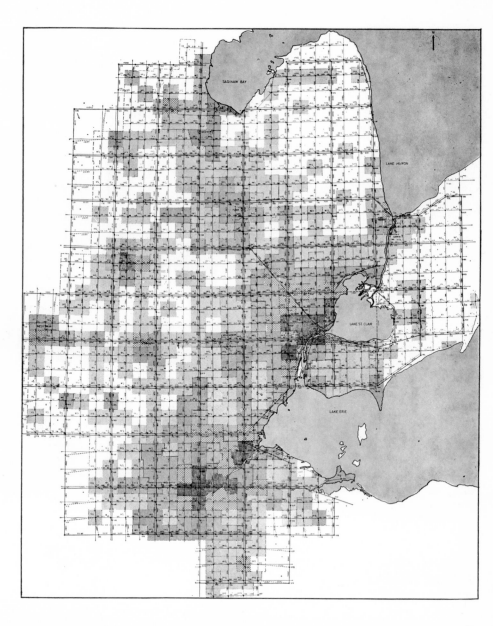

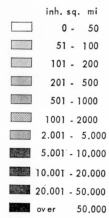

inh. sq. mi

	0 - 50
	51 - 100
	101 - 200
	201 - 500
	501 - 1000
	1001 - 2000
	2.001 - 5.000
	5.001 - 10.000
	10.001 - 20.000
	20.001 - 50.000
	over 50.000

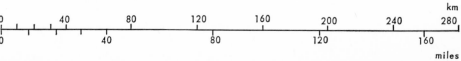

397

**Detroit area project population distribution by
accessibility model for the year 2000**

twin centre in **Port Huron Area** – grid-iron configuration
of the higher order transportation networks – speeds
100 and 250 m.p.h. – maximum travel time
30 minutes

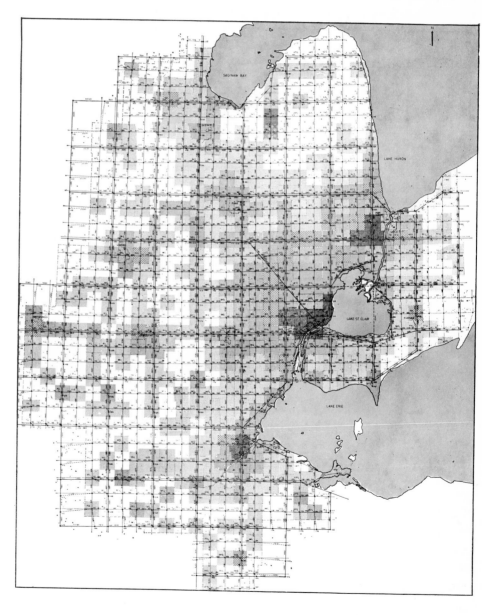

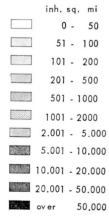

inh. sq. mi

	0 - 50
	51 - 100
	101 - 200
	201 - 500
	501 - 1000
	1001 - 2000
	2.001 - 5.000
	5.001 - 10.000
	10.001 - 20.000
	20.001 - 50.000
	over 50.000

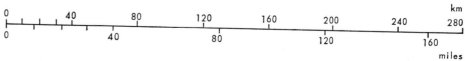

implementation of the I.D.E.A. and C.I.D. methods in an auditorium

one phase of our work

spatial needs of man		personal					social	
		intellect	sight	senses	hearing	body	max density	capacity
criteria	economic					1 person/m²	1 person/m²	2 person/m²
	time							
	psychologic		max. distance 60 m		max distance 40 m			
	safety	balconies of no more than 45°				1 person/m²		

UDA, leading to an increase in the number of alternatives from 28 to 40. The total population assumed for the year 2000 was distributed by means of a mathematical model based on accessibility to employment, and the resulting population and density distribution patterns were evaluated. The evaluation took into account criteria based on the five Ekistic elements, i.e. Nature, Man, Society, Shells and Networks. Seven alternatives represent the output of these steps. Two of these alternatives are shown in figs. 395, 396.

Steps G and H elaborated on the transportation and cost characteristics of the seven alternatives. Criteria such as pressures on the Central Business District of Detroit, cost of transportation networks, cost of urbanisation, etc., were used, leading to one alternative (fig. 397).

It may be asked how this method works for minor settlements, or for single shells. To answer this I will present the case of one auditorium. We must first define the required space. We may then find that this is larger than the scale permitted on the basis of economic criteria. The result may be a multi-level solution with balconies allowing us to respect all the assumptions and stand the test of all criteria. Such action has to take place on a two-dimensional table such as the one on which every phase of the I.D.E.A. Method is based, a table presenting the action in the two movements of assumptions and evaluations, and the tests (fig. 398).

BOOK FOUR

ACTION

*'Zeus, who laid it down that man
Must in sorrow learn and through
Pain to wisdom find his way.'*
AESCHYLUS *Agamemnon*

I am very often asked why I insist on working in theory
and in practice; why I need to travel in both the
rational and empirical worlds; why I insist on action
and I answer: how else can I learn? This book contains
four chapters:

CHAPTER TEN

EKISTIC THERAPY

MEANING OF THERAPY

Therapy, development and evolution

In this book Man is going to take action in his hands. He will decide that description alone constitutes an important but passive attitude and the formulation of laws and theories has meaning only if it helps us to create better human settlements. To achieve this, Man will undertake prescriptive action and develop a prescriptive science or a technology for settlements, especially for minor Ekistic units, an Ekistic art.

His action will mean a therapy for human needs. When transportation in a metropolis is impossible, a corresponding treatment is necessary. When a city does not have enough houses for its citizens, then new houses should be built; when its area is small an expansion is necessary. When there is not enough space for an expansion next to the existing settlement, as happened with the congested ancient Greek cities, then a new city must be created. When a new need cannot be served by existing settlements, a new port-town, or industrial, or administrative city must be created.

In this sense therapy does not mean repair, but real treatment of real human problems; therefore therapy contains the idea of a development of a settlement, and even of its evolution into a settlement, or a system of settlements, of a higher order.

Every Ekistic action, because its aim is to serve the human needs of individuals or societies which exist, or whose future existence has been predicted, has the meaning of a therapy of Ekistic needs, whether they are related to diseases, or to development, and to evolution.

In the same way in which the goal of diagnosis is to understand the real human needs and problems, regardless of their causes, therapy has to treat them in order to serve Man in the best possible way.

I use terms from medicine again and this is not coincidental. The reason is, that not only do I recognise several similarities between the organisms being treated by medicine and settlements which can be wisely exploited; but also feel that it is only medicine which has made the great step forward of not considering the problem or the disease an ontological one, but as a dynamic situation, and has gradually been oriented not to fighting the disease but to supporting the patient. This is what we expect from Ekistic therapy: the support of the patient, that is the settlement, or even better, its content—Man and Society.

In spite of these explanations the use of terms taken from medicine may be dangerous and misleading, if we do not remember that in medicine the task even though very important is limited to the re-establishment of balances which have natural limits, while in settlements, therapy can go beyond this point and treat situations by creating new organs or even organisms and biological individuals of a higher order. The techniques in medicine and Ekistics are in many cases the same but the tasks and the possibilities are to a certain extent different.

Before closing I want to clarify one important point. I said that therapy goes beyond repairs, to development and even to evolution, and it is at this point that I want to insert a note of warning. Evolution in Nature takes place by selection and survival of the fittest; so that in a group of organisms we will recognise changing features in later generations. In settlements, however, even though the case might be the same and we may recognise changed features in later generations of settlements, it may also be different since evolution may take place in the very same settlement which over the years can change not only by developing into a larger and more complex settlement—as it happens with organisms in Nature —but also into a *new* kind of settlement—something which never happens in Nature.

In this respect again human settlements differ from cells and natural organisms. They can develop as they do, but they can also change right there in their original location, out of the same shell into a new species. Such a statement confirms once again our initial attitude, that settlements are biological individuals of a higher order than natural organisms, and of a different order. The difference is that natural organisms must necessarily die while human settlements can avoid death.

Need for proper therapy

The possibility we have of treating a settlement either in order to heal some limited disease and return it to its original condition or its approximate original condition, or to develop it further or even assist it to evolve into a new species, shows that therapy is not a simple action. We cannot say, as we usually do, that a settlement requires therapy answering a need; we have to point out that it needs the right therapy, and that discovering this right therapy is our main task.

In order to achieve this we have to find the balance between continuing the same order and solutions—which may be very wise—and changing them completely—which again may be very wise. The fact is that we need the past; also that, especially in our days, an increasing rate of change may be indispensable. We have to develop the ability to decide to what extent we will respect the past and to what extent we will change it. This is the most crucial point in our act of therapy for human needs through settlements.

In forming his settlements, Man tended, consciously or unconsciously, towards some ideal forms which represented idealisations of the settlements built in every period. As the settlements changed, so did the ideals; but in most cases Man moved ahead with his settlements rather in the way donkeys trot after a carrot hanging from the end of a stick tied to their heads. The ideal was continually being improved upon by Man who was always trying to reach it but always lagged behind, even at the peak of his development in each period.

Beginning in the eighteenth century, and all through the nineteenth century and much more so in the twentieth, Man lost his ability to take satisfactory Ekistic action where his settlements were concerned. He also lost his ability to visualise a total ideal environment. The solutions proposed, such as the garden city, covered only minor parts of the contemporary human settlement. It is characteristic that the two models proposed for the solution of the overall problem, the 'Radiant City' by Le Corbusier and 'Broadacre City' by Frank Lloyd Wright,[1] are actually utopias which cannot and should not be implemented for many obvious reasons.

Ekistic action has been intensified lately, but on the whole it has become more confused. There is an imperative need today for action in the field of human settlements, but many people are confused about the direction it must take. They see much more construction now than during any previous time, larger buildings, larger cities, more complicated networks of communications, and they come to believe that Man is doing his best. It is true that Man is acting in Ekistics much more today (and at a phenomenal speed) than he did in many previous periods. But it is also true that this activity is not being carried out properly.

In absolute figures the present effort is in many respects (the manpower mobilised, the total capital involved and the mechanical means used) much greater than that of the past. But in relative terms it is not. When Athens was reconstructing its city and building the famous monuments on the Acropolis, it was probably using a percentage of the total income of the city, and probably that of its allies, that would be unimaginable today. The same must have been true when cities were completely destroyed and then rebuilt within a very short period of time, in other eras, when Man was a real builder and could mobilise the entire community for construction and development. There is reason to believe that on a relative basis the total effort is weaker today than it was during several important periods of the past.

However, if we do not act wisely in this field today, we will be in great danger. Since everything is on a large scale and taking place at a high speed, a major mistake made in the choice of the course we will take might lead to disaster within a very short time. In the past any new, utopian proposal for cities would have been the subject of careful scrutiny. There was seldom need to hurry in implementing a new idea and indeed, little means for any rapid technical realisation. Today the possibility of realising a quick decision affecting many people and human settlements on a large scale is much greater. Nicholas Berdyaev has said that 'utopias now appear much more realizeable than one used to think. We are now faced with a very different new worry: how to prevent realization'.[2] Utopias in the field of Ekistics have always been dangerous, but they can be even more so today. We have already seen some new cities corresponding to a theoretical utopia being built, which give us plenty of reasons to believe that such utopian conceptions are not at all justifiable.

We behave strangely in the field of human settlements. When we want to build a factory, a school, a university or a hospital, it at once becomes the subject of a very conscientious analysis by all kinds of experts, the subject of long discussions and even of experimental efforts. Even so the results may be discarded as unsatisfactory. But if we regard the man-hours invested in the conception, study and realisation of different types of Ekistic units, we will be amazed at the proportional decrease apparent as we go to larger units. To remodel a room, we may spend as many hours (even days) in the conception, planning, designing and selection of materials as in the actual execution of the project. In other words, the cost of man-hours may be equal in the preparation and implementation stages of the project. For a house, the percentage of man-hours in the preparation stage drops; and for a major building the percentage drops still more. For the larger Ekistic units—cities and metropolitan areas—the amount of effort expended in conception and preparation of the project is infinitesimal in relation to that required for the actual construction effort. It is really unbelievable how small an effort we make for the preparation of the broader Ekistic units of human settlements (fig. 399).

In the small units, we continue to search for something more rational and more suitable for our purposes. Yet in human settlements as a whole, where all specific actions and functions are coordinated, we tend to indulge in sweeping but vague statements, when what we need are the optimum solutions for any given time on the basis of known data, predictions and those ideals which can be rationally justified.

An enlightening example of the extent to which our attitude is confused because of the confusion regarding the scale of phenomena, is that of the therapy that is suggested for different levels of Ekistic units. Physical planning, especially in the highly developed industrialised countries, has lately been taking on non-human qualities. Several people have criticised this type of planning, the most ardent of whom is Jane Jacobs who, in her book, *The Death and Life of Great American Cities*, has given a good example of how planning went wrong in the minor scale of the metropolitan area. I cannot agree with her when she tries, in an analysis of a problem on a micro-scale, to draw conclusions about the middle and macro-scale of the city; and I cannot agree with her when she bases her experience mostly on one type of area and generalises from it. We must understand her book as an appeal to respect qualities and values which the expanding metropolitan areas have not recognised as valid *in the micro-scales*, not as a directive for the totality of 'the Great American Cities'.[3]

The dangers caused by the lack of proper diagnosis of the real disease are accentuated by the fact that we cannot recognise the proper therapy and thus create worse situations. Such is the case with the question of standards: where only one is needed (for example performance standards for building materials), we have many. In other cases we use one standard where several should be employed. For instance, in climates which require special standards of housing ventilation or insulation, people tend to use the standards developed for quite different countries with completely different conditions. This is especially true of standards developed in the more technologically developed countries; very often the less developed countries too readily accept the standards conceived for the others and try to apply them without recasting them according to their own different conditions.

Here is a characteristic example: certain economically developed Western countries have formed building codes and housing standards for their own use which specify one room for a maximum of two persons, a certain number of facilities in each house, etc. These regulations have gradually been codified and have become a 'gospel' being preached to the whole world. So we come to witness phenomena such as that of the city of New Delhi where anyone wanting to build a house must conform to these very strict standards. The result is that while the central part of the town forms a tightly controlled municipality, a great number of people are obliged to live far outside the city simply because they do not have the means to conform to the imposed Westernised standards. Such methods have led to strange results: they no longer serve Man, but serve instead some rather abstract concepts with no justification whatsoever. No one has ever suggested that if people cannot afford to have 2,500 calories

399

effort made for the preparation and implementation of Ekistic action

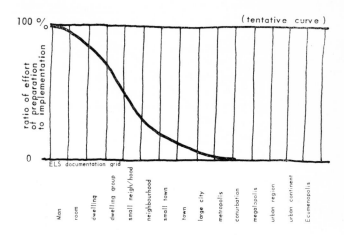

per day they should not eat at all; but in most places in the world people are being told that if they do not have enough money to build what the engineers consider suitable, they must not build at all. These ideas are remnants of an obsolete mentality, a mentality which must be abandoned.

Speaking of the weaknesses due to misuse of the concept of standardisation, it must also be said that an awakening process is beginning. Attempts are being made for a universal standardisation of building materials. This, to a certain extent, is a reasonable measure provided that we are aware of the necessity to standardise dimensions, but not necessarily qualities. There are, for example, areas of the world where economic standards and local conditions justify the use of cast-iron pipes for sewage. In other areas the most reasonable solution may be clay pipes. The attempt to standardise dimensions is reasonable in such a case, but standardising the type of material is unreasonable. It is unreasonable for Middle Eastern countries, with the longest tradition in brick-making, to try to implement British standards of brick quality, the conception of which has been based on completely different criteria. The tendency towards standardisation of building materials is justified, and it will mean great progress provided that in every case we are able to define not only the agreed standards, but also the conditions under which these standards are reasonable. These conditions should be economic, social, biological, technological, etc.

It is perhaps easier to attempt to impose standards on means of transportation and communications, since these depend greatly on machines which are the same the world over. Even though the number of cars may vary from country to country, the same general types of cars exist everywhere. Standardisation of road, railroad and airport dimensions is

400

degree of standardisation in buildings and other parts of human settlements

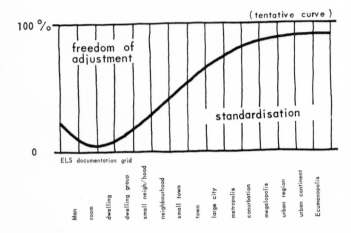

therefore reasonable; but it is wrong to impose identical standards of construction and materials for all types of facilities unless we are sure that these standards give the best performance under all economic and climatic conditions. Again we can say that standardisation is of the greatest importance provided we know how to use it. In this respect the efforts of the International Road Federation—international authorities on airlines and airways—can be seen as a movement in the right direction, but they should not be misunderstood by those attempting to standardise their findings and conclusions.

The standardisation of house types, school buildings and similar facilities is reasonable only when applied to geographically well-defined areas. A house which must have two or three well-insulated and very compact rooms is completely out of place in a hot country where even one room with a good verandah and a courtyard may be of greater value than a two- or three-room dwelling without them. Standardisation in this case has basically local or regional importance.

I think that in terms of the conceptions of Ekistic solutions we are beginning to see how we should carry out our efforts for standardisation; but we are not yet experienced enough to see where we should limit it. In the practice of Ekistic subjects there is great variety in the degree to which we can proceed with standardisation, as can be demonstrated by fig. 400. The smaller the Ekistic unit, the less the degree of standardisation and the greater the freedom for adjustments to specific conditions. The less use of mechanical means for ventilation, climatic adjustment, lighting and transportation, the harder it is to standardise Ekistic solutions. It is difficult and too early to demonstrate these two rules with accuracy, but we have to define the area where Man or the machine are more in control in the sense of the theories presented in

this study. Naturally, standardisation is much more valid in the realm of the machine than in that of Man, where we should proceed with much greater care. The rules defining the construction of an airplane hangar may be set for the whole world, whereas the construction of a small house may vary completely from one part of the world to another.

LEADING TO THERAPY

Predicting the trends

To define the disease through diagnosis is not enough for a proper therapy, since even if we define it with great wisdom, and even if we conceive the proper therapy, by the time it can be applied—and this does take time in human settlements—it may be too late, the situation may have changed to such an extent as will render the therapy meaningless. In order to lead to proper therapy we have to foresee the evolution of the disease—the course that it will follow; only then can we hope that by taking the proper measures we can catch up with it and control it.

But we are afraid to foresee and to predict—we are not used to the idea. What we are really doing is trying to protect ourselves; because we are afraid to attempt predicting the unpredictable, we avoid the predictable. But this is very dangerous. It is not our duty to attempt to make correct prognostications of all events, but to help ourselves in every possible way and on every possible occasion to anticipate and to create a better future, which entails certain predictions and must run the risk of possible failures. After all, life consists of a series of decisions based on predictions. When we go to sleep, we feel confident that our house will not burn down during the night. When we say 'au revoir', we are foreseeing another meeting. We predict certain events at every moment of our lives; why should we be afraid to do this with broader issues?

Obviously predictions are not certainty, but only represent what will probably happen. If we are aware of this difference, predictions present no danger.

'What science observes, what science predicts has all the shortcomings of fact. The facts supply the signal for the future, but the signal is necessarily uncertain and its interpretation against the background of the irrelevant will be inaccurate. The prediction which we base on the signal must be a statistical one. It does not read the future, it forecasts it; and the forecast has meaning only because we couple it with its own estimate of uncertainty. The future is as it were always a little out of focus, and everything that we foresee in it is seen embedded in a small area of uncertainty. It is the human situation and the situation of science. We do not contemplate the facts without error, but because we know what we are doing, we may act upon them without fear'.[4]

401

validity of prediction in relation to time

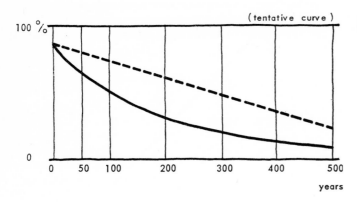

years

402

validity of prediction for different elements or parts of them

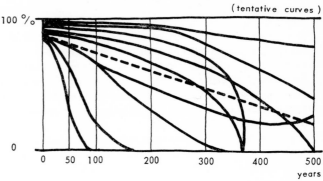

years

All predictions diminish in value the further they venture into the future. It is very probable that a road with many good new houses along it will persist 25 or even 50 years from now. It is less probable that it will be there 100 years from now, and much less probable 200, 300 and 400 years from now. This prediction of diminishing value may occur along a straight or a curved line as shown in fig. 401. If the houses on this road have a possibility of surviving for 25 years, the probability that this road will be changed is very small indeed. If 25 years is the expected amortisation period of most of the houses, the probability of the road being changed increases while the road's curve of survival drops. But if after a certain period of time the houses are renewed, it is quite probable that the road will not change to any great extent, at least not as long as the new groups of houses retain their survival value.

The value of prediction is not the same for all elements of the settlement. I spoke of a road, but how about Man himself? We know that he is undergoing changes; his desires and needs are changing. But we can, for example, be pretty certain that his physical dimensions will not change to any great extent. Even when we take into consideration the possible growth of his body caused by better living conditions, we can predict that the changes will not involve more than, say, 20 per cent of his present dimensions. But what about Man's habits? How about his needs for a different type of environment or for a different type of community life? These may change much more quickly than his physical dimensions. And his ideas: how can we predict these?

The same problem can be observed in other elements of the settlement. In the Shells a street may change on the basis of the curve shown in fig. K3 but the houses alongside it may change at a much faster rate. Even if they remain the same outside, they may need completely new equipment, furniture and decoration inside. And how about the other inhabitants of the settlement, the machines? New types of vehicles may be discovered. However, their implementation may be

delayed because of the economics of their production, the technology of mass production and the needs of nations and individuals to amortise investments made in the older types of vehicles. Thus, even if there is an unexpected discovery of an excellent new means of transportation, we can predict with some certainty that throughout the next generation we will still be dealing basically with the conventional types of vehicles.

So in settlements which consist of many elements that have not been amortised and that create many commitments for us—such as buildings, streets and vehicles—we will be forced to proceed with predictions based on the following considerations:

o Nature, on which we build a settlement, changes in a more or less predictable way—the elimination of hills or forests, air contamination, water pollution and the drying up of rivers, are the result of human activity and can be foreseen;

o we can predict that in the foreseeable future, we will be dealing with a man who will be more or less the same physically, and whose dimensions will not change to any great extent even though his habits may do so;

o Society may change in needs, dimensions and in structure;

o Networks may change to quite a considerable degree, especially in dimension—however, this can be foreseen in most cases;

o the Shells do not change so quickly in many of their parts because of the inertia created by the existing values and the necessity for their amortisation. On the other hand, settlements expand, and in the new areas there are no commitments. Through expansion, they are increasing the pressure on the old parts and this imposes changes even on those areas of the settlements which have not yet been amortised.

From such an analysis, it becomes quite clear that there are some elements of the settlements whose evolution we can predict with reasonable certainty, and others where the pro-babilities of accurate prediction decrease. Such predictions must be compared and combined before we can predict the whole settlement's evolution.

A picture of the value of our predictions can be given by a diagram with many curves, each representing a different element or a different part of an element of the settlement (fig. 402). Our possibility of prediction depends on our ability to isolate the different elements and phenomena within a settlement, to predict separately for each one of them and then, depending on the type of conclusion needed for the phenomenon under study, to combine these completely different curves or predictions.

At this point it may not seem reasonable to proceed with predictions, since it is so difficult and complicated to predict the evolution of so many elements and their combination, which make up human settlements. Not only is it necessary for us to predict, but now we can do so if we are aware of the limitations of our predictions. But all action in Ekistics and the building of human settlements is related to politics in the broadest sense of the word. Politics is the art of the possible, and action in Ekistics is political action. As such it is again based on the art of the possible both in prediction and in implementation.

This prediction is not only necessary, it is also possible, even though more complicated than it was in the past. We reconcile the fact that it is much more difficult and yet at the same time more possible because of Man's ability to face increasingly difficult and complicated problems with his increasing knowledge.

To explain how much more difficult prediction has become, I will take, as an example, the problem of the shape or form of the Shells of the settlement. This results from a synthesis of many factors. Two such factors are, the community which lives in it, and the means by which members of the community are interconnected.

In the past, interconnections between members of a community were based on the movement of Man himself. Animals were used for transportation between settlements, but seldom within the settlements. Today the situation has changed: where the interconnections were once based on Man himself, they are now based on Man and the machine. Therefore, we now have a greater number of variables. Man has a constant speed, but machines change their rate of speed. For example, a car may be designed to go at a speed of 100 miles an hour, but for various reasons, such as the bad quality of a settlement's roads, or congestion of traffic, it may be able to move only at 10 m.p.h. The following figure (fig. 403) shows how complicated the case is even when we consider only these two factors that influence the shape of the Shells (i.e., the community and the method of inter-connections of its members), and even when we take a community inhabited by only two people. In the past there was only one type of line with a limited range of speed

403

variations of a simple interconnection of two people

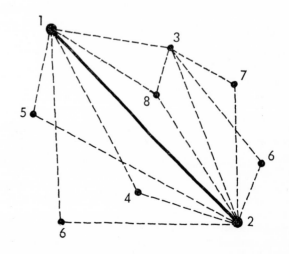

connecting these two people. Now, apart from this constant line, based on Man's own movement, we must include a great number of other lines because we are now dealing with machines and their variable movements. In the past we had only line 1–2. Now we have also line 1–3–2 (which represents one man moving by car at a low speed towards the other man) as well as lines 1–4–2, 1–5–2 and 1–6–2 (representing speed changes) and as many variations of them as there are speeds. But even this is not enough, for a line is seldom as simple as 1–3–2; it is either line 1–3–7–2 or 1–3–8–2 or 1–3–9–2. For every speed we may have a great variety of lines, depending on the means by which it moves. In this way we deal with an enormous number of alternatives even when we limit ourselves to only two people and an analysis of their means of physical interconnection.

In spite of the difficulties we have to acquire the ability to foresee the future. After all whenever we build, we are really building—if only subconsciously—for the future. We invest for the future, and whatever we do today not only commits us for the duration of our project, but also for a long time beyond it. The street called Straight in Damascus has survived for many thousands of years; all over the world there are many streets thousands or hundreds of years old, because of the forces of ownership and the natural, individual, unplanned renewal of the wealth invested in a city. A house is demolished, another is built, usually in the same location, on the same alignment of the street, and it thus perpetuates the notion of a street which may have been created generations, centuries or thousands of years before.

We have to be concerned about the future because we will live in it, and we and our descendants will be committed by actions taken today. Since we live in an era of change, an era of increasing dimensions of phenomena and problems, whatever we build becomes a 'strait jacket' for the future and constitutes a potential danger if we do not understand what will happen to it.

Yet, the fact that we must foresee the future is not enough. We must ask ourselves whether we can achieve this. There is an old Greek saying:

'The gods know things that will happen
and men know what is happening now
but wise men know those things
that are just coming along'.[5]

While we all recognise that the future is in hands which we do not control, humanity, even thousands of years ago, knew that: 'Wise men know those things that are just coming along'. The question is how do they know them?

I will mention two reasons why I believe that it is possible to begin foreseeing the future, especially in the field of human settlements. The first is related to all phenomena and is based on Nature itself. As Loren Eiseley tells us in his book, *The Immense Journey*:

'Considering the innumerable devices by which the mindless root has evaded the limitations of its own stability, however, it may well be that man himself is slowly achieving powers over a new dimension—a dimension capable of presenting him with a wisdom he has barely begun to discern. We cannot know all that has happened in the past, or the reasons for all these events any more than we can with surety discern what lies ahead. We have joined the caravan, you might say, at a certain point; we will travel as far as we can, but we cannot in one lifetime see all that we would like to see or learn all that we would hunger to know'.[6]

We have joined the caravan, and gradually we are beginning to acquire the ability to look further back and further ahead than at any previous time. If even the 'mindless root has evaded the limitations of its own stability' Man has reason to believe that with reasonable and proper action he can develop by foreseeing and acting in the right direction.

The second reason for optimism is connected to the history of our human settlements. While many of Man's products change at a high speed, the human settlement itself changes at a much slower one. For example, in the early Greek civilisation, from the twelfth century B.C. to Homer's time in the eighth century, many things were changing; work, clothing, habits, the use of iron (which changed from a practically precious metal to a common one); yet the houses, the palaces and the furniture remained the same. This is true of almost all historical periods.

So Man's nature and his history show that there is hope that we can come to recognise what lies ahead; for though there will continue to be changes, there is also a constancy which allows us to predict, to a certain extent, many of the characteristics of the future. At this point we must also remember that our responsibility to predict reaches only a certain percentage of what is going to happen because the other percentage depends on our decisions for action in building the future. These very decisions have increased the value of our predictions. If we do not create the future, even our predictions will be more uncertain because we will be trying to predict in an unguided, improperly conceived manner. But if we do decide the future, we know much more about many features of human settlements. Thus, by defining the creation of the future as our task we are increasing our ability to predict, which in turn helps us to serve our goal. It is this positive action that will lead us out of the impasse.

If we consider the development and evolution of settlements and the meaning of our action, we will discover that predicting the future of settlements is almost a descriptive action of a prescriptive human endeavour. It is with this that I will deal in the following part.

Changing the trends

Therapy has to be prescriptive and this means that it has to change those trends which do not serve Man as well as possible. This statement by itself poses many questions and creates a very important dilemma. If we have to change the trends how are we to go about it? Human settlements are for humans, but for how many? For what kind of humans? How should these people live? What kind of settlements can we create? Since Man and settlements are interrelated and the one influences the other, what should we change, Man or the settlement? We must consider how we are going to answer such questions.

One of our major questions concerns Man in human settlements. This question is broken down into many more, one of the most important of which is: how many people will there eventually be on the Earth? We will immediately recognise the difficulty of answering this question, if we only think of the tremendous growth of the world population on the one hand, and the policies of different governments and organisations vis-à-vis this problem on the other. There is a great variety of attitudes. Some say that we must concern ourselves with this problem since it is leading to a world catastrophe. In this context at Darwin's Centennial Celebration in 1959, which took place at the University of Chicago, Sir Charles Darwin and others stated that they foresaw that overpopulation would lead to disaster for our civilisation, and that this trend cannot be reversed. There are other scientists, though, who predict no such catastrophe, and others, like Sir Julian Huxley, who admit the dangers but state that the population explosion can be controlled and stopped if humanity will find ways to do so.

National and international policies reflect the attitudes of these scientists to a great extent. There are governments so concerned that they are implementing very active policies to prevent a further increase in population, such as the

Government of Japan, whose policy has already had important effects. Other governments are either unconcerned, or even indirectly encourage the population increase, as was the case in such a populous nation as China until recently. So there is no universal policy, in spite of the fact that both optimists and pessimists agree on the need to reduce the birth rate, and despite the many movements for birth control and the number of people making appeals for such action, such as Dr. Arnold Toynbee, who declares that there is a maximum beyond which mankind's food supply cannot be expanded.

We do not know if any such limit exists, although it is quite probable that for every phase in the development of technology and civilisation there is such a limit. We are all at the same time trying, through the combined contributions of science, technology and universal education, to push this limit to a very distant future, as B. R. Sen, the Director General of F.A.O., recently stated. Such attitudes do not allow us to speak with any certainty about the possibility of supporting a much greater population, or the possibility of a continuous population growth, or about the attitude mankind will take. We must consider this question of population growth to be still open and try to be as practical about answering it as possible. This means that we must be prepared for growth on the basis of the present-day predictions which lead to assumptions about the stabilisation of the population of the Earth at a level between 12 and 50 billion people, or about 30 billion people for calculations based on probable averages towards the end of the twenty-first century.

The number of people is not the only question related to Man. We must answer another very important question concerning the identity of the Man to be dealt with. We know now that Man has had a biological evolution which has changed him in very considerable ways, enabling him to develop the present civilisation. This development is mainly due to the fact that his brain almost trebles in size very soon after his birth and his childhood has been lengthened in order to allow him to learn from the experience of others. But how are we to know what impact the new forces in the world will have on Man and at what speed? For example, what will be the effect of automation? If some day most of the manual work, if not all, is going to be carried out by machines, what will this mean for Man physically and psychologically? We have already started to witness the necessity of readjustment to this new situation. It was quite interesting to note that in a recent survey among workers, unemployed because of automation in the U.S.A., many were utterly discouraged, but several stated clearly that now they understood that they cannot stop learning.

A recent survey of opinions carried out by an English magazine, the *New Scientist*, which asked several leading scientists about the world in 1984, led to the conclusions that Man by then will be suffering from increased neuroses, he will be using more behaviour-influencing drugs, he may be suffering from malnutrition, from eating the wrong foods and may be gambling with new games not yet invented![7]

To understand better the type of Man we will be dealing with we must think about his way of living. To achieve this we must understand how he spends his time now and how he is going to spend it in the future. For this we must get used to new systems of measuring the values and satisfaction of Man and especially to 'the most convenient measure of organisational time resources' which is that 'of person-time units (the equivalent of man-hours in conventional business computations)'.[8] In this field we have much to achieve.

As an example of this need for a study of the reasonable use of time by Man we can turn our attention to the question of the time he spends moving around during the day, month, year or his lifetime. Such considerations have led to many controversies, the most extreme of which is the conclusion that a permanent settlement is not needed. On the other hand, we can learn from biology. Leading biologists, like Professor C. H. Waddington, speak about a definite nesting problem for Man. In addition to this there is the necessity for a solution for the older people who need a permanent habitat, including those Dr. Margaret Mead has recently termed the 'human vegetables' who are being kept alive. These questions must be answered, and satisfactory solutions should probably be found in the near future. But there are even more difficult questions related to the kind of life that humanity will lead. For example, there are questions related to active and passive participation in sports. Are we going to lead a life that allows everyone to exercise his mind and body, as the ancient Greeks prescribed, or will we have an increase in the number of 'television sportsmen'? What will be the effect on the body of Man, who may increasingly lose opportunities for exercise? Can we not learn a lesson from the fact that the car is already turning many of us into a legless species? Here is another set of questions which cannot be answered definitely.

At present we are unable to answer these questions and to know what attitude we will follow in relation to such problems as sports, art or the type of life now being developed. We must really ask ourselves how we can proceed with the creation of a settlement if we do not have answers to such basic questions. The answer is indeed difficult if we think of the great differences of opinion as to what the real problem in our way of life is. While so many people think of the coming age as one of leisure, an economist, Professor K. Denbigh, in his book *Science, Industry and Social Policy*, supports the idea that the real problem we must face is not that of the age of leisure, but of how we can be satisfied and productive while working.[9] The more we try to understand the real issues related to the type of life we want to develop—which will lead to a certain type of settlement—the more confused we become. This is natural since we have not been able to develop a system of predicting the evolution of the complicated phenomena which concern us.

Similar questions can be raised about art. We are beginning

to understand that art is indeed important in our lives, but we must also begin to understand that the real pleasures in life 'do not consist in consuming the arts, but in producing them, as those who do not produce art are even bad consumers', as Bertrand de Jouvenel recently wrote.[10] Art is important as a framework for life, and cannot be limited for the consumption of the privileged few. It must again become the substance of our settlement and not an item contained within it as it has now become.

More than ever before we should turn to art in the future. The reason is that we shall be obliged to rely on industrial, mass-produced, standardised products; we shall be obliged to follow the rules of an organised society, as regards our movement and production, to an unprecedented degree. This is the reason why we shall find in art the unique possibility for self-expression, one of the most important foundations for a free mind, which in turn is a prerequisite for other freedoms, especially political ones. We must try to strengthen the opportunities for all to express themselves in art. But how will this influence human settlements, which will be threatened by a standardisation that in many respects, will be indispensable for our very survival?

With such considerations our mind turns to the relationship of Man with his culture and the Society to which he belongs. People are now more dependent on Society than ever before. They can survive only in Societies. What kind of Society, however, can we count on for the future, when some people are predicting that the age of leisure will be upon us in a generation from now in several Western countries and in Russia? There are certainly doubts about the possibility of our reaching an age of leisure if we do not face our international, economic, social and political problems with greater wisdom. But this fact merely strengthens our point that we are not able to foresee the type of social order and the type of society we will be dealing with; first because we do not know if the present trends towards a civilisation of leisure will continue, and second, because if they continue, we do not know what kind of problems such a Society will create. We are only at the dawn of such an era and cannot answer these difficult questions.

Even more difficult is the question of the relationship of Man with all types of social groupings formed by modern Society. Is Man going to become more closely connected with his family or less so; and how about his connections with his city, his metropolis, his nation, his religious or racial groups and the world? Every time that we put this question of relationships I cannot help but remember the many types of allegiances which existed in the past and are recommended for the future. The ancient Sanskrit verse comes to mind:

'For the family, sacrifice the individual;
For the community, the family;
For the country, the community;
For the soul, all the world'.[11]

but in juxtaposition we have, as well, the contemporary predictions that we must recognise only the units Man, Family and World. Within these I cannot find any answer more reasonable than a balanced allegiance from individual to family, community, city up to the whole world. We owe allegiances to every Ekistic unit and we must find a balance between them.

Of a similar order are questions relating Man with his Shells. The *New Scientist* survey to which I referred earlier predicts that by 1984 our urban studies will have advanced, and that we will probably have better means of transport or more restrictions on traffic and very cheap buildings leading to impermanence.[12] I do not believe that we should be so pessimistic about it. We will have better means of transport and we will plan for fewer restrictions on traffic. I do not see however this trend for impermanence in our buildings. On the contrary we need greater permanence.

The real question about our Shells is whether by becoming larger and by creating artificial weather conditions they will not alienate Man from Nature and deprive him of the ability to face conditions of life which may at any moment become more adverse for him.

The Networks are going to be much more developed since we will need more water, energy, information much more efficiency distributed and the automatic disposal of waste. There have been doubts expressed about transportation networks because of the present great failures to create better ones; there are even people saying that the

'ratio of motor vehicles to people will be stabilised for the simple reason that cars will be so numerous that the increment of usefulness of additional vehicles will be substantially zero: lack of roads on which to drive them and parking lots and garages in which to leave them will make more cars virtually unwanted'![13]

This will be and perhaps already is so (for example in parts of Manhattan) if we are going to stay idle and will not change the trends in our settlements.

All these questions lead to some more important and basic ones of which one of the most crucial is whether Man should accept Nature as it is and try to adjust himself to it, or whether he should try to make Nature fit his own requirements. This is related to a much broader problem, the attitude of Man's soul versus the world, as Erich Lindermann so ably states in his article 'Mental Health and the Environment'. Should we 'Set the soul right that the world may be right', or should we 'Set the world well that the soul may be sound'?[14]

In order to answer this question a few ideas must be clarified. We must first be certain that Nature, as it is now, is in a normal condition if we are to try to adjust Man to it. But we have no reason to believe that Nature is in a stable condition. On the contrary, as Loren Eiseley tells us in his *Immense Journey* the truth is that 'There is nothing very normal about nature'.[15] At one time there were no flowers at all. Nature is in evolution, and we cannot speak of normality in the conditions of Nature, when they differ so much in different occasions and epochs. We must accept the fact that Nature is much more of a changing element than we think. This entitles us to think of changes in human settlements as natural phenomena, although Nature itself may well be considered as given within the time-scale we are working for.

The same holds true for Man. We have not always tried to adjust Man to Nature; for example, we have not attempted to train Man to survive in any climate without protection. On the contrary, early in our history we tried to create a micro-climate with clothing. We created an artificial climate for Man, who thus became adjusted to Nature, not as a natural organism, but as a combination of the natural organism and the artificial solutions he could invent. Historical evolution therefore shows that Man adjusts himself to natural conditions by creating a different environment for himself on a micro- or macro-scale and that this scale increases as time passes.

We cannot be in any way certain about the future, especially the distant future. I turn again to René Dubos to ask with him

'Who can foretell the distant consequences of the fact that modern man no longer experiences the inclemencies of the weather, need not engage in physical exertion, can use drugs to alleviate almost any form of pain, and increasingly depends on tranquilisers and stimulants to live through the day? These achievements have, of course, made life easier and often more pleasant, but they may bring about an atrophy of the adaptive mechanisms which continue to be essential for the maintenance of health'.[16]

Such threats cannot justify a passive attitude on our part. We are going to initiate changes anyhow; we simply have to go about it as wisely as possible. We must have learned by now that although Nature exercises a great influence on Man by forcing him to create so many artificial conditions, he himself is also beginning to exercise an influence on that part of Nature which he inhabits. Both Man, with his action, and Nature, will be evolving; they will influence each other. We must think of both in proper balance, a balance which will be dynamic and should be the best possible at any given time.

What we must do is frequently re-examine human needs and prospects on the basis of our knowledge at any given time. We must keep in mind that Man and Nature will necessarily continue to develop. In any attempt at answering the great dilemma about our attitudes towards Man and Nature, we must be realistic enough to recognise that we are dealing with dynamically changing forces. To the major questions of whether we should change Man or Nature, Man or Shells, there will be no simple answer. We must understand that Man, Nature, Society, Shells and Networks will be changing

and that we will have the great task of always keeping the most proper balance between these changing elements. In doing so we must always take into consideration all possible alternatives leading to desirable solutions. In other words, in trying to keep the desirable balance or to re-establish it when it has been lost, we must be as objective and scientific as possible.

It is extremely difficult to give one very concrete, or even one-directional answer to all these questions. We must reconcile ourselves to the fact that our answer to the great dilemma of the future of Man, of his relation with Nature and the man-made habitat can be neither specific nor definitive. We are not the builders of this world, much less the creators of styles. We are only tiny agents in the great, long, endless process of evolution.

The subject of how to change the trends for the best and effect therapy is a very difficult one, but we cannot escape from the fact that our settlements do need therapy and our fate and task is to proceed and act in this direction. To the question of whether we should change the trends the answer is definitely yes, since if we do not do it we will be led to disaster. To the question of whether we will do it the answer is yes, because it is necessary. But when? The answer to this is very important: now! How are we going to do it? I do not have any better answer but to say: through careful, reasonable, common sense efforts (which after all is the scientific attitude) leading to a conscious and orderly change which is the best that we can wish. If we fail by such a system we will know by feed-back mechanisms the causes of the failure and we will continue to alter the trends until the end of time.

Against the physical universe's decline to chaos by continuous disorder our action for therapy should lead towards a dynamic order—by changing the trends.

METHODS OF THERAPY

Curative method

The usual procedure of Man and Society in their efforts towards therapy of the diseases of settlements is to attempt the curative method. When 1000 dwellings are missing we try to build them, when a road is too narrow for the corresponding traffic we try to widen it, sometimes through surgery.

By the time this curative method has yielded results the disease may have progressed to a very dangerous extent. The most recent example of failures to relieve settlements from grave stresses by curative methods and surgery is the urban renewal effort in the United States which cannot be mentioned as a successful approach in the way it is usually implemented. It may actually relieve stresses of a certain aspect of settlements but I do not know of cases where it has saved the total biological individual that a settlement is. In many cases it even looks much more like face lifting than a cure—much less a therapy.

However, the situation today in many settlements is such that their central areas and many of their parts are going to disintegrate. If this continues, the destruction will be so great that only their peripheries will survive. This very process took place with the barbarian invasions of the great empires of the past; they aimed at the centres of civilisation and only the forces on the periphery survived.

No matter how good the diagnosis, I do not know of any dynamic settlements that have been saved by the curative method.

Preventive method

Failure of surgery and the curative method leads, in the same way as in Man, to the preventive one. This is a much more reasonable method in any case of therapy since it prevents the disease instead of letting it develop in order to cure it.

Prevention requires greater experience and wisdom and especially the ability to predict and foresee. When, in the past, Man was able to foresee his needs in a city and he planned it, especially within the walls, he could use this same city for several centuries. Only wars created major acute problems for the settlement because of the destruction caused in all elements. What Man was really doing was using preventive therapy of the future needs. This was easy since the rate of growth was not unexpected, it was slow and Man was used to it. His action in planning a whole city was relatively simple and covered the normal changes expected.

This method however lost all its meaning when settlements became dynamic and started changing; Man ceased to be able to foresee, and even when he thought he could, he was overtaken by changes: the preventive method was virtually forgotten.

Development

In the present era the only reasonable method of therapy is through development. It is always bad to find refuge in curative measures and surgery for any biological individual, including settlements, and it is too difficult to implement the preventive method in dynamically growing settlements without foreseeing their development.

It becomes clear, therefore, that in settlements the best method is the preventive one by proper conception of the expected and necessary development. Prevention alone can be useful in static settlements, but in dynamic ones only action for development has a meaning. If we look passively at a settlement growing on the basis of existing trends there is no hope for it. If we can foresee its development and where it may go wrong, then we can take it in our hands and guide it towards the right goals, and development becomes the only reasonable method of therapy.

The great difficulty of this method is that it must start well ahead of the crisis since the forces creating it have been built years, decades or generations earlier. Therapy through development becomes therefore a long-term therapy. For this reason, even though this one is the right method, action for therapy today may have to turn to all three methods since:

- the curative method and surgery may be imperative for immediate and urgent diseases;
- the preventive method may be necessary to avoid the spread of the disease or the stresses to non-affected but easily affectable parts, organs or elements;
- development is the only method which can, in the long run, save the settlement, make surgery and the curative method unnecessary and turn the preventive method into an auxiliary one.

We may not know much about how to proceed by development, but we must be certain that what we know about surgery and the curative method is much less justified and sound. For such cases and for those who are afraid to rely on development I can only repeat the dictum of the experimentalists: 'Don't think, try it'.

CHAPTER ELEVEN
EKISTIC DEVELOPMENT

GOALS

When we are able to understand that Ekistic therapy can be achieved through development, we will be able to reach the conclusion that Ekistic action in general means action for development. Development requires a definition of goals, policies, programmes and physical plans. This is the subject of this chapter.

It may be argued by some that setting goals is not scientific, but this would simply open once again the question of whether science can be prescriptive or not, and I have already dealt with this question. I can only repeat here that it is time for us to turn towards a goal-oriented science and to understand that 'the acquisition of knowledge is intricately interwoven with the pursuit of goals'.[17]

We begin our action by setting goals. Ekistic goals cannot be set by the Ekistician alone; they must be set by those in charge of broader conceptions for the area we are dealing with and of which they are a part. If we are working with a nation, Ekistic objectives must be part of a national development programme. In a city they must be part of its overall programme, although in setting up these objectives we must be certain not to limit ourselves just to the area for which they are intended. If we have to set goals for a city, for example, we must be aware of those existing for the broader area to which the city belongs. If we are setting goals for a region, we must understand that they will be part of those of an even larger region.

So we see that Ekistic goals should be set in the framework of a broader concept, in order to encompass the overall life of which Ekistics is one expression, as well as within a wider geographic space of which our specific area is just a part. Setting Ekistic goals means setting them in the widest conceptual and geographic framework that is necessary and practical in order to obtain accurate and clear definitions. Only then can we be realistic about the relationship of Ekistics with other expressions of life, such as economic, social, political goals, or more specifically, transportation goals, etc. Only then can we understand properly the importance of the universal as opposed to the regional or local

factors, and their combinations. If we study the area we are concerned with within its proper geographic location, and Ekistics in its proper relationship to other sectors from the point of view of contents (fig. 404), we will understand that in spite of the fact that our subject lies where the geographic dimensions and the discipline of Ekistics converge, the area within which we must study it should expand in all directions.

Our goals should be defined as clearly as possible. In war we have very clear goals; in industry we can achieve progress only by setting goals and the same is valid in our private lives. Lately we have become accustomed to goals being set by science (the discovery of the nature and the causes of cancer, for example) and by technology (reaching the moon or Mars). We need to acquire the ability of setting goals for settlements.

Our goals should be defined in as great detail as possible, and therefore should be seen as goals related not only to Ekistic areas but to elements, parts and organs of settlements as well. The best way of defining goals in detail is by defining them in relation to each element. Contrary to the method I used in analysis—starting with Nature and proceeding to Man, Society, Shells and Networks—we must now begin with Man and end with the Networks, since Man is our main goal—after all, we are acting for his benefit. What are we trying to do for him? How do we view him? How can we conceptualise his future role, his future activity, his well-being, the evolution of both his body and his mind? How can we conceptualise his relation to the machine? The settlement will not only serve him, it will necessarily influence him as well. What services should be provided by the settlement and what impact can we expect them to have on Man's evolution?

The definition of goals for Man depends on the criteria we will set. In the past we relied only on economic and safety criteria, but now we have come to understand that the most basic criterion is time; satisfaction follows, then safety. All these criteria should be studied in terms of feasibility on the basis of the economic criterion (Chapter Seven, pages 288–298).

Since the time criterion is the most important one, the goals to be set depend on the length of Man's life and the way in which he spends this life. In this respect it is useful for us to understand that considerable progress has been made during

404

setting of goals within a wider framework

(indicative)

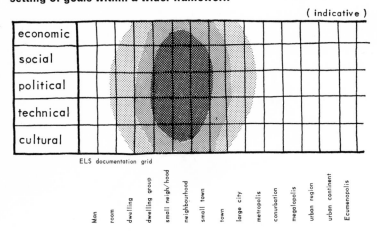

ELS documentation grid

the last generations; also we now have to plan for a life-time which is in some countries 40 per cent longer than at the beginning of our century, and 75 per cent longer than it was one hundred years ago (fig. 405).

In the same way we have to estimate that life expectancy at birth is now completely different from what it was at the beginning of our century and that consequently our tasks have changed in many respects. The subject of our main concern must spend his time in a different way, if for no other reason at least because he has a different type of time-life in relation to his age (fig. 406).

Then we must deal with Society. We cannot isolate any part of it. We must try to understand its entire economic, social, political, administrative and cultural structure. We must understand the whole community we are dealing with, for only then can we set goals for it. We have to define goals for our Society at every level of organisation, from family to Ecumenopolis, and we have to emphasise them for the social units which form our main subject. The interrelation and communication between members of our social groups in relation to their physical locations is one of our main goals —and one that has been largely overlooked so far. There is no reason at all why we should not see Society as we would a group of molecules of, let us say, a gas. This is certainly not the only way of looking at it but it is one which can help us to understand physical relationships which very often are the basis of many resulting phenomena. Such considerations mean that we must consider densities of people and inter-actions as very important goals for Ekistic action.

Next we turn our attention to the third element, to Nature. Here we must be aware that through human settlements we are changing Nature. If we want to set the proper goals for human settlements, we must also set proper goals for the Nature related to them. How far should we exploit natural resources for the creation of settlements? How far should we

use agricultural land? Is it permissible to continue to use natural resources indiscriminately, or are we reaching the point when we must set specific goals for the preservation of natural wealth?

Through such policies we must define, for example, to what extent we may expect human settlements to spread over the Earth's agricultural land. Would it not be more reasonable to consider as an alternative the use of waste land, and should we not define a policy for the construction of human settlements in deserts, or even on the surface of the bodies of water, as some people have suggested? Even though we must first set our goals for Man and his Society, we should be equally careful in setting goals for Nature, which Man quite often does not respect.

We must define goals for the Shells of the human settlement itself. What kind of Shells do we envisage? Ever-expanding ones, compact ones, expensive ones, dynamically growing ones or static ones? Will we be satisfied with Shells consisting exclusively of high buildings, such as are found in the central part of the 'Radiant City', or will we envisage Shells consisting of cottages and private gardens, as in the English garden city? Specific goals must be set for Shells covering every aspect, from overall form to details, from technological to cultural and aesthetic aspects.

Speaking of goals for Shells, I think that I must insist on one basic point: every Man should be entitled to his own personal shell where he can retire and isolate himself when he feels the need, so that the spines of the other hedgehogs cannot hurt him and his cannot hurt the others. This means a minimum of one room per person regardless of the number of common rooms of the family, the community, etc., though it may be more realistic for some countries than for others. It may also mean, depending on the climate, an independent verandah and garden. This alone can be the ultimate human goal for Shells.

415

405

average length of the life of Man from ancient to modern times

406

life expectancy of Man in the U.S.A.

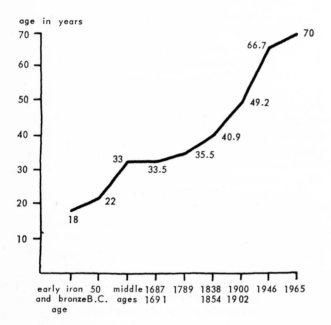

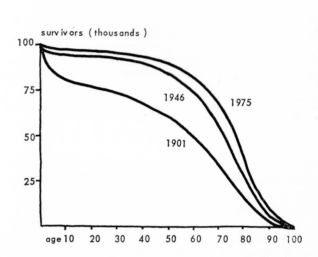

Then goals must be set for all Networks. Today we ignore the importance of this fifth element as a basic factor of human settlements. We allow transportation and communication lines to extend without exercising any control. We allow ourselves to spend our time commuting without thinking of how much we are committing ourselves by creating all these networks without first having set goals for them. This is why it is imperative that, after having set goals for Man, Society and Nature, we set goals for all types of Networks: transportation and communications, water supply and sewage, provision of power, gas, electricity, etc.

After setting these specific goals for the five elements of human settlements, we must then manage to set an overall goal which expresses the interrelationship of these elements. Our goal referring to the use of natural resources is not adequate if it does not correspond to the goals set for Man's expansion over the Earth. In order to set such goals, we must have a proper conception of the interrelationship of these elements and must set proper criteria for their evaluation. We will then reach the point of expressing our goals in a general way which can satisfy every single element as well as their interrelationship.

This stage of our effort will by no means be definitive; for if we set goals without first working them out in detail, we may go wrong, especially where the interrelationship of the

elements is concerned. This is why at first the articulation of goals cannot be but tentative, until by slowly working out policies, programmes and plans, we are able to evaluate the extent to which our goals are realistic; only then can we decide whether the goals should be maintained as initially set, or whether we should revise them in the light of their specific expression in the policies, programmes and plans.

This is why all four stages of our synthesising effort (goals, policies, programmes, plans) towards the realisation of our goals, even though they must be defined separately in sequence, are very closely interrelated, and no decision can be taken on the basis of any one of them until we have—at least theoretically—passed through all of them and have revised each one in terms of the others. The final definition of the course of Ekistic action is a result of the proper synthesis of all our ideas and endeavours in defining the goals, policies, programmes and plans. We can serve them only by guaranteeing a proper balance between the five elements, and this can be achieved only through the proper inter-relationship of the goals, policies, programmes and plans. Correct Ekistic action is possible if we work both through the two-dimensional grid of the human settlement (divided by elements and seen as a whole) and through the process of goals, policies, programmes and plans that guarantees the formation of a rational whole (fig. 407).

407

goals, policies, programmes and plans are interrelated into one system

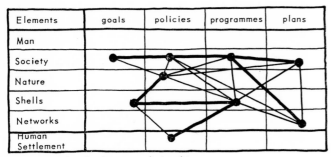

Elements	goals	policies	programmes	plans
Man				
Society				
Nature				
Shells				
Networks				
Human Settlement				

indicative sketch of some relationships

POLICIES

Basic policies

In order to reach our goals we must first define our policies. It is not enough to say that we must have a settlement which makes Man happy and safe, we also have to point out that this will be achieved by way of a conservative policy either respecting private property absolutely, or limiting it to a certain extent or even depriving individuals of the right of ownership. Only then can the goals have a meaning.

In various forms some sort of an Ekistic policy has always existed in every nation and urban settlement even though this policy has almost always been limited to a very few conscious measures, such as town plans and building codes, and many more unconscious principles, such as the construction of houses and buildings in the prevailing manner. Today our policies must be much more complete and must be conceived and implemented much more consciously. This is why a scientific approach to policy-making is needed. The era when we could speak about the art of city building without being conscious of the fact that we need thorough scientific knowledge before expressing ourselves in an artistic way, is over. We must now speak of a science of Ekistics and a scientific approach to policy-making.

From the moment we start speaking about policies instead of theory, we are speaking about the possible and the potential. As long as we work as theoreticians, we can toy with ideas which may be implemented. When we work as scientists, we must try out all ideas which, if successful, can have practical application. But once we become policy-makers, we are limited only to what can really be implemented at that time. Policies up to now have been mainly curative. Our first action was to go about ameliorating settlements when their situation became unbearable. This type of amelioration, the widening

and paving of streets for example, led to the realisation of the necessity for preventive measures. So statutory town-planning was conceived, and community facilities started being determined in advance. But now, due to the fact that the dimensions of settlements and the speed of changes have increased, our problems have been multiplied and Man has completely lost the power of prevention. He is limited to curative measures, which never have the anticipated results since the disease progresses faster than the curative measures can be implemented.

The time is therefore ripe for a revision of all our Ekistic policies, for the realisation that it is necessary to conceive the problem correctly and to proceed with the proper preventive policies, even though we will certainly always need curative policies for the unexpected diseases. But this does not mean that we should not pass through a phase during which a very great effort must be devoted to curative policies.

The importance of preventive policies increases enormously with expanding urban areas. Since the majority of the world population is going to live in urban areas, the degree of preventive policies should be much higher than that of curative ones. We can understand this by looking into the evolution curve of an average urban settlement. Here (fig. 408) we see that the building wealth existing at the moment of major policy-making, programming and planning decreases, thereafter new building wealth increases more and more. If we look at this phenomenon in absolute figures and especially in percentages, we will understand why preventing the evil, even when we cannot cure the present diseases, is of the greatest importance. In order to study the evolution of a settlement taking as an example the number of buildings it contains, we will see that today 100 per cent of its buildings exist; but this percentage will decrease every year until one hundred years from now practically no building which exists today will survive, unless it has some special value (historical, cultural, etc.). On the other hand, the number of new buildings will increase at the rate of 7 per cent, if we assume a 4 per cent increase in urban population, a 2 per cent increase of the value invested in buildings per inhabitant (which is actually low in relation to what we expect) and at least 1 per cent for the replacement of the existing buildings. So, despite the fact that by applying the proper preventive measures we can create a better human settlement for those areas to be developed from today on only, in a generation's time 66 per cent or more of the human settlement will have been created on the basis of proper preventive policies and should satisfy human needs. Two generations from now, the percentage will be extremely high, and three generations from now the building of the total urban settlement will have been guided by preventive policies. However, at this point I must say that illustrating the efficiency of a settlement by the efficiency of its new buildings can be completely misleading if we have limited ourselves to a policy developed only for buildings. In such a case we may have good buildings in the

growth of an average urban settlement

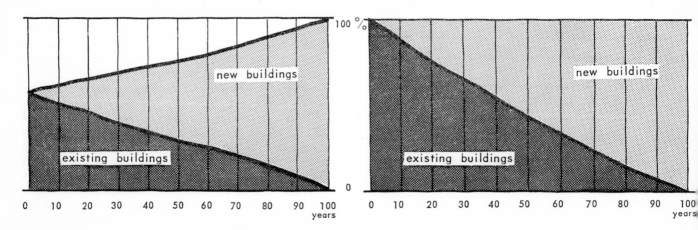

wrong locations, and they might deteriorate not within a hundred years but within five, as has happened in many cities lacking an overall conception. This is why the new building aspect is only one illustration of the overall action we must take in every Ekistic field.

The same diagram also shows why preventive policy is not adequate. For quite a number of years the existing buildings and the existing part of the city play a large role, and this is when curative policies are needed as well. Our policies should be guided also by the lower part of the diagram, but not only for buildings—they should be influenced by all existing elements of settlements—such a diagram shows that whereas in a 100-year period our main concern should be a preventive policy and our secondary one should be a curative one, in a 10-year period (if we can be as short-sighted as that) certainly the curative policy is of the greatest importance. The conclusion is clear: depending on how far ahead we look, we must develop a correct relationship between preventive and curative policies.

Speaking of preventive policies we must also clarify our ideas about their content: how do preventive policies work? The first reaction of humanity to the accumulation of apparently insurmountable problems in contemporary urban settlements was to turn to preventive policies of a negative nature. The first reaction led to the desire for the implementation of police measures. The common reaction ran along the following lines: the city is growing too much, and we can no longer deal with it, so let us stop its growth. This was a childish attitude. Many of the world's large cities declared that their policy was to reach a certain population size, and forbid any more people to move there. It was quite characteristic that the announced size took the existing population into consideration and also allowed for some growth. I have never seen it explained whether keeping the population at a

certain level meant that women would not be allowed to bear more children or that the excess population would be thrown out. This notion of fictitious walls around settlements is a survival of old patterns which have nothing to do with our era. People who devised these policies were intellectually living in the Middle Ages.

An interesting comment on human attitudes is the fact that such policies of negative restrictions on the growth of settlements have been devised and proclaimed by all political systems and by all countries, from the extreme right to the extreme left, from the most conservative to the most liberal theoreticians. Lately there has been a reaction and people have started to speak of controlled growth. Although this is a big step forward, I doubt if it is a new policy in Ekistics. We have learned by now that a proper policy cannot rely simply on controls, since forces are growing too quickly to be controlled. In many ways we should speak of guided growth. A preventive policy should guide growth along broad lines and should control only in detail. For example, when we must plan the expansion of a broader urban area, we cannot implement it by controls. We must conceive the proper areas of expansion and take the initiative by opening the necessary new highways in time and providing for new facilities. Within this area, one can then have controls defining the formation of every single part of the settlement, the policies that will be followed, the programmes and plans. The overall decisions, however, must be taken in advance, otherwise they will never be the correct ones and we shall always be forced to act in a curative way even in areas of expanding programmes.

When policies are preventive, the dimension of time enters into the picture. Certainly, this dimension is expressed in a specific way in the programmes which determine the sequence of development in time, but this should not lead us to believe that time is not inherent in any conception of policy or of

409

**life expectancy in settlements of elements
conceived and created today**

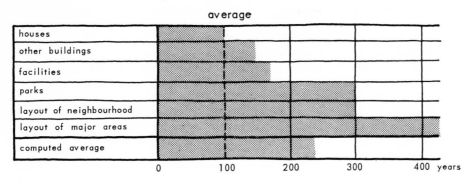

average

houses					
other buildings					
facilities					
parks					
layout of neighbourhood					
layout of major areas					
computed average					

0   100   200   300   400 years

(tentative assumptions for an imaginary case)

goals. Actually, it is a matter of judgment when each new dimension should enter the picture and to what extent. If we say that the goal of an Ekistic policy is to house all families of a certain city, this is very specific; but if we have no notion of when this can be brought into effect, the goal loses much of its importance. When we define a policy as allowing every family to have its own house as quickly as possible, this again is a definite policy. But if we can say that every family should be able to have its own house within a generation's time, or in ten years time, the policy becomes more specific.

Since, in the final analysis, goals, policies, programmes and plans form a total, it is only a matter of system and not of substance when each dimension is allowed to enter the picture.

While speaking about goals we can sometimes avoid the issue of time; but in speaking about policies we can never do so. Thus, though we spoke about the necessity of the proper conception of the goal in the dimensions of geography and its contents, policies must add the idea that the goal must also expand with time. Thus we can set a rule that policies should be expressed as:

- policies in relation to their nature,
- policies in relation to geographic areas,
- policies in relation to time.

An example can run as follows: we want to house every family in a certain metropolitan area, which has a certain relation to its region, within a period of one generation. If we must develop proper preventive policies and include the dimension of time in them, for what period of time should we develop such policies? There was a tendency to recommend five and ten year programmes for many cities. Later there was an attempt to prepare programmes for 20 or 25 years, and lately the target has sometimes been set for the year 2000—an impressive length of time and an impressive date. My own

belief is that even such a period is actually very short. This can be understood when we realise that most of the houses to be built today will survive beyond the year 2000. Infrastructure networks may last several generations, because while some materials may disintegrate, the networks (sewage, drainage, water supply, etc.) will remain. And the general superstructure of the settlement we create may survive, not for generations, but quite often for centuries.

We are dealing with actions being taken today, the results of which will have an impact on Ekistics from one or two generations to a few centuries from now (fig. 409). If this is so, why should we limit our projections and our policy-making to periods which are shorter than the life expectancy of those of our works? This is not reasonable. We must either plan on the basis of the longest life expectancy of the element to be created, or on an average life expectancy, which makes more sense. If the average life expectancy of projects and commitments created today for human settlements were computed in a practical way, it would probably approximate a hundred years. Therefore I think we should develop our policies for this length of time. If we consider a symbolic date, it is again better to set it in terms of a number of years, which remains constant, rather than in terms of a specific date such as the year 2000, because in the latter case the planning period will gradually be shortened, and as we near it, it will be limited to ten or five years.

There can be a major objection to such an assumption: how can we predict for a hundred years from now? This is quite a valid objection. I have already explained in several diagrams that I do not expect us to be able to predict many things with certainty for such a distant period. But since the goal-setting, policy-making, programming and planning process must be continuous, there is no need to stick to today's conceptions when, ten or twenty years later, in the continuous revisions of our efforts, we will come to realise that the situation is different from what we had thought. The process of continuous planning is our guarantee for long-term conceptions and projections.

Before closing this argument, I should mention one more reason why a 100-year period for the definition of a broad framework of policies, programmes and plans makes sense. In physical plans, which are the most specific expression of our action, we must take at least one generation's life into account when designing a specific project. The reason is that the life expectancy of even the cheapest house is at least one generation, and we do not foresee technological changes which can radically upset our designs before a generation's time. I am specifically thinking of the expected changes in our city's traffic systems. There is no possibility of acquiring revolutionary machines which will put those we now depend on out of use within a generation. Even if we do find a new machine there is no chance that highways will be eliminated in this time. One generation is the minimum unit to be reckoned for specific plans. This being so, the period of projection for our more comprehensive plans should be much longer than the period for specific plans, it should be two or three generations long. And if it is three generations long, it might as well be a period of a 100 years.

The contents of the policies should comprise as great a number of aspects as possible. Policies, like goals, must be developed for all five basic elements of human settlements. But this is not enough; this is only the general framework for policies. In order to be worked out in detail, they should follow the complete diagram where work is done in all four dimensions as already explained in previous chapters.

So policies must deal with all geographic dimensions, from the largest to the smallest: nation, region, megalopolis, metropolis, city, village, etc. They must also deal with various factors. In actual practice, no complete Ekistic programmes or policies exist for any country. An attempt at developing policies on a national level, but limited to housing of specific facilities, has been carried out in a few western countries. Other countries, such as Iraq, Pakistan and Lebanon, have developed relatively complete Ekistic policies and their corresponding studies show attempts at a more comprehensive coverage of the whole field. These policies are perhaps the nuclei of the types we will need in the future.

Aspects of policies

We are facing today some problems which urgently demand the development of proper policies. I will mention two of them —the Shells that we are losing and the policies for administrative action in Ekistics.

Many existing Shells consist of two parts: those shells which were satisfactory when they were built, even if they are not so today, and those shells which were unsatisfactory right

from the beginning. Our attitude here should be very cautious. For those shells which were satisfactory when built, we must try to find out what values they still have and what we can learn from them. We must see whether they can be saved. Since they had once been satisfactory but are now under such pressure that they cannot be saved, we must study them as carefully as possible, for the day will come when we will be sorry for having left the satisfactory shells of the past to be gradually eliminated, which is what we are doing today. We must be prepared to change those shells which were unsatisfactory right from the beginning as quickly as possible for these shells certainly have even less value today. We should not worry about changing them, but should guide our policies towards changing mostly those parts of the settlements which were never satisfactory and do not contain any values worth keeping or learning from.

The problem of what type of Shells we shall create is much more critical. We do not know what to do, yet we must do something, and by doing something we will be committing somebody for the future in areas we cannot control. The answer to this dilemma should be that we must plan for the future and build for the present. If we plan properly for the future and look as far ahead as we can, we will be doing our duty by predicting future conditions, and trying to prepare our settlements for what is to come. But by building only for the present, we are committing ourselves and our descendants for as little as necessary. In practice this can be expressed in many ways—by predicting the future expansion of a settlement, and at the same time limiting the construction and development only to those parts which are indispensable now; or by predicting the need for a very wide avenue, but constructing only the lanes indispensable to today's traffic. In this way we are combining the necessity of planning for the future without committing ourselves more than is necessary until we have learned more.

Now, should we be allowed to plan for the future if we are not certain about the right solutions? Yes! Planning for dynamic settlements in a dynamically changing era should be a continuous process. If something went wrong in our planning, we would have the time to change our conception, having made no irrevocable commitment save the effort of planning; this effort is an expenditure which is never wasted, since it entails the recognition of weaknesses and mistakes that eventually helps to find a solution. So planning is an expenditure of intellectual effort indispensable to progress.

The real issue is not whether or not to build; building for the present always takes place. The real issue is whether we should do the building and commit ourselves with or without plans and concepts. The answer is not difficult; seeing that we should commit ourselves to an investment corresponding to certain types of needs, it is better to do it by planning properly, and not allow it to take place haphazardly.

Such considerations lead to the conclusion that a proper policy requires:

420

o an understanding of the existing situation;

o no changes at all in those parts of the settlement which serve their purpose in a relatively satisfactory way;

o a very conservative attitude as regards changing those parts of settlements which did serve their purposes satisfactorily in the past, but no longer do so—we should save these parts as long as possible;

o where change is warranted, freedom to change those parts which do not serve their purposes, especially if they have been unsatisfactory since their inception;

o planning as far ahead as possible;

o committing ourselves and building only for what is indispensable today.

In a proper policy we must respect the past as much as possible, for Man built much better settlements then. In this era of universalism and international forces, about whose values and trends we are not certain, we must protect the local civilisations, expressions and solutions as far as possible until we have reached a point of maturity and are able to test the new trends. By then we will be able to express proper judgements and decide what should remain from the experience and values created in the past, and what we should take over from those of the new trends. We cannot be reasonable in our approach and follow a systematic course unless we understand the necessity of finding the proper balance between the past and the future, and between local and international expressions.

In order to succeed, we should proceed with the following steps:

o be as careful as possible in the creation of the new settlements and the transformation of the existing ones, and act in a systematic and controlled way;

o create broader frames for our future action;

o experiment continuously with whatever we do, follow it up, evaluate it, and feed this information into the planning and creating organisation in order to adjust our thinking;

o maintain whatever values we have and study them;

o develop a new experience on the basis of the new perspectives we are opening, the experiments we are carrying out, and the lessons we are learning from existing settlements;

o build new settlements again and transform the existing ones on the basis of this experience;

o open new perspectives again for this action;

o experiment again, etc.

Administrative action in Ekistics requires great attention and the right policies, which on the whole do not exist today. The greatest defects in the present-day administration of the affairs of human settlements can be classified in the three following categories:

o expanding urban tissues have eliminated many of the community organisations necessary for the proper administration of the lower Ekistic units;

o the expanding urban tissue of metropolitan areas has gone too far without the proper reorganisation of administration on a metropolitan level;

o central governments have had a difficult time recognising the existence of a real problem of human settlements, and in no country are all authorities related to human settlements concentrated in a single ministry, as they should be.

The first of these phenomena has appeared practically everywhere. There were small cities and communities which sometimes had a great tradition of facing their own problems. When these cities grew larger, the municipalities which were created more often than not eliminated the small local institutions which had administered the minor Ekistic units. There is no proper administration at the lowest level of Ekistic organisation in central urban areas today, and I doubt if there is any real awareness in this field. There certainly are religious communities, business groups or school committees or other such expressions related to small Ekistic units, but there is no overall Ekistic administration of the smallest units and this is a great failure.

In metropolitan areas little has been done for the integration of administration at a higher Ekistic level, but we can already speak of an emerging state of consciousness. Several of the newly independent countries which were not committed by previous decisions had the courage to appoint mayors, administrators or development officers for major metropolitan areas. This is the beginning of metropolitan administration even though there is not enough experience in these countries to guarantee the success of such administration. On the other hand, the countries in which large metropolitan areas have developed over the last centuries have faced a great problem since these areas have expanded over the boundaries of many municipalities and communities. Only lately has a real consciousness of the need for proper administration of the broader Ekistic area sprung up. The creation of the London County Council several decades ago was a great step, but its area did not extend far enough. The Miami Metropolitan Area is a first such step in the U.S.A. although its efficacy has not yet been ascertained. The appointment of a high commissioner for the Paris region, covering the broadest possible area around Paris, is as far as I know, the first step in this direction in Western Europe, and it is an important one even though not yet complete.

The movement towards metropolitan governments is spreading, especially in the socialist countries; but this has not yet led to the establishment of the proper metropolitan administration at a high enough level to allow the people of a whole metropolitan area to decide on their broadest interests, while allowing cities and communities of a lower Ekistic level and even minor administrative units for the minor Ekistic areas, to manage their own local affairs.

One major problem which appeared in metropolitan areas is the gradual elimination of the initiative for the administration

421

level of decision taking in Ekistic units

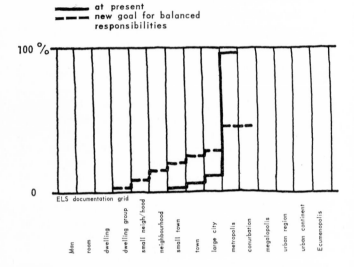

of Ekistic problems in minor Ekistic units. The level of decision making has moved towards major units (even though, as already explained, not to as large units as it should have) at the expense of the minor ones (fig. 410). The result is a very big concentration of responsibilities in a unit not large enough to face the overall problems, and too large to face the minor local ones. A proper policy should tend to create administrative responsibilities at several levels, so that they will form a balanced system.

On the national level several efforts have been made, especially since the war, to delegate all the responsibility of human settlements to one department or ministry. These efforts were mostly influenced by post-war reconstruction needs, so that most of the effort was made in Europe, which had suffered the greatest and most extensive destruction in human settlements. In most of these cases the emphasis was on reconstruction and not on Ekistic development; yet this was a very good beginning because several services of great importance for settlements became united under one central authority. In Greece an attempt was made to bring all services related to human settlements under a central authority, when a ministry was set up first for reconstruction and then for Ekistics. Everything related to human settlements in Greece came under that ministry. But in 1951 the authority of this ministry was divided between several ministries, although its central nucleus remained the Department of Ekistics in the Ministry of Public Works, but several services, including housing, were placed under other ministries, such as Welfare and Labour, and the unified effort was once again divided.

In general there is an increasing recognition of the immediate need to bring all services related to human

settlements under one central ministry; so we are entitled to speak of an awakening where the problem of the administration of human settlements on a national level is concerned.

During the two last decades, and especially during the 60's, several large political parties in the major Western countries have begun to look into the affairs of human settlements in a more pragmatic way although they lay the emphasis on urban settlements, since these are the settlements that create an obviously more critical situation. The fact that in the 1964 conferences and policy statements, the two major political parties in Britain made a point of speaking about the need for several types of solutions for urban settlements and the necessity to plan for them in different ways by using all modern scientific methods, information, control systems, etc., indicates an awareness in those who, as leaders, are concerned with major human problems. The fact that President Johnson, during his 1964 campaign speeches, declared that urban problems deserve the greatest attention of the government and announced that he was preparing action on the national level, further strengthened the optimistic view that an awakening in this field of public interest and national action for human settlements has begun.

To conclude, I think that a consciousness of urban affairs in science, administration and political life is beginning. But the degree of the effort being made is small, and great confusion still exists. Even though there is a beginning, we should not think that something important has taken place. The effort must be intensified and clarified as soon as possible and in all possible directions. Otherwise there will still be great dangers of delay and misguided action.

On the international level there has been no proper recognition of the real issue. The very fact that there are international, specialised agencies of the United Nations in many fields, such as agriculture, education and health, but no corresponding organisation for human settlements (which on the national level are beginning to have their own organisations) is quite characteristic of how little recognition of this problem there is on the international level. The very fact that within the United Nations human settlements come under the section of Social Welfare demonstrates the low level of importance and understanding that this major field of human endeavour receives.

It is a good sign that 1963 saw the first meeting of the first committee to operate on an international level within the United Nations, the Committee on Housing, Building and Planning, on which 21 countries are represented. And in the same year, in the United Nations Conference on the Application of Science and Technology for the Benefit of the Less Developed Areas, a special committee was set up to discuss problems of urbanisation. Yet, even though these two meetings took place in the United Nations during the same month, they both avoided facing the real issue—human settlements. One meeting was on Housing, Building and Planning and tried to circumvent the overall issue in order not to offend other agencies, and the other was a Committee on Urbanisation which tried to concentrate on only one aspect, the movement of more people into urban areas.

The following year, 1964, when the United Nations Committee on Housing, Building and Planning met again, despite the fact that there was a greater recognition of the real issues involved, a move by several countries for the creation of an international agency to face the problems of human settlements at the proper level resulted in a voting draw, thus bringing the effort to a stalemate. Even though for two consecutive years an attempt was made for a better understanding and recognition of the necessity for action, the proposal for a new agency has not risen from the level of the committee. The Secretariat has actually brought the effort to a standstill by proposing that housing, building and planning should come under Welfare; and no other body has tried to facilitate better and wider action than that now being carried out, which deals only with minor areas as compared to the real overall problem of human settlements.

Although at the official level there was no recognition of the necessity for action in the field of human settlements, 1963 was the year when the first unofficial meeting was held of a group of scientists, teachers and administrators concerned with this major human problem. This group met for one week on the island of Delos in the Aegean Sea and came up with the Declaration of Delos—the first document of its nature in which both the real dimensions of the subject and the necessity to face it with a special science are stated. This Declaration states that:

'The city throughout history has been the cradle of human civilisation and progress. Today, like every other human institution, it is profoundly involved in the deepest and widest revolution ever to overtake mankind.

'This revolution proceeds under the sign of dynamic change. In the next forty years, the world's population will rise to seven thousand million. Science and technology determine more and more of the processes of human living. As they advance, Man's social behaviour is profoundly modified. These changes present themselves in every field as a danger matched by an even greater opportunity. Man can use atomic power to reduce every human settlement to the shambles of Hiroshima. It may give him enough energy to fulfil all human needs. The world's population may far outstrip its food supply. Even to keep pace, today's food production must rise threefold by the year 2000. Yet for the first time, we also have the means of securing enough food for everyone.

'We underline with all possible urgency our belief that in every action of ours, in the agencies dealing with these problems on a national or international level, in the institutions of higher learning, whether public or private, our society requires: (a) to establish in its own right a new discipline of human settlements; (b) to initiate basic research of the most far-reaching kind; (c) to bring together specialists from other relevant disciplines to work together on projects in this field; (d) to work out new methods of training the men who can assume leadership and responsibility in the sphere of action; (e) to attract some of the best young minds into this new area of research, development and practice.

'We come from different nations, from different cultural backgrounds. Our politics differ, our professions are various. But we believe that the problem of human settlements is a general and fundamental problem in our new dynamic world and that it must be viewed and studied in such a way that it will, in common with all great scientific disciplines, transcend our local differences. We agree that the practical implementation of policy—in such vital fields as land use, the location of investment or the planning of cities over time—will be determined by domestic policies and needs, and as citizens we pledge ourselves to attempt to bring these issues into the active political dialogue of our local societies. But we are not divided in what we wish most strongly to affirm—that we are citizens of a worldwide city, threatened by its own torrential expansion and that at this level our concern and commitment is for man himself'.[18]

Such a Declaration, although signed by only 34 people, is of great importance since it may inspire more extensive movements in this field, especially if the group continues its activity as a catalytic force which could mobilise public opinion on an international level in order to raise interest in the overall field of human settlements and in coordinated scientific action. Four more meetings in 1964, 1965, 1966 and 1967 (the Delos Symposia Two, Three, Four and Five) have confirmed the belief of all the participants that such action is necessary and that great progress could be achieved by uniting all possible talents and forces in order to lead to the attitudinal change which we so badly need.

The recognition of the real issues even by a small group of people, the beginning of a movement for a better understanding of the problems of human settlements, and the first official meeting on the international level, all point to an awakening in the field of human settlements, even if progress is slow and the movements are only the first signs of a changing attitude. Our generation may be called the generation of awareness in this field. My own effort in the present book is a contribution in this direction.

PROGRAMMES

Ekistic programmes are the specific expression of Ekistic policies in terms of the dimensions of time, expenditures, etc.; they are projections into the future which contain specific measurements and dimensions. They start with the broad conception and description of action in every field and end up as budgets which are programmes that have entered the implementation phase. Goals and policies about which we

423

411

Ekistic programmes expressed in relation to time

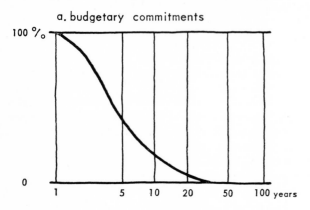

a. budgetary commitments

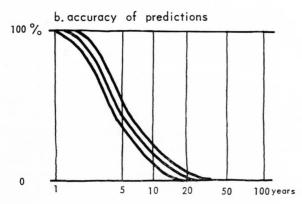

b. accuracy of predictions

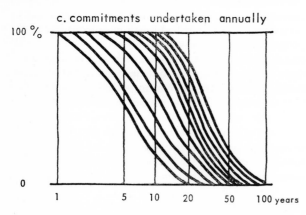

c. commitments undertaken annually

more distant future is very small, since by then many factors will have changed completely. In spite of this, it is necessary to look ahead, because to say, for example, that a city will grow 20 times in 100 years, without defining to some extent what this would mean in terms of investment of facilities, etc., would mean little. Only if we define all known phenomena related to such growth in specific measurements, can we see the reasonability or the absurdity of our assumptions. Thus, a policy should always be expressed in specific dimensions as well as in a general programme.

From the general conception of a programme for 100 years, to the budget which is under execution every fiscal year, there is a variety of programmes, depending on the length of time they cover, and the variety of their detail. We cannot solve the problems of major settlements, especially, with five, ten- and 20-year programmes only, because these problems have been created over many generations and require corresponding periods for their solution. In practice we will need (fig. 411) a whole set of programmes such as:

- a 100-year programme, as a general, vague answer to the magnitude of several phenomena;
- general 50-, 40- or 30-year programmes;
- specific 20-year programmes, including both those commitments already undertaken and the new ones to be undertaken;
- five-year programmes, including such commitments as are definite for this period, and the new items to be created every year;
- one-year programmes expressed in the annual budget, which is to be immediately implemented.

In fig. 411, we can see how to judge these Ekistic programmes. If we are speaking of budgetary commitments, the programme for the first year should approximate what is going to happen. The commitments to be made during the programme for the next five years, however, will be much smaller, and may mean one-third or one-half of the fifth year's budget. They will mean much less for the tenth year's budget, and so on (fig. 411a). In this way, the budgetary commitments undertaken annually will change every year, and we will have the chance to ameliorate our programming on the basis of the new commitments undertaken. If we stop to think that in growing settlements (which means the great majority of important settlements) the annual budgets are going to increase, we see the meaning of the space between curves 1, 2, 3, etc.

The accuracy of prediction of these programmes also varies with their length. During the first year, we can expect to predict correctly on the basis of the year's budget, most of which is going to be implemented, and which creates commitments shown by the first curve in fig. 411b. On the basis of the curves shown in diagram fig. 411c we can now think of the programming process year by year. During the first year we will have the first curve in fig. 411c; in the second year the curve will move into a new location; this will happen annually, and consequently we see that this programming process can

hear so much but are never implemented have not passed through the phase of their expression in concrete terms as programmes.

Programmes can be conceived and worked out for long periods. When a policy is conceived for a hundred years, it should be accompanied by a very general notion of a programme, in order to have some content. Certainly the possibility of implementing this general programme in the

412

**Ekistic programmes expressed in three of their
five basic aspects**

413

**Ekistic programmes expressed in relation to time,
population and income**

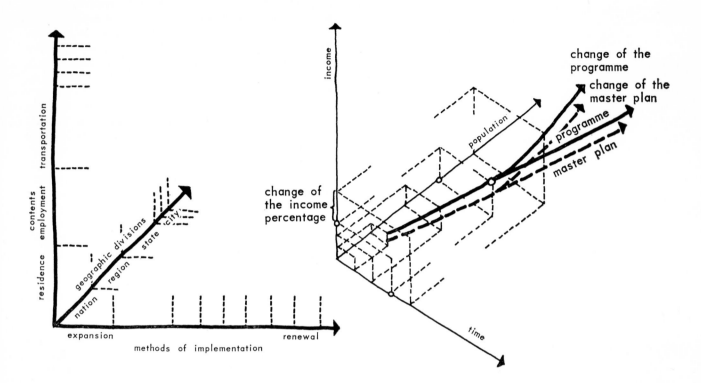

keep ahead of us in such a way as will allow us to carry out a preventive policy, not a curative one, to run ahead of evolution, not behind it, and will allow us a greater degree of prediction, invention and creation in the future. In this way, the existing programme becomes the best foundation for Ekistic development.

Ekistic programmes must be expressed in various dimensions. I have spoken only of the dimension of time. However, they must also be expressed by elements, by geographic divisions, by functions and by methods of implementation, if we deal with expansion, renewal, etc. In every case we should be sure that we interconnect the different aspects of programmes properly by combining them by twos in two-dimensional tables and by threes in three-dimensional conceptions (fig. 412). In fact we are dealing with five aspects, and we must be able to look at one after the other in a systematic way as follows:

- programmes for each kind of Ekistic unit we are dealing with;
- programmes for the five separate elements of the settlements;
- programmes for all functions;
- programmes for all factors;

- programmes related to the methods of implementation, such as the expansion of existing settlements, their renewal, new settlements, etc.

Ekistic programmes will be changing in dimensions and contents, and we should expect them in many cases to increase to a very considerable extent. Let us think of only two changing factors: the population, which is growing, and income, which in most urban areas of the world is also growing. An average Ekistic programme for a metropolitan area may increase by 8 per cent, 10 per cent or more per year for the following reasons:

- the population may be increasing by more than 4 per cent per year;
- the per capita income may be increasing by more than 4 per cent or 5 per cent per year;
- the investment per capita in Ekistic wealth may be increasing even more, since food consumption and other items have reached the point of consumer satisfaction, and after a certain point they will increase to a lesser degree;
- new items such as housing for the underprivileged classes, etc., may have to be added in order to fill up the gaps created in the previous periods.

425

414

meaning of programming

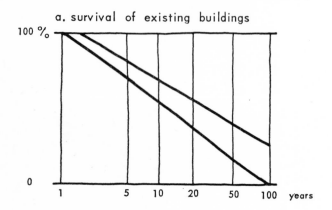

a. survival of existing buildings

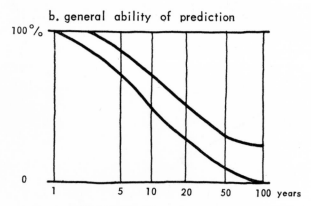

b. general ability of prediction

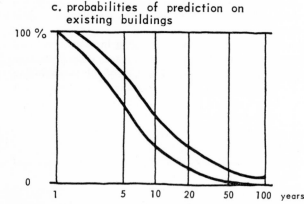

c. probabilities of prediction on existing buildings

It is important to understand how these programmes develop; this can be seen even if we take only the two factors of population and income (fig. 413). If we want now to understand what the meaning of programming for the future would be, we should think in the following way. If we take only the factor of existing buildings and assume an average life expectancy of 100 years, we can draw the curve of the

percentage which will survive (fig. 414a). But we must also look at the problem in a different way, in relation to our general ability of prediction. This is represented by a different curve (fig. 414b). If we now want to speak about the probability of prediction for buildings which exist today, we will be dealing with the curves of fig. 414c which are lower than the previous ones, since on the one hand we are dealing with diminishing wealth, and on the other with a diminishing ability to predict. This probability will increase if we have the proper programmes, for then our ability to predict will increase, and the chances of survival for existing buildings will also increase. Thus, with existing programmes we may be dealing with two curves, which are much higher than the previous ones.

When we now speak about programmes, it becomes clear that, apart from the theoretical knowledge about the overall field of human settlements, we must develop a methodology for the exact evaluation of such complicated programmes. We mentioned the necessity of viewing programmes from five aspects and of thinking of all their possible combinations. As an illustration of one aspect of such programmes, which is the result of a study of all its aspects, I mention those for new houses in Iraq as conceived in 1955 as a part of a national Ekistic programme (fig. 415). This is only an illustration of one aspect which combines the relationship of incomes and house types, and of house types and floors. It is on this basis that the relationship of incomes and densities are estimated for the development of a minor or major community. However, neither the example of several national programmes, nor any other ones have been complete Ekistic programmes. There are many weaknesses in all the efforts that have been carried out up to now. For example, let us think of the need to understand the pressures in the centre of a growing metropolitan area. In order to have a clear view of the real issues involved, we cannot express ourselves in our usual, naïve way by saying that the centre is dying and we must, therefore, build up the periphery. This is a very naïve statement since the centre may well be dying but, it is not the periphery that needs building. The centre must be saved, but we cannot save it if at the same time we continue to increase the pressures being exercised on it. In such a case we must acquire the ability to proceed in the following way, which is only an example:

○ the centre of the city dies;
○ the cause is the increase of pressure on it;
○ the pressure is due to an increased population and increased functions;
○ it is also due to the expansion of the city, which requires better servicing from the centre (better railway stations, bus stations, etc.);
○ there are new demands on the centre;
○ the centre cannot cope with these new demands;
○ if the people want and need the centre, it must be remodelled and access to it should be made easier;

415
comparative table of house types
National Housing Programme
Iraq (1956)

	A			A12	B16	B23	C28	D01	E01	F01	G01
income group	A				B		C	D	E	F	G
north / south	A04	A01	A03					D01	E01	F01	G01
plot — m²	72.00	54.00 72.00	90.00	81.00	108.00	135.00	144.00	162.00	216.00	315.00	720.00
main-rooms — m²	17.90	20.70 20.70	23.50	28.70	38.10	47.70	73.20	56.40	65.00	102.00	155.40
verandah — m²	5.00	9.70 15.50	5.40	7.00	7.00	7.20	15.90	32.40	36.00	71.10	67.90
auxiliary space — m²	2.10	3.10 3.10	1.80	9.90	9.90	9.90	11.80	11.00	17.00	21.30	28.00
courtyard — m²	42.00	11.50 22.90	54.00	21.10	35.20	48.80	41.80	94.50	120.00	172.00	443.20
volume — m³	82.40	111.80 122.70	114.70	169.70	211.70	249.30	381.70	390.80	578.00	776.20	1247.70
cost — I.D	247 / 200	335 / 490 368 / 370	344 / 340	509 / 340	635 / 100	748 / 080	1336 / 055	1563 / 400	2601 / 045	3493 / 170	5614 / 785

income group
access
west - east
north south

plot

main - rooms
verandah
auxiliary space
w.c. shower · kitchen store
bath
courtyard
volume
cost

○ this solution must be judged and compared with other alternatives;

○ when we conclude that it is better to do as we have decided, we must take into consideration the fact that the causes do not cease to exist, the population will continue to increase, pressures will increase also and new functions will be added;

○ we must, therefore, either arrest the new pressure by thinking in a creative way, or remodel the centre continuously, etc.

It is quite clear that such a problem (if indeed we are limited to this one) requires the use of the most modern techniques and equipment. Although we now have the engineers equipped to face such complicated problems, we have not turned to them; neither have we managed to mobilise the available talents which can deal with other similar problems. Ekistics is not the only field which is lagging so in the employment of its means. In medicine, for example, we know that all the vital functions can be measured by electronic devices; but these are used only to a very limited extent. In human settlements this situation is even worse: they are hardly used at all. The few known attempts being made are not concerned with the whole problem, they are only in the phase of data collection and do not proceed to synthesis. It is only in urban traffic studies that modern methods for measurements are being used but even there we fail to achieve as much as we should because of:

○ the lack of coordination of the traffic problem with the overall problem of human settlements;

○ the fact that we approach the problems of traffic through curative policies and not preventive ones;

○ the fact that only lately have we begun to implement such methods, and consequently we do not know how to use them in the best possible way.

Ekistic programmes are now beginning to be created for some urban areas and for a few countries, but we are still in the very elementary stage of programming, especially because we do not connect goals and policies with programmes and we do not clarify every issue related to Ekistic elements and units; we must become aware of this fact.

PLANS

After having set goals and defined policies and programmes, we reach the point of preparing plans, by which I mean in this study physical plans as opposed to non-physical programmes, for all types and sizes of Ekistic units: regional, metropolitan, local plans, neighbourhood layout plans, single project plans, building plans, etc. The fact that the discussion of plans takes place last does not mean that we deal with them only when the other ways and methods for creating the future have ended. On the contrary: on many occasions even in setting the goals we must pay attention to the physical aspects of the whole effort. We cannot set a goal, for example, for the future of a city on an island or in a valley without taking into consideration the limitations imposed by Nature and the physical plan. Some cities have found themselves at the end of their evolution just because their physical formation did not allow for major expansion. Sooner or later, many cities reach this point, and if they are not doomed to stagnation (because lack of growth means the beginning of stagnation), they at any rate face great difficulties concerning their expansion. Thus, while physical considerations are of importance right from the conception of goals, while they influence policies (the policy of housing the people in a country poor in land will be different from the policy of housing them in a country rich in land) they play an even greater role in the formation of programmes. It is only after proper conceptions have been set as goals, policies and programmes that we reach the point of working on specific plans.

When we reach the point of knowing and understanding the settlements and guiding them through proper policies and programmes for their future development, we are confident that we can finalise our opinions about the physical plans—which are a physical expression of conceptions, policies and programmes. They are one, two and three-dimensional projections of an evolving, complicated organism. If we understand this, we can serve the development of our only subject matter—the human settlement as a whole; if not, we create unnecessary hindrances for our settlement, and it may be better to decide not to prepare any plans since this may result either in a delay in its proper development or in improper development. In working out the physical plans, we should not forget that they must change continuously since they are only expressions of an evolving organism which we are trying to guide through corresponding policies and programmes.

In the past there were no regional plans although there were some rules affecting the surrounding region, defining distances between settlements in new settled land or plans for agricultural settlements. There were more town plans and plans for specific buildings and houses, squares, avenues, etc. These plans, when they related to specific projects, were usually accompanied by budgets, and this was in many cases all that guided Ekistic action. In those days the actual conceptions of goals, policies and programmes were either unnecessary because of the low speed of the settlements' evolution, or took place unconsciously.

Our era, however, needs to develop a systematic effort for the future; we must, therefore, see plans only as the three-dimensional projection of four-dimensional goals, policies and programmes. Even though plans are only the final expression of human settlements they are of the utmost importance, for without them no rational construction can take place. This is the reason why, even though plans must now be considered as the outcome of other types of conceptions, which are four-dimensional, they are indispensable for action.

The history of settlements shows that, because of their symbolic value, plans represent the human settlement better in our mind than a goal, a programme or a budget does. Because of this, plans have been considered the only expression of human settlements. This, together with the fact that professions from which most planners begin—architecture, engineering, etc.—are professions which express themselves in drawings, helps plans to acquire in the minds of people much more importance than goals, policies and programmes. This, it must be clear by now, constitutes a great danger, since plans are normally nothing but a three-dimensional projection of the substance of human settlements (fig. 278).

Plans can differ in scale and in their degree of detail, in nature, in contents, etc. How much they can differ in scale and degree of detail can be seen in fig. 26 which presents scales of plans on the basis of the logarithmic scale of Ekistic units. If we are dealing with a room we can present it in scales of 1:1 or 1:2 which are the scales of detail drawings and continue with 1:5, 1:10, 1:50, 1:100 for the general drawings. A house can be shown on the same scales, plus at a 1:200 scale; a major building may have to be shown in the same scales plus at a 1:500 scale; a minor neighbourhood will be shown in scales ranging from 1:50 where details about a small square or a crossing of streets may be shown, to 1:1000; a major neighbourhood may cover the same scales plus that of 1:2000. In the same way we can continue in the whole range of scales which can be as small as 1:100,000 for megalopolitan areas, and one to several millions for regions beyond it. The parameters shown on plans may be of a different nature— physical (including buildings, the bulk of them, the heights, the coverage, the openings, etc.), functional (zoning, land-use, etc.) and also in connection with regulations, codes, by-laws, etc.

The nature of plans differs from case to case. Plans are usually static, since they are finally determined, or they may be flexible if they allow several of the parameters to change.

In such a case, in their own formation they can include the conception of the fourth dimension and become adjustable, evolving plans. This can happen either on a major scale, when for example, there is provision for additions of various communities, or on minor scales, where there may be additions to houses, buildings, facilities, etc. This last can be seen in the case of the growing houses, to which I referred earlier, or to adjustable community facilites, as well as in plans for future roads which show a wide right of way even though in the first stages the road widths will correspond to current traffic needs.

In this spirit we can propose that plans should be gradually turned into four-dimensional ones by always defining the validity of all their elements in time, some of which will be permanent, while others will still be committing the settlement only for a certain length of time. So we can also have a periodic revision of every plan, and we can have long-term and short-term plans in the same manner that we have long-term programmes. In this way we can have revisions of plans every given number of years in the same fashion in which we have to renew our driving licences.

Plans can also be classified according to their contents, and we can have plans for completely new settlements or new parts of existing ones (sometimes the difference is not so clear), or plans for the transformation of settlements (including amelioration plans for slum clearance as well as those providing for major improvements and changes within a part of the human settlement). All such plans, whether for new settlements, or for the transformation of settlements through amelioration or clearance, can belong either to one or a combination of the categories of completely new construction, amelioration or clearance. So, even though we will have plans for completely new settlements or their parts, we may well also have plans for amelioration through the improvement and new expansions of settlements, or plans for the clearance of old, and the addition of new parts of settlements.

CHAPTER TWELVE
NEW TASKS AHEAD

TOWARDS ECUMENOPOLIS

When speaking earlier about Ekistic evolution, I explained that we are heading towards an Ecumenopolis, the universal human settlement. While discussing Ekistic action, we should ask ourselves why we need worry about the Ecumenopolis now at a time when we are struggling unsuccessfully with so many already existing urban problems. The answer is quite simple: what is now taking place is the beginning of the process leading towards Ecumenopolis! We are already on the march towards the universal city.

We have then to answer the question whether or not we should resist the existing trends towards Ecumenopolis. This certainly is a matter of personal opinion, and I believe that to counteract the trends leading towards the Ecumenopolis would be both undesirable and impracticable. It would be undesirable because the Ecumenopolis:

- means the phase in which mankind will be able to operate as one community and since this increases the likelihood of peace, if only for this one reason, we should be all for it;
- will lead to the exploitation of resources for the benefit of the whole of mankind, and this is something which we all need badly.

Counteraction to the trends leading to Ecumenopolis is impracticable also because:

- these are trends of population growth determined by many biological and social forces which we do not even understand properly, let alone dare countermand;
- the great forces shaping the Ecumenopolis, such as economic, commercial, social, political, technological and cultural are already being deployed and it is too late to reverse them.

The eventual creation of the Ecumenopolis should therefore be considered an inevitability which we must accept. Our challenge is to make the Ecumenopolis fit for Man instead of allowing it to choke him to death. This is the great task which lies ahead of us: to make Ecumenopolis a success.

In order to achieve this we must open our eyes and develop an attitude that will allow us to understand what is to come in the next 100 to 200 years. I have explained that while studying a certain geographically limited problem, we must consider the space surrounding it in order to understand its interrelationship with the broader framework within which it is set. And in order to understand this broader concept, we must keep moving on to larger areas until we finally reach the broadest possible, the entire habitable area of the Earth, that is, the ecumenic city. When we study a certain settlement, we should not think only of its expansion in space in order to see how it is set within a geographic framework, we must also consider how it expands in content; only then can we see it in its proper perspective in relation to the economy of the country, its culture, etc. Regardless of how we look at our problem, whether from the whole to the parts or vice-versa, we should set it in its broader perspectives—the universal city.

The universal city has started being built, and it is our task to understand it properly and to guide its present course in the best way. There are those who think that the human settlements are only very small parts of our world, and who may consequently reach the conclusion that the Ecumenopolis is fictitious and will never exist. I need only remind them that human settlements do not consist only of the built-up parts of settlements which are drawn on our maps, but also of a totality of functions which cover much more extensive areas which are indispensable to the survival of the built-up part of the nucleus. Let us not forget that even though Man may live in the built-up area of settlements, he depends on their total vital space.

We should realise that the universal city has already been born and is acquiring dimensions which will eventually cover the entire inhabitable Earth. Let us therefore see where we stand. Though we are heading towards the Ecumenopolis, we have so far ignored this fact. Consequently we have failed in all our efforts to solve our major urban problems. We are simply out of time and out of focus. This is not only happening with human settlements. The same failure is evident in respect to Man. Loren Eiseley says, 'There is something wrong with our world view. It is still Ptolemaic though the sun is no longer believed to revolve around the earth'. And so he continues, 'We teach the past, we see farther; or, at best, we project far into the future idealised versions of ourselves'.[19] In human settlements I doubt very much if what we project is an idealised version. It is simply a projection of the settlements of the present for we have not been able to develop the concepts related to them into an ideal form. We do not even have conceptions of the ideal city of the present.

It is quite clear that by projecting the present form of human settlements into the future, we do not manage to solve any problems since the present form of settlements does not satisfy even our present needs. At least we can say that the man of the present corresponds to the requirements of the present. This is not true of settlements. So with human settlements, much more than with Man, we must understand where it is that we are going, since this is the only way of saving whatever can still be saved. We must change our attitude and try to understand the future, which in turn means trying to understand the Ecumenopolis. An understanding of the Ecumenopolis is necessary if any solution is to be given to any one of our future problems, since the Ecumenopolis creates a new framework, which will have new dimensions and will follow new trends requiring new solutions.

While heading blindly towards an Ecumenopolis we should perhaps ask ourselves if we should try not only to understand it better but should also try to avoid it completely since it may mean a catastrophe for Man. We cannot be sure that evolution leads towards disaster. What we do know is that the solutions we are allowing to take shape during the course of the evolution are leading us to ruin. But this may be a catastrophe limited in time, let us say to a generation or two, which will be remedied later, after many people and urban areas have suffered, after a loss in human life and values has caused a reaction on the part of humanity. This may well be the case. Evolution may follow a path which will save us from overall disaster. Then why take the trouble to act now? Disasters that occur over one or two generations may seem small incidents in the overall life of human settlements; but viewing the same phenomena from our own scale, we cannot be so passive about this evolution. One or two generations are vital to us. They include our children and our grand-children. Besides, it is our obligation to help avoid ruin for any period of time. Also we have no reason to believe that we cannot find a better solution for our new types of problems.

Neither is the general assumption, that an evolution towards a more densely populated Earth may lead to disaster and therefore should be avoided, historically justified. Let us now think what would have happened had the inhabitants of the villages of Attica, which under Theseus joined forces to form the first city of Athens, had protested against this new danger—the creation of a dense urban settlement around the Acropolis of Athens. What would we say today if we were told that the first people who went towards Venice in order to create a major Renaissance urban centre had protested against this unheard of idea of settling in the swamps in order to create a city? Can we not see that we have no experience warranting the rejection of a solution towards a more densely inhabited Earth, towards the universal city?

Our position towards such a problem should be different: assuming that we are on the march towards an Ecumenopolis, how can we ease the difficult phase through which we are now passing, which incorporates elements leading to trouble? In order to find the solutions that will ensure satisfactory conditions we must understand that the Ecumenopolis is the framework within which we must move in the future. It is our task to understand the best solutions which will save this framework and Man from disaster and will make it function as satisfactorily as did the settlements of the past, or perhaps— and why not?—much better.

Actually we have no reason to believe that the forces within the Ecumenopolis necessarily lead towards death, rather than towards rebirth and a new world, towards the most ideal human settlement that Man can conceive and achieve. We need only work towards it; we need to set a goal, develop a policy, a programme and a plan. For all of us it can become an ideal; it can become a belief. There is no logical reason why this cannot be. We need only understand that we must not content ourselves with being the descendants of our fore-fathers; we must also be the forefathers of our descendants.

HUMAN VALUES

Preserving human values

○ *Dangers and needs*

We have not yet the complete experience which will guarantee the best formation of the Ecumenopolis; but we have set goals which can guide specific action and certain solutions. This we can even now attempt to achieve. Our main goal is to make Man happy and safe. As our first target we must set the proper formation of Ecumenopolis; the main danger involved is that it might eliminate Man by suppressing human values. Our second task therefore (first in importance and second only in an orderly presentation of our thoughts) must be the preservation and further development of human values.

In studying the present trends, we have noted and confirmed the necessity of dynamically expanding and changing the overall structure of settlements, but this is no reason why we should not keep its parts as stable as possible. On the contrary it is reasonable and consistent that the smaller the parts, the more stable they will remain. And the closer the scale comes to Man, the more stable it should be. So on a macro-scale the Ecumenopolis will be dynamic, while on a micro-scale it should remain stable and static. This is a difficult problem which we must face by properly conceiving the whole and its relationship to the parts.

While speaking of the necessity for stability in the minor units, I would like to say that this stability is of greater

431

human scale as conditioned by Man

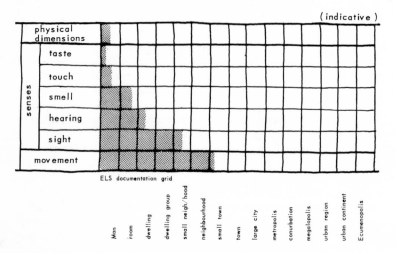

importance for the container, that is Nature, Shells and Networks, which are of a more constant nature and therefore should not change at an unnatural speed. Man and Society will be changing within this container. We cannot keep them stable and static, nor should we; after all, we do not know whether they should be static in the minor parts of settlements, or whether we have the power to keep them static even if we believed it right that we should do so. The only remark to be made about Man and Society is that we are certain that Man needs surroundings of a permanent nature during the 'nesting' period, and that it is better to provide as stable conditions as possible for the younger inhabitants of the community. We have the obligation to achieve this by properly shaping the natural landscape, Shells and Networks. Even if we could contribute also to the stability of Man and Society—which would seem desirable—we would not be at all certain either of the desirability of such stability from every point of view, or the feasibility of the procedure. So Nature, Shells and Networks should tend to be as stable as possible and to constitute a stable environment while the two more mobile elements, Man and Society, should adjust themselves to the others, as long as this seems reasonable in view of the broader aims we are trying to serve.

While we are able to talk about the necessity to keep the three permanent elements in the minor parts of the settlements as stable as possible, we must admit that very little effort is being made in this direction. On the contrary, we are witnessing the following two tendencies:
- destruction of the landscape (this is taking place in most of the organised expansions of new cities; it is also taking place within existing cities where there is a tendency to eliminate the last elements of the natural landscape in the cause of the expansion of buildings,

highways, parking lots, etc.);
- destruction of the stability which used to exist in settlements by the introduction at a continuously higher rate of new elements and new functions everywhere. The fact that we design minor residential roads so as to allow through-traffic for a great number of cars, with no respect for the inhabitants of both sides of the road, shows that we do not understand the necessity of keeping the minor parts of the settlements as stable as possible. And the fact that we are now taking minor squares—which had been the 'breathing spaces' of many settlements serving many social and economic functions—and turning them into parking lots, shows the same lack of respect for the need of stability.

Such action not only destroys stability, but by doing so destroys one of the most important characteristics of human settlements—the human scale which derives from Man himself, and which has been the only scale to influence human settlements until the era of the machine, when railways, automobiles, elevators and airplanes, became parts of our settlements. This human scale is now being destroyed throughout our settlements. It is even being occasionally destroyed within buildings themselves, as when we allow automobiles to enter even the inner courts of palazzos, changing their function and scale completely. It is being destroyed when we allow automobiles to approach monuments and enter squares and streets which have been designed for Man. It is being destroyed when we design minor parts of settlements according to the scale of automobiles despite the fact that it is not necessary.

The way this scale is being destroyed can be seen in most of the settlements of the world which have a major archaeological, cultural or aesthetic value; and it can be seen in the

human scale as conditioned by hearing

normal bubbles   extended bubble

confidential talk   normal talk   distant talk or normal call

design of almost all our new projects and in the neighbourhoods of all our cities.

We must keep our settlements human and preserve the human scale. This is one task which is even more important that that of organising settlements in a rational way in order to allow them to function and not die. We must serve both basic elements of the settlement, content and container. For the former we must keep the settlements human or else Man will suffer. And we must serve the latter in a way that will allow it to function, for otherwise the settlement will die. If we do not in the first case it will not be human, in the second it will be eliminated.

If we want to preserve the human scale, we must understand it. In order to do this, we may act in two ways:

○ learn as much as we can about it by studying the way in which the scale is derived from Man;

○ learn as much as possible by studying what kind of human scale Man has created during the six-thousand-year-old history of permanent human settlements.

The meaning of the human scale

I have often mentioned the human scale, now I must also define it. As I have already said, one way of learning about it is through analysis, which means understanding the derivation of the human scale. The human scale can be derived only from Man (fig. 416). But how is Man related to this scale? We could answer this by pointing out that Man is related to his physical environment in several ways such as:

○ through his physical dimensions;

○ through his senses;

○ through his movements.

In the first case we can easily say that a chair is part of the human scale if it enables Man to sit, without being either too narrow for his needs or unnaturally large. For example, a chair meant for one Man yet large enough to seat two ceases

to be on the human scale. The same holds true for a table, a bed, a family dining-room, a school-room, etc. These should correspond to the physical dimensions of the people using them. In the first case (furniture) we are dealing with the physical dimensions of Man himself, in the second (rooms) with the physical dimensions of the 'bubbles' surrounding Man, as already explained in Chapter Seven.

In the case of our senses, the situation is more complicated since there are five of them; so we should make distinctions between them. For example, I do not see how taste can be related to the human scale in space; for the time being I cannot see any relation. With touch, the human scale is related mainly to the quality of materials Man touches—materials can be soft or hard, pleasant or unpleasant for his hands, feet, elbows or knees; materials should be suited to Man's touch, and this includes their temperature when Man touches them. In this way we can define the human scale from the point of view of touch. We are not concerned about the quality of a ceiling from the point of view of touch, while we care a lot about the surface of the furniture and walls, and in a different way about the surface of the floor.

There is a direct relationship between the human sense of smell and the odour of our surroundings. We cannot permit the use of materials whose odour is unbearable or even unpleasant; nor can we bear rooms which are not well ventilated. We should create the proper human scale in terms of smell, and in a complete synthesis we should take into consideration the fact that the human scale in relation to our nose should not simply be inoffensive, that is, of a negative value, but on the contrary it should be of a positive one. Let us compare our awareness of human scale on entering a factory to that of being in a street, or entering a small courtyard full of flowers, or a room full of stagnant and decaying flowers, and we will find ways of satisfying our sense of smell and providing a satisfactory human scale in terms of it.

With hearing we must take into consideration distances,

418

**human scale as conditioned by eyesight
perception of forms in a public square**

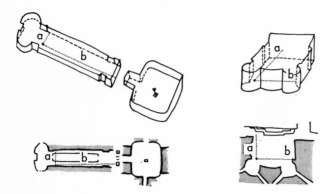

intensities, qualities of sounds, as well as reflections and other problems related to acoustics. There are spaces which, because of their shape, form and materials, are on a human scale from the point of view of hearing, and other spaces which are unsatisfactory. We can, by proper analysis, differentiate between those which are satisfactory, and those which are not. In the case of hearing, the human scale can be expressed in forms and in distances. When the form of a room causes an echo it is not at all satisfactory. When the distances are such that we cannot speak to others—that is, when our hearing 'bubbles' do not meet—we have lost the human scale (fig. 417). When, for example, about 100 years ago, the authorities of the city of Athens decided to widen some central streets, the inhabitants protested that the streets would be so wide that they would not be able to speak to one another if they were walking on opposite sidewalks. The planners were inclined to laugh at this attitude. But they were incorrect because we should be aware that by widening a street across which people have been used to talking to one another, we are depriving them of an element which encompassed the human scale. I do not say that we can keep all streets as narrow as that. Unfortunately we cannot in many cases, but there are cases where we must and can. We must be aware of the scale that exists in hearing.

Finally, sight is the sense which most clearly defines the relationship of Man to space. When we want to be able to see people, we can say that they should not be located farther than a certain distance in the open and in an enclosed space. This is what defines the maximum distance in a theatre or in a city square. When we want to speak to people, however, the scale is different. When we want to look at an object closely, we know now that we should not look at it at an angle of more than 30° with a maximum of 45°. Looking at it at a greater angle tires our eyes. This angle in many ways defines the human scale where what we want to create is related to

what we want to see. Such angles also define those spaces desirable for our purposes. For example, we do not want a very elongated square as we could not easily see in all directions without tiring our eyes. The adjustment between 'a' and 'b' (fig. 418) is very difficult if the square is elongated, while it is very easy and not tiresome at all if both sides of the square do not differ by more than a 1:2 ratio. This, apart from other reasons for which the second type of square is preferable to the first, is directly related to our eye-sight. The human scale of our sight defines not only forms, but distances as well. If we want to see an object very clearly, we must keep it at a certain distance; if we want to see it as a whole, we must keep it at a different distance; according to its dimension, we can define the distance of the object.

In this way we can define several distances which do not go beyond certain limits depending on the type of relationship we want to develop. If we want to sit with somebody and speak to him, the distance cannot be a few centimetres, it should be about a metre or more, but it cannot go beyond five or six metres. If two people in a room select their seats in order to speak, they will sit neither very close nor very far apart. If, however, we are concerned with the relationship of a man to a monument, we will find that this relationship is given by the angle at which he can view it; if it is large he will stand at a greater distance, if it is small he has to be very close in order to see it properly. The distance can range from a few metres, for a very small statue, to hundreds of metres for a large building. If the relationship is one with the landscape, the distance may be thousands of metres instead of hundreds. I know of no cases in which the human scale relates Man to landscape in distances greater than a few kilometres. This shows that we have a variation of human scales, depending on our purposes and the elements with which we want to be related, ranging from a metre to a few thousand metres.

If we now relate all these remarks about the senses to the Ekistic Logarithmic Scale we can see that there are different expressions of the notion of human scale; depending on whether we want to see, hear or both see and hear, and so on. In this way we can express ourselves properly and specifically in terms of the human scale related to our senses (fig. 419). In any case, all types of scales derived from our senses have a maximum limit.

The human scale is also related to our movements, to our ability to reach something with our hands, to our ability to walk, etc. For example, our ability to reach something defines the height of our furniture—the height of a bookcase for example. Even if we want to use a ladder, we will be introducing an extension of the human scale, and we will find a second limit to it. Our ability to walk in different ways and to different degrees of fatigue defines the scale in length. Within the corridor of a hospital we can walk up to a certain point; within a square which we want to enjoy we can walk up to a certain limit; within a neighbourhood, a community or a city,

419

human scale of the senses

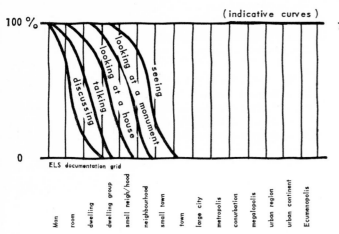

420

human scale as conditioned by movement

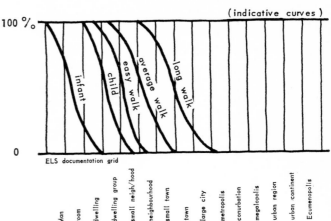

we can walk up to a certain distance depending on our age, health and purpose for walking. All these combined define scales in movement. The same is valid for movement on one level, vertical movement, etc. In this way we can define the scales of a nursery, a square meant for Man, or a community where Man is supposed to walk, by defining the maximum, minimum and average limits. We can in this way define the dimensions of Ekistic space in relation to the movement of Man. Here we find that the maximum distances we can cover constitute the dimensions of a small city, while for other purposes the dimensions and the human scales are much smaller.

If we complete such an analysis of what Man needs and likes in relation to his senses, to his movement and to his physical dimensions, we will reach the point where we will be able to define the human scale on the basis of analytical experience, and then proceed to define it for the different kinds of space and needs (fig. 420).

We could even proceed further in our research in order to define more carefully questions related to our psychological reaction to different types of Ekistic space. Psychology could help us define the influence Ekistic space can have on the self-image of Man. The way this question could be answered should be based on the previous analysis; then we can ask ourselves how we want this concept of the self-image to be interpreted, how we want it to be projected; for example, do we want Man to be aware that he is enclosed in a very small place and consequently feel afraid? Do we want him to get a feeling of wildness, or of self-importance, etc.? Depending on what we want to do, we can use different types of human scales in the formation of space. On the basis of the world that we want to create for our senses and movements, we can define the Ekistic scale. We will always find that as long as Man's life and movements are concerned, the scale should be limited to the lower parts of the entire Ekistic space.

Learning from experience

The analytical method by which we try to define the human scale can be supplemented by what we can learn empirically from the experience gained in six thousand years of human history. We need only look at the streets and squares which were made for Man in order to understand how far Man wanted to develop space on a human scale because in the past only the human scale existed, with a few exceptions of scales created for animals such as hippodromes, etc. Looking back we can learn from every period of history and can then compare our findings and come to conclusions of major importance. Minor squares do not exceed a few dozen metres in length; the same is true of internal courtyards. Major squares seldom exceed one hundred metres in one of their dimensions, and much more seldom are they more than this distance in both dimensions. Even the very large squares are very seldom two hundred metres in one direction, and this only if they contain very important monuments.

This feeling of a human scale existed in all periods and was accompanied by an appropriately developed architecture. The most characteristic examples can be drawn from ancient Greece, the Italian Renaissance and the works of the great Moguls either in India or Pakistan. These periods convince us that the concept of the human scale was not expressed only subconsciously, but also by a very conscious and well-studied method. The most characteristic examples are in Greece, where certain relationships existed not only between distances, but between the angles at which Man looked at various monuments as well (fig. 421). We can be sure that on the Acropolis of Athens there was an attempt to create a synthesis that allowed the eye to understand its main elements more easily. When we look at the Parthenon at an angle of 30°, we understand that the relation of Man entering the Acropolis

435

human scale as conditioned by eyesight and movement   in ancient Greek monumental syntheses

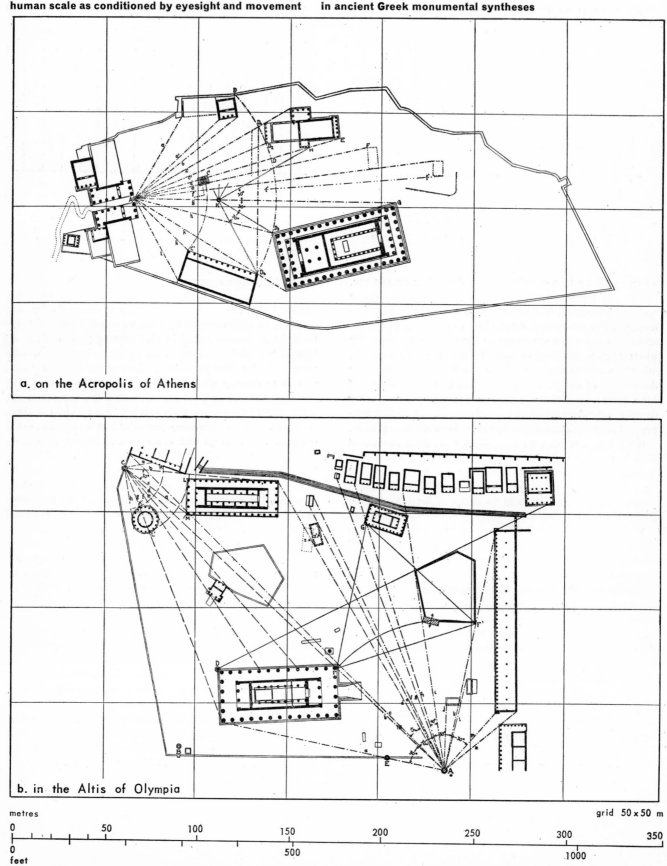

a. on the Acropolis of Athens

b. in the Altis of Olympia

metres   grid 50 x 50 m

0   50   100   150   200   250   300   350

0   500   1000
feet

422

(right) human scale in a small pedestrian street
Mosul, Iraq (1958)

423

(below) human scale in a small square
Mosul, Iraq (1958)

424

(below right) human scale in a market square
Korangi, Pakistan (1964)

to its main monument was intentionally organised so as to allow Man to see this monument at the best possible angle. We can make similar remarks about the other synthesis, based on a 36° angle, which was used mostly in Ionia. In continental Greece and some islands the 30° angle prevailed. Such examples can convince us of what we can learn by studying the experience gained in the past.

Present efforts

I have tried to re-establish the human scale in minor units of many of the projects I was related with. As examples of such efforts I can mention the creation of minor roads in many projects where people did not own an automobile, or would not do so in the foreseeable future. Such is the case of roads in projects in the Middle East, Pakistan, Africa, as well as in countries where people may own or may expect to own an automobile but should still leave it a certain distance from the entrances to their houses, in the same way in which an inhabitant of a high-standard block of flats leaves his car some distance from the entrance to his own flat. Why should we allow ourselves to walk a certain distance from our automobiles if we live in multi-storey buildings and not if we live in one-storey houses? Certainly this can stir up arguments, but the point I want to make here is that we can establish the human scale in minor residential and other streets (fig. 422). Whether we want to reach our house by car or not, there are always ways of preserving the human scale in minor spaces even if machines must enter them.

On the basis of such ideas I have tried to make the public squares of minor communities inaccessible to cars, and to derive their dimensions from distances which are satisfactory to a man who is looking, shopping, talking and walking. As examples of this there is a small gossip square in similar projects in Iraq (fig. 423) and a market square in Pakistan (fig. 424).

425

relationship of the human and non-human scales

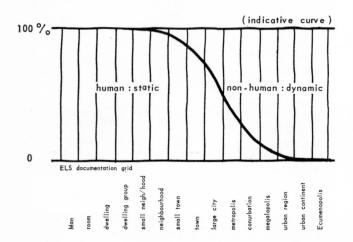

FROM THE NON-HUMAN TO
THE HUMAN SCALE

Definition by physical dimensions

Up to now I have developed the case for the Ecumenopolis and the necessity that we move towards it by rational thinking. I have also spoken of the necessity of preserving human values so as to allow Man to survive within this expanding man-made landscape. So, we are at the point where we can state that we are consciously creating a man-made landscape which is controlled by new forces which are non-human; this is the Ecumenopolis with all of its parts (megalopolis, metropolis, etc.) at related scales. But at the same time we want to create this major man-made landscape in a way that will correspond to human values.

How can we now reconcile this necessity for the non-human scale of the Ecumenopolis with the necessity to preserve human values? The answer is the same as that given when I was speaking about the need for a dynamically growing settlement with stable parts: the human settlement of the future should be dynamic in its macro-scale and as stable as possible in its micro-scale. The same holds true both for the non-human and human: the settlement of the future will necessarily remain non-human in its macro-scale and human in its micro-scale. In this way we arrive at what could be called the synthesis of opposites (fig. 425). This rule, which provides for a human, basically static space in the minor units of the whole Ekistic scale and a non-human or dynamic space in its major units, shows how we can proceed towards the creation of the whole range of space we need in order to survive within the Ecumenopolis. At first, there was

only a human scale; then came the machines, which imposed their non-human scale, and other forces which imposed dynamic growth. Overwhelmed by these forces, we allowed them to enter into the realm of the human and static, and the non-human and dynamic. We live in both, and both have to serve us, only the first has to serve Man as he is, while the second has to first serve its parts, then, as a whole, serve Man as he is supplemented by artificial extensions. In the first we live as free agents, moving around and imposing the human scale, in the second we are going to be protected by bubbles corresponding to Man's dimensions. Be they airplanes, rockets, new types of automobiles or railways, these bubbles will contain completely human dimensions while moving in non-human, dynamic space.

So we arrive at a system of units with corresponding human spaces:

Units	*Human Spaces*
room	room
dwelling	living room
dwelling group	major hall, minor square
small neighbourhood	square
neighbourhood	square
small town	major public square
town	central monumental square
large city	not solved
metropolis	,, ,,
conurbation	,, ,,
megalopolis	,, ,,
urban region	,, ,,
urbanised continent	,, ,,
Ecumenopolis	,, ,,

As we move from one end of the scale to the other, the more the static turns into the dynamic, the human into the non-human. Certainly, these concepts of static, dynamic, human and non-human are of a relative and not of an absolute value, as has already been explained. But if we want to compare phenomena on the whole Ekistic scale, we can find our way through such a broad distinction and definition of the two trends.

It now becomes clear that we are dealing with several sets of forces which have a different value in the various parts of the Ecumenopolis. In rooms and small squares we can re-establish the human scale completely. In larger areas the motor scale will begin to intrude till we reach the major areas where the motor scale prevails.

An important point that we must keep in mind is at what stage of the transfer from minor to major parts does the motor scale or the machine scale begin to prevail. We can gradually discover this by proper surveys such as those being carried out at the Athens Center of Ekistics, one of which deals with the definition of the variables in the dimensions of the human community, and the other with the dimensions which prevailed in all ancient Greek cities. Both studies lead to the same conclusion in reference to the maximum distance over which Man liked and still likes to walk.

We began accumulating and implementing this experience in 1946, when in the Greek Government's Ministry of Reconstruction and Ekistics, we had the opportunity of designing the first human community near Athens—the reconstruction of an experimental housing scheme in the demolished areas of the city of Piraeus. From that time on we have had opportunities to study the human scale and its operation in more than 20 countries in several areas of the world. These continuous surveys have allowed us to reach some conclusions about the distances in which Man likes to walk and beyond which he does not want or does not need to. Such surveys have found that Man easily walks up to one kilometre (or 10–12 minutes) and many people like to walk this distance. As far as a maximum distance is concerned, I believe we are very close to the average desire and possibilities.

So we see that both studies mentioned, as well as the surveys we have carried out in more than 20 countries in relation to specific projects, prove that one kilometre is the maximum average urban walking distance for Man. This means that we must have corresponding units not crossed by automobiles, in which people can walk freely up to the distance of one kilometre. Such a community can be surrounded by highways at distances of about two kilometres. Since many people do not want to walk or cannot walk this distance, automobiles should be able to enter these communities, but not cross them, or, at least, cross them as little as possible. Certainly there are people who do not want to walk this distance just as there are others who like to walk greater ones. For these last we can interconnect our communities with pedestrian bridges or underpasses.

Such a community can be implemented regardless of what type of regulations we are working with. It has been tried in the U.S.A., Africa, Asia and Europe both in the planning and designing stage or in actual construction. Depending on the case, the number of inhabitants and automobiles, the density of the population and size of investment, such a community may reach dimensions of two by two kilometres (corresponding to the maximum dimension in both directions) or may be as small as one sixteenth of the maximum, that is, 500 metres to 1,000 metres. However, this creates difficulties if we do not want it crossed by automobiles for we cannot comply with many countries' regulations, many of which are quite reasonable. This is why if we decide to use this maximum community size we should allow it to be crossed by automobiles moving towards the centres, with the provision that a person coming from the outlying houses or neighbourhoods towards the central ones should not cross the car-lines more than once. This can easily be effected and leads to a division of the community into a central part or nucleus, and the surrounding communities or neighbourhoods. What is important is that this overall community should not be

divided by through-lines, since this will break its continuity. Cars should be able to reach the nucleus without passing through to the other side of the community; they should instead move around the central nucleus in order to cross the community. This means that anyone wanting to pass beyond the community would not select this line, since it would be much more practical to take the outlying through-lines designed for this purpose. But these internal motor-vehicle roads do divide the overall communities into minor ones, the basic communities.

Here in the basic community the machine scale ends and the human scale begins. This community corresponds to the lowest limit of the non-human scale, which starts at the Ecumenopolis and should not enter the human scale. In practice, it was found through a great number of projects that in many countries the human community corresponds for many categories of income to a class IV community, in other cases where incomes are higher and plots are larger to a class III community and in some others, it may approach a class V community. Thus, we conclude that the limits between the non-human and human scale are to be found in a human community, and this community, depending on many factors, is either class III, IV or V.

Thus, we can now describe the human community as that corresponding to three factors as in fig. 426:
o walking distance,
o human scale, and
o social groupings,
and having the following physical characteristics:
  o it is surrounded by highways imposing the non-human scale, but these are restricted to the borders of the communities;
  o it is connected with adjoining communities by controlled passages for pedestrians, or by bridges or underpasses;
  o it is not crossed by the automobile, but is served by it;
  o it is designed on a human scale in all its elements, with emphasis placed on the requirements of the pedestrian in design, movement, spatial dimensions, etc.

It becomes clear that in class I, II and III communities, we can definitely have a human scale. Beyond class III communities, we may have a human scale on rare occasions; this occurs in most cases in class IV communities and in some extreme cases in class V. From class III or IV or V on up, we have mechanical connections based on the automobile, train or airplane, of which the latter is prevalent in even larger community sizes. However, these mechanical, non-human dynamic scales are not always the same. If we have the introduction of the mechanical scale around the class III community size, this scale is of a relatively low degree of intensity. If the mechanical scale starts around a class IV community, its intensity is greater. Beyond class V it is even greater; and the further we go beyond the scales of a higher order, the more intense the mechanical non-human scale becomes. If we allow automobiles to enter a community at

439

human community

definition by dimensions

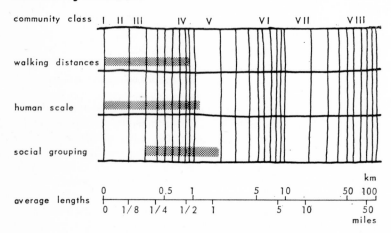

scales related to Man's speed of 5 kilometres (3.1 miles) an hour, i.e. 10 kilometres (6.3 miles) in a small residential street and 20–30 kilometres (12.5–18.8 miles) in the streets within the communities, the speeds could be 50 kilometres (31.3 miles) around a community class III, or 60–70 (37.5–43.8 miles) or 80 (50 miles) around a community class IV, 70–100 (43.8–62.5 miles) around a community class V, 80–120 (50–75 miles) around a community class VI, etc.

The blending of the human and the non-human

Having reached the definition of the human community, we must now see how we can blend the non-human and human communities in practice. We have tried this on several occasions. I will first present three examples demonstrating how this idea was implemented in areas within existing urban tissues, as in the development of Western Baghdad in Iraq and of Eastwick, Philadelphia. Then I will demonstrate how this system works in a new urban area—as in the case of Islamabad.

In Western Baghdad an extension of the city had to be created in an area surrounded by several highways and including two built-up areas (fig. 427). The dimensions were such that there was a need for a major conception including human communities. Studies of the whole of Baghdad had proved that the realistic dimensions of the human community were of a length of close to 800 metres as proved by many naturally growing schemes. This was the basic community unit which led to the design of community class IV. Thirteen such communities had their own centres and were designed as human communities of different categories of income, varying from very low to middle class. All these communities were interconnected to form a major community class V which had

its own central area. This major community was surrounded by highways, and divided by two of them crossing each other at a right angle approximately at the community's centre of gravity, where the major commercial and administrative centre lies. Around it, old and new communities were designed and built on a human scale.

A similar example in a country with different conditions in many respects was the Eastwick redevelopment project in Philadelphia, Pa. (fig. 428). Here within the urban tissue of Philadelphia a slum and marsh area had to be completely remodelled while many of the existing features, such as railways, several highways, houses and installations, had to be respected. This was done in a way allowing the formation of several human communities class IV, some of which were smaller than necessary and others larger than the maximum required. These variations, from what was considered to be the optimum size with a length of approximately 1,500 metres (4,920 feet) and a width of approximately 1,200 metres (3,936 feet) were imposed by the existing conditions in the surrounding areas. In spite of that, several communities come close to the optimum size and the entire redevelopment project combines the non-human scale of the major railway networks, major highways and industry, with the human scale of all residential communities. In addition, these are interconnected so that people can walk from one community to another by passing over the highways on pedestrian bridges.

Islamabad in Pakistan offered another occasion for combining the non-human with the human scale. Islamabad as a Dynapolis has already been presented in previous chapters. Here we will see (fig. 429) how the non-human scale of the major transportation and communication networks that pass between the sectors with dimensions of 1,800 metres (5,094 feet), are gradually yielding to minor communication networks entering the sectors without crossing

427

human and non-human scales

western Baghdad, Iraq (1955)

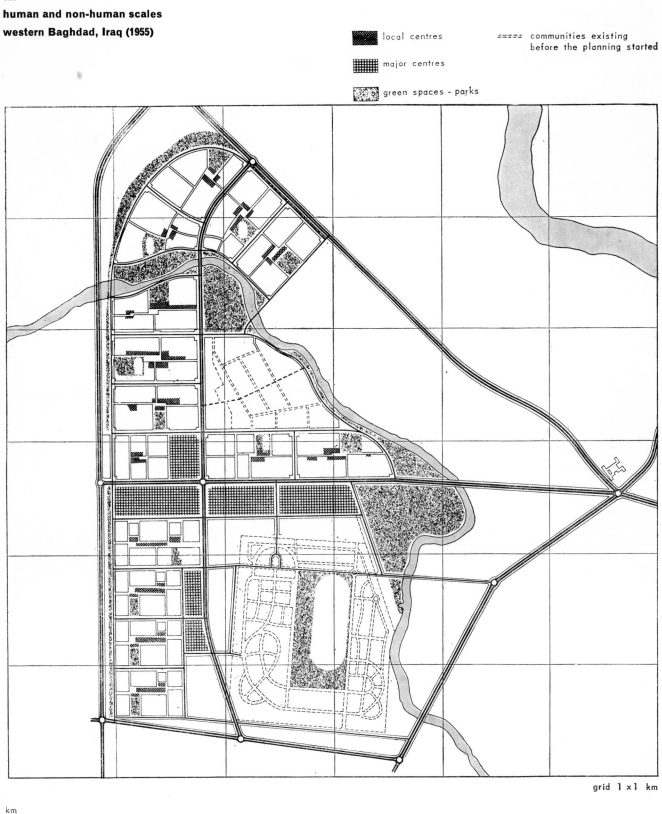

local centres

major centres

green spaces - parks

communities existing
before the planning started

grid 1 x 1 km

km

0   1   2   3   4   5   6

0   1   2   3

miles

Action

428

human and non-human scales
urban renewal project
Eastwick, Philadelphia, U.S.A. (1960)

industrial area

green areas

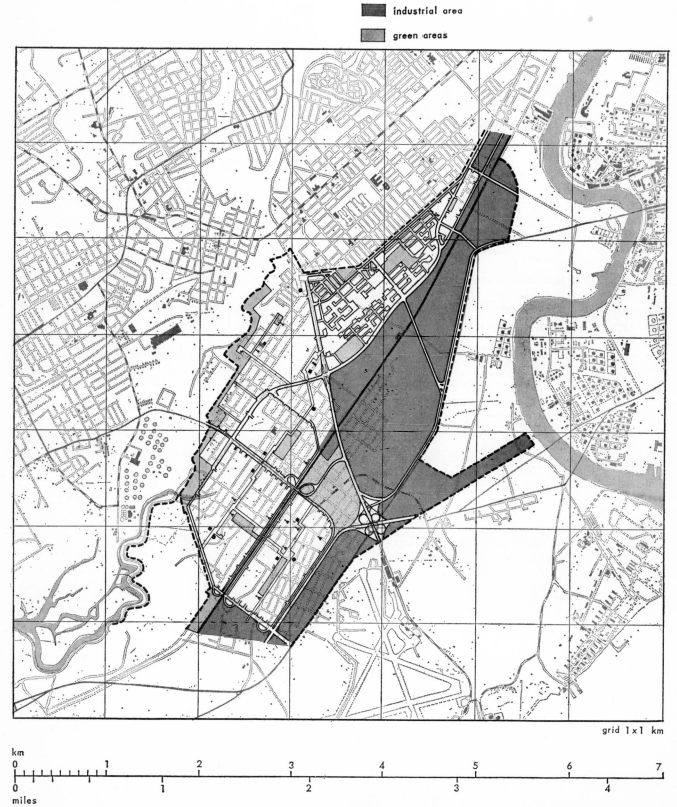

grid 1 x 1 km

km
0   1   2   3   4   5   6   7

0   1   2   3   4
miles

429
human and non-human scales
model of a sector forming community class V
Islamabad, Pakistan (1960)

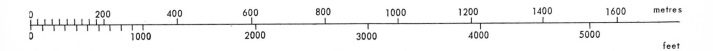

them and in a way not attracting through-traffic, thus defining three or four human communities within each sector.

In all these examples we have seen how we can achieve a gradual transition from the non-human scale of the Ecumenopolis or of a metropolitan area to the human scale, and how we have been led to the connection of the human community with surrounding urban tissues.

The human community

The fact that I had the opportunity to carry out research on the meaning of the human dimensions which led to the definition of a human community, and was able to implement our finding in several countries with various types of people, income and habits, strengthens my conviction that the human community has always existed, has suffered great losses during the last few generations (especially in over-developed urban areas) and on several occasions has nearly been lost. But it still has great significance for people everywhere.

I therefore believe that we can keep the human community as the basic cell of the urban settlements to be created in the future. The same holds true for urban settlements which will have to be remodelled in order to survive, as well as for rural settlements, those few which must survive or be rebuilt in order to meet future needs.

These cells of the human settlements of the future will serve all types of functions. They will be purely residential cells or cells combining several functions such as residence and employment, residence and leisure. If the human communities or the cells to be built should combine employment opportunities with residence, the residential area will necessarily be in the middle so as to be far away from the highways and the machine scale, while minor workshops or factories will be located on the periphery of the community near the highways so as not to disturb the residents. I first proposed such communities for the new plan of Washington D.C. in order to shorten the long commuting trips of a certain number of residents, who would thus find in their own community greater opportunities of employment and would have less reason to move across the city.

In presenting several related ideas I have already shown plans of such communities in several cities, and even gave an analysis of several of their characteristics. Here I want to present the case of one such community built, not as a typical residential community of a city, but as a special function representing the same idea and formed accordingly. In the university of the Punjab, which is already building a campus for 20,000 students, I thought it reasonable to create a human scale throughout the university by not allowing automobiles to enter among classroom buildings. This was one of the reasons why all educational buildings were interconnected in a way allowing people to walk from one to the

other through corridors and internal courtyards. In this way the human scale which had been preserved within buildings only has been extended over the entire educational institution (fig. 430).

Such communities can also contain other types of single functions including central ones if these are large enough to justify a cell of their own, such as a big plant with related facilities, a military camp, etc. In all these cases the cell can have the dimensions and characteristics of the human community. If the density of these communities is too high, as in the central areas of cities, the human scale can be preserved by keeping the functions of Man's movements on a higher level and those of the machines on a lower one. Such is the case of the Accra downtown area, where all automobiles move at a high speed around the community and enter parking lots within it. If these parking lots are near the periphery of the community, they can be in the open and shaded with trees. But if they are in the very heart of the community, they must be on a lower level so that Man can move on a higher level without being disturbed (fig. 431).

These cells, which will form the urban tissue of the future, can and should be of various sizes. Their sizes would depend on many factors such as location, function and the scale of the whole synthesis. Cells near the centre of the city should be smaller than those of its periphery. There are many reasons for this. The central functions justify closer approach by automobiles; higher traffic density justifies smaller distances between through highways, for if the distances are too great the number of automobiles will be too large to be accommodated by one highway. Functions also justify different dimensions. If the functions require a great number of trips by automobile every day, as will a hotel area or large office blocks, then we must have smaller cells. If the functions are purely residential and densities are low, we can have much larger cells, bearing in mind that the scale of the whole also defines the dimensions of the cells. If we are dealing with a very large urban area, we may have relatively larger cells, up to the maximum allowed on the basis of the analysis already made. If the urban area is small, there is no reason why its cells should be of maximum size. If we are dealing with a city like Islamabad, which will have a population of several million quite soon, we are entitled to have the largest cells, i.e. approximately 2 km. by 2 km. large. But if we are dealing with an urban area of a city which, though it may become a part of a major urban tissue, may by itself reach a maximum population of 200,000–300,000 people, there is no reason to divide it into cells of 2 km. by 2 km. which may contain up to 40,000–50,000 people for in such a case the whole city could be divided into six sectors only. In such cases even minor communities of 1,500 metres (4,920 feet) or 1,000 metres (3,280 feet) could do a much better job without creating more complicated problems which would arise if the cells were to be of maximum dimensions.

All these considerations lead to the conclusion that the

430

human scale preserved in a major synthesis
University of the Punjab, Lahore, Pakistan (1959)

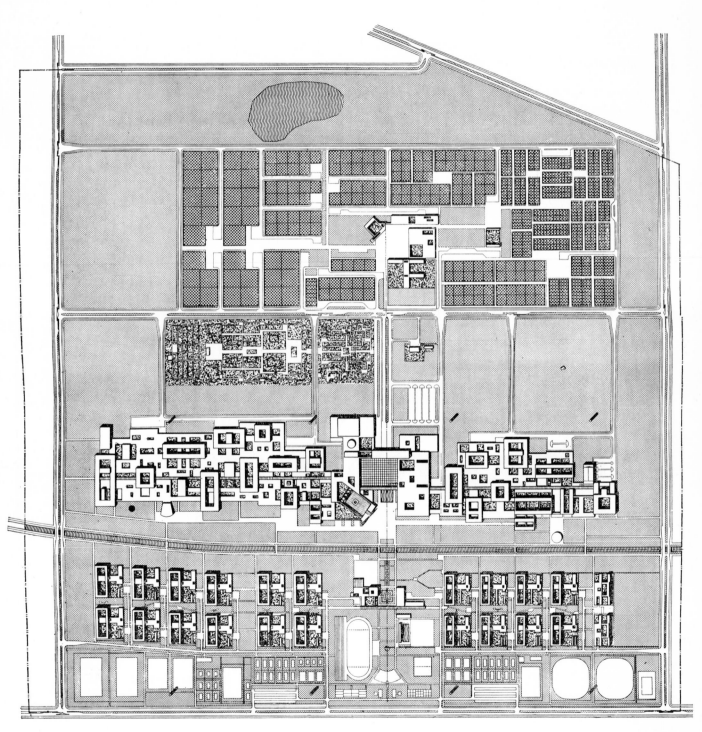

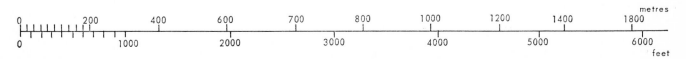

metres

0	200	400	600	700	800	1000	1200	1400	1800

0	1000	2000	3000	4000	5000	6000

feet

human scale in a downtown area
two level synthesis for the Accra civic centre
Accra, Ghana (1962)

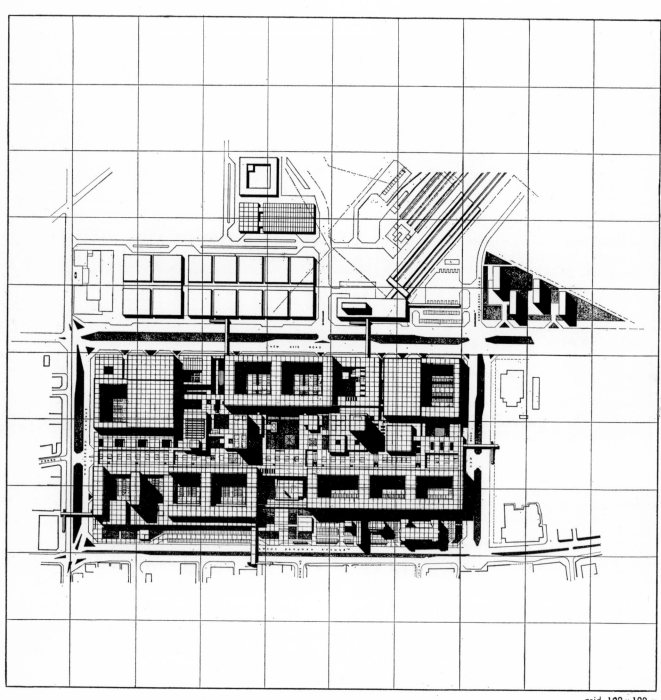

grid 100 x 100 m

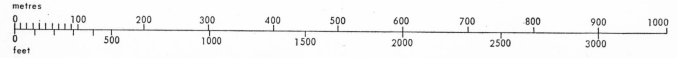

metres

0   100   200   300   400   500   600   700   800   900   1000

0   500   1000   1500   2000   2500   3000

feet

entire urban tissue can consist of cells corresponding to human dimensions, cells to be called human communities, the exact functions, structure and dimensions of which will be defined in accordance with the local requirements based on location, function and the scale of the entire synthesis.

NEW NEEDS AND NEW SOLUTIONS

New dimensions

Within the Ecumenopolis, the proper formation of which is our first task, where human values have to be preserved in cells forming human communities, we are going to have many new needs which will require new solutions. To conceive and implement them is our third basic task.

The greatest new need will be created by new physical dimensions of all our five elements. The population of the Earth will be at least 10–12 billion, and will very probably be even more. And we should not forget that even by the year 2000 the population of the Earth can easily reach seven billion. Society is going to be organised by the formation of very big communities, whereas now there are only a few megalopolitan areas which are beginning to be formed with a few tens of millions of people and three metropolitan areas with more than 10 million people, we must expect in the future to have many more megalopolitan areas with more than a hundred million, many other metropolitan areas with several millions, which will not be isolated but interconnected. Networks are going to be multiplied by enormous coefficients (we need only think of what is going to happen with transportation, power transmission, etc.). The same is going to be true of the dimensions of the Shells. By the end of this century (i.e. in a generation's time), the investment in human settlements may be equal to or even higher than the total investment since the beginning of civilisation, 6000 years ago.

These new dimensions of four of the elements—of Man, Society, Shells and Networks—are going to have a great impact on the dimensions and availability of the fifth element, Nature. If Nature has already presented some difficulties for the expansion of major settled areas—forcing several of them to be limited in size, as, for example, the settled areas of minor and later even of major islands—this phenomenon will be increased to a considerable extent. The four expanding elements are soon going to begin disputing the surface of the Earth and the available natural resources to a degree which will become dangerous for certain areas and eventually for the entire Earth.

Because of this conflict—the outcome of which will depend on many factors, mainly on expanding technology and the ability of Man to implement it for the interest of humanity—we cannot be certain of the final dimensions of the Ecumeno-

polis. There are only a few things of which we can be certain.

In size the Ecumenopolis will be the largest settlement ever created, covering as much of the Earth as humanity can afford to build on. In order to illustrate this, let us assume that an Ecumenopolis of several billions of people is going to require around 40 million square kilometres (15 million sq. miles) for the built-up parts alone, approximately equal to the total habitable surface of the Earth at present. This means that an Ecumenopolis of this size would cover the entire habitable area of the Earth. What would happen then? Would the Ecumenopolis acquire this huge population, or would it be limited to much less? If it reaches such high numbers, where is its food going to be produced? Will it be produced in a different way, let us say in the sea? Is the settlement going to expand into those areas of the world which are at present uninhabitable? These are questions which cannot be answered now. We can only give the dimensions of the framework for the Ecumenopolis. The total surface of the Earth is 510 million sq. km. (196.9 million sq. miles). If we subtract the oceans and those uninhabitable areas covered by ice and deserts, the usable area is 73.9 million sq. km. (28.5 million sq. miles): 13.0 million sq. km. is arable land (5.0 million sq. miles), 21.3 million sq. km. (8.2 million sq. miles) is covered with pastures, 35.3 million sq. km. (13.6 million sq. miles) by forests, 3.9 million sq. km. (1.5 million sq. miles) is potentially usable for cultivation and 0.4 million sq. km. (0.15 million sq. miles) by built-up parts of settlements. Of this 73.9 million sq. km. (28.5 million sq. miles) only 40 million sq. km. (15 million sq. miles) are considered to be habitable today (fig. 432).

Such is the framework of dimensions within which we may expect the universal city to grow. There is a great variety of probabilities in its dimensions, population, investment, area to be covered, etc. Depending on these, there may be universal settlements of different values. There are people who are quite ready to propound limitations to the expansion of our present settlements. They speak in terms of the availability of food, energy, ores, solar energy, etc. Personally I see no reason for a negative attitude in Ekistics in the trends towards the universal city. We must be prepared for the foreseeable expanding universal settlement, which will have around four to five times more population than at present—a very probable low figure for a century from today which is the time set as the target for our projections. Unless we can prove that there are no solutions beyond certain dimensions, we must be ready for this figure. In such a case we are entitled to ask for a limitation of one of the other dimensions of settlements, either population, the use of natural resources or the area to be utilised. Here we can look at the Ecumenopolis in a different way, demanding more expansion in certain agricultural or other areas. For example, we may decide that those areas with a greater amount of sunshine are more important than the agricultural land of the present. If so, we must select for preservation areas which may be of no use today or which

breakdown of the surface of the Earth

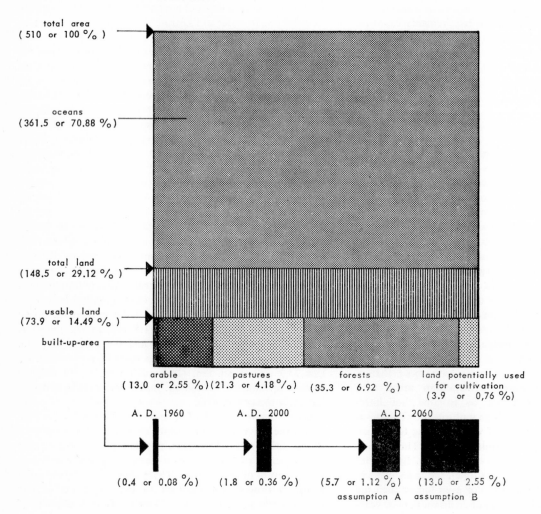

total area
(510 or 100 %)

oceans
(361.5 or 70.88 %)

total land
(148.5 or 29.12 %)

usable land
(73.9 or 14.49 %)

built-up-area

arable
(13.0 or 2.55 %)

pastures
(21.3 or 4.18 %)

forests
(35.3 or 6.92 %)

land potentially used
for cultivation
(3.9 or 0,76 %)

A. D. 1960

A. D. 2000

A. D. 2060

(0.4 or 0.08 %)

(1.8 or 0.36 %)

(5.7 or 1.12 %)

(13.0 or 2.55 %)

assumption A   assumption B

all areas in million km^2

may be of low value for present-day agriculture as are some deserts. We cannot however decide in advance which area should be preserved until we know to which of the resources we attribute more value. Until we manage to set limits based on specific calculations of the resources of the world to come, we are obliged to work out solutions for expanding settlements.

The idea of expanding forces, so basic to the understanding of the Ecumenopolis, leads us to envisage another eventual limitation. We may say that although we have not yet reached a limit in the use of our resources, the speed at which we are moving is such as not to allow us to provide proper solutions for the increasing dimensions of settlements. If it is proved that, even if we mobilise the rest of our resources, we cannot

easily shorten the gap existing today between increasing requirements and the solutions provided for them, we will be entitled to envisage an Ecumenopolis growing at a lower rate than that of the present. In such a case we will not tend towards a limitation of growth, but towards a limitation of the rate of growth.

If we prove neither the existence of a higher limit in the dimensions of settlements nor a higher limit in the speed of development, we can work out solutions for both the increasing dimension and the rate of increase in the following way:

o by not allowing the gap which exists between Man and his settlements at present to increase;

o by stabilising this gap;

by working out methods which will allow us to decrease it within a reasonable time.

Thus, the question of dimensions in the Ecumenopolis should remain open, and we should understand first that, for the time being and for quite some time to come, we must face the fact that we will be on the march towards the Ecumenopolis, and secondly that we must be prepared for much larger dimensions of problems which will create new trends and will require new solutions.

NEW TRENDS

The second greatest new need is created by new trends in many of the forces that shape settlements. Since many dimensions are going to change completely in the Ecumenopolis, and since the speed at which these changes take place is increasing, we should be prepared for changes of trends of the elements which form human settlements as well as changes in their interrelationship. Needless to say, an enormous number of changes will have to be faced and regardless of which element we look at, we should expect many new trends.

Let us take the case of Man and Society. We should expect much greater numbers of people to live together. What impact will this 'togetherness' have on the many problems separating or connecting Man—such as the problems of social classes, religion and race? Man and Society may be quite different in these new dimensions of the future human communities. The population explosion may have a very great impact on Man as an individual and as a part of Society. Actually, even the very term 'population explosion' is already beginning to be disputed by some; Marshall McLuhan, for instance, says that we are living in an era of implosion because we are expanding in space, while at the same time reducing the notion of time, meaning that we are coming closer together and that we are much more interconnected, which is leading to much more complicated interrelationships, to an implosion of Man.[20]

Considering the relation of Man to the Ecumenopolis, we must also be prepared for many new trends. We are already witnessing completely new movements in the arts, and I think we must be prepared for many new trends not only in our material needs, but also in our aesthetic ones. Today we are beginning to mix all types of space in our human settlements, for instance hearing, only one of our senses, needs many qualities of space within Ecumenopolis. We need such types as:

- completely quiet landscape areas, which, though open and exposed to Nature, are not vulnerable to any man-made noises (if we are told that this exists today, I can ask how about the noise of jets, which may spoil the aesthetic value of even a remote landscape?);

- on the other hand we will need Shells, a completely man-made space which will be completely quiet;
- we will need a natural open space where all natural sounds and noises prevail—those of birds and insects and the noises of forests;
- we may also need artificial space with proper acoustics where music can be played and can follow us while we move (We must confess here that research in this field has not been satisfactory at all and we may have to fulfil completely new requirements. What is today offered to us as music in many public spaces is not what we should want, first because we have not asked for this music and secondly because very often it is of low quality, especially in its transmission).

In the same way I could continue to describe various kinds of spaces which must be guaranteed in the Ecumenopolis because we can no longer take anything for granted, either in the realm of natural landscape, which is being continuously spoilt, or in man-made landscapes. Let us not forget the effects of insecticides on flowers and birds, which may lead to their complete extinction. As Rachel Carson says in *Silent Spring*, the number of nesting birds in general has declined as much as 90 per cent in some 'sprayed' areas.[21]

Returning to the sense of hearing, we must confess that we do not yet know which sound or noise is going to make us feel happier and more secure. Since on the one hand we do not know what satisfaction can be derived from new types of sounds and the relationship of space to sound, while on the other hand we are not allowed to eliminate any type of natural landscape, we must realise that, in terms of hearing alone, the Ecumenopolis must have all types of natural and man-made space: from the quietness of the insulated study room to the silence of the desert, including the whole spectrum of Nature and man-made space helping us to receive as many natural and man-made sounds as we may need, every type to be found in a specially provided area.

We can see quite clearly that the lack of specific knowledge of the types of space we should preserve (as they may be needed for our survival) as well as of our requirements in new types of space, forces us to demand that the universal city provide all types of space to satisfy all our aesthetic needs. The same certainly is valid not only for our aesthetic needs, but for all other needs as well.

From the point of view of shape and structure, the Ecumenopolis is tending towards a much more complicated system of human settlements. It seems that we are entering an era during which many of our expressions are turning towards major systems. William James, for example, foresaw this for the unified knowledge of Man, and it is true of many other expressions. Gradually it is going to become true of the universal settlements. At the beginning, and this is already happening, there will be major centres in some areas and some intermediate and minor ones in others. Later we may witness the creation of many major centres in many

systems of human settlements

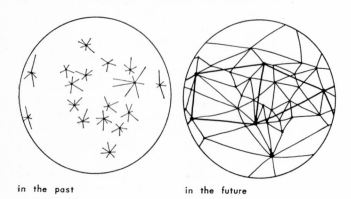

in the past   in the future

other parts of the world which are favoured by location, even if at present they are not so because of historical development (fig. 433).

In the past human settlements were minor 'islands' within a sea of natural landscape. In the universal city quite often the natural landscape will be nothing but a small 'island' although these 'islands' will sometimes be very large surrounded only by thin branches of the Ecumenopolis.

Within this ecumenic city we will witness many new trends and problems. For example, as I have already explained, there are three forces which are going to shape the Ecumenopolis: concentric economic forces, forces attracting many elements towards the main lines of transportation and aesthetic ones attracting the same elements towards the coastal and aesthetically pleasing areas. These forces will create new problems in the already existing human settlements, like the ones that are strangling the centres. No centre will survive under the impact of such strong forces and no communication line will be able to function normally unless relieved of this great pressure. New trends are going to force us to look at this problem in a much more imaginative way.

New centres may have to be created out in the open, where no settlements exist, so as to acquire an efficient form. New areas for settlements may have to be created in the desert, and perhaps (in the long run) human settlements will experience what takes place in Nature, as the paleontologist Edward Drinker Cope has stated with the 'law of the unspecialised'[22]: in the next period the best solutions leading to dominant forms may arise from lower types of animals of the previous period, and not from the most developed ones. If this is true of human settlements, the centres of the Ecumenopolis may not be near Tokyo, New York or London, which are the major urban areas of the world today, but somewhere in Canada, Central America, Latin America, Africa, Siberia or Mongolia, in an area where there are much

smaller settlements today. Should this occur, it will not be the first time in human history. But this time it will have greater importance as it is quite probable that once the Ecumenopolis takes shape, it will not change very easily, at least not during a predictable length of time (figs. 434 and 435).

This assumption is not as unrealistic as it may seem. If we let the present human settlements expand as they are doing today, the great cities will be choked to death and others might have to take over their functions. This might take place through peaceful evolution, or through war, which cannot be excluded even though it should be. In any case, if the situation continues as at present, the big cities will not be able to stand up to their requirements and will have to be replaced by other centres somewhere else. Our real challenge, therefore, is not to allow this change to take place too late and coincidentally, but to take the evolution into our own hands and plan for the gradual creation of new centres in these locations which will benefit the existing centres and thus prevent the new ones from growing out of the decay of the former.

NEW SOLUTIONS

The need for new solutions does not necessarily imply the exclusion of old solutions. On the contrary, there is reason to believe that in many respects old solutions may be indispensable for the survival of the Ecumenopolis. Nevertheless we must look at the same time for new solutions.

New solutions can be exemplified by looking into one of the aspects of the universal city—physical expansion over major areas. From this single example we can understand that major changes in many areas of the world can be expected. If we take, for example, a country such as Greece, we should expect the Ecumenopolis to follow the trends of the forces already described; that is, to gradually fill the more important coastal areas and the interconnected major valleys. How this system works can be seen in the present traffic chart of the highways of Greece (fig. 436). A study of the next 100 years shows that we should expect the Greek branches of the Ecumenopolis to be continuous and to follow approximately the present major transportation networks (fig. 437). It is quite clear that in countries like Greece the Ecumenopolis, if left alone, will fill up many important valleys where today a major portion of agricultural production is taking place. It will not exercise enormous pressure only on the city of Athens, but on the entire geographic area of Attica, which will become one continuous urban settlement, whereas in the days of ancient Greece it was an entire state.

In England (fig. 438) the Ecumenopolis may take shape as one basic continuous settlement connecting the Greater London area with Manchester and Liverpool, but we should certainly expect minor branches leading to many other minor centres. Seen on a larger scale, the branches of the Ecumenopolis in continental Europe and the U.S.A. will (figs. 439, 440 and 441) cover wide areas of both continents. It should be understood that these predictions are not the result of detailed studies, but they are indicative of the types of urban areas which may come to be a century from today in regions of various dimensions. If we look at all of them, from the minor area of Greece to the major one of the U.S.A., we will find some areas with great concentrations of people taking shape around major existing settlements. If this actually happens, we can expect disaster, for we know that the present-day settlements cannot withstand this pressure.

Let us turn our attention for a moment to the following problem: during the process of the formation of the Ecumenopolis some centres, be they minor or major, are going to reach the limits of the area of which they are at present the centre. In such a case they will approach the boundaries of other settlements, first reaching their outer or 'soft' part, and then their central built-up area. Since some of these settlements will also be expanding simultaneously with the central settlements of their region, after a certain time there will be no possibility of continued expansion.

We must consider the possible courses to be followed. One possibility is that a central expanding settlement will break into the areas of neighbouring settlements, change their structure, destroy their texture and continue to expand, thus creating on the way more problems than it is solving. If this expanding centre had been conceived for a certain range of functions in the past, for a certain volume of traffic, etc., it will probably not serve the new needs. If this trend continues, it will mean disaster for both the centre and the entire surrounding areas.

A second possibility is based on a realisation that the centre cannot bear any more pressure and can therefore grow only up to a certain limit. But if the urban area is still growing it will need a new centre to take over the pressure which the older one cannot stand. If we look into the eastern part of the U.S.A. and think of the megalopolis now taking shape between Boston and Washington (figs. 81 and 82), and if we understand that this area will not only expand in an elliptical way around the Appalachian mountains as Jean Gottmann foresees, but will also suffer from pressure of a very high order, we must realise that its major cities are going to be choked to death unless we create a new system of centres and highway networks to relieve the pressure from the existing ones as has already been explained.

Such an analysis shows that if we allow the Ecumenopolis to continue growing as far as space allows, which may be possible in the macro-scale, it may lead to destruction in the intermediate and micro-scales. In order to avoid such a fate we must understand that our passive action, which allows the Ecumenopolis to grow by itself, should become active and should lead to the following new solutions.

o We must define the maximum area within which existing settlements can grow and we must make a decision as to

434
evolution of systems   new lines of transportation outside the existing settlements growth creates one unit out of many

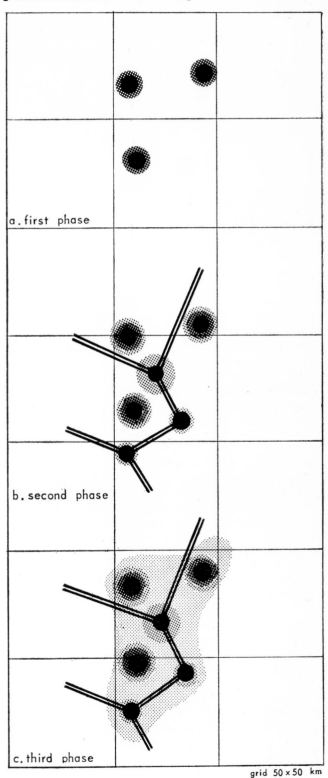

a. first phase

b. second phase

c. third phase

grid 50 x 50 km

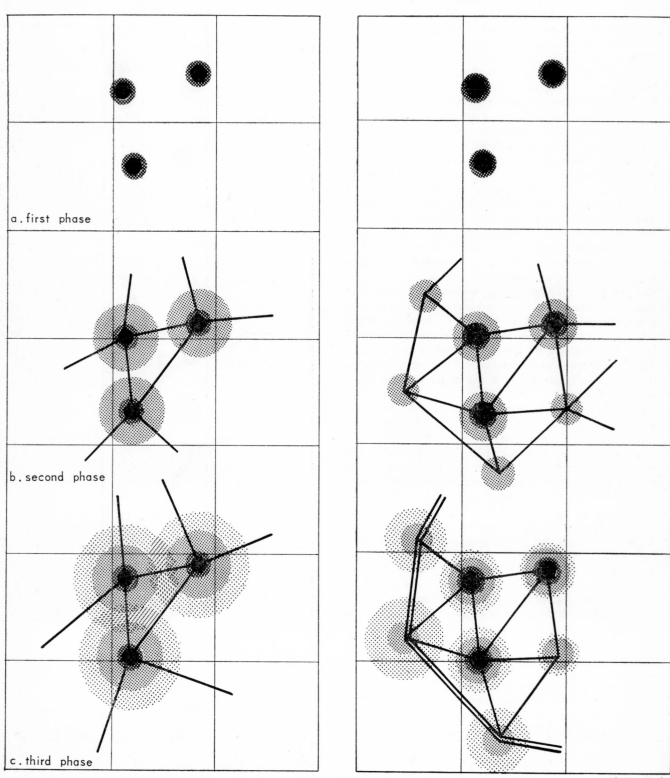

**evolution of systems   lines of transportation lead to the existing settlements (first column) or to
new ones (second column)   new lines of transportation outside the existing settlements
growth does not affect them**

a. first phase

b. second phase

c. third phase

grid 50 × 50 km

436
pattern of traffic
Greece 1952, 1953 and 1958

cars in 1952-1953

cars in 1958

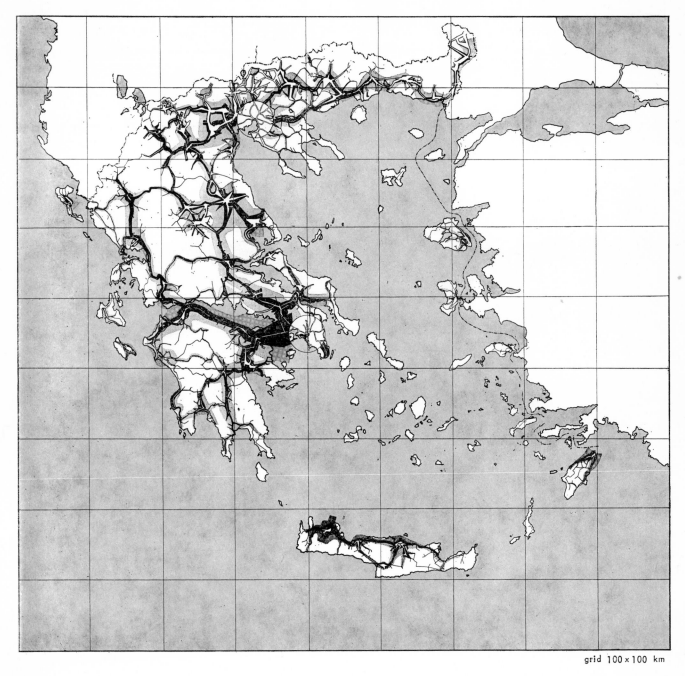

grid 100 x 100 km

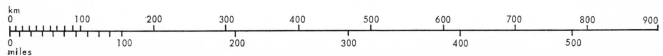

Action

437

Greek branch of Ecumenopolis

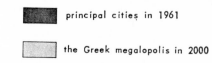

principal cities in 1961

the Greek megalopolis in 2000

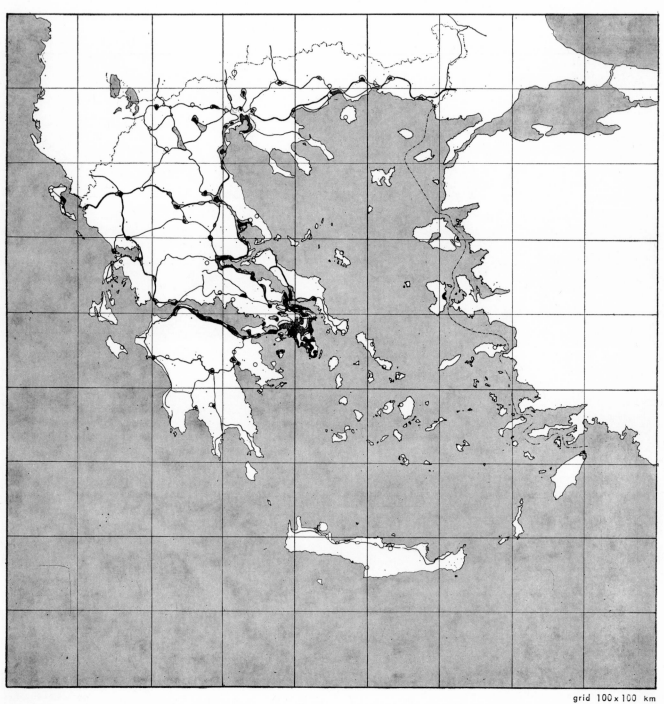

grid 100 x 100 km

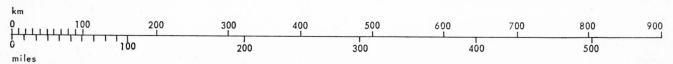

438

British branch of Ecumenopolis

N. Ireland not included

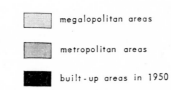

megalopolitan areas

metropolitan areas

built-up areas in 1950

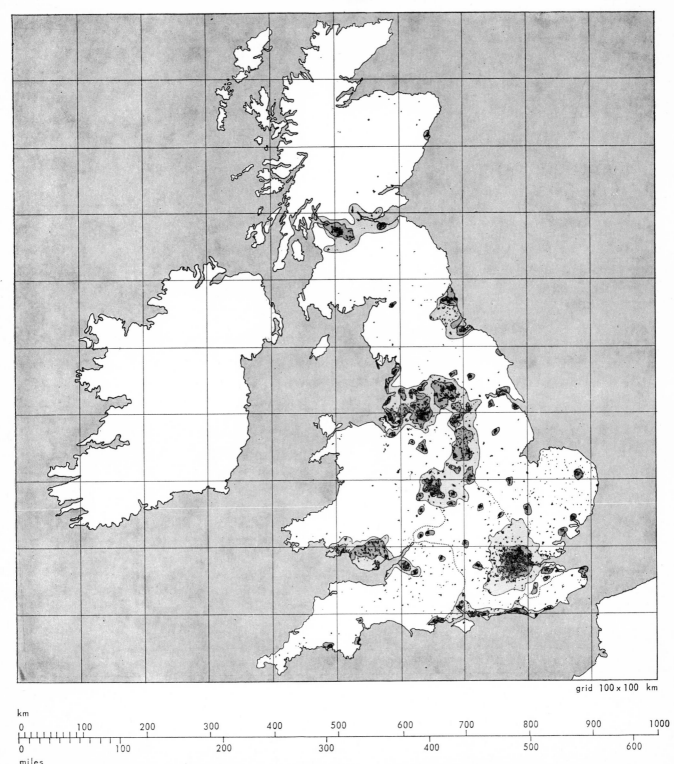

grid 100 × 100 km

km
0   100   200   300   400   500   600   700   800   900   1000

0   100   200   300   400   500   600
miles

continental European branch of Ecumenopolis
a very tentative approach

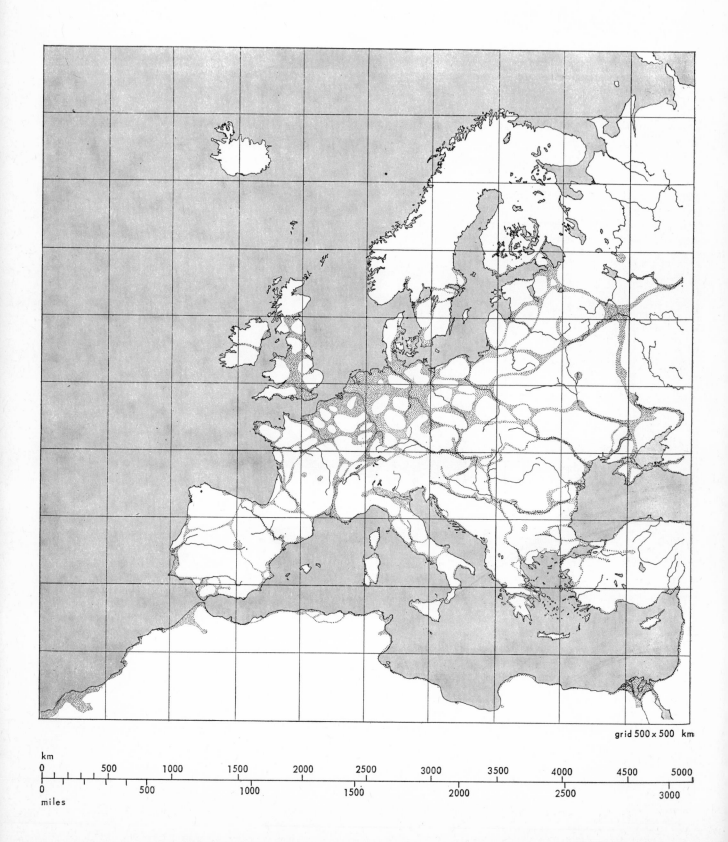

grid 500 x 500 km

north-eastern American branch of Ecumenopolis

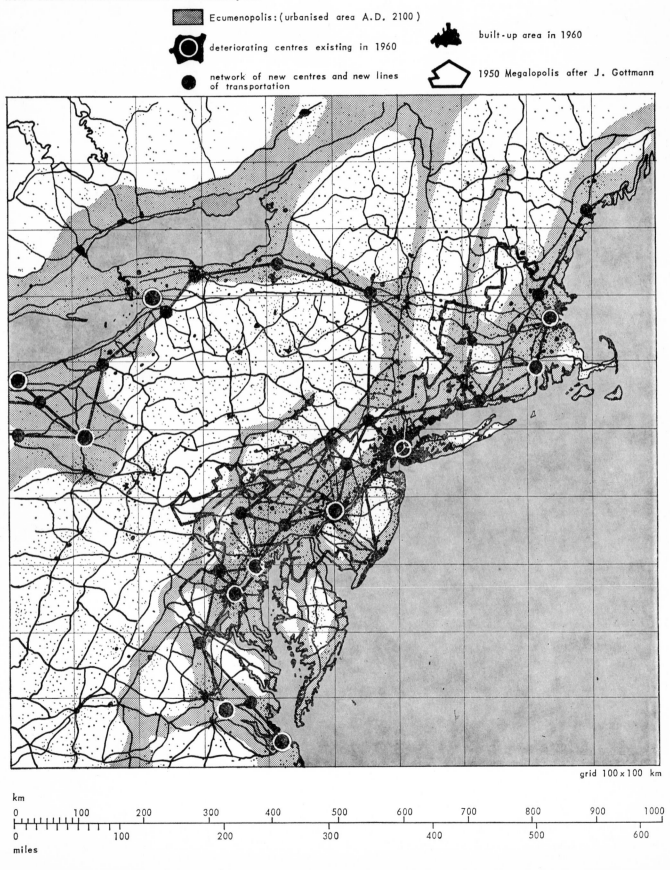

Ecumenopolis:(urbanised area A.D. 2100)

deteriorating centres existing in 1960

network of new centres and new lines of transportation

built-up area in 1960

1950 Megalopolis after J. Gottmann

grid 100 x 100 km

km
0   100   200   300   400   500   600   700   800   900   1000

0   100   200   300   400   500   600
miles

Action

441

northern American branch of Ecumenopolis
a very tentative approach

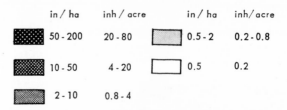

in / ha	inh / acre		in / ha	inh/acre
50 - 200	20 - 80		0.5 - 2	0.2 - 0.8
10 - 50	4 - 20		0.5	0.2
2 - 10	0.8 - 4			

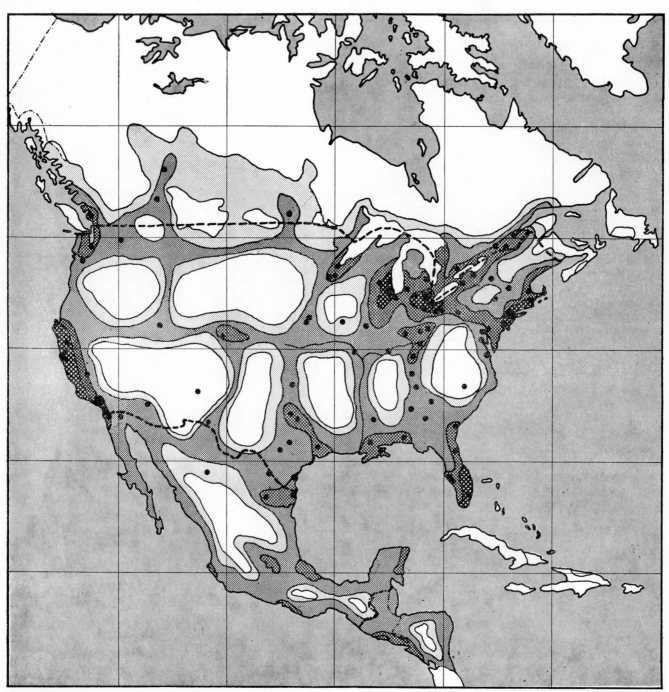

grid 1000 x 1000 km

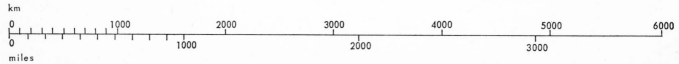

km

0   1000   2000   3000   4000   5000   6000

0   1000   2000   3000

miles

442

new types of settlements within Ecumenopolis

C.D. existing settlements which can grow up to a certain limit

E. new settlement of higher order

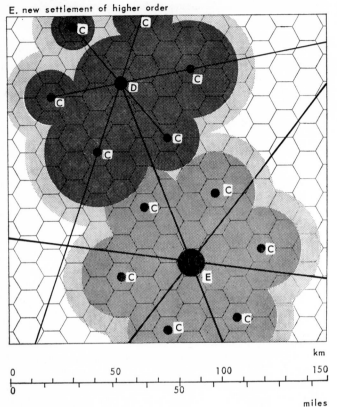

km

| 0 | 50 | 100 | 150 |

| 0 | 50 |

miles

for the creation of many centres of an order higher than that of the existing ones, not in order to limit the freedom of the latter, but to allow them to survive within an expanding system. How this system works can be seen in fig. 442 where the centres of 'C' order reach a point beyond which they cannot grow, unless they invade each other's area to their common detriment, or the 'D' area to its own detriment. The 'D' centre on the other hand, which is central to all the others, has already been blocked by its own minor centres and can no longer expand unless it begins eating into the areas of its subordinate settlements.

Thus our system will either be self-destroying, until its central parts are choked to death, or become static leaving its leadership to a new centre of higher order 'E', which is created in the open land where it can expand, assume in the long run the necessary dimensions, become connected by communication lines of a higher order, and lead the whole system to survival and a successful functioning. If such a policy is followed, the Ecumenopolis most likely can be turned into a successfully functioning settlement and our passive and negative policies can change into active and positive ones.

The implementation of such ideas should lead to the formation of a continuous system which will be rational and meaningful and will consist of the proper elements and transportation and communication networks—a system within which every settlement will have a pre-defined role. Otherwise no settlement would survive if left to work under all types of pressure. Actually the implementation of such new types of solutions depends on a new conception of transportation networks. It is very interesting for us to note that movements for such changes have been started on several occasions by either private industry or governments. Characteristic of this last case is the new legislation in the United States which authorises research and studies in high speed connections within the north-eastern megalopolis. Also characteristic are the studies by statesmen, such as the recent one *Megalopolis Unbound* by Senator Claiborne Pell.[23]

We must understand that we will need completely new networks of transportation in which the maximum speeds will be of the order of hundreds of kilometres or miles per hour. If we turn to the circulatory system of mammals we find that while the speed in the capillaries is 0.5–1 mm/sec., in the veins it is 20 cm/sec., in the carotids 33 cm/sec. and in the aorta 44 cm/sec. or about 700 times more than in the capillaries. Could not the Anthropocosmos which has speeds of 5 kilometres per hour in its capillaries reach this level of organisation and come to have central aortas with speeds of 3,500 kilometres per hour?

It may be argued that this is not realistic since such speeds would have to be in underground tunnels—as in the mammals; but we should not forget that 'between 1930 and 1960 the cost of tunnelling dropped 46 per cent (from $6.7 million to

their role, which can be defined in accordance with the maximum area they can cover and the maximum number of functions they can serve. Such an idea sets a new solution for the definition of the maximum role a settlement can play. This is not the same as the negative policy of limiting the growth of a settlement for the sake of the planning process, even if the settlement has not reached its maximum area. On the contrary, this is part of a creative policy by which the settlement will become a rational part of a whole system in which it is assigned a major role. It does not say 'Do not let the settlement grow'. It says, 'Let it grow as long as necessary, as much as possible, perhaps until it touches the next settlement; but at some stage it should cease to grow so as not to disturb the built-up areas of the other settlements in its vicinity'.

o In order not to make the previous decision negative, we must conceive new centres in the proper locations, playing a role of a higher order than the previous ones, the growth of which has been limited. This is a new conception by which the government takes the initiative

$3.8 million per lane mile) while the cost of the cheapest city freeway rose from $210,000 to $1,000,000 per lane mile' and that according to expert predictions in the middle seventies tunnels will be cheaper than highways.[24]

The new solution of our transportation problems may be a turn towards a new system of Deepways. If we realise the necessity that we start thinking in this way about new solutions and if we follow such policies, we can hope that the Ecumenopolis will be a success and will survive for the period of time during which the factors leading to its birth will exist.

The Ecumenopolis should at all times tend to achieve a balance between the man-made and natural parts of its landscape for it will have made a clear distinction between them. The man-made landscape will be an urban landscape and the natural landscape will be devoted to agricultural production or to contact with Nature. Both should preserve the best qualities of a natural landscape. The best lands on the plains should be given over to agriculture and the most productive and beautiful forest, river and mountain areas should be free from any type of settlement. The less productive and less interesting areas will be covered by the built-up parts of the Ecumenopolis. We shall therefore have the new task of turning the less interesting parts of the natural landscape into a man-made landscape of a cultural value. It will thus be our duty to preserve the best that has been created by Nature and turn the worst of it into a fine cultural landscape. The largest parts of the Ecumenopolis may therefore be built on the more arid, less productive areas.

The Ecumenopolis will be hierarchical in structure. It will probably have one centre of administration for all international affairs. However it will certainly contain many others of great international importance as well as many completely specialised centres for research, the care of health, philosophy, etc. It will then have centres of a different order, from large to very small, serving the people in their various neighbourhoods. It will have facilities of different orders, from the ecumenic highways and networks of communications down to the small residential roads and parks, from large natural parks, down to small local parks at short distances from every house. The centres, facilities, highways and parks will be classified into international, national (although now with a different meaning) regional, or local centres of several classes. It is quite probable that we shall have something between 10 and 13 orders of magnitude for these centres and facilities. On the basis of such ideas the Ecumenopolis will be divided into communities of several orders, each one having the corresponding structure including a centre serving the entire community, as well as industries and facilities, parks and gardens.

The Ecumenopolis will be renewed on the basis of a well-conceived programme and plan. It will be a self-renovating city, a city always prepared for renewal. This renewal will have a different content, not forced by unexpected evolution; it will be a gradual movement towards the creation of better areas from those which have become amortised economically or culturally. No areas will be demolished until they have actually served all the useful purposes for which they were originally created.

Above all the Ecumenopolis will have to be a city built on a human scale, the city of Man that Lewis Mumford urges us to build, a city for all humanity. We now have a new task before us, for the moment has come for us to create a city for all humanity. Indeed, it is the main characteristic of our century that for the first time we have the ability to make modern technology serve not only the privileged classes, but all mankind. Such a city will have one main goal: to serve Man and offer him a better way of life. This will be the city which, according to the old definition of Aristotle, will give its inhabitants security and happiness.

We can now see that a proper Ekistic policy for the creation of the Ecumenopolis should be divided into two types of action:

- growth by new settlements, since the present ones will not survive if we do not create new ones of the right order in the proper location;
- transformation of settlements, since the existing ones, which are suffering from present pressure and the pressure to come, cannot survive unless properly transformed. This is also valid for all those suffering from pressure in a negative way, which means that they are areas of depression and are losing life, thus needing special care.

With these two types of action I will deal in the next chapter on Ekistic practice.

CHAPTER THIRTEEN
EKISTIC PRACTICE

DEVELOPMENT THROUGH GROWTH

Process

Two basic types of development leading towards Ecumeno-polis exist today and these are the two basic types of Ekistic action: growth and transformation. Therefore, the different cases we come up against in practice should be studied as examples in accordance with these basic categories, since in Ekistic practice there are very few cases where development can be considered as belonging to one type exclusively. The forces of growth or expansion and those of change are inherent in all cases though sometimes only one may be at work for a limited period of time. Actually I know of no settlement which in the long run could be listed as having developed through only one of these forces.

In the broadest sense of the word we must classify almost all types of newly created settlements, under the term 'growth', whether they are completely new and physically isolated from others, or physical expansions of built-up areas. In the past it could perhaps be argued that these were two completely different phenomena. But in those times it was possible for new settlements to remain isolated. Now, this is impossible for—as we have said—a settlement consists of more than its built-up part, and we know that settlements are very quickly merging with one another. So, regardless of whether a settlement has a new nucleus and a new centre of a higher order than the surrounding one, or a new centre of a lower order at a certain distance from the old one, or whether the settlement is simply a physical continuation of existing settlements, it belongs to the same basic category of growth through the expansion of the existing texture. A settlement belongs to one of two groups: one consists of those new settlements which have their own centre and periphery, and the other of those which form the physical expansions of already existing settlements.

The examples I shall now give are mostly drawn from projects I have worked on. I have drawn on them because:

o I know their cases better and am able to take a clear-cut position in relation to them, and

o they correspond to the theory I am presenting.

In dealing with the development of settlements through expansion, we must consider both urban and rural settlements. We must bear in mind that urban settlements are almost all dynamic, and that this is always true of the major ones, even though they might ultimately reach a point of physical saturation or of full satisfaction of all the needs which can be served in that area, in which case they might become static. From this phase on, their development will continue through amelioration, if they have inherent forces keeping them alive; otherwise they may pass through a negative period and become depressed areas. Generally the larger the urban settlements, the more dynamic they are. Rural settlements however are almost always static since they depend upon a limited area; and even though this area may become more productive, because of technological advances, there will seldom be a need for a larger population. So, rural settlements normally develop through transformation, which can be either positive or negative. In rare cases, they may enter a new phase of development (a change of cultivation from dry to irrigated farming or the mechanisation of cultivation) in which case they may undergo development through expansion; but this will last for only a very short transitional period. So, most cases of development of settlements through expansion are those of urban settlements. Very few belong to the category of the rural settlements; and if so, it is only for a very short period.

Since the Ecumenopolis is going to need much larger areas for settlements, there will be a great expansion of almost all intermediate and major settlements, as well as the creation of new ones. This expansion is now taking place—with no regard for land values—mostly around major cities, close to the main transportation lines and in the most beautiful areas, near the sea, lakes, etc. Part of this expansion is also taking place in new areas where there is a need for new activities (such as new administrative or industrial centres) or in areas which offer good possibilities for low-cost urban land. These areas are sometimes necessary for defence industries, which require a lot of space and must have no settlements close by for reasons of safety or security, as well as for other industries which need large areas with a small labour force. Lately, such

greater Athens area

increase of the economic potential in 10 years

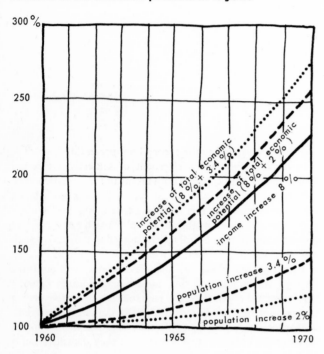

industries have been moving into desert areas. It is characteristic that several large countries have selected such areas for the creation of new settlements, such as Texas (the expansion of El Paso is quite characteristic) and Arizona, as well as others in Siberia, Australia, etc.

The accelerated speed with which we shall be moving towards the Ecumenopolis will lead to the formation of many more such settlements in relatively unattractive areas, although, for many decades to come, the bulk of the expansion will still be in the most densely inhabited areas of the world. A major effort will be needed to accelerate the speed of movement towards the neglected areas in order to save precious land needed for other purposes. Thinking along these lines, we must remember that countries with a scarcity of land resources—islands such as Great Britain and Java—are beginning to take measures to control the expansion of existing settlements and especially the use of agricultural land for urban purposes. Such measures, which will be intensified in the future in several more countries, will create a greater movement towards the wide open spaces with settlements with a very low population density although they may well have a very high level of investment.

Considerations related to the expansion of settlements raise the question of optimum size. It has already been

explained that it is not reasonable to have an optimum size for dynamic settlements since this can correspond to certain conditions only, and as long as conditions continue to change, the optimum size can exist only for a certain time and under certain conditions. We cannot say that settlements should not expand in order to fulfil the requirements of the optimum size, since this size will have changed the moment there was a need for new expansion. There may be cases where, in order to save the settlement, we must limit its growth since its own structural texture cannot stand greater pressures. In this case we are not speaking of optimum size, but of the maximum expansion it can bear in accordance with its present physiological condition. Actually, if a settlement reaches a point beyond which it should not grow because it has reached the limits of the other settlements and may break their texture or may break its own texture, we must consider how much it could expand within its own area. This is related to certain economic conditions. In this case we would look into the problem of the physical expansion of the Shells to the limit permitted by the congested and saturated area.

Such considerations may lead to the conclusion that it is necessary to decrease the population in order to allow the functions to operate properly, Man to be happy, and the Shells to be satisfactory. Such an analysis may prove not only that expansion is impossible, but that on the contrary, a decrease in population, functions, etc., may be necessary. This is actually what is already happening in the central areas of many cities. Because of the great pressure, and because of the inability of the central city's texture to withstand it, some of the functions and people are moving out. This is erroneously called 'natural evolution'. In some cases it may be that, but in others it may be the wrong solution leading the city centre to destruction. But it may be the only way out left for individuals, if the community has not conceived a constructive policy to guide development by defining those areas which can withstand pressure and to what extent, and those which cannot withstand any more pressure. When the maximum dimension of a settlement saturated because of pressure has been reached, it is time to determine the method by which the transformation should take place; whether by changes in building heights, by the replacement of existing buildings with new ones providing for higher densities, etc.

How this pressure works physically has already been explained and can now be demonstrated in a specific example from the district of Greater Athens. In 1960, a study was made of the trends to be expected in the next 30 years, and it was found that the expected rate of population growth is 3.4 per cent, while the expected increase of income is 8 per cent annually. If we add these together, even if we overlook some other forces, the increase of the total economic potential of Greater Athens in 30 years will be equal to 200 per cent of its present potential, and there will be an increase of 100 per cent only in 16 years. Even if we assume that the rate of population growth will have to slow down to the minimum imaginable

444

greater Athens area

evolution and urban renewal

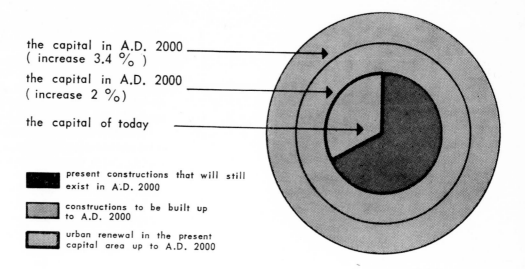

the capital in A.D. 2000
(increase 3.4 %)

the capital in A.D. 2000
(increase 2 %)

the capital of today

present constructions that will still
exist in A.D. 2000

constructions to be built up
to A.D. 2000

urban renewal in the present
capital area up to A.D. 2000

under present conditions, 2 per cent (this may be caused by emigration plus difficulties in housing, etc., but is not very probable), then again the total potential will be doubled in six and a half years and will be three times larger in ten years (fig. 443). With such trends, the increase of the wealth of Greater Athens in houses and buildings is very impressive as we can see in fig. 444 where, at the end of the century only a very small percentage of the Greater Athens area will consist of buildings which exist today, that is areas already committed to certain patterns.

Such calculations clearly demonstrate how great the forces developing within settlements are at this moment, and how they compel us to think more seriously about the problems of expansion. In practice, this serious consideration of problems is not taking place either in Athens or in any major area of the world. We know of no one who has foreseen these major trends in advance and has managed to prepare himself with programmes and plans in order to afford the best possible solutions to the present crisis. During the last ten years, we have become more aware of this need and several urban areas have started conceiving and implementing such plans. However, this is only the beginning of such an effort, and we must be aware that we are only starting this process and that a lot must be learned on the way.

New settlements

Today only a very small number of new settlements is being created, so small that the chances of transforming the overall pattern of human settlements are very limited. There are only

very few places where the effort for completely new settlements is being carried out, and this is the most dangerous phenomenon on our road towards an Ecumenopolis. For, even though there are so few new settlements, they are very seldom conceived in the proper regional context or in the proper dynamic or static form. Almost all the new urban settlements are based on the image of the settlements of the past, that is, static settlements. On the other hand, new rural settlements are very seldom conceived statically, but are built under the influence of the ideas of urban settlements—wide squares, streets, etc.—which is just the opposite of what people settling in rural areas need.

The weaknesses of such new creations are intensified by the fact that there is practically no connection between these new settlements and the regional conceptions about the future of settlements over a wider area. This certainly does not contribute to a satisfactory solution and the formation of a proper Ekistic system. It is natural that only a proper regional conception, as has already been explained, can define the role of every settlement exactly, so that it will fulfil its requirements satisfactorily. I will now give two examples of settlements which have been conceived as new ones on the basis of the ideas represented in this study; one is in a rural and the other an urban area.

The rural settlement is the area of Greater Mussayib, south-west of Baghdad in Iraq (fig. 445a). The plan for its creation provided for utilisation of the land to its maximum capacity in accordance with present economic, social and technological conditions. On the basis of this, the optimum area for every farming village was selected and plans made for its full utilisation through agriculture and cattle breeding.

445

new rural settlements

Greater Mussayib area, Iraq (1958)

community class A
community class B
community class C

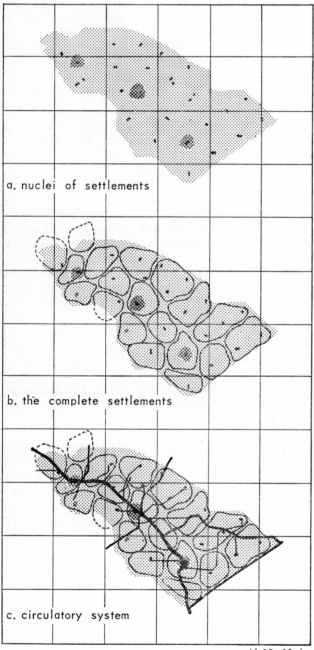

a. nuclei of settlements

b. the complete settlements

c. circulatory system

grid 10 × 10 km

These farming villages (Class A) are properly interconnected and lead to the formation of centres of a higher order which will have some additional central functions (Class B) calculated on the basis of the requirements of the area. Then, this whole system was calculated so as to lead to the formation of one (Class C) centre of a higher order, which again comes under the influence of an existing city (Class D) which is of an even higher order and serves a wider area. In fig. 445b we can see the full utilisation of the entire space leading to the conception of relatively static settlements, while in fig. 445c we see the interrelationship of the different settlements and the functional coverage of all the space.

The second example is of a new urban settlement. Islamabad is the new capital of Pakistan, a nation of close to 90 million people. After separation from India and independence, Pakistan found itself with a temporary capital, Karachi, and had to create a permanent one. Proper Ekistic studies determined where this capital should be located geographically and topographically, and these studies, continued on a microscale, gradually led to the formation of the first regional conception for such a plan (fig. 446).

Islamabad was conceived within the framework of its region in a position which serves the following purposes:

- o it is near the crossroads of important national highways along the axes of the age old Grand Trunk Road, which connects East and West, and the other old road to the north passing through the mountains and Kashmir;
- o it is near the crossroads of the highways, but not on them as these highways cross at a distance of more than four kilometres from the city's centre;
- o it has the best location from the point of view of climate and landscape, being at the foot of a series of hills from which it receives a cool draught in the summer, and which protect it from the cold winter winds;
- o the maximum benefit is obtained from the surrounding landscape by incorporating into its regional conception Lake Rawal, other lakes to be created and all the hills, which will become a national park;
- o the city's position allows for its continuous growth into the less important and low fertility areas (fig. 447).

Thus, the regional conception of Islamabad is such as to allow it to become an important nucleus of major metropolitan areas close to the crossing of the nation's major highways without having these highways in its very heart, which would have led to Islamabad being a traffic centre and not the capital. How this system will work in detail is demonstrated in fig. 448, where Islamabad is shown as it was conceived, as a typical Dynametropolis. There is already one city in this region, Rawalpindi, which at the outset is being used as the 'mother' to feed the young child-to-be in order to make the whole operation more natural and more economic for a country which cannot afford to waste its natural resources. There was a great danger that Rawalpindi would interfere with Islamabad's development. The problem to be faced was

446

new urban settlements

Islamabad region in Pakistan (1960)

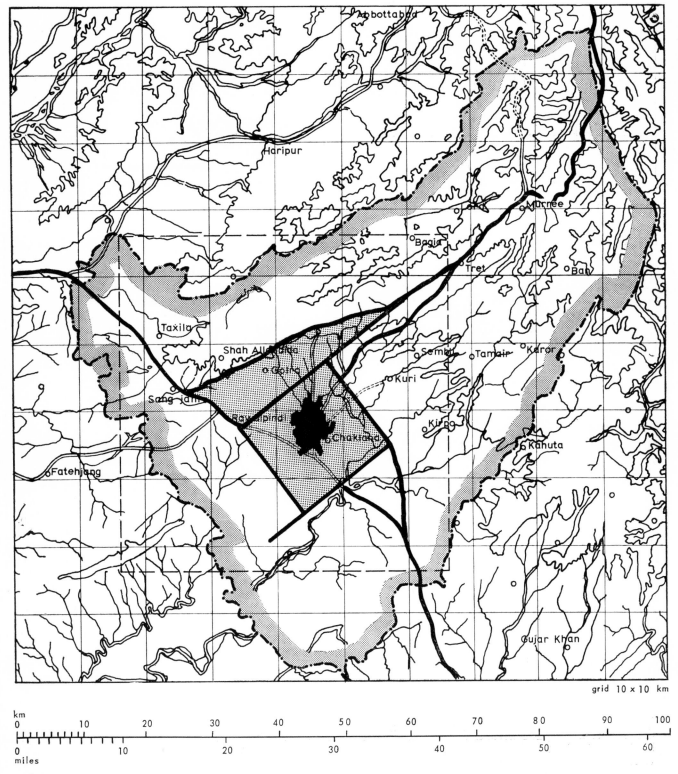

grid 10 x 10 km

km
0   10   20   30   40   50   60   70   80   90   100

0   10   20   30   40   50   60
miles

H1

dynamically growing Dynametropolis
Islamabad, Pakistan (1960)

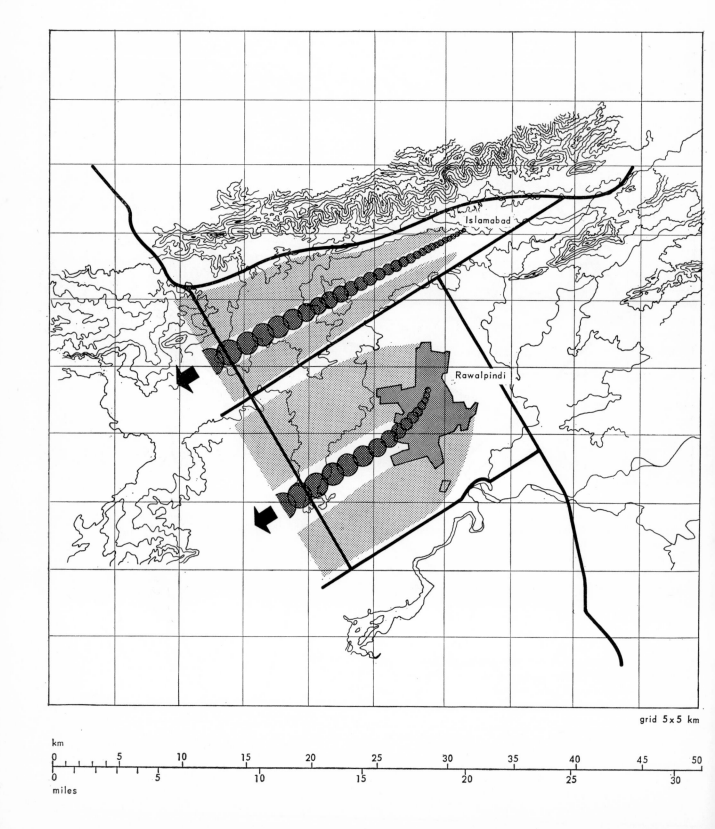

grid 5 x 5 km

km
0   5   10   15   20   25   30   35   40   45   50

0   5   10   15   20   25   30
miles

that Rawalpindi should be strengthened in order to become a natural city itself and remain the capital of the region and aid the growth of Islamabad; but how could it be prevented from interfering with Islamabad's development? This is why Rawalpindi has been planned as a Dynapolis developing towards the south-west, which is also the direction suggested by an analytical study of the landscape. Then Islamabad itself, with its back to the hills (where the capital area and the administrative part of the city is situated) could also grow to the south-west, parallel to the growth of Rawalpindi. So here we have two dynamic cities. Rawalpindi already exists as such, and will grow in the future with several types of functions—industry (which it already has), an army (of which it is the headquarters) and regional administration (of which it is the centre). At the same time the new city of Islamabad, now under construction, will grow into a Dynametropolis.

As a result of such a conception on a regional and metropolitan scale, we are led to the formation of the metropolitan plan of Islamabad (fig. 449) which is a quite typical example of a Dynametropolitan area, with the parallel growth of its several centres. The principles of the Ecumenopolis have been adhered to in Islamabad as faithfully as was possible; the area, apart from having been conceived as growing dynamically, is separated into sectors which correspond approximately in dimension to the cities of the past to which Man was accustomed in Pakistan, India and practically the whole world—that is, cities with ten to fifty thousand inhabitants, depending on their densities. The sectors will function within the metropolitan area of Islamabad as centres of urban life of a lower order to which Man is accustomed. Beyond them the new scale enters into the picture, where Man moves at high speeds on the spinal roads which cross the entire metropolitan area. How the city of Islamabad will function, and how it is already taking shape, is demonstrated in figs. 450, 451 and 452 showing the first sectors.

Uni-directional growth

The ideal form for a uni-nuclear dynamic city is the uni-directional form of expansion which leads to a parabolic solution, as already explained in the theory of urban growth. This certainly cannot be implemented on every occasion. It cannot be utilised when the patterns are too complicated as was also explained in theory. Also, it cannot be implemented when the local and topographic conditions, for one reason or another, do not allow for the development of a uni-directional pattern of expansion as has been demonstrated in the cases of Baghdad and Athens. There are other cases, however, where it is possible to work out solutions on the basis of the pattern of the ideal Dynapolis. In this chapter I am going to present some solutions I have worked out for several cities; some of the solutions were approved and are already in the

448

dynamically growing Dynametropolis

relationship between Rawalpindi (existing) and Islamabad (created)

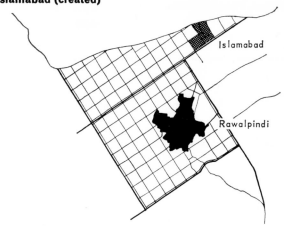

stage A : new-born Islamabad is fed by Rawalpindi

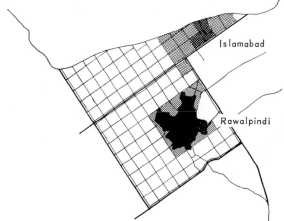

stage B : new-born Islamabad grows
both cities are serving each other

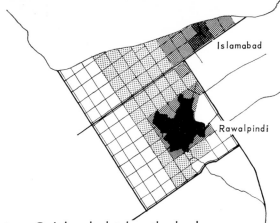

stage C : Islamabad takes the lead
both cities serve each other

Action

449

typical Dynametropolis

master plan of the metropolitan area

Islamabad, Pakistan (1960)

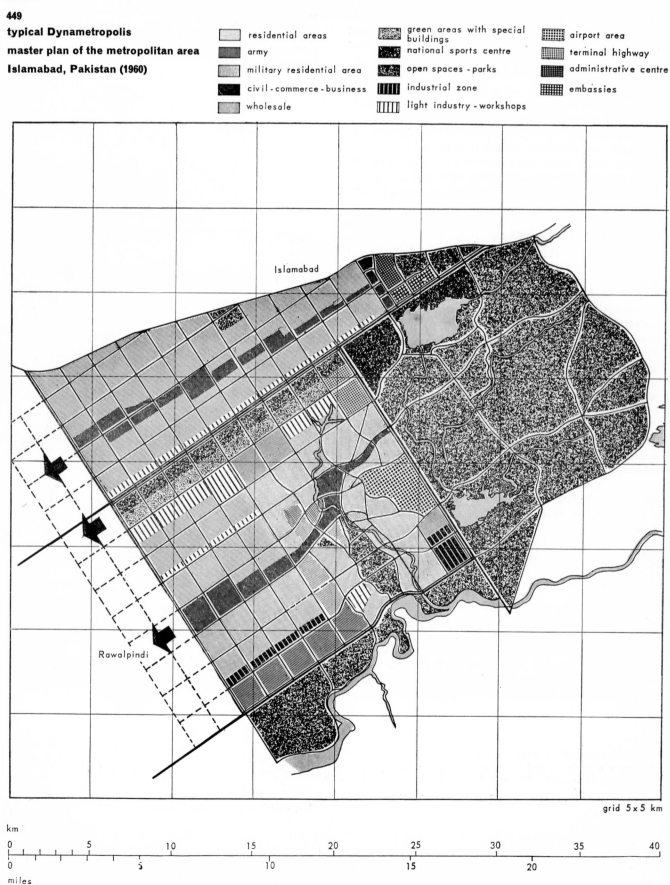

residential areas	green areas with special buildings
army	national sports centre
military residential area	open spaces - parks
civil - commerce - business	industrial zone
wholesale	light industry - workshops
	airport area
	terminal highway
	administrative centre
	embassies

Islamabad

Rawalpindi

grid 5 x 5 km

km

0   5   10   15   20   25   30   35   40

0   5   10   15   20

miles

450
circulatory network of Dynametropolis
the first four sectors (communities class V)
Islamabad, Pakistan (1960)

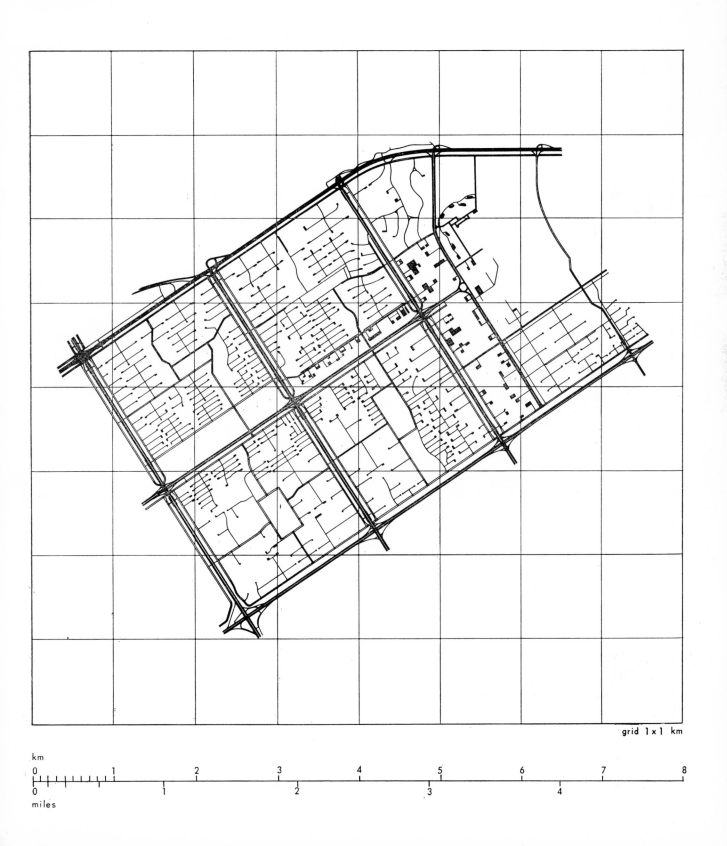

grid 1 x 1 km

km
0   1   2   3   4   5   6   7   8

0   1   2   3   4

miles

Shells and Networks of Dynametropolis
the first four sectors (communities class V)
Islamabad, Pakistan (1960)

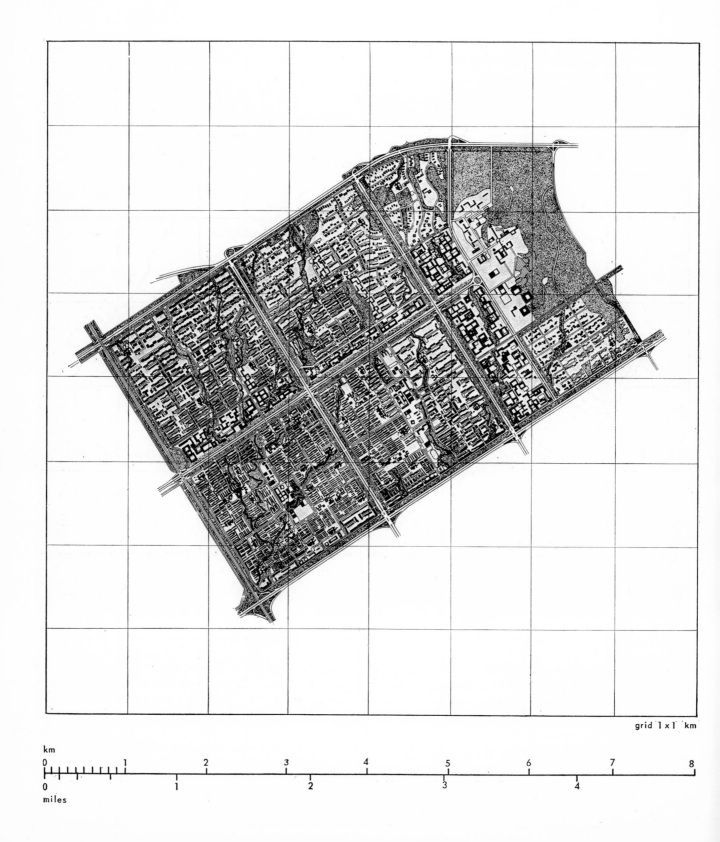

grid 1 x 1 km

km
0   1   2   3   4   5   6   7   8

0   1   2   3   4
miles

452

Shells and Networks of Dynametropolis

model of administrative centre and first sectors
(communities class **V**)

Islamabad, Pakistan (1960)

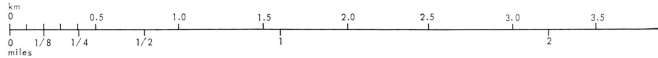

km
0   0.5   1.0   1.5   2.0   2.5   3.0   3.5

0   1/8   1/4   1/2   1   2
miles

Action

453

future of a Dynametropolis

suggestions for the year 2060 plan

Copenhagen, Denmark (1963)

**large space conception allows for the normal
evolution of the settlement on the basis of the forms
shaping Ecumenopolis**

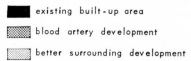

- existing built-up area
- blood artery development
- better surrounding development

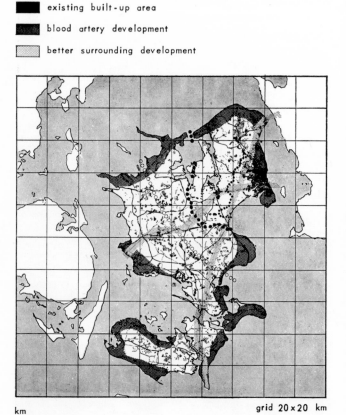

km

| grid 20×20 km |
| 0 | 20 | 40 | 60 | 80 | 100 | 120 | 140 | 160 | 180 | 200 |
| 0 | 20 | 40 | 60 | 80 | 100 | 120 |

miles

454

future of a Dynametropolis

suggestions for the year 2060 plan

Copenhagen, Denmark (1963)

- existing built-up area
- blood artery development
- better surrounding development

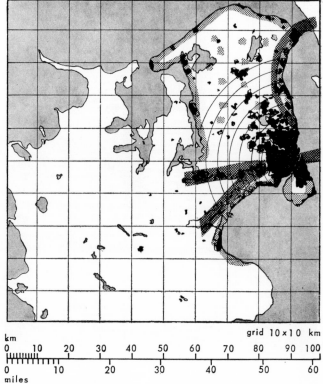

km

| grid 10×10 km |
| 0 | 10 | 20 | 30 | 40 | 50 | 60 | 70 | 80 | 90 | 100 |
| 0 | 10 | 20 | 30 | 40 | 50 | 60 |

miles

implementation phase; others were not approved but had an impact on the evolution of later ideas; and finally, some had no impact at all.

The most characteristic case of the implementation of the ideal Dynapolis conception is Islamabad, which has already been presented. It is quite natural that in a totally new city we should come closer to our ideals. In two of the cases which have accepted a star-fish development (Copenhagen and Washington D.C.), I have worked out suggestions of plans in order to demonstrate how the idea of an ideal Dynapolis could influence their pattern of expansion. In Copenhagen, my effort followed the submission of the official plan; in

the case of Washington D.C., however, it preceded it.

A macro-scopic (in the sense of space and time) projection of the Copenhagen area shows that we should expect many forces of growth to work on its peninsula as shown in fig. 453. These forces can be found along the main highways, along the coastal areas and radiating out from the centre of Copenhagen (fig. 454). Such growth, seen on an even larger scale, shows that we should expect a centre of gravity and a transportation centre to be created south-west of the present city, where the major growth will probably take place (fig. 455). If these are the natural trends, we should expect the centre to move gradually from a location very close to the

472

455

future of a Dynametropolis

suggested uni-directional growth of centre for the year 2060 plan

Copenhagen, Denmark (1963)

a. nearest centre in an open area

b. centre of transportation

c. centre of gravity

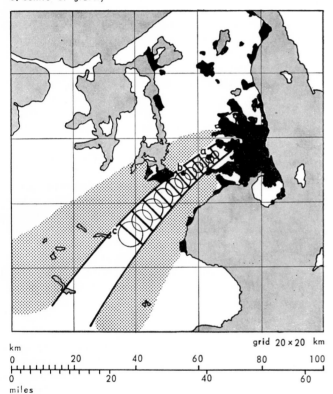

km

0   20   40   60   80   100

0   20   40   60

miles

grid 20 x 20 km

existing city towards the centre of transportation, towards the centre of gravity. A centre will guarantee the uni-directional expansion of the main functions of the city although several of them will spread around the countryside because of the forces already mentioned. Only through such a solution could we expect to relieve present-day Copenhagen and save it for its own sake and for the sake of the megalo-politan area or the branch of Ecumenopolis which will pass through Denmark.

In the case of Washington D.C., a survey carried out in 1959 led to the realisation of the relief needed for the area of the present centre of the capital because:

○ there was no more space for the central functions of the federal capital, as the case of the Pentagon, which had to be built far out, demonstrates;

○ the centre was already suffering from over-congestion and the city not functioning properly.

Because of this, a general approach to the solution of the problem was worked out by the conception of uni-directional growth of the centre, and the idea was suggested that the Potomac river could be used as an axis which, because of its width, would offer the following advantages:

○ a gradual transfer of the new functions of the centre to the south just outside the over-congested area where most of the government land lies;

○ future transportation along this axis, both for the commuters and the tourists;

○ growth on both sides of the Potomac of new areas which would lead to easier development and would relieve all other radial highways from the great pressure they now bear (fig. 243b).

Two other similar proposals were worked out for the cities of Beirut and Caracas, which are both over-congested. In both, the only possible solution for an over-congested centre which was already functioning very badly was found to be the creation of a new centre outside the existing one since that was already surrounded by such development that it could not be broken through in the theoretical pattern of the Dynapolis. This centre would then develop in one direction on the basis of the pattern of the Dynapolis and would allow the new residential areas and other areas to be developed on both sides of it, as seen in figs. 456 and 457.

In another case I had the opportunity to work on the idea of a uni-directional Dynapolis which could have been of great help for the solution of a complicated situation. This was the case of Karachi which had grown out of a small city of a few hundred thousand people into a city of millions in less than a decade. There was a possibility of implementing the scheme parallel to that of the ideal Dynapolis' uni-directional growth because:

○ the sea to the south would block one area of expansion;

○ the hills, the airport and the military installations to the west and north would make it easy to avoid major expansions in that direction;

○ the Malir river, the special formation of the ground and other developments would allow controlled growth to the east.

Thus, the expansion of the centre of the metropolitan area of Karachi towards the north-east (as already occurred in the past in the old city of Karachi, which is already a big metro-politan area and will expand into a much larger one), seemed the only reasonable one and became the basis of the plans for expansion already approved and executed in areas B and D, which are conceived as parts of a major area depending on the expanding centre in one direction (fig. 458).

456

future of a Dynametropolis

suggested uni-directional growth

Beirut, Lebanon (1958)

new residential areas

growth of the city

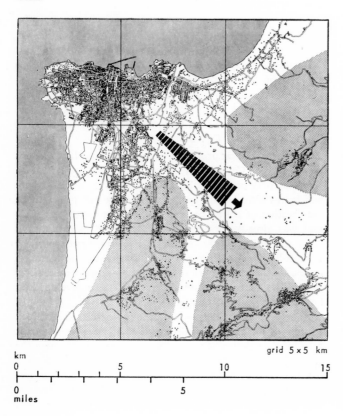

km
0   5   10   15

grid 5 x 5 km

0   5
miles

More difficult cases can be found in metropolitan areas which do not have only one nucleus able to expand in one direction but contain more than one nucleus. These cases are much more complicated and they can very seldom be solved by way of the principles of the ideal Dynapolis. They have to be based on the principles of the ideal Dynametropolis, which is much more complex and requires much more extensive analysis of all the possibilities. In some cases, however, there is a possibility for expansion of a metropolitan area which has more than one nucleus in one direction, a possibility connecting the Dynapolis with the Dynametropolis conceptions. We have already seen one such case in Islamabad,

which is a new city next to an old city, thus creating a two-nuclei city. Two more cases are the Greater Khartoum and the Accra-Tema metropolitan areas.

In the case of Greater Khartoum, there were specific reasons which did not simply allow, but actually enforced uni-directional growth. In addition to the known reasons leading to the conception of the parabolic uni-directional plan, there was another one which would impose such a solution: Greater Khartoum is built on the three parts of the land which are divided by the Blue and White Niles. The width of the river and the foundation conditions are such that the cost of bridges is very high in relation to the city's income. It would have been high even for cities of a higher income. If Greater Khartoum continued to grow on all three sides of the rivers, the need for many people and cars to cross the rivers would increase at such a rate that almost the entire budget of the city would be committed to bridge construction in order to allow the inhabitants of the three parts to communicate. This is why there was an imperative need that the two minor sections, the older part of Omdurman and the new and industrial one of Greater Khartoum be limited in their growth so as not to perpetuate the existing problems of the city. If this is achieved, growth will take place where it is most natural—out of present-day Khartoum towards the south, where the best area for the city's expansion lies—this growth would allow the city of Khartoum to become an area expanding in one direction, with two parts on the other sides of the rivers which will stop growing as soon as possible. A master plan submitted in 1959 was approved and is now under execution (fig. 459).

The question related to Khartoum is no longer that of a physical plan, but of its implementation. The first new features, such as a large new bridge on the Nile, follow the plan. Whether or not uni-directional growth is going to be successfully implemented depends on the rate at which investment takes place in the main city of Khartoum, and especially to the south of it. The attraction of the main functions of the basic development to the south must be facilitated by a policy of slowing down the rate of growth of Omdurman and North Khartoum. This is one more characteristic case when physical plans alone are meaningless unless they are parts of overall, well-conceived policies and programmes tending to one very specific direction, as physically exemplified by the plan. If the programme of investment facilitates this trend, this plan can turn the Greater Khartoum area—which was a multi-nuclei, multi-directional expanding city—into a uni-directional city, which will mean a great change in its evolution and will guarantee a much better future. Khartoum has become the first major metropolitan area to approve a plan on the basis of the ideal Dynapolis conception of uni-directional growth. One complicated case of a Dynametropolis with three nuclei can be solved on the basis of the principle of uni-directional ideal growth by leading the two other nuclei towards static forms.

457

future of a Dynametropolis

suggested uni-directional growth

Caracas, Venezuela (1960)

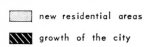

☐ new residential areas

▨ growth of the city

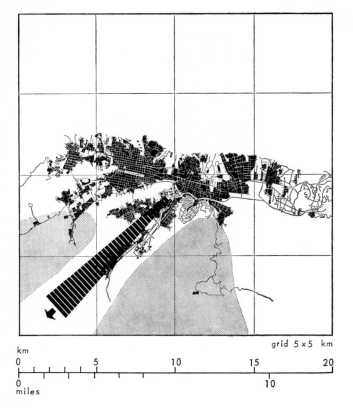

grid 5 x 5 km

km
0   5   10   15   20

0   10
miles

458

future of a Dynametropolis

suggested uni-directional growth

greater Karachi, Pakistan (1959)

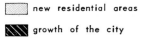

☐ new residential areas

▨ growth of the city

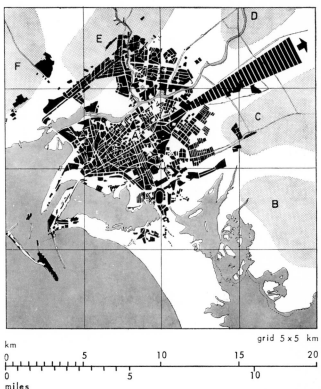

grid 5 x 5 km

km
0   5   10   15   20

0   5   10
miles

The other such problem is presented by the Accra-Tema metropolitan area (fig. 460). Accra, the capital of Ghana, is a one-nucleus city which naturally expands inland in one direction. But its future depends on other factors—transportation, a port and industry—and these had to be created in the new location of Tema, many miles away. This new city of Tema required a new centre the normal future of which would again be to expand inland in one direction (fig. 461). Therefore, there was a need for two centres expanding uni-directionally at a right angle to the sea and parallel to each other. A study of the area has proved that these two centres could not serve the entire region which

would gradually be built, so a master programme and a master plan were prepared for the entire metropolitan area. This plan proves that to serve the whole metropolitan area only through the centre of Accra and Tema is unreasonable. The distance between them is too great, and an area in the middle of the metropolitan area would have been left without proper services. Analysis has shown that a centre similar to those of Accra and Tema must be created near the sea and must move parallel to the other centres inland. Thus, we have a third dynamic centre to be created on the basis of the same principle, and the Accra-Tema metropolitan area will turn, therefore, into a typical Dynametropolis with three parallel

475

future of a Dynametropolis

plan for two static centres and one dynamic centre

approved master plan of greater Khartoum, Sudan (1959)

residential areas

local centres

commerce-business administration

sewage disposal area

industrial areas

green areas with special buildings

open spaces

railway station

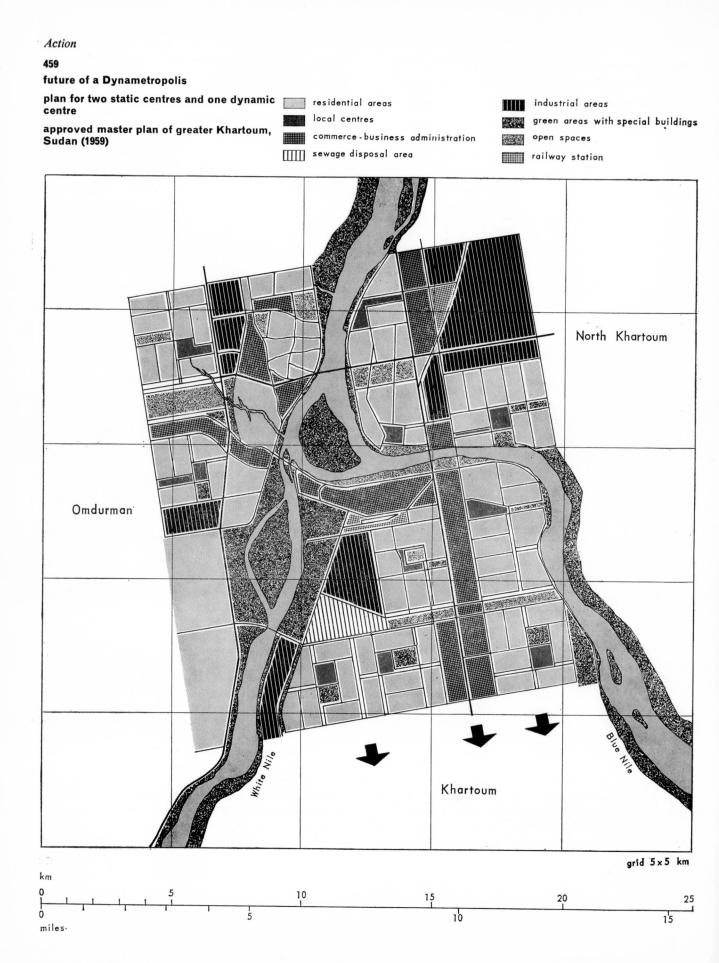

North Khartoum

Omdurman

Khartoum

White Nile

Blue Nile

grid 5 x 5 km

km
0   5   10   15   20   25

0   5   10   15
miles·

460

future of a Dynametropolis

plan for three dynamic centres

approved master plan of Accra-Tema, Ghana (1960)

- residential area
- existing city
- civil-commerce-business
- institutions
- administration
- industrial zone
- military area and civil aviation
- open spaces-parks-green areas
- green spaces with special buildings
- radio relay stations
- academic area
- harbour
- light industry workshops

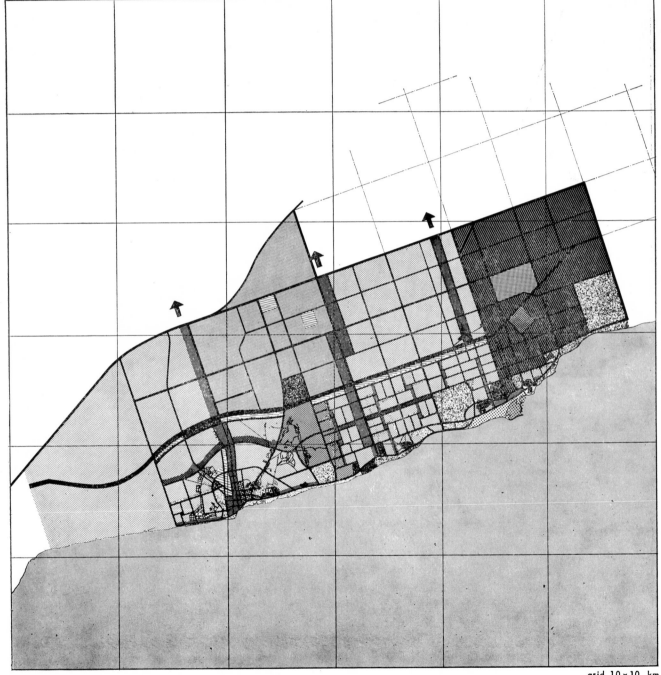

grid 10 x 10 km

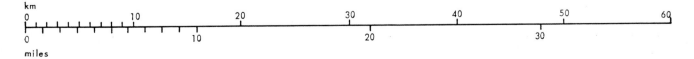

km
0 ... 10 ... 20 ... 30 ... 40 ... 50 ... 60

0 ... 10 ... 20 ... 30

miles

Action

461

typical Dynametropolis

Tema, Ghana (1964)

residential areas	radio relay stations	green areas
civil-commercial-business	light industry-workshops	special recreations.
institutions and other functions	industrial area	fishing harbour
hospital	open spaces-parks	

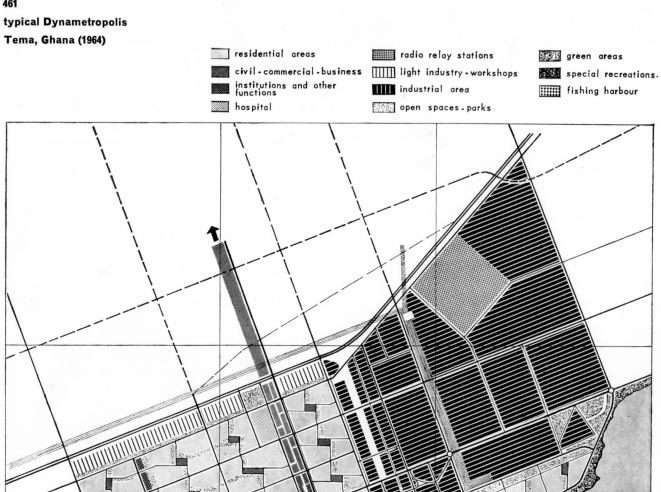

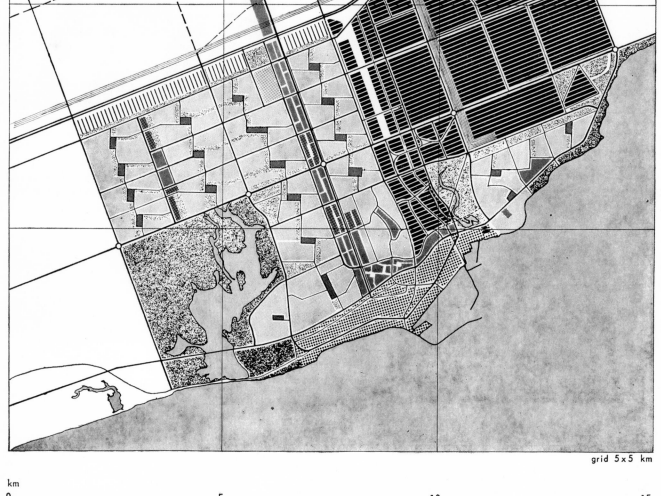

grid 5x5 km

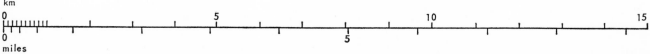

km

0   5   10   15

0   5

miles

uni-directional lines of expansion—those of Accra, Tema and the new community to be created between them (fig. 460). Such a conception leads to a pattern of a Dynametropolis which, though expanding along the coast, will have three centres growing inland and several connecting lines with functions of different orders between them, as shown in fig. 460.

This is the occasion to mention that all these solutions are very often already imposed when the expert arrives on the scene and the wisest thing he can do is to understand the right trends and then serve them. In the case of Baghdad the solution is provided by the river, in the case of Athens by the valley, in the case of Accra by the sea which could not attract the centre since it was a solid wall which has led the expansion of facilities onto the main inland road. This is something that we must always understand and remember: the solution is very often already there, and we need only open our eyes to see it.

Multi-directional growth

In most cases I know of, growth of settlements takes place from an existing nucleus outwards. Most human settlements today expand with no real overall plan, growing out of a nucleus in concentric circles or along several axes, depending on the structure and texture of the settlement, as has already been explained in the Ekistic theory of the growth of human settlements. Because of this trend and because of the tradition of concentric growth, almost all human settlements which have prepared or are preparing plans for their future growth through expansion, provide ring-roads within and outside the built-up area as a pattern of expansion. Since this tendency is so strong, almost all plans prepared to relieve over-congested central areas of cities provide a succession of ring-roads. How wrong this is can be understood on the basis of the theory already developed. Sooner or later, these settlements will be choked to death.

Only during the last two decades have any efforts been made to break up the ring-roads and to create star-shaped or star-fish patterns of expansion.

Star-shaped expansions

The first and most characteristic effort was begun by the city of Copenhagen, which in the year 1951 approved the so-called 'five finger plan' providing for expansion in five main directions. The idea was to allow the city to grow only along the axes of the main transportation lines, thus blending the natural with the man-made landscape. Ten years later the results were such that it was quite clear that the actual expansion of the city was not taking place on the main transportation lines but also in between them, and the gaps between the 'fingers' were beginning to be filled. This led to a second multi-

directional conception of expansion, based on lines of high speed traffic, which was worked out in 1960. We can make the same remarks about this conception as the previous one: there will be a tendency to fill the gaps between the protruding elongated, high-speed 'fingers'.

A very characteristic example of how our prognostication of urban trends is being continuously improved is given by the city of Copenhagen's report presenting this last plan. It is a prediction prepared from 1958 to 1960 of the number of cars the Copenhagen area will have in the year 1980 (fig. 462). Within that period of only two years, the estimated number of cars by 1980 rose from slightly over 200,000 (estimate prepared by a commission investigating the possibility of a bridge over the Great Belt in 1958) to close to 340,000 (revised estimate by a national motoring organisation which in 1959 had estimated the number of cars for 1980 to be lower than 280,000). These changes in the estimates of the numbers of cars should not be considered as miscalculations due to a lack of proper understanding of the problems. They were all probably very conscientious efforts for the best possible estimate, but they are characteristic of the changes of our attitudes or our beliefs about the importance of the machine in the city and its dynamic character.

The continuous revision of the estimate of the number of cars is in no way a failure on the part of the city of Copenhagen; on the contrary, it is a proof of the desire for the best solution, and it was a courageous act to present this difference in estimates, which shows an increase of 70 per cent in a period of two years.

The same thing is still happening in almost all cities. The estimates, when properly prepared are being continuously raised—not only for cars, but for many other elements of the city as well. The difference is that few cities still make systematic attempts to reach such estimates, and are very seldom prepared to admit their previous failure. It is also characteristic that the only realistic estimates of growth of traffic that have been made during the last ten years are in the United States, which has suffered from a greater number of cars and thus, greater pressures in settlements. This is why this experience has, during the last two or three years, been exported to European countries and other continents. The Americans were the first to face the necessity of very careful calculations. It is also characteristic that because of the pressure from cars, the emphasis is placed on studies related to the importance of machines and their system of transportation, when studies of other functions should have preceded them and the entire framework should have been set upon this basis.

It is just this failure to admit the existence of all factors that retarded the development of Ekistics as a scientific field of knowledge. It is only when we have the courage to observe all phenomena, make all necessary estimates, revise them continuously and be prepared for a criticism of our own action, that we can develop the right attitude which will

462

(below) prognosis prepared between 1958-1960 of the number of cars in Copenhagen

463

(right) growth of a Dynametropolis
Washington D.C., U.S.A.

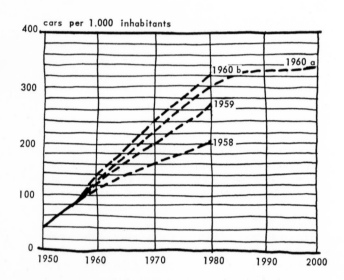

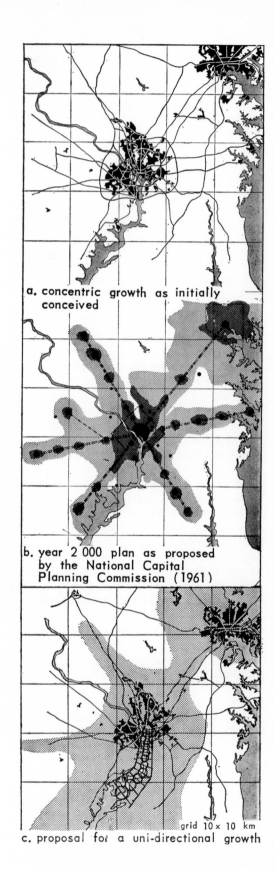

a. concentric growth as initially conceived

b. year 2 000 plan as proposed by the National Capital Planning Commission (1961)

grid 10 x 10 km

c. proposal for a uni-directional growth

lead us to scientific knowledge and to scientific solutions of these major problems.

The second important case of a city which decided to follow a plan of multi-directional expansion without introducing the concept of ring-roads (that is, initiating a star-like plan), is Washington D.C. In 1959, when reviewing the growth of the city for the Redevelopment Land Agency of Washington D.C., I had the opportunity to speak against the ring or loop system—which was partially under execution and was supposed to be the basic pattern of the city's growth—and to stress the necessity for a uni-directional growth to the south. This report of mine, although it became a subject of discussion, was not endorsed by the planning authorities. In 1961 the 'Year 2000 Plan' was published which practically abandoned the loop system, was definitely a multi-directional plan of expansion providing not for five 'fingers' as in Copenhagen, but for six along the main highways of the country (fig. 463). In this respect, it was a break with the tradition of ring-roads, and provided new opportunities for growth; but it did not give an answer to the danger that the filling up of the gaps between the 'fingers' might result in a choking of the centre.

Speaking of these two major contributions to the creation of star-like or star-fish plans, we should note that if the lines of transportation they create are of a much higher speed than the previous ones, they will provide temporary relief for those people who move along these lines; they will provide a temporary balance between the built-up areas which expand only in several directions and the natural landscape which can survive in the first period between them. These plans, however, give no answer at all either to the problem related to the centre—which suffers from the same pressure as in the case of the ring-roads, if not worse—or to the problem of what is going to happen in the gaps between the 'fingers', which in the past have tended to be filled.

The theory already explained, that we should expect a filling up of the gaps between 'fingers' and a tendency towards a circular form, is now fairly widely understood although I do not know whether it is accepted as such. Recent evidence was given by John R. Borchert in his presentation, 'The Twin Cities Urbanized Area'.[25] Both proposals given therein are important contributions to the effort of developing major urban areas. Although the step made by this courageous plan is great, I do not believe that it offers the necessary solutions. In 1900 the twin cities of Minneapolis and St. Paul in Minnesota began showing a tendency towards two-directional growth. In 1940 this tendency was strengthened, but minor 'fingers' were beginning to spread around in the countryside (fig. 464). By 1956 the gaps between the 'fingers' were filling up and the twin cities tended to fill a circle. Borchert foresees that by 1980 this movement towards a circle will increase so much that the plan will no longer retain any characteristics of a linear or star-fish expansion[26] (fig. 464). If the theory of urban growth and the projections about the universal city to come are correct (and to the best of my knowledge they are as close as we can come with our present-day knowledge), the future of such urban areas depends on the recognition of the following important facts:

○ major urban areas cannot survive as such under the pressures to come—they will either be choked to death or gradually transform their central core, with all its values, into an enormous meeting place of highways and cars;

○ in order to save such urban areas and in order to serve the future inhabitants and functions, we must conceive a plan for a much broader area and project it over a much longer period;

○ in order really to help these urban areas, such a plan should not be one of satellites, no matter how well conceived their form, dimensions and shape—for though these satellites may solve their own internal problems, they can never solve those of the centre from which they derive their life and which they serve—satellites will not relieve centres from the enormous pressures which are built up;

○ the only way to save these urban areas is to conceive an overall plan with a new centre of a higher order (If these areas are communities class VII, the new centre to be created should be of class VIII.);

○ this centre will have new types of functions which

present-day cities are inadequate to serve, functions which are of the greatest importance for a population of several millions.

In the light of such considerations, all new areas to be created for the expansion of the city must be looked upon as functional parts of the future city and not only of the present one. Although at first they may be directly and strongly connected with the original centre, in the future they will gradually become the appendices of the new one, appendices which will be added to the centre of the original urban areas only to serve such functions as remain in that centre. These will be functions which will serve and preserve the original centre instead of gradually choking and killing it.

Two-directional growth

The star-like conceptions are not the only ones leading to the abandonment of the ring-road pattern. In order to avoid many of the weaknesses of the star-like plans, we can work with two-directional growth patterns. The answers which they provide for the two problems of star-fish development are:

○ because development takes place along one axis, there are no gaps tending to be filled left between 'fingers' and there is no danger of reverting from a new pattern to the age-old one of concentric circles and ring-roads;

○ because a very specific line of the centre's development is given, it becomes elongated, which may slightly relieve the core from the danger of over-congestion.

While the first of these answers can lead to satisfactory results, I doubt if the second can do so, for the danger of an over-crowded centre would remain, since most of the outlying areas would continue to converge on it. Yet there are cases where the implementation of a uni-directional pattern of growth as developed by the theory of a Dynapolis is impossible, and this is why we must be prepared to work with the conception of expansion which, although not ideal, is at least theoretically better than others since it provides answers for most of the problems created in major urban areas (fig. 465).

In two cases, I personally was forced to implement this pattern because local conditions reasonably imposed it. The first was the Baghdad Master Plan. Baghdad was, in the past (fig. 466), a city developing in a two-directional way along the river, because:

○ it was only along the river that the land lent itself to better living conditions because it had better soil, was close to the water and was cultivated (mostly with palm trees);

○ the river created a micro-climate which was much better than the desert climate beyond it;

○ water supply, rain and sewage disposal were more convenient.

Nineteenth century Baghdad was a two-directional city and was forced to grow on the basis of the same basic pattern.

growth of urban settlements

tendency towards a circular form

twin cities, Minneapolis-St. Paul, Minnesota, U.S.A.

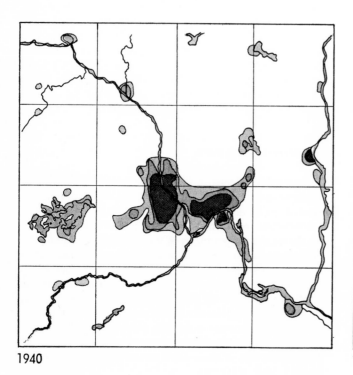

1940

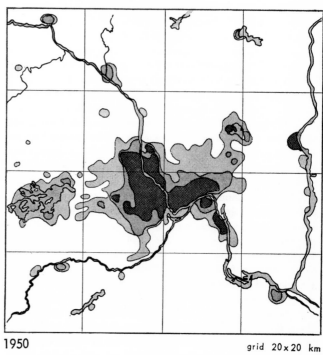

1950   grid 20 x 20 km

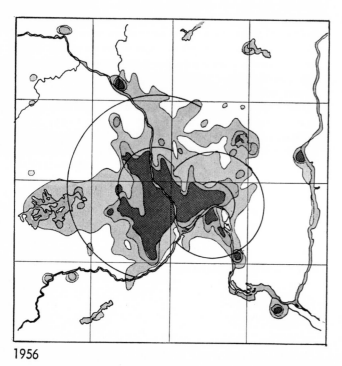

1956

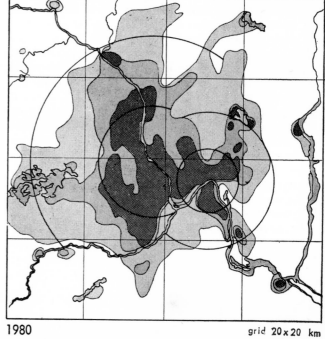

1980   grid 20 x 20 km

465

two-directional expansion

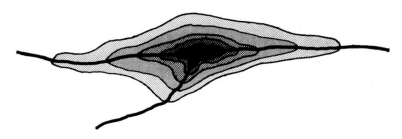

To turn Baghdad into a uni-directional city would have been unnatural: why should the movement of a settlement up-river or down-river be excluded? So, the enlarged Baghdad was conceived as a two-directional city for exactly the same reasons as those which forced the nineteenth-century Baghdad to follow this pattern (fig. 467).

In order to maintain the advantages given by the river, a proposal was made for a new master plan along these lines incorporating a proposal for a big canal A to the east of the city connected to the Tigris river. This canal has already been built and creates an area of climatic conditions equally as good as those along the river. Then another provision was made for a second canal B which would create another such area. Consequently, the city of Baghdad would be built on the basis of the following principles:

○ two-directional growth along the spinal axis of the river, since that is the natural solution imposed by the landscape;

○ a two-directional main centre parallel to it;

○ parallel canals to the main axis, creating areas of similar climate;

○ vertical connections providing for special functions of the centre depending upon whether these connections were of purely internal importance or led to several important functions (such as the airport) or to other parts of the country.

The second case requiring two-directional growth was Athens. The centre of present-day Athens has been built between the main hills of the city, the Acropolis and Lycabettus, and it has become so congested with blocks of flats during the last generation that it is not possible for the centre to expand properly in any way that would save the city (as shown in fig. 468). Because of the topographic formation, the centre is already blocked by a ring of building investment which is spreading at a higher rate in all directions and does not allow a break-through. There is no solution for this centre but to keep it as it is with minor ameliorations, and create a new one of a higher order somewhere out in the open where it will still be possible for the city to expand.

As the topography of the city shows, expansion is possible mostly to the north, where the last undeveloped areas remaining between the city and the surrounding mountains (which cannot and should not be built upon) exist. This is where the new axis connecting the metropolitan area with the whole country can be built and where a new centre can be created.

If we also look at fig. 437, showing how the branches of the Ecumenopolis within Greece are going to take shape in the vicinity of Athens, we will realise the great importance of the location which is on the crossroads of the axes of the country and the future Ecumenopolis. This centre cannot develop in one direction in accordance with the requirements of the ideal Dynapolis. It is, therefore, necessary to admit that two-directional growth is the only natural solution; this will create the spinal axis of the whole valley of Athens, which will also be the spinal axis of the continental part of the Greek Ecumenopolis (fig. 469).

We have seen two examples of how a two-directional road is the only natural solution because of topographic conditions even though these conditions are completely different in each case. In the first case we have open land all around, but only one relevant topographic element, a river, which is a very important element in a desert climate. To overlook this river in favour of any schematic conception of uni-directional growth—which is theoretically more justified—would have been disastrous. This is why two-directional growth was the only natural solution; it was imposed by the open landscape, which contained a strong two-dimensional element.

The other case is completely different. In Athens the landscape, contrary to that of Baghdad, is absolutely limited by the surrounding mountains. It is really a small valley overlooking the sea. In the centre of this valley is the city of Athens whose centre is already surrounded by high investment and is choked; the centre cannot expand. The part of the valley which is free allows for the creation of a new centre which, because of the formation of the landscape, will grow along the valley as a two-directional centre. Here the limitations enforced by the mountains have imposed on the valley of Athens a similar solution to that imposed by the river on the past and future of Baghdad.

483

Action

466

growth of urban settlements

natural two-directional expansion

Baghdad, Iraq (1955)

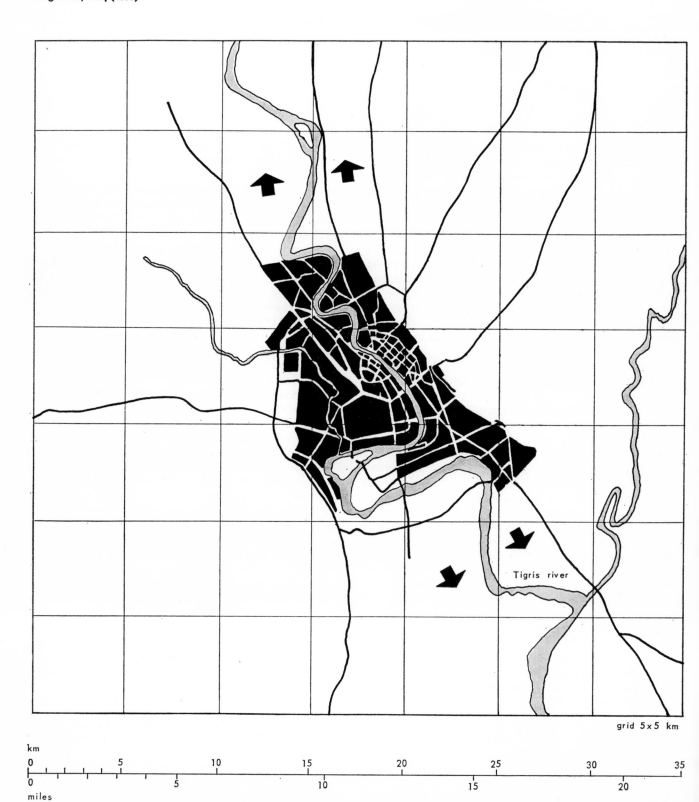

grid 5 x 5 km

Tigris river

km

| 0 | 5 | 10 | 15 | 20 | 25 | 30 | 35 |

| 0 | 5 | 10 | 15 | 20 |

miles

467

growth of urban settlements

planned two-directional expansion

proposed and partially implemented master plan

Baghdad, Iraq (1955)

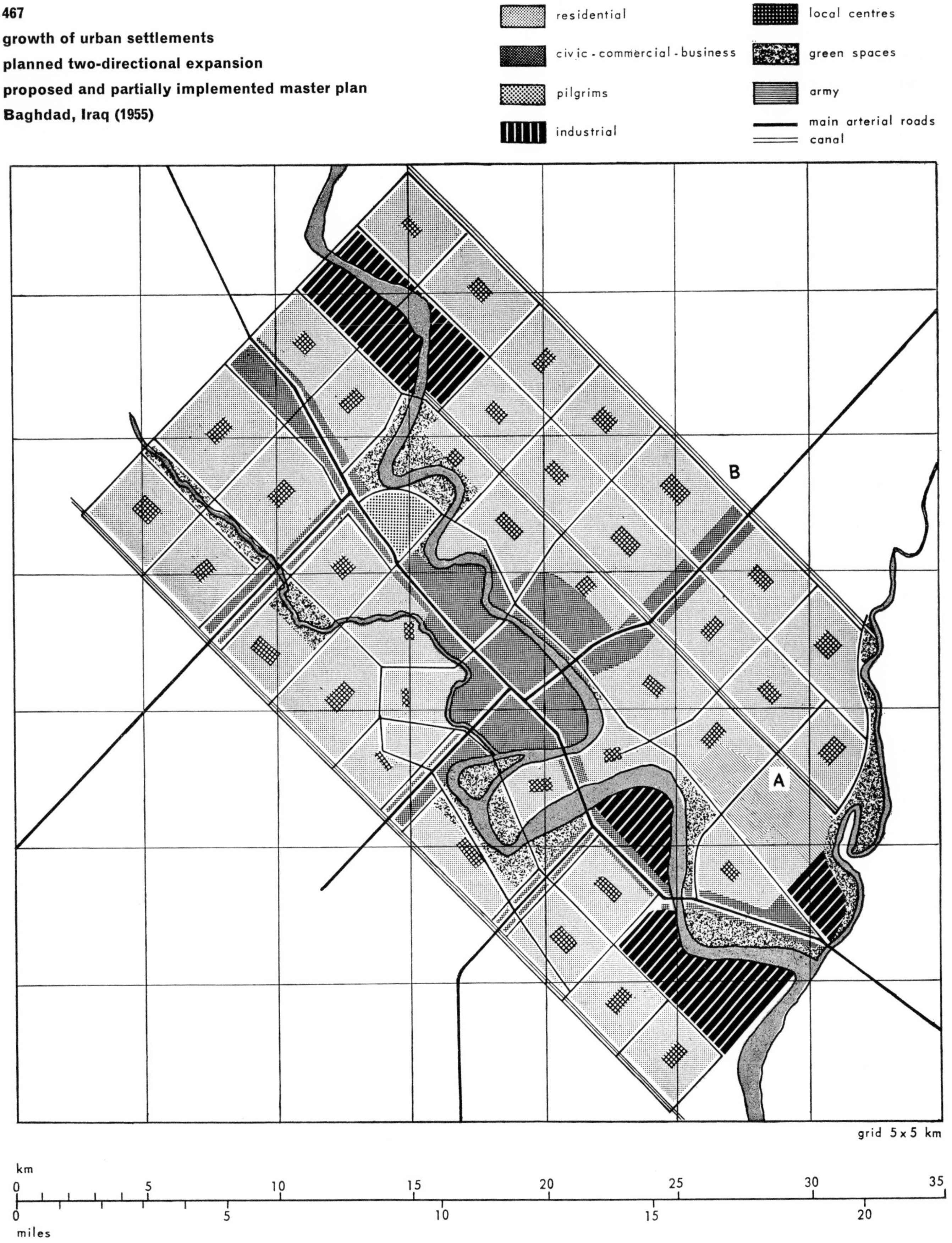

residential		local centres	
civic - commercial - business		green spaces	
pilgrims		army	
industrial		main arterial roads	
		canal	

grid 5 x 5 km

km
0   5   10   15   20   25   30   35

0   5   10   15   20
miles

growth of a Dynametropolis
creation of a new centre
as proposed for Athens, Greece (1959)

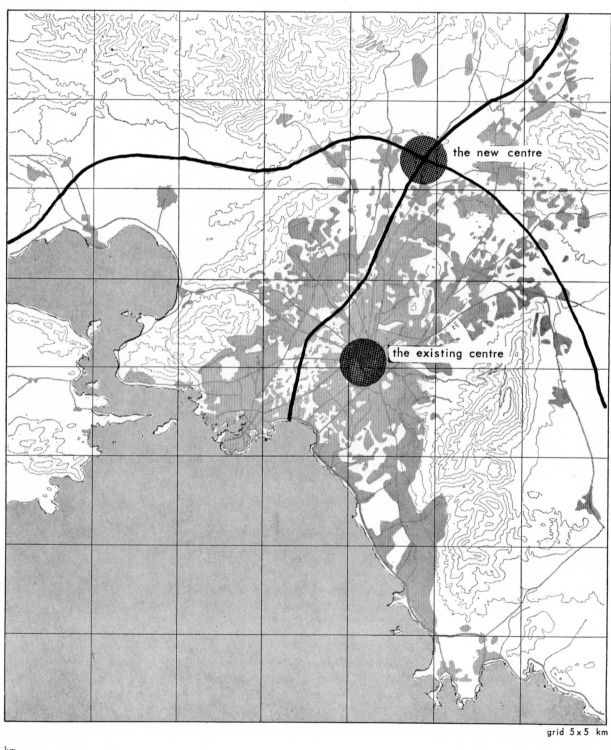

built-up area

main axis of circulation

the new centre

the existing centre

grid 5 x 5 km

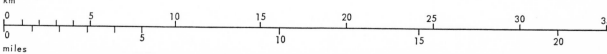

km

0   5   10   15   20   25   30   35

0   5   10   15   20

miles

469

growth of a Dynametropolis

two-directional development of a new centre

as proposed for Athens, Greece (1959)

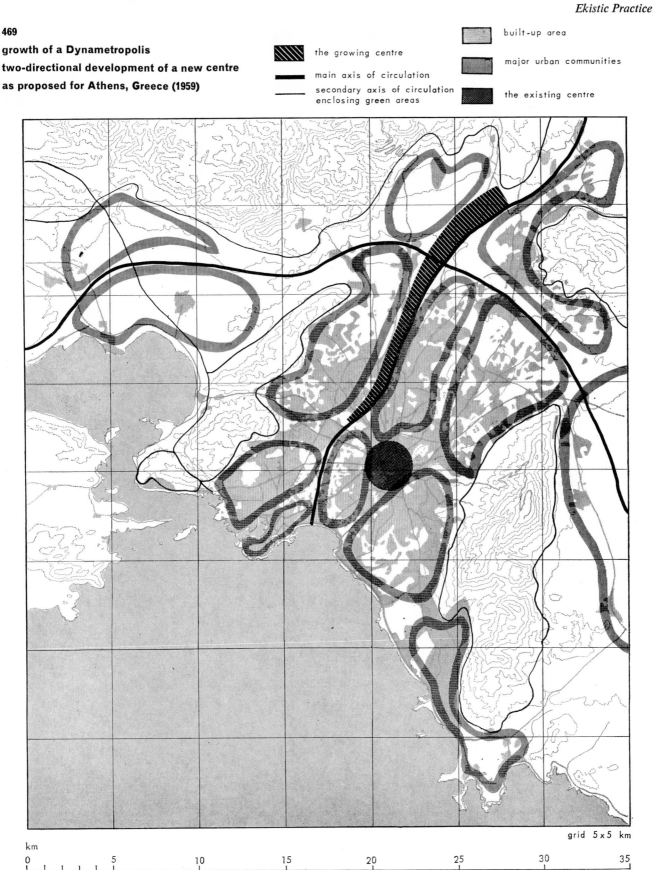

the growing centre

main axis of circulation

secondary axis of circulation
enclosing green areas

built-up area

major urban communities

the existing centre

grid 5 x 5 km

km

0   5   10   15   20   25   30   35

0   5   10   15   20

miles

DEVELOPMENT THROUGH TRANSFORMATION

Process

Development also takes place through the transformation of the structure of existing settlements. This is actually the age-old process of development, which some day may well be the only type. This will become possible if and when we achieve a stable Ecumenopolis with a stable population, by which time there will be no need for major expansion, but for a continuous transformation of the tissue of urban and rural settlements in order to increase its value and its efficiency for its inhabitants.

Transformation is also a very normal process since it is a more common form of development than growth and expansion. Expansion occurs in every location only once, that is, only once in every major cultural phase of a settlement, while transformation may take place a great number of times. For example, a house which has been built in the outskirts of a city and has contributed to its expansion may be changed many times during the lifetime of that part of the city; the same holds true of other elements of the overall settlement.

Development through transformation is valid in all types of settlements—rural and urban, small and large. To understand its importance, we need only realise that even in non-expanding settlements transformation—be it positive or negative—takes place continuously. This was especially true in the past. For many centuries the city was confined within walls, but it was continuously changing; the buildings, the roads and the squares were in a constant state of alteration. If we assume an average life span of five centuries for a city with walls and 70 years for most of the buildings in it, we can state that development through transformation was roughly seven times greater than through expansion.

Because we are now living in an era of explosion, which is expressed by a population explosion, as well as an explosion of the Shells, this ratio has changed. Even so, we are continuously witnessing changes and transformations within the built-up areas, which means that even today development through transformation in the average settlement takes place at a higher rate than development through expansion, even though this is not necessarily true of all settlements some of which are now expanding very rapidly over short periods of time. But on the whole, if we take into consideration all those forces that lead to the increase of the rate of transformation of settlements over longer periods, we will see that development through transformation occurs much more often and is much more important than development through expansion which has only become significant today.

Development through transformation takes place through the amelioration of the existing Shells and through natural or planned changes. Some minor parts of the Shells—houses, roads and squares—are repaired, maintained and improved upon. Others are replaced in a natural way; a house which is getting too old and no longer serves its purpose may well be replaced. The same is true of water supply networks, sewers, transportation lines, etc. Finally, projects for the clearance of depressed areas are an example of planned transformation.

Because we have now entered an era when major changes in the tissue of human settlements are necessary, we quite often define policies in relation to the transformation of settlements. What was happening in a natural way in the past must now take place through planning. And very often we must face such questions as: do we need a new settlement, or can we cope with the existing one? And if we can manage with the existing one, are we going to maintain it as it is, or should we change it? If we decide to change it, are we going to repair, ameliorate or rebuild it? By answering such questions, we define a policy for development through transformation which is then expressed, as all other policies, in programmes and plans. In this respect we must admit that although such policies are now beginning to take shape in different countries, we are not at all certain that they are sound. Actually, it is only in the present generation, especially in the post-war years, that several countries have been concerned with the planned transformation of settlements on a major scale. Before that, any measures taken were very limited in scope as well as in purpose.

The purpose of transformation in the past was usually the beautification of a city: building a new road or square, sometimes even clearing slum areas. This, however, was almost always very limited in scale, an important exception being the slum clearance which Nero probably conceived and carried out in a rather brutal manner in ancient Rome. Only after the last war has the necessity of development by way of planned transformation become evident because:

- the destruction caused by the war was of such magnitude that it opened the eyes of humanity to the necessity and possibility of creating better human settlements;
- the pressure created within the tissue of expanding settlements was such that many parts were completely unable to fulfil even a part of their initial functions.

While planned transformation is now becoming a necessity, we are completely unprepared for it, since we lack experience. Our policies are usually very feeble in conception and quite vague. Our plans are not at all consistent with the overall development and are limited in area and scope. For these reasons they quite often do not lead to success but contribute to greater confusion in urban affairs. Such plans tend to eliminate existing wealth because the area no longer fulfils its initial purposes properly. Only lately have we realised that conservation of created wealth may be a very important factor. Why, after all, do we develop policies and programmes for the conservation of natural resources and not for man-made resources in urban areas? We are trying to save whatever we can for future generations, in order to leave them a better natural habitat, while at the same time we allow the urban habitat, which has been created through the hard labour and efforts of many generations to be destroyed. Moreover, we create conditions for an unsuitable habitat, the improvement of which will take its toll on the entire community.

A careful analysis of the present situation in urban settlements compels us to realise that, aside from the knowledge we must acquire for the sound expansion of human settlements, we must learn a lot more about the necessity to conserve as much of our investment in existing settlements as possible. In order to achieve this, we must work in two directions.

- We must understand the process of irrational growth, decay, decline and death of the human settlement and its parts. Only when we understand the natural process can we adjust ourselves to every occasion and realise the specific requirements of all or a part of the settlement we are dealing with. Only then can we understand its future growth and plan for it accordingly.
- We must develop criteria to help us evaluate the degree of satisfaction which every settlement or part of a settlement provides for Man. After having conceived its future within the whole pattern as explained above, we must be able to understand how much satisfaction every area affords, whether it is worth investing more in this area in order to preserve it, or whether it is worth ameliorating or remodelling or even eliminating and rebuilding it to serve the same or another function.

The definition of satisfaction must have many aspects. We must discover to what degree the existing part of the settlement satisfies the daily human needs for which it has been built. This should be estimated under all conditions if we are to understand how this settlement satisfies our present needs and how well it can satisfy them in the future—under normal and exceptional conditions of evolution, in emergencies, in peace and in war. This last point should not be excluded. For example, it has been estimated that if all the registered cars in Paris circulated in the streets at the same time, there would be no possibility of movement. Is this a normal condition for a human settlement—not to be able to function in an emergency? We take so many measures to ascertain that people can abandon a building in an emergency, but we do not think of how we can abandon a city in such a case. This is an important factor to be taken into consideration together with the others.

The policy I recommend for a definition of our attitude towards development through transformation consists of two parts. The first should tend to clarify the role of every settlement or part of it and how it will function within the overall system. To do this we must:

- study the population increase in both large and minor

areas in order to know what population is to be expected in every area;
- do the same with regard to the surface and the physical characteristics of settlements;
- ascertain the mobility of every person within the settlement, how much income the settlement has, how many cars, how many kilometres per person, how many telephones per person, connections per person, etc.

If the findings of the above are combined, we can calculate for every area:

- the amount of pressure in the centres and peripheries of settlements;
- the degree of importance and the types of functions which will be carried out by every such part;
- the problems which arise in relation to the development of every part of a settlement, especially as far as their structure and texture are concerned.

We will then have a picture of the role to be played by every part in the expanding texture and can proceed to the second point—the estimation of the degree of satisfaction provided to us by every such part. By combining the results of the estimate of the role with that of the degree of satisfaction provided, we can find the existing divergencies, which will help us decide:

- whether the area we are dealing with is going to become depressed because it will suffer greater pressures which will create higher demands where the satisfaction is already low;
- whether the area will be stable because the functions we expect it to fulfil are the same as the original ones, and whether the degree of satisfaction is quite reasonable, so that there will be no need for a major change;
- whether the area where the functions are carried out or are to be carried out will grow. This, compared with the degree of satisfaction of these functions, will reveal that there may be a need for major changes.

Thus combining our findings concerning the role with those concerning the degree of satisfaction provided, we can classify the settlement into one of three categories which lead to different policies and attitudes from the point of view of development through transformation. How such a system of ideas is implemented can be seen in fig. 470, where an old settlement A, which was central to C, D, E and F, is now expanding towards B, where it is easily connected with the new line of transportation G–H. Such a development created the following areas in accordance with the transformation they are undergoing:

- D, which is a depressed area because it is at a distance from the new lines of communication and is connected only through settlement A, which provides great hindrances;
- C, E and F, which are stable because they are not on the main lines of development but are properly connected with them so that their inhabitants have the same

489

development through transformation

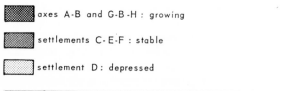

axes A-B and G-B-H : growing

settlements C-E-F : stable

settlement D : depressed

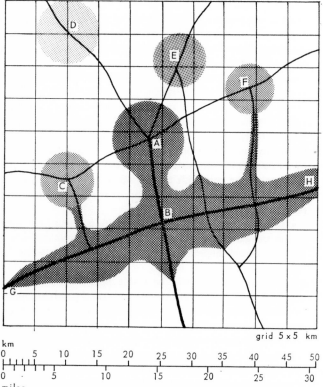

grid 5 x 5 km

km

| 0 | 5 | 10 | 15 | 20 | 25 | 30 | 35 | 40 | 45 | 50 |

| 0 | 5 | 10 | 15 | 20 | 25 | 30 |

miles

physical expression of depression its real substance and cause. What is actually wrong in depressed areas is that the people in them are no longer as satisfied as they once were, and this is why they are apt to abandon the areas. This then means that the elements and their interrelationship are receiving insufficient attention. Man is unhappy, Society is disintegrating, the Networks are declining and, therefore, poorly run, and the Shells are beginning to be abandoned.

A proper policy for depressed areas should not concentrate on the Shells; we cannot keep the Shells of depressed or dying settlements intact unless we make a great effort requiring huge expenditure which a nation undertakes usually only if it concerns itself with important historical monuments. The important thing is to understand what is really happening in the settlement through the methodology described in the preceding sections. If the process shows that it is natural for a settlement to be depressed, then we must be able to decide what should be done: should this area be saved, and how? If so, it is a matter of taking the necessary measures to turn it into a stable or expanding settlement; our policies should be concerned with the transformation of a depressed settlement into a non-depressed one. We should study Man, Society and the landscape, then the Shells and the Networks. Proper policies should lead to the formation of much better Shells not through unnatural methods, i.e., expenditure leading only to the preservation of the Shells—but through those measures which will re-create life in this depressed area.

If, on the other hand, study shows that the depressed area should not be returned to normal life because it has been left behind by evolution, the physical aspect no longer plays a role, unless it is of historical value, in which case it can be preserved as a monument. The key factor here will be the definition of a proper policy to relieve the inhabitants from a long period of depression by helping them to abandon the area in time. In such a case we should bear in mind that the Shells of the settlement act as a force of inertia on its inhabitants and the better the Shells the more valid this is. It is difficult for a community which has invested for generations in houses, buildings, facilities, churches and monuments to abandon them overnight just because the function which was maintaining the community is beginning to decline. Even if employment is low, a man's decision to abandon his work may correspond to the investment of his life in the Shells of the settlements; to move somewhere else is a very difficult decision to make. This is why policies for the condemnation of settlements should be decided on only after a very careful evaluation of the whole situation and in full recognition that such action will mean the eventual loss of great economic, historical, cultural and aesthetic values.

At present there are three categories of depressed areas.

○ In the countryside there are depressed areas where economic changes or various national security conditions force people to move towards areas which were not previously favoured. In feudal eras (and there are still

facilities as they had earlier in relation to the major communication lines and the major centres;

○ the area along axis A–B, which is suffering from growing pressure; for to the A functions which remain the same, new functions have been added because of the broader area developed not only on G–H, but also on the A–B axis, which was very sparsely built with residential areas and now has to turn into an axis of central functions.

Depressed areas

It is wrongly thought that in depressed areas, be they urban or rural, the important problem is that of the disintegrating Shells. Certainly it is the Shells we see when we visit these areas, but it would be completely erroneous to consider the countries which are only now emerging from them), or in periods of foreign occupation, many people avoided living near those areas which exercised power over the others. They even preferred to live in remote places in order to have, if not greater actual security at least the feeling of such. Since many countries are changing completely now and becoming independent we are witnessing a movement of people towards the abandonment of such areas (mountainous, remote, etc.) in order to gain employment in the plains, near the coastal areas and the large centres. Therefore a great variety of depressed areas of this type appears in the countryside.

o Special settlements which have been providing specific types of functions are no longer necessary. Small market towns 20 or 30 kilometres from one another no longer play the same role, for with new highways people can reach centres 100 kilometres away and return to their own settlements the same day, having expended no more energy than they would have had they gone to the market towns. There is a great category of such settlements which are becoming depressed. The case is similar with many mining centres which are becoming uneconomic because they were based on local consumption, and cannot now compete with international prices. This category of settlement is going to continue increasing, for the more international the exchange of goods becomes, the less important will such centres be. And the greater the progress of transportation, the more older market centres will decline.

o Areas and parts of settlements within broader urban built-up settlements, because of the forces already explained, may remain in locations without the proper services, or may suffer from their proximity to the negative pressure of expanding centres such as warehouses, factories, etc.

It is for these depressed areas that proper policies, programmes and plans should be developed to guide either their transformation in order to serve new needs, or their eventual elimination. But in all these efforts we should always keep in mind that the real contents of the settlements are Man and Society, and that the Shells are only one of the elements—that is, the skin—and the external expression of what is vital.

Stable areas

Areas which remain stable, with no major changes in the size or structure of the population or in the functions which are taking place in them, present no special problems. They show no signs of depression or expansion. Their transformation therefore takes place through a natural renewal of their elements, and a certain amelioration takes place continuously. These stable areas are not problems for their citizens or the government. We do not know whether these stable

conditions aided Man's evolution and it will take us time to find out. But the fact is they have not harmed Man up to now, and we have no reason to avoid them. On the contrary, there are many reasons why we should seek them and try to utilise them.

We need these stable areas so as to have some order in the affairs of human settlements, an order which will allow us to concentrate on the problem areas. How we can turn many depressed or growing areas suffering from negative or positive pressures into stable ones should be the concern of most of the broader policies related to the transformation of settlements. In view of the fact that old cities, which are now becoming the central parts of major metropolitan areas, are suffering from too much pressure and being practically asphyxiated by cars, and that these areas are gradually being abandoned by business firms and by their residents, we must think of ways of turning them into stable areas in order to retain their values for as long as possible and their citizens as content as possible.

Stable areas are not only satisfactory because they do not present any acute problems; they are also so because Man is used to taking care of them in a natural way. A stable area means stable income, a tradition of proper municipal or communal budgets, a tradition in services and administration, an ability in the development of programmes and plans which will gradually add conveniences until the settlements, even if they do not have a high income, will provide the maximum degree of services and satisfaction to their inhabitants. The continuity and the accumulation of wealth which takes place within a settlement comprises much more satisfaction than high incomes when there is constant change. Only the continuous effort of generations has created satisfactory settlements up to now. Let us not forget that in a traditional farmer's house, for example, there are dimensions and costs which cannot be justified by his income. His house is simply the product of accumulated effort of many generations. The same is true of minor settlements not greatly affected by evolution. The continuous investment of many generations has turned them into very satisfactory settlements, with all their houses well maintained, all their streets paved, their squares and gardens in very good shape and many expressions of art, not bought and added to the settlement, but created as an organic part of normal life.

It could perhaps be asked how we can speak of dynamic settlements and at the same time ask for stability in them. The answer lies in the proper conception of the overall settlement, a conception which will allow for its overall growth while guaranteeing the stability of as many of its parts as possible. It is because the tensions of an expanding settlement are allowed to be transferred into its every part that the whole organism is suffering. We must conceive the method whereby the whole will expand while the parts, or most of them at least, will be stable. After all, how does a plant expand, how does a tree grow? By the expansion and

471

growth of a tree

eight year old pear tree under normal conditions

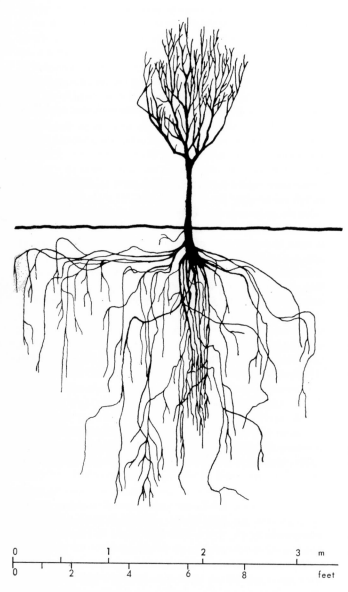

0		1		2		3	m
0	2	4	6	8			feet

growth of its branches and leaves and root system. The changes in its main part, its trunk, are very small, just the addition of one annual ring (fig. 471). It is this wisdom of nature which must be transferred to our settlements so as to enable us to retain as many of their parts as possible and to keep them as stable as we can.

Expanding areas

○ *General considerations*

Of all the areas which develop through transformation, those which grow as well present the major problems; and if the rate of development and change is great, these problems will be even more acute. It is in these areas that everything changes almost constantly, which in itself is a tragic event for there is a conflict between:

○ static buildings and works which, once built, must remain for a certain time as they have been initially conceived and, even if repaired and ameliorated, they must remain long enough for the investment in them to be amortised, and

○ changing requirements which continuously create new functions in and around the already developed parts.

It is this conflict between the Shells and Networks which are able to change only at certain periods on one side and Man, Society and functions which change continuously on the other that creates a tragedy in our urban affairs.

Many of the changes which take place within growing and changing areas of high positive pressure are, up to a certain degree, natural. These changes are caused by the necessity for maintenance, repair and amelioration as in every stable area. These are, therefore, not the changes which create problems. Those which do create problems are the completely unnatural, very often unexpected changes which occur in many parts of the tissue of settlements mainly caused by the fact that we continue to maintain the existing settlements as centres of growing functions which may be ten or 20 times larger than the settlements we inherited and already suffering from pressure. Where it would have been reasonable to create new Shells for completely new functions, we stick to the existing ones, and consequently these have to undergo changes at a rate that makes even the very existence of part of a settlement or a construction within it unreasonable in itself.

In the earlier parts of this study, in speaking of the evolution of settlements and their theory, I demonstrated why these areas of changes within major settlements are necessarily going to continue to undergo many more changes. It is not reasonable, therefore, for us to say that we want to carry out development projects in them unless we can estimate the reasonable life expectancy of these projects in the light of their changing functions. When we have done this, we must follow one of two courses:

○ if we can demonstrate that a certain area which is unsatisfactory and should be changed is going to have the same requirements for a long period—let us say 20 years—it is reasonable to plan this area in such a way as will satisfy the needs for the next 20 years and build only constructions which can be amortised within the same period;

○ if the above is not possible—that is, if we see that the

changes are not going to occur in 20 years, but in ten or five years or that the projects we are going to build will not be amortised within 20 years although we expect that they will satisfy needs for only 20 years—then we must admit that the problem cannot be solved in this area, but must be faced as part of a much broader one.

Such conclusions mean that these are problems of a much wider area; and unless we change our policies concerning this whole area so as to achieve the necessary effects on the minor one under study, there is no hope for a solution. The fact is that regardless of the case, we come to a conclusion similar to the one we reached about the areas of negative pressure (depressed areas); this is that as soon and as reasonably as possible we must try to turn this growing area into a stable one. We must realise that the less change there is, the greater our investment and happiness. We cannot build and change everything, for change defeats the idea of building anything of permanent value. This is the only conclusion we need draw in order to avoid the conflict between stable Shells and their changing components.

It is desirable to leave as many such areas as possible stable, or let them change at a slow rate in order to make the conflict between Shells and contents bearable; this will justify any Ekistic action in these areas, which again leads to the conclusion we reached earlier (although we began with different conditions) that in a changing area we should lead its parts towards stable or near-stable conditions in order to allow the major part of the existing settlements to survive while diverting the pressure only in certain other parts of the settlements. The whole has to be conceived dynamically and the parts statically. This is the only way in which they can survive, and the only way in which Man can strive for investments and worthwhile transformation in his settlements.

If we want to evaluate the problem within every area, we must calculate to what extent this area satisfies its present needs and will meet those of the future—the latter being possible only for certain times. This can be found on the basis of the specific conditions and the satisfaction afforded to the different elements separately and as a whole. We should say, for example, that the natural landscape is, under present conditions, being preserved, or on the contrary is changing and becoming worse. We should think of Man within these changing areas and we should be able to evaluate his problems as well as those of Society. The same process should be carried out with regard to the functions as well as the Shells and Networks. It is here that we will see the results of the changes we are speaking of, and will discover that there are several reasons necessitating changes.

Whereas in the past the need for changes in the Shells was due to the age and decay of buildings and other structures, and very occasionally to the decline of a neighbourhood, in our time the speed of change is due to location, and ownership conditions, as well as to age. How this takes place is shown in fig. 271, where out of eight categories of buildings and

projects within a city, it is quite probable that seven will have to undergo changes. For example, some buildings may be useless because of age or location, or because of changes in the city structure. In such a case the owners may be able to rebuild and take the initiative for reconstruction. However, when buildings become useless because of their location or age, regardless of whether the owners are able to rebuild, they cannot be allowed to do so since an entire area has completely changed its structure and not the individual building only. The situation is even worse when the owners are unable to rebuild. In this case even useful buildings must be studied by the city, and eventually they too will be altered. Since all the other categories of buildings in this area have owners who are also unable to rebuild, we come to the conclusion that in six out of eight categories there is a need for planned urban action. This alone shows how great are the real dimensions of the urban renewal problems.

Such an analysis, together with our knowledge of the causes underlying the need for such changes forces us to realise that in order to face this problem of change through transformation—that is renewal—we must widen the subject. This will enable us to cover a major urban area and to properly classify the types of problems, solutions and areas and to interrelate all these within a reasonable system. We will thus guarantee:

o the possibility of classifying every area in accordance with the magnitude of its problem;

o a new Ekistic programme and plan which will help stabilise as many areas as possible;

o that on the basis of this, it will be possible to clarify the programme and plan to be carried out in every area, and should the new Ekistic programme and plan mentioned above be successful, they can be considered reasonable and justifiable;

o after all this is carried out, we can proceed with the specific programmes and plans for every such area.

This suggestion of widening the subject may seem strange to those who are used to regarding private initiative or a study of every area separately as the proper approach to urban renewal. This is no longer possible, for neither private initiative nor the study of the suffering area alone can lead to a solution.

If we widen the subject we will certainly come up against much more difficult problems; but it is no use avoiding them—they are there, and we had better be aware of them and face them. These problems will often be problems of space for normal traffic. They will have been created for reasons already explained and can be faced only when we understand that since we allowed the Shells to develop in height and depth we should have done the same thing for the Networks. Normally this should happen in the schematic way shown in fig. 472, that is by the pyramidal construction of Networks *under* the surface so that their pyramid will correspond to that of the Shells.

**pyramidal expansion of Networks in depth
corresponding to the pyramid of Shells**

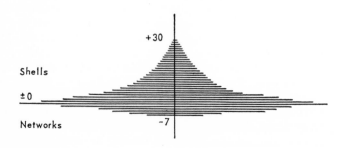

If such a solution is not possible, because of cost, or physical conditions, then, in existing settlements we may also need multi-storey constructions for the Networks. Such a solution was worked out by our team for the new master plan of Rio de Janeiro (fig. 473).

○ *Urban renewal efforts*

Since the problems leading to the need for planned action to transform urban areas are beginning to be important only in those metropolitan areas which have grown beyond expectations since the turn of the century, the U.S.A. which has more metropolitan areas than any other country, has been the first nation to realise this need for action. This action, called 'urban renewal', began to take shape in the U.S.A. in the 'thirties as a programme directly related to slum clearance and public housing.

In 1941, the Illinois Neighborhood Redevelopment Corporations' Law and the New York Urban Redevelopment Corporations' Law marked the first official action in the field of urban renewal although the term was not used then. The Housing Act of 1949 set broader goals. It dealt especially with 'the elimination of substandard and other inadequate housing through the clearance of slums and blighted areas, and the realization, as soon as feasible, of the goal of a decent home and a suitable living environment for every American family, thus contributing to the development and redevelopment of Communities'. This was the first time the word 'redevelopment' was used in Federal legislation.

In 1953, a committee of experts recommended broader, more comprehensive renewal. This concerned 'programs for slum redemption, for rehabilitation of existing houses and neighborhoods and for demolition of worn-out structures and areas which must advance along a broad unified front to accomplish the renewal of our towns and cities'. In 1954 such advice was incorporated in the Housing Act. By 1960, more than 400 communities had an average of two urban renewal

projects each, ranging from very small ones related only to a handful of families up to very large ones affecting more than ten thousand families.

The conception of urban renewal was confined to the achievement of physical urban renewal. But if we remodel a community we must set an ideal of life within it. If the redevelopment of the community is our goal, we should not limit ourselves to physical renewal; this should be an expression of a broader redevelopment of community life. We should, therefore, not consider urban renewal as an ultimate goal but as one of our goals, and at the same time as one of the means of achieving better community life and more vigorous community economic development.

I think it is true to say that, as conceived by most of the people concerned, urban renewal was interpreted mainly as the need for the creation of a better physical urban environment, and only incidentally as an occasion for the creation of a better way of life. In short, there was no proper conception of a way of urban life which could be achieved through an urban renewal programme. Assuming a proper conception of an urban way of life, we should then have an ideal physical form for the urban frame to serve such a conception. This means that we should have a sound notion of the physical form of our cities.

This has not come about in urban renewal, any more than it has in any other aspect of our planned efforts for our cities. But this is not a phenomenon confined to the United States; it has general validity for our era as a whole. We are afraid to conceive the proper forms for our urban life and the correct physical expressions of these forms. In a word, we have no model of an ideal city. Not only have we no specific goals for the area of a complete settlement; we have not even decided on the appropriate size for the typical urban renewal unit. If we want to proceed with urban renewal, we must determine the size of the minimum unit to be considered as an urban renewal unit. Neither do we have a sound estimate of the total extent of the urban renewal problem.

If we cannot even estimate our present needs accurately, how can we proceed to determine those of the future? While carrying out a special survey on urban renewal in the United States in 1960–1961, I asked several of those responsible for urban renewal in many cities to define the specific goals of urban renewal. Their answers gave the following order of priority: slum clearance, blighted areas, substandard houses, downtown or city centre remodelling, public buildings, traffic problems and house preservation.[27]

If we try to understand the criteria for these specific goals we will not be able to specify them, for why, as an example, should substandard houses come third in relation to slum clearance, and why should traffic problems have less priority than slum clearance? Thus, while many local public agencies have set goals and priorities, there seem to be no specific rules or goals which have established a rational system of priorities in the definition of problems. Thus I came to

473

multi-level structures for highways and other networks

Rio de Janeiro, Guanabara State, Brazil (1965)

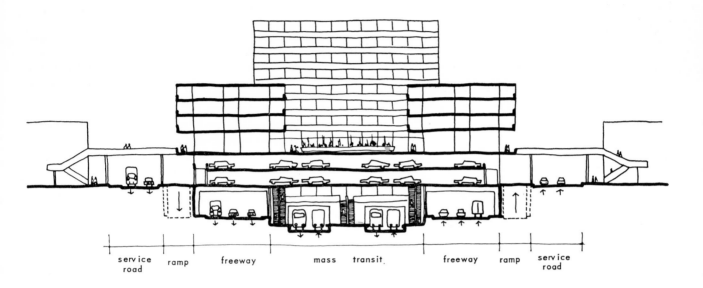

service road | ramp | freeway | mass transit | freeway | ramp | service road

conclusions about urban renewal which were later confirmed by my personal findings in areas where I was given the opportunity to contribute in planning for urban renewal projects.

Some of the conclusions I reached then are quite interesting. Although the majority of those concerned answered that an overall analysis of the urban area was carried out which led to urban renewal projects, only 25 per cent of those asked had prepared a budget of the required expenditures for these programmes, which means that most of the programmes prepared are still very general in nature and cannot be considered satisfactory in the light of the real requirements of the settlements in need of urban renewal. The same holds true for the questions related to the evolution of our present problems. While more than half of the experts answered that this has been studied, in only 11 per cent of the cases had a budget been prepared to correspond to the problems created by this evolution. This led to the conclusion that only 11 per cent have approached national long-term programmes and the exact evaluation of those problems created and those which can be solved.

Due to the lack of specific goals, urban renewal as a whole has developed neither a definite methodology for the formulation of policies and programmes, nor particular critieria allowing for an accurate estimate of problems in relation to potentialities. There can be no overall policies and programmes until specific goals are set for them and a

definite method is agreed upon for the proper estimate of the total size of the problem. Only then can the size of the problem be interrelated with the financial potentials of the community which is to undertake the project and with the results to be expected from the implementation of this programme. The Community Renewal Programs (CRP) tend to develop such programmes for wider areas. They have not yet led, however, to the formulation of an overall policy.

In all the hundreds of programmes which have been implemented, there is a great variety of methods followed in order to attain the goals set on each occasion. Because of the lack of general goals, every authority has in practice set its goals with the emphasis on slum clearance, or downtown or city centre remodelling, or the preservation of houses, or the solution of traffic problems, etc. What is more, every local public agency has followed a different course towards the attainment of its goals, whether in the development of policies and programmes or in the methodology of the implementation of every project, from the selection of a sponsor to the selection of a plan or design.

The fact that so many different methods have been followed for the implementation of the urban renewal effort has by now given us a great deal of valuable experience, but it has not yet led to the development of a methodology able to help everybody concerned to select his own road in a systematic way. However, the difficulties created during the implementation phase are caused not only by the lack of a specific

495

474

urban renewal in central areas
solution of a cellular project
Washington D.C., U.S.A. (1962)

■ major streets
▨ grand avenues
▨ local streets
▨ downtown core

▨ existing special places
▨ proposed special places
▨ predominantly pedestrian streets

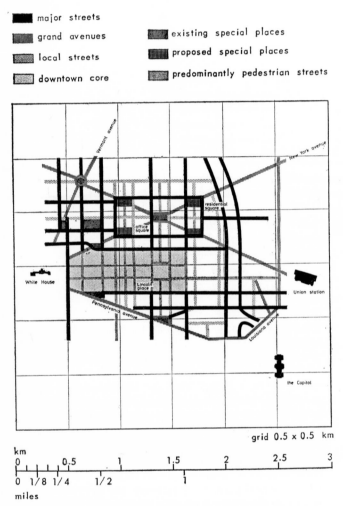

grid 0.5 x 0.5 km

km
0   0.5   1   1.5   2   2.5   3

0 1/8 1/4   1/2   1
miles

methodology, but also by the limited responsibility of local public agencies. Local public agencies in many cases have no responsibility for planning, are limited to only one part of the real physical settlement and are very often separated from the responsibility for housing, all of which greatly limits any possibility of implementing their programmes properly.

There are several hundred local public agencies struggling to conceive and implement their urban renewal programmes. Some of these efforts are important, others are meaningless. Their importance is measured with respect to the size of the effort and the method followed, and also in relation to the experience gained from these efforts. However, regardless of the degree of success and experience gained through every

project, we can definitely state that on the whole local public agencies are following a rather random course. They may solve partial problems, but will certainly never solve the overall problem of urban renewal. Local public agencies may—and I want to lay emphasis on the word 'may'—solve their present problems in this way, but they certainly will not solve those of the future.

During this study I was led to believe that no exact estimate of the total dimensions of urban renewal in the U.S.A. has yet been made. But if we do not know the total size of the urban renewal problem, how can we be certain that the policies we are conceiving, the programmes we are preparing and the projects we are carrying out are, in fact, solving any part of our problem? How can we be certain that, in spite of our efforts, we will not be worse off tomorrow than we are today? If we have no specific goal and no definitive system for estimating needs and programmes, we cannot be certain that while cutting down trees to make a road we are not cutting in the wrong direction; so that instead of finding ourselves in open country, we have in fact penetrated even deeper into the jungle.

I have, therefore, come to the following conclusions:
o Urban renewal in the U.S.A. has had a slow start. This is justifiable since it is the beginning of a new effort in which humanity has no experience at all; but this slow start has unfortunately resulted in disappointing most of the people concerned.
o Urban renewal has not followed a programme conceived in a systematic and detailed way. As a result, its problems cannot be assessed accurately and its programmes cannot yet follow a well-defined road.
o The relatively few projects which have been initiated have not yet led to any results which can convince us of the impact of such efforts on the future of our urban areas.

It is therefore quite natural even now that we turn our attention to the need of developing a sound methodology. After all, it is in the U.S.A. that the first efforts for planned urban renewal were started, and it is there that the greatest experience can be gained. Since the effort is still in its initial stage, a lot can be learned from the start which has been made, even though it is slow, and what has been learned can lead us to much more specific policies, programmes and plans.

As I have pointed out earlier, in order to solve the problems of a growing area, we must first look into the broader area of which it is a part. If this problem area happens to be a central one where unexpected and unreasonable pressure is exercised, this area will be suffering so much that no change would be reasonable, since any calculation will prove that by the time the changes take place, there will be a need for new ones. In such cases, it is of the greatest importance to have a study of the entire surrounding area made in order to find ways of relieving those parts suffering most from pressure. Such a policy has been implemented in Karachi.

Karachi, the capital of the province of Sind in the days of the British Empire in India, in 1947 turned overnight into the capital of the new country of Pakistan. Many new pressures were exercised on it, such as those added by functions created by the people coming as refugees from India. The result was an overcongested centre which could not function properly. When the time came for the development of a rational policy, it became quite apparent that there could be no solution to the problem of the centre of Karachi unless this could be relieved at least of the pressure which grew more and more every day. This led to a survey of the overall situation which concluded that the most important part of a programme for the relief of Karachi's centre from pressure was not its remodelling, nor any project in it, but just the opposite: many projects far from it which would relieve the centre from new pressure. Thus a programme was implemented for the creation of communities of a lower order in several new outlying areas of the city, with most of their corresponding services provided, so that people would go to Karachi's centre only for services of a very high order (fig. 458).

This programme was conceived and carried out from 1959 on, and two major areas have already been developed, the result being that the centre has been relieved to a great extent from pressure from which it formerly suffered. Then, the policy followed in Karachi was one of relief from pressure, which could thus lead to a reasonable plan allowing for a remodelling of the centre at a suitable time. We operate on a man's heart only after having diverted his blood circulation to an artificial heart for a few hours, then we allow it to return; it is in the same way that we relieve the heart of a city from pressure in order to be able to 'operate' on it.

○ *Urban renewal projects*

Several urban renewal projects have been carried out in the U.S.A. I will present some that are characteristic in their illustration of the process through which we are now passing in our attempt to face this new difficult category of problems.

One was the Downtown Washington project initiated by Downtown Progress and executed by Doxiadis Associates, Inc. It aimed at a revitalisation of the central part of the American capital. The effort made entailed:
○ preventing new functions from entering the area;
○ separating the through traffic from the local in order to facilitate the local traffic;
○ ameliorating the layout and the appearance of the central core in order to make it more attractive.

The substance of this plan is shown in fig. 474. It is a plan based on the idea that as little as possible should be changed in order not to upset the existing ownership or land use pattern. I consider it one of those projects which I would call

'cellular' for it does not deal with the structural difficulties of the whole urban area, does not face long-term programmes of increasing pressures and is not extended over wider areas in order to seek relief through the amelioration of the whole texture, but it tends rather to achieve the best that is possible within the area concerned. In a way these projects could be called 'first aid projects' for only one small suffering part of the city.

A completely different project was conceived and designed for the city of Philadelphia by its own Planning Services. It provides for a complete remodelling of the centre in order to permit it to absorb all the pressure of the city. A good idea of this project can be acquired from fig. 475, which illustrates the centre conceived on many levels—on, under and above the ground, with transportation lines at four levels and parking at even more. Such a conception is radical and tends to solve the problems of the centre on the basic assumption that the pressure on the city of Philadelphia is going to remain relatively constant. The meaning of such a project for the overall structure of the metropolitan area of Philadelphia is different, however, for it leads to much greater pressure on the city itself, and by that time the conception of its centre might have to be changed.

Such a project exemplifies the tendency to solve the problem of a city centre suffering from great pressure by creating within it a mechanism that can withstand certain pressure up to a certain extent. It is a radical solution for the centre of a city for it basically assumes that it can be turned into a stable area.

A project which aims at the same target, but tries to achieve it in a different way, is the Downtown Louisville urban renewal project, where in a completely depressed area covered by warehouses and parking lots, an effort is being made by the city of Louisville to create a community that can survive regardless of the pressure which will be exercised on it from the outside (fig. 476).

In some ways it is a project related to the Downtown Washington one especially because it is a cellular one, it tries to face only problems within its area rather than change the overall structure of the city. On the other hand, it is completely different from that of Washington since it is not based on a conservative wish to ameliorate and beautify only the existing area at a minimum cost and without causing any changes in the ownership pattern, but is founded on the idea that everything that exists today is worthless and cannot remain since it is already being surpassed by evolution. The entire project must therefore be considered as a new conception, providing for the creation of a community turned inwards, and connected both with downtown and the river. Thus the community will retain its human values while diverting its 'harder' functions—parking, shopping, etc., to the outside in order to be properly connected with the city.

Urban renewal of a different character exists again in Philadelphia, not in its centre but in the outlying areas. It is

475
urban renewal in central areas
solution by multi-level construction
Philadelphia, Pa., U.S.A. (1959)

476
urban renewal in central areas
solution of a cellular project on the riverfront
Louisville, Ky., U.S.A. (1965)

477
urban renewal
Eastwick, Philadelphia, Pa., U.S.A. (1960)

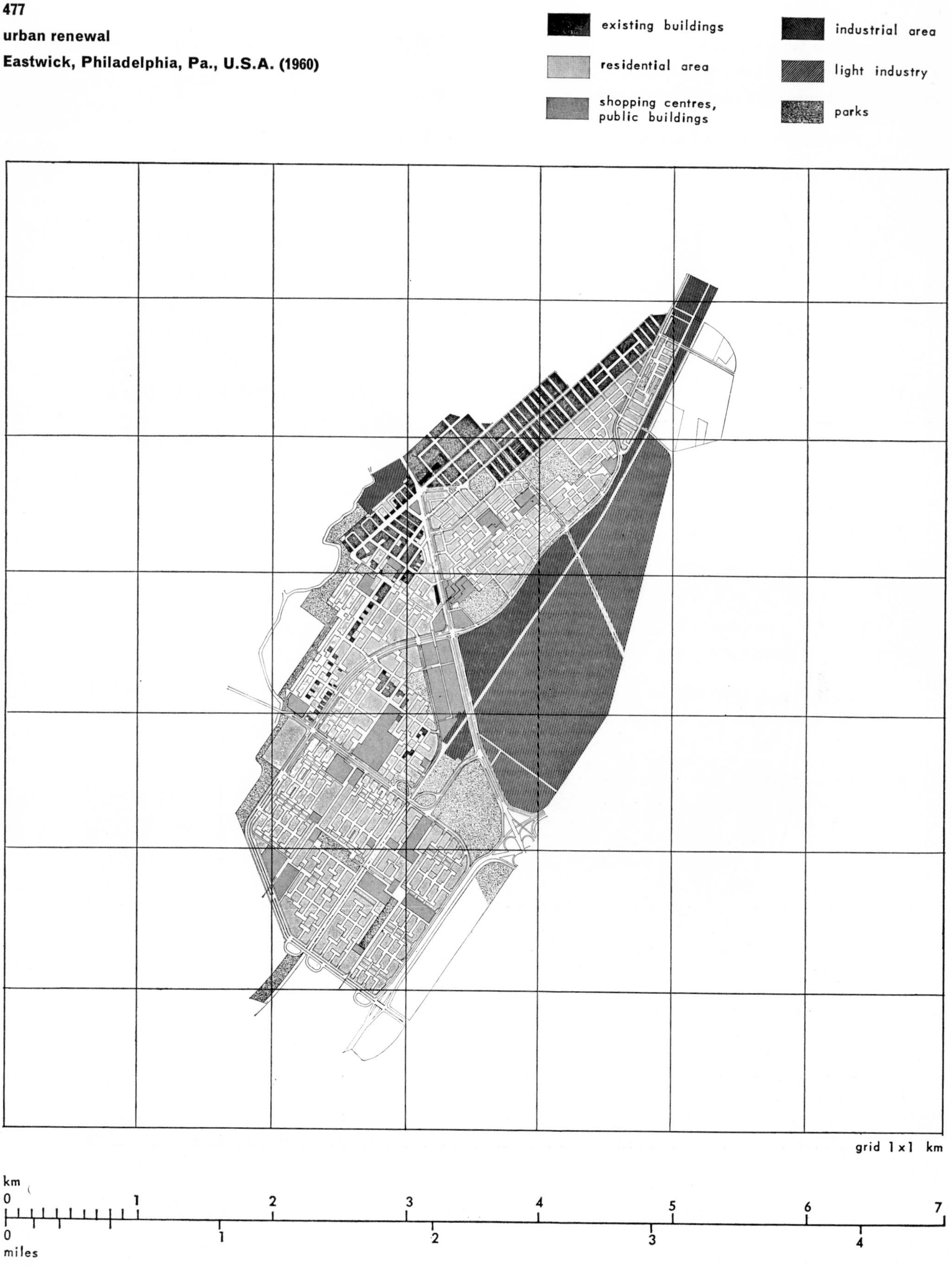

existing buildings

residential area

shopping centres,
public buildings

industrial area

light industry

parks

grid 1 x 1 km

km
0   1   2   3   4   5   6   7

0   1   2   3   4
miles

478

urban renewal in outlying areas

solution by creation of human communities

two of the first communities combining old and
new developments

Eastwick, Philadelphia, Pa., U.S.A. (1960)

■ built-up area   ▨ public spaces

▨ existing residential   ▨ pedestrian sidewalks

▨ proposed residential

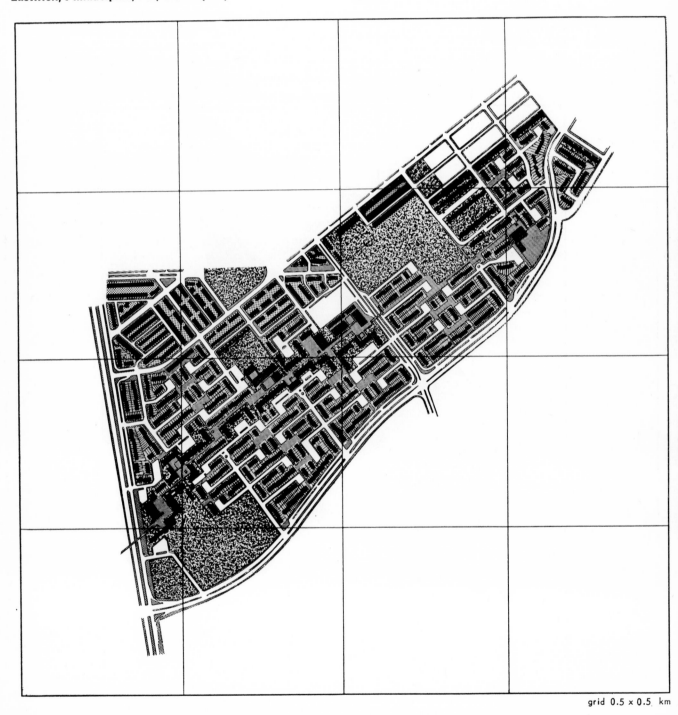

grid 0.5 × 0.5 km

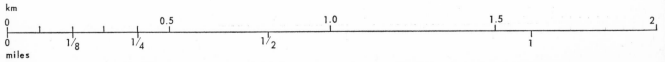

km
0   0.5   1.0   1.5   2

0   1/8   1/4   1/2   1
miles

479

urban renewal re-establishing the human scale

highways are turned into Deepways

Georgetown riverfront, Washington D.C., U.S.A.
(1966)

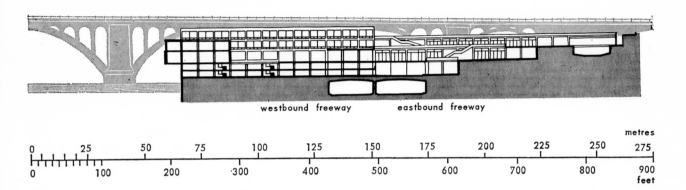

westbound freeway   eastbound freeway

metres

| 0 | 25 | 50 | 75 | 100 | 125 | 150 | 175 | 200 | 225 | 250 | 275 |

| 0 | 100 | 200 | ·300 | 400 | 500 | 600 | 700 | 800 | 900 |

feet

a project mainly initiated because of the desire to make a slum and swamp area habitable. This project was conceived in 1959, and its construction has already been started on a large scale providing for:

- complete remodelling of an area of 10–12,000 houses, including many completely new communities in several of which some of the old houses will be preserved;
- commercial, educational, religious and other facilities;
- an industrial area for 400 plants providing employment close to the new residential areas.

This project has been worked out on the assumption that the area can and should preserve its own new character for a very long period, since there will be no possibility of expanding new functions over it, and the expansion of the centre of Philadelphia, even if it is not going to be limited to the dimensions provided at present, may not reach it for quite some time (figs. 477 and 478).

Finally, a project which is worth mentioning because it involves creating *Deepways* out of highways, is the one studied for the riverfront of Georgetown in Washington D.C. There the previously spoiled area on the surface of the Earth is being remodelled, and its scale is being changed to the human scale, and all present and future highways are being turned into Deepways (fig. 479).

EPILOGUE

Our responsibility

We are living through a crisis; and because we have failed to respond properly, we are heading towards disaster. Our settlements are lagging behind the world's overall progress, our ideas are confused, we are moving without coordination and adjustment and we have not even defined our role. However, we do have a historic responsibility, and that is to understand the crisis and develop a new approach in order to face it. In concluding this study, I feel that I must raise some final questions.

It is obvious that we must act in a more efficient way and on a much larger scale. In this regard I ask whether we have the right to interfere with Nature through our settlement. Man has been doing so for thousands of years, but now he must do so on a larger and more intensive scale. This is the reason why he has to act differently. Up to now, Man has justified himself. Because he once created something worthy, the Acropolis of Athens, the Piazza di Campidoglio in Rome, the mosques of the Great Moguls, Man has the right to believe that he can now create better settlements. Nobody can say absolutely whether they must remain small or should be larger. Small and large are concepts directly related to the individual with no absolute value whatsoever. The justification for our action can be given only as it was given for the work of the past, that is, by the quality of our creation.

The question is not whether we should interfere, not whether we should act, but how we are going to do so. In this respect we must remember our historical phase. Many thousands of years ago the Earth appeared barren of human settlements with the exception of small isolated compounds housing very few people. Then, about ten thousand years ago these isolated compounds merged into larger ones, the villages, and later into even larger ones, the cities, which from a distance looked like the original settlements only larger. For the last few centuries these larger cells have been merging to form more complex organisms. This is a phase resembling the one of hundreds of millions of years ago when the cells of organic life started merging into biological individuals of a higher order. It took Nature millions of years of trial and error to arrive at properly functioning organisms. Now we do not have that much time because we are not dealing with chemical compounds but with humans.

We have the right and the obligation to interfere with Nature in order to save Man. We have always been doing it, but now we must do it wisely since much more is at stake. We need a more careful approach, a scientific one.

My second question is: in developing a science and by acting properly, can we hope to make Man happy and secure? And this really means: is there a satisfactory solution to our problem?

We are dealing with a very complex system, even the molecules of which always consist of five elements, Nature, Man, Society, Shells and Networks. We cannot control all of them in all their dimensions although the degree of our control is increasing. It is more probable that we can and will control their relationship since some of these elements depend on us. I agree with René Dubos when he says 'It is futile to hope that the environment can be controlled sufficiently to assure passive health and happiness. More and more adaptation will be an active process demanding continuous efforts.'[28] Settlements will never change the fate of Man completely, but by being better they will help him to be happier and more secure. They will make his necessary adjustments an easier task, for these adjustments will be for his benefit and not opposed to his needs.

We will have to develop ourselves in order to be able to adjust to new conditions. From the very beginning of our lives we should be able to adjust ourselves, and since our life begins in human communities, they should give us the opportunities to adjust properly to Nature, and the Society, Shells and Networks of the settlement. In this way the human community will become a school where we will be taught how to live with all the elements. In the same way in which the Japanese symbolically bring the whole world into their gardens, we must bring the whole world into the human community so that within this micro-cosmos we can prepare ourselves to meet life.

Thinking in such terms we can now build an entire system starting with the private room, for in an ideal community every person needs to have a micro-space of his own. The next step is the family living room, the smallest unit of cohabitation. Then we go beyond this to the space where Man meets on a small scale with some of his neighbours, and beyond this to larger and larger spaces. While in the smallest space all functions coincide—a man can sleep, relax, dream, work and dress in his own room—the larger the space, the more specialised the functions. In the living room some functions are already excluded. Members of the same family would not be naked and would not wish to sleep in the living room. In the larger unit of a public square only a certain type of social gathering takes place, while reading in common takes place in the community library. Thus, the functions gradually grow and become specialised.

By acting in this way we do not have to answer the great dilemma whether we should build a static and more Aristotelian human settlement, or a dynamic and more Heraclitan one. This is the question since we need minor units much closer to the Aristotelian conception of a harmonious world and complexes of them leading to continuously growing organisms which are changing ones and consequently closer to the Heraclitan philosophy. Our world needs both static and dynamic moments and areas as does our life. Our whole system must provide for both.

In order to attain our goals of a systematic complex of settlements we must act on the elements and their relationships. If we have the right to interfere with any of the five elements of the settlement, it is with the Networks and the Shells more than with anything else. After all, we are a part of Nature, and if we do not come to understand it we may easily destroy it. Man and Society are too precious to be tampered with without complete knowledge. It is the structure we can interfere with more easily, that is the Shells and the Networks of the settlement—which are man-made. The reason is that they are the youngest and least developed of the elements; and of the two we can interfere more with the Networks which are the youngest and still in a primitive stage. They have been changing lately in a revolutionary way, and they will change even more, which gives us a margin for better conception and remodelling. Shells, on the other hand, while not as valuable or as old as Man, Society and Nature, are older than the organised elaborate Networks and contain values which we should not lose without developing a better system of values or better solutions than the existing ones. Therefore, Networks should be changed first and Shells, next. It is with much greater care that we should deal with the other elements, especially Man, whom we should not touch unless we are very certain of what we are doing.

My answers to the previous question about the ability of Man to attain his goals and build a better systematic human settlement, presuppose that he can act wisely in defining his goals and rationally in order to attain them. Thus I have the obligation to ask the third question, whether Man can act rationally and wisely. I must confess that when I visit the great cities of the present or when I see the proposals of some architects for the buildings we are to live in, I must answer in the negative. Also when I think of the obscure motivations of Man, of his aggressiveness or of the beliefs of such experts in Man's nature as Karl Menninger stating that:

> We want to believe that man is a rational creature but there is so much evidence that he is not. No one can know all the reasons for his behavior, and yet almost anyone can give *many* reasons for specific acts. Over and beyond the reasons he gives, there are many reasons which he doesn't give. There are reasonable but unmentioned reasons and there are unmentioned and unreasonable reasons, reasons depending upon emotions or biological processes of which the individual has no full knowledge.[29]

I would have answered my question in the negative, but on the other hand I do see the Parthenon and the cathedrals, and Oxford and Venice and Williamsburg and I do know that while Man's behaviour is very often unpredictable, when he has to build he begins to act more reasonably, as the great dams and bridges and the use of rockets not for destruction but for the conquest of the Cosmos prove. My answer—definitely influenced by an inborn optimism and my wishes, but also definitely based on common and personal experience—is that we can count on Man's ability to act wisely and rationally and we must plan for it in the proper scale.

In this way I reach my fourth question. The problems involved are very difficult and complex; we are in the middle of a crisis which is getting worse. We recognise our right to intervene, and we believe that we can work in the direction of the creation of rational human settlements. But, can we accomplish anything? Is there any possibility of coping with such difficult problems? We are dealing with a part of human endeavour which is so backward that it is natural for it to be the slowest to improve. This is a field in which we are going to meet with more difficulties than we expect. But, we also have the right to hope that we can face these problems because we now have the means at our disposal. Man possesses a new technology which he must now make available to the field of human settlements. We have more people who are much more extensively educated than at any previous time. Let us not forget that 90 per cent of all the scientists in human history are now alive. Humanity has never had such an intellectual force at hand. True, this force has not been turned towards Ekistics, but there is no reason why it should not move in this direction. Also, our human potential is increasing at a very high speed, in numbers, education and abilities.

Problems are difficult and human settlements very complicated, but we should not forget that they are very simple in relation to Nature. If we compare human settlements with the human body as a whole, or even the DNA molecule, we can understand how much less complicated human settlements still are as organisms. We will learn some day from Nature, which has solved much more complicated problems, how to solve the problems of human settlements. Therefore, my

503

answer to the fourth question is a definite 'yes'. There is no reason why we cannot cope with these problems.

I must now ask my fifth question. Can we cope with our problems immediately in order to avoid the crisis? My answer has to be a firm 'no'. We are not prepared to do so, which is one more reason why we should mobilise our forces and act as quickly as possible. But we can and must act immediately. If we continue to develop greater skills, as we have in the past, we can hope that in the seventies there will be full recognition of the problems. If this statement seems strange, I need only mention that there was no such recognition in the fifties; indeed, people very often laughed at the very idea of a crisis in human settlements. If recognition is achieved in the seventies, we can hope to have the first rational systems developed in the eighties, and in the nineties we can have them implemented, tried and remodelled, so that by the end of the century Man will be in a position to know what he is doing in human settlements and to be in control of the situation. Therefore we can hope that by then he will be able to direct both the growth and transformation of his settlements for his own happiness and safety.

Programme of Action

In order to attain our goals and respond properly to the present challenge, we need a proper programme of action:

One: We must set our goals. Human happiness is our goal. We may never achieve it completely, but we can work towards it through human settlements.

Two: We must develop Ekistics, the science of human settlements. The closer we come to a scientific approach, the better we will serve our goals. We will attain our goals through the full use of human knowledge in other fields and disciplines and through the development of new approaches and a new methodology.

Three: We must develop Ekistics as a prescriptive discipline and develop proper policies and programmes of action which are going to work for the mobilisation of all the resources at our disposal.

Four: In developing a descriptive science and a prescriptive discipline, we should not forget that we should also develop our ability for better technology, better engineering, and better art. They should be seen as a total; they should not tend towards different directions, but should be unified.

Five: We must carry out an extensive programme of research. We do not know the truth, and we will never learn it if we continue to devote such a small percentage of research to human settlements. Since the gap between the study of human settlements and other fields of knowledge is going to increase, as the latter have made much greater progress, we must spend at least as much as they spend for research. We must devote huge amounts to research. We should not forget that humanity now has many possibilities for research and progress in many directions. Progress will be made only in those fields where the

best and maximum research is carried out. This will be the deciding factor.

Six: We should develop a proper programme for education, since there are very few people who know enough about human settlements. Some are beginning to learn, the others must follow. These people will learn much more through proper research. They, in turn, should educate the others. It is now thought that with the present state of technology, we can have an impact in practice if we train teachers properly, and these teachers in turn train the generation of new workers. We will need ten years to train teachers, and they will need ten years to train those who are going to carry out our task. So even under the best conditions we need 20 years for action on a large scale. We cannot afford to waste time; we must develop the best possible educational programme.

Seven: Public opinion must be mobilised. Scientists must be trained to inform public opinion. Sir Robert Watson-Watt is right when he states that:

When the scientist will not (or cannot) achieve this combination in writing directed to the ordinary reader, he should seek the cooperation of those whose career is based on the serious journalist's trusteeship for truth in plain language.[30]

We must have people who can mobilise public opinion for we need everyone's support.

Eight: In order to achieve all this, we must organise ourselves in the best possible way. In order to set goals, develop a science, carry out research, educate people and mobilise public opinion, we will need good organisation on every level: international, national, local, public and private. We must be organised to carry out our task.

And now, we should ask ourselves the final question: have we the courage to undertake this battle for an ideal? Have we the courage to go uphill and not downhill? Have we the courage to prepare ourselves and our settlements for the urban settlements which will form the Ecumenopolis while preserving human values, or are we going to stick to our present patterns with the resultant deterioration and abandonment of our cities even within the framework of the urban settlements to come? Are we going to allow the small areas which are now deteriorating to be enlarged and then try to modernise them, or will we have the courage to reverse this trend? I think the answer must be that we should have the courage to reverse the trend, and this is something that can be done if we set an ideal, if we set targets for achievement.

How are we going to attain such difficult goals? When for the first time I was confronted by the magnitude of this problem, I felt discouraged and said to myself, 'Churchill was right; we think that we are shaping our buildings, but in reality the buildings are shaping us, for we are unable to reshape them'. When I wake up every morning and go into the streets and see the same street, the same buildings which have shaped my life, I gradually come to consider them as the only natural habitat for myself and my descendants. In all my thinking, I end up doing nothing but mentally projecting into the future the type of village or city I have been living in all my life, and with this attitude, there is certainly no hope for a change.

The situation really seems grim until we realise that we can reverse these trends in a very simple way. We need only realise that we should begin to look critically at everything we see around us, that we should not consider any part of our human habitat to be sacred. We must understand that instead of thinking of what our fathers and grandfathers and great-grandfathers have done and whether they have acted rightly or wrongly, we should think of our own children and grand-children and great-grandchildren. We must really reverse our thinking, switch our thoughts from the past to the future,

turn our heads in the other direction. Only then will we have the ability and the vision to lead ourselves, our cities and our nations towards the creation of the city to come, the city which can justify our existence and our efforts.

Our attitude will change when we understand that instead of thinking of ourselves as the descendants of our grandfathers we must think of ourselves as the forbears of our grand-children; only then will we be able to connect their lives with the lives of our ancestors. The commitments the past has created for us are so strong that we cannot forget them and cannot disentangle ourselves from them. They are there, in brick, stone, steel and concrete. Let us not think of them any more. Let us think of the future and acquire the imagination and the ability to connect the ideal forms of the future with the cities of the present. This is the only way.

List of human settlements shown by plans in the present book, giving actual, estimated, or planned-for size of population

Except where otherwise stated all population data are for actual settlements. The year given refers to the population which existed or is anticipated by the plans to exist at that date. The table numbers correspond to those given on pp 510 and 512, and serve to identify the settlements.

Name of settlement	Area	Actual or planned	Year	Population	Table No.	Source
Accra, Ghana	city	master plan	1980	380,000	1	Doxiadis Associates
Accra-Tema, Ghana	metrop. area	"	1985	1,324,000	2	"
Athens, Greece	city	"	5th cent. B.C.	50,000		Various sources
	incl. Piraeus		1839	26,000		
	" "		1853	36,594		The City of the Future
	" "		1896	179,755		Research Project, Athens
	" "		1907	254,410		Center of Ekistics
	" "		1920	457,550		
	central area		1940	1,165,000	3	
	greater Athens		1961	641,307	3	
			2000	1,940,500	4	
			2060	5—5,500,000	5	
				9—14,000,000		
Atlantis	city	Plato's conception	5th cent. B.C.	100,000		Based on Plato, *Critias*, 277
Baghdad, Iraq	metrop. area	master plan	1980	2,000,000	6	Doxiadis Associates
	community class IV	plan		6,000	6	" "
West Baghdad development	community class V	master plan		100,000	6	" "
Beirut, Lebanon	metrop. area	proposal	2000	1,200,000	7	J.B. Bury, *History of the Later Roman Empire*, vol. 1, 1923, p. 53
Byzantine Empire			4th cent. A.D.	70,000,000	8	Doxiadis Associates
						Estimate on the basis of a density of 200 inh./ha.
Caracas, Venezuela	metrop. area		1980	2,500,000	9	J.B. Bury, *History of the Later Roman Empire*, vol. 1, 1923, p.88
Cyrene	town	"	4th cent. B.C.	16,000	10	*Statesman's Yearbook* for 1965–1966
Constantinople	city		5th-9th cent. A.D.	1,000,000	11	The City of the Future Research Project, Athens Center of Ekistics
Copenhagen, Denmark	metrop. area		1960	1,370,000	12	Doxiadis Associates
	" "	"	2000	2,000,000	13	" "
Copenhagen Urban Area	central city	projection	"	5,500,000	13	Doxiadis Associates
Detroit, U.S.A.			1960	1,670,000	14	Doxiadis Associates
Urban Detroit Area		projection	1960	7,106,000		
		"	2000	15,000,000	15	" "
Eastwick, Philadelphia, U.S.A.	community class V	master plan	1961	50,000	16	" "
	community class IV	" "	"	5,000	16	The City of the Future Research Project, Athens Center of Ekistics
Ecumenopolis	world	projection	late 21st cent.	high estimate: 50,000,000,000	17	
			" " "	middle " 35,000,000,000		
			" " "	low " 20,000,000,000		
Ecumenopolis branches in: Britain			1980	57,250,000	18	*Provisional Report on World Population Prospects* (1963), U.N.
Greece		"	2000	9,000,000	19	

Name of settlement	Area	Actual or planned	Year	Population	Table No.	Source
Greece		projection	2060	high estimate: 24,000,000	20	The City of the Future Research Project, Athens Center of Ekistics
				low " 18,000,000		
Europe		"	2000	610—640,000,000		
			2060	1,090—2,420,000,000		
U.S.A.			"	high estimate: 2,330,000,000		
			"	middle " 1,440,000,000		
			"	low " 1,060,000,000		
North and Central America		"	"	high " 2,900,000,000	21	The City of the Future Research Project, Athens Center of Ekistics
			"	middle " 2,360,000,000		
			"	low " 1,750,000,000		
E. Pappas, Greece	town		1961	1,600	22	Estimate on the basis of a density of 80 inh./ha.
Great Lakes Area			1960	36,200,000	23	Doxiadis Associates
Great Lakes Megalopolis	incl. Canada, Mohawk, Cincinnati portions	"	2000	75,000,000	24	The City of the Future Research Project, Athens Center of Ekistics
			1960	37,500,000		
Great Lakes Megalopolis	main portion only		1960	22,700,000		The City of the Future Research Project, Athens Center of Ekistics
Gournia	part of town		1700 B.C.	250	25	Estimate on the basis of a density of 200 inh./ha.
Guipuzcoa, Spain	region		1960	478,337	26	Doxiadis Associates
Homs, Syria	town		1962	164,302	27	"
Houston, Texas	urbanised area		1960	1,139,678	28	*Statesman's Yearbook* for 1965–1966
Ideal Cities: Sforzinda, Italy		plan	A.D. 1460	120,000	29	Estimate on the basis of a density of 200 inh./ha.
Ideal city by Dürer		plan	A.D. 1527	6,000	30	"
Ideal city by Scamozzi		plan	A.D. 1615	12,000	31	"
Ioannina, Greece	town		1961	34,997	32	*Statistical Yearbook of Greece*, 1966
Islamabad, Pakistan	metrop. area	master plan	1960	100,000	33	Doxiadis Associates
	community class IV			5–15,000	33	"
	community class V			50,000	33	"
Islamabad-Rawalpindi area		projection	2020	2,500,000	34	Estimate on the basis of a density of 150 inh./ha.
Jkerra, Libya	nomadic settlement		1966	300	35	Doxiadis Associates
Karachi, Pakistan	metrop. area	proposal	2000	4,000,000	36	Estimate on the basis of density of 200 inh./ha.
Karlsruhe, Germany	town		1834	20,000	37	Doxiadis Associates
Karpenissi, Greece	town		1961	3,523	38	*Population of Greece*—1961 census
Greater Khartoum, Sudan	city	master plan	1980	793,000	39	Doxiadis Associates
Khirokitia	town		3700–3400 B.C.	5–7,000	40	P. Dikaios, *Khirokitia*, estimated from number of houses
Koropi, Greece	town		1961	7,862	41	*Population of Greece*—1961 census
Kranidi, Greece	"		"	3,942	42	*Population of Greece*—1961 census
Larissa, Greece	"		"	55,391	43	*Statistical Yearbook of Greece*, 1966
Leipzig, Germany	city		1963	588,135	44	*Statesman's Yearbook* for 1965–1966
Limassol, Cyprus	"		1961	47,000	45	*Statesman's Yearbook* for 1965–1966
London, England	metrop. region		"	12,466,000	46	*London Traffic Survey*, London County Council, 1964

list of human settlements shown by plans in the present book, giving actual, estimated, or planned-for size of population

Except where otherwise stated all population data are for actual settlements. The year given refers to the population which existed or is anticipated by the plans to exist at that date. The table numbers correspond to those given on pp.510 and 512, and serve to identify the settlements.

Name of settlement	Area	Actual or planned	Year	Population	Table No.	Source
Los Angeles, California, U.S.A.	city		1960	2,479,015		Statesman's Yearbook for 1965–1966
Lyon, France	downtown city		1962	885,944	47 48	Statesman's Yearbook for 1965–1966
Maresa	town		Hellenistic period	400	49	Estimate on the basis of a density of 200 inh./ha.
Marsa el Brega, Libya	city	master plan	2000	100,000	50	Doxiadis Associates
Megalopolis of Eastern Coast, U.S.A.			1960	37,000,000	51	Jean Gottmann, Megalopolis, The Urbanized Northeastern Seaboard of the United States
Metsovo, Greece	town		1961	2,976	52	Population of Greece—1961 census
Miletus, Greece	city		4th century B.C.	30,000	53	K. Freeman, Greek City-States, 1950
Minneapolis—St. Paul, Minn., U.S.A.	twin-city		1960	1,950,000	54	Statesman's Yearbook for 1965–1966
Mongol Empire of China			13th century A.D.	59,847,000	55	T. R. Treagor, A Geography of China, 1965
Mussayib, Iraq	region	regional plan	1970	51,800	56	Doxiadis Associates
Myconos, Greece	town		1961	2,797	57	Population of Greece—1961 census
New York, U.S.A.	urbanised area		1960	14,114,927	58	Statesman's Yearbook for 1965–1966
Olynthos, Greece	city		5th century B.C.	15,000	59	Lewis Mumford, The City in History, 1961
	residential blocks		" " "	200	59	Estimate on the basis of a density of 200 inh./ha.
Palaiokastro, Crete	part of the town		Minoan period	500	60	Estimate on the basis of 200 inh./ha.
Palma Nuova, Italy	town		1593	7,000	61	Estimate on the basis of a density of 200 inh./ha.
Paris, France	metrop. area		1962	7,439,110	62	Villes et Agglomérations Urbaines —recensement de 1962
Paros, Greece	town		1961	1,886	63	Population of Greece—1961 census
Patras, Greece	city		"	95,364	64	Statistical Yearbook of Greece, 1966
Peking, China	city		13th century A.D.	over 1,000,000	65	W. Schneider, Babylon is Everywhere, Hodder and Stoughton, London, 1963
Priene, Asia Minor	city		4th century B.C.	4,000	66	R. E. Wycherley, How the Greeks Built Cities, 1962
Psychico, Greece	suburb of Athens		1961	7,209	67	Statistical Yearbook of Greece, 1965
Punjab, Pakistan	university	plan	1966	20,000	68	Doxiadis Associates
Rethymno, Greece	town		1961	15,000	69	Statistical Yearbook of Greece, 1966
Rio de Janeiro, Brazil	metrop. area		2000	4,673,000	70	Doxiadis Associates
	megalop. area	master plan	"	19,000,000	71	
Roman Empire			1st century B.C.	60,000,000	72	J. B. Bury, The History of the Later Roman Empire, vol. 1, 1923, pp. 53, 62
Rome	city		imperial period	approx. 1,000,000	73	Various sources

Name of settlement	Area	Actual or planned	Year	Population	Table No.	Source
St. Gall, Switzerland	town		1963	77,400	74	*Statesman's Yearbook for 1965–1966*
Salonica, Greece	city		1961	378,444	75	*Statistical Yearbook of Greece, 1966*
Somanya, Ghana	town		1960	9,300	76	Doxiadis Associates
Thrace, Greece	region		1951	336,954	77	*Statistical Yearbook of Greece, 1966*
Timgad, Algeria	town		2nd century A.D.	approx. 6,000	78	M. Rostortzeff, *The Social and Economic History of the Roman Empire*, 1926 pp. 328–9
Tema, Ghana	city	master plan	1980	170,000	1	Doxiadis Associates
		"	1985	234,000		"
Tokyo, Japan	metrop. area incl. Yokohama and Kawasaki		1960	12,000,000	79	"
Tübingen, Germany	town		13th century A.D.	5,000	80	Estimate on the basis of a density of 200 inh./ha.
TURA	city	plan	1965	1,000,000	81	Doxiadis Associates
Venice, Italy	"		1963	355,661	82	*Statesman's Yearbook for 1965–1966*
Washington D.C., U.S.A.	metrop. area incl. Maryland and Virginia		1961	2,230,000	83	*Statistical Abstract of the United States*, 1964.
Zagliveri, Greece	town		"	2,800	84	*Population of Greece*—1961 census
Zamosc, Poland	"		1578	1,500	85	Estimate on the basis of a density of 200 inh./ha.

table of human settlements shown by plans in the present book classified by Ekistic unit

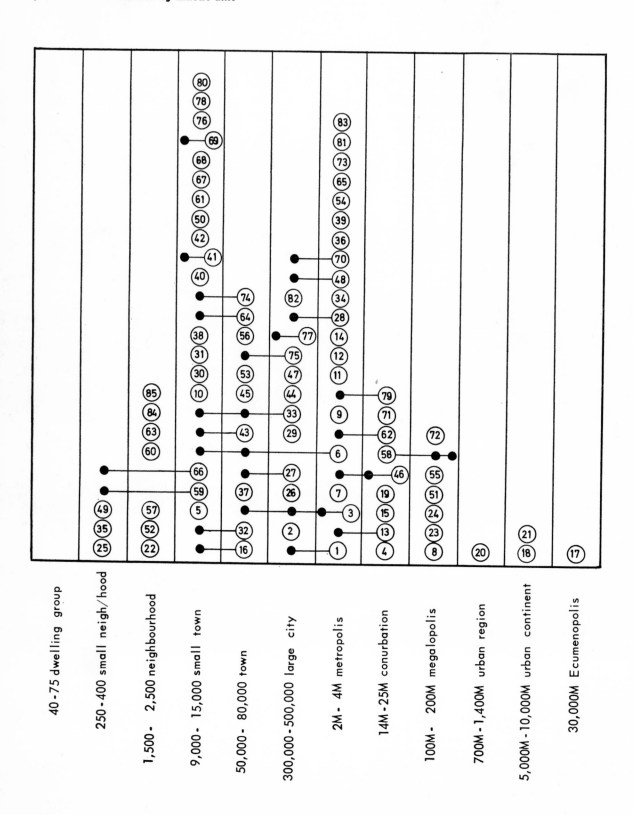

In this table all the human settlements whose plans are shown in the book are given by size in accordance with the Ekistic Logarithmic Scale. In this way we have an index of settlements by the size of Ekistic units which can aid the reader in a comparative study of the settlements of similar size presented in the book.

In the preceding list each settlement has been given a number, which is here used to identify it. The lines connecting the circled numbers with the black dot indicate that the same settlement has been presented in different scales in order to show a part of the settlement as well as the whole or in order to show the settlement as part of a larger urban region.

The sum total of the circles and dots in every column shows the sum total of Ekistic units of a certain order given in the book, regardless of whether they form complete settlements or simply parts of settlements. There are 85 whole settlements and 115 Ekistic units and whole settlements or parts of settlements given in the entire table.

511

table of human settlements shown by plans in the present book classified by Ekistic unit and date

The eighty-five settlements tabulated on pp. 506–9 are here classified according to population size and date. As would be expected, most of them belong to our own era, since human settlements of the past are dealt with mainly in a single chapter, although the present-day phenomena covered in the rest of the book are related to their historical setting.

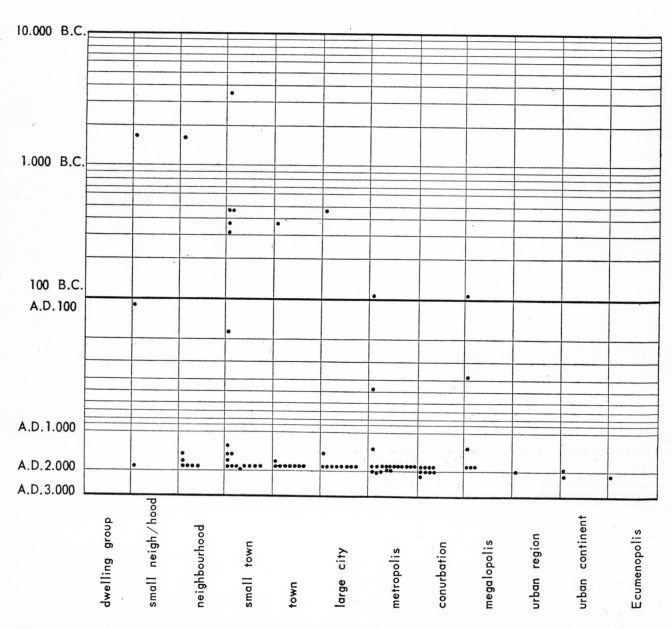

512

NOTES

PREFACE

1 C. A. Doxiadis, *Ekistic Analysis*. Department of Reconstruction Series, Athens, 1946.
   C. A. Doxiadis, *Ekistic Policies for the Reconstruction of the Country with a 20-year Program*. Department of Reconstruction Series, Athens, 1947.
2 Vannevar Bush, *Science Pauses*, page 167.
3 C. A. Doxiadis, *Architecture in Transition*, Hutchinson of London, 1963.
   C. A. Doxiadis and Dr. Truman B. Douglass, *The New World of Urban Man*, United Church Press, Boston, 1965.
   C. A. Doxiadis, *Urban Renewal and the Future of the American City*, Public Administration Service, Chicago, 1966.
   C. A. Doxiadis, *Between Dystopia and Utopia*, the Trinity College Press, Hartford, Conn., 1966.

INTRODUCTION

1 Dennis Gabor, *Inventing the Future*, page 50.
2 Rachel Carson, *Silent Spring*, dedication.
3 Ibid, page xviii.
4 Ibid, page xviii.
5 Lewis Mumford, *The Highway and the City*, page 66.
6 John Rader Platt, *The Excitement of Science*, page 1.
7 Paul Valéry, *Eupalinos*, pages 119–25.
8 Henry Moore, *Sculpture and Drawings*, page xli.

BOOK ONE

1 Edward T. Hall, *The Hidden Dimension of Man*, 1966.
2 Le Corbusier, *La Charte d'Athènes*, 1957.
3 Edward T. Hall, *The Hidden Dimension of Man*, page 100.
4 Paul Valéry, 'La soirée avec M. Teste', from George Seferis, *Antigraphes*, Ikaros, Athens, 1965, page 23.
5 Karl Menninger, *The Vital Balance*, page 3.
6 J. Bronowski, *The Common Sense of Science*, pages 53–4.
7 Ibid, page 57.
8 Ibid, page 62.
9 Karl Menninger, *The Vital Balance*, pages 12–14.
10 Auguste Rodin, *L'Art*, page ix.
11 Bertrand de Jouvenel, *The Pure Theory of Politics*, page 39.
12 Sir Julian Huxley, *The Uniqueness of Man*, page 245.

13 Fred L. Whipple, during his address at the Smithsonian Bicentennial, September 1965, as noted by the author.
14 Patrick Geddes, *Cities in Evolution*, 1949.
15 A. E. Brinckmann, *Platz und Monument als Künstlerisches Formsproblem*, 1923.
16 Camillo Sitte, *Der Städtebau nach seinen Künstlerischen Grundsätzen*, 1922.
17 Walter Christaller, *Die Zentralen Orte in Süddeutschland*, 1933.
18 Plato, *Theatitus*, 151E–152A.
19 Loren Eiseley, *The Mind as Nature*, page 36.
20 World Health Organisation, *Preamble to the Constitution*, Geneva, 1946.
21 George Orwell, *Nineteen Eighty-Four*, 1959.
22 Aldous Huxley, *Brave New World*, 1960.
23 Aldous Huxley, *Island*, 1962.
24 J. Bronowski, *The Common Sense of Science*, page 135.
25 Ibid, page 105.
26 Ibid, page 75.
27 Loren Eiseley, *Francis Bacon*, page 45.
28 Theodosius Dobzhansky, *Mankind Evolving: The Evolution of the Human Species*, page 334.
29 Hans Selye, *Stress*, preface.
30 Rachel Carson, *Silent Spring*, pages 226–7.
31 Sir Robert Watson-Watt, *Man's Means to His End*, page 75.
32 Ibid, pages 207–10.
33 John Rader Platt, *The Excitement of Science*, page 10.
34 René Dubos, *Can Man Keep up with History?* page 6.
35 Ibid, page 9.
36 Dennis Gabor, *Inventing the Future*, page 26.
37 Walter Christaller, *Die Zentralen Orte in Süddeutschland*, 1933.
38 The Regional Science Association, *Papers and Proceedings*, vol. 4, 1958, page 5.
39 C. A. Doxiadis, *Ekistics, Regional Science and Urban Geography*, Second European Congress, Sept. 3–6, 1962.
40 Doxiadis Associates, Document R–GA 307, page 37.
41 *Ekistics*, a monthly publication of the Athens Center of Ekistics, Athens Technological Institute, Athens, Greece.
42 F. Fraser Darling, 'The Unity of Ecology', *Ekistics*, May 1964.
43 Leonard J. Duhl (ed.), *The Urban Condition*, 1963.
44 C. A. Doxiadis, *Architecture in Transition*, 1963, page 177.
45 Ibid.
46 C. A. Doxiadis, 'Ekistics and Traffic', *Traffic Quarterly*, July 1963.

Notes

47 George Politis, *Eklogai apo Tragoudia Ellinikou Laou,* No. 64, page 71, Athens, 1932.

48 Sir Robert Watson-Watt, *Man's Means to His End,* page 97.

49 The Editors of *Fortune, The Mighty Force of Research,* page 289.

50 Richard Llewelyn-Davies and Peter Cowan, *How Much Research?* 1963.

51 Delos Symposia One, Two, Three and Four (1963–1966); *Ekistics,* the October issues for 1963–1966.

52 Dennis Gabor, *Inventing the Future,* 1963.

53 René Dubos, *Can Man keep up with History?* page 9.

54 Paul Valéry, *Eupalinos,* 1944.

55 René Dubos, *Can Man keep up with History?* page 9.

BOOK TWO

1 J. Bronowski, *The Common Sense of Science,* page 84.

2 *City of the Future,* Research Project, Athens Center of Ekistics, 1964.

3 Jean Gottmann, *Megalopolis, The Urbanized Northeastern Seaboard of the United States,* page 26.

4 *City of the Future,* Research Project, Athens Center of Ekistics, 1964.

5 Jean Gottmann, *Megalopolis, The Urbanized Northeastern Seaboard of the United States,* page 26.

6 *City of the Future,* Research Project, Athens Center of Ekistics, 1964.

7 For examples of a similar type of basic architecture in primitive and more advanced settlements, the reader may refer to *Architecture in Transition.*

8 See pages 27–31 for a definition of community classes.

9 Claude Bernard, *Leçons sur les phénomènes de la Vie commune aux animaux et aux végétaux,* (2 vol. Paris 1878) vol. I, pages 6–7 as translated by Bertrand de Jouvenel in *The Pure Theory of Politics,* New Haven, 1963, page 39.

10 Walter Christaller, *Die Zentralen Orte in Süddeutschland,* 1933.

11 René Dubos, *Mirage of Health,* page 28 (from Aristotle's *Politics*).

12 Ian McHarg, 'Man and his Environment' *The Urban Condition,* 1963.

13 Sir Julian Huxley, *The Uniqueness of Man,* page 141.

14 Ian McHarg, 'Man and His Environment', *The Urban Condition,* pages 48–9.

15 A small static city of several thousand people called Megalopolis existed in ancient Greece in the Peloponnesus. It was called megalo-polis (large city) because it was created in an area that had previously had no other cities.

16 Richard L. Meier, 'Is Birth Control Enough', reprinted from the *Humanist,* page 74.

17 *City of the Future,* Research Project, Athens Center of Ekistics.

18 C. A. Doxiadis, *Architecture in Transition,* pages 136–42.

19 Jean Gottmann, *Megalopolis, The Urbanized Northeastern Seaboard of the United States,* fig. 7, page 36.

20 Ibid, page 659.

21 P. B. Medawar, *The Uniqueness of the Individual,* page 108.

22 Ibid, page 110.

23 C. A. Doxiadis, *Architecture in Transition,* 1963.

24 René Dubos, *Can Man keep up with History?* page 7.

25 Ibid, page 6.

26 For greater details on the author's views on urban renewal, see *Urban Renewal and the Future of the American City,* 1966.

27 Karl Menninger, *The Vital Balance,* page 10.

28 P. B. Medawar, *The Uniqueness of the Individual,* page 74.

BOOK THREE

1 Leonard J. Duhl (ed.), *The Urban Condition,* page 69.

2 Marshall McLuhan, *The Gutenberg Galaxy, the Making of Typographic Man,* page 27.

3 Hans Selye, *Stress,* preface.

4 See documents series B presented at the Delos Symposion, 1966—Delos Four; and the address given by the author upon receipt of the Aspen Award, July 1966.

5 Karl Menninger, *The Vital Balance,* page 111.

6 International Seminar on Ekistics, Athens Ekistics Month, 1966.

7 Edward T. Hall, *The Hidden Dimension,* page 10.

8 Ibid.

9 Edward T. Hall, *Silent Assumptions in Social Communication,* page 45.

10 I owe the credit for this idea to a colleague and associate of mine, the architect Savvas Kondaratos.

11 P. B. Medawar, *The Uniqueness of the Individual,* page 113.

12 Alexis Carrel, *Man, the Unknown,* pages 56–7.

13 Ibid.

14 Ezra Pound *Canto XIII.*

15 See author's work, *Between Dystopia and Utopia,* 1966.

16 J. Z. Young, *Doubt and Certainty in Science,* cited by Sir Julian Huxley in *Evolution in Action,* page 15.

17 René Dubos, *Can Man keep up with History?,* page 7.

BOOK FOUR

1 Le Corbusier, *La Ville Radieuse,* 1964, and Frank Lloyd Wright, *The Living City,* 1958.

2 Quoted in Aldous Huxley, *Brave New World,* page v (translation by the Author).

3 Jane Jacobs, *The Death and Life of Great American Cities,* 1961.

4 J. Bronowski, *The Common Sense of Science,* page 134.

5 Philostratus, *Life of Apollonius,* Book VIII, chapter VII.

6 Loren Eiseley, *The Immense Journey,* page 12.

7 Nigel Calder (ed.), *The World in 1984,* vol. 2, page 197.

8 Wilbert E. Moore, *Man, Time and Society,* page 9.

9 K. Denbigh, *Science, Industry and Social Policy,* 1964.

10 Bertrand de Jouvenel, *Efficacité et Savoir-Vivre,* pages 8–13.

11 Rabindranath Tagore, *Towards Universal Man,* page 85.

12 Nigel Calder (ed.), *The World in 1984,* vol. 2, page 197.

13 Ibid, page 142.

14 Erich Lindermann, 'Mental Health and the Environment', *The Urban Condition,* pages 3–10.

15 Loren Eiseley, *The Immense Journey,* page 57.

16 René Dubos, *Can Man keep up with History?* page 7.

17 René Dubos, *Mirage of Health,* page 227.

18 *Declaration of Delos,* Athens Center of Ekistics, Greece, July 1963.

19 Loren Eiseley, *The Immense Journey*, page 57.
20 Marshall McLuhan, *The Gutenberg Galaxy, the Making of Typographic Man*, 1962.
21 Rachel Carson, *Silent Spring*, page 90.
22 Loren Eiseley, *The Immense Journey*, page 55.
23 Senator Claiborne Pell, *Megalopolis Unbound*, Praeger, New York, 1966.
24 *Civil Engineering Magazine*, October 1965.

25 John R. Borchert, *The Twin Cities Urbanized Area*, pages 47–50.
26 Ibid.
27 C. A. Doxiadis, *Urban Renewal and the Future of the American City*, 1966.
28 René Dubos, *Mirage of Health*, pages 31–56.
29 Karl Menninger, *The Vital Balance*, page 110.
30 Sir Robert Watson-Watt, *Man's Means to his End*, page 117.

GLOSSARY OF TERMS

Accessibility model: mathematical model for the distribution of population among the zones of a study area based on the concept of accessibility.

Anthropics: total discipline covering the whole knowledge about Man, or the Science of Man as suggested by Alexis Carrel in *Man, the Unknown*. We need Anthropics, the science based on the wholeness of Man, *anthropos*, to help us study and develop him, since we cannot achieve this by simple coordination of his separate aspects. Term coined by the author, first used in the Delos Symposion of July 1966 and his speech delivered at the Aspen Institute for Humanistic Studies on July 29, 1966.

Anthropocosmos: world of Man as distinguished from the great world or cosmos beyond Man's reach. Term coined by the author, from the Greek words *anthropos* and *cosmos*, 'man' and 'world'; first used in his lecture at the Swarthmore College Centennial Year Celebrations in 1964, entitled *The Human Crust of the Earth*.

Community class: based on a systematic classification of human communities expressed in the Ekistic Logarithmic Scale (ELS), starting from class I which corresponds to building group and ending with class XII, corresponding to Ecumenopolis.

Continuously Increasing Dimensionality Method (C.I.D.): the process of the gradual increase of scale in the application of the I.D.E.A. method, in order to permit the introduction of more dimensions in the search for the best alternative.

Deepways: the whole system of underground lines of transportation for private or mass-transportation vehicles, few or many, travelling at all speeds, which is indispensable for the solution of our urban problems. Term coined by the author, first used in his studies of 1965 and 1966 and in his book *Between Dystopia and Utopia*, 1966.

Directional forces: forces of attraction or repulsion that exist in or around human settlements and influence their structure, form and pattern of development.

Dynametropolis: a metropolis which exhibits continuous growth like the Dynapolis. A Dynametropolis contains all the phenomena that characterise a Dynapolis, only intensified in scale and complexity. In some respects Dynametropolis may, in addition to its major urban areas, contain examples of all types of settlements, including agricultural and nomadic. Term coined by the author.

Dynapolis: dynamic 'polis' or dynamic city. The ideal Dynapolis depends on the type of city we are dealing with. Term coined by the author, and used since the early fifties in teaching and writing; used in his book *Architecture in Transition*, 1963.

Ecumeni: entire space inhabited by Man. It is the Greek word *Oikoumeni* meaning inhabited land, i.e., the settled part of the Earth.

Ecumenopolis: the coming city that will, together with the corresponding open land which is indispensable for Man, cover the entire Earth as a continuous system forming a universal settlement. Term coined by the author and first used in the October 1961 issue of *Ekistics*.

Ekistics: science of human settlements. Term coined by the author, from the Greek words οἶκος, 'home' and οἰκῶ, 'settling down'; first used in his lectures of 1942 at the Athens Technical University.

Ekistic Logarithmic Scale (ELS): classification of settlements according to their size presented on the basis of a logarithmic scale, running from Man (unit 1) as the smallest unit of measurement to the whole Earth (unit 15). The Ekistic Logarithmic Scale can be presented graphically, showing area or number of people corresponding to each unit, etc., so that it can be used as a basis for the measurement and classification of many dimensions in human settlements. Scale developed by the author, first presented in 1961, published in *Architecture in Transition* (1963) and elaborated by the Athens Center of Ekistics.

Ekistic unit: based on classification of parts or whole human settlements. From unit 4, which corresponds to community class I, to unit 15, which corresponds to community class XII, the Ekistic units coincide with the classification of human communities expressed in the Ekistic Logarithmic Scale (ELS), which starts from unit 1 corresponding to Man and ends with unit 15 corresponding to Ecumenopolis.

Entopia: place that is practicable—that can exist. Term coined by the author, from the Greek words *en* and *topos*, 'in' and 'place'. First used in the Trinity College Lectures, Hartford, Conn., 1966, and published in his book *Between Dystopia and Utopia*, 1966.

Force-mobile: the interplay created by all forces which act and evolve in the human settlements. A heuristic model based on the forces of attraction of functions of several classes depending on the type of problem which is faced. It is used for the evaluation and comparison of alternatives.

Functions: all types of activities within a human settlement, such as movement of people or industrial activities, research and education activities, and so forth, as distinct from *structure* such as roads and highways or an industrial zone, university campus, and so forth.

516

Human Community: is designed on a human scale in all its elements, with emphasis placed on the requirements of the pedestrian in design, movement, spatial dimensions, etc.; the non-human machine scale being restricted to the borders of the community.

Ideal city: mentioned by several authors especially in relation to the physical aspects of the city and the disciplines of architecture and physical planning in distinction to utopia which seldom refers to these aspects.

Isolation of Dimensions and Elimination of Alternatives Method (I.D.E.A.): the method devised for the gradual isolation of dimensions and the selection, by elimination, of those alternatives, among the great number conceived, that satisfy certain Ekistic criteria. It is an attempt to eliminate arbitrariness in the search of the many-dimensional parameter space of the urban system for the optimum alternative.

Man: term with many meanings depending on the discipline concerned. Used in the present book to indicate the individual with his own characteristics and problems as distinct from society.

Megalopolis: greater urbanised area developed by the gradual merging of many metropolises and cities into one urban system. Its population is calculated in the tens of millions. It is distinct from the metropolis, either because its population exceeds ten million people, in which case it also covers a vast surface area, or because it has incorporated more than one metropolis. Term used since ancient Greece when a city called Megalopolis was created in Arcadia. Jean Gottmann gives a special meaning to this ancient term in 1961 in his book *Megalopolis, The Urbanized Northeastern Seaboard of the United States*.

Nature: term with many meanings depending on the discipline concerned. Used in the present book to indicate the natural environment of Man as it exists before he starts remodelling it by cultivation or construction. It provides the foundation upon which the settlements are created and the frame within which they function.

Networks: term with many meanings depending on the discipline concerned. Used in the present book to indicate the man-made systems which facilitate the functioning of the settlement, such as, roads, water supply networks, electricity, etc.

Shells: term with many meanings depending on the discipline concerned. Used in the present book to indicate all types of structures which Man uses to live in or to put animals, machinery, produce, etc., in; the structures within which Man lives and carries out his different functions; the structures that cover Ekistic functions.

Society: term with many meanings depending on the discipline concerned and also on different schools of thought. Used in the present book to indicate human society with all its characteristics, needs and problems; individuals are examined only as parts of it.

Standard Metropolitan Statistical Area (SMSA): human settlements containing at least one city with 50,000 inhabitants or more and having close economic and social relationships with contiguous settlements of a metropolitan character. For a more detailed definition see the introduction to any of the *1960 Census of Population* reports, U.S. Bureau of the Census.

Texture forces: forces that exist in human settlements, which spread around humans, animals, machines, Shells or Networks, or in an abstract way around points, lines, areas or volumes and cannot be expressed as directional forces. They influence the structure and form of settlements but mainly their density and size.

Urban areas: areas of an almost completely urban character, with overall density of 1,000 persons or more per square mile.

Urban Detroit Area: consists of the area of immediate urban influence of Detroit, which extends roughly within a hundred-mile radius from the city.

Urbanised areas: human settlements containing one or more central cities, with 50,000 inhabitants or more, as well as the remainder area of the urban fringe which consists either of incorporated places of at least 2,500 inhabitants or 100 housing units or of unincorporated areas with a density of 1,000 inhabitants and over per square mile. For a more detailed definition see the introduction to any of the *1960 Census of Population* reports, U.S. Bureau of the Census.

Utopia: an imaginary and indefinitely remote place, a place or state of ideal perfection, especially in laws, government, and social conditions. First used by Sir Thomas More for an imaginary and ideal country in his book *Utopia*, 1516; it is a Greek word, a combination of *ou*, 'not', and *topos*, 'place', meaning no-where or no-place.

BIBLIOGRAPHY

AESCHYLUS. *Agamemnon*, trans. by George Thomson in *The Oresteia Trilogy*, The Laurel Classical Drama, Dell Books, New York, 1965.

BORCHERT, J. R. 'The Twin Cities Urbanized Area: Past, Present, Future', *Geographic Review*, vol. LI, 1961.

BRINCKMANN, E. A. *Platz und Monument als Künstlerisches Formproblem*, Ernst Wasmuth A. G., Berlin, 1923.

BRONOWSKI, J. *The Common Sense of Science*, Penguin Books, Baltimore, Md., 1966.

BURY, R. G. *Plato*, W. Heinemann Ltd., Cambridge, Mass., Harvard University Press.

BUSH, V. 'Science Pauses', *Fortune*, May 1965.

CALDER, N. (ed.) *The World in 1984* (2 vols.), Penguin Books, Middlesex, England, 1965.

CARSON, R. *Silent Spring*, Hamish Hamilton, London, 1962.

CARREL, A. *Man, the Unknown*, Hamish Hamilton, London, 1961.

CAWS, P. *The Philosophy of Science*, D. van Nostrand, Inc., Princeton, N. J., 1965.

CHOAY, F. *Le Corbusier*, distributed by Pocket Books, Inc., George Braziller, Inc., New York, 1960.

CHRISTALLER, W. *Die Zentralen Orte in Süddeutschland*, Gustav Fischer, Jena, 1933.

DARLING, F. F. 'The Unity of Ecology' *Ekistics*, May 1964. *Declaration of Delos*, Athens Center of Ekistics, July 1963.

DE CHARDIN, P. T. *Building the Earth*, Dimension Books, Wilkes-Barre, Pa., 1965.

DENBIGH, K. *Science, Industry and Social Policy*, Dufour Editions, Chester Springs, Pa., 1964.

DE JOUVENEL, B. 'Efficacité et Savoir-Vivre', extrait de la *Revue Economie et Humanisme*, No. 135, Sept.–Oct. 1961, pp. 8–13.

DE JOUVENEL, B. *The Pure Theory of Politics*, Yale University Press, New Haven, 1963.

DOBZHANSKY, T. *Mankind Evolving: The Evolution of the Human Species*, Yale University Press, New Haven and London, 1962.

DUBOS, R. 'Can Man keep up with History?', *Horizon*, November 1962.

DUBOS, R. *Mirage of Health: Utopias, Progress and Biological Change*, Harper and Bros, New York, 1959.

DUBOS, R. *Man Adapting*, Yale University Press, New Haven and London, 1965.

DUHL, L. J. (ed.) *The Urban Condition*, Basic Books, Inc., New York, 1963.

The Editors of *Fortune*, *The Mighty Force of Research*, McGraw-Hill, New York, 1956.

EISELEY, L. 'Francis Bacon', *Horizon*, Winter, 1964.

EISELEY, L. *The Immense Journey*, Vintage Books, A Division of Random House, New York, 1957.

EISELEY, L. *The Mind as Nature*, Harper & Row, New York, 1962. *Ekistics*, a monthly publication of the Athens Center of Ekistics, Athens Technological Institute, Athens, Greece.

ELLUL, J. *The Technological Society*, Alfred A. Knopf, New York, 1964.

GABOR, D. *Inventing the Future*, M. Secker & Warburg, Ltd., London, 1963.

GEDDES, P. *Cities in Evolution*, Williams and Norgate, Ltd., London, 1949.

GERKAN, A. VON. *Griechische Städteanlagen*, Walter de Gruyter & Co., Berlin & Leipzig, 1924.

GIBBERD, F. *Town Design*, The Architectural Press, London, 1955.

GIEDION, S. *The Eternal Present: The Beginning of Architecture*, Bollingen Series XXXV.6.11, Pantheon Books, 1964.

GIEDION, S. *Space, Time and Architecture*, 3rd ed., Oxford University Press, London, 1956.

GOTTMANN, J. *Megalopolis, The Urbanized Northeastern Seaboard of the United States*, The M.I.T. Press, Cambridge, Mass., 1961.

GROPIUS, W. *Scope of Total Architecture*, Allen & Unwin, Ltd., London, 1956.

GUTKIND, E. A. 'Urban Development in Central Europe', *International History of City Development*, vol. I, The Free Press of Glencoe Collier-Macmillan, Ltd., London, 1964.

HALL, E. T. *Silent Assumptions in Social Communication*, reprinted from *Disorders of Communication*, vol. XLII, Research Publication A.R.N.M.O., 1964.

HALL, E. T. *The Hidden Dimension*, Doubleday & Co., Inc., New York, 1966.

HARRISON, R. J. *Man, the Peculiar Animal*, Pelican Medical Series, A412, Penguin Books, Ltd., Harmondsworth, Middlesex, 1958, pages 145–53.

HILBERSEIMER, L. *The Nature of Cities*, P. Theobold & Co., Chicago, 1955.

HILBERSEIMER, L. *Mies Van der Rohe*, P. Theobold & Co., Chicago, 1956.

HUXLEY, A. *Brave New World*, Chatto & Windus, London, 1960.

HUXLEY, A. *Island*, Chatto & Windus, London, 1962.

HUXLEY, SIR JULIAN *The Uniqueness of Man*, Chatto & Windus, London, 1941.

HUXLEY, SIR JULIAN *Evolution, the Modern Synthesis*, George Allen & Unwin, Ltd., London, 1955.

HUXLEY, SIR JULIAN *Evolution in Action*, Chatto & Windus, London, 1953.

Institut d'Aménagement et d'Urbanisme de la Région Parisienne, *Paris et Huit Metropoles Mondiales*, vol. 2, 1965.

JACOBS, J. *The Death and Life o* ¦*Great American Cities*, Random House, New York, 1961.

JASPERT, F. *Vom Städtebau der Welt*, Safari Verlag, Berlin, 1961.

JASPERS, K. *The Future of Mankind*, trans. by E. B. Ashton, The University of Chicago Press, Chicago, 1961.

LAVEDAN, P. *Histoire de l'Urbanisme: Renaissance et Temps Modernes*, Henri Laurens, Paris, 1959.

LAWRENCE, A. W. *Greek Architecture*, Penguin Books, 1957.

LE CORBUSIER. *La Ville Radieuse*, Editions Vincent Fréal & Cie., Paris, 1964.

LE CORBUSIER. *Towards a New Architecture*, trans. by Frederick Etchells, The Architectural Press, Paris, 1959.

LE PLAY. *La Reforme Sociale en France* (2 vols., 1864; 7th ed., 3 vols., 1887) republished by the Librairie Plon, Paris, after 1940.

LLEWELYN-DAVIES, R. and COWAN, P. 'How much Research?', R.I.B.A. Journal, April 1963.

LLEWELYN-DAVIES, R. and COWAN, P. 'The Future of Research' (extracts from a paper given before the Royal Institute of British Architects), *Architectural Record*, September 1964.

MCLUHAN, M. *The Gutenberg Galaxy: The Making of Typographic Man*, University of Toronto Press, 1962.

MEDAWAR, P. B. *The Future of Man*, Basic Books, Inc., New York, 1960.

MEDAWAR, P. B. *The Uniqueness of the Individual*, Basic Books, Inc., New York, 1957.

MEIER, R. L. *Implications of the Population Size of the Ecumenopolis*, R–ERES 42, Athens Center of Ekistics, Athens, 1962.

MEIER, R. L. 'Is Birth Control Enough?' reprinted from the *Humanist*, 1958, No. 2, The American Humanist Society, 1958.

MENNINGER, K., with M. MAYMAN and P. PRUYSER. *The Vital Balance*, 'The Life Process in Mental Health and Illness', The Viking Press, New York, 1965.

MOORE, H. *Sculpture and Drawings*, Zwemmer Ltd., London, 1944.

MOORE, W. E. *Man, Time and Society*, John Wiley & Sons, Inc., New York & London, 1963.

MUMFORD, L. *The City in History*, Harcourt, Brace & World, Inc., New York, 1961.

MUMFORD, L. *The Highway and the City*, Harcourt, Brace & World, Inc., New York, 1963.

MUMFORD, L. *The Story of Utopias*, Peter Smith, Gloucester, Mass., 1959.

MYRDAL, G. *Population, a Problem for Democracy*, Peter Smith, Gloucester, Mass., 1962.

The Nation's Capital, a Plan for the Year 2000, prepared by National Capital Planning Commission, National Capital Regional Planning Council, 1961.

ORTMANN, W. *Städtebau früher und heute*, Werner-Verlag, Düsseldorf, 1956.

ORWELL, G. *Nineteen Eighty-four*, New American Library, 1959.

PAPAIOANNOU, J. *Overall Estimates of World Population Since the Appearance of Man*, Athens Center of Ekistics, R–ERES 41, Athens, 1964.

PELL, C. *Megalopolis Unbound*, 'The Supercity and the Transportation of Tomorrow', Praeger, New York, 1966.

PHILOSTRATUS, E. *Life of Apollonius*, trans. by F. C. Conybeare, Loeb Classical Library, London, 1912, book VIII, chapter VII.

PLATO. *Theatitus*, 151E–152A.

PLATT, J. R. *The Excitement of Science*, Houghton Mifflin Company, Boston, The Riverside Press, Cambridge, 1962.

Principsketse til Egnsplan, for Byudviklingen Indtil I Kobenhavn, Frederiksorg og Roskilde Amter. Egnsplansekretariatet for Storkøbnhavn, Dec. 1960, January 1961.

RATTRAY, T. G. *The Science of Life*, Thames and Hudson, London, 1963.

The Papers and Proceedings, of the Regional Science Association, vol. IV, 1958.

RIDER, B. C. *Ancient Greek Houses*, Chicago, Argonaut, 1964.

ROBERTSON, D. S. *A Handbook of Greek and Roman Architecture*, 2nd ed., Cambridge, at the University Press, 1959.

RODIN, A. *L'Art*, Bernard Grasset, Paris, 1911.

ROSTAND, J. *Can Man be Modified?* Basic Books, Inc., New York, 1959.

RUSSELL, B. *The Impact of Science on Society*, George Allen & Unwin Ltd., London, 1952.

SCHNEIDER, W. *Babylon is Everywhere*, trans. from the German by Ingeborg Sammet and John Oldenburg, Hodder and Stoughton, London, 1963.

SCHWEITZER, A. *Civilization and Ethics*, Unwin Books, published in association with Adam & Charles Black, London, 1961.

SITTE, C. *Der Städtebau nach seinen Künstlerischen Grundsätzen*, 5th impression, Wien, 1922.

SELYE, H. *The Physiology and Pathology of Exposure to Stress*, ACTA, Inc., Medical Publishers, Montreal, Canada.

TAGORE, R. *Towards Universal Man*, Asia Publishing House, Bombay, 1961.

TRAVLOS, J. *City Planning Development of Athens*, Athens, 1960.

The Town Planning Review, edited at the Dept. of Civic Design, The Liverpool School of Architecture, The University of Liverpool, Quarterly, vol. XXI, no. 3, October 1950.

TOYNBEE, A. *Civilization on Trial and the World and the West*, Meridian Books, Inc., New York, 1960.

VALÉRY, P. *Eupalinos, l'Ame et la Danse, Dialogue de l'Arbre*, Gallimard, Paris, 1944.

VALÉRY, P. 'La Soirée avec M. Teste', from G. Seferis, *Antigraphes*, Ikaros, Athens, 1965.

VAN MILLINGEN, A. *Byzantine Constantinople*, John Murray, London, 1899.

WATSON-WATT, SIR R. *Man's Means to his End*, Clarkson N. Potter, Inc., New York, 1961.

WOOD KRUTCH, J. *The Measure of Man*, Grosset & Dunlap, New York, 1953.

WORLD HEALTH ORGANISATION. *Constitution*, Geneva, 1946, Preface.

WRIGHT, F. L. *The Living City*, Horizon Press, New York, 1958.

WYCHERLEY, R. E. *How the Greeks Built Cities*, Macmillan & Co., Ltd., London, 1962.

BOOKS AND PUBLICATIONS
by the author

BOOKS

Raumordnung im Griechischen Städtebau, (in German) Vowinckel, Berlin, 1937.

Ekistic Analysis, (in Greek) Dept. of Reconstruction Series, Athens, 1946.

Economic Policy for the Reconstruction of the Settlements of Greece, (in Greek) Dept. of Reconstruction Series, Athens, 1946.

Ekistic Policies for the Reconstruction of the Country with a 20-year Program, (in Greek) Dept. of Reconstruction Series, Athens, 1947.

The Administrative Reorganization of the Country, (in Greek) Dept. of Reconstruction Series, Athens, 1948.

Our Capital and its Future, (in Greek) Athens, 1960. Printed in English by Doxiadis Associates, Doc. R–GA 202, August 1961.

Architecture in Transition, Hutchinson, London; Oxford University Press, New York, 1963; (in Spanish) Editiones Ariel S.A., Barcelona, 1964; (in Portuguese) Armenio Amado, Ceira-Coimbra, 1965; (in German) Econ Verlag, Düsseldorf-Wien, 1965.

The New World of Urban Man, (co-author Dr. Truman B. Douglass), United Church Press, Philadelphia, Boston, 1965.

Urban Renewal and the Future of the American City, prepared for the National Association of Housing and Redevelopment Officials, Public Administration Service, Chicago, Illinois, 1966.

Between Dystopia and Utopia, the Trinity College Press, Hartford, Conn., 1966.

Emergence and Growth of an Urban Region, 'The Developing Urban Detroit Area', volumes one and two, a project of the Detroit Edison Company, Wayne State University and Doxiadis Associates. Published by the Detroit Edison Company, 1966 and 1967.

PUBLICATIONS

No More Regional Planning. A paper prepared for discussion at the United Nations Seminar on Regional Planning in South East Asia, Tokyo, Japan, summer, 1958. Printed by Doxiadis Associates.

The Rising Tide and the Planners. An address given before the American Institute of Planners, October 29, 1958, and published in *Ekistics*, January 1959. Also printed by Doxiadis Associates, as R–GA 146, November 14, 1958.

The Science of Ekistics (and in Greek). Printed by Doxiadis Associates, R–GA 159, April 10, 1959.

Ekistics, the Science of Human Settlements. Reprint of a paper presented to the Town and Country Planning Summer School, Southampton, September 2, 1959 and printed by Page Bros. (Norwich) Ltd., Norwich.

Ekistics, The Key to Housing in Developing Areas. A report prepared for the CIB Congress, Rotterdam, September 21–25, 1959, and published in *Ekistics*, November 1959. Printed by Doxiadis Associates as R–GA 169, July 1959.

Dynapolis: The City of the Future. A lecture at the Oslo Arkitektforening, Oslo, March 3, 1960. Printed by Doxiadis Associates, R–GA 185, February 15, 1960.

The Death of our Cities. Speech delivered to the Fifth Working Conference on Urban Renewal, NAHRO, at Chapel Hill, North Carolina, U.S.A., March 21, 1960; and published in *Ekistics*, November 1960. Also printed by Doxiadis Associates, R–GA 190, April 15, 1960.

Architecture in Evolution. Annual Discourse at the Royal Institute of British Architects, London, March 10, 1960. Printed in Great Britain by Unwin Bros. Ltd., Woking and London. Published in *Ekistics*, February 1961. Also reprinted from the *R.I.B.A. Journal* of Sept.–Oct. 1960 by Doxiadis Associates as R–GA 209.

The Arab Metropolis. An address delivered at the Seminar, The New Metropolis in the Arab World, Cairo, December 21, 1960. Printed by Doxiadis Associates, R–GA 212.

The Future of our Cities. An address delivered at the NAHRO Southwest Regional Conference, El Paso, Texas, May 29, 1961; and published in *Ekistics*, October 1961. Printed by Doxiadis Associates, R–GA 219.

Ecumenopolis, Towards the Universal City. Lecture to NAHRO's 28th National Conference, Washington D.C., October 30, 1961; and published in *Ekistics*, January 1962. Printed by Doxiadis Associates as DOX–UA–4, October 1961.

Aid to Underdeveloped Countries. An address delivered to the NATO Defence College, Paris, November 23, 1960. Printed by Doxiadis Associates, R–GA 222.

The City of the Future. Lecture at the Graduate School of Ekistics, Athens, July 1961, comprised in DA–GSE Lecture Series, vol. I. Printed by Doxiadis Associates, R–GA 264, August 20, 1962.

Ekistics and Regional Science. A paper presented to the Second European Congress of the Regional Science Association, Zürich, Switzerland, September 3–6, 1962; and published in *Ekistics*, November 1962. Printed by Doxiadis Associates, R–GA 265, August 1962.

Ekistics as a Tool for the Solution of Problems in Human Settlements. A paper for the United Nations Conference on the Application of

Science and Technology for the Benefit of the Less Developed Areas, Geneva, Switzerland, February 4–20, 1963. Printed by Doxiadis Associates, Doc. R–GA 272 (October 1962). (And in Spanish, French and Russian) E/CONF. 39/G/11.

The Future of Copenhagen: 'Considerations in the Abstract'. Article published in the Danish magazine *Arkitekten*, February 26, 1963, and in *Ekistics*, April 1963. Printed by Doxiadis Associates, R–GA 289, November 18, 1963.

Slum Clearance and Public Housing in Underdeveloped Countries. A study submitted to the Subcommittee on Housing, Committee on Banking and Currency, United States Senate, 88th Congress, 1st Session, April 1963. Published in *Study for International Housing*, US Government Printing Office, Washington DC, March 1963.

Ekistics and Traffic. An article published in the magazine *Traffic Quarterly*, July 1963 and in *Ekistics*, November 1963. Printed by Doxiadis Associates, R–GA 299, April 1963.

Ekistics: New Problems and New Solutions in Human Settlements. An article published in the Spanish magazine *Revista de Occidente*, March 1964. Printed by Doxiadis Associates, R–GA 304, June 1963.

Ecumenopolis, Towards a Universal Settlement. Study based on several lectures given to various universities, organisations and professional societies. Printed by Doxiadis Associates, R–GA 305, June 1963.

Ekistics, Regional Science and Urban Geography. A comparative study based on a paper presented to the Second European Congress, Regional Science Association, Zürich, Switzerland, September 3–6, 1962, and published in *Ekistics*, November 1962. Printed by Doxiadis Associates, R–GA 307, June 20, 1963.

The Course to Synthesis, Human Settlements in East and West. Printed by Doxiadis Associates, Doc. R–GA 311, August 1963.

A New Role for the Architect. An address given before the I.U.A. International Symposium on Architecture, organised by the Mexican Union of Architects, Mexico City, October 9, 1963. Printed by Doxiadis Associates, R–GA 316 (November 1963). Also printed in Greek by Doxiadis Associates, R–GA 319 (December 1963), for the Third Conference of the Greek Union of Architects at Nauplion, December 13–15, 1963.

The Ancient Greek City and the City of the Present. Based on C. A. Doxiadis' presentation at the VIth Congress of the European Cultural Foundation. Printed by Doxiadis Associates as R–GEN–A 330, May 1964. Also published (abridged) in the July–August issue of the magazine *Architectoniki*.

The Generation of Change. Address to the Graduating Class of Mills College, Oakland, California, June 7, 1964. Printed by Doxiadis Associates as R–GEN–A 331, June 1964.

The City of Man. Address to Wayne State University on March 5, 1964. Printed by Doxiadis Associates as R–GEN–A 323, June 10, 1964.

Art and the Human Scale in the City. Lecture at the Institute of Contemporary Arts, Washington, January 31, 1964. Printed by Doxiadis Associates as R–GEN–A 333, June 12, 1964.

The Human Crust of the Earth. Lectures delivered at the Swarthmore College Centennial Celebrations, March 1964. Printed by Doxiadis Associates as R–GEN–A 334, June 15, 1964.

Social Planning and Ekistics. Lecture at the XIIth Conference of Social Work, September 14, 1964.

Towards Ecumenopolis (in Greek). Lecture organised by the Varvakion Alumni Association (April 11, 1964). Printed by Doxiadis Associates as R–GEN–A 344, October 1964.

On the Measure of Man. Address to the Mayo Clinic Symposium, Rochester, Minnesota (September 17, 1964). Printed by Doxiadis Associates as R–GEN–A 345, October 1964, and published in the Mayo Clinic Proceedings (vol. 40, no. 1, January 1965).

Islamabad: The Creation of a New Capital. An article appearing in *The Town Planning Review* (vol. 36, no. 1, April 1965). Edited by the Dept. of Civil Design, The Liverpool School of Architecture, The University of Liverpool.

Resisting the Forces of Inertia. An article appearing in *Ekistics* (vol. 19, no. 114, May 1965).

The Master Builders. A lecture to the Edinburgh Architectural Association (May 13, 1965). Printed by Doxiadis Associates as R–GEN–A 378, October 1965.

How a City Can Grow Without Growing Pains. An article appearing in the *Washington Post*, October 3, 1965.

Learning How to Learn. An article appearing in the *Saturday Review*, vol. XLIX, no. 1, January 1, 1966, edited by Norman Cousins.

A Technique to Control Technique. A lecture given at the Symposium on the Technological Society, The Center for the Study of Democratic Institutions, Santa Barbara, California, December 19–23, 1965. Printed as R–GEN–A 383 (January 1966); also published in *Main Currents in Modern Thought*, May–June 1966, volume 22, no. 5.

Anthropocosmos: The World of Man. Address delivered at the Aspen Institute for Humanistic Studies on July 29, 1966 upon the occasion of the receipt of the Aspen Award. Also printed in the *Congressional Record* (Proceedings and Debates of the 89th Congress, Second Session) as proposed by the Representative from New York, James H. Scheuer, August 29, 1966. Published by *Saturday Review*, March 18, 1967, pp. 214–221, as *The Coming Era of Ecumenopolis*.

Human Settlements: Challenge and Response. Published in the Hearings before the Sub-committee on Executive Reorganization of the Committee on Government Operations, United States Senate, 89th Congress, Second Session, December 2 and 5, 1966, Part 8. Article abstracted from evidence submitted by the author on December 5, 1966, in support of an address in the series of United States Senate Hearings on Problems of Cities, before the Committee on Government Operations, Subcommittee on Executive Reorganization. Published in *Ekistics*, February 1967.

Water and Human Environment. Prepared for the International Conference on Water for Peace, Washington D.C., May 23, 1967. Printed by Doxiadis Associates as R–GEN–A 410, 1967.

INDEX

growth, rings and star-shaped, 244
  of Ecumenopolis, 447
  prediction, 244
  dynamic growth, significance of, 249
  guided growth, 418
Guipuzcoa, Spain, 383

habitation, average density of, 126
happiness, 47, 50–51, 289
health, definition, 50, 265
hexagonal form of community, 204–205, 343
  see also Christaller, hexagonal patterns
hexagonal patterns, 132–140, 146
  types, 140–141
  dimensions, 141–144
  size, 145
hierarchical systems, in Ecum., 150, 307, 309, 460
Hippodamian settlements, 347–348
Hippodamos of Miletus, 14, 45
H.U.C.O. (Human Community Research Project), 116
human community, the, 438–447
  description, 439
  and non-human scale, 440
human settlements, definition, 21–23, 25–26, 41–43
  basic parts, 26, 109–119
  basic categories, 233
  evolution, 14, 44–46, 54, 220
  growth, 242–244, 293
  prediction of growth, 244
  as living organisms, 41–43, 254, 265, 291, 403; *see also*, biological
    individuals
  numbers and sizes, 81–82, 145, 302–303; *see also*, size
  goals, 47, 289
  life and death, 219–220: *see also*, disease, death, decline
  and war, 489
  percent of urban renewal, 417
hypothesis, 279, 284
  definition, 287

I.D.E.A. (Isolation of Dimensions and Elimination of Alternatives),
    386
  see also, I.D.E.A.—C.I.D.
I.D.E.A.—C.I.D., 386–400
  phases, 386
  implementation, 394
ideal, fear of and search for, 353, 404
ideal city, 353
  see also, utopia, and under Dynapolis, megalopolis,
    Ecumenopolis, etc.
ideal Dynapolis
  „ Dynametropolis } *see*, Dynapolis, Dynametropolis,
  „ Dynamegalopolis }   megalopolis, etc.
implosion, 449
inductive method, 283
inertia, 227, 297, 298, 490
International Road Federation, 406
investment, total in settlements, 85, 292
  related to income, 152–153
Islamabad, Pakistan, 48, 243, 358, 440, 444, 464/467
islands, success of settlements on, 222
isochronic distances, 148

Jacobs, J., 405
Karachi, Pakistan, 473, 497
Khan-I-Meamaran, 45
Khartoum, Sudan, 474

knowledge, decrease of in relation to settlements, 69–70, 72–73
kutcha settlements, 87

law, definition, 287
  causal laws, 288
  laws of chance, 288
  statistical laws, 288
  laws of development, 288–298
    of internal balance, 298–301
  of physical characteristics, 301–316
Le Corbusier, 9, 48
  'L'unité d'habitation', 9
leisure, age of, 411
linear forces, 311, 328, 335, 339
  see also, directional forces, forces
Linnaeus, 32
local civilizations, 268
location, 189, 291, 301–302
  see also, Networks, hexagonal patterns, laws
London, first modern city to reach one million mark, 44, 213
  megalopolis, 214–215
Louisville, Kentucky, urban renewal project, 497

Man, the element, 5, 21, 34–35, 101, 385
  as a unit, 29
  danger for, 210/212
  future, 407, 410
  and Ecumenopolis, 449
  and Nature, 411–412
  and Society, 411
  and Shells, 411; *see also*, Shells
  goals, 414
  choice of contacts, 189
  choice of location for residence, 189
  occupation of time, 210/212
  ability to attain goals, 502–503
  ability to act wisely, 503
measurements, 116
  of efficiency, 116
megalopolis, 82, 87, 101
  population and number, 157
  ideal Dynamegalopolis, 374–376
*Megalopolis, The Urbanized Northeastern Seaboard of the United
    States*, 82, 101, 232, 242
metropolis, 91/101, 212–213
  see also, Dynametropolis
mixed static-dynamic settlements, 190
mixed urban-agricultural settlements, 87
models, (abstract theoretical) use, 66–67
modulus, ideal Dynapolis, the sector, 367
monumental settlements, 348/353
morphology, static settlements, 345–353
  dynamic settlements, 353
multi-directional growth, 479–483
  star-shaped, 479–481
  two-directional, 481/483
multi-storey apartments, 249
  hostility, 276–277
Mumford, L., 48
  see, Bibliography for list of works
myths, *see*, satellites, 'New Towns', densities,

'natural' settlements, 87, 88, 347
Nature, the element, 21, 34–35, 46, 385
  and Man, 286, 411–412